Violence: Patterns, Causes, Public Policy

Neil Alan Weiner
Sellin Center for Studies in Criminology and Criminal Law
The Wharton School, University of Pennsylvania

Margaret A. Zahn
Northern Arizona University

Rita J. Sagi
Temple University

Under the General Editorship of
Robert K. Merton
Columbia University

Harcourt Brace Jovanovich, Publishers
San Diego New York Chicago Austin Washington, D.C.
London Sydney Tokyo Toronto

Dedication

To the memory of of my mother and father, Bertha and Isidore Weiner.

NAW

To the memory of my father Ted Zahn; to my mother, brother, and sisters who have been my anchor for many years; to my husband Steve for his loving support; to my son Christopher for whom I wish a world of nonviolence; and to the students in my classes on violence who were the inspiration for this project.

MAZ

To family and friends for their sustained encouragement, and to academic collegiality that helped us survive a collaborative effort.

RJS

ISBN: 0-15-594915-2
Library of Congress Catalog Card Number: 89-84241

Printed in the United States of America

Copyrights and Acknowledgments appear on pages 464–467 which constitute a continuation of the copyright page.

Preface

The origin of this volume was simple. As teachers and researchers, we know there is great interest in the subject of American violence. Yet, no single volume has provided an array of historical, theoretical, research, and public policy perspectives on both interpersonal and collective violence. For this reason, we undertook to fashion a textbook that captures the diversity and complexity of violent phenomena. We trust that this volume accomplishes this and serves the needs of students, colleagues, policy analysts, and other interested readers.

The completion of this book was more difficult. There were massive amounts of material, of varying qualities and lengths, to review and evaluate in order to provide a substantial and balanced account of violent behavior. The process took considerable time, often leading to heated discussions about how to conceptualize violent phenomena and about what criteria should be employed in selecting among rival articles. This volume represents the culmination of these joint efforts and decisions.

We also were guided by many colleagues who kindly recommended topic areas and articles for inclusion. Only the space constraints that always accompany book preparation prevented us from taking full advantage of their suggestions.

We begin with an introduction that asks the basic question, "What Is Violence?" We invite the reader to review the variety of behavioral vignettes presented there and to reflect upon the definitional elements needed to form a meaningful and useful conception of violence. Part 1 presents an overview of American violence that highlights major trends, both historical and contemporary. Part 2 explores the major types of interpersonal violent crimes and details their patterns and impacts on the lives of victims. Part 3 focuses on collective and political violence and includes narratives of labor and racial strife and discussions of modern terrorism. Part 4 examines the topic of violent behavior within organizational settings. Part 5 reviews theoretical explanations of interpersonal and collective violence and discusses some important correlates. Part 6 concludes with articles on public policy that examine prevention and treatment programs, some of which are controversial.

Some topical omissions are due to space limitations and others to sparse or insufficient writing in given areas. For example, we had hoped to include a radical or conflict theoretical perspective on interpersonal violence, but were unable to locate completed pieces, although some colleagues are now writing in these areas. Future editions of this volume will surely benefit from these efforts and from other new theoretical and research contributions.

We have tried to bridge the gap between the immediate experiences of interpersonal and collective violence to which we are all at some risk and the detached analyses of these incidents which are chronicled in theoretical and research papers. For this reason, we have included some graphic depictions of violence alongside the analytical ones.

The pages that follow document an affliction of major proportions. We hope not only to present a balanced assessment of our present knowledge about violent behavior but also to promote continuing investigations into the nature and consequences of this behavior. These investigations are a necessary point of departure for exploring the extent to which we might feasibly reduce the levels of violence in our nation.

Neil Alan Weiner
Margaret A. Zahn
Rita J. Sagi

Acknowledgment

The editors wish to give special thanks to Selma Pastor, formerly librarian at the Sellin Center for Studies in Criminology and Criminal law at the University of Pennsylvania, who recommended and helped locate articles for inclusion and provided substantial technical advice and whose careful and thoughtful reading and organization of the entire manuscript resulted in significant improvements.

Margaret Zahn also wishes to acknowledge a one-semester sabbatical leave sponsored by Temple University which helped provide time to complete this project.

Contents

Part 4
Organizational Structure and Violence / 219

Part 5
Causes, Correlates, and Contexts / 277

Part 6
Prevention, Treatment, and Public Policy / 333

Introduction

What Is Violence?

Defining violence and then identifying behaviors that fit the definition are difficult matters. Several vignettes are presented below which describe diverse incidents and behaviors. These vignettes underscore the complexity and variety of behaviors that might be classified as violent. When reading the vignettes, consider what characteristics they exhibit that would fall within an acceptable definition of violence.

> Billy knocked over and broke the living room lamp after his mother had warned him not to play there. Billy's mother grabbed him by his arm, turned him around, and spanked him softly.
>
> Gerry had been selling heroin for more than two years. This was the first time he had sold goods to Eddie. The next day the word was on the street. Eddie had died of a heroin overdose.
>
> Donna was walking home from the train stop after work, at about midnight. As she turned the corner onto her street, a young man with a knife approached her from behind. He forced her to walk to a nearby vacant lot where he repeatedly raped her at knifepoint.
>
> Jessie had just left the factory where he worked. On the way to his car, two young men whom he did not recognize approached him. The one holding the knife demanded Jessie's wallet. Jessie refused. The two men ran away.
>
> Donna and Ted had been introduced through mutual friends at their college. This was their first date. After dinner at an expensive restaurant, they returned to Donna's apartment, where they had some drinks. Donna and Ted kissed several times. Then, despite Donna's protests, Ted proceeded to have sexual intercourse with her.
>
> Freddie had suffered through another bad day at the office. When he got home, he fixed himself a drink and sat down in his favorite chair. Freddie's golden retriever, Rolf, came running from the kitchen and jumped onto Freddie, who pushed Rolf away. Rolf jumped back onto Freddie. Freddie threw the glass down, shattering it, smacked Rolf across the nose, and threw him hard across the room into the wooden desk legs.

Officer Canova stopped Amanda after she had run a red light at a busy intersection in her neighborhood. Amanda denied that the light was red. She got out of the car and became verbally abusive. A crowd formed and began siding with Amanda, yelling at and taunting Officer Canova, who then requested backup assistance. The crowd grew larger and nastier, physically attacking Officer Canova just before the backup units arrived.

Ginger dreaded showing her report card to her parents who had excelled at school. She was certain that her parents would yell at her for the average grades, as they had done in the past. Ginger was right. Ginger's mother screamed: "You know that your father and I are Phi Beta Kappas. You're just not trying. How can you do this to us?"

Gus needed the insurance money to rescue his garment business from a second year of sales losses, so he contracted with a professional arsonist to torch his factory. A week later the factory burned to the ground from "accidental" causes.

Ben falls, knocking out a tooth and fracturing his jaw.
Ben knocks out his own tooth and fractures his jaw after banging his head against the wall in a fit of self-directed rage.
Ben's dentist extracts an abscessed tooth and, in the process, fractures Ben's jaw.
Ben is punched in the mouth in a barroom brawl, resulting in a lost tooth and a fractured jaw.

Mike had been out of work for more than a year. His last unemployment check had come months ago. He just could not face his wife and daughter again without a paycheck and a job. Mike walked into the garage, shut the door, blocked off the fresh-air vents, and turned on the car engine.

Pete strongly believed in the right to bear firearms. City Councilwoman Oliver had sponsored for a long time a municipal ordinance to restrict the purchase of handguns. Pete had written her progressively more abusive letters about her stance. In the last letter, Pete threatened ". . . to look her up . . . and show her firsthand why good upstanding people need guns."

Arnie fired two shots at Senator Bromfield, hitting him in the forearm with the first round, missing with the second. He later told the police that "they" controlled the Senator's every move and that the "conspiracy" had to be stopped.

The Chief Executive Officer (CEO) of the Trust-Us Motor Company had just been told by his engineering staff that the standard transmissions in their hot-selling new line-up of cars could lock when in first gear causing potential injuries. The CEO decided that the risk of the transmission locking was too small to warrant the great cost of a car recall. Notifications were not mailed to buyers. The danger was greater than projected. Many serious injuries occurred.

In August 1984, in Bossier City, Louisiana, Edward Byrne Jr., age 24, robbed and murdered Roberta Johnson, repeatedly hitting her over the head with a hammer. He was subsequently found guilty of capital murder and sentenced to death. On June 14, 1988, Edward Byrne Jr. was executed by electric chair by the state of Louisiana, becoming the one-hundredth person executed in the United States since 1976 when capital punishment was reintroduced in the nation.

As the foregoing vignettes suggest, a number of elements need to be considered when formulating a definition of violence: (1) the degree and type of injury; (2) the intent of the participant(s) to apply or to threaten to apply force; (3) the object of the attack (i.e., a person, property, or an animal); (4) the causes of and motivations and justifications for the behavior; (5) the numbers of persons involved in the incident; and (6) whether the harm is the result of behavior that is committed or omitted. In the following discussion, we explore the significance of each of these elements.

A concept is a way of looking at a phenomenon such as violence. Useful concepts characterize the phenomenon's main elements. A suggested definition of **violence**, which incorporates some of the above elements, is *the threat, attempt, or use of physical force by one or more persons that results in physical or nonphysical harm to one or more other persons.*

The use of physical force includes behaviors such as a blow or wound to the body by a fist, blunt object, knife or other sharp instrument, or a firearm. Poison, fire, rope for strangulation, and other related technologies are also mechanisms for the application of physical force. The use of force can result in injuries ranging from minor bruises, punctures, gashes, and lacerations to lethal wounds. Threats of violence can be both face-to-face (e.g., speech or gestures) and indirect (e.g., letter, telephone, other person), expressing the intent to employ physical force against another person.

Threats to apply physical force can result in psychological damage and trauma ranging from minor apprehension and stress to pathologically immobilizing fear and anxiety leading to varying degrees of withdrawal from social relationships. (Of course, psychological trauma and damage can also follow in the aftermath of a forceful assault or attack.)

In addition to psychological harm, nonphysical economic and social losses can occur—for example, the loss of valuables sustained as the result of a completed robbery or the loss of social face that occurs when one is verbally abused in the presence of peers, family members, or fellow workers.

Intent

The definition used here focuses on behaviors (i.e., the use of physical force or the threat of the same) and behavioral outcomes (i.e., physical or nonphysical harm and losses). It does not address whether the behavior or the outcome was intended. A behavior is not violent only if the harm was intended and planned well in advance of or even just prior to the time of its infliction. To cite an example, robbers who murder usually neither intend nor plan to harm their victims fatally. Nevertheless, fatalities may occur when robbery victims aggressively resist armed felons or when robbers unintentionally discharge handguns in the absence of resistance.

Even if one were to subscribe to a definition of violence which includes intent, proving intent presents formidable problems. The criminal law has grappled for some time with the evidentiary substance of this requirement; and it is still somewhat ambiguous. However, we have not omitted the intent criterion from the definition simply because it is often so difficult to establish in practice. Rather we have omitted intent because it distinguishes different kinds of violence from one another rather than being an essential component of the violence itself. Intent partly distinguishes, for example, criminal from noncriminal violence, and nonaccidental (intentional) from accidental (nonintentional) harm.

Criminally violent behavior involves those acts which are in violation of legislatively enacted criminal statutes and which are subject to a punitive legal response by duly authorized governmental agencies.[1] One of several necessary legal elements of criminal behavior is "criminal intent" (*mens rea*), which is considered present in those infractions that are performed intentionally, knowingly, and willingly or that entail recklessness or negligence. The presence of criminal intent differentiates criminally violent behavior from noncriminally violent behavior, not violent behavior from nonviolent behavior. Recall the earlier example of the state execution. Lethal force is intentionally used but not criminally so because the force is legally sanctioned.

Unintentional injuries are not commonly called violent acts. Consider the vignette presented earlier in which the dentist fractures Ben's jaw while extracting a tooth. According to our definition, a violent act has taken place because the dentist used force which resulted in physical injury. However, the absence of intent to use physical force for purposes of inflicting injury usually results in the social designation of the behavior as an "unintentional" or "accidental" injury—one that could not have been avoided through any prudent course of action—rather than as a violent behavior.

The shift in terminology from "violent" behavior to "unintentional" or "accidental" injury certainly represents a consequential shift in social and legal attributions of blame, responsibility, and accountability. However, this social convention notwithstanding, definitional rigor and consistency require that we classify the dentist's behavior as a violent act, albeit one that was not intended to be so. Classifying it thusly avoids confusing violent behavior with associated social attributions and definitions of that behavior.

Objects of Violence

The foregoing definition excludes attacks against physical property or animals. We have restricted the definition to human subjects and targets for both theoretical and practical reasons. Understanding and explaining individual, interpersonal, and collective human violence casts a wide theoretical and substantive net. Focusing on violence by and against humans concentrates theory and research on a substantively self-contained and manageable domain. Expanding the theoretical focus to include violence against animals and property could yield an integrated theory of violence that acknowledges continuities in violence dynamics across varying targets and species. However, this tenable wider focus will not be included in the definition used here.

Attributions for Violent Behavior

The definition leaves unstated the kinds of motivations that violent persons themselves attribute to their behavior or which researchers, legislators, and others attribute to their violent behavior. Attributions for violence are innumerable and may be related to the origins, development, maintenance, and cessation of the behavior. However, behavior is not violent by virtue of the fact that it exhibits a specific motivation. These motivations do play an important role in theoretical explanation and are important with respect to how others (e.g., police, family, neighbors, and public and mental health professionals) will respond. For example, in theory, the absence of criminal intent shields a violent person from criminal liability and prosecution.

A variety of audiences are usually involved in determining whether a behavior is violent and, if this determination is affirmed, in understanding the reasons for the violence. The participants themselves certainly do this. Criminal justice professionals are responsible for making judgments about the legality of, and their official responses to, the behavior. Mental and public health professionals may be required to make clinical judgments and to decide whether to deliver treatment and support services. And scientists seek systematic explanation and understanding. Competing behavioral assessments by these different audiences often arise. The viewpoint that prevails depends upon several factors, including the relative powers and credibilities of these audiences.

Consider the vignette involving Ted and Donna presented earlier. To Ted, the final sexual engagement might be viewed as a natural and nonviolent end to a romantic evening in which the female is expected to "resist" as part of the erotic foreplay script. Ted believed he had simply exerted the "usual" and "acceptable" force that is part of the male's role. However, from Donna's perspective, her protests belied no hidden message of eventual consent.

Characterizing an incident as violent or nonviolent, like the hypothetical one involving Ted and Donna, may not always be straightforward. Whether others will define the incident as violent and, importantly, as criminally violent will depend, for example, upon evidence which established Ted's direct role in the sexual engagement, the degree of his intent to apply force, and the levels of threatened and applied physical force. Friends and family may judge the incident to be violent based on these same criteria, if they have access to this information, but they are also likely to base their judgments on other considerations, such as their personal knowledge of, and their histories of interacting with, the two participants. Has Ted used or been accused of using force in the past? If so, then perhaps this incident establishes Ted's penchant for engaging in sexually violent behavior rather than romantically assertive behavior. Has Donna been involved in similar incidents in which she has neither complained nor considered herself victimized? If so, then perhaps this encounter does not reflect her usual response.

In order to operate scientifically, the research investigator must identify violent acts independently of the subjective viewpoints and attributions of those persons who have some direct or peripheral relationship to the violent actors and the violent incident. Personal history information can be quite useful in understanding the origins of the violence but not in determining whether the incident was violent. For this reason, the attributions made by audiences, although an extremely important issue, are not included in the definition of violence used here.

Unit of Analysis

Violence can be classified as individual (against the self), interpersonal, or collective. Interpersonal and collective violence, the foci of this volume, are often differentiated by their respective numbers of participants; the participants' goals; the character of the norms that govern the interaction; the frequency and duration of interaction among the participants and, consequently, the degree of continuity, permanence, and solidarity of the interaction.

Interpersonal violence involves numerically few people whose forceful exchanges are a function of influences largely limited to that setting and its proximate social surroundings and whose goals are similarly so limited. The social impetus to become violently involved originates, therefore, in a temporal and spatial context that is not far removed from the violent setting itself. Collective violence, on the other hand, involves large numbers of people who are typically influenced by broadly and historically shared group experiences of social structural or political injustices and inequities. Collective violence represents forceful efforts to remove, or otherwise respond to, the sources and consequences of these unacceptable disparities.

The immediate substance of the incident does not differentiate interpersonal from collective violence. Rather the difference is conceptual and explanatory, depending upon the purposes and functions of the violence and its causal dynamics. For example, twenty men using physical force against four men clearly indicates the presence of violence. On the one hand, the violence is interpersonal if it involves participants who orient mainly toward one another for the duration of the confrontation and whose goals are primarily restricted to the interaction itself or directed at proximate social settings. A barroom brawl set off by a rude remark that pits twenty men against four men fits this pattern. On the other hand, the violence is collective if it involves participants who share common and long-standing group experiences, interests, and beliefs that shape the course of the encounter and, furthermore, who are influenced by objectives beyond the physical and social boundaries of the encounter. A confrontation between twenty politically disenfranchised activists and four politically enfranchised opponents fits this pattern.

Acts of Commission or Omission

One final point needs to be addressed. Violent behavior can comprise acts that are either committed or omitted. The application or threatened application of physical force can be accomplished by an overt behavior, which people most commonly associate with violence, or physical force may be applied or threatened by withholding or delaying a behavior. For example, corporate failure to correct product defects might constitute a violent act: bodily injury resulting from the force generated by the defective product is a direct outcome of the corporate decision to refrain from responsible corrective actions.

Conclusion

The working definition presented earlier in this discussion highlights some salient aspects of violence and, in this capacity, functions as a heuristic for violence classification, analysis, and discussion. We expect that theorists and researchers will modify the definition in response to research problems and expanding knowledge.

While there are scholarly discussions over points of definition and typology, there is generally agreement that there is too much violence in America. The selections which follow are intended to widen and deepen our understanding of the causes and correlates of interpersonal and collective violence and, as a byproduct, to enhance our understanding of prudent, feasible, and ethical ways to reduce this violence.

Note

1. Although there is jurisdictional variation in terminology and statutory definition, criminally violent behaviors usually fall under the following headings: homicide, forcible rape and other sexual assaults, robbery, and aggravated and simple assaults. For purposes of compiling national crime statistics, the Federal Bureau of Investigation, under its Uniform Crime Reporting Program, has developed the following definitions of these violent crimes:

   criminal homicide (comprising murder and nonnegligent manslaughter): "the willful (nonnegligent) killing of one human being by another" (U.S. Department of Justice, FBI, *Uniform Crime Reports, 1986* [Washington, DC: U.S. Government Printing Office, 1987] p. 331).
   forcible rape: "the carnal knowledge of a female forcibly and against her will" (p. 331).

   robbery: "the taking or attempting to take something of value from the care, custody, or control of a person or persons by force or threat of force or violence and/or by putting the victim in fear" (p. 331).

   aggravated assault: "an unlawful attack by one person upon another for the purpose of inflicting severe or aggravated bodily injury. The type of assault usually is accompanied by the use of a weapon or by means likely to produce death or great bodily harm" (p. 331).

   other assaults (simple): "assaults and attempted assaults where no weapon was used and which did not result in serious or aggravated injury to the victim" (p. 331).

Part 1

Patterns and Trends in Violence

A central symbol of the American dream, inscribed in the Preamble to the Constitution, has been to "ensure domestic tranquillity." Understood in its literal sense, this tranquility comprises the right and aspiration to civil peace and order. Despite this national right and aspiration, American history is a panoply of interpersonal and collective violence: the national Union was born of revolutionary violence and was later preserved through the fratricide of civil war. The dream of a tranquil Union has had a much darker side.

Historical Patterns of Collective Violence

Richard Maxwell Brown delivers precisely this message of a darker side to our nation in "Historical Patterns of American Violence," underscoring that "violence has accompanied virtually every stage and aspect of our national existence." In gripping narrative style he depicts our national heritage of collective violence, including the rural guerrilla fighting of the revolutionary and civil wars, in the battles against Native Americans, in interfamilial feuding, and interpersonal assaults and murders.

Brown notes that the patterns in American political and collective violence reflect the distinguishing features of the American experience. For instance, political assassination, although it has exacted a heavy toll at the national apex—the presidency—has been mainly absent as an instrument of choice in the political toolbox when compared with other countries. Similarly, other forms of collective violence—including racial, labor, and urban—have not been the preferred and routine means to deal with long-standing social injustices or to settle festering political and social scores, even though each of these forms of violence has periodically exploded on the American scene.

To understand American violence, we must recognize our ambivalent attitudes toward it. Although collective violence is publicly avoided or rejected in the political and civil pronouncements of the nation, Brown notes that such violence has been a central aspect of some of the most significant and productive events in our history. Both those persons who wield and those who aspire to wield democratic power have often employed incendiary words and deeds, destroying the domestic tranquility even as they would preserve it. Violence is then an American norm and behavioral motif.

Historical Patterns of Interpersonal Violence

To complement Brown's discussion of collective violence, Ted Robert Gurr's "Historical Trends in Violent Crime: A Critical Review of the Evidence" is presented. Gurr's panoramic survey examines Western European and American historical records with respect to patterns and trends in homicide, robbery, and assault and places, in historical context, the contemporary experience of increasing levels of interpersonal violence since the mid-1960s. Beginning with medieval and early modern England and other Western European cities and societies, Gurr traces the extent of these interpersonal violent acts through the twentieth century. Some evidence suggests that contemporary levels of serious interpersonal violence in Western society are at a low ebb in comparison to corresponding rates during the medieval period. Violent upswings over the last two decades are merely vertical spikes in the long-term trough. Generally, the overall historical trend has been toward lower levels of violence.

Gurr points to "the civilizing process" as partly responsible for the downward spiral in serious interpersonal violence. Over time, the advancement and subsequent embracement of humanistic values, which originated in the cultural elites, has resulted in widening normative constraints on aggressive and violent conduct in everyday life. Confrontations, that at one time may have resulted in physical injury, have been reduced through socialization processes that promoted a pacifistic ethic. Gurr suggests that the sporadic upsurges in violence can be attributed to the influences of an adolescent and young adult culture that sometimes extols violence, to the socially disruptive early stages of urbanization and industrialization, and to the desensitization to violence that arises from the upheavals of warfare.

To Americans who fear walking today's streets because of violent crime, it may be small comfort to know that recent rising levels of serious interpersonal criminal violence—homicide, rape, robbery, and aggravated assault—are merely minor oscillations in a long-term historical decline in these behaviors in Western and American societies.

The Extent and Character of Violent Crime

Neil Alan Weiner and Marvin E. Wolfgang review "The Extent and Character of Violent Crime in America, 1969 to 1982" by analyzing official statistics compiled by the Federal Bureau of Investigation's *Uniform Crime Reports (UCR)* and victimization statistics published by the U.S. Department of Justice in the National Crime

Survey (NCS). The authors conclude that "on balance . . . violent crime has increased—but less so than indicated by the *UCR* . . ."; and, moreover, "that these rates are disturbingly high and would be viewed as such even without evidence of their increase."

American criminal violence exhibits its unique national character, reflecting the underlying social and cultural roots from which it partly springs. Violent offenders, as well as victims of interpersonal violence, are mainly young disadvantaged males residing in urban areas. The similarities in personal characteristics between these two groups suggest that social forces converge and interact in ways that place the members of some social groups at high risk either to initiate violent acts or to be the target of these acts.

Evidence presented by Weiner and Wolfgang indicates that a small cadre of individuals, the "chronic" violent offenders, is frequently involved in physically explosive exchanges, accounting for a disproportionate number of these incidents. In broader perspective, comparisons of violent interpersonal crime rates in America with those of other nations indicate that "America has experienced levels of criminal violence that either far exceed or are among the highest of nations most similar to our own. . . ." Why this is so is the subject of much speculation.

The Risk of Violent Crime

A special report on "The Risk of Violent Crime," by Patrick A. Langan and Christopher A. Innes for the Bureau of Justice Statistics of the U.S. Department of Justice, documents the annual rates from 1978 to 1982 of interpersonal violent victimizations. During this period, nearly three percent of Americans, aged twelve or over (six million persons) had been victimized at least once by rape, robbery, or aggravated or simple assault. Overall, assaults, particularly simple assaults, dominated the violence risks, followed by aggravated assault, robbery, and rape. The report shows that, although the annual risk of suffering a lethal encounter is modest, lifetime risks can be substantial and, furthermore, are unevenly distributed across America's social and economic structures.

Summary

America the Beautiful is also America the Violent. By documenting clearly and acknowledging widely this ignominious legacy the nation may be propelled to change. Part 1 addresses this first major concern, namely the identification and description of major patterns of interpersonal and collective violence in American society.

Chapter 1

American Violence: An Overview

Historical Patterns of American Violence

Richard Maxwell Brown

Violence has accompanied virtually every stage and aspect of our national existence. Our most heroic episode, the Revolution, was shot through with domestic violence in both its origins and its progress. During the Civil War, when the slave gained freedom and the unity of our country was preserved, internal violence flared behind the lines of the bloodily contending Northern and Southern armies. Nor did the violence pale in the postwar period, which turned out to be one of the most turbulent epochs in American history.

One significant feature of the Revolution is that the example of violent resistance to the mother country, and all the acts of violence associated with that great event, served as a grand model for later violent actions by Americans in behalf of any cause—law and order, for example—deemed good and proper, for a salient fact of American violence is that, time and again, it has been the instrument not merely of the criminal and disorderly but of the most upright and honorable. Thus, in our two great national crises—the Revolution and the Civil War—we called on violence to found and to preserve the nation.

Apart from its role in the formation and preservation of the nation, violence has been a determinant of both the form and the substance of American life. The threat to the structure of society mounted by the criminal and the disorderly has been met energetically by the official and unofficial violence of the forces of law and order. Often perceiving a grave menace to social stability in the unsettled conditions of frontier life and racial, ethnic, urban, and industrial unrest, solid citizens rallied to the cause of community order. They did this indirectly by granting to the police and other duly constituted agents of the community the power to commit violence to preserve order. Not confining themselves to passive approval of police action, these upright citizens revealed their deep commitment to community order by their own violent participation in lynch mobs and vigilante movements and related extralegal bodies. Violence, thus employed, has been socially conservative. Whether employed legally or extralegally, it has been used to support the cohesive, three-tiered structure of the American community with its upper, middle, and lower classes and its underlying social values of law and order and the sanctity of property. . . .

Much American violence has related not only to the structure of the community but to the substance of the American experience—the nature and content of our society. In this connection, violence has characterized the struggle of American groups in conflict from the colonial period to the present. Group hostility has often escalated to the level of violence in white-Indian wars, white-black confrontations, ethnic rivalries, religious vendettas, agrarian uprisings, and the struggles of laborers against industrialists. Here, too, the violence has been tinctured with social conservatism. Established groups have been quick to resort to violence in defense of the status quo they dominate.

In one way or another, much of our nineteenth- and twentieth-century violence has represented the attempt of established Americans to preserve their favored position in the social, economic, and political order. . . . Conversely, the unsympathetic and unyielding stance of established power in the face of rightly aggrieved groups has frequently incited insurgent violence that stretches from the afflicted yeomanry and lower gentry, who enlisted in Bacon's Rebellion in late seventeenth-century Virginia, to the distressed urban black rioters of our own generation.

Our nation was conceived and born in violence—in the violence of the Sons of Liberty and the patriots of the American port cities of the 1760s and 1770s. Such was the Boston Massacre of 1770, in which five defiant Americans were killed by British officers and troops who were goaded by patriotic roughnecks. The whole episode was a natural continuation of nearly a century of organized mob violence in Boston. The same was true of the Boston Tea Party, wherein the ancient, organized South End Mob of Boston was enlisted in the tea-dumping work. . . .

With the decision in 1774 to resist the British by military means, the second round of revolutionary violence began. The main goal of revolutionary violence, in the transitional period from 1774 to 1777, was to intimidate the Tories who lived in fairly large numbers in seaport cities and the hinterland. The countrywide Continental Association of 1774 was drawn up to interrupt all trade between the colonies and the mother country, but a related purpose was to ferret out Tories, expose them to public contumely and intimidation, and bring them to heel or to silence. . . . The old American custom of tarring and feathering was mainly a product of the patriotic campaign to root out Toryism.

Aside from the regular clash of the Continental and British armies, the third and final phase of revolutionary violence was the guerrilla activity all the way from the Hudson to the Savannah. Wherever strong British occupying forces were to be found—as in New York City, Philadelphia, and Charleston—in opposition to an American-dominated hinterland, the result was the polarization of the population and the outbreak of savage guerrilla warfare, desperate hit-and-run forays, and the thrust and counterthrust of pillage and mayhem. . . .

Two things stand out about the Revolution. The first, of course, is that it was successful and immediately became enshrined in our tradition and history. The second is that the meanest and most squalid sort of violence was from the very beginning to the very end put to the service of revolutionary ideals and objectives. The operational philosophy that the end justifies the means became the keynote of revolutionary violence. Thus, given sanctification by the Revolution, Americans have never been loath to employ the most unremitting violence in the interest of any cause deemed a good one.

Violence was interwoven with the creation of the American nation. By the same token, it became the handmaiden of American salvation in the era of Civil War and Reconstruction, for the Civil War was not only a time of pervasive violence in its own right but had an almost incalculable effect in the following decades. The latter part of the nineteenth century was one of the most violent periods of American history—an era of Ku Kluxers, lynch mobs, White Caps, Bald Knobbers, night riders, feudists, and outlaws—and much of that violence is traceable to the Civil War and to the earlier legitimizing effect of the revolutionary war.

The years before the Civil War were years of mounting violence in both North and South. Feeling against the Fugitive Slave Law in the North gave rise to vigilance committees concerned with protecting runaway slaves and to increasingly fervent abolitionism. Below the Mason-Dixon Line, abolitionists had long since ceased to exist in anything save the minds of slaveholders and Southern nationalists, but from this delusion were formed vigilante movements to deal with nonexistent abolitionists. . . . Bleeding Kansas was truly just that as marauding bands of slaveholder and antislaveholder sympathizers surged through the territory. . . .

. . . The struggle between the armies of the North and the South still stands as the most massive military bloodletting in American history, but almost forgotten is the irregular underwar of violence and guerrilla conflict that paralleled military action by the regulars. In numerous localities throughout the North, resistance to the military draft was continuous and violent. The apogee of resistance to the draft occurred in New York City with the massive riots of 1863, when the city suffered through three days of fierce rioting. Related troubles occurred throughout the war years in southern Indiana, southern Illinois, and southern Iowa, where widespread Copperhead feeling caused large-scale disaffection, antidraft riots, and guerrilla fighting between Union soldiers and deserters and Copperhead sympathizers. The guerrilla war along the Kansas-Missouri border has seldom been equaled for unmitigated savagery. . . .

Among [the] legacies of the Civil War was a surge of domestic violence. Racial strife and Ku Klux Klan activity became routine in the old Confederate states. Regulator troubles broke out in central Kentucky and the Blue Grass region. Outlaw and vigilante activity blazed up in Texas, Kansas, and Missouri. As late as the closing years of the century, white capping, bald knobbing, and night riding, while spurred by particular social and economic conditions, remained as legacies of the violent emotions and methods bred by the Civil War. Especially prominent, too, in the violent heritage of the Civil War was the surge of local feuding in southern Appalachia and in Texas during the postwar period. . . .

The evidence is convincing that southern mountain feuding was triggered by animosities generated by the Civil War. The mountains were divided country, where Confederate and Union sympathizers fought in rival armies and slew each other in marauding guerrilla bands. After the war, old hatreds did not die out but, fueled anew by political partisanship and moonshine whiskey in a region bedeviled by isolation, poverty, and minimal education, burned on as never before. The formal law barely operated; its power was manipulated for selfish purposes by close-knit political and family factions. . . .

As in so many other instances of American violence, the Civil War forms the "great divide" in regard to the phenomenon of political assassination. Not one important American assassination occurred before the Civil War (an 1835 attempt on Andrew Jackson's life by a crazed individual failed). The role of the Civil War vis-à-vis political assassination is partly cause and partly coincidence. . . .

. . . [O]ur twentieth-century assassinations clearly spring from the problems of modern America. Even the assassinations of our time refer back, ultimately, to the example of the acts of assassination so prevalent in the post-Civil War era.

The Civil War marked the replacement of the two-man personal duel by assassination as the main mortal hazard to the American politician and statesman. The duel, involving nonpolitical as well as political gentlemen, was common before the Civil War. Most famous of all was Alexander Hamilton's death in a duel with Aaron Burr. . . . Dueling faded after the Civil War, as state antidueling laws began to be obeyed rather than ignored and as leading men came to see no dishonor in rejecting challenges to participate in what public opinion had come to view as an outmoded, barbarous practice.

With the lapse of dueling, political assassination came to the fore. In quantitative terms, assassination has not been conspicuous in the history of American violence, but, at the highest level of our political system, the presidency, it has had a heavy impact. In a hundred-year span (1865-1965) four presidents (Lincoln, Garfield, McKinley, and Kennedy) fell to assassins' bullets, and others were the intended objects of assassination. One of the victims, Lincoln, was the target of an assassination conspiracy. The other three victims—Garfield, McKinley, and Kennedy—were the prey of freelance assassins in varying states of mental instability. . . .

Although the mortality rate of American presidents in the last century has been a high one at the hands of assassins, some comfort can be taken in the fact that assassination has not become a part of the American political system as it has elsewhere in the world, in the Middle East, for example. None of the major political parties have resorted—even indirectly—to assassination at the national level. Notable, also, is the immunity other high political officials—vice-presidents, Supreme Court justices, and cabinet officers—have enjoyed from assassination.

Despite some prominent cases, assassinations at the state and local level have, on the whole, been few and far between with the exceptions of the New Mexico Territory . . . and the South during Reconstruction. . . .

In our own time, two notable political assassination attempts below the presidential level were successfully aimed at Senator Robert F. Kennedy of New York in 1968, and unsuccessfully at Governor George C. Wallace of Alabama in

1972. In the 1960s, three outstanding black leaders—Martin Luther King, Malcolm X, and Medger Evers—perished at the hands of assassins as did the white leader of the American Nazi Party, George Lincoln Rockwell. . . . Much earlier, one of the most famous assassinations in American history took the life of Senator Huey Long of Louisiana at the height of his flourishing national political career on September 8, 1935. . . . Apparently the only place in America where assassination became an integral part of the political system was the New Mexico Territory from the end of the Civil War down to about 1900. . . . Virtually all political factions in New Mexico accepted and used assassination as a way of eliminating troublesome opponents. . . .

II

An examination of American criminal violence reveals four noteworthy facts: (1) Organized interstate (or, earlier, intercolonial) gangs of criminals are an old story, going well back into the eighteenth century. (2) Before the Civil War, the most prevalent type of criminal activity—especially in frontier areas—was horse theft and the counterfeiting of the myriad number of private banknotes then in circulation. (3) After the Civil War, a new era of crime began with the popularization of train robbery by the Reno brothers of Indiana and bank robbery by the James-Younger gang of Missouri. (4) The modern era of big-city organized crime with its police and political connections began to emerge in the early twentieth century.

America has long been ambiguous about crime. Official condemnation of the outlaw has been matched by social adulation. The ambiguity is not restricted to America, for the British historian, E. J. Hobsbawm, has shown the existence in European history of the "social bandit." By social bandit, Hobsbawm means largely what we have come to denote by a "Robin Hood," i.e., an outlaw whom society views as its hero rather than its enemy. . . .

There have indeed been American social bandits. Jesse and Frank James gained a strong popular following in Mid-America after the Civil War. . . . Other social bandits have been Henry Berry Lowry (a hero to his people—the Lumber River Indians of southeast North Carolina—during a period of harassment by the dominant white faction during the Reconstruction era), Billy the Kid (the idol of the poor Mexican herdsmen and villagers of the Southwest), Pretty Boy Floyd (Public Enemy No. 1 of the 1930s, who retained the admiration of the sharecroppers of eastern Oklahoma from which stock he sprang), and John Dillinger (the premier bank robber of the Depression Era). . . . The rural-small-town era of American crime came largely to an end with the demise of John Dillinger, Pretty Boy Floyd, Clyde Barrow and Bonnie Parker, and other "public enemies" of the 1930s. With them the American tradition of the social bandit declined.

While the tradition of the rural American social bandit was waxing and waning, urban crime was increasing in importance. The first urban criminal gangs arose in New York and other cities in the pre-Civil War decades, but these gangs were limited in significance and restricted to such ethnic "slum" neighborhoods as Five Points and the Bowery in New York City. Murder, mayhem, and gang vendettas were a feature of the proliferation of these gangs. Meanwhile, in the early decades of the twentieth century the present pattern of centralized, citywide criminal operations under the control of a single "syndicate" or "organization" began to take shape in New York under Arnold Rothstein. Converging with this trend was, apparently, the Mafia tradition of criminal organization, which Sicilian immigrants seem to have brought into East Coast port cities in the decades around 1900. During the 1920s and 1930s, the two trends merged into the predominant pattern of centralized operations under Mafia control. . . .

In contrast to the relatively impersonal, well-organized criminal gangs and the widely admired exploits of the American social bandits has been a type of personalized violence, historically, that has aroused deep emotions of horror in the populace: freelance multiple murder. . . . It was the summer of 1966 that made Americans wonder whether the freelance multiple murder was becoming the characteristic American crime, for, in the space of a few weeks, two shocking mass murders occurred. First, in Chicago, Richard F. Speck murdered, one by one, eight student nurses. Then, less than a month later, Charles Whitman ascended to the top of the tower of the University of Texas library in Austin and left tower and campus strewn with 13 dead or dying and 31 wounded as a result of his unerring marksmanship. . . .

The threatening presence of the criminal and disorderly in American life has incurred the violent riposte of the forces of law and order, ranging from the police and associated legal bodies to lynch mobs, vigilantes, and related extralegal groups. . . .

Undue violence in the course of enforcing the law has long been a matter of concern. In an earlier generation, the public worried about the employment of the "third degree" to obtain criminal confessions. In our own time, the concern is with "police brutality," often against blacks. The use of violence by police in the pursuit of their regular duties has been related to the large measure of violence associated with the incarceration of prisoners in jails and prisons.

Police brutality, police riots (in which large numbers of police rage out of control in a law-enforcement situation, as happened in Chicago at the 1968 Democratic National Convention), and the violence in penal institutions all illustrate the paradoxical but intimate and all too common connection between lawfulness and lawlessness. Heightening the paradox is the contradictory coupling of lawlessness in behalf of lawfulness to be found, historically, in lynch law and vigilantism.

Lynch law has been defined as "the practice or custom by which persons are punished for real or alleged crimes without due process of law." The first organized movement of lynch law in America occurred in the South Carolina back country in 1767–1769. It appeared again in the Virginia Piedmont near the present city of Lynchburg during the latter years of the Revolution. The Virginia movement was initiated by Colonel Charles Lynch (from whom "lynch law" gained its name) and was employed against Tory miscreants. Well into the nineteenth century, lynch law meant merely the infliction of corporal punishment—usually 39 lashes or more well laid on with hickory withes, whips, or any readily available frontier instrument. By the middle of the nineteenth century, lynch law had come to be synonymous, mainly, with hanging or killing by illegal group action. The term lynch mob refers to an organized, spontaneous, ephemeral mob that comes together briefly to do its work and then breaks up. The more regular vigilante (or regulator) movements engaged in a systematic usurpation of the functions of law and order. . . .

. . . In the post[-Civil War] period (down to the first World War), lynch-mob violence was employed frequently in all sections of the country and against whites as well as against blacks, but in this period it was preeminently directed against the Southern black. From 1882 to 1903 the staggering total of 1,985 blacks were killed by Southern lynch mobs. . . .

Although predominant in the South, lynch-mob violence was far from being restricted to that section. In the West, the ephemeral "necktie party" was often foregathered for the summary disposal of thief, rapist, rustler, murderer, or all-around desperado. Frenzied mobs also worked their will in the North and East, where (as in the West) villainous white men were the usual victims.

The phenomenon of vigilantism appears to be native to America. . . . Vigilantism arose in response to a typical American problem: the absence of effective law and order in a frontier region. . . .

The first phase of American vigilantism occurred mainly before the Civil War and dealt largely with the threat of frontier horse thieves and counterfeiters. Virtually every state or territory west of the Appalachians possessed well-organized, relentless vigilante movements. We have tended to think of the vigilante movement as being typical of the Western plains and mountains, but, in actuality, there was much vigilantism east of the Missouri and Mississippi rivers. The main thrust of vigilantism was to reestablish in each newly settled frontier area the community structure of the old settled areas along with the values of the sanctity of property and law and order. Vigilante movements were characteristically in the control of the frontier elite and represented the elite's social values and preferences. . . .

Although the typical vigilante movements were dominated by social conservatives who desired to establish order and stability in newly settled areas, there were disconcertingly numerous departures from the norm. Many vigilante movements led not to order but to increasing disorder and anarchy. . . . Frequently the strife between vigilantes and their opponents (exacerbated by individual, family, and political hatreds) became so bitter and untrammeled that order could be restored only by the governor calling out the militia. . . .

The elite nature of nineteenth-century vigilante leadership is revealed by the prominent men who figured in vigilante movements; they included U.S. senators and congressmen, governors, lawyers, and capitalists. Even presidents of the United States were attracted to vigilantism. President Andrew Jackson once approved the resort of Iowa pioneers to vigilante methods pending the clarification of their territorial status. As a young cattle rancher in North Dakota, Theodore Roosevelt begged to be admitted to a vigilante band that was being formed to deal with rustlers and horse thieves. . . .

America changed from the basically rural nation it had been in the antebellum era to an urban, industrial nation after the Civil War. The institution of vigilantism changed to match the altering character of the nation. From a generally narrow concern with the classic frontier problems of horse thieves and counterfeiters, vigilantism broadened its scope to include a variety of targets connected with the tensions of the new America: Catholics, Jews, blacks, immigrants, laboring men and labor leaders, political radicals, advocates of civil liberties, and nonconformists in general. . . .

III

Unquestionably the longest and most remorseless war in American history was the one between whites and Indians that began in tidewater Virginia in 1607 and continued, with intermittent truces, for nearly 300 years down to the final event, the massacre of the Sioux by U.S. troops at Wounded Knee, South Dakota, in 1890. Nor has white-Indian conflict disappeared. Such conflict is ordinarily nonviolent, but that was not the case in early 1973 when a violent confrontation between militant members of the American Indian Movement (AIM) and white federal agents, which took place, again, at Wounded Knee, led to fatalities.

Bitter, implacable white-Indian hostility was by no means inevitable. The small Indian population that existed in the continental United States allowed plenty of room for white settlement. The economic resources of the white settlers were such that the Indians could have been easily and fairly reimbursed for the land needed for occupation by the whites. In fact, a model of peaceful white-Indian relations was developed in seventeenth-century New England by John Eliot, Roger Williams, and other Puritan statesmen. The same was true in eighteenth-century Pennsylvania. . . . Racial prejudice and greed in the mass of New England whites finally reaped the whirlwind in King Philip's War of 1675–1676, which shattered the peaceful New England model. . . .

. . . Indian wars proliferated during the seventeenth and eighteenth centuries, nor did the pace of the conflict slacken in the nineteenth century. It is possible that no other factor has exercised a more brutalizing influence on the American character than the Indian wars. The struggles with the Indians have sometimes been represented as being "just" wars in the interest of promoting superior Western civilization at the expense of the crude stone-age culture of the Indians. The recent ethnohistorical approach to the interpretation of white-Indian relations has given us a more balanced understanding of the relative merits of white and Indian civilizations. The norms of Indian warfare were, however, more barbaric than those of early modern Western Europe. Among the Indians of eastern America, torture was an accepted and customary part of war-making. In their violent encounters with Indians, the white settlers adopted the cruel practices of Indian conflict. Scalping had not been prevalent in Europe since the Dark Ages, but in the new world white men—responding to the Indians' widely (but not universally) practiced habit of scalping—reverted to this savage form of warfare. Down to the battle at Wounded Knee, lifting the hair of an Indian opponent was the usual tactic among experienced white fighters. Broken treaties, unkept promises, and the slaughter of defenseless women and children all, along with brutal warfare, continued to characterize the white American's dealings with the Indian. The effect on our national character has not been a healthy one; it has done much to further our proclivity to violence.

In the realm of intergroup conflict, racial violence between whites and blacks, extending far back into the eighteenth century, is unequaled in persistence as a factor in the history of American violence. The first slave uprising occurred in New York City in 1712 and was put down with great ruthlessness. In 1739, there was the Stono Rebellion in South Carolina, and, in 1741, New York City was again wracked with fears (apparently justified) of a slave conspiracy. The result was that New York white men went on a hysterical rampage in which scores of blacks were burned, hanged, or expelled. . . . The rebellion of Nat Turner, although a failure, is better known than the single successful instance of large-scale violent resistance to slavery by American blacks: the case of the Florida Maroons, who, in coalition with the Seminole Indians, successfully fought down to 1838 to maintain their status as freed men or escapees from white servitude. . . .

With the end of slavery and its conjoined slave patrols and black codes, the white people of the South developed a special organization for dealing with the blacks: the Ku Klux Klan. The latter has been one of the most consistent features in the last 100 years of American violence. There have been three Ku Klux Klans: the first Ku Klux Klan of Reconstruction times, the second Ku Klux Klan of the 1920s, and the third, current, Ku Klux Klan of the 1950s to 1970s. The first Ku Klux Klan was employed to intimidate the Radical Republicans of the Reconstruction Era and, by violence and threats, to force the freedman to accept the renewed rule of Southern whites. The second Ku Klux Klan differed significantly from both its predecessor and successor. Although the second Ku Klux Klan was founded in Atlanta in 1915, its greatest growth and strength actually took place beyond the borders of the old Confederacy. During the early 1920s it became a truly national organization. . . . The second Ku Klux Klan surely belongs to the violent history of America, but, unlike either the first or the third Klans, blacks were only a secondary target for it. Although denunciation of Catholics and Jews ranked one-two in the rhetoric of the second Klan, recent students of the movement have shown that Klan violence—whippings, torture, and murder—were directed less against Catholics, Jews, and blacks than against ne'er-do-wells and the allegedly immoral of the very same background as the Klansmen: white, Anglo-Saxon Protestant. . . . The [third] Ku Klux Klan resurgence . . . has been largely restricted to the South; it is only too well known for acts of violence against the civil rights movement and against desegregation.

Paralleling the Ku Klux Klan has been a host of other movements of racial, ethnic, and religious malice. Before the Civil War, the Northeastern United States was marked by convent burnings and anti-Catholic riots. This "Protestant Crusade" eventually bred the political Know Nothing movement. Anti-Chinese agitation that often burst into violence became a familiar feature in California and the West as the nineteenth century wore on. In 1891, eleven Italian immigrants were the victims of a murderous mob in New Orleans. The fear and loathing of Catholics (especially Irish and Italians), which often took a violent form, was organized in the nonviolent but bigoted American Protective Association (A.P.A.) of 1887. Labor clashes of the late nineteenth century and early twentieth century were in reality, often, ethnic clashes with native, old stock Americans ranged on one side as owners, foremen, and skilled workers against growing numbers of unskilled immigrants—chiefly Jews, Slavs, Italians, and others from southern and eastern Europe.

The arena of violent racial, ethnic, religious, political, economic, and industrial group conflict in American history has frequently been the urban riot. The situation seemed at its worst in the late 1960s when the country was widely believed to be on the verge of some sort of urban apocalypse, but the fact is that our cities have been in a state of more or less continuous turmoil since the colonial period. . . .

Economic and political conditions brought more urban turmoil in the postrevolutionary period of the 1780s and 1790s, and, by the midnineteenth century, with industrial and urban expansion occurring by leaps and bounds, the cities of America found themselves in the grips of a new era of violence. . . . Ulcerating slums . . . and severe ethnic and religious strife stemming from the confrontation between burgeoning immigrant groups and the native American element made the 1830s, 1840s, and 1850s decades of sustained urban rioting, particularly in the great cities of the Northeast. It may have been the era of the greatest urban violence America has ever experienced. During this period, at least 35 major riots occurred in Baltimore, Philadelphia, New York, and Boston. . . . Among the most important types of riots were labor riots, election riots, antiabolitionist riots, antiblack riots, anti-Catholic riots, and riots of various sorts involving the turbulent volunteer firemen's units. . . .

The prototype of the antiblack urban race riot was established in the North as far back as the 1820s and 1830s, and after the Civil War it was replicated in such major Southern outbreaks as the riots in Wilmington, North Carolina (1898) and Atlanta (1906). These earliest riots were, in effect pogroms—one-sided attacks on urban blacks by whites. By the era of the First World War, however, the pogrom-type race riot was eclipsed by the appearance of the "communal" riot, in which, with whites still usually dominant, mobs of counterrioting blacks and whites raged through city streets. Among a number of communal riots from 1917 to the 1940s, the greatest were those of Washington, D.C. and Chicago in 1919 and Detroit in 1943. In the 1960s, two long-term trends combined to reverse the typical pattern of white primacy in rioting: one was a demographic revolution, in which, during the course of the twentieth century, American blacks made the transition from being a predominantly rural, Southern people to a predominantly urban people heavily concentrated in black ghetto areas of Northern and Western cities; the other was a comparable revolution in black consciousness, resulting in a mood of black pride and aggressiveness that became stunningly evident in Los Angeles's Watts riot of 1964, the first of the black superriots of the 1960s.

Violent America group conflict has by no means been restricted to the urban sector with its manifold racial, ethnic, and economic antagonisms. . . . The tree of liberty in America has been nurtured by a series of movements in behalf of the ever-suffering farmer or yeoman. Often these movements—generally considered to be liberal in their political character—have been formed for the purpose of redressing the economic grievances of the farmer; at times they have been land-reform movements. . . .

The insurgent farmer movements have . . . formed one of the longest and most enduring chronicles in the history of American reform but one that has been blighted again and again with violence. Nathaniel Bacon's movement became a full-fledged rebellion that resulted in the burning of Jamestown. The New Jersey land rioters used violence to press their claims against Jersey land companies. The New York antirent movement frequently used force against dominant landlords. The North Carolina Regulators rioted against the courthouse rings that ground them down under the burden of heavy taxes and rapacious fees. The Paxton Boys of Pennsylvania followed their massacre of Indians with a march on Philadelphia. The followers of Daniel Shays in Massachusetts broke up court sessions in order to forestall land foreclosures. The farmers of Pennsylvania rebelled against taxes on liquor and land in the Whiskey and Fries uprisings. The Western Claim Clubs (which, paradoxically, were sometimes dominated by land speculators pursuing their own interests) used intimidation to protect "squatters' rights." The land reform movement in California spawned a night-rider league in Tulare County (1878–1880) to resist railroad land agents. . . . The New Mexican White Caps fought the land-enclosure movement with a reign of terror. The Working Class Union of Oklahoma fomented the Green Corn Rebellion. . . . The Farmers' Holiday Association dumped milk cans, blocked roads, and roughed up opponents. Farmer grievances were serious, and, repeatedly, farmers used a higher law—the need to right insufferable wrongs, the very justification of the American Revolution—to justify the use of violence in uprising after uprising.

The labor movement in American history—like the farmers'—has been bathed in the same sort of glory that anointed the agrarian uprisings. Most would agree that by raising the health and living standards of the working man the American labor movement has been a significant factor in advancing the social well-being of the nation. But the labor movement reveals the same mixture of glorious ends with inglorious means—violence—that has characterized the agrarian movement.

IV

By now it is evident that, historically, American life has been characterized by continuous and often intense violence. It is not merely that violence has accompanied such negative aspects of our history as criminal activity, political assassination, and racial conflict. On the contrary, violence has formed a seamless web with some of the most positive events of U.S. history: independence (revolutionary violence), the freeing of the slaves and the preservation of the Union (Civil War violence), the occupation of the land (Indian wars), the stabilization of frontier society (vigilante violence), the elevation of the farmer and the laborer (agrarian and labor violence), and the preservation of law and order (police violence). The patriot, the humanitarian, the nationalist, the pioneer, the landholder, the farmer, and the laborer (and the capitalist) have used violence as a means to a higher end.

All too often unyielding and unsympathetic, established political and economic power has incited violence by its refusal to heed and appease just grievances. . . . The possessors of power and wealth have often been arrogant in their refusal to share their advantages until it has been too late. Arrogance is indeed a quality that comes to unchecked power more readily than sympathy and forbearance.

By the same token, one can argue that the aggrieved in American history have been too quick to revolt, too hastily violent. We have resorted so often to violence that we have long since become a trigger-happy people. Violence is clearly rejected by us as a part of the American value system, but so great has been our involvement with violence over the long sweep of our history that violence has truly become part of our unacknowledged (or underground) value structure. . . .

Historical Trends in Violent Crime: A Critical Review of the Evidence

Ted Robert Gurr

. . . It is generally accepted by criminologists and other social scientists that the real incidence of serious crimes against persons and property increased substantially in the United States and most Western European societies during the 1960s and 1970s, though skepticism remains about the accuracy of official data on the precise magnitude of change. What is less widely recognized is a growing body of historical evidence, some of it examined by Lane . . . (1980), that the incidence of serious crime has traced an irregular downward trend for a much longer period of time, in some places for a century or more. When the historical and contemporary evidence are joined together, they depict a distended U-shaped curve.

The thesis that rates of serious crime in Western societies have traced a reversing U-shaped curve is a simplification of a much more complex reality. It characterizes some but not all offenses. The evidence for it is substantial in some societies, especially the English-speaking and Scandinavian countries, but either lacking or contradictory in others. There are severe problems in the interpretation of official data on crime compiled in different eras. Even where a reversing trend is clearly present, as in England and Wales during the past 150 years, there are substantial short-term deviations around it. For these and other reasons, the

U-shaped curve is used here as a hypothesis, not received wisdom, against which to evaluate diverse evidence on trends in violent crime. . . .

This essay is limited mainly to evidence about trends in homicide and assault, with occasional reference to robbery. . . . From the perspective of the social and cultural historian, the distribution of these offenses across time, space, and social groups is of particular interest because of what it tells us about interpersonal aggression and the complex of social attitudes toward it. . . .

. . . I suggest these general guidelines for interpreting long-term trends in violent crime, with special reference to the putative period of decline that ended in the mid-twentieth century. (1) The declining historical trend in *homicide* probably is understated somewhat, because of closer official attention and a stretching of definitions to include more cases of manslaughter. Since the establishment of modern, centralized systems for recording crime and death data, official homicide data are the most accurate of all data on interpersonal violence. . . . (2) Data on robberies known are second, albeit a rather distant second, to homicide data in reliability. . . . (3) Long-run trends which show increases in assault are suspect because of increasing concern about these offenses. Long-run declining trends in assault are convincing if based on "offenses known," or on trial data for all courts, higher and lower. . . .

. . . [W]e can be more confident about the underlying trends in interpersonal violence to the extent that there is converging evidence from different studies and different indicators. Conclusions about the directions and magnitude of change in violence are convincing to the extent that they are supported by any of the following kinds of parallel evidence: (1) Similarity in trends of indicators of an offense obtained from two different sources, for example police and coroner's records of homicides. (2) Similarity in trends of indicators of an offense registered at different stages in the criminal justice process, for example offenses known versus committals to trial or convictions. (3) Similarity in trends of indicators of an offense from different cities or regions. (4) Similarity in trends of different offenses, for example homicide and assault, or assault and robbery. . . .

The Long-Term Trend in English Homicide

. . . The general trend which emerges from the evidence is . . . unmistakable: rates of violent crime were far higher in medieval and early modern England than in the twentieth century—probably ten and possibly twenty or more times higher. The estimates . . . are displayed graphically in figure 1-1. Each estimate for a county and city prior to 1800 is represented by a dot, even though the estimate may represent a period of several decades. A speculative trend curve is fitted to these data points. Elizabethan Essex and the period 1820 to 1975 are represented by five-year moving averages.

There are two problematic features of the trends traced in figure 1-1. One is the extraordinarily high incidence of homicide in fourteenth-century cities by comparison with the preceding century. If the handful of estimates are not grossly in error, there evidently was a tremendous upsurge in violent crime in England (or at least its cities) during the early fourteenth century. Hanawalt suggests as

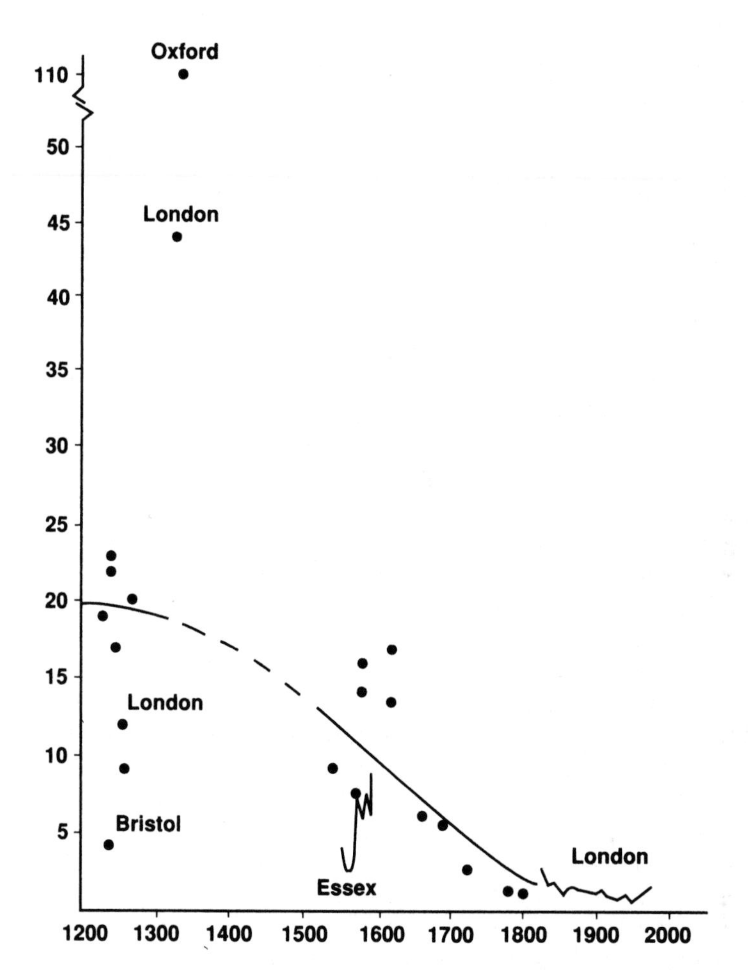

Fig. 1-1.
Indicators of homicides per 100,000 population in England, thirteenth to twentieth centuries. Each dot represents the estimated homicide rate for a city or county for periods ranging from several years to several decades. The sources of the data are referred to in the text, with two exceptions. The estimate of 20 for ca. 1270 is the mean of high and low figures for Bedfordshire, as calculated by Hair (1971, p. 18) using minimum and maximum estimates of population. The estimate for ca. 1550 is the mean of high and low figures for Nottinghamshire for 1530–58, also calculated by Hair (1971, p. 17). Hair's estimates of London homicide rates for the seventeenth through nineteenth centuries, based on the London bills of mortality, are not shown because the source is highly suspect.

much [1979, p. 260]. In general the fourteenth century was more disorderly than the thirteenth. The Hundred Years War, which began in 1337, and the Black Death, which killed perhaps one-third of the population, precipitated social and economic crises of major proportions. . . .

The evidence thus clearly favors the possibility . . . that the nineteenth- and early twentieth-century decline in violent crime in England was the latest phase in a substantially longer trend. The seemingly high rates of homicide in early nineteenth- and late twentieth-century London were actually very low when contrasted with the more distant historical experience. The possibility of cyclical or wavelike movements away from the underlying trend is not ruled out, however. There probably was a surge in violent crime in fourteenth-century England. Violent crime also evidently increased in Elizabethan times. More certainly, Beattie (1974) offers evidence of several such waves during the period from 1660 to 1802, and it is likely that violent crime rates were unusually high in early nineteenth-century London.

Most of the evidence surveyed here relates only to homicide. Did assaults also decline over the long run? For the medieval and early modern period we simply cannot say because the court data on assaults are either nonexistent or unreliable. In Elizabethan times they appear in court records less often than homicide, but a century later assaults were much more numerous. Since most homicides of this period resulted from violent altercations, the real incidence of assault was presumably much higher. The infrequency of assaults in early court records almost surely reflects the fact that it ordinarily was not thought serious enough to warrant indictments unless someone died as a consequence of the assault. The higher assault rates of the period studied by Beattie, from 1660 to 1802, very likely reflect increased concern by victims and courts, not a real long-term increase in assault. During the last 150 years, however, trends and peaks in official data on assault in London and all of England have closely paralleled those for murder and manslaughter. Thus for this period we can be reasonably confident that the incidence of assault, like murder, declined for most of the period but increased after ca. 1950.

TRENDS IN VIOLENT CRIME IN THE UNITED STATES

The Long-Term Trend in American Homicide

The composite picture of violent crime in nineteenth-century America is a stable or declining trend with a pronounced upward swing which began shortly before the Civil War and persisted into the 1870s. The evidence is summarized . . . in figure 1-2. It is limited to cities, mainly on the eastern seaboard and in the Midwest, which may not be representative of what was happening in towns or on the frontier. The trends in violent crime before the Civil War are especially problematic because only Philadelphia and Boston have been studied prior to 1850. After 1900 there was a sustained rise in violent crime to the early 1930s, a thirty-year subsidence, and another increase since 1965. Current national homicide rates are higher than any recorded previously, though only slightly greater than those of the 1920s. They are also greater than any indicated by the fragmentary nineteenth-century evidence.

There is also evidence, summarized . . . in figure 1-3, that the two waves in twentieth-century homicide rates may be attributable mainly to increases in killings among blacks. White homicide rates have varied much less. The trends in black homicide arrests in Washington, D.C., are especially suggestive in this regard. . . .

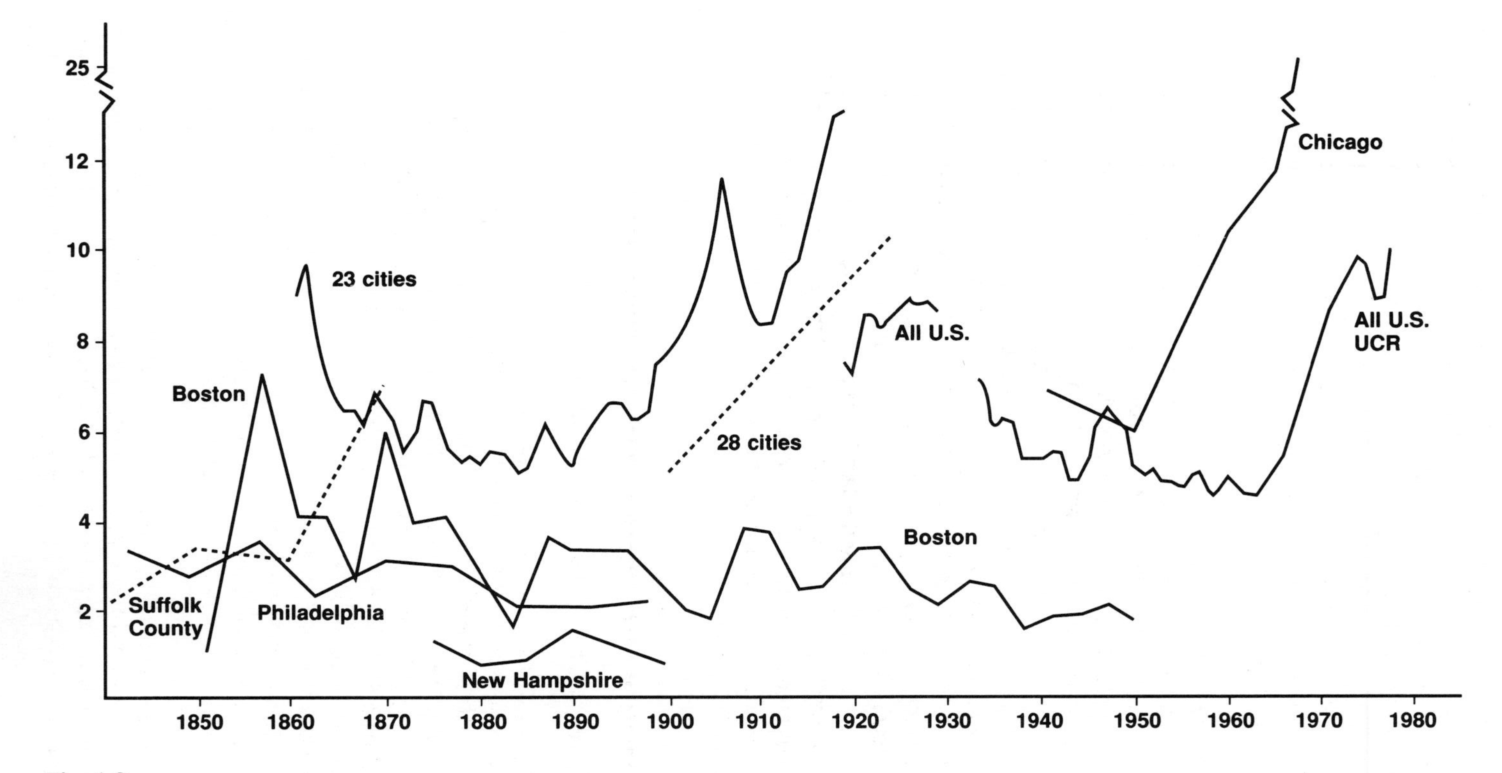

Fig. 1-2.
Indicators of homicides per 100,000 population in the United States, 1840–1980. *Types of data:* indictments: Suffolk County, Philadelphia, New Hampshire; arrests: Boston, 23 cities; homicide registrations: 28 cities, all U.S. 1919–29; offenses known: all U.S. 1933–77, Chicago 1940–75.
Sources: [Block 1977, Brearley 1932, Ferdinand 1967, Hindus 1980, Hoffman 1925, Lane 1979, Monkkonen 1981, and Nutt 1905.]

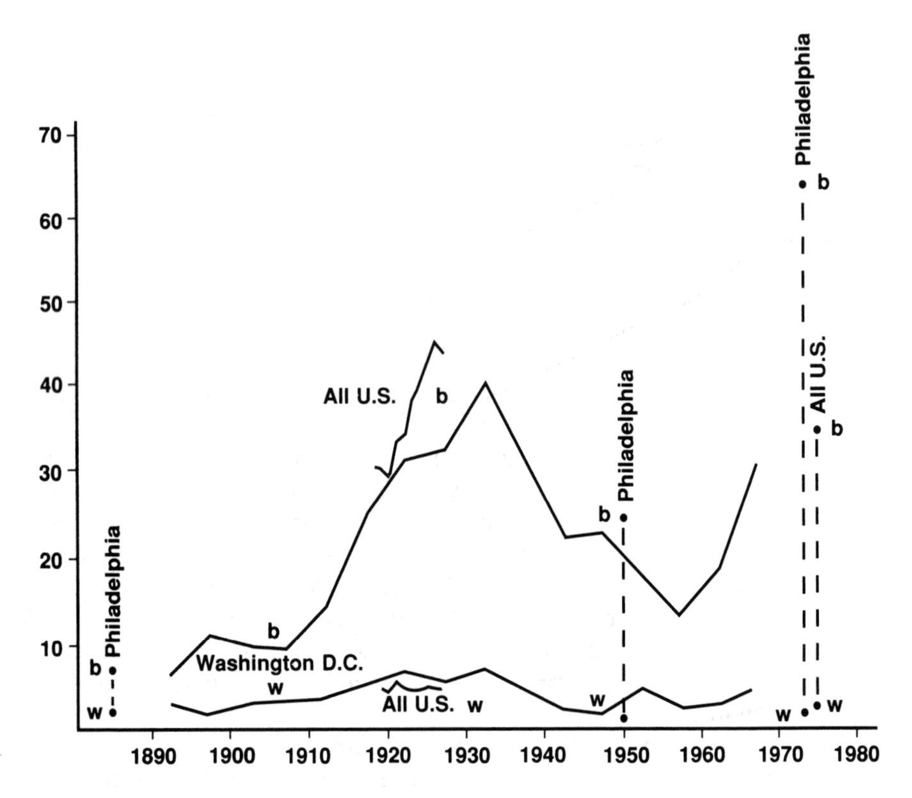

Fig. 1-3.
Differences in homicides per 100,000 by race in the United States, nineteenth century to 1980. *Types and sources of data:* Philadelphia: race of victims in homicide indictments in 1838–1901 (mean), 1948–52, and 1972–74 (Lane 1979); Washington, D.C.: arrests for homicide by race (Count–van Manen 1977); all U.S., 1918–27: homicide mortality rates by race (Brearley 1932); all U.S., 1976: calculated by the author from *UCR* data on arrests for murder and nonnegligent manslaughter.

In conclusion, we may ask to what extent the American evidence is consistent with the reversing U-shaped curve proposed at the outset of this essay. The dominant feature of crime trends in the United States is the occurrence of three pronounced upsurges of interpersonal violence which began roughly fifty years apart: ca. 1860, 1900, and 1960. These waves or cycles are of such amplitude that we cannot say conclusively whether the cycles are superimposed on a longer-run decline. To the extent that North America from settlement to industrialization was an extension of British culture and society, I suspect that the underlying trend was downward. At least it was for Anglo-Americans. But as Lane points out (personal communication), non-English immigrants have unquestionably added to the violence of American cities: the Irish, especially from the 1840s through the 1860s; possibly the Italians, in the early twentieth century; and in-migrating blacks throughout. In culturally heterogenous societies the aggregate trends and cycles of interpersonal violence are instructive only about how disorderly society is, not about the social behavior of its constituent groups. . . .

SOME OBSERVATIONS

How well does the U-shaped curve of declining, then rising violent crime fit the evidence reviewed here? The English evidence on homicide covers the longest timespan and is the most convincing in documenting a sustained decline of substantial magnitude. By the same token it makes the post-1960 upturn appear to be a minor perturbation, proportionally no greater than upward swings in homicide rates in Elizabethan times and during the Napoleonic wars—swings which proved to be temporary. In the United States the occurrence of three great surges in violent crime, beginning ca. 1850, 1900, and 1960, makes it impossible to say whether these increases are superimposed on a long-term decline. My reading of the evidence is that the long-term trend in homicide rates among whites has been generally downward until recently, whereas homicide rates among blacks not only have been higher and more variable but have moved generally upward since the beginning of the twentieth century, perhaps earlier. Declines in homicidal violence also are established for nineteenth-century Stockholm, New South Wales, France, and—beginning late in the century—Germany. In general we have not seen any evidence from any country or jurisdiction that there was a sustained increase in homicides during the nineteenth century—with the important codicil that most of the time-series studies span only the second half of the century. An increase in homicide rates since the 1960s is also a common though not universal phenomenon in Western societies. . . .

The evidence on assault and robbery is more limited but in general parallels the trends in homicide. That is strikingly evident in countries which experienced the post-1960 increase in crime: robbery and assault rates usually increased much more than homicide. In the nineteenth century, however, assault rates moved contrary to homicides in France, Germany, and some American jurisdictions. There is reason to attribute this to increased official attention to minor offenses, not to real and sustained increases in assault.

The discussion of trend evidence has touched on a number of explanations for trends and variations around them. There are two separate questions for which explanation is needed. One is, What social dynamics underlie the long-term decline in violent crime? The other is, What accounts for the big deviations of crime above this trend, especially those sustained upwellings of violence that persist for ten or twenty or more years before subsiding again? I think that there is a simple and singular answer to the first question, but multiple and complex answers to the second. I also think that no special, *sui generis* explanation is needed for the late increase in violent crime. Its explanation should follow from an understanding of the dynamics of the long-term decline and of the deviations from it. In other words I propose to regard the upturn of the U-shaped curve as simply the latest, and best-documented, deviation from the underlying trend.

A plausible explanation for the long-term decline in interpersonal violence is what Norbert Elias calls "the civilizing process" (1978) and all that it implies about the restraint of aggressive impulses and the acceptance of humanistic values. By their own accounts, medieval Europeans were easily angered to the point of violence and enmeshed in a culture which accepted, even glorified, many forms of brutality and aggressive behavior (see Given 1977, chap. 1 for a summary; also Elias 1978, pp. 191–205). The progress of Western civilization has been marked by increasing internal and external controls on the show of violence. . . . The process is in essence a cultural one and like most cultural change had its origins in the changing values of social and intellectual elites. . . .

The cultural process of sensitization to violence, to use Soman's phrase (1980, pp. 20–23), has not been uniform. It took root first among the urban upper and middle classes and only gradually and selectively was promulgated among rural people and the lower classes. It has been suggested, for example, that one significant social function of the new nineteenth-century police forces was to serve as missionaries of upper and middle class values to the theretofore dangerous lower classes (see for example Silver 1967 and Monkkonen 1975). Be that as it may, the thesis that sensitization to violence spread from the social center to the periphery and from upper to lower classes is intrinsically plausible as an explanation of some basic features of nineteenth-century and contemporary criminality. Interpersonal violence historically may have been higher in rural than urban areas—the evidence is mixed—because of the persistence there of traditional patterns of interpersonal behavior. It tended to increase in cities during the early stages of urbanization and industrialization because new immigrants from the countryside, or from overseas, only gradually assimilated the lifeways of the city. Violence declined overall during the nineteenth century and the first half of the twentieth because Western societies became increasingly urban and formal education became universal. The further down the class and status ladder, past and present, the more common is interpersonal violence, because the lower classes did not assimilate and still have not wholly assimilated the aggression-inhibiting values of the middle and upper classes. . . .

There is one other group that may become *de*sensitized to violence: youth. The historical process of sensitization to violence must be replicated in the socialization of each new generation of children in each Western society. To the extent that socialization fails, or is incomplete because it is not reinforced by other social institutions, youth are susceptible to other kinds of values, including those which celebrate violence. . . .

The long-run downslope of interpersonal violence is irregular and some of the irregularities take the form of sharp and sustained increases. . . . [S]tudies of France and Germany [indicate] that violent crime tends to rise in the early stages of industrialization and urbanization, though there is little evidence that the pace of urban growth in general has affected rates of violent crime. Modernization may have been one of the sources of high rates of violent crime in early nineteenth-century England and in the United States in the 1860s and 1870s. But urbanization and industrialization usually are gradual processes, not likely of themselves to create a single tidal wave of disorder except in regions and cities experiencing very rapid change.

The connection between warfare and waves of violent crime is more precise. In fact, war is the single most obvious correlate of the great historical waves of violent crime in England and the United States. Civil and foreign war contributed to the crime peak of the 1340s (Hanawalt 1979, pp. 228–39). . . . The upsurge of crime at the onset of the nineteenth century began while Britain was enmeshed in the Napoleonic wars, from 1793 to 1815, and continued through the severe economic depression which followed their end. In the United States the peak of urban crime in the 1860s and 1870s coincides with the social and political upheavals of the Civil War. . . . The second high wave of violent American crime crested during the decade after World War I. The third began near the onset of the Vietnam war. . . .

War may lead to increased violent crime for a number of reasons, reviewed and tested by Archer and Gartner (1976). I opt for the interpretation, consistent with their evidence, that it does so mainly because war legitimizes violence. It does so directly for young men who become habituated to violence in military service; it does so indirectly for others who find in the patriotic gore of wartime a license to act out their own feelings of anger. . . . [I]f the civilizing process has been accompanied by sensitization to violence, then war, including internal war, temporarily desensitizes people to violence. If there is such an effect it is probably greatest among youth who are at the most impressionable age during wartime. . . .

Another basic factor that influences the extent of personal crime is the size of the youthful population. If their relative numbers are high in a particular city or era, its crime rates are likely to be higher than in times and places where the population is older. . . .

The strands of this speculative discussion can be brought together by concluding that each great upsurge of violent crime in the histories of the societies under study has been caused by a distinctive combination of altered social forces. Some crime waves have followed from fundamental social dislocation, as a result of which significant segments of a population have been separated from the civilizing institutions which instill and reinforce the basic Western injunctions against interpersonal violence. They may be migrants, demobilized veterans, a growing population of disillusioned young people for whom there is no social or economic niche, or badly educated young black men locked in the decaying ghettoes of an affluent society. The most devastating episodes of public disorder, however, seem to occur when social dislocation coincides with changes in values which legitimate violence that was once thought to be illegitimate. Historically, wars seem to have had this effect. There is also the possibility that other factors, such as the content of popular culture or the values articulated in segmented groups, may have the same consequences. . . .

REFERENCES

Archer, Dane, and Rosemary Gartner. 1976. "Violent Acts and Violent Times: A Comparative Approach to Postwar Homicide Rates," *American Sociological Review* 41:937–63.

Beattie, J. M. 1974. "The Pattern of Crime in England, 1660–1800," *Past & Present* 62 (February): 47–95.

Block, Richard. 1977. *Violent Crime: Environment, Interaction, and Death.* Lexington, Mass.: Lexington Books.

Brearley, H. C. 1932. *Homicide in the United States.* Chapel Hill: University of North Carolina Press.
Elias, Norbert. 1978. *The Civilizing Process: The History of Manners.* New York: Urizen. (Originally published 1939.)
Ferdinand, Theodore N. 1967. "The Criminal Patterns of Boston since 1869," *American Journal of Sociology* 73:688–98.
Given, James Buchanan. 1977. *Society and Homicide in Thirteenth-Century England.* Stanford: Stanford University Press.
Hair, P. E. H. 1971. "Deaths from Violence in Britain: A Tentative Secular Survey," *Population Studies* 25:5–24.
Hanawalt, Barbara A. 1979. *Crime and Conflict in English Communities, 1300–1348.* Cambridge, Mass.: Harvard University Press.
Hindus, Michael Stephen. 1980. *Prison and Plantation: Crime, Justice, and Authority in Massachusetts and South Carolina, 1767–1878.* Chapel Hill: University of North Carolina Press.
Hoffman, F. L. 1925. *The Homicide Problem.* Newark: Prudential Press.
Lane, Roger. 1979. *Violent Death in the City: Suicide, Accident, and Murder in Nineteenth-Century Philadelphia.* Cambridge, Mass.: Harvard University Press.
———. 1980. "Urban Police and Crime in Nineteenth-Century America," *Crime and Justice* 2:1–44.
Monkkonen, Eric. 1975. *The Dangerous Class: Crime and Poverty in Columbus, Ohio, 1860–1885.* Cambridge, Mass.: Harvard University Press.
———. 1981. *Police in Urban America, 1860–1920.* New York: Cambridge University Press.
Nutt, Harry G. 1905. "Homicide in New Hampshire," *Journal of the American Statistical Association* 9:220–30.
Silver, Allan. 1967. "The Demand for Order in Civil Society: A Review of Some Themes in the History of Urban Crime, Police, and Riot." In *The Police: Six Sociological Essays*, ed. David J. Bordua. New York: John Wiley and Sons.
Soman, Alfred. 1980. "Deviance and Criminal Justice in Western Europe, 1300–1800: An Essay in Structure," *Criminal Justice History: An International Annual* 1:1–28.

The Extent and Character of Violent Crime in America, 1969 to 1982

Neil Alan Weiner and Marvin E. Wolfgang

SOME PRELIMINAR[IES] . . .

This overview of violent crime in the United States during the last decade and a half will be developed from . . . the *Uniform Crime Reports (UCR)*, prepared annually by the Federal Bureau of Investigation (FBI), and the "National Crime Survey" (NCS), prepared annually for the Bureau of Justice Statistics by the U.S. Bureau of the Census. The *UCR* information is based on records collected and maintained each year by approximately fourteen thousand local and state law-enforcement agencies about offenses established by these agencies as having occurred and about persons arrested for these offenses. These data are submitted to the FBI either directly or through state *UCR* programs according to standardized reporting procedures. . . .

The *UCR* presents an official statistical picture of criminal violence. NCS data, on the other hand, comprise information about crime that is obtained by structured interviews with the victims of crime.[1] . . . Since 1973, when the NCS was initiated, data have been collected annually. To ensure that comprehensive information is obtained about criminal victimization in the United States, a national sample of households and commercial establishments was selected. Persons aged 12 and over in the sample have been interviewed twice yearly about their victimization experiences, including questions about the type, frequency, and effects of crime as well as about the characteristics of the offender(s) and of the victim(s). . . .

VIOLENT CRIME IN AMERICA: 1969 to 1982

The four serious violent crimes considered here—criminal homicide, forcible rape, robbery, and aggravated assault—together with the serious property crimes—burglary, larceny-theft, and motor-vehicle theft—constitute what the *UCR* designates as "index crimes." The term *index* implies that because these crimes are serious, they are most likely to be reported to and recorded by law-enforcement agencies and therefore can serve as a valid barometer of changing patterns and trends in crime.

In its discussion of the levels and trends of criminal violence, the [National Commission on the Causes and Prevention of Violence (hereinafter the] Violence Commission[)] made two important observations: (1) the rates of serious violent crimes were substantially below those of serious property crimes, and (2) the rates of serious violent and property crimes were on the increase.

The discrepancy between the rates of violent index crimes and property index crimes is so great that the combined violent crime rate has almost always been lower than the rate of each of the three property index crimes.[2] . . . Violent index crimes, although dwarfed in incidence by property index crimes, are[, however,] the more grievous offenses because of the potential physical and emotional harm to the victims.

The Violence Commission reported that the rates of both serious violent crimes and serious property crimes were rising in a parallel and dramatic fashion. The commission concluded that the rates of violent crimes in the 1960s compared "unfavorably, even alarmingly, with those of the 1950s" and that there was good reason to believe, even on the basis of "fragmentary information," that these rates were higher than at any other time in this century, except perhaps for the earliest decades. Drawing upon *UCR* data, the commission showed that the national rates of criminal homicide, forcible rape, and most notably, robbery and aggravated assault had been on the upswing. Between 1958 and 1968 the national rate of criminal homicide had jumped from 4.6 to 6.8 per 100,000 population, that of forcible rape from 9.3 to 15.5, that of robbery from 54.9 to 131.0, and that of aggravated assault from 78.8 to 141.3. The combined violent crime rate had jumped from 147.6 to 294.6 in a matter of just ten years. In percentage terms, the increase was 48 percent for criminal homicide, 67 percent for forcible rape, 139 percent for robbery, and 79 percent for aggravated assault, for an increase in the combined violent crime rate of nearly 100 percent.

UCR data for 1969 to 1982 indicate that throughout this period violent index crimes constituted a modest (approximately 10 percent) but stable portion of all index crimes.[3] . . . NCS statistics present a strikingly similar picture.[4] When victimizations against the person are grouped with criminal incidents committed against households, a composite category is created that is roughly the same as the *UCR* index offenses. (The most notable difference is that the NCS does not include criminal homicide.) For the years 1973 to 1980 major violent crimes against the person (forcible rape, robbery, and aggravated assault) constituted between 7.8 and 8.8 percent of all crimes. . . .

The relatively low representation of serious violent crimes among all serious crimes can be examined in a different way by comparing the rates of violent index crimes to the rates of property index crimes. The rate discrepancies in the *UCR* noted by the Violence Commission persisted into the 1970s. The rate of aggravated assault, which was generally highest among the violent offenses, was nevertheless still well below the rate of motor-vehicle theft, which had the lowest rate among the property offenses (table 1-1). Indeed, even when the violent index crimes are grouped together, their combined rate historically had been below that of motor-vehicle theft until 1975.

When the gravity of different types of offenses is considered, however, violent crime is probably the most salient of all crimes in the minds of Americans because of its potential for serious physical and emotional harm. We now focus on these particular offenses.

The rate increases in serious violent crimes documented by the Violence Commission have continued.[5] *UCR* data show that between 1969 and 1982 the rate of murder and nonnegligent manslaughter rose from 7.3 to 9.1 per 100,000 population; the rate of forcible rape climbed from 18.5 to 33.6; and the rates of robbery and aggravated assault jumped from 148.4 to 231.9 and from 154.5 to 280.8, respectively (table 1.1). These rates represent substantial percentage increases: 25 percent for criminal homicide, 82 percent for forcible rape, 56 percent for robbery, and 82 percent for aggravated assault. The combined violent crime rate, which is dominated by robbery and aggravated assault, soared from 328.7 to 555.3, an increase of 69 percent in fourteen years. Criminal homicide, forcible rape, and aggravated assault all reached their highest levels in 1981, and robbery did so one year later. Aggravated assault exhibited the highest rates, followed closely by robbery. If both the levels and the increases in violent crime reported in the *UCR* were cause for alarm in 1969, then these more recent data are cause for even greater alarm.

Since the 1980s began, the nation has witnessed declines in the official rates of every violent crime. . . . Whether this downswing represents the beginning of a

Table 1-1.
Index Crimes: United States, 1969 to 1982 (Offense Rate per 100,000 Population)

	Violent Index Crimes						Property Index Crimes		
Year	Total Violent Index Crimes	Murder and Nonnegligent Manslaughter	Forcible Rape	Robbery	Aggravated Assault	Total Property Index Crimes	Burglary	Larceny-Theft	Motor-Vehicle Theft
1969	328.7	7.3	18.5	148.4	154.5	3351.3	984.1	1930.9	436.2
1970	363.5	7.9	18.7	172.1	164.8	3621.0	1084.9	2079.3	456.8
1971	396.0	8.6	20.5	188.0	178.8	3768.8	1163.5	2145.5	459.8
1972	401.0	9.0	22.5	180.7	188.8	3560.4	1140.8	1993.6	426.1
1973	417.4	9.4	24.5	183.1	200.5	3737.0	1222.5	2071.9	442.6
1974	461.1	9.8	26.2	209.3	215.8	4389.3	1437.7	2489.5	462.2
1975	481.5	9.6	26.3	218.2	227.4	4800.2	1525.9	2804.8	469.4
1976	459.6	8.7	26.4	195.8	228.7	4806.8	1439.4	2921.3	446.1
1977	466.6	8.8	29.1	187.1	241.5	4588.4	1410.9	2729.9	447.6
1978	486.9	9.0	30.8	191.3	255.9	4622.4	1423.7	2743.9	454.7
1979	535.5	9.7	34.5	212.1	279.1	4986.0	1499.1	2988.4	498.5
1980	580.8	10.2	36.4	243.5	290.6	5319.1	1668.2	3156.3	494.6
1981	576.9	9.8	35.6	250.6	280.9	5223.0	1632.1	3122.3	468.7
1982	555.3	9.1	33.6	231.9	280.8	4997.8	1475.2	3069.8	452.8
Percentage Change, 1969 to 1982	(+68.9)	(+24.7)	(+81.6)	(+56.3)	(+81.8)	(+49.1)	(+49.9)	(+59.0)	(+3.8)

Source: Adapted from U.S. Department of Justice, Federal Bureau of Investigation, *Uniform Crime Reports for the United States, 1978* and *1982: 1978*, Table 2, p. 39; *1982*, Table 2, p. 43.

long-term trend or only a short-term depression cannot yet be ascertained. [It has been short-term: The rates are once again on the rise.]

NCS statistics tell a somewhat different story. Forcible rape, personal robbery, and aggravated assault have not shown striking changes between 1973 and 1980. The rate (per 100,000 population aged 12 and over) of forcible rape was 100.0 in 1973 and 90.0 in 1980; the rate of personal robbery was 700.0 in 1973 and 650.0 in 1980; the rate of aggravated assault was 1,000.0 in 1973 and 920.0 in 1980; and the combined violent crime rate was 1,800.0 in 1973 and 1,660.0 in 1980 (table 1-2). These rate differences represent a decrease in forcible rape of 10 percent and decreases in personal robbery and aggravated assault of 7 and 8 percent, respectively. The combined violent crime rate fell by 8 percent over the eight-year period. In contrast to the *UCR*, which shows violent crime to have risen through the 1970s, reaching its highest levels in the first two years of the 1980s, the NCS shows no regular incline for forcible rape or aggravated assault, and for robbery it shows higher rates in the early 1970s.

For a fair comparison to be made between the *UCR* and the NCS, they should be examined for at least the years in which they overlap, 1973 to 1980. In this period, the *UCR* indicates an increase in forcible rape of 49 percent, whereas the NCS shows a decrease of 10 percent; the *UCR* shows that aggravated assault increased by 45 percent, but the NCS indicates only an 8 percent increase; the *UCR* shows that robbery increased by 33 percent, whereas the NCS indicates a 7 percent decrease (table 1-3).

Table 1-2.
Victimization by Violent Personal Crimes: United States, 1973 to 1980 (Rate per 100,000 Population Aged 12 and Over)

Year	Total Violent Personal Victimization	Rape	Personal-Sector Robbery	Aggravated Assault
1973	1800.0	100.0	700.0	1000.0
1974	1840.0	100.0	710.0	1030.0
1975	1710.0	90.0	670.0	950.0
1976	1720.0	80.0	650.0	990.0
1977	1710.0	90.0	620.0	1000.0
1978	1660.0	100.0	590.0	970.0
1979	1730.0	110.0	630.0	990.0
1980	1660.0	90.0	650.0	920.0
Percentage Change, 1973 to 1980	(−7.8)	(−10.0)	(−7.1)	(−8.0)

Source: Adapted from U.S. Department of Justice, National Criminal Justice Information and Statistics Service, *Criminal Victimization in the United States, 1973*, Table 1, p. 67; *Criminal Victimization in the United States, 1974*, Table 1, p. 17; *Criminal Victimization in the United States, 1975*, Table 1, p. 17; *Criminal Victimization in the United States, 1976*, Table 1, p. 22; *Criminal Victimization in the United States, 1977*, Table 1, p. 20; U.S. Department of Justice, Bureau of Justice Statistics, *Criminal Victimization in the United States, 1978*, Table 1, p. 18; *Criminal Victimization in the United States, 1979*, Table 1, p. 22; *Criminal Victimization in the United States, 1980*, Table 1, p. 22.

Table 1-3.
Rate Comparisons Between the *UCR*[a] and the NCS[b]: Rape, Robbery, and Aggravated Assault (Rate per 100,000: Total Population, *UCR*; Population Aged 12 and Over, NCS)

	Rape		Robbery		Aggravated Assault	
Year	*UCR*	NCS	*UCR*	NCS[c]	*UCR*	NCS
1973	24.5	100.0	183.1	700.0	200.5	1000.0
1974	26.2	100.0	209.3	710.0	215.8	1030.0
1975	26.3	90.0	218.2	670.0	227.4	950.0
1976	26.4	80.0	195.8	650.0	228.7	990.0
1977	29.1	90.0	187.1	620.0	241.5	1000.0
1978	30.8	100.0	191.3	590.0	255.9	970.0
1979	34.5	110.0	212.1	630.0	279.1	990.0
1980	36.4	90.0	243.5	650.0	290.6	920.0
Percentage Change, 1973 to 1980	(+48.6)	(−10.0)	(+33.0)	(−7.1)	(+44.9)	(−8.0)

[a]These rates were obtained from table 1-1.

[b]These rates were obtained from table 1-2.

[c]NCS rates include only personal-sector robbery.

These discrepancies between the two systems between 1973 and 1980 are just part of the picture, however. The annual rates show, according to the *UCR*, that forcible rape and aggravated assault increased consistently, whereas robbery first increased, then decreased, and subsequently increased again (table [1-3]). The NCS, on the other hand, shows that forcible rape and aggravated assault remained fairly stable, whereas robbery was generally on the decline until the most recent years.

Turning from trend comparisons to magnitude comparisons, the NCS always registers substantially higher rates. Between 1973 and 1980, the NCS rates of forcible rape and robbery were 2.5 to 4 times higher than the corresponding *UCR* rates, and the rate of aggravated assault was 3.5 to 5 times higher (table [1-3]). These figures should invite heightened concern over the levels of violent crime in America. . . .

Though much work remains to be done to bolster the reliability of these two important sources of criminal statistics, on balance we can conclude from them that violent crime has increased—but somewhat less than is indicated by the *UCR*—and that these rates are disturbingly high and would have to be viewed as such even without evidence of their increase.

When *UCR* violent offense rates are used to compute victimization probabilities (by dividing each offense rate into the population base of 100,000 used to calculate it), we find, as expected, that the probability of being victimized violently has increased between 1969 and 1981 (table 1-1).[6] The chances of being murdered were 1 in 13,699 in 1969 compared to 1 in 10,989 in 1982; the chances of being forcibly raped were 1 in 5,405 in 1969 compared to 1 in 2,976 in 1982; the chances of being robbed were 1 in 674 in 1969 compared to 1 in 431 in 1982; and the chances of being assaulted seriously were 1 in 647 in 1969 compared to 1 in 356 in 1982. These figures represent unsettling upturns of 34 percent for criminal homicide, 92 percent for forcible rape, 69 percent for robbery, and 82 percent for aggravated assault. . . .

We can obtain a rough estimate of the number of persons responsible for acts of criminal violence in the nation by using a procedure outlined by the Violence Commission. In 1969 there were approximately 1,972 seriously violent offenders for every 100,000 Americans; in 1981 this figure had climbed to 3,461. Viewed alternatively, approximately 1 in 50 Americans may have been involved in a violent crime in 1969 compared to 1 in 30 Americans in 1981, an increase of 76 percent. In terms of absolute numbers, more than 4 million people in 1969 and almost 8 million people in 1981 appear to have committed a criminally violent act, staggering numbers to say the least.

In the 1960s and persisting throughout the 1970s, disparities were observed in rates of violent crimes between city areas, areas adjacent to the city, and rural areas and between cities of different sizes.[7] *UCR* data indicate that cities continued to suffer higher rates of violent crime than rural areas by factors of about 1.5 for criminal homicide, 2–2.5 for both rape and aggravated assault, and 12–20 for robbery. . . . This pattern is confirmed by the NCS data, which show that metropolitan areas (both central cities and the adjacent areas) have consistently higher rates of forcible rape, personal robbery, and aggravated assault than nonmetropolitan areas. . . . Cities exceeded both rural and nonmetropolitan areas to a much greater extent in robbery rates than was the case for any of the other serious violent crimes, indicating that robbery, more than these other crimes, is a city phenomenon.

Cities most plagued by violent crime are the larger ones. . . . For example, cities with populations greater than 250,000 experienced substantially higher rates of violent crime than cities with populations of less than 10,000. Criminal homicide rates were about 6 times higher; forcible rape rates were between 4 and 6 times greater; robbery rates were between 15 and 25 times higher; and aggravated assault rates were about 2 to 3 times higher. . . .

Data collected by the *UCR* indicate that all regions—the Northeast, North Central, South, and West—sustained rate increases between 1969 and 1982, a continuation of the upward trend noted by the Violence Commission.[8] . . . The Northeast experienced the highest rate increase in robbery and aggravated assault and the second highest rate increases in criminal homicide and forcible rape, which together produced the highest overall rate increase among the four regions. During both the 1960s and the 1970s, the Northeast suffered some of the most dramatic upturns in the levels of violent crime in the nation.

The South continued to have the highest rates of criminal homicide (between 10.4 and 13.3 per 100,000 population), nearly 2 times greater than the rates of the Northeast and North Central regions. For the first half of the 1970s, the South also registered rates of criminal homicide that were nearly twice as high as those of the West, but rates in the West began to rise in the second half of the decade, and by the decade's end they were not far below those of the South. Although the South had the highest rates of aggravated assault throughout the 1960s, from 1973 on the West displayed the highest rates, ranging from 234.6 per 100,000 population in 1973 to 371.4 in 1980.

During the 1970s, the West displayed the highest rates of forcible rape, as it did during the 1960s. These rates, which ranged between 28.9 and 51.9 per 100,000 population, were approximately one and one-third to two times greater than those of the other regions. When robbery was considered, a clear shift in pattern obtained across the last two decades. Whereas the West and North Central regions had the highest robbery rates during the 1960s, the Northeast was so burdened during the 1970s, followed by the West. Between 1969 and 1982, the robbery rate in the Northeast shot upward from 188.6 to 348.5. Considering the total violent crime rate, from a closely clustered field in 1969 the West and the Northeast have emerged as the most beleaguered regions, mainly because of their relatively high rates of robbery and aggravated assault. . . .

Work conducted for the Violence Commission showed that young male members of minority groups had been responsible for a disproportionately high share of the serious violent crimes during the 1960s. *UCR* and NCS statistics for the 1970s indicate that these patterns have remained stable. *UCR* data further indicate that the rates of violent crime among young males and among members of minority groups are increasing almost without exception. . . .

Disparities between males and females in the commission of serious violent crime can be highlighted by comparing their respective arrest rates. *UCR* data for the 1970s show that male rates far outstripped those of females for each type of violent crime: by a factor of between 5 and 6 for criminal homicide, by a factor of close to 7 for aggravated assault, and by a factor of between 13 and 16 for robbery. . . . When the four violent crimes are combined, male arrest rates are about ten times greater than those of females.

During the past decade, both males and females sustained rate increases for robbery and aggravated assault—almost equal increases for aggravated assault but greater increases for females than for males for robbery. . . . Male rates also increased for criminal homicide and forcible rape, but the female rate of criminal homicide displayed almost no change. . . .

UCR data show that young adults (aged 18 to 24) and older juveniles (aged 15 to 17) have been responsible disproportionately for acts of criminal violence. . . . Striking results appear when arrest rates for the different age groups are computed from *UCR* data. Examination of the rates for violent index crimes combined indicates that young adults (aged 18 to 24) had the highest overall rates, followed fairly closely by older juveniles (aged 15 to 17) and then, far behind, by older adults (aged 25 and older) and, still further behind, by younger juveniles and children (below age 15). . . . Furthermore, young adults and older juveniles registered the highest rates regardless of the type of violent crime. When these two age groups were compared, young adults recorded higher arrest rates for three of the four violent offenses: criminal homicide by a factor of about two, forcible rape by a factor of about one and one-third, and aggravated assault by a factor of about one and one-quarter. Robbery, however, was committed more often by older juveniles, especially since the middle of the past decade, when their arrest rates began to exceed those of young adults by about one and one-third. . . .

After World War II, the country entered a period of about a decade (1946 to 1956) in which the birthrate soared. The first of these large baby-boom cohorts entered its peak arrest ages (15 to 25) for violent crimes about 1963, the time at which the violent crime rate began to rise sharply in the nation. The last of these cohorts entered its peak arrest ages in the early 1970s and matured out of this high-risk period in about 1980. The high and increasing levels of violent crime witnessed in the 1960s and the 1970s are attributable in part to these birth cohorts. As the last of these cohorts has passed out of the high-risk ages, we might expect a decline in the level of violent crime during the latter part of the 1980s. The decline is likely to be modest, however, for those demographic groups that exhibit the highest arrest rates for violent crimes tend also to have the highest birthrates. As a result, even after the baby-boom cohorts have moved out of their high-risk ages, these age groups will nevertheless in forthcoming years still have a high proportion of persons most likely to engage in violent crimes.

Examination of *UCR* statistics on race indicates that although blacks have constituted approximately 12 percent of the nation's population,[9] they have accumulated 50 to 60 percent of the arrests for criminal homicide, about 50 percent of the arrests for forcible rape, close to 60 percent of the arrests for robbery, and between 40 and 50 percent of the arrests for aggravated assault. . . . NCS data also show that blacks are responsible for a disproportionate amount of serious violent crime. . . .

Race specific arrest rates computed from *UCR* figures show the size of these disparities in an alternative way. Relative to whites, blacks sustained criminal homicide rates that were between 7 and 13 times greater, forcible rape rates about 7 times higher, robbery rates 10 to 17 times higher, and aggravated assault rates between 4 and 7 times greater. . . . Over the span of the decade, whites exhibited more pronounced increases in their arrest rates than did blacks for forcible rape, robbery, and aggravated assault. For criminal homicide, the white rate increased substantially, whereas the black rate decreased slightly.

That victims are very much like offenders in terms of social and demographic characteristics had been established by the Violence Commission; that this has remained the case is confirmed by the NCS. Victimization rates were higher for males than for females (with the exception of forcible rape), for the young than for the old, for blacks than for whites, and for the poor than for the more affluent.

Males figure more prominently than females as victims of both robbery and aggravated assault, sustaining victimization rates that were more than 2 times as high for robbery and about 3 times as high for aggravated assault. . . . Not surprisingly, females were much more likely to be forcibly raped than were males, by a factor of about 8.

Older juveniles (aged 16 to 19) and young adults (aged 20 to 24) have been found to be disproportionately the targets of violent crimes. NCS data firmly support the currency of this finding. Persons in these age groups experienced the highest and roughly comparable chances of being raped, which were approximately 2 times as high as those of other age groups. Older juveniles and young adults also suffered the highest and roughly comparable risks of being assaulted seriously. They were about twice as likely to be assaulted as their two closest rivals, the 12- to 15-year-olds and the 25- to 34-year-olds. Robbery victims also fell, for the most part, into the younger age brackets: 12- to 15-year-olds, 16- to 19-year-olds, and 20- to 24-year-olds all shared a similarly high risk of being robbed, which was 2 to 3 times higher than that of older age groups.

Victimization rates by race indicate that blacks have continued to sustain the highest risks. Focusing just on disparities between blacks and whites, NCS data show that blacks ran a risk of forcible rape that was one and one-half to two times greater, a risk of robbery two to three times higher, and a risk of aggravated assault more than one and one-third times higher, yielding an overall risk that was nearly twice as great. . . .

Economically disadvantaged persons were most often victims of serious violent crimes. NCS data indicate that persons who belonged to families earning less than $3,000 annually bore the brunt of violent crime, for they were more than twice as likely as any other income group to be forcibly raped, more than one and one-half times more likely to be robbed, and more than one and one-third times more likely to be assaulted seriously. As annual family income increased, the ravages of violent crime generally decreased.

The NCS presents information for the years 1973 and 1979 that relates the victim and the offender by their respective races. The only other personal characteristic for which similar information is presented is sex, but only for 1976. Forcible rape, robbery, and aggravated assault were predominantly intraracial; in general, more than seven out of every ten serious violent offenses committed against a black were committed by a black, and between three-fifths and four-fifths of the forcible rapes and assaults committed against whites were committed by whites. Robbery, however, was the exception to this pattern, as it has been historically: more than the other violent offenses, robbery was an interracial affair in which blacks were more likely to victimize whites. Although whites robbed other whites in substantial proportions, in more than half of the incidents involving a single offender and in more than one-third of the events involving multiple offenders, blacks also robbed whites in substantial numbers.

Looking at NCS data on the involvement of the sexes as victims and offenders in violent crimes, the overwhelming majority of these incidents were committed by males regardless of the sex of the victim: virtually all forcible rapes, more than four-fifths of the robberies, and more than two-thirds of the aggravated assaults. When females offended violently, they were most likely to engage in robbery and aggravated assault and were more likely to select a female victim than a male victim.

NCS data show that when a violent crime erupts the victim is likely to be alone: in more than nine out of every ten forcible rapes and robberies and in more than eight out of every ten aggravated assaults. These data also show that a victim is most likely to be faced by a single offender in cases of forcible rape (about 80 percent of the incidents), is somewhat less likely to be so confronted in cases of aggravated assault (between 65 and 70 percent of the time), and is least likely to be confronted by a single offender in cases of robbery (50 percent of the incidents).

A significant part of the fear of violent crime is the fear of being victimized by a stranger. NCS data indicate that a majority of violent crimes have been committed historically by strangers: four-fifths of the robberies, two-thirds of the forcible rapes, and three-fifths of the aggravated assaults. Rates computed for these data tell the same story but in a different way: robberies were about six times more likely to be committed by a stranger than by someone who was known to the victim; forcible rapes were twice as likely to be carried out by a stranger; and aggravated assaults were about one and two-thirds times more likely to be performed by a stranger. . . .

Much violent crime occurred outside the home and [in] its immediate vicinity. Approximately three-fifths of the robberies and two-fifths of both the forcible rapes and the aggravated assaults occurred in open public places, such as the street or a park. . . . More intimate environments, the home and places nearby, were not immune from these events, however, for about one-third of the forcible rapes and about one-fifth of the robberies and aggravated assaults were committed there. Forcible rapes occurred about as often in the victim's home or close by as in an open public place. Robbery and aggravated assault, on the other hand, occurred more often in an open public place than in the home or nearby: robbery about three times more often and aggravated assault about twice as often. Robbery and aggravated assault have been violent street phenomena more than has forcible rape.

Central to the enigma of criminal violence is the outcome. In precisely how many incidents is the victim physically harmed? NCS data indicate that one of every three victims of personal robberies and assaults sustained an injury. . . . Males and females were injured equally often. When age was examined, no clear pattern appeared, for the victims of both personal robberies and assaults had similar risks of injury across the age spectrum. Nor did the race of the victim bear strongly on the likelihood of injury. Interestingly, injuries were sustained more often by victims who knew their assailants in cases of personal robbery and assault than by victims who did not.

Americans have not behaved passively toward those who would victimize them violently: eight out of every ten victims of forcible rape, more than one out of every two robbery victims, and seven out of every ten victims of aggravated assault initiated some type of self-protective measure. Firearms and knives were used rarely for self-protection—in less than 4 percent of the personal robberies and aggravated assaults and almost never in cases of forcible rape. Victims of forcible rape most often attempted to get help or to frighten their attacker (about 30 percent of the time); somewhat less often, they used physical force or a weapon other than a firearm or knife or tried to threaten or to reason with their assailant (between 20 and 25 percent of the time). Robbery victims most often tried to use physical force or a weapon other than a firearm or knife (about 30 percent of the time); about equally often they tried to get help, to frighten the robber, to threaten or reason with the robber, or to use some other kind of nonviolent resistance like evasion (about 20 percent of the time). Use of physical force, a weapon other than a firearm or knife, or nonviolent resistance was the most favored tactic of persons subjected to serious assaults (between 25 and 30 percent of the time). . . .

In the past decade, considerable work has been done to determine whether a core group of offenders exists who repeatedly commit serious violent crimes and who, as a consequence, are responsible for the bulk of these acts. Efforts along this line have yielded the finding that the vast majority of violent crime is committed by a relatively few repetitively violent persons. Research conducted on two large birth cohorts born in Philadelphia in 1945 and 1958 indicates that chronic male offenders (those who compiled five or more police contacts) represented small segments of the offender populations: 18 percent of the offenders in the 1945 birth cohort and 23 percent in the 1958 cohort. These offenders accounted, however, for a disproportionately large share of the offenses: 52 percent in the 1945 birth cohort and 61 percent in the 1958 cohort.[10] More significant, the chronic offenders in each cohort were responsible for the major portion of serious violent offenses: 71 percent of the criminal homicides, 73 percent of the rapes, 82 percent of the robberies, and 69 percent of the aggravated assaults in the 1945 birth cohort; and 61 percent of the criminal homicides, 76 percent of the forcible rapes, 73 percent of the robberies, and 65 percent of the aggravated assaults in the 1958 birth cohort. Furthermore, offenders with five or more police contacts were most likely to injure their victims, for they compiled 58 percent of the injurious offenses in the 1945 birth cohort and 66 percent in the 1958 cohort.[11] A similar pattern of a high concentration of serious offenses among a small minority of offenders has been reported in other research. Within already high-risk offender populations—urban, young, male, minority-group members—there is, then, a small group that is at even greater risk to do harm to others.

INTERNATIONAL COMPARISONS

An accurate appraisal of the dimensions of criminal violence in America requires a comparative treatment at the international level. . . . To minimize . . . hindrances to cross-cultural analysis, we limit our discussion to nations that bear the greatest similarity to the United States in their history and institutions: the urban and industrial European nations and those non-European nations that share this cultural tradition.

The Violence Commission relied on data published by the United Nations in its analysis of criminal homicide and on data compiled by Canada, Denmark, England, and Wales for the UN investigation of forcible rape, robbery, and aggravated assault. These data clearly document that levels of violent crime in the United States were well above those of the comparison nations. Statistics collected by the commission indicated that between 1955 and 1966 the rate of criminal homicide in the United States, which varied between about 4.5 and 6.0 per 100,000 population, was at least twice as high as the rates of the other nations: Australia, Austria, Belgium, Canada, Denmark, England, Finland, France, Germany, Italy, Norway, and Switzerland. Furthermore, whereas the rate of criminal homicide in the United States showed a consistent incline over the twelve-year period, the rates of the other nations were either relatively stable or erratic, or they increased only modestly.

Similar disparities obtained when the rates of forcible rape, robbery, and aggravated assault were compared for the United States, Canada, Denmark, England, and Wales. U.S. rates in each of these categories exceeded those of each of the comparison countries by a factor of at least one and one-half. As the Violence Commission pointed out, "For each major violent act, the reported American average rate [for the years 1963 to 1967] is greater than the reported average rate for the other three countries *combined*."[12]

Cross-national patterns in homicide observed in 1969 continued throughout the 1970s. The United States still suffered a homicide rate at least three times higher than the rates sustained by European nations. . . . Furthermore, for the early portion of the comparison period, 1970 to 1975, the United States experienced a much steeper incline in its homicide rate than did the other nations.

Data on robbery for the first half of the 1970s also conform to what we would expect, given the findings of the Violence Commission. Relative to European countries, the United States exhibited by far the highest mean robbery rate (191.2 per 100,000 population), exceeding its closest rival, Canada, by a factor of almost 3. . . .

Traditionally, then, America has experienced levels of criminal violence that either far exceed or are among the highest of nations most similar to it in culture and history. . . .

NOTES

1. For a review of the NCS, see James Garofalo and Michael J. Hindelang, *An Introduction to the National Crime Survey* (Washington, D.C.: U.S. Government Printing Office, 1977).
2. Donald J. Mulvihill, Melvin M. Tumin, and Lynn A. Curtis, *Crimes of Violence*, a Staff Report Submitted to the National Commission on the Causes and Prevention of Violence (Washington, D.C.: U.S. Government Printing Office, 1969), 11: 53.
3. *UCR* data reviewed in the following discussion were obtained from U.S. Department of Justice, Federal Bureau of Investigation, *Uniform Crime Reports for the United States, 1969–82* (Washington, D.C.: U.S. Government Printing Office, 1970–83).
4. NCS data reviewed in the following discussion were obtained from U.S. Department of Justice, National Criminal Justice Information and Statistics Service, *Criminal Victimization in the United States, 1973–77* (Washington, D.C.: U.S. Government Printing Office, 1976, 1977, 1977, 1979, 1979); U.S. Department of Justice, Bureau of Justice Statistics, *Criminal Victimization in the United States, 1978–1980* (Washington, D.C.: U.S. Government Printing Office, 1980, 1981, 1982).
5. Mulvihill, Tumin, and Curtis, *Crimes of Violence*, 11: 53–59.
6. For a brief statement about the procedure, see Mulvihill, Tumin, and Curtis, *Crimes of Violence*, 11: 56, 130, fn. 21.
7. Mulvihill, Tumin, and Curtis, *Crimes of Violence*, 11: 62–69.
8. Ibid., pp. 69–80. The regional breakdowns by states are as follows: *Northeast:* Connecticut, Maine, Massachusetts, New Hampshire, New Jersey, New York, Pennsylvania, Rhode Island, Vermont; *North Central:* Illinois, Indiana, Iowa, Kansas, Michigan, Minnesota, Missouri, Nebraska, North Dakota, Ohio, South Dakota,

Wisconsin; *South:* Alabama, Arkansas, Delaware, District of Columbia, Florida, Georgia, Kentucky, Louisiana, Maryland, Mississippi, North Carolina, Oklahoma, South Carolina, Tennessee, Texas, Virginia, West Virginia; *West:* Alaska, Arizona, California, Colorado, Hawaii, Idaho, Montana, Nevada, New Mexico, Oregon, Puerto Rico, Utah, Washington, Wyoming.

9. U.S. Bureau of the Census, Current Population Reports, *Preliminary Estimates of the Population of the United States*, Table 2, pp. 26–43. . . . U.S. Bureau of the Census, Current Population Reports, *Estimates of the Population of the United States*, Table 2, p. 2.

10. Marvin E. Wolfgang and Paul E. Tracy, Jr., "The 1945 and the 1958 Birth Cohorts: A Comparison of the Prevalence, Incidence, and Severity of Delinquent Behavior," paper presented at the Conference on Public Danger, Dangerousness, Dangerous Offenders, and the Criminal Justice System, sponsored by Harvard University and the John F. Kennedy School of Government, Boston, February 11–12, 1982, tables 6a–b, pp. 16–18.

11. Ibid., tables 8a–b, pp. 16–18.

12. Mulvihill, Tumin, and Curtis, *Crimes of Violence*, 11: 124; emphasis in original.

The Risk of Violent Crime

Patrick A. Langan and Christopher A. Innes

THE CRIME RISK INDEX

. . . [T]he Bureau of Justice Statistics (BJS) sponsors an ongoing nationwide survey (National Crime Survey) of the American people to measure personal and household victimization. Through this survey interviews are conducted at 6-month intervals with all occupants age 12 and older of about 60,000 households (approximately 128,000 persons).

Each year BJS publishes the results of the National Crime Survey in two forms. One is the "victimization rate," which shows the number of criminal victimizations for various major offenses per 1,000 members of the general population age 12 and older or per 1,000 households. The offenses which constitute the violent crime victimization rate are rape, robbery, and assault (both simple and aggravated). The other measure of the crime problem published by BJS is "households touched by crime." Unlike the victimization rate, this indicator measures the percentage of all households in which a member was victimized by crime at any time during the year. Since crime affects household (usually family) members as well as the immediate victim, this "household touched" indicator is a useful complement to the standard victimization rate for gauging the impact of crime on the public.

As informative as these two measures of criminal victimization are, neither one tells us what percentage of persons in the United States were victimized by the various crimes measured by the National Crime Survey during the course of a year. For example, the question "what percentage of women in the United States were raped last year?" cannot be answered by reference to either of these measures.

The "households touched" indicator does not help because it measures the prevalence of crime only among household units. The victimization rate measure also will not show the percentage of the population victimized because it counts the total number of "victimizations" whether or not the same person was victimized more than once. Unless no one is victimized more than once, the number of victimizations will be greater than the number of distinct persons victimized.

For example, in 1982 the violent crime victimization rate was 34.3 for every 1000 persons age 12 and over in the general population. This is the same as 3.4 violent crime victimizations for every 100 persons. This could mean that 3.4% of the population was victimized by violent crime, with no one victimized more than once; or it could mean that 1% was victimized, with the typical victim averaging 3.4 victimizations. Unless we know the average number of victimizations per victim, the standard victimization rate can tell us nothing about the number of distinct persons victimized.

The Crime Risk Index introduced in this report solves this problem. It measures the proportion of the population victimized by violent crime by dividing the total number of distinct crime victims in a given year by the size of the population. . . .

When the Crime Risk Index is calculated . . . it shows that 3.2% of the population was victimized by violent crime in 1982. Since this figure is only slightly lower than the victimization rate measure of 3.4 victimizations per 100 persons, we can conclude that the great majority of violent crime victims suffered only one violent crime victimization during 1982. This new Crime Risk Index can also be compared to the "households touched by crime" measure. The three BJS measures of violent crime victimization during 1982 are summarized here:

Crime Risk Index:	3.2 persons victimized by violent crime per 100 persons
Victimization Rate:	3.4 violent crime victimizations per 100 persons
Households Touched:	5.6 households touched by violent crime per 100 households

FINDINGS

Table 1-4 . . . present[s] the detailed findings for the Crime Risk Index. . . .

Overview

In 1982 an estimated 3.2% of the Nation's population (or about 1 out of 31 persons age 12 and older) was the victim of rape, robbery, or assault. This is equivalent to approximately 6 million Americans. Assault victims were the majority of violent

Table 1-4.
Percentage of U.S. Population Victimized by Violent Crime, 1978–82

Offense and Characteristic	Year				
	1978	1979	1980	1981	1982
All violent	2.94%	3.23%	3.00%	3.21%	3.15%
Sex					
Male	3.91	4.23	3.99	4.17	4.07
Female	2.04	2.31	2.11	2.34	2.31
Race					
White	2.89	3.14	2.97	3.04	3.05
Black	3.51	4.06	3.39	4.55	4.04
Other	2.17	3.11	2.62	3.80	2.78
Rape	.09	.11	.09	.09	.07
Sex					
Male	.01	.03	.02	.01	.00[a]
Female	.17	.18	.16	.17	.14
Race					
White	.08	.10	.09	.09	.07
Black	.17	.19	.11	.14	.10
Other	.16[a]	.04[a]	.03[a]	.17[a]	.03[a]
Robbery	.53	.62	.60	.70	.72
Sex					
Male	.75	.85	.81	.93	.98
Female	.33	.41	.40	.49	.49
Race					
White	.46	.56	.54	.59	.62
Black	1.15	1.18	1.15	1.60	1.45
Other	.30[a]	.55	.24[a]	.86	1.12
Assault	2.39	2.59	2.40	2.53	2.46
Sex					
Male	3.25	3.45	3.26	3.36	3.22
Female	1.59	1.80	1.61	1.77	1.77
Race					
White	2.42	2.56	2.42	2.47	2.46
Black	2.29	2.82	2.22	3.00	2.67
Other	1.70	2.65	2.43	2.80	1.72
Aggravated assault	.89	1.01	.91	.96	.89
Sex					
Male	1.33	1.53	1.36	1.40	1.30
Female	.49	.53	.49	.57	.51
Race					
White	.87	.96	.87	.90	.84
Black	1.13	1.39	1.14	1.49	1.31
Other	.45	1.29	1.25	.93	.50
Simple assault	1.61	1.72	1.60	1.68	1.69
Sex					
Male	2.09	2.13	2.05	2.13	2.09
Female	1.16	1.34	1.18	1.27	1.32
Race					
White	1.66	1.75	1.66	1.68	1.73
Black	1.28	1.55	1.15	1.65	1.49
Other	1.24	1.50	1.31	2.06	1.25

[a]Estimate, based on about 10 or fewer sample cases, is statistically unreliable.

crime victims: 2.5% of the population was assaulted (about 1 out of 40). Robbery victims were the next most numerous: 0.7% of Americans were robbed (or 1 out of 143). Of the three violent crimes measured, rape was the least prevalent: 0.07% of the population was raped (or roughly 1 out of 1,400 Americans). The proportion of females victimized by rape was about twice as high (0.14%—1 out of 700 females), reflecting the fact that nearly all rape victims are females.

About two-thirds of those assaulted were victims of simple assault; the balance were victims of aggravated assault. . . . About 1.7% of the population was the victim of simple assault in 1982 (approximately 1 of every 59 Americans); and 0.9% was the victim of aggravated assault (or 1 out of 111 persons).

Victim Characteristics

Sex. In 1982 a higher proportion of the Nation's males than females were victimized by violent crimes. Males were more likely than females to be robbed or assaulted and females more likely than males to be raped. Specifically, about 3% of males were assaulted and about 1% were robbed. In contrast, about 1.7% of females were assaulted and 0.5% were robbed. The proportion of males who were raped was too small to measure with much confidence, while about one-tenth of 1% of females were raped. Altogether about 1 of every 25 males age 12 and over was the victim of a violent crime and about 1 of every 43 females.

Race. Among all races, blacks were most often victimized by violent crime in 1982. Four percent of the Nation's black population (or about 1 in 25 blacks) was the victim of one of the violent crimes, as compared to about 3% of whites and 2.7% of persons of all other races. The greater risk of a violent victimization among blacks in comparison with whites was largely because robbery victimization was more widespread among blacks (1.4% of blacks were robbed compared to 0.6% of whites). . . .

Age. Among the different age groups in the population, the young were the most likely to be victims of violent crime in 1982. The risk of a violent victimization for each of the three youngest age groups (ages 12–15, 16–19, and 20–24) was greater than that for any of the three oldest age groups (ages 35–49, 50–64, and 65 and older). Not only was this true for the population as a whole, it was also true for each of the four major race and sex divisions of the population: white males, white females, black males, and black females. For each of these divisions the differences in likelihood of violent crime victimization were particularly great between those 16–19 years old and those 65 and older:

	Percent Victimized	
	16–19 years old	65 years and older
White males	8.5%	0.7%
White females	4.6	0.4
Black males	8.3	1.5
Black females	5.0	1.2

Although blacks generally were more likely to be victims than whites, during the ages when risks are highest (16 to 24) nearly equal percentages of black males and white males were victims of violent crime. The nature of their victimizations differed nevertheless. Black males ages 16–24 were more likely than their white male counterparts to be robbed; white males ages 16–24 were more likely than their black male counterparts to be assaulted.

Marital Status. For both males and females, married persons were less likely to be victims of violent crime in 1982 than were the never married or the separated or divorced. For example, 2.3% of married males were victims of violent crime as compared to 7.1% of males who had never been married and 5.8% of males who were separated or divorced. Similarly, 1.2% of married females were victims of violent crime as compared to 3.9% of females who had never been married and 5.5% of females who were separated or divorced. Widowed members of both sexes had the lowest likelihood of victimization (1.4 of males and 0.9 of females), probably reflecting their relatively older ages.

Income. For both whites and blacks there was a direct relationship between family income and the likelihood of violent victimization in 1982: the lower the income the greater the victimization. . . . Similar proportions of the wealthiest whites and blacks (family incomes $25,000 and over) were victimized by violent crime (2.5% and 2.7% respectively). These percentages are about half of those for the poorest whites and blacks (family incomes less than $3000), who were victimized by violent crime at the rates of 6.3% and 5.6% respectively.

Trends: 1978–82

As table [1-4] shows, the proportion of the population victimized by violent crime remained fairly constant from 1978 to 1982. This was true for males as well as females and for whites as well as blacks. This fairly constant level of victimization was also true for each of the crimes examined separately, with the exception of robbery. Unlike rape, assault, and the subcategories of simple and aggravated assault, robbery showed a statistically significant increase in the proportion of the population victimized during the 5-year period studied: from 0.5% in 1978 to 0.7% in 1982. During the same period there were statistically significant increases in the proportions of males, of females, and of whites who were victimized by robbery. . . .

The Risk of Being Murdered

Coroner and medical examiner reports compiled by the National Center for Health Statistics show that during the years 1978–82 the prevalence of homicide reached its highest level in 1980: in that year 1 of every 10,000 Americans was murdered. Although a 1 in 10,000 chance of being murdered may seem remote to most people, it would be wrong to conclude from the statistic for a single year that the chance of *ever* becoming a homicide victim is equally remote. When the annual homicide reports are analyzed to determine the lifetime probability of being murdered, the likelihood jumps to 1 in 133. Black males, who have the highest probability of all, have a 1 in 21 lifetime chance of becoming a homicide victim. The results of this lifetime probability analysis are summarized here:

BJS Estimates of Life-Time Risk of Becoming a Victim of Homicide: 1 out of:

U.S. total	133
Male	84
White	131
Black	21
Female	282
White	369
Black	104

A comparable study conducted by the FBI reported similar results. Each year the FBI publishes a statistical series called the *Uniform Crime Reports*, which presents a variety of measures of the crime problem, including an annual measure of the prevalence of murder victimization. The measure is based on information collected from police departments throughout the Nation and covers the number of murders known to them during the year. Over the past 10 years, the highest level the measure reached was in 1980: the FBI reported 1 out of 10,000 Americans was murdered that year. For their special study, the FBI analyzed averaged 1978–80 murder victimization data to see what annual data might indicate about the lifetime risk of being murdered. In sharp contrast to the (at most) 1 out of 10,000 murder probability found for a single year, the FBI found a 1 out of 153 lifetime chance of becoming a murder victim in the United States. More complete results are shown below:

FBI Estimates of Life-Time Risk of Becoming a Victim of Homicide: 1 out of:

U.S. total	153
Male	100
White	164
Nonwhite	28
Female	323
White	450
Nonwhite	117

The homicide example illustrates why annual crime victimization data must be viewed with caution. Since annual violent crime victimization rates are relatively low compared to other life events, there may be a tendency to think that only an unlucky few are ever victimized by violent crime. As the homicide example illustrates, however, a person's lifetime risk of becoming a crime victim is far greater than annual victimization statistics might suggest.

Part 2

Interpersonal Violence

Interpersonal violence is the most frequently encountered and feared form of violence in America. This part elaborates on the major types: homicide, aggravated assault, rape, robbery, domestic violence, and child abuse. The following selections span a wide range of issues, from violence patterns and dynamics to the physical and psychological harm incurred by those who suffer from its aftermath.

The Behavioral Aspects of Homicide

Homicide—the taking of another person's life—is perhaps the most widely studied form of interpersonal violence. In "Homicide: Behavioral Aspects" Marvin E. Wolfgang and Margaret A. Zahn first distinguish criminal from noncriminal forms and then describe basic social, demographic, and spatial patterns in criminal homicide. Homicide rates are highest in Latin American countries and lowest in northern and western European countries. In recent decades homicide rates in the United States were lowest in the 1950s, rose substantially in the 1970s, peaked in 1980, and then declined somewhat in subsequent years. Black males have consistently sustained the highest victimization rates, and the Southern region of the United States has almost invariably led the nation in homicide rates. The typical deadly clash involves a male lethally assaulting another male of the same race and age with whom he is acquainted. Familial killings were more frequent in the 1950s than in other periods, and stranger killings have accelerated in the 1980s.

Patterns and Trends in Black Homicide

Patrick W. O'Carroll and James A. Mercy, in reviewing demographic "Patterns and Recent Trends in Black Homicide," reiterate the little-known but grim statistic that murderous attacks are the leading cause of death among blacks aged 15 to 34. Almost two-thirds of all black homicides are the result of arguments or some other nonfelony situation. Although the majority of white homicides are not felony related, felony homicide still accounts for a greater proportion of lethal attacks on whites than blacks. Despite the decline in black homicide rates between 1976 and 1984, these rates nevertheless outpaced those of other racial and ethnic groups, including those of whites, which have risen over this period.

Situational Aspects of Criminal Homicide

In narrative detail David F. Luckenbill describes how lethal exchanges between intimates and acquaintances unfold in "Criminal Homicide as a Situated Transaction." Murder is often the outcome of a "character contest" between rivals who are aggressively trying to save face socially. The interpersonal contest advances down a deadly pathway: the early stages involve behavior which the murderer views as insulting or which is noncompliant with a request. Each antagonist attempts to protect and defend his honor, with the use of lethal force as the final arbiter. The "typical" murder represents the final recourse of deadly foes who, in their interpersonal transaction, have developed "a working agreement that violence is a useful tool for resolving questions of face and character."

Mass Murder

Jack Levin and James Alan Fox describe a much less common but universally abhorred form of homicide in "Mass Murder: America's Growing Menace." On the average, three mass murders occur each month in the United States. The serial killer, that is, a murderer who slays victims on different occasions, is distinguished from the simultaneous killer, that is, a murderer who slays victims at the same time or in a single incident. Levin and Fox profile both types of killers and their victims. The simultaneous murderer is typically a white male in his late twenties who kills people he knows with a handgun or a rifle. The serial killer lethally attacks innocent strangers who possess triggering physical characteristics or who are socially or physically vulnerable, such as prostitutes, hitchhikers, or children. Public reaction to this vicious and shocking mass killing often translates into public support for capital punishment.

Comparisons of Homicide, Assault, and Suicide

Alex D. Pokorny reviews a wide spectrum of violence in "Human Violence: A Comparison of Homicide, Aggravated Assault, Suicide, and Attempted Suicide." Suicide and homicide are most dissimilar with respect to selected victim and offender characteristics and the settings in which participants confront one another. Criminal homicide and aggravated assault are most similar in their time and place of occurrence and in victim and offender characteristics. Pokorny concludes that aggravated assault and homicide are essentially the same types of behavior, with chance or unforeseen circumstances determining which incidents will be gravely assaultive and which will be murderous. For example, the presence and types of weapons, the interactive patterns between victim and offender, and the availability and quality of medical care figure prominently among the conditions which result in different levels of physical harm.

The Behavioral Aspects of Rape

A. Nicholas Groth, in "Rape: Behavioral Aspects," maintains that only since the 1970s has the crime of rape received the serious and systematic attention it deserves. Rape is gradually becoming more widely recognized as a manifestation of sexual pathology, behavioral disorder, and aggression. Clinical studies reveal that rape serves mainly nonsexual needs. As Groth notes, "rape is not summarily the aggressive expression of sexuality but rather the sexual expression of aggression." Rape must be understood as nonsexually motivated so that effective responses can be organized. Legalizing prostitution or banning pornography are misguided "solutions" because they inappropriately shift causal determination from the offender to an external source of sexual stimulation. By doing so, the internal pathological dynamics of the rapist are ignored or discounted.

Groth formulates three categories of rape based on different causal processes: anger, power, and sadism. Distinguishing among these three types can assist in isolating prior dynamics that differentially result in sexual assaults that are similar only in the gravity of their consequences.

Sexual assaulters exhibit common psychological characteristics, including low self-worth, doubts about manhood, and the tendency toward involvement in distant and superficial personal relationships. Groth further reports that identified sexual offenders were very often themselves victims of sexual abuse. Intergenerational transmission of sexual violence may be operating, but more research is needed. The author endorses several approaches to prevent or curtail sexually assaultive behavior, including reeducation, resocialization and counseling.

Recovery from Rape

Ann Wolbert Burgess and Lynda Lytle Holmstrom developed one of the more influential models for rape-crisis intervention centers, and their article, "Adaptive Stages and Recovery from Rape," examines the cogency of their model. The authors conducted a follow-up study of ninety-two adult rape victims who were contacted during a counseling-research project in the emergency room of Boston City Hospital. Of those interviewed, almost two-fifths felt that they had recovered within months, a similar proportion within years, and one-quarter not at all. Burgess and Holmstrom detail the many factors that govern the pace of recovery from serious sexual assault. Certain actions taken by the victim, such as changing residence, traveling, and becoming better educated about rape, appear to be related to improved prospects of recovery. Clinicians must be made aware of these and other factors so that services can be marshalled and tailored to the needs of those victims most in jeopardy of making a poor recovery.

Robbery in the United States

Philip J. Cook's article on "Robbery in the United States: An Analysis of Recent Trends and Patterns" reviews the harm resulting from this crime, including possible loss of life, economic losses, and criminal justice costs. He also describes major demographic patterns: robbery is mainly an urban problem which typically involves several males confronting a single victim who shares similar characteristics with the offenders. Although some robbers commit these offenses at high rates, most robberies are committed by offenders whose criminal careers are marked by eclectic criminal involvements. Cook concludes with a discussion of proposals to diminish robbery levels: making the apprehension and prosecution of armed robbers a criminal justice priority; inaugurating neighborhood watch programs; and reducing youth access to drugs, alcohol, and guns.

Robbery at Convenience Stores

Dennis C. Duffala studied thirty-nine commercial establishments to determine which of their characteristics are associated with an increased risk of robbery, reporting his findings in "Convenience Stores, Armed Robbery, and Physical Environmental Features." Although the effect of any one characteristic on vulnerability is not substantial, those convenience stores most at risk of robbery were located on streets with light vehicular traffic and few other commercial establishments nearby. Vulnerability appears, therefore, to be related to a lack of adequate surveillance.

The Mugging

Morton Hunt depicts "The Mugging" and the grim potential for lethal violence that can sometimes result from robbery. While returning home from the grocery store, an elderly man is tracked by a gang of youthful predators who, with furious speed, rush into his apartment, ransack it, and leave the frail and trembling man to die of knife wounds. It is precisely this type of apparently random violence that has progressively heightened levels of fear in our cities and led to the fortification of some urban neighborhoods.

Domestic Criminal Violence

We fear the unprovoked attacks of strangers; but violence by family members also occurs frequently, transforming the family circle into a battleground. As the victims of family violence emerge from behind closed doors, these domestic batterings are increasingly being treated as a public problem rather than a private issue. The selections on domestic violence document the scope of the problem, identify offender characteristics and victim vulnerabilities, and suggest remedial and coping strategies.

Richard J. Gelles presents an overview of "Domestic Criminal Violence," discussing patterns and identifying factors associated with familial abuse and attacks. These factors include growing up in a violent household, low socioeconomic status, social isolation, and financial and other types of stresses. The relationship between race and domestic violence is not clearly established. However, preliminary findings indicate that while blacks have higher rates of familial violence than whites, both groups exhibit similar rates of violence against children. Physical punishment by parents of children appears to be socially acceptable, with more than eight of nine parents admitting its use. Gelles closes by reviewing major theories of family violence. He concludes that a vigorous program of longitudinal and cross-sectional research must be pursued before we can satisfactorily explain domestic violence.

Changes in Society and Family Violence

Murray A. Straus and Richard J. Gelles investigate "Societal Change and Change in Family Violence from 1975 to 1985 as Revealed by Two National Surveys." Comparisons of their 1985 national sample of 6,002 persons with their 1975 national sample of 2,143 persons showed declines in the physical abuse of children and wife battering by husbands. Straus and Gelles suggest various reasons for the declines: increased reluctance to report these behaviors to authorities; more social service alternatives for battered women, such as shelters and family counseling and treatment programs; shifts in police guidelines for dealing with family violence; and basic changes in family structure. Whatever the reasons for the declines, they are encouraging and indicate that changes in public policy and the structures of social relationships can reduce brutal domestic abuses.

Battered Women and Spousal Homicide

In "When Battered Women Kill," Angela Browne compares 42 women who killed or seriously injured their mates with 205 women who had been in abusive relationships but who did not take lethal action. While women who killed were somewhat older and came from a higher socioeconomic class than women in the nonlethal group, the major differences between the groups were not their personal and social characteristics but rather the men with whom they were involved. For example, men in the homicide group used alcohol and drugs more frequently than men in the comparison group, engaged in more threatening and actually assaultive behavior, were likely to abuse children as well as their partners, and engaged in sexual assault.

In effect, women who kill do so mainly because they are involved in prolonged, intensely abusive relationships which they can neither control nor flee from. These women fear for both their own lives and the lives of their children. The lethal exchange is unplanned, often punctuating an assaultive violent confrontation or a failed attempt to escape. Deadly violence is the irrevocable act of last resort after long-endured battering.

Children at Risk of Sexual Violence

David Finkelhor and Larry Baron attempt to develop a profile of "High-Risk Children," those who are at great risk of being sexually abused. Children are most vulnerable between the ages of 8 and 12, with girls more likely targets than boys. Current studies suggest that sexual abuse and social class are unrelated; and there do not appear to be significant differences between black and white families.

Familial background factors show the strongest relationship to sexual abuse: parental absence during childhood, poor relationships with the mother, and conflict between parents.

Violent and Serious Victimization

Victims of interpersonal violence are too frequently viewed as mere statistical casualties. Gary D. Gottfredson provides balance to the statistical portrait in "The Experiences of Violent and Serious Victimization." He argues that the customary legal and criminal justice focus on the crime and criminal diverts attention from the immediate and long-term needs of victims. The victims' movement has sought to redress this imbalance by reiterating that the victim is the wronged and injured party who deserves humane and respectful treatment by criminal justice and other social service agencies.

Gottfredson begins by examining the unequal risks of victimization in different social groups and identifying victim populations most in need of assistance. Most vulnerable to violence are adolescents or young adult males who are poor urban residents. Corollary evidence suggests that many persons who might benefit from victim services live or work in our central cities.

Although our present knowledge about recovery from violent attacks is limited, Gottfredson offers some generalizations drawn from available research evidence: "the more varied and supportive a victim's resources—that is, friends, money, housing, safety—the more easily and rapidly the victim recovers from the victimization." The author concludes with a discussion of how to design and implement programs that best meet the urgent needs of victims whose personal and social circumstances have been frequently ignored or subordinated to the interests of the offender.

The Aftermath of Mugging

Despite the fact that many urban residents live with a general anticipation of violent street crime, it is nonetheless an unexpected and harrowing event when it happens to them. "On Being Mugged: The Event and its Aftermath," by Robert Lejeune and Nicholas Alex, probes the mugging and its social and psychological consequences.

City residents routinely conduct their lives based on tacit assumptions of personal invulnerability and interpersonal trust and, as a result, often misdefine the initial phase of a mugging. The confrontation is commonly seen as a joke rather than as an actual intimidation that is a prelude to violence. The violent encounter typically begins in a familiar setting that has been routinely nonthreatening. Furthermore, because the assailant's demeanor and attire are often disarming because so conventional, the violence may assume the unusual character of unreality due to disbelief.

The mugging may be followed by an abrupt psychological conversion manifested by a heightened sense of vulnerability and distrust. These reactions are bolstered and maintained as the result of social exchanges that often follow the mugging. The victim will usually talk with family, friends, and acquaintances about the attack, crystallizing and consolidating the awareness that protective measures must be adopted in public places. Feelings of vulnerability can be further exacerbated by the police when they reveal how little assistance they can (or will) provide. As a result, the mugging may force the victim into the defensive posture of acquiring personal armaments and becoming "adept at evasion . . . and as ruthless as the victimizers." While the aftermath of interpersonal violence can certainly result in grievous harm and even in death to the victim, we also are beginning to realize how the pervasiveness of interpersonal violence in our society corrodes and imperils the quality of life for all of us.

Chapter 2

Homicide and Aggravated Assault

Homicide: Behavioral Aspects

Marvin E. Wolfgang and Margaret A. Zahn

Homicide is the killing of one human being by another. As a legal category, it can be criminal or noncriminal. Criminal homicides are generally considered first-degree murder, when one person causes the death of another with premeditation and intent, or second-degree murder, when the death is with malice and intent but is not premeditated. Voluntary manslaughter usually involves intent to inflict bodily injury without deliberate intent to kill; involuntary manslaughter is negligent or reckless killing without intent to harm.

Noncriminal forms include excusable homicide, usually in self-defense, and justifiable homicide, as when a police officer kills a felon or when a convicted offender is executed by the state. The classification of any homicide as either criminal or noncriminal, or of a death as either a homicide, an accident, or a natural death, is not uniform across all time periods or across legal jurisdictions. What is considered a homicide death varies over time by the legal code of given jurisdictions and by the interpretations and practices of agencies responsible for reporting deaths. When cars were first introduced into the United States, for example, deaths resulting from them were classified by some coroners as homicides, although now they are generally labeled accidental deaths unless caused by negligence. An abortion may be considered a criminal homicide or the exercise of women's reproductive choice. Homicide statistics, like those of many other crimes, reflect definitions and legal interpretations that vary over time and space. . . .

SOURCES OF DATA ON HOMICIDE

Homicide data generally derive from either health or police agencies. There are two major sources of international data, one compiled by the United Nations in *World Health Statistics Annual* and the other by the International Criminal Police Organization (Interpol), which was established in 1950. In addition, the national police agency of each country reports the number of that country's homicides for every two-year period. *World Health Statistics Annual* publishes the causes of death, including homicide, for each reporting country. These statistics, which have been collected since 1939, are the joint product of the health and statistical administration of many countries and the office of the United Nations and the World Health Organization. Problems in the use of these sources include lack of consistent definitions and interpretations across jurisdictions and lack of consistent reporting by all countries. Some countries, including many Communist ones, do not routinely report.

Within the United States there are two major national sources of data on homicide: the National Center for Health Statistics (NCHS) and the Federal Bureau of Investigation's *Crime in the United States* (known as the Uniform Crime Reports and published annually). The NCHS data derive from coroners and medical examiners, who forward death certificates to the center's Division of Vital Statistics. These data focus solely on the homicide victim and generally include information on the cause of death and the age, race, and sex of the victim. Data about offenders, victim-offender relationships, and motives are not included. The various states entered this national reporting system at different times. Prior to the 1930s, when the system became fully national, the data available depended on which states and cities were included. Boston was the first entrant, and in general, there were data from East Coast cities very early. Boston had death data in 1880, Pennsylvania in 1906, and Washington, D.C. in 1880. Other states, such as Georgia and Texas, entered the registry much later—in 1922 and 1933, respectively. In establishing trends, then, there is difficulty in obtaining national data before 1930.

The Uniform Crime Reports, a voluntary national data-collection effort, began in 1930 and gradually accumulated reporting police districts. Homicide reports are detailed and include information on both victims and offenders and, since the 1970s, on victim-offender relationships. This system is the only national one with information on homicide offenders and includes information on crimes classified by size of population, state, county, and Standard Metropolitan Statistical Area. Although there are some problems with the use of the Uniform Crime Reports data, they are commonly used in studies of homicide. . . .

CROSS-NATIONAL PATTERNS OF CRIMINAL HOMICIDE

Although there are problems in using international crime statistics because of differing definitions and methods in classifying the phenomenon, both Interpol and United Nations data nonetheless offer useful information on homicide rates in different countries. Of the two, data from the United Nations are more frequently used for cross-national studies. Marvin Wolfgang and Franco Ferracuti, for example, used these data in their discussion of the subcultural determinants of homicide. . . . Basing their study on data from the late 1950s and early 1960s, they found that in general, the highest rates of homicide were in Latin America and the Caribbean. Among the fifteen countries and legal dependencies constituting the top quartile, ten were Latin American; the top three were Colombia, Mexico, and Nicaragua. The lowest rates were found in northern and western European countries. Nine northern and western countries were found in the bottom quartile.

Wolfgang and Ferracuti hypothesized that the relatively high homicide rates in Latin American and Caribbean countries, as well as in urban communities and southern states in the United States, are related to subcultural values supporting violence as a means of interpersonal dispute resolution. . . . In countries with relatively weak normative supports for the resolution of violent disputes—as in many northern European, western European, and Asiatic countries—low homicide rates are found. These findings are reported for sixty-one countries and do not include many Islamic, African, and Communist countries. The last have not provided, or do not have, reportable data; hence, comparative findings reflect a select set of countries.

Marshall Clinard and Daniel Abbott, using United Nations data, presented international homicide rates for the late 1960s. Of twenty-five countries examined, nine of the thirteen highest were Hispanic; of the five lowest, three were northern or eastern European. Clinard and Abbott explained this observed variation by means of different theories of homicide. Subcultural theory was used to explain homicides in Hispanic countries that result from personal insult and extramarital involvements. . . . Homicides resulting from long-standing interfamilial or intertribal disputes were explained primarily as a function of normative or power conflicts. The authors applied this perspective to homicide in India, Ceylon, and sections of Africa . . . , introducing the concepts of tradition, obligation, and responsibility. Their formulation was used to account for certain kinds of homicide observed in tradition-bound sectors of African society—for example, those that are the outcome of failure to pay the bride-price attached to the ritual marriage contract.

Dane Archer and Rosemary Gartner compared selected cross-national homicide rates drawn from their comparative crime data file of 110 nations. Their data confirmed previous findings: Latin American and Caribbean countries are represented among the high-rate countries, and European countries are among the low-rate ones. Of the ten high-rate countries, five are Latin American, Caribbean, or Hispanic; of the ten low-rate countries, eight are northern, eastern or western European.

Insufficient cross-national data exist on the basic demographics of criminal homicide—that is, age, sex, race, and socioeconomic distributions. The existing data, however, suggest that criminal homicide is more prevalent among the young, among males, and among racial, ethnic, and religious minorities (Connor). The United States scores substantially higher than European countries, but lower than most Latin American ones, in the rate of criminal homicide. The rate in the United States is relatively high, especially when compared to other countries of similar levels of development, affluence, and cultural heritage.

PATTERNS OF CRIMINAL HOMICIDE IN THE UNITED STATES

. . . Trend studies in the United States (Klebba; Farley) and comparative analyses in different time periods (Zahn) reveal that the overall homicide rate increased from 1900 to the early 1930s. The rate declined slowly after 1933 and was low in the 1940s and 1950s. Homicide in the United States was at a minimum in the 1950s (Farley) but was followed by a modest rise and then a steep rise from 1963 through the late 1970s. The pattern held for blacks and whites and for males and females, although homicide has always been much more common among blacks and males. Reynolds Farley has reported that age-adjusted homicide rates are about six times greater for nonwhites than for whites, and four times higher for men than for women. Homicide victimization rates are highest for young adults: the highest rates generally occur between the ages of twenty-five and thirty-five. . . . There are also differences in geographic patterns of homicide, with higher rates of violence in the South. . . .

Victim–Offender Relationships

Literature on homicide since the 1960s has attempted to describe the relationship between the victim and offender and the motive for the slaying. Although many relationships occur in human affairs, only some seem to be persistently associated with homicide. Seldom, for example, is an employee-employer relationship associated with homicide, but frequently a husband-wife relationship is. . . .

In the 1940s and 1950s, the percentage of homicides between husbands and wives was more pronounced [than previously], [and] homicides between two males known to one another as friends and acquaintances were still significant. In the late 1960s and the 1970s, victims who were strangers to the offenders . . . appeared to be more prevalent than in the past. . . . [Homicides between two friends or acquaintances—usually a male killing another male within the same racial group—was the largest category in a recent study of homicide in eight major cities (Zahn and Riedel, 1982).] . . . Males tend to be close to the same age, generally in the early thirties, with the victim slightly older than the offender. . . .

SOCIOLOGICAL EXPLANATIONS OF VIOLENCE

There are three sociological approaches to explaining homicide: the cultural-subcultural, the structural, and the interactional. Cultural theorists explain homicide as resulting from learned, shared values and behavior specific to a given group. The basic causes are the norms and values, transmitted across generations, that are learned by members of a group. Certain subgroups exhibit higher rates of homicide because they are participants in a subculture [in which] violence [is] a norm. . . . [T]his position asserts that there is a subculture of violence—that is, a subculture with a cluster of values that support and encourage the overt use of force in interpersonal relations and group interactions. . . .

. . . The structuralist position . . . asserts that broad-scale social forces such as lack of opportunity, institutional racism, persistent poverty, demographic transitions, and population density determine homicide rates. These forces operate independently of human cognition and do not require individual learning to explain their impact. . . . In general, structural explanations suggest variables that influence homicide rates. They do not specify, however, the conditions under which these variables lead to homicide rather than to other possible outcomes, such as passivity. With few exceptions, the explanations fail to examine whether structural forces work the same way for rates of family, friend, and stranger-to-stranger killings. . . .

Interaction theory focuses on the character of relationships that escalate into homicide. Interaction theorists see homicide as resulting from the [social] interaction process itself; they examine how the act of a participant precipitates the acts of another and how escalating [interpersonal] conflict culminates in homicide.

REFERENCES

Archer, Dane, and Gartner, Rosemary. "Homicide in 110 Nations: The Development of the Comparative Crime Data File." *International Annals of Criminology* 16 (1977): 109–139.

Block, Richard. *Violent Crime: Environment, Interaction, and Death*. Lexington, Mass.: Heath, Lexington Books, 1977.

Clinard, Marshall B., and Abbott, Daniel J. *Crime in Developing Countries: A Comparative Perspective*. New York: Wiley, 1973.

Connor, Walter D. "Criminal Homicide, USSR/USA: Reflections on Soviet Data in a Comparative Framework." *Journal of Criminal Law and Criminology* 64 (1973): 111–117.

Farley, Reynolds. "Homicide Trends in the United States." *Demography* 17 (1980): 177– 188.

International Criminal Police Organization. *Statistiques criminelles internationales*. St. Cloud, France: INTERPOL, biennially.

Klebba, A. Joan. "Homicide Trends in the United States, 1900–1974." *U.S. Public Health Service Public Health Reports* 90 (1975): 195–204.

United Nations, World Health Organization. *World Health Statistics Annual*. New York: WHO, annually.

Wolfgang, Marvin E. *Crimes of Violence: Report Submitted to the President's Commission on Law Enforcement and Administration of Justice*. Washington, D.C.: The Commission, 1967.

———. *Patterns in Criminal Homicide* (1958). Reprint. New York: Wiley, 1966.

———, and Ferracuti, Franco. *The Subculture of Violence: Towards an Integrated Theory in Criminology*. Translated from the Italian. London: Tavistock, 1967.

Zahn, Margaret A. "Homicide in the Twentieth-century United States." *History and Crime*. Edited by James A. Inciardi and Charles E. Faupel. Beverly Hills, Calif.: Sage, 1980, pp. 111–131.

———, and Riedel, Marc. "Homicide in Eight American Cities." Unpublished book manuscript, 1982.

Patterns and Recent Trends in Black Homicide

Patrick W. O'Carroll and James A. Mercy

*H*omicide among black Americans has emerged as one of the most important public health issues today. . . . [It] is the fifth leading cause of death among blacks overall and is actually the leading cause of death among blacks age 15 to 34 (Centers for Disease Control, 1985). The U.S. Department of Health and Human Services Secretary's Task force on Black and Minority Health notes that a large proportion of the disparity in health status between blacks and whites is due to high levels of homicide victimization in the black population. Indeed, for black males under age 45, homicide accounted for a greater proportion of this disparity than any other cause of death ([U.S.] Department of Health and Human Services, 1985).

Homicide has traditionally been considered a criminal justice problem, and the term "homicide" in that context connotes the commission of a criminal act. In this essay, however, homicide is considered as a cause of death, in the same sense that heart disease or cancer are causes of death. The term "homicide" in this context refers to victimization, rather than perpetration, and a "homicide rate" refers to the rate at which persons die from homicide, rather than the rate at which homicides are committed. . . .

HOMICIDE MORTALITY DATA

Homicide is defined [here] . . . as death resulting from the killing of one person by another, excluding death caused by law enforcement officers or legal execution. The information on homicide . . . is drawn primarily from the Federal Bureau of Investigation's Supplementary Homicide Reports (FBI-SHR). . . .

[(H]omicide victims are classified into two race categories, black and white. The white racial category includes homicide victims reported as white, Mexican, Puerto Rican and all other caucasians. Not included in either the black or white category are Native Americans, Asians and Pacific Islanders.[)] . . .

RATES BY AGE, SEX, AND REGION

During the period 1976 to 1984, over 75,000 black Americans lost their lives to homicide. Blacks experienced by far the highest homicide victimization rates of any racial group, with a combined nine-year rate of 31.7 homicide deaths per 100,000 persons per year. The risk of dying from homicide was six times greater for blacks than whites during this period.

Homicide is often considered primarily a "male" problem, because rates for males are consistently much higher than they are for females. Indeed, the risk of homicide was much higher for black males than black females . . . (53.6 vs. 11.9). However, the rate for black females was higher than the rate for white males. . . . Thus, although homicide rates are higher by far for black males than for any other race-sex group, black females also represent a group at high risk. . . .

For both males and females in 1983, black homicide rates were highest among young adults age 20 to 39 (Table 2-1). Homicide rates for black males peaked at 99.8 for those age 25 to 29; for black females, rates also peaked in the 25 to 29 year age group, at 20.5. Black male rates were four to five times greater than black female rates in almost all age groups. A similar pattern is seen among whites in terms of the high risk among young adults and the consistently greater male

Table 2-1.
Homicide Rates* by Race and Age of Victim, United States, 1983

	Black			White		
Age Group	**Male**	**Female**	**Both**	**Male**	**Female**	**Both**
Under 1	12.8	14.2	13.5	3.3	3.8	3.6
1–4	6.9	5.9	6.4	1.7	1.2	1.5
5–9	2.2	1.4	1.8	0.8	0.7	0.7
10–14	4.1	1.5	2.8	1.1	0.7	0.9
15–19	42.6	10.6	26.7	7.5	2.9	5.2
20–24	85.2	20.2	52.0	14.6	4.4	9.5
25–29	99.8	20.5	58.1	15.3	4.6	10.0
30–34	98.5	19.1	56.0	13.7	3.5	8.6
35–39	84.0	16.2	47.2	12.3	3.4	7.8
40–44	76.0	12.9	41.4	11.9	3.5	7.7
45–49	61.7	11.6	34.1	9.6	3.3	6.4
50–54	54.7	7.5	28.4	8.4	2.5	5.4
55–59	50.0	8.1	26.5	6.8	2.4	4.5
60–64	45.6	4.4	22.5	5.9	2.0	3.8
65–69	30.6	8.8	18.0	4.8	2.1	3.3
70–74	27.3	5.3	14.2	4.5	1.8	2.9
75–79	29.9	11.9	18.9	4.3	3.0	3.5
80–84	31.9	8.7	17.1	4.6	3.2	3.7
85+	50.5	9.4	16.1	5.7	3.9	4.4
Total	50.6	11.3	29.9	8.4	2.8	5.6

*Rates per 100,000 population

than female rates in each age group. However, the ratio of male to female rates is not quite so great for whites, with white male rates generally ranging between two to three times white female rates.

The risk of homicide victimization varies among the different regions of the country (Table 2-2). In 1980, 43% of all homicides occurred in the South. . . . [W]hen blacks and whites were considered separately, the West had the highest homicide rate for each race group. . . .

WEAPON USE, VICTIM-ASSAILANT RELATIONSHIP, AND CRIME CIRCUMSTANCE

Two-thirds of all homicides of blacks during the period 1976 to 1984 were committed with firearms . . . 77% of which were handguns. Indeed, homicides committed with handguns accounted for over half of all homicides of blacks. A similar but less pronounced pattern is seen for whites: 60% of homicides of whites were committed with firearms, most of which were handguns. . . .

There is a common misconception that most homicides are committed by strangers in the act of perpetrating some other felony crime, such as rape or robbery. In fact, most homicide victims know their assailants. . . . During the period studied, 60% of homicides of blacks were committed by acquaintances or family members, and only 12% were committed by strangers. This pattern varies by sex. Of black male homicide victims, 44.9% were killed by acquaintances, while 13.2% were killed by family members. Of black female homicide victims, 37.2% were killed by acquaintances and 28.4% were killed by family members. . . . [H]omicides committed by family members are proportionately two times more important for black females than for black males. On the other hand, acquaintance homicide and stranger homicide are proportionately more important for black males. . . .

Almost two-thirds of all homicides of blacks occurred in the context of arguments or some other non-felony circumstance. . . . Only 13% to 17% of black victims were killed by assailants committing some other felony crime, such as robbery. The majority of homicides of whites also occurs under non-felony-associated circumstances, but felony . . . homicides account for a greater proportion of homicides among whites.

Table 2-2.
Homicide Rates by Geographic Region of Occurrence and Race of Victim, United States, 1980

	Total	White	Black
United States	10.6	6.8	38.4
Northeast	8.2	5.1	36.0
North Central	8.1	4.3	46.6
South	13.5	8.9	33.7
West	11.4	9.2	50.3

TEMPORAL TRENDS IN BLACK HOMICIDE

Overall blacks experienced a 20.4% decrease in homicide rates during the period under study. . . . Rates for black males declined by 20.4%, from 53.4 in 1976 to 42.5 in 1984. Rates for black females declined by 19.4%, from 12.4 . . . to 10.0. . . . Almost all age groups experienced some decline in homicide rates. During the same period, white homicide rates increased by 6.5%. Declining black rates and increasing white rates narrowed the gap in homicide risk between blacks and whites, but in 1984 blacks were still 5.2 times more likely to die from homicide than whites. . . .

DIRECTIONS FOR RESEARCH AND PREVENTION

In every year of the 9 year period studied, in every region of the country, for both sexes and for every age group, blacks were many times more likely to die from homicide than whites. Black males consistently experienced the highest homicide rates of any race/sex group, and young black males were at especially high risk of homicide victimization. These dramatic differences in the risk of homicide victimization must be explained, and factors which place blacks at such high risk of homicide must be identified. . . .

COMMON PATTERNS OF HOMICIDE

Considered in light of the dramatic differences noted . . . in the risk of homicide victimization for blacks and whites, it is perhaps remarkable that in a number of ways the patterns of homicide in the two race groups are very similar. Specifically, for both blacks and whites:

- males were many times more likely to die . . . than females;
- for both males and females . . . rates were highest among young adults, peaking among those age 20 to 39;
- . . . rates were highest in the West;
- at least half of all . . . victims were killed with firearms, most of which were handguns;
- the majority of homicides occurred during the course of an argument or some other non-felony circumstance; only a small proportion . . . occurred during the perpetration of another crime (e.g. robbery);
- at least half of all . . . victims were killed by persons whom they knew;
- a greater proportion of female . . . victims were killed by family members than male . . . victims; conversely, a greater proportion of male . . . victims were killed by acquaintances or strangers.

This commonality in . . . patterns among blacks and whites suggests that, despite dramatic differences in risk of victimization, the fundamental causes of homicide may be much the same regardless of race. Differences in . . . rates presumably arise because those factors which increase the risk of homicide victimization are experienced more frequently or more intensely by blacks than they are by whites. Patterns . . . that are common to all race groups also suggest that preventive interventions developed for high risk groups may ultimately be applicable to the general population.

The fundamental causes of homicide may indeed be related to such pervasive societal influences as poverty and prejudice. To the extent that this is true, this is yet another reason to work toward the elimination of these evils. But there is much that can be done on a more immediate scale as well that may be effective in the prevention of homicide. Since most homicides are not associated with the commission of some other felony crime (e.g. robbery) and since most homicide victims are killed by acquaintances or family members, preventive strategies must include, but also go beyond, the purview of the criminal justice system. Community leaders and health and social service professionals must work together with law enforcement agencies if we are to reduce the tremendous, tragic toll exacted by homicide.

REFERENCES

Centers for Disease Control. Homicide Among Young Black Males—United States, 1970–1982. Morbidity Mortality Weekly Rep 1985; 34; 629–33.

U.S. Department of Health and Human Services. 1985. Report of the Secretary's Task Force on Black and Minority Health. Washington, D.C.: Department of Health and Human Services, August.

Criminal Homicide as a Situated Transaction

David F. Luckenbill

The present data were drawn from all cases of criminal homicide over a ten-year period, 1963–1972, in one medium sized (350,000) California county. . . .

All official documents pertaining to these cases were secured. The character of the larger occasion as well as the organization and development of the fateful transaction were reconstructed from the content analysis of police, probation, psychiatric, and witness reports, offender interviews, victim statements, and grand jury and court testimony. . . .

THE SOCIAL OCCASION OF CRIMINAL HOMICIDE

Criminal homicide is the culmination of an intense interchange between an offender and victim. Transactions resulting in murder involved the joint contribution of the offender and victim to the escalation of a "character contest," a confrontation in which at least one, but usually both, attempt to establish or save face at the other's expense by standing steady in the face of adversity (Goffman, 1967: 218–219, 238–257). Such transactions additionally involved a consensus among participants that violence was a suitable if not required means for settling the contest.

Before examining the dynamics of these transactions, it is useful to consider the larger context in which they were imbedded. A "situated transaction" refers to a chain of interaction between two or more individuals that lasts the time they find themselves in one another's immediate physical presence (Goffman, 1963: 167). A "social occasion," in contrast, refers to a wider social affair within which many situated transactions may form, dissolve, and re-form (Goffman, 1963: 18). And, as Goffman aptly demonstrates, social occasions carry boundaries of sorts which establish what kinds of transactions are appropriate and inappropriate.

Social occasions which encompassed transactions ending in murder shared several features. First, all such transactions occurred in occasions of non-work or leisure-time (cf. Bullock, 1955; Wolfgang, 1958: 121–128; Wallace, 1965). The majority of murders occurred between the leisure hours of six p.m. and two a.m. and especially on weekends. More important, they were always found in leisure settings: almost half the cases occurred while members engaged in leisure activities at home; fifteen percent occurred while members frequented a favorite tavern; another fifteen percent occurred while members habituated a streetcorner or "turf;" little over twelve percent occurred while the offender and victim drove or "cruised" about the city, highway, or country roads; the few remaining cases occurred while members engaged in activities in some other public place such as a hotel room.

Second, occasions of murder were "loose," informal affairs permitting a wide range of activities definable by members as appropriate (cf. Goffman, 1963: 198–215). In contrast to work and such tighter occasions of leisure as weddings and funerals, where members are bound by rather strict sets of expectations, occasions of murder were permissive environs allowing the performance of various respectable and non-respectable activities. . . .

In the sample, members engaged in a variety of activities within such loosely structured occasions. In about seventy-five percent of the cases, the offender and victim were engaged in pleasurable pursuits. They sought to drop serious or work roles and pursue such enjoyable activities as drinking alcoholic beverages, dancing, partying, watching television, or cruising main street. In the remainder of the cases, members were engaged in reasonably serious concerns. Here, conversations of marital or relational futures, sexual prowess, beauty, trustworthiness, and integrity were central themes about which members organized.

A third feature of such occasions was their population by intimates. In over sixty percent of the cases, the offender and victim were related by marriage, kinship, or friendship. In the remaining cases, while the offender and victim were enemies, mere acquaintances, or complete strangers, at least one, but often both were in the company of their family, friends, lovers, or co-workers.

DYNAMICS OF THE SITUATED PERFORMANCE

These are the occasions in which situated transactions resulted in violent death. . . . In almost half the cases there had previously occurred what might be termed rehearsals between the offender and victim. . . . [I]t was possible to derive a set of time-ordered stages of which each shares certain basic properties. . . . In discussing the first five stages, the labels of offender and victim will be used to refer to the statuses that emerge in the course of interaction and not the statuses resulting from the battle. . . . In the discussion of the sixth stage the labels of offender and victim will be used to refer to the statuses resulting from the battle.

Stage I

The opening move in the transaction was an event performed by the victim and subsequently defined by the offender as an offense to "face," that image of self a person claims during a particular occasion or social contact (Goffman, 1967:5). . . .

While the form and content of the victim's move varied, three basic types of events cover all cases. In the first, found in over forty-one percent of the cases, the victim made some direct, verbal expression which the offender subsequently interpreted as offensive. . . . Included were everything from insults levied at some particular attribute of the offender's self, family, or friends to verbal tirades which disparaged the overall character of the offender:

> *Case 34* The offender, victim, and two friends were driving toward the country where they could consume their wine. En route, the victim turned to the offender, both of whom were located in the back seat, and stated: "You know, you really got some good parents. You know, you're really a son-of-a-bitch. You're a leech. The whole time you were out of a job, you were living with them, and weren't even paying. The car you have should be your father's. He's the one who made the payments. Any time your dad goes to the store, you're the first in line to sponge off him. Why don't you grow up and stop being a leech?" The offender swore at him, and told him to shut up. But the victim continued, "Someone ought to come along and really fuck you up."

A second type, found in thirty-four percent of the cases, involved the victim's refusal to cooperate or comply with the requests of the offender. The offender subsequently interpreted the victim's action as a denial of his ability or right to command obedience. This was illustrated in transactions where parents murdered their children. When the parent's request that the child eat dinner, stop screaming, or take a bath went unheeded, the parent subsequently interpreted the child's activity as a challenge to rightful authority. . . .

The third type of event, found in twenty-five percent of the cases, involved some physical or nonverbal gesture which the offender subsequently defined as personally offensive. Often this gesture entailed an insult to the offender's sexual prowess, and took the form of affairs or flirtation. . . .

Stage II

In all cases ending in murder the offender interpreted the victim's previous move as personally offensive. In some cases the victim was intentionally offensive. But it is plausible that in other cases the victim was unwitting. . . . [F]or instance, the victim, a five-week old boy, started crying early in the morning. The offender, the boy's father, ordered the victim to stop crying. . . . The victim was too young to understand the [father's] verbal order [and continued to cry]. . . . [Whatever the child's motive for continued crying, the] child's father defined it as purposive and offensive. . . . What the victim intends may be inconsequential. What the offender interprets as intentional, however, may have consequences for the organization of subsequent activity.

In sixty percent of the cases, the offender learned the meaning of the victim's move from inquiries made of victim or audience. In reply, the offender received statements suggesting the victim's action was insulting and intentional. In thirty-nine percent of the cases, the offender ascertained the meaning of the impropriety directly from the victim. . . .

Stage III

The apparent affront could have evoked different responses. The offender could have excused the violation because the victim was judged to be drunk, crazy, or joking. He could have fled the scene and avoided further interaction with the victim. . . .

In countering the impropriety, the offender attempted to restore the occasioned order and reaffirm face by standing his or her ground. To have used another alternative was to confirm questions of face and self raised by the victim. . . . Two basic patterns of retaliation were found. In eighty-six percent of the cases, the offender issued a verbal or physical challenge to the victim. In the remaining cases, the offender physically retaliated, killing the victim. . . .

This third stage is the offender's opening move in salvaging face and honor. In retaliating by verbal and physically nonlethal means, the offender appeared to suggest to the victim a definition of the situation as one in which violence was suitable in settling questions of face and reputation.

Stage IV

Except for cases in which the victim has been eliminated, the offender's preceeding move placed the victim in a problematic and consequential position: either stand up to the challenge and demonstrate strength of character, or apologize, discontinue the inappropriate conduct, or flee the situation and thus withdraw questions of the offender's face while placing one's own in jeopardy. Just as the offender could have dismissed the impropriety, fled the scene, or avoided further contact with the victim, so too did the victim have similar alternatives. Rather than break the escalation in a manner demonstrating weakness, all victims in the remaining sample came into a "working" agreement with the proffered definition of the situation as one suited for violence. In the majority of cases, the victim's move appeared as an agreement that violence was suitable to the transaction. In some cases, though, the offender interpreted, sometimes incorrectly, the victim's move as implicit agreement to violence. A working agreement was struck in several ways.

The most prominent response, found in forty-one percent of the cases, involved noncompliance with the offender's challenge or command, and the continued performance of activities deemed offensive:

> *Case 54* The victim continued ridiculing the offender before friends. The offender finally shouted, "I said shut up. If you don't shut up and stop it, I'm going to kill you and I mean it." The victim continued his abusive line of conduct. The offender proceeded to the kitchen, secured a knife, and returned to the living room. She repeated her warning. The victim rose from his chair, swore at the offender's stupidity, and continued laughing at her. She thrust the knife deep into his chest.

Similarly, a spouse or lover's refusal, under threat of violence, to conciliate a failing marriage or relationship served as tacit acceptance that violence was suitable to the present transaction. . . .

Just as the victim contributed to the escalation toward violence, so too did the audience to the transaction. Seventy percent of all cases were performed before an audience. In these cases, onlookers generally engaged one or two roles. In fifty-seven percent of these cases, interested members of the audience intervened in the transaction, and actively encouraged the use of violence by means of indicating to opponents the initial improprieties, cheering them toward violent action, blocking the encounter from outside interference, or providing lethal weapons. . . .

Stage V

On forging a working agreement, the offender and, in many cases, the victim appeared committed to battle. . . . They placed their character on the line, and alternative methods for assessing character focused on a working agreement that violence was appropriate. . . .

Commitment to battle was additionally enhanced by the availability of weapons to support verbal threats and challenges. . . . In about thirty-six percent of the cases, offenders carried handguns or knives into the setting. In only thirteen percent of these cases did offenders bring handguns or knives into the situation on the assumption that they might be needed if the victims were confronted. In the remainder of these cases such weapons were brought in as a matter of everyday routine. . . . In sixty-four percent of the cases, the offender either left the situation temporarily to secure a handgun, rifle, or knife, or transformed the status of some existing situational prop, such as a pillow, telephone cord, kitchen knife, beer mug, or baseball bat, into a lethal weapon. . . .

Stage VI

Once the victim had fallen, the offender made one of three moves which marked the termination of the transaction. In over fifty-eight percent of the cases, the offender fled the scene. In about thirty-two percent of the cases, the offender voluntarily remained on the scene for the police. In the remaining cases, the offender was involuntarily held for the police by members of the audience. . . .

When there is no audience, the offender appeared to act on the basis of his relationship to the victim. When the offender and the victim were intimately related, the offender typically remained on the scene and notified the police. Sometimes these offenders waited for minutes or hours before reporting the event, stating they needed time to think, check the victim's condition, and make arrangements on financial matters, the children, and work before arrest. In contrast, when victims were acquaintances or enemies, offenders typically fled the scene. Moreover, these offenders often attempted to dispose of their victims and incriminating evidence.

Seventy percent of the cases, however, occurred before an audience, and offenders' moves seemed related to audience reactions to the offense. Bystanders seemed to replace the victim as the primary interactant, serving the offender as the pivotal reference for his exiting orientations. The audience assumed one of three roles: hostile, neutral, or supportive. In the hostile role, . . . , bystanders moved to apprehend the offender, assist the victim, and immediately notify police. . . .

[In the neutral role], . . . people appeared as shocked bystanders. Having witnessed the killing, they stood numb as the offender escaped and the victim expired.

[In the supportive role, bystanders] . . . encouraged the offender during the pre-battle stages. Supportive bystanders rendered assistance to the offender in his escape, destroyed incriminating evidence, and maintained ignorance of the event when questioned by the police, breaking down only in later stages of interrogation. . . .

CONCLUSION

On the basis of this research, criminal homicide does not appear as a one-sided event with an unwitting victim assuming a passive, non-contributory role. Rather, murder is the outcome of a dynamic interchange between an offender, victim, and, in many cases, bystanders. The offender and victim develop lines of action shaped in part by the actions of the other and focused toward saving or maintaining face and reputation and demonstrating character. Participants develop a working agreement, sometimes implicit, often explicit, that violence is a useful tool for resolving questions of face and character. . . .

REFERENCES

Bullock, Henry A.
1955 "Urban homicide in theory and fact." Journal of Criminal Law, Criminology and Police Science 45 (January–February): 565–575.
Goffman, Erving
1963 Behavior in Public Places: Notes on the Social Organization of Gatherings. Glencoe: Free Press.
1967 Interaction Ritual: Essays on Face-to-Face Behavior. Garden City, N.Y.: Doubleday.
1969 Strategic Interaction, New York: Ballantine.
Wallace, Samuel E.
1965 "Patterns of violence in San Juan." Pp. 43–48 in Interdisciplinary Problems in Criminology: Papers of the American Society of Criminology, 1964, edited by Walter C. Reckless and Charles L. Newman. Columbus: Ohio State University Press.
Wolfgang, Marvin E.
1958 Patterns of Criminal Homicide. Philadelphia: University of Pennsylvania Press.

Mass Murder: America's Growing Menace

Jack Levin and James Alan Fox

Since 1980, the number of mass murders that have made headlines in the newspapers has grown noticeably, even as the rate of homicide itself on a national level is beginning to subside. The nation is faced, if by this time not shocked, by an average of three mass murders each month. The state of Texas alone was hit recently with three mass slayings in one month. . . .

Some mass killers are so despicably evil that we can feel no compassion, while others are understood to be expressing impulses that they cannot control. Some mass murderers kill so obtrusively that their crimes are featured in the news across the country; others hardly disturb the night as they massacre their entire sleeping families and so are renowned only in their own communities.

Even with the many features that make each mass murder unique, there is one distinction among mass killings that . . . is central to understanding the motives, the detection, and the punishment of this crime. The fundamental dichotomy is between serial killers—mass murderers who slay their victims on different occasions—and simultaneous killers—those who murder their victims at the same time or in one episode. . . .

The popular view of the mass killer closely fits the likes of one Edward Gein, a man whose name is not widely known but whose misdeeds have become ingrained in our minds.[1]

The break of dawn on November 16, 1957 heralded the start of deer hunting season in rural Waushara County, Wisconsin. The men of Plainfield went off with their hunting rifles and knives but without any clue of what Edward Gein would do that day. Gein was known to the 647 residents of Plainfield as a quiet man who kept to himself and his aging, dilapidated farmhouse. But when the men of the village returned from hunting that evening, they learned the awful truth about their 51-year-old neighbor and the atrocities that he had ritualized within the walls of his farmhouse.

The first in a series of discoveries that would disrupt the usually tranquil town occurred when Frank Worden arrived at his hardware store after hunting all day. Frank's mother, Bernice Worden, who had been minding the store, was missing; so was Frank's truck. But there was a pool of blood on the floor and a trail of blood leading toward the place where the truck had been garaged.

The investigation of Bernice's disappearance and possible homicide led police to the farm of Ed Gein. . . . Methodically scanning the barn for clues, the sheriff's light suddenly exposed a hanging figure, apparently Mrs. Worden. As Captain Schoephoerster later described[2]:

> . . . Mrs. Worden had been completely dressed out like a deer with her head cut off at the shoulders. Gein had slit the skin on the back of her ankles and inserted a wooden rod, 3-1/2 feet long, and about 4 inches in diameter, and sharpened to a point at both ends, through the cut tendons on the back of her ankles. Both hands were tied to her side with binder twine. The center of the rod was attached to a pulley on a block and tackle. The body was pulled up so that the feet were near the ceiling. We noticed that there was just a few drops of watery blood beneath the body on the dirt floor, and not finding the head or intestines, we thought possibly the body had been butchered at another location.

Apparently, "deer" season had begun in the mind of Edward Gein too. . . .

In the months that followed, more of the macabre practices of Ed Gein were unveiled. Not only was he suspected in several other deaths, but Gein admitted to having robbed corpses and body parts from a number of graves. Gein used these limbs and organs to fashion ornaments, such as a belt of nipples and a hanging human head, as well as decorations for his house, including chairs upholstered with human skin and bed posts crowned with skulls. A shoe box containing nine vulvas was but one part of Gein's grim collection of female organs. On moonlit evenings he would prance around his farm wearing a real female mask, a vest of skin complete with female breasts, and woman's panties filled with vaginas in an attempt to recreate the form and presence of his dead mother. . . .

The most dramatic characteristics of simultaneous multiple killings are their suddenness and their ferocity: the speed with which so many lives are destroyed. . . . [F]ew episodes remain so fixed in the minds of Americans, epitomizing the horror of mass murder, as the ninety-one-minute outburst that shook the nation in August of 1966. . . .

On August 1, 1966, [Charles] Whitman had climbed atop the 307-foot tower on the campus of the University of Texas in Austin and had opened fire on the campus from a vantage point behind the tower's huge clock. Ninety-one bloody minutes later, fourteen were dead or dying. Thirty more lay injured in a sixteen-block area surrounding the tower which, strewn with casualties, looked more like a war zone than a college campus. Another victim of Whitman's rampage was the fetus of a woman eight months pregnant that was stillborn. In addition to these casualties, Whitman had killed his mother and his wife the night before, and Whitman himself was gunned down by a team of four officers at the top of the tower.

To those who knew Charlie casually, he was the "all-American boy," certainly not the popular image of a deadly killer. A committed and hard-working student, he had earned all A's during his final semester at the University of Texas. . . . He also seemed to be a friendly and caring fellow. After having been an eagle scout in his youth, Whitman as an adult served as a scoutmaster, and impressed the scouts' parents as being good with the children. Being a bright student and a respected member of the community, he seemed to have a promising future. But his parents, his wife, and his friends knew the real Charles Whitman, a troubled man who, according to his psychiatrist, was "oozing with hostility."[3] Whitman had in fact told the doctor that he thought about "going up on the tower with a deer rifle and start shooting people," but the therapist considered this to be merely one of the many idle fantasies that depressed college students entertain about the tower.[4] Whitman also beat his wife on occasion, as reportedly his father—whom he hated passionately—had done to the mother Charles so passionately loved. . . .

Despite the extreme nature of his crime, the mass killer appears to be extraordinarily ordinary. He is indistinguishable from everyone else. Indeed, he may be the neighbor next door, a co-worker at the next desk, or a member of the family. Because of his ordinary role in the community, those who know him best are astonished when they learn of his murderous behavior.

No one can predict who will turn out to be a mass killer. Beyond personality and background, there are significant elements in a setting—the availability of weapons, obedience to authority, membership in a group whose theme is murder—that encourage "normal" people to kill.

Like murder generally, few mass murderers prey on total strangers. The extent to which the victims of mass murder are specifically chosen by the killer or are simply unfortunate to be "in the wrong place at the wrong time" depends on the type and motivation of the crime. Simultaneous slaughters rarely involve total strangers. . . .

The serial killer typically picks on innocent strangers who may possess a certain physical feature or may just be accessible. Nearly without exception, serial killers select the vulnerable—prostitutes who willingly enter cars of strangers and subject themselves to submissive roles, hitchhikers who similarly place themselves within the domain controlled by the killer, old women who live alone and are defenseless, and children whose trusting nature or lack of strength make them easy marks. . . .

Do mass killers really get away with murder? This depends on the type of killing. Simultaneous massacres usually leave behind a houseful of evidence leading a trail to the perpetrator. . . .

The police have far more difficulty with serial killers. In the first place, some time may pass before law enforcement investigators realize that a series of seemingly unrelated homicides is actually the work of a single individual—by that time, he may be long gone. The Justice Department is taking initiatives to try to stem the tide of serial murders in the United States. Both psychological profiling of the unknown killer from clues at the scene of the crime and computerized linking of crimes in separate jurisdictions hold some promise. Besides their intrinsic limitations, however, these methods must challenge the cunning and skill of the most successful of all killers. . . . [W]hen a serial murderer is caught, it is often more a result of luck or the cooperation of snitches than of the matching skill of the investigators.

When mass killers are caught and prosecuted, they rarely get treated with leniency. Very few benefit from the insanity plea—if in fact such is a benefit—and most get extremely severe penalties: either death or life imprisonment. Under recent laws, many states employ sentences for mass killers that explicitly prohibit their release on parole. . . .

Public support for the execution of mass killers is now overwhelming. Gallup polls indicate that two of every three Americans now approve of the death penalty for murder.[5] Furthermore, we found in a survey of almost four hundred Bostonians even stronger support for the death penalty in the case of mass murder than in the case of other forms of murder.[6] . . .

Based on our study of forty-two mass killers and FBI data on simultaneous homicides, we have developed a composite profile of a mass murderer. . . . He is typically a white male in his late twenties or thirties. In the case of simultaneous mass murder, he kills people he knows with a handgun or rifle; in serial crimes, he murders strangers by beating or strangulation. His specific motivation depends on the circumstances leading up to the crime, but it generally deals directly with either money, expediency, jealousy, or lust. Rarely is the mass murderer a hardened criminal with a long criminal record, although a spotty history of property crime is common. The occurrence of mass murder often follows a spell of frustration when a particular event triggers sudden rage; yet, in other cases, the killer is coolly pursuing some goal he cannot otherwise attain. Finally, though the mass killer often may appear cold and show no remorse, and even deny responsibility for his crime, serious mental illness or psychosis is rarely present. Most unexpectedly, in background, in personality, and even in appearance, the mass murderer is *extraordinarily ordinary*. This may be the key to his extraordinary "talent" for murder: After all, who would ever suspect him?

NOTES

1. Much of the information about the case of Edward Gein came from Judge Robert H. Gollmar, *Edward Gein: America's Most Bizarre Murderer* (Delavan, Wisconsin: Chas. Hallberg and Company, 1981).
2. ". . . Mrs. Worden had . . ." *ibid.*, p. 32.
3. "All-American Boy," *Newsweek*, August 15, 1966, p. 24.
4. *Ibid.*
5. George H. Gallup, *The Gallup Report*, No. 187 (Princeton, New Jersey: The Gallup Poll, April 1981), pp. 18, 19 reprinted in Bureau of Justice Statistics, United States Department of Justice, *Sourcebook of Criminal Justice Statistics—1982* (Washington, D.C.: United States Government Printing Office, 1983), p. 264.
6. The survey of Bostonians was conducted at the College of Criminal Justice, Northeastern University.

Human Violence: A Comparison of Homicide, Aggravated Assault, Suicide, and Attempted Suicide

Alex D. Pokorny

SUICIDE-HOMICIDE

One of the most familiar themes in discussions of suicide and homicide is that these behaviors are closely related. Not only do they both represent the taking of human life by a human, but it is held that they are related in their motivation, that they spring from the same soil.

Perhaps the best known of these views is that suicide is a kind of inverted or retroflexed homicide[1]: "Nobody kills himself who had not intended to kill somebody else."[2] . . . Suicide and homicide are seen as having similar underlying and often unconscious motivations. Karl Menninger has emphasized that persons who commit suicide have a wish to kill as one of the necessary components. . . .

A contrasting view is that suicide and homicide are just the opposite of each other.[3] Durkheim . . . expresses doubt about the universality of this inversion, but he lists a number of observations which are compatible with it: (1) With regard to rates in European countries, there is a good fit; Spain, Ireland, and Italy are the three countries with the least suicide, yet they have the most murders, whereas France and Prussia are just the reverse; (2) Wars tend to decrease suicides but to increase homicides, and political crises have the same effect; (3) Suicide is more urban than rural, with homicide the opposite; (4) Catholic countries have high homicide and low suicide rates, whereas Protestant countries are just the opposite.[4] . . .

HOMICIDE-AGGRAVATED ASSAULT

. . . Homicide has a related, larger category of Aggravated Assault. This has been defined as an attempt to deprive an individual of his life or to cause him serious injury.[5] Is Aggravated Assault properly viewed as a bungled or unsuccessful Homicide, with the same motivations and characteristics? . . .

It has been stated that homicide offenders have, as a long-term characteristic, greater impulsivity, less ability to control emotions.[6] It has been found . . . that in many instances of homicide fierce arguments precede the murder, with progressive escalation in emotion and violence.[7] It may therefore be largely a matter of chance that an offense becomes a homicide or an assault. . . .

PROCEDURE

Data for individual cases of Suicide, Attempted Suicide, and Criminal Homicide were abstracted from the files of the Houston Police Department.[8] . . . This yielded a total of 400 Attempted Suicides (the round number is fortuitous), 320 Suicides, and 438 Homicides. . . .

RESULTS

1. Place:
   a. *Place of Occurrence*. . . . Suicides and Attempted Suicides occur typically at home, whereas Homicides occur more typically away from home, in public places such as bars, streets, and sidewalks, places where suicides and suicide attempts are virtually unknown. This is consistent with the idea that Suicide is a "private affair", whereas Homicide requires a partner. In this respect Attempted Suicide seems more like suicide.
2. Time:
   a. *Hour of Occurrence*. . . . Homicides and Aggravated Assaults are quite similar, with the offenses bunched in the periods from 5:00 p.m. to 2:00 a.m. The hourly distribution for Suicide is strikingly different, with a peak in the morning and tapering off in the afternoon and evening. The hourly distribution of Attempted Suicide is approximately midway between the others; the peak hours of Attempted Suicide do fall into the "after work" period of the day, suggesting that presence of other people was a factor. All four types of behavior fall off during the hours of 2:00 to 6:00 a.m.

b. *Day of Week.* . . . Homicide and Aggravated Assault show the astonishingly high correlation of .997; both tend to occur on weekends with a peak on Saturday. Attempted Suicide likewise is more frequent on weekends and shows some positive (though non-significant) correlation with Homicide and Assault. In this series Suicide is more common in the middle of the week, so that the relationship to the other behaviors is a negative one. . . .

3. Persons:
   a. *Race and Ethnic Groups, Rates.* [I]t is apparent that Negroes are greatly overrepresented in the Homicide and Aggravated Assault columns, while being sharply underrepresented in the Suicide and Attempted Suicide columns. Just the opposite is true for the "Other White" group. The Latin-American group shows by far the fewest Suicides, and they are moderately low in Suicide Attempts. Thus, with regard to race and ethnic grouping, Suicide and Attempted Suicide are similar, and the same is true for Homicide and Aggravated Assault.
   b. *Sex.* . . . [M]ales account for about three-fourths of the cases in all columns (including victims in Aggravated Assault and Homicide cases) except for Attempted Suicide; here the proportions are about reversed. Thus in terms of this one factor, Attempted Suicide does not appear to resemble any of the other behaviors.

DISCUSSION

In practically all of the characteristics studied, Suicide and Homicide are the opposite of each other. Suicide tends to occur at home, homicide away from home. The areas of residence of persons involved tend to be in different census tracts of the city. The hours of the day and days of the week are clearly different. The age distribution of the persons involved is distinctly different. Homicide is much more common in Negroes, whereas Suicide is much more common in Whites; in both cases, the Whites with Spanish surnames are in an intermediate position. The only similarity of these behaviors in the characteristics examined is in the sex distribution: both are more common in males.

Thus most of the findings here support the view that these are polar opposites, rather than that they are directly related. At least this appears to be true of the groups as a whole. . . .

. . . Criminal Homicide and Aggravated Assault seem to be similar in all of the analyses. They tend to occur in the same census tracts of the city. The distributions for the hour of the day and day of the week are remarkably similar. They have a very similar age distribution, with regard to both victims and offenders. The race and ethnic proportions in the two categories of offenses are quite similar. So is the representation of the sexes, in both victims and offenders. These findings suggest that Aggravated Assault and Criminal Homicide are basically the same category of behavior, and that it may be mainly a matter of chance that an assault becomes a homicide. . . .

NOTES

1. Jackson, *Theories of Suicide*, in Schneidman & Farberow, Clues to Suicide (New York: McGraw-Hill, 1957).
2. Fenichel, *The Psychoanalytic Theory of Neurosis* (New York: W. W. Norton & Company, Inc., 1945).
3. Wolfgang, *Patterns in Criminal Homicide* (Philadelphia: University of Pennsylvania Press, 1958).
4. It should be noted that the United States has a far higher homicide rate than any of these European countries. Dublin & Bunzel, "Thou Shall Not Kill, A Study of Homicide in the United States," 24 *Survey Graphic* 127 (1935).
5. Menninger, *Man Against Himself* (New York: Harcourt, Brace & Company, 1938).
6. Brearly, *Homicide in the United States* (Chapel Hill, NC: University of North Carolina Press, 1932).
7. Berg & Fox, "Factors in Homicide Committed by 200 Males," 26 *J. Soc. Psy.* 109 (1947).
8. The author wishes to express his appreciation to the Houston Police Department, and particularly Inspector Larry W. Fultz of the Records Division for their cooperation, and to Dr. Fred B. Davis for his assistance in data collection and analysis.

Chapter 3

Rape and Sexual Offenses

Rape: Behavioral Aspects

A. Nicholas Groth

An individual who forces another person to submit to or to commit a sexual act against that person's will through intimidation, threat, or physical force and without the person's consent, has committed the act of rape. . . .

Rape is a behavioral act. It does not in itself constitute a diagnostic category but may occur across the whole spectrum of conventional psychiatric disorders. At one extreme, the act of rape may reflect a transient reaction to extraordinary stresses that temporarily overwhelm the offender's coping resources. . . . At the other extreme, rape may result from an internal state of affairs in which the offender's psychological resources and skills are developmentally defective or insufficient to cope with ordinary life demands in a mature and responsible fashion. The offense may occur as a single exception to an otherwise law-abiding and responsible life, or it may be a characteristic pattern of behavior reflecting [a] chronic maladaptive personality. . . . It is never an appropriate act, and whether a single occurrence[,] . . . or a chronic behavior pattern, the act of rape [is] . . . equivalent to symptom formation that serves to express a conflict, defend against anxiety, and partially gratify an impulse.

Since rape is a sexual offense, it is commonly, but mistakenly, assumed to be prompted by sexual desire. This basic misconception gives rise to a number of . . . myths and misconceptions about the offender, the offense, and the victim. One basic impression about the offender is that he is an adult male. . . . [A]lthough it is true that the majority of identified offenders are adult men. . . . [t]here have been [some] cases reported of female offenders committing sexual assaults. . . . More important, clinical work with convicted male offenders has revealed that the majority of adult rapists attempted or committed their first sexual offense by the age of sixteen. The majority of these juvenile offenses went undetected, and those cases that were discovered were typically dismissed as merely representing normal adolescent sexual curiosity and experimentation. For most offenders, then, the age of conviction for sexual assault did not coincide with the age at which such sexual pathology first manifested itself.

The contrasting stereotypes of the rapist as either a normal, sexually aggressive male who is the victim of a provocative but punitive female, or as an oversexed, demented, predatory monster ravishing innocent victims, have in common the underlying assumption that the offense is sexually motivated. . . . Neither stereotype corresponds to the reality.

. . . [C]linical study of offenders reveals that rape serves essentially nonsexual needs in the psychology of the offender. Rape is not primarily the aggressive expression of sexuality but rather the sexual expression of aggression. It is a pseudosexual act prompted more by retaliatory and compensatory motives than by sexual ones. It is complex and multidetermined, but involves issues of control and hostility more than those of passion and desire. The rapist is not assaulting because he is sexually frustrated or deprived, any more than the alcoholic is drinking because he is thirsty. Failure to appreciate this has resulted in blurring rape and sex in the minds of the general public, with the unfortunate consequence that the victim is often held more responsible than the perpetrator. Moreover, the existence of a psychosexual disorder in the offender, one that requires intervention, goes unrecognized and neglected, putting others at risk of sexual victimization.

Since it is commonly assumed that the offender is committing his offense to gratify a sexual need, and since he is directing his sexual assault toward a particular victim, it is further assumed that the victim must have done something, either deliberately or inadvertently, to arouse such desire in the offender. Victim credibility is impeached, and offender accountability is diminished, by focusing on the sexual aspects of the victim's appearance and behavior: how she looked, how she was dressed, and how she acted. One of the most persistent and insidious stereotypes regarding rape is that of the seductive or provocative female who "only got what she asked for." In reality, victim selection is determined primarily by availability and vulnerability rather than sexual desirability, and anyone could be a victim of sexual assault. Rape happens not only to young adult women but to both sexes and all age groups, from infants to the aged.

It is also commonly believed that a victim, if she really wanted to, could usually prevent a rape. The fact is that much rape occurs through intimidation or incapacitation. . . . Different motives operate in different offenders, and what might serve to discourage one type of assailant may only aggravate the situation with a different type. Rape is a complex act, and there is no single infallible strategy to cope with all such assaults.

Finally, the misconception of rape as a sexually motivated offense may result in pursuing ineffective measures to combat it. Suggested "solutions" such as legalizing prostitution, banning pornography, or castrating offenders all imply that the problem to be solved is one of sexual stimulation.

These misconceptions reduce a complex, multidetermined behavior to the product of a single motive—uncontrollable sexual desire—and shift responsibility from the offender to something external. Consequently, efforts to combat rape are diverted into nonproductive channels. As with any type of behavior, . . . rape cannot be understood apart from its sociocultural context. This article will examine rape from a psychological perspective, concentrating on the dynamics of the offense and the characteristics of the offender. Rape, however, is more than a psychological issue; it is a cultural, social, legal, moral, economic, and educational issue [that] must be . . . understood from all these perspectives if it is to be effectively combated.

THE SEXUAL EXPRESSION OF AGGRESSION

The defining element in rape is coercion, and therefore, rape can be conceptualized as the sexual expression of aggression. In some offenses the aggression is expressed in the form of anger and violence; in other cases, in the form of control and domination. In a third pattern, aggression itself becomes an erotic experience. In every act of rape, there is present a combination of all these facets of aggression, but one will usually predominate. . . .

Anger rape

. . . [S]exuality has become a means of expressing and discharging feelings of pent-up anger and rage. The assault is characterized by physical brutality. Far more actual force is used in the commission of the offense than would be necessary if the intent were simply to overpower the victim and achieve sexual penetration. Sex becomes the means by which the offender can degrade his victim; through rape he retaliates for what he perceives to be wrongs experienced at the hands of others. Rather than seeking sexual gratification, he is seeking to hurt, punish, and humiliate his victim. . . .

Such offenses appear unplanned and impulsive, and the offender, while recognizing that he is in an angry and depressed frame of mind, generally does not anticipate committing a sexual assault. Typically, the anger rapist will report that he was not sexually aroused at the time of the rape and may even have experienced difficulty in achieving or maintaining an erection. . . . [T]he assault itself is of relatively short duration, sometimes completed within a few minutes. The assault discharges the offender's pent-up anger and provides temporary relief from his inner turmoil. . . . His anger spent, it will take time for it to build again to the critical point at which he is prone to strike. . . .

Power Rape

In a second pattern of rape, power appears to be the paramount factor motivating the offender. In these assaults it is not the offender's intent to harm his victim but to dominate her sexually. Sexuality becomes a means of compensating for underlying feelings of inadequacy, and serves the need to express a sense of mastery, strength, control, authority, and identity. Rape here allows him to feel strong, powerful, and in control. He wants his victim to welcome and be impressed by his sexual embrace, so that he may be reassured that he is a sexually desirable person. . . .

Such offenses are planned, although the actual assault may be opportunistic in origin. Adult sexuality is threatening to such an offender because it confronts him with issues of adequacy and competency, and his mood at the time of the assault is usually one of anxiety. The power rapist, like the anger rapist, does not find the offense sexually satisfying. . . . [H]is modus operandi is one of capture, control, and conquer. Having no sense of control over his own life, the power rapist attempts to compensate and deny his feelings of helplessness and vulnerability by gaining sexual control of someone else.

Sadistic Rape

. . . [S]exuality and aggression become fused into a single psychological experience known as sadism. Aggression itself is eroticized. If the power components of aggression are eroticized, the offense is typically characterized by symbolic and ritualistic acts, such as bondage. If the anger components are eroticized, the offense is characterized by sexual abuse and torture. In some cases, the offender is an individual who cannot achieve sexual satisfaction unless his victim physically resists him. He becomes aroused or excited only through aggression or violence, finding pleasure in taking a woman against her will and tormenting her. He may even use an object or instrument to sexually assault her, such as a stick or bottle. The victims of a sadistic rapist often have symbolic representation for him; that is, they may share some common characteristic with regard to their appearance or profession.

Sexual Dysfunction During Rape

The pseudosexual nature of rape is reflected in the significantly high incidence of sexual dysfunction evidenced by the perpetrator during the assault. . . . [O]ne out of every three offenders experiences some type of sexual dysfunction during the rape; such dysfunction is specific to the assault and not evident in the offender's consenting sexual encounters. Among such dysfunctions, difficulties in maintaining erection and in ejaculating appear equally common. For these and other reasons . . . the absence of semen in the victim may be more typical than its presence, and the absence of semen does not in itself indicate the absence of a sexual assault. . . . The observation that sexual dysfunction is more prominent in coerced than in consenting sexual activity lends support to the concept of rape as primarily an act of aggression.

The Role of Alcohol Abuse

. . . The crime of rape is frequently associated with alcohol or drug abuse. . . . [I]t appears that both the sexual abuse and the alcohol abuse are parallel but separate symptoms of the offender's state of psychological distress. Unable to cope with the demands and stresses of adult life and seeing others as the cause of such distress, the rapist resorts to alcohol and assault to relieve his turmoil, but it is not his drinking that causes him to rape. At most, in some cases, the use of alcohol may be contributory, but it is never causative. . . .

PERSONALITY CHARACTERISTICS OF OFFENDERS

. . . Although there is a wide range of individual differences among men who rape, such offenders do tend to share some common psychological characteristics. . . .

Self-Image

The rapist tends to possess little sense of self-worth. Low self-esteem is coupled with a sense of vulnerability and helplessness, and the offender feels only tenuous control over himself and his life. . . .

Masculine Identity

Failure in most areas of personal realization, such as work, love, and friendship, makes the rapist experience severe doubts about his manhood. He compensates for his inability to achieve an adequate sense of masculine identity by placing a premium on sexuality and aggression to assert his identity [and] validate his manhood. . . . Since he is insecure in regard to his own masculinity, sexuality becomes a particularly threatening and conflict-ridden aspect of his life. . . .

Social Relationships

The offender's underlying sense of inadequacy and low self-esteem result in his keeping others at a distance. Intimacy produces anxiety, since it poses the risk of exposing his inadequacy. Consequently, he tends to be a loner and fails to develop the social skills necessary to establish and maintain successful interpersonal relationships. Trust, reciprocity, and empathic identification are noticeably deficient; rather, a quality of detachment and a self-centered orientation tend to characterize interactions with others. . . .

Mood State

The offender's sense of personal inadequacy and interpersonal ineffectiveness combine to create a state of chronic unhappiness. He feels unable to cope with the responsibilities of adult life, which fill him with anxiety. His unfulfilled needs for acceptance, affection, and intimacy result in depression, and his perception of others as depriving, rejecting, or taking advantage of him cause feelings of anger and hostility. A sense of isolation from others produces a feeling of emptiness. The offender tends to find little satisfaction or meaning in his life. Consequently, humor, happiness, and warmth are noticeably absent and his characteristic mood state is one of distress, frustration, and resentment.

Management of Aggression

The offender's feelings of personal inadequacy and betrayal by others prompt him to channel his aggression into . . . retaliatory actions (assaults) as a way of denying his vulnerability, asserting his power, and avenging his "honor." Self-centered but lacking self-respect, and feeling outside of community life, he experiences no need to neutralize, modulate, or redirect his aggression into appropriate or constructive outlets. Instead, he sees aggression as necessary for psychological survival and deploys it in the form of domination, intimidation, exploitation, and physical force in order to achieve control or exact revenge. . . .

Men who rape, then, experience the world as one filled with overwhelming stresses, perceive others as adversaries, and believe that aggression is necessary for survival. . . . Although the rapist is not psychotic, his ability to perceive, comprehend, and respond accurately to real situations . . . becomes impaired or undependable when his aggression is aroused. . . .

ETIOLOGY OF SEXUAL ASSAULTIVENESS

. . . No one yet completely understands what developmental factors are needed, in what combinations, and at what critical points in time, to produce a proneness to rape. One significant factor that appears in the developmental history of men who have a high risk of committing sexual assaults, however, is sexual trauma or sexual abuse of which they themselves were victims during their formative years. . . .

Since most males are socialized to be aggressive, it appears that one way in which the sexually abused boy may attempt to deal with the helplessness of being sexually victimized is to become a sexual victimizer. That is, rather than forming an empathic identification with the role of the victim, he identifies with the role of the aggressor. He is oversensitive to any situation in which he does not feel in control. . . . A sexual assault may result when this unresolved trauma is reactivated by an event in the offender's life, generally one that involves a challenge by a female or a threat from a male. . . . Through rape, he attempts both to regain control and to retaliate for such perceived abuse. . . . [T]he offender's sense of himself as victim rather than victimizer can be understood to stem from the abuse, neglect, abandonment, or other maltreatment generally found in the developmental histories of men who rape. . . .

As the psychologically abused male child moves into adolescence and adulthood and finds that he is unequipped to fulfill the demands of this phase of development, he experiences an internal crisis. His sexual assaultiveness is symptomatic of this crisis. . . . When life events and personal encounters activate the offender's deep-seated feelings of helplessness, worthlessness, and rejection, sexual assault becomes his defense against the resulting psychological distress. Depression is converted into aggression. . . .

Adaptive Strategies and Recovery from Rape

Ann Wolbert Burgess and Lynda Lytle Holmstrom

Being raped generates an enormous amount of anxiety in the victim. This anxiety is the basis for an acute traumatic reaction called the rape trauma syndrome. [Burgess and Holmstrom 1974]. . . . [W]e will look at a . . . spectrum of adaptive behaviors aimed at reorganization and the ways . . . victims deal with their rape [trauma]. [This study consisted of 81 adult rape victims from a larger group of 92 women seen during a counseling research project based in the emergency department of Boston City Hospital in 1972–73.] . . .

We used a standard schedule of questions that were flexible and open ended. . . . The classification of length of recovery [Burgess and Holmstrom 1978] was developed by looking at the answers to two major questions: Do you feel back to normal, that is, the way you felt prior to the rape? and, Has the rape interfered in your life and, if so, in what areas? These data are victims' subjective reports of their own recovery over the intervening 4–6 years. . . .

ADAPTIVE RESPONSES TO RAPE

Self-Esteem

Self-esteem is the evaluative component of an individual's self-concept and implies a personal assessment of worth or competence. . . .

The spontaneous comments made by 45 of the victims were coded as positive or negative and categorized by length of recovery time. There was a clear association between self-esteem and length of recovery. Among the victims who gave a positive statement 65% recovered in months, but among those with a negative statement none recovered this quickly. In contrast, among victims who gave a positive assessment none was still not recovered, but among those who gave a negative assessment 50% were not yet recovered. . . .

Positive Self-Assessment. Victims who made a positive statement reflected acceptance and approval of either behavior or approach to situations and/or people. Examples of positive terms included "strong" ("I'm a strong person mentally"), "calm" ("I remain calm in difficult situations"), and "high tolerance for stress" ("I was glad I cooperated with the guys and didn't get hurt"). . . .

Negative Self-Assessment. Victims who made a negative statement did not affirm or approve of their behavior. The negative terms included "doubt" ("gave me another self-doubt about myself"), "not functioning adequately" ("I have never been normal"), "regret" ("I regret not yelling . . . maybe I could have done more"). . . .

Defense Mechanisms

. . . [I]t seemed important to analyze the conscious cognitive strategies that victims used to master the anxiety generated by the rape. Four types of defense mechanisms were identified: explanation, minimization, suppression, and dramatization. Table 3-1 illustrates the frequency with which victims used these mechanisms and their length of recovery. Adult rape victims who use any or all of these mechanisms are more apt to recover in months or years than to be unrecovered 4–6 years after the rape. . . .

Explanation. The mechanism of explanation helps the victim cope with the anxiety by providing some reason for the rape. Coming up with an explanation gives some understanding for the bizarreness of the acts and aids in returning some degree of control to the victim. . . .

Explanations victims gave for the rape divide according to whom the victims assigned responsibility, the assailant or the victim. Victims who assigned responsibility to the assailant gave such reasons as sex ("He said he was horny"), revenge ("He enjoyed it in that he was getting back at me. He could get sex for a dime"), pathology ("He is sick . . . he needs help"), and exploitation of the victim's vulnerability ("He saw me drunk").

Victims also have explanations focusing on themselves: their decisions ("If I hadn't gone, it wouldn't have happened"), self-reflection ("I was dumb," "I was

Table 3-1.
Defense Mechanisms Used by 81 Rape Victims[a]

Length of Recovery	Explanation	Minimization	Suppression	Dramatization
Months (N=30)	20	10	8	4
Years (N=30)	13	7	8	1
Not yet recovered (N=21)	4	0	0	1
Total (N=81)	37	17	16	6

[a]Some victims used more than one defense mechanism, and some used none.

idealistic," "I was conned," and "For 20¢ I was raped. I hitchhiked to save 20¢"), and being forewarned ("I went to a fortune teller a long time ago who said a disaster was coming. When this happened, I said to myself, The disaster has happened").

Victims who use the mechanisms of explanation may make themselves more vulnerable to judgmental reactions from others. Explanations often have a self-blaming quality to them. . . . [A]lthough victims may blame themselves for their decisions or behavior, they do not necessarily feel guilty about their actions. Their anxiety is decreased by providing a reason, which serves as a self-correcting mechanism. This contrasts with victims who feel guilty, which increases anxiety about the rape. . . .

Minimization. Minimization helps cope with the anxiety by reducing the anxiety to a smaller, more manageable context. Minimization decreases the terrifying aspects and allows the person to think of it in tolerable amounts. . . .

Victims often have a perception or image of what it is like to be raped and if the rape does not match the image, they feel fortunate to have survived so well. Victims perceive rape as fatal ("I got off lucky . . . there could have been a bullet in the gun"), perverted ("Even though they had a knife, I kept thinking they were kids and they weren't going to use it . . . they didn't do anything perverse"), involving additional violence ("scared they were going to kill me . . . or take me out of the city or to a place with older men . . . all I had to do was lie there . . . didn't ask me to do anything unnatural"). . . .

Victims may compare themselves to other victims and minimize their anxiety that way. . . . One 62-year-old victim, who had been badly beaten, almost smothered by a pillow, and cut in the stomach with the assailant's knife, compared age and sexual experience:

> I guess you see worse victims than me. I know it must be awful for some of these young girls. I know what sex is all about. I've been married and had kids. It would have been really awful if I was a virgin. Something like that would have really bothered me.

Prior experience with upsetting events may give victims a clue to what must be done in terms of coping. Victims with this strategy talked of accepting the rape ("It's over . . . it must be accepted. There is nothing else I can do about it. It's better to be raped than die").

Suppression. Suppression provides cognitive control over thoughts of the rape. The person tries to put the memory of the rape completely out of her mind through a conscious effort. Victims using this mechanism do not like the subject of rape to be brought up. . . .

Dramatization. According to sociologist Zola, the defense mechanism of dramatization "seems to cope with anxiety by repeatedly overexpressing it and thereby dissipating it" [Zola 1966, 627]. Victims using this mechanism usually have a small group of friends with whom they discuss the rape. . . . [A] victim who recovered within months said, "I don't cry much and when this happened I cried a lot. . . . I got everything out plus talked about it with so many people."

Action

In response to their rapes, victims exhibited three patterns of behavior: increased action, no change in action, or decreased action. Increased action was associated with faster recovery.

Of the victims who increased their action, 45% had recovered in months, but of those with decreased action none recovered that fast. . . .

Increased action. The most common action taken by victims was to change residence or to travel. Eight victims traveled outside the country within the first year after the rape. An important consideration in this type of action was the economic resources of the victim. Victims who had financial resources were able to travel and change residence. . . .

Victims with less economic independence moved in temporarily with relatives and/or friends. . . . When they did move, they commented on the positive component. . . . One victim who could not afford a move stayed with relatives and then rearranged her home. She had been raped in her bedroom and describes the change as follows,

> Wouldn't sleep in my own bed. Stayed with friends for a while. Have changed my bedroom around and got a new bedroom set.

There were other types of increased action that victims took. First, changing telephone numbers or getting an unlisted telephone number helped to provide some environmental control. . . . Second, reading, watching television talk shows, or writing about rape helped victims gain intellectual control. Third, some victims became active in rape crisis centers to assist other victims. . . .

One-third of the victims reported no specific change in their actions. A minority of victims (17%) described a marked decrease in action. Victims talked of withdrawing from people ("I shut people out"), life events ("I hibernated"), or the world ("I disappeared and my family covered"). Victims talked of becoming substantially immobile ("I just lay on the couch for two weeks," or "I went to bed for a month").

MALADAPTIVE RESPONSES

Victims do not always cope with the anxiety of rape in adaptive ways. Some victims fail to cope with the stress of the rape and develop maladaptive responses. Eighteen (22%) of the victims reported either making a suicide attempt and/or seriously abusing alcohol or drugs after the rape.

The abuse of drugs or alcohol and/or acting on suicidal thoughts was associated with longer recovery. . . . Nine victims reported making some attempt at suicide. Sometimes the suicidal behavior is present before the rape. . . . Or the suicidal behavior may be a response to the failure to renegotiate a partner relationship after the rape. . . .

QUALITY OF LIFE AFTER RAPE

Social Task Performance

Women in our society generally have one or more of three major social tasks: to be a housewife and/or parent, to be employed, and/or to be in school. On follow-up the majority of victims (81%) reported meeting at least one of these social tasks. . . .

Recovery was most obvious in the resumption of social task functions. . . . [Fourteen] women (17%) . . . had completed some type of formal school program during the years after the rape. . . . It was clear that women saw starting or completing an educational program as a positive aspect of their life. . . .

. . . Victims who felt recovered within months and who did not identify a social task . . . were either under psychiatric aftercare supervision, . . . were retired or disabled and on pension funds . . . , or were in a social support network group. . . . In contrast, all victims who were not yet recovered and did not identify a social task had no strong social network ties and were socially drifting. In the years after the rape, they had been unsuccessful in gaining any personal achievements. . . .

Partnership Stability

The stability of partnership relationships is associated with length of recovery. . . . Three patterns of partnership stability were noted after the rape. The most common pattern (. . . 59%) was disruption of the relationship, followed by no disruption of the relationship (. . . 27%), followed by semi-disruption of the relationship (. . . 14%). Victims with partnership stability had a faster recovery than victims who did not have partnership stability. . . .

Sexual Functioning

The majority of victims who were sexually active at the time of the rape . . . reported disruption in sexual functioning within the 6 months after the rape. Changes . . . reported in their frequency of sexual activity [were] . . . abstinence (38%), decreased activity (33%), increased activity (10%). Only 19% reported no change in sexual activity. . . .

DISCUSSION

Recovery from rape is complex and influenced by many factors. These factors include prior life stress . . . , style of attack . . . , relationship of victim and offender (and whether it is an inter-or intraracial rape), number of assailants, language used by the assailant . . . , the amount of violence or the sexual acts demanded . . . , and postrape factors of institutional response to the victim . . . , social network response . . . , and subsequent victimization. . . . Clinicians should consider all of these factors in identifying victims who are at high risk for a slow recovery from rape and will remain vulnerable to many life stresses for a long time. . . .

REFERENCES

Burgess A.W., Holmstrom L.L.: Rape trauma syndrome. Am J. Psychiatry 131:981–986. 1974

Burgess A.W., Holmstrom L.L.: Recovery from rape and prior life stress. Research in Nursing and Health 1:165–174. 1978

Zola I.K.: Culture and symptoms—an analysis of patients' presenting complaints. Am Sociol Rev 31:615–630. 1966

Chapter 4
Robbery

Robbery in the United States: An Analysis of Recent Trends and Patterns

Philip J. Cook

DEFINITIONS AND RECENT TRENDS IN THE ROBBERY RATE

Definitions

Robbery is defined as theft or attempted theft, in a direct confrontation with the victim, by force or the threat of force or violence. . . . A child "rolled" for his school lunch money and a bank teller confronted by a gang of shotgun-toting bandits are both robbery victims. . . . Purse snatching and pocket-picking incidents are not classified as robbery unless the victim resists and is overpowered. . . .

Recent Trends in the Robbery Rate

The National Crime Survey (NCS, 1980) estimated that there were about 1.2 million noncommercial robberies in the United States in 1980, or 6.5 per thousand residents aged 12 and over. The NCS estimated there were 279,000 commercial robberies in 1976, the last year the commercial survey was conducted (NCS, 1976); this number corresponds to a rate of 38.5 per 1000 commercial establishments. . . .

Annual data on robbery is available from both the UCR and the National Crime Survey for 1973–1980. Table 4-1 presents these data. Despite the fact that these two robbery counts are estimated from entirely different sources, and the fact that the NCS excludes commercial robberies, the two series exhibit similar patterns between 1975 and 1979; both show a 12 percent decline between 1975 and 1978, and an increase in 1979. There is a rather large discrepancy in the two series in the 1973–75 interval, however, and also between 1979 and 1980. . . .

Table 4-1.
Annual Robbery Rates, 1973–1980

	Rate Per 100,000								
	1973	1974	1975	1976	1977	1978	1979	1980	1981
UCR	182.6	208.8	218.2	195.8	187.1	191.3	212.1	243.5	250.6
NCS	528.0	567.2	538.2	517.6	500.6	476.0	507.0	523.2	n.a.
	Index (1975 = 100)								
UCR	84	96	100	90	86	88	97	112	115
NCS	98	105	100	96	93	88	94	97	n.a.

Note: The Uniform Crime Reports (UCR) include commercial robberies in their total, whereas the National Crime Survey (NCS) does not. NCS also excludes victims aged less than 12 years old. However, the same denominators were used in calculating the 2 rates in each year.
Source: NCS data are taken from the Bureau of Justice Statistics' National Crime Report SD-NCS-N-21, NCJ-80838, issued July, 1982. U.S. population figures used to calculate the NCS rates were taken from various issues of the UCR, to make them as comparable as possible with UCR rates.

Reported robbery rates tripled between 1965 and 1975, and began growing again in 1978 after a brief decline. Year-to-year changes in the UCR and NCS series have usually been in the same direction between 1973 and 1980, but for the period as a whole there is substantial disagreement; the UCR indicates a 24 percent increase in the robbery rate during these 8 years, whereas the NCS indicates a slight reduction. . . .

Robbery is a property crime, in the sense that most robbers are motivated by economic gain. . . . It is of course the violent nature of robbery that makes it such a serious crime in the eyes of the public and the criminal law. The million plus robberies that occur each year result in psychological and physical trauma for hundreds of thousands of victims, and several thousand deaths. Perhaps even more important, the urban public's fear of robbery causes widespread anxiety and defensive behavior. . . . Race relations are perhaps also harmed by the urban public's fear of robbery—youthful black males commit the majority of robberies, which may cause some people to be suspicious and fearful of all members of this group (Silberman, 1978). . . .

Robbery Murder

Criminal homicide rates doubled between 1965 and 1974. A concomitant change occurred in the nature of homicide, with disproportionate increases in felony murders and other killings by strangers (. . . Block, 1977; Zimring, 1977). Increases in robbery killings played an important role in these changes. . . .

Developing an accurate measure of the robbery murder rate is difficult because a large percentage of robbery murders go unsolved. . . . [A]bout 10 percent of criminal homicides have been assigned to the "robbery" category in recent years; other homicides that in fact occurred in a robbery context may have been classified in the "suspected felony" or "unknown motives" categories. . . .

[A]t least 2160 robbery murders occurred in 1979, and the true number may have been as much as twice that large. . . .

A conservative estimate of the likelihood that the victim will be killed in a robbery [is] . . . about 1.5 per 1000 robberies [using NCS and UCR data]. Thus, the probability that any one robbery victim will be killed is quite small. . . .

[A]bout one-fifth of all law enforcement officers killed in the line of duty in the last decade were killed while attempting to stop a robbery or pursue a fleeing robber.

Robbery Injury and Theft Losses

While robbery always includes force or threat of violence as one element, only about one-third of victims of noncommercial robbery were actually injured in 1979. . . . Only 2.6 percent of victims were injured seriously enough to require inpatient care in a hospital. . . .

Cook (1976) used victimization survey data in 26 cities (collected in the early 1970s) to compute medical costs incurred by robbery victims. For all noncommercial robberies in these cities, 6.2 percent of victims incurred medical costs, which averaged $291 . . . [o]nly 0.5 percent incurred costs which exceeded $1000.

. . . The value of the stolen items was less than $50 in 37 percent of successful [noncommercial] robberies, and exceeded $250 in only 16.5 percent of such cases. . . . By way of comparison, about 23 percent of household burglaries resulted in a theft of items valued at more than $250.

Commercial robbery losses were naturally somewhat larger. . . . [A]bout 14 percent [of the successful robberies] resulted in a theft of less than $50, and 36 percent in a theft of more than $250. . . .

The statistics . . . indicate that less than 20 percent of all noncommercial robberies inflict serious economic losses and/or significant physical injury on victims. We have no measure of the extent to which victims suffer serious psychological trauma, but a good many surely do. It is clear, in any event, that robberies differ widely in terms of the seriousness of their immediate consequences.

Table 4-2 presents an estimate of the total direct cost of nonlethal robbery to victims in 1978. This total of $333 million excludes any valuation of pain and psychological trauma, and makes no effort to assign an economic value to the lives of the robbery murder victims. . . .

Table 4.2.
Direct Economic Costs of Robbery to Victims (Excluding Robbery Murder), 1978

	(millions)
Medical Expenses	$ 36.8
Property Loss, Noncommercial	115.8
Property Loss, Commercial	148.3
Days Lost from Work	32.5
	$333.4

Criminal Justice System Costs

A complete accounting of the costs that robbery inflicts on society must include the cost to the criminal justice system of investigating robberies, processing defendants in the courts, and punishing convicts. A dramatic indication of the importance of robbery cases in the felony courts is the fact that 23 percent of all state prisoners (in 1974) were there on a conviction for robbery. . . . Robbers constituted the largest category of prisoners in that year. . . .

There is no easy method for allocating the appropriate share of the total costs of the CJS to robbery cases, but the correct figure is on the order of several billion dollars. Supposing 75–100 thousand robbery convicts currently in prison, at an annual cost of at least $10,000 per prisoner, yields a total of about one billion dollars just for imprisonment. The total allocatable costs of police, courts, juvenile corrections, probation and parole, etc., no doubt exceed this figure by a wide margin.

Conclusions

The total cost of robbery to society is hard to measure. . . . Robbery may well be a $7–10 billion problem, especially when criminal justice system costs are taken into account. James Q. Wilson [and Barbara Boland] (1978, p. 183) assert that robbery is "the most costly of all common crimes," due to its "psychic and communal costs."

WEAPON[S] USE IN ROBBERY

Distribution by Weapon[s] Type

. . . [A]bout half of all robberies are unarmed, and only one-quarter involve firearms. There is a dramatic difference between commercial and noncommercial robbery in this respect, with half of the former involving firearms, and only one-sixth of the latter. . . . [G]un robberies are much more likely to be reported to the police than other types of robbery. . . .

. . . It appears that the relative frequency of gun use in robbery increased between 1967 and 1975 (from 36 percent to 45 percent) and has declined slightly [from 1976 to 1981].

Seriousness and Weapon[s] Type

A recent survey of 900 assistant prosecutors found that they perceived gun robbery as substantially more serious than robbery with a blunt object or physical force (Roth, 1978). These judgments receive support from several empirical studies. First, the likelihood that a robbery will result in the victim's death is closely related to the lethality of the robber's weapon. . . . [T]he fraction of robberies committed with a gun is a major determinant of the robbery murder rate. . . .

Gun robberies also tend to be more serious in the sense that they are more likely to be successful, and the "take" is larger on the average if successful. Unarmed robberies have the lowest chance of success, and the smallest "take" if successful (Cook, 1976, p. 182), when compared with robberies involving other weapons.

One set of results tends to confuse the relationship between weapon lethality and robbery seriousness; a number of studies (. . . Cook, 1976; Skogan, 1978; Cook, 1980) have found that the likelihood of victim injury is related *inversely* to the lethality of the weapon. It is unusual for the victim to be physically attacked in a gun robbery, while most unarmed robberies include such an attack. If there is an attack, however, the likelihood of serious injury or death increases with the lethality of the weapon.

GEOGRAPHIC DISTRIBUTION OF ROBBERIES

City Size

Robbery is the quintessential urban crime. . . . UCR robbery rates increase rapidly with city size. . . . The largest cities have a collective robbery rate that is 36 times greater than in rural areas. . . . [In 1981 t]he six largest cities (with eight percent of the population) had 33 percent of the robberies, and New York City alone had 18 percent. Robbery is more highly concentrated in large cities than any of the other index crimes. . . .

Among the nation's largest cities, it appears that population size may be a less important correlate of robbery than population density. . . . Cook (1979) found that the principal explanatory variables were population density and the fraction of the city population that were youthful black males. . . .

Large cities differ from small cities not only with respect to overall robbery rates, but also location patterns. Fifty-nine percent of robberies in the largest cities (250,000 or more) occur on the street; this fraction declines steadily with city size, and only 28.6 percent of robberies in the smallest cities are on the street (UCR, 1981, p. 18). On the other hand, the relative importance of commercial robberies is inversely related to city size, increasing from 19 percent for the largest cities, to 41 percent for the smallest cities. . . . "The establishments which have the highest commercial robbery rates are those which tend to locate independently of other businesses" ([Feeney and Weir 1973,] p. 59). . . .

The distribution of robberies within cities is concentrated to some degree in poverty districts and the central business district. . . .

The typical distribution of robberies within a large city can be explained by two reasonably well documented observations: (1) Most robbers reside in poverty areas, and typically operate close to home; (2) The most lucrative targets are in the commercial areas of the city, and robbers who do travel tend to seek out such targets. . . .

ROBBERY SITES

Residential Robbery

Residential robberies . . . may involve a confrontation at the entrance, or a robbery committed by someone who has a right to be in the house (e.g., as an invited guest at a party). One piece of evidence suggests that this last circumstance dominates the residential robbery statistics—54 percent of all residential robberies are committed by acquaintances (NCS, 1979). This is the only category of robbery for which acquaintances figure importantly. . . .

Robberies in Schools

The NCS estimates that 3.2 percent of noncommercial robberies occur in schools. . . . The *Violent Schools–Safe Schools* report characterizes the robberies this way:

> They are not stickups or muggings for the most part, but instances of petty extortion—shakedowns—which for some student victims become an almost routine part of the school day (p. 60).

. . . [F]ew of these robberies involve much property loss; in 76 percent of these incidents, the loss was less than one dollar (p. 60).

Perhaps even more disturbing than these high robbery rates for students is equally high victimization rates for teachers. In a typical month, 0.6 percent of both junior and senior high teachers reported being robbed at least once on school property. The implied annual victimization rate of over five percent exceeds that for other adults by an order of magnitude.

Taken together, these results suggest that there are about one million school-related robberies per year. . . . If the *Violent Schools–Safe Schools* survey results are valid, then school-related robberies constitute a large portion of the robbery "problem." While most of these robberies are not serious, it is disturbing that such an important institution, for which attendance is required by law, is in many cases doing such a poor job of protecting the more vulnerable students against intimidation and extortion.

Robberies of Banks and Convenience Stores

In 1957, there were 278 bank robberies in the U.S. In 1980, there were 6515. . . . These growth rates far outstrip the rates of growth for any other major category of robbery. . . . Bank robbery tends to be less violent than other forms of robbery and involves much greater property losses on the average.

The most common method of bank robbery is a threat with a visible firearm. . . . Most of the remaining robberies were perpetrated by use of a demand note passed to the teller. The vast majority of bank robberies were committed by individuals acting alone. . . .

Why have bank robbery rates increased so rapidly in recent years? Surely part of the answer lies in the increase in the number of small branch banks, which tend to be designed and located in such a way as to be highly vulnerable to robbers. But there are no complete, well-documented explanations available at present.

The other fast-growing category of robbery during recent years is robbery of convenience stores. Between 1970 and 1974, the annual number of such robberies more than doubled. . . . Currently convenience stores are the target for more than one quarter of all commercial robberies. . . .

Summary

Three robbery sites were singled out for special comment. Residential robberies are unusual in that most of them involve perpetrators who are acquainted with their victims. School robberies are notable for their pettiness, and for their prevalence; if the *Violent Schools–Safe Schools* report is accurate, there are as many robberies in schools as in all other noncommercial sites combined. However, there is a gross discrepancy between this survey and the NCS findings on school robbery. Finally, bank robbery is notable for the large financial losses typical of this crime, and because of its unparalleled rate of growth over the last 25 years.

CHARACTERISTICS OF ROBBERS AND THEIR VICTIMS

Number of Offenders and Victims Per Incident

Most robberies involve two or more offenders (58 percent) and a single victim (92 percent). [Thirty] . . . percent of robberies actually involve three or more offenders, and about one percent of these incidents involve large gangs of ten or more robbers.

Zimring (1981) reports that the propensity to commit robbery in groups is age-related to a substantial degree; adult robbers are much more likely to work alone than youthful robbers. . . .

Age, Race, and Sex

Most robberies are committed by youthful males. Blacks commit more than half of all robberies. About 75 percent of all offenders are less than 25 years old, and more than 90 percent are males. Blacks are most overrepresented among youthful offenders; 62 percent of youths younger than 18 who are arrested for robbery are black. . . . Just as for offenders, victims are disproportionately youthful, black, and male. . . . None of these tendencies [is] nearly as pronounced for victims as for offenders.

Interactions between Victims and Offenders

When the demographic characteristics of robbers are compared with their victims, a strong "similarity pattern" emerges for each of the dimensions: race, sex, and age (Cook, 1976). . . . [T]here is some tendency for robbers to choose victims who are similar to themselves with respect to demographic characteristics. Nevertheless, there are a substantial number of racial cross-over robberies.

Blacks committed 70 percent of the noncommercial robberies in the 26 cities covered by special National Crime Panel victimization surveys in the early 1970s. Despite the fact that their victims were also blacks to a disproportionate degree (the similarity pattern), it was nevertheless true that a majority of their victims were whites. Whites were three times as likely to be robbed by nonwhites as by whites. . . . Thus interracial robbery is common—much more so than for other crimes of violence. . . .

ROBBERY CAREERS

The Rand Studies

A series of studies by the Rand Corporation (Greenwood, 1980) have gathered considerable information on robbers and other criminals through intensive interviews with prisoners concerning their careers in crime.[2] . . . Based on information collected from these surveys and other sources, the discussion below considers activity levels, crime specialization, motivation, sophistication, and involvement with drugs and alcohol.

Activity Levels

The distribution of robberies among active offenders fits the "J-curve" model . . .: in any one year, a few offenders have a very high rate of commission, whereas most active robbers only commit one or two. . . .

The . . . results [of various studies] can be summarized as follows; about one-third of all active adult male street criminals commit at least one armed robbery in a year; of those who do commit at least one, and are incarcerated subsequently, the median person commits about five in that year; the distribution of activity levels among active robbers is very skewed, with the top ten percent committing a large fraction of all robberies; it is quite possible that the average robbery activity level is substantially less the year following an arrest than it was the year before. . . .

Specialization

Rand Inmate Survey I and numerous other longitudinal studies . . . have found that most active offenders do not specialize in any one type of crime. Peterson and Braiker (1980, p. x) report that a typical group of 100 adult male California prison inmates convicted of robbery will have committed 490 armed robberies, 310 assaults, 720 burglaries, 70 auto thefts, 100 forgeries, and 3400 drug sales in the previous year of street time. Of the almost 200 respondents who reported committing a robbery in Inmate Survey I, only about 10 (five percent) were robbery "specialists"—men who committed robbery frequently and to the exclusion of other types of crimes. (The other high rate robbers were also very active in other types of criminal activity.) While one-third of all respondents had committed a robbery, only 11 percent named robbery as their main crime (p. 84).

The basic picture, then, is one of considerable diversification. Nevertheless, men who commit robbery in one year are more likely than other street criminals to commit robbery in subsequent years. . . .

Motivation

Robbery is similar to other property crimes with respect to its principal motive. Rand's Habitual Offenders Survey of 49 California Prisoners imprisoned for robbery . . . found that a majority of respondents' careers had progressed from auto theft and burglary to an increasing proportion of robbery and forgery. "The majority said they had switched to robbery because it required little preparation and few tools, was easy to do, seldom required hurting anyone, and offered unlimited potential targets" (Petersilia, Greenwood, and Lavin, 1977, p. vii).

Respondents in the Habitual Offenders Survey were queried concerning the main reasons for their crimes at different phases of their criminal careers. "Expressive" needs (thrills, peer influence) were the most important during the juvenile period, whereas financial need and desire for "high living" (drugs, alcohol, women) became much more important in later years (pp. 75–79). . . .

One question that has received enormous attention in recent years has been the role of alcohol and drugs in crime. About 70 percent of respondents in the Habitual Offenders Survey were involved in alcohol or drugs at some point in their careers. Thirty percent of all respondents listed obtaining money for alcohol or drugs as their main motivation for crime since reaching adulthood (Petersilia, Greenwood, and Lavin, 1977, p. 76). Rand's Inmate Survey I found that street criminals who were regular users of hard drugs were no more likely than others to commit robbery; however, among those who do rob, the drug users had a robbery offense rate almost twice that of non-drug users (p. 150).

Interviews with over 10,000 inmates of state correctional institutions found that 39 percent of all those incarcerated for robbery reported that they had been drinking at the time of their offense (Roizen and Schneberk, 1978). This percentage is lower than for other crimes of violence. . . .

This survey found that the amount of planning was greater during the respondent's adult career than their juvenile careers. It was also found that the tendency to use partners declined markedly with age (p. 66), apparently in part because of a concern that a partner might inform on them at some point.

Conclusions

The most interesting lesson from this review is that any attempt to create a typology of robbers must deal with the fact that most robberies are not committed by "robbers" (people who specialize in robbery), but rather by street criminals who commit a wide variety of crimes. Nevertheless, at any one time it appears that a small fraction of street criminals commit the majority of all robberies—robbery commission rates differ enormously among active robbers, and the most active group are very active indeed (several robberies each week). Because of this disparity in commission rates, valid generalizations about *robbers* may not be valid generalizations about *robberies*, particularly if the most intensive group differs in important respects than others. . . .

Summary

The primary motivation for robbery is to obtain money, although juvenile robbers are also motivated by peer influence and the quest for "thrills." Drug and alcohol use are common among street criminals, and may influence criminal career patterns—robbers who use drugs are twice as active as those who do not.

Robbery's advantages relative to other crimes are that it is quick, easy, and requires little planning or preparation.

AN OVERVIEW OF THE ROBBERY PROCESS

Determinants of Robbery Rates and Patterns

Motivation and Personality What factors influence street criminals' crime-related choices? The various types of crime included in the hustler's "portfolio" differ in a number of respects. Robbery is a quick, uncomplicated way of obtaining cash, that does not require making any arrangements with other people such as fences, drug buyers, etc. Its drawbacks are a relatively high probability of arrest, typically low "take" (in street robbery), and the possibility of being injured by the victim (in commercial robbery) (Petersilia, Greenwood, and Lavin, 1977, pp. 64–65). The necessity for physical confrontation and possible attack of the victim may be a drawback for some, but not for others who have more of a taste for violence. Indeed, street robberies committed by large gangs of youths may be more of a violent "sport" than a way of making money (Cook, 1980).

There are no interventions that have been demonstrated to be effective in reducing robbery by changing street criminals' tastes, skills, or special circumstances. The special "circumstance" that has received the most attention during the last decade is drug addiction, a concern that has elicited massive law enforcement efforts to reduce the availability of illicit drugs and bring addicts into rehabilitation programs (Gandossy et al., 1980). While it seems reasonable that addicts in search of a quick fix would find robbery a particularly attractive crime, Rand's

Inmate Survey I found otherwise—regular users of hard drugs were about as likely as other respondents to have been active in robbery.

Drunkenness may also play an important role in robbery. Drunks may be more likely to commit an impulsive robbery and also to serve as especially vulnerable victims.

Opportunities A robbery "opportunity"—potential victim—has a variety of characteristics of relevance to the street criminal, such as location, potential take, capability of defending against robbery, likelihood of intervention by bystanders, and the presence of alarms, cameras, and guards. From the criminal's viewpoint, these features determine the perceived attractiveness of the target, and particularly the following: (1) The amount of preparation required; (2) The likelihood of success given the weapons, skills, and accomplices available to the criminals; (3) The expected "take" if the robbery is successful; (4) The likelihood of injury at the hands of the victim; (5) The likelihood of arrest and conviction; and (6) The expected severity of punishment if convicted. . . .

Gun Availability To complete a robbery successfully, the offender must find the means to intimidate or overpower the victim, and prevent intervention by bystanders. The inherent difficulty of this task depends on the nature of the victim and the circumstances. The most vulnerable victims are the elderly and the very young when they are by themselves. The least vulnerable targets are commercial places which have armed guards and other means of protection. The observed patterns in robbery clearly reflect the tendency of offenders to take victim vulnerability into account (Cook, 1976 and 1981; Skogan, 1980); commercial targets, especially those with several employees, are typically robbed by gun-toting adults, whereas female victims on the street are typically robbed by unarmed youths. The age, sex, and number of robbers, together with the lethality of their weapons, determine their capability; there is a strong tendency for the robber's capability to be inversely related to the vulnerability of his victim.

The principal intervention suggested by these observations is the regulation of gun commerce and use. Gun control measures, if they are effective in depriving some street criminals of guns, should reduce the commercial robbery rate by reducing the robbers' capability.

Gun control measures may also have some effect on the injury and death rate in robbery. . . .

Robbery Consequences

Robbery is such a serious crime in part because of the large number of robbery-related injuries and deaths. Some of these injuries and deaths are an inescapable by-product of the robbery process, and most any intervention that reduced the overall robbery rate would probably also reduce the number of victim casualties. There is considerable evidence, on the other hand, that there exists a good deal of "excess violence" in robbery—gratuitous violence that is not the consequence of victim resistance (Cook, 1980). For this reason, it is conceivable that interventions could be designed that would reduce the amount of violence in robbery without reducing the overall robbery rate. The felony murder rule is an example of such an intervention. Other possibilities for reducing robbery murder include strengthening legal controls on gun commerce and adopting special sentencing provisions for robbers who use guns.

Interventions that are oriented towards reducing gun use will not reduce the injury rate in robbery, since gun robberies are much less likely to result in victim injury than other types of robbery. One possible intervention focused on robbery injury is to single out robbery defendants who are also chargeable with injuring their victims for high priority handling in the courts. . . .

Summary

There are a number of interventions available to the criminal justice system that have the potential for reducing either the rate or the seriousness of robbery.

First is the traditional strategy of devoting greater effort . . . to arresting, convicting, and incarcerating robbers. Given limited resources, the problem is to set appropriate priorities for the allocation of prosecution and prison capacity among robbery defendants. One aspect of this problem is to develop means for identifying that subgroup of robbery defendants who are most likely to pursue active criminal careers and/or inflict serious injuries on their future victims. Criminal careers research is directly relevant in this context. A second aspect of the priority setting problem is to determine which types of robbery induce the greatest harm and hence should be most actively discouraged. One traditional distinction in this regard is between armed and unarmed robbery; many jurisdictions have recently created an additional distinction between robbery with a gun and robbery committed with another weapon. . . .

A second type of intervention is to encourage robbery targets to protect themselves, and to cooperate with the criminal justice system investigation and prosecution of robbery suspects. The possibilities here include everything from the formation of neighborhood watch associations to the installation of hidden cameras and methods for limiting the amount of readily available "loot." Reliable evaluation of such measures is difficult due to the resistance of public agencies to conducting experiments. . . .

A third type of intervention applies specifically to schools. If the robbery problem is anywhere near as severe in junior and senior high schools as indicated by the *Violent Schools–Safe Schools* report, then it warrants immediate attention. It is possible that a good deal can be accomplished to reduce inschool robberies through internal policies implemented by school officials. . . .

The fourth and final type of intervention is to modify policies directed at controlling youth's access to drugs, alcohol, and guns. Despite years of research on the drug/crime nexus, it is still not clear whether a more active policy in controlling illicit drugs would reduce or increase the robbery rate. The causal role of alcohol use in robbery has not been evaluated. The relationship between gun availability and robbery patterns is better understood, but certainly not resolved.

NOTES

1. In this report, references . . . to the annual reports of the Uniform Crime Reports (the FBI's *Crime in the United States*) and the National Crime Survey are referenced with the abbreviations "UCR" and "NCS" respectively, followed by the year to which their data refer; thus, "(NCS, 1980)" indicates the report of the National Crime Survey results for 1980.

2. Conklin (1972) was the first to conduct an interview study of this sort. His work has been superceded by the far larger efforts of the Rand researchers.

REFERENCES

Block, Richard (1977). *Violent Crime*. Lexington, Mass.: Lexington Books.

Cook, Philip J. (1976). "A Strategic Choice Analysis of Robbery." From *Sample Surveys of the Victims of Crime*, by Wesley G. Skogan. Cambridge, Mass.: Ballinger Publishing Co.

——— (1977). "Punishment and Crime: A Critique of Current Findings Concerning the Preventive Effects of Punishment," *Law and Contemporary Problems* 41, pp. 164–204.

——— (1979). "The Effect of Gun Availability on Robbery and Robbery Murder: A Cross Section Study of Fifty Cities," in Robert H. Haveman and Bruce Zellner, eds., *Policy Studies Review Annual* 3. Beverly Hills: Sage.

——— (1980). "Reducing Injury and Death Rates in Robbery," *Policy Analysis* 6, No. 1, pp. 21–45.

——— (1981). "The Effect of Gun Availability on Violent Crime Patterns," *The Annals of the American Academy of Political and Social Science*, May, pp. 63–79.

Feeney, Floyd and Adrianne Weir (1974). "The Prevention and Control of Robbery: A Summary." Center on Administration of Criminal Justice, University of Calif., Davis, mimeo.

Gandossy, Robert P., Jay R. Williams, Jo Cohen, and Henrick J. Harwood (1980). *Drugs and Crime: A Survey and Analysis of the Literature*, Washington, D.C.: National Institute of Justice.

Greenwood, Peter W. (1980). "Rand Research on Criminal Careers: An Update on Progress to Date," Santa Monica, Calif.: Rand Corporation.

Petersilia, Joan, Peter Greenwood, and Marvin Lavin (1977). *Criminal Careers of Habitual Felons*. Santa Monica, Calif.: Rand Corporation.

Peterson, Mark A. and Harriet B. Braiker (1980). *Doing Crime: A Survey of California Prison Inmates*. Santa Monica, Calif.: Rand Corporation.

Roizen, J. and D. Schneberk (1978). "Alcohol and Crime" in M. Aarens et al. (eds.) *Alcohol, Casualties, and Crime*. Berkeley: Social Research Group.

Roth, Jeffery A. (1978). "Prosecutor Perceptions of Crime Seriousness," *Journal of Criminal Law and Criminology* 69, No. 2.

Silberman, Charles E. (1978). *Criminal Violence, Criminal Justice*. New York: Random House.

Skogan, Wesley G. (1978). "Weapon Use in Robbery," in *Violent Crime: Historical and Contemporary Issues*, by James A. Inciardi and Anne E. Pottieger. Beverly Hills, Calif.: Sage Publications, Inc.

Violent Schools–Safe Schools (1978). The Safe School Study Report to the Congress, Vol. I and II, Department of Health, Education and Welfare, National Institute of Education, Washington, D.C.: Government Printing Office.

Wilson, James Q. and Barbara Boland (1978). *Effect of the Police on Crime*. Washington, D.C.: Urban Institute.
Zimring, Franklin E. (1976). *Crime, Demography and Time in Five American Cities*. Croton-on-Hudson, N.Y.: Hudson Institute.
——— (1977). "Determinants of the Death Rate from Robbery: A Detroit Time Study," *The Journal of Legal Studies* VI, No. 2, pp. 317–332.
——— (1979). "American Youth Violence: Issues and Trends," in Norval Morris and Michael Tonry, eds., *Crime and Justice: An Annual Review of Research* I. University of Chicago. pp. 67–107.
——— (1981). "Kids, Groups, and Crime: Some Implications of a Well-Known Secret." *Journal of Criminal Law and Criminology* 72(3), pp. 867–885.

Convenience Stores, Armed Robbery, and Physical Environmental Features

Dennis C. Duffala

Convenience stores, along with liquor stores and service stations, are known . . . as natural crime targets. They get "hit" at a much higher rate than would be anticipated on the basis of chance. Convenience stores are also very much a part of urban design and development, especially city growth as is reflected in transportation systems, suburban development, and the usage of streets. . . .

THE RESEARCH DESIGN

The purpose of this research is to test whether or not the vulnerability of convenience stores to armed robbery is associated with certain environmental characteristics. Four hypotheses will be tested:

1. a convenience store is more vulnerable to armed robbery when located within two blocks of a major transportation route;
2. a convenience store is more vulnerable to armed robbery when located on a street(s) with only a light amount of vehicular traffic;
3. a convenience store is more vulnerable to armed robbery in a residential and/or vacant land use area; and
4. a convenience store is more vulnerable to armed robbery when located in an area of fewer surrounding commercial activities. . . .

Vulnerability refers to the actual number of times each store has been robbed during the time frame [of] January 1, 1973, . . . through April 30, 1975; a store . . . robbed five times will be considered more vulnerable than one . . . robbed only twice. . . . [R]obbery information was obtained from . . . the Tallahassee Police Department and the Leon County Sheriff's Office official records. . . . The difference between strong armed robbery and armed robbery is that the latter takes place when a weapon is used and consequently increases the risk of injury to the victim. Armed robbery was chosen . . . to investigate in this study. It is assumed . . . that the use of a weapon indicates premeditation. . . . This premeditation would at least suggest a rational planning process . . . probably in conjunction with a "casing," regardless how superficial. . . . Even a superficial casing must have a criteri[on] on which to judge the likelihood of success; . . . at least part of that criteri[on] would include the environmental characteristics of the immediate area. It should be noted that all the robberies that occurred during the time frame of this study were armed robberies and not strong armed robberies. The convenience stores chosen for this study were selected for . . . two reasons: . . . the relatively high number of such stores existing within and just . . . outside . . . the Tallahassee city limits, and . . . the design and layout similarities of all these stores both externally and internally. Within an individual chain (Majik-Market, Jr. Food Stores, and so on) the layout is almost exactly alike down to the merchandise displays, hours of operation, clerk and cash register location, singulation entrance, parking area, and distance to adjacent street. Between chains, [these] . . . physical characteristics are still surprisingly similar. . . . The 39 stores selected for this study include the following number of stores from each particular chain: 24 Majik-Markets, nine Jr. Food Stores, five Sing Stop and Shop Stores, and one Li'l Essex Store. . . .

Because the stores were all so similar, . . . they were considered identical, thus controlling for the physical edifice. With all stores being alike, only the physical environmental settings surrounding these stores were dissimilar[;] . . . these settings were looked at to see if any type, or types, of . . . environmental features [were] related to high numbers of robberies. . . .

The first environmental characteristic looked at in this study was proximity to major transportation routes: a store is assumed to be more vulnerable to armed robbery when located within two blocks of a major transportation route. . . .

The second environmental characteristic . . . was the amount of traffic on the adjacent street(s): a store is assumed to be more vulnerable to armed robbery when located on a street(s) with only a light amount of vehicular traffic. . . . Traffic counts[,] . . . obtained from the Florida Department of Transportation and calculated over a two-year period, . . . were divided into . . . light and heavy: light was up to ten thousand vehicles per 24-hour period, and heavy was greater than ten thousand. . . .

A third environmental characteristic . . . was the type of land use immediately adjacent to each store: a store is assumed to be more vulnerable to armed robbery in a residential and/or vacant land use area. . . .

The fourth . . . environmental characteristic . . . was the number of surrounding commercial activities: a store is assumed to be more vulnerable to armed robbery when located in an area of fewer surrounding commercial activities. The . . . criterion used in determining what was "surrounding" . . . was . . . surveillance. . . . If an activity was within one block in any direction . . . of a convenience store from the most heavily traveled entrance and/or exit (usually the front) . . . , it could be considered as a surrounding activity. . . . [F]urther, if the activity . . . cater[ed] to a heavy amount of pedestrian and vehicular traffic which came through an adjoining parking facility and walking area which did have a line of vision to the front of the convenience store, that activity could be included as a surrounding one. . . .

Hypothesis: A convenience store is more vulnerable to armed robbery when located within two blocks of a major transportation route. . . . [T]he data show no significant relationship between variables. . . . [O]ne of the greatest concerns of the "convenience store" . . . is easy access for the customer. Consequently, in the Tallahassee area, just over half of all convenience stores are located on or within two blocks of a major transportation route. . . .

. . . [W]hile only eight of 24 stores within two blocks of major routes fell into the "robbed three or more times" category, three store were robbed three times, three stores were robbed four times, one store was robbed seven times, and one store was robbed eleven times. . . . [N]oteworthy is that 66.6% of all those stores robbed three or more times were on or near major routes. [Nevertheless, the overall relationship is not significant.] . . .

Hypothesis: A convenience store is more vulnerable to armed robbery when located on a street(s) with only a light amount of vehicular traffic. . . . The . . . data . . . show a significant relationship[;] . . . [52]% of the stores located on streets with a light flow of traffic (less than 10,000 vehicles in 24 hours) [were] . . . robbed three or more times [in contrast to just 6% of the stores on streets with higher vehicular traffic.] . . .

Hypothesis: A convenience store is more vulnerable to armed robbery when located in a residential and/or vacant area. . . . The . . . data . . . show no significant relationship between residential and vacant land uses and vulnerability. . . . [F]or those stores robbed never, once, or twice, . . . 37% were located in a predominantly residential or vacant surrounding. Of those stores robbed three times or more, 66.6% were located in a residential and/or vacant area. . . .

Hypothesis: A convenience store is more vulnerable to armed robbery when located in an area of fewer surrounding commercial activities. . . . [This hypothesis is sustained] when there is a high number of surrounding commercial activities there is a low incidence of robbery. . . .

The . . . importance of this study . . . is not how significant any one relationship is but rather how important all four hypotheses are when considered in concert for any one store. . . .

When considering . . . the twelve stores that were robbed three times or more, . . . [we observe] . . . that a variable that does not relate highly to vulnerability in and of itself may still be extremely important . . . [when it is] considered with . . . [just] one other factor. Of [the] twelve stores . . . robbed . . . 61 times . . . nine were located within two blocks of a major transportation route; ten were located on a street(s) with only a light amount of traffic; eight were located in a residential and/or vacant land-use area; and twelve had fewer than two surrounding commercial activities. . . . [I]t is possible to combine the data [to show] . . . how many stores simultaneously experience all of the environmental conditions presented in the four hypotheses. . . . The data . . . show that of the twelve stores having the highest incidence of robbery, nine are found on or within two blocks of a major transportation route. Of those nine stores on or near a major route, eight are located on an adjacent street with fewer than ten thousand vehicles passing by in a 24-hour period. Of those eight stores on a major route and an adjacent street with a light amount of vehicular traffic, six are located in a residential and/or vacant land-use area. Of those six stores found to be located on a major route and on an adjacent street with a light amount of vehicular traffic and in a residential and/or vacant land-use area, all six have two or fewer surrounding commercial activities.... It seems that the relationship of any one variable to store vulnerability is not too important. . . .

REFERENCES

Angel, S. (1968) Discouraging Crime Through City Planning. University of California Institute of Urban and Regional Development, Center for Planning and Development Research Working Paper No. 75.

Brantingham, P. J. and P. L. Brantingham (1974) "Housing patterns and burglary in a medium-sized American city." Paper read at 1974 Meeting of the American Society of Criminology, Chicago.

Curtis, L. A. (1974) Criminal Violence. Lexington, Mass.: Lexington.

Harries, K. (1974) The Geography of Crime and Justice. New York: McGraw-Hill.

Jacobs, J. (1961) The Death and Life of Great American Cities. New York: Random House.

Jeffery, C. R. (1971) Crime Prevention Through Environmental Design. Beverly Hills, Calif.: Sage.

Letkemann, P. (1973) Crime as Work. Englewood Cliffs, N.J.: Prentice-Hall.

Luedtke, G. and Associates (1970) "Crime and the physical city: neighborhood design techniques for crime reduction." Springfield, Va.: National Technical Information Service.

Newman, O. (1972) Defensible Space. New York: Macmillan.

Pyle, G. F. (1974) The Spatial Dynamics of Crime. University of Chicago Department of Geography Research Paper No. 159.

The Mugging

Morton Hunt

THE VICTIMAL BEHAVIOR OF A. HELMER

On nearly all counts (aside from the time of day) Alexander Helmer was a more than ordinarily good candidate for a mugging that Friday noon; indeed, the fact that it was Friday partly balanced out the time element, since robbery or theft accompanied by violence is more common on weekdays than on Saturdays or Sundays. In most respects he was not at all to blame for his victimal tendencies, but in at least two ways he was distinctly complicitous. . . . First, due to vanity, he had imprudently heightened his visibility as a target, for, despite his paranoid secrecy where his landlady and neighbors were concerned, he had been something of a braggart and blabbermouth with casual acquaintances, boasting of his stock-market holdings to half a dozen or more neighborhood people he knew only slightly, and making it plain that he lived alone and had no heirs—information which, passed along as idle gossip, could considerably increase his chance of victimization. Second, he had continued to live and to wander around in an area where predators were coming to abound, and where his personal traits marked him out as potential prey. The Melrose neighborhood had become distinctly dangerous during the past five to ten years, particularly that part of it a few blocks to the south of his residence, but he stubbornly (or perhaps blindly) remained in the apartment he had been in for twenty-five years and, in search of his meager ration of social contact and his bargain groceries, kept taking long walks down Melrose Avenue, past the decaying side-streets, past groups of street-corner loungers, and past the dark, urinous doorways and vacated stores that were the hangouts of local pushers and junkies.

Which is precisely what he did on this day. At the A&P, by noontime or a little after, Helmer had collected the things he needed and wheeled his shopping cart up to a checkout line being handled by Miss Annette Odierno, a tiny, dark-haired woman in her late thirties who had been punching an A&P register for twenty years, and who, without looking up, swiftly and mechanically checked out Helmer's little purchases—a quart of milk, a pint of ice cream, a few tomatoes and a couple of apples, a loaf of bread, half a dozen eggs, and a few other things—ringing up a total of $4.20 and stowing his purchases neatly in a medium-sized bag. Helmer left, and turned north, up Melrose Avenue, walking leisurely toward an unsuspected rendezvous.

MELROSE: THE STREET, THE AREA, THE SYNDROME

Melrose Avenue is moderately broad and busy: buses run both ways on it, there is a good deal of automobile traffic, and all day long a fair number of people are walking or lounging on the sidewalks, a welcome sight for a man who spends most of his waking hours alone at home. It had never been a beautiful thoroughfare—it was lined on both sides by four- to six-story brick tenement buildings with little shops at the ground level and tangles of iron fire-escapes hanging overhead, and the sidewalks had been built without allowance for grass or trees at the curbside, or room for shrubbery in front of the buildings—but in Helmer's earlier years the avenue had at least been neat, orderly, busy, and interesting. It was one of the several main north–south thoroughfares of that part of the south Bronx known as Melrose—a lower-income residential district very much like those established in many large American cities half a century or more ago which, though until recently sound and peaceful, are now rapidly succumbing to physical and social decay and turning into festering slums. . . .

HELMER AT THE THRESHOLD OF SAFETY

. . . Alexander Helmer, for one, paid little attention to the street-corner loungers he was passing, and must not have been especially fearful of being attacked by such people, for in his wallet that day he was carrying $189 for no particular reason except that he liked to. Even if the thought of robbery did occur to him from time to time, he had little personal reason to think of it as involving physical brutality, for years ago, in his rounds as a milkman, he had been robbed twice without being hurt. Whatever he thought of the dark and alien-looking newcomers to his neighborhood, he did not greatly fear them or worry about the increased amount of crime that had come with them into formerly safe and peaceful Melrose. . . .

Even the youths idling in front of the Vega-Baja Self-Service Grocery on the south side of 160th Street, directly across from Helmer's building, did not look particularly malevolent or vicious. Had anyone been watching them, he would probably have noticed nothing particularly ominous about their behavior; even when Helmer, carrying his bag of groceries, suddenly appeared at the corner, they did little more than whisper to each other and assume a broad air of nonchalance. They watched with no evident interest as the old man crossed the street at the corner, turned west, and walked toward the front door of his building; they made no move as he pushed open the heavy glass door with its iron grillwork, mounted several steps inside the tiny foyer, and fished a bunch of keys out of his pocket; they stayed where they were as he unlocked the wooden inner door and pushed his way in, letting it close slowly by itself as he disappeared, out of the sight of the enemies he had not even noticed and into the safety of the building that had been his home so many years. . . .

. . . Had anyone been watching Helmer and the youths across the street that day—no one was, in all likelihood, for 160th Street was relatively quiet much of the time, and almost deserted at that particular moment—he would have seen a pattern with which police have become all too familiar in recent years. As Helmer went through the inner door and disappeared, there was a moment or so of waiting and urgent whispering; then one youth darted across the street and through the front door into the foyer, where he punched a button at random on the panel in the right-hand wall. As soon as the buzzer sounded, unlocking the inner door, he pushed it open and held it ajar, turning and waving to the others across the street to come on; they came running, burst into the foyer and rushed through the door he was holding open, and bounded up the stairs Alexander Helmer had just climbed.

THE HIGH COST OF FEAR

None of the tenants of the building had seen them run in, and none saw them go rushing up the stairs, but this is not unusual; muggers pick their moment to strike and are rarely or only fleetingly observed. And even if anyone at 399 East 160th Street had seen them, he would neither have recognized them nor been able to give a useful description of them, for none of the invaders had ever been in the building before, and although they all lived nearby, people in a crowded tenement area can be total strangers to others who live only half a block away. Moreover, when the victim or witnesses are white and the attackers are black or Puerto Rican (whom whites are notoriously poor at perceiving and recognizing as individuals), there is little chance that any eyewitness report will be of much help to the police. Such reports almost always fit hundreds of persons within walking distance of the scene of the attack, a typical description reading something like this: "Negro, male, early twenties, medium height and build, dark-skinned, wearing gray windbreaker."

In many robberies, and especially in hit-and-run muggings, the situation is hopeless; there are no clues, no web of personal connections, no motives leading inexorably to one person who has been involved with the victim. . . .

Thus muggings, in addition to their other dismaying and alarming characteristics, seem all but uncontrollable by the police and the courts. Victims of muggers—and virtually all who fear they might someday become victims—feel helpless, unprotected, and without any means of redress. . . .

It is for such reasons that robberies, and muggings in particular, have so powerfully corrosive an effect upon American life, for, over and above everything else they do to us, they cause a loss of faith in our society, and a pervasive and demoralizing fear. Other things which might be expected to cause far greater fear do not, and have no such demoralizing effect. Automobiles, to take but one example, killed 56,400 Americans and injured two million in 1969—roughly 20 times as many deaths, and 25 times as many injuries, as were caused by muggers. Yet in comparison to our fear of muggers, our fear of automobiles is almost nonexistent. This does not mean that we are fools, but that we far better tolerate the thought that an accident may harm us than that another human being—a total stranger to whom we have done no wrong—may suddenly and viciously attack us.

The effects of our fear have been disastrous. Throughout the 1960s the quality of daily life in American's major cities, particularly for the scores of millions who live in or near high-crime areas, has grown ever more impoverished and barren. Out of fear of walking in the streets at night, such people have increasingly given up many of the activities that used to enrich and vary their lives. Each year during the decade, the nighttime use of public libraries in many large cities declined, attendance dwindled at PTA meetings, and parks and public recreation facilities were less used. . . .

HELMER PLAYS HIS PART IN A NEFARIOUS SYMBIOSIS

Certainly, nothing the police were doing in 1964 and nothing they have done since then would have forestalled the criminal behavior of the youths who had decided to pull a score on Alexander Helmer. At the most, a patrolman on the corner of 160th Street and Melrose might have made them decide to choose another place in which to attack him, or deflected their aim to another target altogether; but even for such limited benefits one would need patrolmen on every block of the city at all times, or perhaps ten times as many as all those now in the New York Police Department, even assuming every one of them could be assigned to street duty—a level of policing not even the most repressive dictatorship in Europe or South America has come close to. . . .

[One] pattern of attack—much like that decided upon by the little band that was after Helmer—involves trailing an old and single person home, unobtrusively following him (or her) until he unlocks his front door, and then rushing him on inside, where the mugging can take place unobserved and uninterrupted.

It happens very fast—too fast, usually, for the victim to be aware of what is going on except in that vague, surprised, and disbelieving way in which one perceives himself to be in the middle of an automobile accident. Helmer had climbed two flights of stairs and was at the front door of his apartment, Number 2-B—the 2-series apartments were on the third floor, two levels up from the street—unlocking it with his right hand, the bag of groceries cradled in his left arm. As he got the door open, he put the bunch of keys back in his pocket and started on in; then from the stairway, to his left and behind him, there was the sound of racing feet, and in an instant he was violently propelled inside and shoved, stumbling, half a dozen steps along the narrow hall to the kitchen doorway on the right side.

Here he lurched into the doorway and turned, gasping in astonishment and fear. The shapes of two young men were hard upon him, and a third was at the front door, in the background. Inexplicably and wordlessly, as if preparing to do something to him, one of the two took the bag of groceries from his unresisting hands and set it on the floor just outside the kitchen. The other, meanwhile, slipped into the kitchen behind Helmer, who wheeled around in panic, beginning to shout in a cracked, aging voice and flailing out at the intruder with his feeble old arms. Behind him, whoever had taken the groceries from him now pinioned his arms to his sides, at which Helmer shouted all the louder. Then suddenly the man in front of him had a knife in his hand, with which he struck Helmer backhandedly and powerfully, hitting him in the left side and pulling the knife out, and striking again and yet three more times, the blade disappearing into Helmer for an instant each time, then reappearing, bright red.

Helmer abruptly stopped shouting and grew limp; the arms holding him from behind let go and he pitched forward onto the kitchen floor, landing heavily on his face, his brown hat flying off and falling to the floor a couple feet away, and the flesh-colored hearing aid popping out of his ear and landing close to his face, still connected to him by its fine wire. He lay there without moving, the warm blood soaking his clothes beneath him and beginning to seep out onto the floor. He did not see them step around him to search the kitchen, or hear their hurried footsteps around his apartment or the opening and slamming shut of bureau drawers and lids of boxes. The grayness and the silence closed in; he was unaware of what they said to each other, and did not hear the front door slam shut as they left, running pell-mell down the two flights of steps, splitting up, and disappearing in opposite directions, unnoticed by anyone, their faces fading even from the memory network of Helmer's brain as it slowly cooled and its circuits shut down for the first time in seventy-two years.

Chapter 5
Domestic Violence and Child Abuse

Domestic Criminal Violence

Richard J. Gelles

. . . As the victims of family violence came out from the closets and from behind the closed doors of the home in the late 1960s and early 1970s, the issue of family violence was transformed from a private issue into a public problem. . . . Star (1980) claims that the silence, which traditionally surrounded the issue of family violence, was attributable to three factors: (1) lack of awareness, (2) general acceptance, and (3) denial.

Official reporting systems for recording incidents of family violence were first nonexistent and then slow to develop. . . . While the child welfare movement of the late nineteenth century uncovered incidents of the abuse and exploitation of children (Taylor and Newberger, 1979), it was not until 1968 that all fifty states had legislated mandatory child-abuse-reporting statutes. . . .

. . . Violence between family members has enjoyed a long tradition of legal legitimization. In 1824, the Mississippi Supreme Court was the first of several states to grant husbands immunity from assault and battery charges for moderately chastizing their wives (Calvert, 1974; Star, 1980). . . . Such legal support . . . can be traced back to English common law, which gave husbands the right to strike their wives with sticks no wider than their thumbs—hence the classic "rule of thumb" (Calvert, 1974; Davidson, 1978). Similarly, historical evidence indicates legal precedents allowing for the mutilation, striking, and even killing of children as part of the legal parental prerogative (Radbill, 1974). . . .

Star (1980) believes that . . . denial . . . was the most widely held defense against acknowledging either the prevalence or the severity of family violence. Doctors, lawyers, social workers, and teachers often preferred to see a child's injury as caused by a fall or accident rather than as inflicted by a parent or caretaker. . . .

FAMILY VIOLENCE AND THE LACK OF A CRIMINAL PERSPECTIVE

Definitions: Violence and Abuse

The first form of domestic violence that was . . . recognized as a social problem was the abuse of children. While the victimization and exploitation of children was a problem seen and treated by members of the social service and child welfare community since the mid-nineteenth century, it was not until physician C. Henry Kempe and his colleagues published their seminal paper, "The Battered Child Syndrome," in 1962 that general attention was drawn to the problem of the abuse of children. Kempe and his colleagues narrowly defined the battered-child syndrome as willfully inflicted injury caused by a parent or caretaker. The definition was limited to acts of physical violence that produced injury and thus was consistent with the normal criminal definition of assault and battery. But the term "battered-child syndrome" quickly gave way to the terms "child abuse," "child abuse and neglect," and "child maltreatment." The definitions of these terms added conditions such as malnutrition, failure to thrive, sexual abuse, educational neglect, medical neglect, and mental abuse. . . .

The same general pattern that occurred with the broadening and politicalization of the definition of child abuse also occurred with the definition of wife abuse. Initial definitions of wife abuse (Gelles, 1974; Martin, 1976) focused on acts of damaging physical violence directed toward women by their spouses or partners. As wife abuse became recognized as a social problem, the definition was sometimes broadened to include sexual abuse, marital rape, and even pornography (London, 1978). . . .

Official Responses to Family Violence

Child Abuse: A Child Welfare Problem Perhaps the first publicly identified case of child abuse was that of a badly abused foster child named Mary Ellen who was discovered by church workers in New York City in 1874. When the church workers tried to get aid for Mary Ellen, they found that the only available agency was the Society for the Prevention of Cruelty to Animals. Thus, they founded the first chapter of a similar society for children (Ross, 1977). For nearly the next century the child welfare community was virtually the only institution available to identify and treat cases of battered children.

The Kempe et al. paper (1962) introduced the problem of child abuse to the medical community and was instrumental in establishing mandatory reporting laws in all fifty states. Such laws vary, but the modal strategy is that the key agencies charged with the responsibility of initiating contact with reported abusive families and providing services are protective service agencies (Nelson et al., 1980). While the police are frequently included as part of an overall reporting and service plan in state child-abuse laws, the criminal justice system is clearly placed on the periphery of the system of social control and social services (Rosenthal, 1979). . . .

While some child abusers are officially charged with crimes (ranging from child abuse to assault or murder), and many are convicted, most instances of officially reported child abuse are confined to the child welfare system, with the involvement of the criminal justice system limited to the granting of temporary restraining orders or family or probate court proceedings bearing on the custody status of the child.

Wife Abuse: The Struggle for Recognition The battered wife, who remained behind closed doors for a decade after the "discovery" of child abuse, found no official social service agency available to turn to for help, protection, or prevention. No "Society for the Prevention of Cruelty to Wives" was formed. . . .

The criminal justice system, beginning with the role and actions of the police, tended to view the problem of battered women from various perspectives. . . . One view of the police and the criminal justice system is that they positively sanction violence against women by failing to treat such behaviors as criminal assault. . . . [L]aws which "allowed" for some violence toward women were matched by informal procedures used by police, such as "stitch rules," which provided that a husband could not be arrested for assaulting his wife unless she had a wound that required a certain number of sutures (Field and Field, 1973). Prosecutors were castigated for not taking women's claims seriously and failing actively to pursue prosecution of assaultive husbands (Truninger, 1971).

On the other hand, the police and public prosecutors point to the actions of battered wives as "handcuffing" the effectiveness of the criminal justice system. Police frequently point to the women who attack and even kill police officers who intervene in domestic violence incidents. Other police officers point to the numerous instances of women who fail to file charges against their husbands or who return to their husbands time after time. Some prosecutors also point to numerous examples of women who fail to follow through in pressing charges against assaultive husbands or who drop charges at a trial and announce that "husbands are supposed to hit their wives, aren't they?" (Parnas, 1967).

The ten years since the identification of wife abuse as a social problem have seen a major effort on the part of organized groups advocating for battered women to obtain what they see as equal protection from the police. Three class-action suits best illustrate this struggle for a criminal perspective on wife-battering. In December 1976, wives in New York City filed a class-action suit (*Bruno v Maguire*) against the New York Police Department, probation officers, and family court employees for failing to prosecute abusive husbands. The police settled the case out of court in 1977. In 1974, a class-action suit was filed against the Cleveland district attorneys for denying battered women equal protection under the law by not following through on prosecution of abusive husbands. That suit was settled by a consent decree ordering the prosecutors to change their practices. In Oakland, the police department was accused of illegal conduct in its pattern and practice of discouraging arrests in cases of domestic violence. Similar proceedings followed these three cases, all with the goal of "criminalizing" violence against women. . . . Nevertheless, one thing remains clear. Husband-to-wife violence is neither uniformly nor completely recognized as an instance of criminal violence.

Husband Abuse: All Rhetoric and No Data? In 1978 Steinmetz published an article designed to demonstrate that husbands as well as wives were the victims of violence in the home. [She] . . . went on to claim that it was husband and *not* wife abuse that was the most underreported form of family violence. Steinmetz was immediately challenged and attacked by feminists and scholars alike for misreading, misinterpreting, and misrepresenting her findings (see Pleck et al., 1978). . . . What the actual extent of the battering of husbands is remains muddied, if not unknown. Any criminal justice concern for battered husbands was lost amidst the vociferous claims by those concerned with battered women that the issue of battered men was a red herring (Jones, 1980).

Other Forms of Family Violence: Little Notice Discussion of violence toward children has been subsumed under the heading of child abuse; domestic violence has become a concept that refers only to violence toward wives . . . and despite the effort of some scholars (for example, Straus et al., 1980) to define the problem as one of *family* violence, the other forms of violence in the home are largely unrecognized by the public, the scientific community, and the criminal justice system. Violence between siblings is perhaps the best example of a form of family violence that gets no criminal justice attention, with the obvious exception of criminal homicides. Abuse of the elderly was recently discovered. . . . Twelve states have passed "adult protective service" laws which attempt to increase the identification and servicing of elderly victims of family abuse (Mancini, 1980). . . .

FROM PRIVATE ISSUE TO PUBLIC PROBLEM

The prevailing public and social scientific attitude toward family violence through the mid-1970s was that family violence was rare and, when it did occur, was the product of mental illness or a psychological disorder. By the end of the 1970s, there had been a major revision of this line of thinking. . . .

Straus (1974a) attempted to explain the shift from family violence as a private issue to a high-priority public social issue by positing that the emergence of family violence as an important research topic was the result of three cultural and social forces. First, social scientists and the public alike became increasingly sensitive to violence—including a war in Southeast Asia, assassinations, civil disturbances, and increasing homicide rates—in the 1960s. Second, the emergence of the women's movement played a part—especially by uncovering and highlighting the problems of battered women. . . . The third factor postulated by Straus was the decline of the consensus model of society employed by social scientists, and the ensuing challenge by those advancing a conflict or social action model.

Perhaps a fourth factor should be added. Someone had to demonstrate that research on family violence could be conducted. . . .

THE EXTENT OF FAMILY VIOLENCE

Physical Punishment

One of the more widespread and better documented forms of family violence is also the form that is most controversial to label "violent." General social surveys indicate that physical punishment is used by 84 to 97 percent of all parents at some time in their children's lives (Blumberg, 1964; Bronfenbrenner, 1958; Erlanger, 1974; Stark and McEvoy, 1970). . . . [I]t is parent-to-child hitting that is perhaps the most widely practiced and socially accepted form of family violence.

Violence toward children does not cease when the children are old enough to walk, talk, and reason with. Four different studies of college and university students found that half of the parents of the students threatened or used physical punishment on their children while the students were seniors in high school (Straus, 1971; Steinmetz, 1971; Mulligan, 1977). . . .

Child Abuse

. . . In 1967, Gil (1970) conducted a nationwide inventory of reported cases of child abuse. . . . He found 6,000 confirmed cases of child abuse. Gil also reported on an opinion survey which asked a representative sample of 1,520 individuals if they had knowledge of families where incidents of child abuse had occurred. Forty-five, or 3 percent of the sample, reported knowledge of 48 different incidents. Extrapolating this number to a national population of 110 million adults, Gil estimated that between 2.53 and 4.07 million children were abused the year prior to his study. . . . Gil's data were analyzed by Light (1974) to correct for possible instances where the same abuse incidents were known by more than one person. Light's refined estimate of child abuse was 500,000 abused children in the United States during the survey year. . . .

Homicide

Homicide . . . is the one aspect of intrafamily violence on which there are reasonably reliable data. . . . Researchers generally report that intrafamilial homicide accounts for between 20 and 40 percent of all homicides (Curtis, 1974).

Applicants for Divorce

Studies of couples applying for divorce also provided some early data on the extent of husband–wife violence. Levinger (1966) found 22 percent of the middle-class and 40 percent of the working-class applicants for divorce whom he interviewed discussed "physical violence" as a major complaint. . . .

A National Survey of Family Violence

One study that was based on a nationally representative sample of families . . . was conducted by Straus et al. (1980). . . . These investigators based their estimates of violence and abuse on self-reports of a nationally representative sample of 2,143 individual family members. . . .

Parent-to-Child Violence: Child Abuse The national survey [showed] . . . 3.8 percent of American children 3 to 17 years of age . . . were victims of severe or abusive violence each year. . . . Projected to the 46 million children [aged] 3 to 17 who lived with both parents during the year of the survey, . . . between 1.5 and 2 million children were abused by their parents (Gelles, 1978; Straus et al., 1980).

Marital Violence and Spouse Abuse Focusing on violence between marital partners, . . . 16 percent of those surveyed reported some kind of physical violence between spouses during the year of the survey, while 28 percent . . . reported marital violence at some point in the marriage (Straus, 1978; Straus et al., 1980).

In terms of acts of violence that could be considered wife-beating, the national study revealed that 3.8 percent of American women were victims of abusive violence during the twelve months prior to the interview (see Table 5-1). The same survey found that 4.6 percent of the wives admitted or were reported by their husbands as having engaged in violence. . . .

Violence between Siblings It is rare that someone considers a fistfight between siblings as violence. Stark and McEvoy (1970) found that 70 percent of a nationally representative sample of adults thought that it was important for a boy to have a few fistfights when growing up. . . .

Table 5-1.
Comparison of Husband and Wife Violence Rates (in percentages)

	Incidence Rate		Frequency*			
			Mean		Median	
	H	W	H	W	H	W
Wife-Beating and Husband-Beating (N to R)	3.8	4.6	8.0	8.9	2.4	3.0
Overall Violence Index (K to R)	12.1	11.6	8.8	10.1	2.5	3.0
K. Threw something at spouse	2.8	5.2	5.5	4.5	2.2	2.0
L. Pushed, grabbed, shoved spouse	10.7	8.3	4.2	4.6	2.0	2.1
M. Slapped spouse	5.1	4.6	4.2	3.5	1.6	1.9
N. Kicked, bit, or hit with fist	2.4	3.1	4.8	4.6	1.9	2.3
O. Hit or tried to hit with something	2.2	3.0	4.5	7.4	2.0	3.8
P. Beat up spouse	1.1	0.6	5.5	3.9	1.7	1.4
Q. Threatened with knife or gun	0.4	0.6	4.6	3.1	1.8	2.0
R. Used a knife or gun	0.3	0.2	5.3	1.8	1.5	1.5

Source: From Murray A. Straus, "Wife Beating: How Common and Why?" *Victimology*, 1978, 2(3/4), p. 446. Reprinted with permission.
*For those who engaged in each act (i.e., omits those with scores of zero).

Given this attitude, it is not surprising that violence between siblings is *the most common form of intrafamilial violence*. Of the 733 children who lived with siblings in the national sample, four out of five were involved in at least one violent act in the survey year. Twenty percent . . . reported that one child "beat up" a sibling in the previous twelve months. . . . Three children in 1,000 used a gun or a knife on a sibling in the previous 12 months. Extrapolating this figure to the 36 million children aged 3 to 17 years old who live with a sibling, 109,000 American children used a gun or a knife against a sibling. . . .

Child-to-Parent Violence Another form of family violence rarely mentioned in public discussions of family violence, and virtually ignored by researchers (with the recent exceptions of Steinmetz, 1978c, and Harbin and Madden, 1979), is children's use of violence against their parents. Subjects in the national survey were asked to report on whether their children had ever used violence against them. Sixteen percent of the parents reported they had been struck at least once during the previous twelve months. . . . These figures, however, tend to exaggerate the extent of parent abuse, since much of the so-called abusive violence (such as kicking, biting, punching) was carried out by children 3 or 4 years old. . . . A better illustration . . . [is] . . . abusive violence used by teenagers. More than 3 teenagers (aged 15 to 17 years of age) in 100 (3.5 percent) were reported as kicking, biting, punching, hitting with an object, beating up, threatening, or using a gun or a knife against a parent in the survey year. . . .

National Crime Survey Report

A second source of data on the extent and patterns of domestic violence is the National Crime Survey. The National Crime Survey estimates the amount of crime, whether reported or unreported to the police, committed against persons aged 12 and over and against households.

. . . "Intimate Victims: A Study of Violence Among Friends and Relatives" (U.S. Department of Justice, 1980) reported on events occurring between 1973 and 1976. . . .

1. There were about 3.8 million incidents of violence among intimates in the four-year period of the survey. Nearly a third (1.2 million) were committed by offenders related to the victims.
2. More than half (55 percent) of incidents of intimate violence went unreported to the police.
3. An analysis of the single-offender incidents revealed 1,055,000 incidents between relatives. Of this number, 616,000 (58 percent) were between spouses or ex-spouses; 57,000 victims (5 percent) were parents; 38,000 victims (4 percent) were the offender's own children; 76,000 victims (7 percent) were attacked by siblings; and the remaining 268,000 victims (27 percent) were other relatives. Thus, the most common form of violence between relatives was interspousal.
4. Of the single-offender incidents, 80.9 percent of the spousal victims reported injuries, the most common being bruises, black eyes, cuts,

scratches, or swellings. Of the parent victims, 89 percent reported injuries; 79.6 percent of the children reported injuries; 77.3 percent of the siblings reported injuries; and 70.4 percent of the other relatives reported injuries.

5. More than half of the spouse victims (56.8 percent), child victims (58.8 percent), sibling victims (53.6 percent), and other relative victims (56.2 percent) reported their victimization to the police. Less than 50 percent of all the parent victims (47.3 percent) reported their situation to the police. Of all the victims of intimate violence, relatives were most likely to make police reports. . . .

Violence between Unmarried Intimates

. . . [I]ntimate violence neither is confined to legally married couples nor is necessarily more common among those who are married. . . . Yllo and Straus (1978) examined data from the national family violence survey (Straus et al., 1980) and found that cohabitating couples reported more violence than married couples. However, cohabitators who were over 30, had been together for more than 10 years, had high incomes, and were divorced had very low rates of violence.

FACTORS ASSOCIATED WITH FAMILY VIOLENCE

Early research and writing on family violence was dominated by the psychopathological model (Gelles, 1973; Spenetta and Rigler, 1972). Child-abuse researchers discounted social factors as playing any causal role in violence toward children (see, for example, Steele and Pollock, 1968, 1974). Rather, the explanation was thought to lie in personality or character disorders of individual battering parents (Steele and Pollock, 1968; Galdston, 1965; Zalba, 1971). . . .

The similarity of theoretical focus in early studies of family violence was probably a product of the similar methods of procedure employed by investigators. Nearly all published work on child abuse and family violence was based on clinical samples (such as hospitalized children and patients of psychiatrists or social workers) or officially reported cases of child abuse. Early studies of family violence typically failed to employ control or comparison groups, based conclusions on post-hoc explanation, and were based on small, nonrepresentative samples (Spinetta and Rigler, 1972). . . .

Gender and Violence

Research on child abuse frequently reports that mothers are at least as abusive toward their children, if not more so, than are fathers (Bennie and Sclare, 1969; Steele and Pollock, 1974; Gil, 1970; Parke and Collmer, 1975; Straus et al., 1980). The simple explanation for mothers' violence is that they spend more time with their children than do fathers. The actual explanation of mothers' slightly greater use of violence is probably more complex. First, the mother role is invested with the greatest degree of responsibility for child rearing. Second, because mothers are viewed as more responsible, and child rearing is such a central aspect of the female family role, children are more likely to interfere with mothers' plans and self-concepts than with fathers' activities or sense of self. Mothers, then, are the parents with the highest degree of role commitment to parenting, the greatest role investment, and thus, probably experience the most stress and frustration in raising children. . . .

In terms of sibling violence, boys were found to be slightly more violent than girls (83 percent compared to 74 percent) in the national survey of family violence (Straus et al., 1980). More interestingly, all male sibships were found to have the highest rates of sibling violence (67 percent), followed by mixed-sex sibships (52 percent), with all female sibships being the least violent—40 percent (Straus et al., 1980).

The data on the relationship between gender and family violence are of interest because violence in the home, especially violence toward children, is the exception to the rule in studies of criminal violence that find males to be the predominant offenders and victims of violence outside of the home.

The Cycle of Violence

One of the consistent conclusions of domestic-violence research is that individuals who have experienced violent and abusive childhoods are more likely to grow up to become child and spouse abusers than individuals who experienced little or no violence in their childhood years (Spinetta and Rigler, 1971; Parke and Collmer, 1975; Kempe et al., 1962; Straus, 1979a; Steinmetz, 1977; Gayford, 1975; Owens and Straus, 1975; Byrd, 1979; Gelles, 1974; Flynn, 1975). . . .

Data from the national survey of family violence also lend support to the hypothesis that "violence begets violence" (Straus, 1979a; Straus et al., 1980). . . . Those who said their mothers had used physical punishment twice or more a year reported, as parents, a child abuse rate of 18.5. This rate is 57 percent greater than the rate (11.8)) for parents in the survey who had experienced less physical punishment at age 13. . . .

Observing parents hit each other was also found to be related to violence as an adult. . . .

[E]xperiencing violence as a teenager was related to marital violence reported by subjects. Husbands who were categorized as being reared in the most violent homes had a rate of wife abuse 600 times greater than husbands reared in the least violent homes.

Socioeconomic Status

. . . [R]esearch [has] supported the hypothesis that domestic violence is more prevalent in low-socioeconomic-status families (Byrd, 1979; Gelles, 1974; Levinger, 1966; Gayford, 1975; Maden and Wrench, 1977; Elmer, 1967; Gil, 1970;

Parke and Collmer, 1975; Straus et al., 1980). This conclusion, however, does not mean that domestic violence is confined to lower-class households. Investigators reporting the differential distribution of violence are frequently careful to point out that child and spouse abuse can be found in families across the spectrum of socioeconomic status (Steinmetz, 1978b).

Race

Examinations of the relationship between race and family violence have yielded mixed results. Data from official reports of child abuse indicate child abuse is greater among blacks than whites (Johnson, 1974; Thompson et al., 1971; Gil, 1970). Other studies have reported that blacks do not have a significantly higher rate of child abuse and violence than whites (Billingsley, 1969; Young, 1964; Elmer, 1967). Byrd's review of research on interspousal violence concluded that race was not related to intersexual assault in the home (1979–citing Gelles, 1974; Martin, 1976; Ball, 1977; Parker and Schumacher, 1977; and Gaquin, 1977–1978).

Data from the national survey of family violence (Straus et al., 1980) indicate no difference in the rates of abusive violence toward children among black and white families (15 percent in black families, 14 percent in white families). Cazenave and Straus (1978), in a more detailed examination of the national survey data, concluded that the aid and support, especially child care, provided by black extended family kin seem to reduce the risk of abusive violence directed toward children. . . .

The . . . *National Study of the Incidence and Severity of Child Abuse and Neglect* (Westat, Inc., 1980) found that black children were *underrepresented* in all child-abuse categories. . . . [This] family violence survey found that rates of abusive violence among couples, toward wives, and toward husbands was higher in black than in white families. Black couples reported a rate of abusive violence more than double the rate for whites (11 percent as opposed to 5 percent). Finally, black females' rates of abusive violence were twice the rate for white wives (8 percent as opposed to 4 percent).

While the picture of the relationship between race and family violence is far from clear, it does appear that, in terms of marital violence, the differences between blacks and whites parallel differences found in studies of criminal violence. The two most recent national surveys of violence toward children and reported child abuse are exceptions to the trend of higher rates of criminal violence among blacks.

Stress

A third consistent finding of most domestic-violence research is that family violence rates are directly related to social stress in families (Gil, 1970; . . . Straus et al., 1980). . . . [I]nvestigators report associations between . . . family violence and . . . *unemployment or part-time employment of males* (Gil, 1970; Parke and

Collmer, 1975; Prescott and Letko, 1977; Straus [et al.,] 1980); *financial problems* (Prescott and Letko, 1977); *pregnancy*, in the case of wife abuse (Gelles, 1975b; Eisenberg and Micklow, 1977); and *single-parent family*, in the case of child abuse (Maden and Wrench, 1977).

Social Isolation

A fourth major finding in the study of both child and spouse abuse is that social isolation raises the risk that there will be severe violence directed at children or between spouses (Gil, 1970; Maden and Wrench, 1977; Parke and Collmer, 1975; Gelles, 1974; Ball, 1977; Borland, 1976). . . .

. . . [T]here have been [other] studies directed at identifying specific factors related to child *or* spouse abuse. In the case of violence toward children, some of the factors are larger-than-average family size (Light, 1974; Gil, 1970; Maden and Wrench, 1977; Parke and Collmer, 1975; Elmer, 1967; Straus et al., 1980); low birth weight of the child (Parke and Collmer, 1975); prematurity of the child (Elmer, 1967; Maden and Wrench, 1977; Parke and Collmer, 1975; Steele and Pollock, 1974); and lack of attachment between mother and child, sometimes as a result of low birth weight or prematurity (Klaus and Kennell, 1976). In addition, females are found to be slightly more likely to abuse their children (Maden and Wrench, 1977), and males are slightly more likely to be the victims of child abuse (Gil, 1970; Maden and Wrench, 1977). Last, researchers have proposed that children who are handicapped, retarded, developmentally delayed, or perceived by their parents as "different" are at greater risk of being abused (Friedrich and Boriskin, 1976; Gil, 1970; Steinmetz, 1978b). . . .

THEORIES OF INTRAFAMILY VIOLENCE

Family violence has been approached from three general theoretical levels of analysis: (1) the intraindividual level of analysis, or the psychiatric model; (2) the social-psychological level of analysis; and (3) the sociological or sociocultural level of analysis (Burgess and Conger, 1978; Justice and Justice, 1976; Gelles and Straus, 1979; Steinmetz, 1978b; Parke and Collmer, 1975).

The Psychiatric Model . . . focuses on the offender's personality characteristics as the chief determinants of violence and abuse. . . . [This] model includes theoretical approaches that link mental illness, alcohol and drug abuse, and other intraindividual phenomena to acts of family violence.

The Social-Psychological Model . . . assumes that violence and abuse can be best understood by a careful examination of the external environmental factors that impact on the family. In addition, this model considers which everyday family interactions are precursors to violence. Theoretical approaches that examine stress, the transmission of violence from one generation to another, and family interaction patterns fit into [this] . . . model. . . .

The Sociocultural Model . . . provides a macro-level analysis of family violence. Violence is considered in light of socially structured inequality and cultural attitudes and norms about violence and family relations. . . .

Five Theories of Family Violence

Goode's Resource Theory of Intrafamily Violence (1971) was the first theoretical approach applied explicitly to family violence. Goode states that social systems "rest to some degree on force or its threat." . . . [W]ithin a social system, the greater the resources a person can command, the more force he or she can muster. However, the more resources a person can command, the less that person will *actually deploy* violence. Thus, violence is used as a last resort when all other resources are insufficient or lacking. Applying this set of assumptions to the family, Goode explains that a husband who wants to be the dominant family member but has little education, job prestige, or income and lacks interpersonal skills may be likely to resort to violence to be the dominant person. . . .

. . . Straus's General Systems Theory (1973) . . . attempts to account for violence in the home by viewing the family as a purposive, goal-seeking, adaptive social system. Violence is viewed as a system product, or output, rather than an individual pathology. Straus specified "positive feedback" in the system, which can create an upward spiral of violence, and "negative feedback," which can maintain, dampen, or reduce the level of violence. . . .

Garbarino (1977) proposed an "ecological model" to explain the complex nature of child maltreatment. The ecological, or human development approach, focuses on the progressive, mutual adaptation of organism and environment. . . . [T]he model assesses the political, economic, and demographic factors that shape the quality of life for children and families. Garbarino identified cultural support for the use of physical force against children, and the inadequacy and inadequate use of family support systems as two necessary conditions for child maltreatment. . . . [M]altreatment is believed to arise out of a mismatch of parent to child and family to neighborhood and community. . . .

Burgess (1979) proposed an evolutionary perspective for understanding child abuse. . . . Using the concept of "parental investment," [he] explains that in situations such as lack of bonding and parental uncertainty, the risk of child abuse would be increased. . . . Burgess also proposes that an inadequate parenting resource base would decrease the probability of parental investment and thus raise the risk of abuse. Lack of parental resources would then explain the inverse relationship proposed between abuse and social class and the proposed positive relationship between family size and abuse. Last, Burgess (1979) points to problems with children that decrease parental investment and increase the risk of abuse—such as developmental problems, retardation, and Down's syndrome. . . .

Dobash and Dobash (1979) . . . attempt to make the case that throughout history, violence has been systematically directed at women. Their central thesis is that economic and social processes operate directly and indirectly to support a patriarchal social order and family structure. . . . [P]atriarchy leads to the subordination of women and contributes to a historical pattern of systematic violence directed against wives. . . .

LOOKING AHEAD

The development of knowledge about the nature and causes of domestic criminal violence has been hampered by definitional problems, methodological inadequacies and errors, and failures in logic. . . . We still have difficulty in precisely defining child abuse, wife abuse, and family violence. Controversy still surrounds estimates and research concerning the incidence and prevalence of domestic violence. Our knowledge about the causes of family violence is largely limited to research that is able to establish associations between psychological or sociological variables and family violence. The magnitude of the relationships, even those that are consistently found, are most often quite modest, although the magnitude is frequently inflated by reports on family violence that are more journalistic than social-scientific.

The theoretical work on family violence has been even more modest and primitive than the research on either incidence or associations of factors. . . . Few investigators attempt to establish a theoretical model and then test the model or propositions derived from the model. . . .

While investigators have demonstrated that certain social factors are related to family violence and abuse, many of the associations found could be symmetrical. In other words, stress could lead to abuse or abuse could create family stress. A major gap in research in family violence is that there have been no longitudinal studies that can be used to reduce the number of plausible rival hypotheses concerning time order and causal direction. . . .

Cross-Cultural Research. Another shortcoming of current research on domestic violence is that it is largely confined to . . . the United States. . . . There is a need to cast the net more widely and examine whether or not domestic violence occurs with less, equal, or greater frequency in other countries and in other societies. . . .

NOTE

1. Space precludes providing a complete and exhaustive reference list of articles and papers documenting each relationship. We have chosen to cite key studies and major review articles to document each relationship. The review articles (Maden and Wrench, 1977; Parke and Collmer, 1975; Byrd, 1979; Steinmetz, 1978b) should be consulted for the exhaustive documentation.

REFERENCES

Ball, M. Issues of violence in family casework. *Social Casework*, 1977, 58(January), 3–12.

Bennie, A. B., and Sclare, A. B. The battered child syndrome. *American Journal of Psychiatry*, 1969, 125(January), 975–979.

Billingsley, A. Family functioning in the low income black community. *Casework*, 1969, 50, 563–572.

Blumberg, M. When parents hit out. *Twentieth Century*, 1964, 173(Winter), 39–44.

Borland, M. (Ed.). *Violence in the family*. Atlantic Highlands, NJ: Humanities Press, 1976.

Boudouris, J. Homicide and the family. *Journal of Marriage and the Family*, 1971, 33(November), 667–682.

Bronfenbrenner, U. Socialization and social class through time and space. In E. Maccoby, T. Newcomb, and E. Hartley (Eds.), *Readings in social psychology*. New York: Holt, Rinehart & Winston, 1958. 400–425.

Bruno v. Maguire. New York Supreme Court, City of New York, Index No. 21946/76, consent decree.

Burgess, R. L. Family violence: Some implications from evolutionary biology. Paper presented at the annual meetings of the American Society of Criminology, Philadelphia, 1979.

Burgess, R. L., and Conger, R. D. Family interaction in abusive, neglectful, and normal families. *Child Development*, 1978, 49(December), 1163–1173.

Byrd, D. E. Intersexual assault: A review of empirical findings. Paper presented at the annual meetings of the Eastern Sociological Society, New York, 1979.

Calvert, R. Criminal and civil liability in husband–wife assaults. In S. Steinmetz and M. Straus (Eds.), *Violence in the family*. New York: Harper & Row, 1974, 88–90.

Cazenave, N. A., and Straus, M. A. The effect of social network embeddedness on black family violence attitudes and behavior: A search for potent support systems. Paper presented at the National Council on Family Relations Meetings, Philadelphia, October 19–22, 1978.

Curtis, L. *Criminal violence: National patterns and behavior*. Lexington, MA: D.C. Heath, 1974.

Davidson, T. *Conjugal crime: Understanding and changing the wifebeating pattern*. New York: Hawthorn Books, 1978.

Dobash, R. E., and Dobash, R. *Violence against wives*. New York: Free Press, 1979.

Eisenberg, S. E., and Micklow, P. L. The assaulted wife. "Catch 22" revisited. *Women's Rights Law Reporter*, 1977, 3/4(Spring/Summer), 138–161.

Elmer, E. *Children in jeopardy: A study of abused minors and their families*. Pittsburgh, University of Pittsburgh Press, 1967.

Erlanger, H. Social class and corporal punishment in childrearing: A reassessment. *American Sociological Review*, 1974, 39(February), 68–85.

Field, M., and Field, H. Marital violence and the criminal process: Neither justice nor peace. *Social Service Review*, 1973, 47(2), 221–240.

Flynn, J. P. Spouse assault: Its dimensions and characteristics in Kalamazoo County, Michigan. Unpublished Field Studies in Research and Practice, School of Social Work, Western Michigan University, Kalamazoo, Michigan, 1975.

Friedrich, W. N., and Boriskin, J. A. The role of the child in abuse: A review of literature. *American Journal of Orthopsychiatry*, 1976, 46(4), 580–590.

Gaquin, D. A. Spouse abuse: Data from the National Crime Survey. *Victimology*, 1977–1978, 2(3/4), 632–643.

Garbarino, J. The human ecology of child maltreatment. *Journal of Marriage and the Family*, 1977, 39(4), 721–735.

Gayford, J. J. Wife battering: A preliminary survey of 100 cases. *British Medical Journal*, 1975, 1(January), 194–197.

Gelles, R. J. Child abuse as psychopathology: A sociological critique and reformulation. *American Journal of Orthopsychiatry*, 1973, 43(July), 611–621.

Gelles, R. J. *The violent home*. Beverly Hills, CA: Sage Publications, 1974.

Gelles, R. J. Violence and pregnancy: A note on the extent of the problem and needed services. *Family Coordinator*, 1975, 24(January), 81–86. (b)

Gelles, R. J. Violence towards children in the United States. *American Journal of Orthopsychiatry*, 1978, 48(October), 580–592.

Gelles, R. J., and Straus, M. A. Determinants of violence in the family: Toward a theoretical integration. In W. R. Burr, R. Hill, F. I. Nye, and I. L. Reiss (Eds.), *Contemporary theories about the family*. New York: Free Press, 1979, 549–581.

Gil, D. *Violence against children: Physical child abuse in the United States*. Cambridge: Harvard University Press, 1970.

Goode, W. J. Force and violence in the family. *Journal of Marriage and the Family*, 1971, 33(November), 624–636.

Harbin, H. T., and Madden, D. J. Battered parents–A new syndrome. *American Journal of Psychiatry*, 1979, 136(October), 1288–1291.

Johnson, C. L. Child abuse in the Southeast. An analysis of 1172 reported cases. Athens, GA: University of Georgia, Athens Welfare Research, 1974.

Jones, A. *Women who kill*. New York: Holt, Rinehart & Winston, 1980.

Justice, B., and Justice, R. *The abusing family*. New York: Human Sciences Press, 1976.

Kempe, C. H., Silverman, F. N., Steele, B. F., Droegemueller, W., and Silver, H. K. The battered child syndrome. *Journal of the American Medical Association*, 1962, 181, 107–112.

Klaus, M. H., and Kennel, J. H. Maternal-infant bonding. St. Louis: C.V. Mosby, 1976.

Levinger, G. Sources of marital dissatisfaction among applicants for divorce. *American Journal of Orthopsychiatry*, 1966, 26(October), 803–897.

Light, R. J. Abused and neglected children in America: A study of alternative policies. *Harvard Educational Review*, 1974, 43(November), 556–598.

London, J. Images of violence against women. *Victimology*, 1978, 2(3/4), 510–524.

Maden, M. F., and Wrench, D. F. Significant findings in child abuse research. *Victimology*, 1977, 2, 196–224.

Mancini, M. Adult abuse laws. *American Journal of Nursing*, 1980, 80(April), 739–740.

Martin, D. *Battered Wives*. San Francisco: Glide Publications, 1976.

Mulligan, M. A. An investigation of factors associated with violent modes of conflict resolution in the family. Unpublished M.A. Thesis, University of Rhode Island, 1977.

Nelson, G. K., Dainauski, J., and Kilmer, L. Child abuse reporting laws: Action and uncertainty. *Child Welfare*, 1980, 59(2), 203–212.

Owens, D., and Straus, M. A. Childhood violence and adult approval of violence. *Aggressive Behavior*, 1975, 1(2), 193–211.

Parke, R. D., and Collmer, C. W. Child abuse: An interdisciplinary analysis. In M. Hetherington (Ed.), *Review of child development research* (Vol. 5). Chicago: University of Chicago Press, 1975, 1–102.

Parker, B., and Schumacher, D. N. The battered wife syndrome and violence in the nuclear family of origin: A controlled pilot study. *American Journal of Public Health*, 1977, 67(August), 760–761.

Parnas, R. The police response to domestic disturbance. *Wisconsin Law Review*, 1967, 914(Fall), 914–960.

Pittman, D. J., and Handy, W. Patterns in criminal aggravated assault. *Journal of Criminal Law, Criminology and Police Science*, 1964, 55(4), 462–470.

Pleck, E., Pleck, J., Grossman, M., and Bart, P. The battered data syndrome: A comment on Steinmetz's article, *Victimology*, 1978, 2(3/4), 680–683.

Prescott, S. and Letko, C. Battered women: A social psychological perspective. In M. Roy (Ed.), *Battered women*. New York: Van Nostrand Reinhold, 1977, 72–96.

Radbill, S. A history of child abuse and infanticide. In R. Helfer and C. Kempe (Eds.), *The battered child* (2nd Ed.). Chicago: University of Chicago Press, 1974, 3–24.

Rosenthal, M. P. Physical abuse of children by parents: The criminalization decision. *American Journal of Criminal Law*, 1979, 7(2), 141–169.

Ross, C. J. Society's children: The care of indigent youngsters in New York City, 1875–1903. Unpublished doctoral dissertation, Yale University, 1977.

Spinetta, J. J., and Rigler, D. The child abusing parent: A psychological review. *Psychological Bulletin*, 1972, 77(April), 296–304.

Star, B. Patterns of family violence. *Social Casework*, 1980, 61(June), 339–346.

Stark, R., and McEvoy, J. Middle class violence. *Psychology Today*, 1970, 4(November), 52–65.

Steele, B. F., and Pollock, C. A psychiatric study of parents who abuse infants and small children. In R. E. Helfer and C. H. Kempe (Eds.), *The battered child*. Chicago: University of Chicago Press, 1968, 103–147.

Steele, B. F., and Pollock, C. A psychiatric study of parents who abuse infants and small children. In R. E. Helfer and C. H. Kempe (Eds.), *The battered child* (2nd Ed.). Chicago: University of Chicago Press, 1974, 89–134.

Steinmetz, S. K. Occupation and physical punishment: A response to Straus. *Journal of Marriage and the Family*, 1971, 33(November), 664–666.

Steinmetz, S. K. *The cycle of violence: Assertive, aggressive, and abusive family interaction*. New York: Praeger, 1977.

Steinmetz, S. K. The battered husband syndrome. *Victimology*, 1978, 2(3/4), 499–509. (a)

Steinmetz, S. K. Violence between family members. *Marriage and Family Review*, 1978, 1(3), 1–16. (b)

Straus, M. A. Some social antecedents of physical punishment: A linkage theory interpretation. *Journal of Marriage and the Family*, 1971, 33(November), 658–663.

Straus, M. A. A general systems theory approach to a theory of violence between family members. *Social Science Information*, 1973, 12(June), 105–125.

Straus, M. A. Foreword. In R. J. Gelles, *The violent home: A study of physical aggression between husbands and wives*. Beverly Hills, CA: Sage Publications, 1974, 13–17. (a)

Straus, M. A. Wife beating: How common and why? *Victimology*, 1978, 2(3/4), pp. 443–458.

Straus, M. A. Family patterns and child abuse in a nationally representative American sample. *Child Abuse and Neglect: The International Journal*, 1979, 3(1), 213–225. (a)

Straus, M. A., Gelles, R. J. and Steinmetz, S. K. *Behind closed doors: Violence in the American family*. New York: Doubleday/Anchor, 1980.

Taylor, L., and Newberger, E. H. Child abuse in the International Year of the Child. *New England Journal of Medicine*, 1979, 301(November 29), 1205–1212.

Thompson, E. M., Paget, N. W., Morris Mesch, D. W., and Putnam, T. I. *Child abuse: A community challenge*. East Aurora, NY: Henry Stewart, 1971.

Truninger, E. Marital violence: The legal solutions. *Hastings Law Review*, 1971, 23(November), 259–276.

U.S. Department of Justice. *Intimate victims: A study of violence among friends and relatives*. Washington, DC: Government Printing Office, 1980.

Westat, Inc. *Recognition and reporting of child maltreatment: Findings from the National Study of the Incidence and Severity of Child Abuse and Neglect*. Rockville, MD: Westat, Inc., 1980.

Yllo, K., and Straus, M. A. Interpersonal violence among married and cohabitating couples. Paper presented at the annual meetings of the National Council on Family Relations, Philadelphia, 1978.
Young, L. *Wednesday's child: A study of child abuse and neglect*. New York: McGraw-Hill, 1964.

Societal Change and Change in Family Violence from 1975 to 1985 as Revealed by Two National Surveys

Murray A. Straus and Richard J. Gelles

. . . The purpose of this paper is to report the results of a 1985 replication of [a] 1975–76 study. This replication enables the first comparison of rates of family violence from surveys at two time points.

DEFINITION AND MEASUREMENT OF VIOLENCE AND ABUSE

The term *abuse* is a source of considerable difficulty and confusion because it covers many types of abuse, not just acts of physical violence, and because there is no consensus on the severity of violence required for an act to be considered "abuse." . . .

Violence [as used in this article] is defined as an act carried out with the intention, or perceived intention, of causing physical pain or injury to another person.[1]

The term *abuse* is restricted to *physical* abuse. . . . It does not [include] other types of abuse, such as psychological abuse and sexual abuse. . . .

Operationalizing Violence and Abuse

Violence was measured by the Conflict Tactics Scales (Straus, 1979; 1981a). . . .

Format of the CTS. The introduction to the Conflict Tactics Scales asks respondents to think of situations in the past year when they had a disagreement or were angry with a specified family member and to indicate how often they engaged in each of the acts included in the CTS. The 1975 version of the CTS consisted of 19 items, 8 of which were acts of violence.

Violent Acts. The violent acts in the version of the CTS we used for this study are: threw something at the other; pushed, grabbed, or shoved; slapped or spanked; kicked, bit, or hit with a fist; hit or tried to hit with something; beat up the other; threatened with knife or gun; used a knife or gun.

Violence Indexes. . . . The following [violence index] measures are used in this study:

1. *Overall violence.* This measure indicates the percentage of parents or spouses who used *any* of the violent acts included in the CTS during the year covered by the study.
2. *Severe violence. . . .* was defined as acts that have a relatively high probability of causing an injury. Thus, kicking is classified as severe violence because kicking a child or a spouse has a much greater potential for producing an injury than an act of "minor violence" such as spanking or slapping.[2] The acts making up the severe violence index are: kicked, bit, punched, hit with an object, beat up, threatened with a knife or gun, and used a knife or gun . . .

THE TWO NATIONAL SURVEYS

Sample and Administration of the 1975 Study

A national . . . sample of 2,143 currently married or cohabiting persons was interviewed. . . . If the household included a child or children between the ages of 3 and 17 years, a "referent child" was selected by a random procedure. . . . [H]alf of the respondents were women and the other half men. . . .

The 1985 National Family Violence Re-survey[3]

Data on a national . . . sample of 6,002 households were obtained by telephone interviews conducted by Louis Harris and Associates. To be eligible for inclusion, a household had to include two adults, a male and female 18 years of age or older, who were: (a) presently married, or (b) presently living as a male-female couple; or a household might include one adult 18 years of age or older who was either (c) divorced or separated within the last two years, or (d) a single parent living with a child under the age of 18. When more than one adult was in the household, a random procedure was used to select the gender and marital status of the respondent. When more than one child under the age of 18 was in the household, a random procedure was used to select the "referent child" as the focus of the parent-to-child violence questions. . . .

VIOLENCE AGAINST CHILDREN IN 1975 AND 1985

Table 5-2 enables one to compare the 1975 and 1985 rates per thousand children for each violent act as well as three summary indexes of violence. The data . . . show that, with the exception of the most unusual and severe forms of violence

Table 5-2.
Parent-to-Child Violence: Comparison of Rates in 1975 and 1985

Type of Violence	Rate per 1,000 Children Aged 3 through 17[a] 1975 $n = 1{,}146$[b]	1985 $n = 1{,}428$[c]	t for 1975–1985 Difference
A. Minor Violence Acts			
1. Threw something	54	27	3.41**
2. Pushed/grabbed/shoved	318	307	0.54
3. Slapped or spanked	582	549	1.68
B. Severe Violence Acts			
4. Kicked/bit/hit with fist	32	13	3.17*
5. Hit, tried to hit with something	134	97	1.41
6. Beat up	13	6	0.26
7. Threatened with gun or knife	1	2	0.69
8. Used gun or knife	1	2	0.69
C. Violence Indexes			
Overall Violence (1–8)	630	620	0.52
Severe Violence (4–8)	140	107	2.56*
Very Severe Violence (4, 6, 8) ("child abuse" for this article)	36	19	4.25**

[a]For two-caretaker households with at least one child 3 to 17 years of age at home.
[b]A few respondents were omitted because of missing data on some items, but the *n* is never less than 1,140.
[c]A few respondents were omitted because of missing data on some items, but the *n* is never less than 1,418.
*$p < .01$; **$p < .001$ (two-tailed tests).

(Items 7 and 8: threatening and using guns and knives), *the occurrence of each form of violence toward children declined in the last 10 years.* However, only two of these differences are statistically significant. . . .

Child Abuse Rate

. . . [W]e used the Very Severe Violence Index . . . as the measure of child abuse. . . . This is the same as the Severe Violence Index, except that it omits hitting with an object and is therefore the index that comes closest to the public conception of child abuse. The rate of such indubitably abusive violence declined from 36 per thousand children to 19. This is *a decline of 47% in the rate of physical child abuse since 1975.*

VIOLENCE BETWEEN SPOUSES IN 1975 AND 1985[4]

Table 5-3 summarizes the findings on violence between married or cohabitating couples in the form of three indexes. . . . All but one of the nine comparisons in Table 5-3 show that the rate of violence was lower in 1985 than in 1975. However,

Table 5-3.
Marital Violence Indexes: Comparison of 1975 and 1985

Violence Index	Rate per 1,000 Couples 1975	Rate per 1,000 Couples 1985	t for 1975–1985 Difference
A. Husband-to-Wife			
Overall Violence (1–6)	121	113	0.91
Severe Violence (4– 8) ("wife beating")	38	30	1.60
B. Wife-to-Husband			
Overall Violence (1–6)	116	121	0.57
Severe Violence (4– 8)	46	44	0.35
C. Couple			
Overall Violence (1–6)	160	158	0.20
Severe Violence (4–8)	61	58	0.46
Number of cases[a]	2,143	3,520	

[a]A few respondents were omitted because of missing data on some items, but the n is never decreased by more than 10.

as compared to the changes in parental violence, the decreases from 1975 to 1985 are much smaller.

Husband-to-Wife Violence

. . . [T]he Overall Violence rate of violence by husbands declined from 121 to 113. . . . [T]he husband-to-wife violence rate declined by 6.6%, which is not statistically significant.

. . . [T]he rate of Severe Violence by husbands—our measure of "wife beating" shows that the rate declined from 38 per thousand couples to 30 per thousand couples in 1985. . . . [R]elative to the 1975 rate, it represents a 26.6% decrease in the rate of wife beating, and the difference comes close to being significant. . . .

Wife-to-Husband Violence

Although the trend for husband-to-wife violence is encouraging, the situation for wife-to-husband violence is at best mixed. . . . [T]he Overall Violence rate actually increased slightly. The rate for Severe Violence against a husband decreased, but only slightly. . . . [T]he [wife-to-husband] violence rates . . . reveal an important and distressing finding about violence in American families—that, in marked contrast to the behavior of women outside the family, women are about as violent within the family as men. This highly controversial finding of the 1975 study is confirmed by the 1985 study. . . .

Although the two national surveys . . . leave little doubt about the high frequency of wife-to-husband violence, the meaning and consequences of that violence are easily misunderstood. For one thing, . . . the greater average size and strength of men, and their greater aggressiveness (Maccoby and Jacklin, 1974;

Tavris and Offir, 1977), mean that the same act (for example, a punch) is likely to be very different in the amount of pain or injury inflicted (see also Greenblat, 1983). Even more important, a great deal of violence by women against their husbands is retaliation or self-defense (Straus, 1980; Saunders, 1986). One of the most fundamental reasons why some women are violent within the family, but not outside the family, is that the risk of assault for a typical American woman is greatest in her own home (Straus, Gelles, and Steinmetz, 1980: chapters 1 and 2). . . .

PREVENTION AND TREATMENT PROGRAMS AND CHANGE IN FAMILY VIOLENCE

Child Abuse

. . . Since 1971, every state has adopted compulsory reporting laws, and an extensive educational effort has developed across the country. In comparison to other forms of domestic violence, the largest share of financial resources has been allocated to child abuse. . . .

Wife Beating

The campaign against wife beating, by contrast, began a decade or more later and has been less intensive, and far fewer resources have been invested. Providing shelters has mostly been a private endeavor of the women's movement. Even the feeble effort of the federal government in the form of an information clearinghouse was abolished early in the Reagan administration. Many bills to provide funds for shelters have been introduced and defeated. . . .

Violence by Wives

Violence by wives has not been an object of public concern. There has been no publicity, and no funds have been invested in ameliorating this problem because it has not been defined as a problem. . . .

Physical Punishment of Children

Not only has physical punishment of children not been a focus of a public effort, but most Americans consider it morally correct to hit a child who misbehaves (Straus, Gelles, and Steinmetz, 1980). Consistent with this, we found only small and nonsignificant differences between 1975 and 1985 in the overall rate of parent-to-child violence.

Overall, the findings of this study are consistent with the idea that the longer an aspect of violence has been the object of public condemnation, and the more resources that are put into the effort to change that . . . , the greater the reduction in the . . . behavior.

ALTERNATIVE INTERPRETATIONS OF THE FINDINGS

We have presented some startling and controversial findings. . . . Three possible explanations for the findings follow.

Methodological Differences between the Two Surveys

Data for the 1975 survey were collected by in-person interview, while the 1985 survey was conducted over the telephone. . . . The difference in interview method . . . should have produced *higher*, not lower, rates of reported violence in 1985. . . .

Another methodological difference is that, in the 1975–76 survey, respondents were handed a card listing the response categories for the Conflict Tactics Scales. All possible answers, including "never," were on the card. For the 1985 telephone survey, . . . [r]espondents had to volunteer "never" or "don't know" responses. Experience has shown that rates of reported sensitive or deviant behavior are higher if the subject has to volunteer the "no" or "never" response (see, for example, Kinsey, Pomeroy, and Martin, 1948).

These differences in methodology between the two studies should have led to higher, not lower, rates of reported violence. Since the rates of child abuse and wife beating decreased, it seems unlikely that the change is due to the different methods of data collection.

Reluctance to Report

A second plausible explanation for the decline in the rate of child abuse and wife beating is that respondents may have been more reluctant to report severe violence in 1985 than in 1975. As indicated above, the last 10 years have seen a tremendous increase in public attention to the problem of child abuse and wife beating. . . . [This] decrease . . . may reflect a "moral passage" (Gusfield, 1963), as family violence becomes less acceptable and consequently fewer parents and fewer husbands are willing to admit to participating in violence. . . .

Change in Behavior

The third explanation is that there has indeed been a decline in child abuse and wife beating. This explanation is consistent with changes in the family and other developments during the last 10 years. . . .

Change in Family Structure. There have been changes in a number of aspects of the family that are associated with violence, including: a rise in the average age at first marriage, an increase in the average age for having a first child, a decline in the number of children per family, and therefore, a corresponding decrease in the number of unwanted children (Statistical Abstract, 1985: Tables 120, 92, 63, 97). Parents in 1985 are among the first generation to be able to choose a full range of planned parenthood options (including abortion) to plan family size. All these factors are related to lower rates of child abuse and may have an indirect effect on spouse abuse by lowering the level of stress. . . .

The fact that . . . American marriages are becoming more equalitarian (Thornton, Alwin, and Camburn, 1983) has important implications for family violence because previous research shows that male-dominant marriages have the highest, and equalitarian marriages the lowest, rate of violence (Coleman and Straus, 1986; Straus, 1973; Straus, Gelles, and Steinmetz, 1980). . . .

Economic Change. Both child abuse and wife beating are associated with unemployment and economic stress. . . . The one-year referent period used for the 1985 survey coincided with one of the more prosperous years in the past decade. Thus, the lower level of economic stress in 1985 may have contributed to the decline in severe violence.

Alternatives for Battered Women. . . . [T]here were only a handful of "safe houses" or "shelters" for battered women in 1975, as contrasted with about 700 in 1985 (Back et al., 1980; Warrior, 1982). The existence of shelters provides an alternative that did not exist in 1975. In addition, the fact that shelters provide an alternative may have emboldened more women to tell their partner that his violence is unacceptable, and to make this more than an idle threat. Similarly, the tremendous growth in paid employment of married women in the 1975–85 period not only helped rectify the imbalance of power between spouses, but also provided the economic resources that enable more women to terminate a violent marriage (Kalmuss and Straus, 1982). Finally the increased acceptance of divorce probably also helped more women to terminate violent marriages.

Treatment Programs. New and innovative prevention and treatment programs for child abuse and wife beating proliferated during or immediately before the 1975–85 decade. . . . Only a small percentage of the cases they deal with are the gory (and difficult to treat) cases that make the newspaper headlines. Most are parents at their wits' end who can and do benefit from the help and the additional resources that state social service departments provide. . . .

[F]amily therapy of all types has grown tremendously. It was probably the fastest-growing human service profession in the 1975–85 decade. The increased use of family counseling and the increasing proportion of therapists who directly raise the issue of violence may have had a part in reducing intrafamily violence.

Deterrence. . . . Extensive efforts have been made to alert the public to the problem of child abuse and wife beating. In addition, shelters for battered women may have an indirect effect. The process of publicizing the availability of a shelter can contribute to a husband's redefining "I just slapped her a few times" to "I was violent." Each of these activities probably contributed to a changed perception of the legitimacy of violence against children and wives and therefore plays a preventative or deterrent role. Public opinion poll data suggest that those programs seem to have been effective. . . . It is not implausible to suggest that the advertising campaigns and media attention have had some effect in making parents more cautious about assaulting children and husbands more cautious about severely assaulting wives.

Another important change affects the certainty and severity of legal sanctions for wife beating. The police are gradually changing methods of dealing with wife beating. . . . [The] manual [of the International Chiefs of Police (1976)] . . . now recommends dealing with all assaults on the same basis, irrespective of whether they are in the home or elsewhere. . . . A growing number of police departments are doing that. To the extent that this change in police policy was known to potential offenders, it is not implausible to think that it has had an effect. Indeed, a study comparing three different methods used by the police to deal with domestic violence suggests that there is a lower recidivism rate when wife beating is treated as a criminal act rather than a private problem (Sherman and Berk, 1984).

NOTES

1. As pointed out in a previous theoretical article (Gelles and Straus, 1979), the fact of a physical assault having taken place is not sufficient for understanding violence. Several other dimensions also needed to be considered. However, it is also important that each of these other dimensions be measured separately so that their causes and consequences and joint effects can be investigated. Among the other dimensions are the seriousness of the assault (which can range from a slap to stabbing and shooting); whether a physical injury was produced (which can range from none to death); the motivation (which might range from a concern for a person's safety, as when a child is spanked for going into the street, to hostility so intense that the death of the person is desired); and whether the act of violence is normatively legitimate (as in the case of slapping a child) or illegitimate (as in the case of slapping a spouse), and which set of norms are applicable (legal, ethnic, or class norms, couple norms, etc).
2. It should be recognized that in most instances, being kicked, although painful, does *not* result in an injury. However, the absence of injury does not make it less abusive an act. Our distinction between minor and severe violence parallels the legal distinctions between a "simple assault" and an "aggravated assault." An aggravated assault is an attack that is likely to cause grave bodily harm, such as an attack with a knife or gun, irrespective of whether the object of the attack was actually injured.
3. The 1985 survey differs from the 1975–76 study in a number of important ways. It includes several groups that were omitted from the first survey, such as single parents; and it includes additions to the CTS Violence Index. However, the instrumentation was designed to permit the comparable questions to be selected, and the sample was chosen in a way that permits selection of a comparable part of the 1985 sample to be used for the 1975-to-1985 change analysis. Unless otherwise indicated, the material reported in this article is restricted to the comparable parts of the 1985 sample and the comparable parts of the instrumentation.
4. For convenience and economy of wording, terms such as *marital, spouse, wife*, and *husband* are used to refer to couples, irrespective of whether they are married or nonmarried cohabiting persons. For an analysis of differences and similarities between married and cohabiting couples in the 1975–76 study, see Yllö (1978); Yllö and Straus (1981).

REFERENCES

Back, Susan M., Judith Blum, Ellen Nakhnikian, and Susan Stark. 1980. Spouse Abuse Yellow Pages. Denver, CO: Denver Research Institute, University of Denver.

Coleman, Diane H., and Murray A. Straus. 1986. "Marital power, conflict, and violence." Violence and Victims 1: 139–153.

Gelles, Richard J., and Murray A. Straus. 1979. "Determinants of violence in the family: Towards a theoretical integration." Chapter 21 in Wesley R. Burr, Reuben Hill, F. Ivan Nye, and Ira L. Reiss (eds.), Contemporary Theories about the Family (Vol. 1). New York: Free Press.

Gelles, Richard J., and Murray A. Straus. 1985. "Is violence toward children increasing? A comparison of 1975 and 1985 national survey rates." Paper presented at the Seventh National Conference on Child Abuse and Neglect, Chicago.

Greenblat, Cathy. 1983. "Physical force by any other name . . . : Quantitative data, qualitative data, and the politics of family violence research." In David Finkelhor, Richard J. Gelles, Gerald T. Hotaling, and Murray A. Straus (eds.), The Dark Side of Families: Current Family Violence Research. Beverly Hills, CA: Sage.

Kalmuss, Debra S., and Murray A. Straus. 1982. "Wives' marital dependency and wife abuse." Journal of Marriage and the Family 44: 277–286. Also reprinted in Bert N. Adams and John L. Campbell (eds.), Framing the Family: Contemporary Portraits. Prospect Heights, IL: Waveland Press, 1985.

Kinsey, Alfred C., Wardell B. Pomeroy, and Clyde E. Martin. 1948. Sexual Behavior in the Human Male. Philadelphia: W. B. Saunders.

Maccoby, Eleanor Emmons, and Carol Nagy Jacklin. 1974. The Psychology of Sex Differences. Stanford, CA: Stanford University Press.

Saunders, Daniel G. 1986. "When battered women use violence: Husband-abuse or self-defense?" Violence and Victims 1: 47–60.

Sherman, Laurence, and Richard A. Berk. 1984. "The specific deterrent effects of arrest for domestic assault." American Sociological Review 49: 261–272.

Straus, Murray A. 1973. "A general systems theory approach to a theory of violence between family members." Social Science Information 13: 105–125.

Straus, Murray A. 1979. "Measuring intrafamily conflict and violence: The Conflict Tactics (CT) Scales." Journal of Marriage and the Family 41: 75–88.

Straus, Murray A. 1980. "Victims and aggressors in marital violence." American Behavioral Scientist 23: 681–704.

Straus, Murray A. 1981. "Re-evaluation of the Conflict Tactics Scale." Paper presented at the National Conference for Family Violence Researchers, University of New Hampshire (July).

Straus, Murray A., and Richard J. Gelles. 1986. "How violent are American families: Estimates based on two national surveys and other studies." Paper in progress.

Straus, Murray A., Richard J. Gelles, and Suzanne K. Steinmetz. 1980. Behind Closed Doors: Violence in the American Family. Garden City, NY: Doubleday, Anchor Press.

Tavris, Carol, and Carole Offir. 1977. The Longest War: Sex Differences in Perspective. New York: Harcourt Brace Jovanovich.

Thorton, Arland, Duane F. Alwin, and Donald Camburn. 1983. "Causes and consequences of sex-role attitudes and attitude change." American Sociolog[ical] Review 48: 211–227.

Warrior, Betsy. 1982. Battered Women's Directory (8th ed.). Cambridge, MA: Author, 46 Pleasant Street, Cambridge, MA 02139.

Yllö, Kersti. 1978. "Nonmarital cohabitation: Beyond the college campus." Alternative Lifestyles 1: 37–54.

Yllö, Kersti, and Murray A. Straus. 1981. "Interpersonal violence among married and cohabiting couples." Family Relations 30: 339–345.

When Battered Women Kill

Angela Browne

STUDYING WOMEN WHO KILL

Results of the study are based on interviews with 42 women who were charged with a crime in the death or serious injury of their mates. The women came from 15 states; seven of them were incarcerated awaiting trial at the time of the interview. Initial contact was made with the women when their attorneys requested an evaluation based on evidence that the woman had been physically abused by her partner prior to the homicide incident. Thirty-three of the women were charged with murder, three with conspiracy to commit murder, and six with attempted murder. (In reporting these findings, no distinction is made between cases involving attempted murder and the homicide cases, since the same dynamics applied to both types of events.) Of the women who went to trial after the interview, twenty (about half) received jail terms, 12 received probation or a suspended sentence, and nine were acquitted. In one case, the District Attorney's office determined that the killing was justified on the grounds of self-defense and dropped the charges. Jail sentences generally ranged from six months to 25 years; one woman was sentenced to 50 years.

The purpose of the study was to understand more about the relationships of abused women who kill their husbands, and to identify the dynamics that lead up to the commission of a homicide. Thus, the inquiry focused on the women's actions—e.g., the killing of a mate—in the context of their position as victims, and investigated the impact that violence and threat from a romantic partner, as well as other situational and societal variables, had on their perception of danger and of alternatives. In an effort to understand more about battered women who kill, and to identify the factors that characterize their relationship with their abusers, reports from women in the homicide group were later compared to those of 205 women who had been in abusive relationships but did not take lethal action against their partners.

Women in the comparison group came from a six-state region, and from both urban and rural areas. They were recruited through public-service announcements, newspaper ads, and posted notices, as well as through referrals from physicians, emergency-room personnel, and battered-women's shelters. The women in the comparison group were self-identified and self-referred . . . and were considered eligible to participate in the study if they reported being physically abused at least twice by a man with whom they had had an ongoing intimate relationship. . . . [W]omen in the comparison group were limited to those either still with the abusive partner or out of the relationship less than one year.

Definition of Abuse

When studying violent relationships, it is important to define what is meant by the labels being used.... "[B]attered women" are those who have been struck repeatedly, often experiencing several different kinds of physically violent actions in one incident, and usually, by the time they are identified, having experienced a series of such incidents, each consisting of a cluster of violent acts.... "[P]hysical abuse" was defined as *any physically assaultive act by one person against another, with or without evident resultant physical injury....*

The problem of violence between partners, once considered of little importance, is now known to affect thousands upon thousands of people in our society, to account for millions of injuries, and to be implicated in a substantial proportion of the homicides occurring between women and men. Figures from nationally representative samples reveal that over 1 1/2 million women in the United States are physically assaulted by a male partner each year. Many of the acts involved in these assaults, including punching, kicking, hitting with an object, beating up, and assaults with a knife or a gun, are quite serious, and many result in injuries to the victims. We now know that attacks by family members are actually more serious, in terms of injuries, than the attacks by strangers we have geared our system to defend against. Men are more likely to assault their female partners than women are to assault male partners, and assaults by husbands appear to involve more of the dangerous and injurious forms of violence—and more repetition of these acts—than do assaults by wives. In studies of injurious assault involving couples, 95 percent of the time it is the woman who gets hurt.

Studies of severely battered women suggest that they are not typically violent toward their mates, either in initiation or response. However, lack of effective legal intervention in cases of wife abuse, and the lack of adequate and established alternatives to protect victims from further aggression, leaves many of these women alone with a danger from which they cannot escape. Homicides that result from abusive relationships remind us of the seriousness of "domestic" violence, and highlight how the lack of adequate intervention and response by all segments of society exacerbates the danger already present in these situations. A society that allows violence against wives to continue by forcing the individual woman to stop the perpetrator's behavior runs the risk that victims may eventually take action that the society does not condone. Homicides resulting from abusive relationships must be examined within the context from which they developed, if the event is to be accurately understood—especially if that homicide is perpetrated by a previously nonviolent individual. Knowing the history of the relationship between the partners then becomes critical, both from a legal and a psychological standpoint.

In focusing on women who kill their abusers, it is important to remember that these cases are the exceptions to the general pattern: In a lethal altercation between partners, it is more typically the woman who loses her life. In 1984, two-thirds of the homicides between partners were of husbands killing wives, while one-third were of wives killing husbands. Given the finding that women are more likely than men to kill in self-defense, and that physical abuse by the man precedes many spousal homicides regardless of the perpetrator, it seems probable that a high proportion of these cases represented the culmination of a battering relationship. As Susan Jacoby points out, in many homicides between partners, the woman kills as a "desperate, final response" to physical threat and attack, whereas the man kills as a "logical extension of the . . . abuse he has been dispensing for years."[1]

Still, it is an extreme reaction for a woman, even a battered woman, to kill. In the current study, battered women charged with the death or attempted murder of their mates were compared to women from abusive relationships in which no lethal incident had occurred, to see if differences between the two groups could be identified. Women in the homicide group were somewhat older than women in the comparison group, and came from a slightly higher class background; however, their level of education and their employment patterns were not significantly different. Although nearly three-quarters of the women in the homicide group had been exposed to violence in childhood, and over half had been the victim of at least one completed or attempted sexual assault, this also did not differentiate them from abused women in the comparison group.

Significant differences appeared primarily between the men with whom the women were involved. Men in the homicide group used drugs more frequently than did men in the comparison group, and they became intoxicated much more often. They were also more frequently given to threats and assaultive behavior. Significantly more men in the homicide group threatened to kill someone other than themselves; more of them abused a child or children, as well as their women partners; and their abuse of their mates was more frequent, more injurious, and more likely to include sexual assault.

Like victims of other types of trauma, women in the homicide group responded to these assaults with reactions of depression, denial, shock, and a sense of helplessness and fear. They typically withdrew after the initial assaults and did not attempt escape, or left the assaulter but were talked into returning by his contrition and assurances that the violence would not be repeated. . . . [M]ost women spent a great deal of time attempting to understand why the violence occurred and making adaptations to avoid it. They continued to attach importance to maintaining their relationships with the abusers, responding with care and concern, and attempting to reason and work things out. Yet their responses had no positive effect on the aggressive behavior of their mates. In fact, for most women in the homicide group, the violence they experienced became both more frequent and more severe over the course of their relationships.

As the assaults became more brutal and the abusers seemed increasingly unconcerned about the harm they were inflicting, the women's focus shifted from attempts to understand to an emphasis on survival. Subjected to frequent attacks and living with a constant awareness of danger, their perceptions of alternatives to their violent situations narrowed. . . . Like other victims, they chose responses that seemed most likely to minimize the immediate danger, attempting to appease their mates and avoiding actions that might trigger a renewed attack. Many women attempted to leave their partners, but were found and beaten, or intimidated into returning home. Some women did succeed in leaving their abusive partners, but were still experiencing assaults and threats by them months or even years later. The abusers' power to constrain and punish was strengthened by a lack of societal awareness of the women's plight and by the legal barriers against prosecution and effective protection from attack by a mate. This lack of safe alternatives for the women, combined with the men's threats of retaliation if they left and/or prior failed escape attempts, convinced most of these women that they could not escape their partners and survive. Yet the violence within the relationships became increasingly harder to endure. Most of the women began to live with almost an expectation of death.

The women's perception of entrapment in a desperate situation led to increasingly extreme degrees of adaptation. . . . Yet, eventually, the violence escalated beyond the point to which the women could adapt. One attack would be so much more severe, or so far beyond the range of what she was willing to assimilate, that a formerly passive woman would suddenly take action in her own defense or in the defense of a child. Typically, the killing of the abuser was unplanned and occurred during the period of threat before an assault, in the midst of a violent episode, or during a failed escape attempt. In most cases, the homicide weapon was a gun; often, it was the same gun the man had threatened his mate with earlier.

The violence in severely abusive relationships, and the homicides that occur as a culmination of this violence, often seem inexplicable and bizarre. Yet, the phenomenon can be effectively studied and, as our findings indicate, important variables and patterns can be identified. . . . [F]indings in the homicide study suggest that it *is* possible to identify couples at particularly high risk for a lethal incident (at least one perpetrated by the female victim), based on a cluster of reported factors: frequency of assaultive incidents by the man, severity of injury, frequency of alcohol intoxication or other substance abuse by the man, forced or threatened sexual assaults of the woman partner, the man's threats to kill, and suicide ideation by the woman. . . .

In assessing risk in violent relationships, it is important to take seriously the woman's fears and perceptions of the danger. Despite abused women's tendencies to understate the severity of their experiences and to skip the details of the more bizarre or embarrassing incidents, they are extremely knowledgeable about the patterns of violence in their relationships. Professionals confronted with these cases should make use of the woman's expertise; her ability, when encouraged, to assess the degree of risk she is facing; and her experience in predicting when another assault seems imminent. Without some knowledge of the history of violence, recommendations or interventions by outsiders may be highly inappropriate for the situation, and may actually serve to exacerbate the aggression and further endanger the lives of those involved. . . .

Based on the documented frequency with which battered women ask for help prior to killing their abusive mates, more active responses by the agencies and individuals to whom these women turn could undoubtedly prevent many of the homicides that are eventually committed in desperation. Given . . . the tendency for abuse to escalate over time and the potential for the violence in some relationships to assume lethal proportions, the importance of informed, effective responses during early contacts with domestic violence cases cannot be overemphasized. Even "mild" abuse must be taken seriously, and assaults by partners treated with the same stringency as are attacks by strangers. Research to date suggests that the most effective method of reducing assaults by abusive husbands toward their mates involves . . . treating a man's assault of his wife as a criminal offense; and immediate, specialized counseling for the offender in the context of a group designed for men who physically abuse their intimates.[2] . . .

Early interventions in abusive relationships in which the level of assault is less serious than that documented here would avert at least some of the serious injuries and deaths that occur when the violence is left to run its course. . . .

We still know relatively little about men who perpetrate violence against their partners—their motivations and perceptions, and the distinguishing features in their lives that cause them to turn to violence as a response to daily events and emotions. . . . [Because] characteristics of the woman herself, are the best predictors of a woman's chances of victimization, it is imperative that we make a systematic effort to understand more about the aggressors. The men's aggression seems to be more in response to internal triggers than to the realities of current relationships with others.

Men who are assaultive toward their women partners may actually be striking out in an attempt to connect with another person, to break through a sense of alienation engendered by a neglectful or violence-scarred childhood. Yet repeated perpetration of aggression against others produces alienation, and such a misguided attempt at connection can only result in a worsening cycle of abuse and despair. Descriptions of violent men . . . suggest a violence-prone personality pattern, originating in childhood and becoming progressively more severe as the men practice aggression.[3] Yet we do not know what factors determine which individuals, exposed to violence in childhood, will later become violent, and what variables mitigate against this outcome in some children. . . .

Earlier [psychological] theories suggest[ed] pathology in the female victim [and] ignored the man's initiation of violence and its effects on the woman. Though experiences of victimization have a major impact on women's choices and behaviors while they are with their abusers, behaviors specifically related to victimization tend to disappear over time when the threat of violence is no longer present. . . .

It is important to identify these women's strengths as survivors—the depth of their compassion, their willingness to try again, their endurance in the face of pain and terror—in order to encourage them to go on. Although previously applied in an increasingly hopeless situation, these are the strengths an abused woman needs to leave a violent partner and begin a new life, even in the face of threat and danger. As society clearly identifies the abuse these women experience as outside the bounds of *societal* acceptability—and demonstrates that in outrage and in sanctions—abused women will also come to share that view and refuse to accept violence in their relationships.

NOTES

1. Jacoby, 1983, p. 185.
2. E.g., Dutton, 1986; Ganley, 1978, 1981; Sherman & Berk, 1984.
3. Walker & Browne, 1985; Hotaling & Sugerman, 1986.

REFERENCES

Dutton, D. (1986). Wife assault: Social Psychological Contributions to Criminal Justice Policy. *Applied Social Psychology Annual, 4*.

Ganley, A. (1981). "Counseling programs for men who batter: Elements of effective programs." *Response, 4*(8), 3–4.

Ganley, A. L. & Harris, L. (1978). "Domestic violence: Issues in designing and implementing programs for male batterers." Paper presented at the annual meeting of the American Psychological Association. Toronto, Canada.

Hotaling, G. T. & Sugarman, D. B. (1986). "An analysis of risk markers in husband to wife violence: The current state of knowledge." *Violence and Victims, 1*(2), 101–124.

Jacoby, S. (1983). *Wild Justice*. New York, NY: Harper & Row.

Sherman, L. W. & Berk, R. A. (1984). "The Minneapolis domestic violence experiment." *Police Foundation Reports 1*. Washington, D.C.: The Police Foundation.

Sherman, L. W. & Berk, R. A. (1984). "The specific deterrent effects of arrest for domestic assault." *American Sociological Review, 49*, 261– 272.

Walker, L. E. & Browne, A. (1985). "Gender and victimization by intimates." *Journal of Personality, 53*(2), 179–195.

High-Risk Children

David Finkelhor and Larry Baron

*I*n responding to the problem of child sexual abuse, one of our most pressing tasks is to identify any group of children who may be at high risk. . . . Th[is] task . . . is not a simple one, however. Because much sexual abuse is hidden, so are the risk factors. Any characteristic that appears to be common to victims who come to public attention may not apply to the vast number of victims who do not. If most reported sexual abuse victims are from impoverished, disorganized families, for example, is it because these children are at higher risk or simply because these victims are more readily detected? . . .

In the following review of findings concerning risk factors,[1] we will rely exclusively on studies that employed samples of the general population—either whole communities or students. One crucial feature of these studies is that they also contain built-in comparison groups. . . . The whole notion of a "risk factor" requires such a comparison between characteristics of abuse victims and characteristics of nonvictims from the same samples. We will from time to time make reference to a few studies without comparison samples, particularly when these studies are large in scope, but it will be primarily for supporting evidence. . . .

SEX

Virtually all studies that included men as well as women found higher abuse rates for women. . . . The mean ratio of . . . the eight random sample community surveys that interviewed both men and women (Badgley et al., 1984; Burnam, 1985; Finkelhor, 1984; Keckley Market Research, 1983; Kercher & McShane, 1984; Lewis, 1985; Miller, 1976; Murphy, 1985) is 2.5 women for every man. This would translate into an expectation that among all victims 71% are females and 29% males. . . .

. . . In more recent years, the number of boys appearing in agency-based studies has increased somewhat. The National Incidence Study of Child Abuse and Neglect (NCCAN, 1981), based on cases known to professionals, and the American Humane Association study (1981), based on agency-identified cases, have reported about 5 girls for every boy, or a distribution of about 83% girls and 17% boys.

However, the degree to which these agency surveys reveal a smaller proportion of boys than the community studies strongly suggests that the abuse of boys is still quite underreported. This is also what clinicians have hypothesized (Woods & Dean, 1984). Boys, it is speculated, are reluctant to admit victimization because it clashes with the expectations of masculinity. The homosexual character of most abuse of boys may also inhibit disclosure. And the fact that public stereotypes have focused primarily on the risk to girls may have made parents and professionals less apt to identify abused boys.

The fact that abuse of boys is underreported has led some to speculate that boys may, in fact, be abused just as frequently as girls (Kempe & Kempe, 1984; Plummer, 1984). However, the consistent data from the surveys cast doubt on this assertion. . . .

Because girls are at higher risk, they have been subject to more attention, study, and analysis. This is unfortunate because it may have contributed to an already mistaken public impression that boys are rarely abused at all. It has resulted also in the collection of substantially fewer data about the abuse of boys. Although some of the studies that we review here had samples of boy victims, most did not analyze risk factors pertaining to boys.

AGE OF CHILD AT ONSET

Almost all studies report statistics showing that children are more vulnerable to sexual abuse starting in the preadolescent period between ages 8 and 12. . . . The pattern . . . shows an increase in vulnerability at ages 6–7 and another very dramatic increase at age 10. Ages 10 through 12 appear to be years of particularly acute risk, when children are victimized at more than double the average rate. . . . [T]he distribution for age of onset is affected by what types of experiences are being counted.

All the studies agree about lower rates of vulnerability for children under 6–7. Here again, however, methodological considerations urge some caution. Clinicians have pointed out how easy it is for the memories of early sexual abuse experiences to be forgotten and repressed, especially when they occur to children without a cognitive framework for interpreting their experiences. It is possible that the lower rates for younger children may simply reflect a greater loss of memory of these experiences.

In discussing the age distributions for victims of sexual abuse, it is also important to include some comment about statistics that come from studies of reported cases. In general such studies show much higher means or median ages for abused children than do the studies using survey methodology. For example, in the National Incidence Study of Child Abuse and Neglect, 60% of the sexually abused children were 12 or older. It must be remembered, though, that most studies using reported cases record the age of the child *at the time of the reporting*, which is in a great many cases some years after the *onset* of the abuse. Moreover, it is probable that older children are more likely to reveal abuse, thus biasing upward the ages of children in studies of reported cases. Thus the discrepancies between the clinical and survey studies are less contradictory than they might seem.

SOCIAL CLASS

Child abuse in general has been thought to be more prevalent in lower social classes. But child welfare advocates generally have found this a politically unappealing stereotype and have tried to emphasize the fact that child abuse occurs in all social strata. For some writers, this emphasis has turned into a claim that child abuse is *unrelated* to social class. Empirical studies repeatedly have undercut these claims, however, finding rather strong associations between class and physical abuse (Pelton, 1981; Straus, Gelles, & Steinmetz, 1980). Although abuse is certainly not limited to the lower classes, as the stereotype might suggest, to most researchers it makes sense that the frustrations of poverty, joblessness, lack of education, and inadequate housing contribute to the conditions that increase violence toward children.

Child *sexual* abuse, however, may be an entirely different story. The most representative surveys of child sexual abuse in the community have been unable to find any relationship between sexual abuse and the social class of the family in which the victims grew up. . . .

Other retrospective community studies looked at victimization rates according to respondents' *current* social class standing and also failed to find any higher rates in lower social statuses. Unfortunately, current SES measures (such as current income or education) are not the best way to see if social class is a risk factor for abuse, because the issue . . . is whether . . . coming from a lower-class background as a child (better measured by parents' education, occupation, or income) raises the risk for sexual abuse. If anything, having been abused might be a cause of downward social mobility as an adult, creating a misleading association between abuse and social class. Nonetheless, studies looking at current measures do not find such an association. The Nashville telephone survey (Keckley Market Research, 1983) showed a nonsignificant trend for higher rates not among low-income, but among the middle-income, $15,000–$35,000 group. The *Los Angeles*

Times survey (Lewis, 1985; Timnick, 1985a) found somewhat higher rates among high school graduates and people with white-collar jobs. Although Finkelhor (1984) found somewhat higher rates among those adult women with current family incomes under $10,000, the finding was not quite significant. The conclusion from these community-based studies is that sexual abuse is not disproportionately prevalent in lower social classes. . . .

A positive relationships exists between sexual abuse and social class among reported cases, . . . but here again the data are not well suited for determining the class linkages. It is generally acknowledged that the child welfare system is heavily biased toward identifying abuse in lower social strata. The data, of course, show this bias. The National Incidence Study of Child Abuse and Neglect (NCCAN, 1981) found that 38% of all sexual abuse cases known to professionals came from families with annual incomes less than $7,000, whereas only 17% of American families had incomes in this category. This is about the same lower-class bias as for physical abuse (35% of cases from incomes less than $7,000), but not as much as for child neglect (53% of cases are from the poorest bracket). Similarly, the American Humane Association (Trainor, 1984) reports that, although only 11.9% of U.S. families were receiving public assistance in 1980, 29.3% of officially reported sexual abuse cases in 1982 came from such families. Interestingly, the report notes that there has been a marked decline since 1976 (from 39.8%) in the percentage of sexual abuse cases that involved welfare recipients. . . .

The currently available data on sexual abuse suggest that sexual abuse and social class are unrelated. The most representative community surveys suggest little connection (Russell, 1986; Miller, 1976; Peters, 1984). The strong overrepresentation of the poor among reported cases is readily accounted for as a reporting bias in that system.

An argument could be made that the surveys are masking a social class connection. It is possible that women from higher social classes are more candid with middle-class interviewers and report more of their abuse, thus creating an artificial parity with less candid lower-class women. But there is no evidence for this specific effect, and not much inferential support for it from the methodological studies of survey research.

ETHNICITY

Across the board, studies have consistently failed to find any black-white differences in rates of sexual abuse. Even among reported cases, in which it is thought that blacks suffer from a labeling bias (O'Toole, Turbott, & Nalepka, 1983), the percentage of black cases is no more than the percentage of blacks in the population as a whole (NCCAN, 1981). . . .

Although studies have found no black-white differences, there are hints of possible differences for other ethnic groups. Kercher and McShane (1984), for example, in a mail survey of Texas driver's license holders, found victimization rates of 21.7% for Hispanic women, compared to 9.8% for whites and 10.4% for blacks. Russell's (1986) findings concerning Hispanic women give some possible support to the Texas study. Although not statistically significant, Russell's overall rates for incestuous victimization for Hispanic women are somewhat higher than for the sample as a whole (20% versus 16% for the whole sample), and in the case of father-daughter incest, Hispanic women have a rate of 7.5% compared to 4.5% for the sample as a whole. Russell's data also show low rates (this time statistically significant) for Asian and Jewish women, only 8% and 10% of whom were incestuously victimized. Ethnic differences should be the subject of further analysis.

SOCIAL ISOLATION

Social isolation is a risk factor of interest to sexual abuse researchers for two reasons. First, there are anecdotal reports of concentrations of sexually abusive families in rural areas (Summit & Kryso, 1978). Second, social isolation has proven to be correlated in some research with other forms of child abuse and neglect (Garbarino & Stocking, 1980).

However, rural residence has been associated with more sexual abuse in only one study, and in two it has actually been associated with less. . . . So the idea that sexual abuse is more common in rural areas seems doubtful.

However, another aspect of social isolation has been confirmed empirically by three studies: Sexual abuse victims appear to be isolated among their peers. Finkelhor (1984) found that women with two or fewer friends at age 12 had more experiences of sexual abuse. Fromuth (1983) confirmed this in her student sample with the exact same question. Peters (1984) found higher rates associated with women who reported either lack of closeness with peers or lack of closeness with siblings. . . .

A plausible hypothesis is that social isolation is related to abuse. If children have few friends, this may create a need for contact and friendship on which sexual abusers can capitalize. Friendless children may be easy marks. However, the friendlessness found in the three studies may, unfortunately, be the *result* of having been victimized rather than a risk factor. Children who are being abused by family members are often prohibited from having friends. Children who are feeling shame and stigma as a result of having suffered victimization often isolate themselves from others. At age 12, the year asked about in both the Finkelhor and the Fromuth studies, more than half of the respondents had already suffered their victimizations. This casts doubt on whether the friendlessness was truly a risk factor. . . .

PARENTAL ABSENCE AND UNAVAILABILITY

In general, the background factors that have shown the strongest connection to sexual abuse, both across and within studies, have been those relating to parents and family. We have subdivided these into four categories: (1) parental absence and unavailability, (2) poor relationship with parents, (3) parental conflict, and (4) presence of a stepfather. . . .

In regard to parental absence, seven studies have found higher vulnerability to sexual abuse among women who *lived without their natural mothers or fathers* at some time during childhood. In Finkelhor's (1984) student study, having lived apart from a natural mother was the most powerful risk factor, resulting in an almost threefold higher risk. Herman and Hirschman (1981) found separation from mother to be a serious risk for father–daughter incest. However, these findings were not replicated by Fromuth (1983) or Peters (1984). Finkelhor, Fromuth, and Peters all found that girls who had ever lived without their natural *fathers* were at higher risk, although Peters's finding applied only to white women. Russell (1986) also found higher rates among girls living with their biological mothers and no fathers, but the finding applied only to extrafamily abuse. Similarly, Miller (1976) found elevated risk for adolescents who were currently living without their fathers or without both natural parents. Bagley and Ramsay (in press) found that any separation from either parent for a period of six months or more before the age of 16 was correlated with the likelihood of being a victim. This is an impressive number of studies with positive findings on the question of parental absence.

Another variable that in some of its forms might be related to parental absence is the *mother's employment outside the home*. At least four studies have found this related to sexual abuse (Fromuth, 1983; Landis, 1956; Peters, 1984; Russell, 1986). . . .

Parental unavailability may also be indicated by a *disabled or ill* parent. Finkelhor (1984) found higher rates of sexual victimization among girls who reported that their mothers were often ill. Peters (1984) reported somewhat higher rates . . . for girls with one parent who was disabled by substance addiction, emotional problems, or physical ailments. Looking specifically at father–daughter incest families, Herman and Hirschman (1981) found significantly more mothers who were seriously ill (most commonly due to alcoholism, depression, or psychosis) and also mothers who were burdened with many children and pregnancies. However, Fromuth (1983), using the same variables as Finkelhor, did not confirm any association between sexual abuse and mother's illness.

POOR RELATIONSHIP WITH PARENTS

As impressive as the findings concerning parental absences are the findings concerning poor relationships with parents, particularly with the mother. This has been substantiated also by a large number of studies (six) and is one of the most consistent findings to date. Landis (1956) was one of the first to observe that molested women reported a more distant relationship with their mothers. Such women also were less likely to mention their mothers as their primary source of sex information. Finkelhor (1984) found in his sample of college students that those women at higher risk were the ones who said they were not close to their mothers or received little affection from their mothers or fathers. The same was true if they rated their mothers high on a scale of sexual punitiveness. All of these factors, except maternal affection, made an independent contribution. . . . Peters

(1984) found . . . that not being close to mother was the variable that was most predictive of sexual abuse. Miller (1976) also used multivariate analysis and found that poor relationships with either parent were potent correlates of abuse. . . .

CONFLICT BETWEEN PARENTS

Besides reporting poor relationships *with* their parents, sexual abuse victims are also more likely to report poor relationships *between* their parents. Five out of five studies confirm such a risk factor. Landis (1956) found a high proportion of unhappy marriages in the families of victims of what he called "child participated" experiences. Gruber and Jones (1983) . . . found poor parental relations to be the most potent predictor of sexual abuse among their group of delinquent girls. Finkelhor (1984) found that rates of sexual abuse were higher among the college student women who reported that their parents either had unhappy marriages or showed little mutual affection. Fromuth (1983) and Peters (1984) both confirmed Finkelhor's findings.

All of these findings—on parental absence, poor relationships with parents, and conflict between parents—seem to point strongly toward the idea that sexually victimized girls have disturbances in their relationships with their parents. . . .

One hypothesis that has to be taken very seriously is that when victimization occurs, it alienates a girl from her parents. . . . If the alienation is the result of the abuse, then it can hardly be considered a risk factor.

Other findings may also be interpreted as a result of abuse rather than a risk factor, particularly with intrafamily abuse. Girls who are abused may be more likely to live without a parent if they, or an offending parent, are removed from the home. If a father is removed, a mother may have to go out to work. If a girl is being abused by a father, she may certainly perceive her parents as having an unhappy relationship.

However, many of the associations related to family disturbances—parental absence, parental conflict, and poor relationships to parents—also make a great deal of sense as risk factors. . . . It is unfortunate that more of the studies have not made sure that the family condition under question existed prior to the time that the abuse occurred.

If these clusters of variables are risk factors, there are at least two major dynamics that explain the relationship. One concerns supervision. When a child is missing a parent, has a poor relationship with a parent, or has parents who are hostile to one another, the child may be less well supervised and thus less well protected from predatory adults. . . .

A second possibility is that the poor parental relationships are connected to sexual abuse through emotional disturbances in the child. If a child is unhappy, emotionally deprived, or needy, then she may be more conspicuous and more vulnerable to an adult interested in molesting her. She may be more amenable to the offers of friendship, appreciation, and the material rewards that the offender makes, and she may be less able to stand up for herself. Moreover, she may be more afraid to tell her parents about the abuse, because she has reason to believe she will not be supported. This second dynamic does not necessarily preclude the first. . . .

STEPFATHER FAMILIES

Besides parental absence, conflict, and lack of support, another parental factor—the presence of a non-biologically related father—has been discussed as a risk factor for sexual abuse. Four out of six studies examining this factor have confirmed its significance. Three of these studies—Miller (1976), Finkelhor (1980), and Gruber and Jones (1983)—found that having a stepfather increased a girl's risk for all types of sexual abuse. [See also Russell (1986), Fromuth (1983), and Peters (1984).] . . . Although most of these studies . . . indicate that simple father absence is a risk factor, both Finkelhor (1984) and Gruber and Jones (1983) . . . showed that the presence of a stepfather further augmented the risk.

Russell's (1986) dramatic figures on the higher rate of abuse at the hands of stepfathers are illustrative of the risk. Whereas only 2.3% of daughters growing up with natural fathers had been abused by them, 17% of the daughters growing up with stepfathers had been abused by them. Moreover, the types of abuse committed by stepfathers were more serious (involving more intercourse, fellatio, cunnilingus, analingus, and anal intercourse) and more violent. . . .

These studies appear to point to higher risk for girls who have stepfathers, and several explanations for this risk have been offered. One is that the taboos against stepfather–stepdaughter sexual contact are less stringent and therefore have less of a deterrent effect. Another is that natural fathers are more inhibited from incestuous contact as a result of a period of parent–child bonding that occurs when the child is quite small. . . . The intense dependency of the child during this period or perhaps the father's involvement in diapering and bodily care may block later sexualization of the relationship. Stepfathers who have not experienced this type of bonding may be more apt to see the child as a possible sexual partner.

Nonetheless, studies are not clear on whether or not the higher risk for girls with stepfathers is explained entirely by the greater predatory behavior of these stepfathers. In Finkelhor's (1980) research, girls with stepfathers were victimized at greater rates by other men as well. Finkelhor suggested that dating mothers may bring home sexually opportunistic men who exploit the daughters. Stepfathers may also bring steprelatives into the family who do not feel so constrained about becoming sexually involved with daughters. And perhaps stepfathers are less concerned and protective of stepdaughters when friends or relatives make sexual overtures to them. . . .

One caution about some of the findings reported here is that they may be historically outdated. They are based mostly on studies of women who grew up before the 1970s, when fewer children had stepfathers. It may have been very different to live in a stepfather family in an era when there were few such families compared to the current era, when such families are much more commonplace. Assuming that this vulnerability does show up even in studies of current cohorts of children, it would support a crucial new direction for social policy. A case might be made that families containing stepfathers should be the target of sexual abuse prevention efforts.

SUMMARY OF RISK FACTORS

This review of findings concerning risk factors has been fruitful in identifying some emerging consistencies across studies. A number of background factors seem to be associated clearly with higher risk in several studies. . . .

Not surprisingly, girls are at higher risk than boys. Also, preadolescents appear to be more at risk than either younger or older children. Girls with few friends in childhood report more abuse, but this may be an effect of abuse and not a risk factor. The strongest and most consistent associations across the studies concerned the parents of abused children. Girls who are victimized are (1) more likely to have lived without their natural fathers, (2) more likely to have mothers who were employed outside the home, (3) more likely to have mothers who were disabled or ill, (4) more likely to witness conflict between their parents, and (5) more likely to report a poor relationship with one of their parents. Girls who lived with stepfathers were also at increased risk for abuse. . . .

The studies also seem to agree that two factors do *not* increase risk for abuse. Blacks have no higher rates for abuse than whites; and girls from lower social strata are at no more risk than others. In fact, sexual abuse appears to be very democratic in its social class distribution. The studies have demonstrated strong agreement on these points. . . .

Studies of Child Populations

Virtually all of the risk factor studies that have been done so far have been of adults or young adults looking back on their childhoods. These studies have some important limitations, however. For example, it is very hard to get detailed and accurate information about parent–child relationships and other childhood variables from somebody who has been out of his or her family for 20 years. . . .

There is an obvious need for more contemporaneous studies that gather information on families immediately after the abuse has occurred to assess how these families and children may differ from others. Questions about supervision, parental relationships, and parental conflict may be much more reliably evaluated in these immediate studies. Of course, one problem with such studies now is that only a small portion of abuse comes to public attention. As a result, they may not tell us about risk factors for sexual abuse so much as risk factors for sexual abuse that gets detected.

The optimal kind of [research] design . . . is a longitudinal study that would gather information early in the family life cycle on families with young children, and then follow them and the children until the children become adults. Then it might be possible to ascertain from self-reports in interviews whether or not sexual abuse had occurred, even if it had never been reported. The data gathered early in the study would give fairly unbiased information on possible predictors of subsequent abuse. . . .

A Final Caveat: Blaming the Victim

Risk factors always require cautious handling, but this is particularly so when dealing with child sexual abuse, which has been fraught with myth and misunderstanding. In the past there have been those who have taken findings such as the fact that children without friends are at higher risk and used those findings to hold victims responsible for being abused. Others have taken findings such as the fact that children with working mothers are at higher risk and used them to hold mothers responsible for abuse.

Conclusions such as these are particularly likely when victims are studied without simultaneous study of offenders. All the data in this review are based on victim surveys, which, because they gather detailed information on victims and their families, and correspondingly little about offenders and their backgrounds, tend to overemphasize the role of victims and obscure the contributions of the perpetrators.

It is important to emphasize that true causal responsibility for abuse lies with offenders. All the research suggests that it is offenders who initiate the sexual activity. . . .

NOTE

1. "Risk factor" is a concept used widely by epidemiologists and defined by Mausner and Bahn (1974) as "factors whose presence is associated with an increased likelihood that disease will develop at a later time." Thus, although the risk factors are presumed to precede the disease temporally, they are not necessarily causal factors, but simply markers of higher susceptibility. Thus sex, age, or ethnicity may be risk factors without having any direct connection to etiology.

REFERENCES

American Humane Association. (1981). *National study on child neglect and abuse reporting*. Denver, CO: Author.

Badgley, R., Allard, H., McCormick, N., Proudfoot, P., Fortin, D., Ogilvie, D., Rae-Grant, Q., Gelinas, P., Pepin, L., & Sutherland, S. [Committee on Sexual Offences Against Children and Youth] (1984). *Sexual offences against children* (Vol. 1). Ottawa: Canadian Government Publishing Centre.

Bagley C., & Ramsay, R. (in press). Disrupted childhood and vulnerability to sexual assault: Long-term sequels with implications for counselling. *Social Work and Human Sexuality*.

Burnam, A. (1985). Personal communication concerning the Los Angeles Epidemiological Catchment Area Study.

Finkelhor, D. (1980). Risk factors in the sexual victimization of children. *Child Abuse and Neglect, 4*, 265–273.

Finkelhor, D. (1984). *Child sexual abuse: New theory and research* New York: Free Press.

Fromuth, M. E. (1983). *The long term psychological impact of childhood sexual abuse.* Unpublished doctoral dissertation, Auburn University.

Garbarino, J., & Stocking, S. H. (1980). *Protecting children from abuse and neglect.* San Francisco: Jossey-Bass.

Gruber, K., & Jones, R. (1983). Identifying determinants of risk of sexual victimization of youth. *Child Abuse and Neglect, 7*, 17–24.

Keckley Market Research. (1983, March). *Sexual abuse in Nashville: A report on incidence and long- term effects.* Nashville, TN: Keckley Market Research.

Kempe R., & Kempe, C. H. (1984). *The common secret: Sexual abuse of children and adolescents.* New York: W. H. Freeman.

Kercher, G., & McShane, M. (1984). The prevalence of child sexual abuse victimization in an adult sample of Texas residents. *Child Abuse and Neglect, 8*, 495–502.

Landis, J. (1956). Experiences of 500 children with adult sexual deviants. *Psychiatric Quarterly Supplement, 30*, 91–109.

Lewis, I.A. (1985). [*Los Angeles Times Poll* #98]. Unpublished raw data.

Miller, P. (1976). Blaming the victim of child molestation: An empirical analysis (Doctoral dissertation, Northwestern University). *Dissertation Abstracts International.* (University Microfilms No. 77-10069).

Murphy, J. E. (1985, June). Untitled news release. (Available from St. Cloud State University, St. Cloud, MN 56301).

National Center on Child Abuse and Neglect (NCCAN). (1981). *Study findings: National study of incidence and severity of child abuse and neglect.* Washington, DC: Department of Health, Education and Welfare.

O'Toole, R., Turbett, P., & Nalepka, C. (1983). Theories, professional knowledge and diagnosis of child abuse. In D. Finkelhor, R. J. Gelles, G. T. Hotaling, & M. A. Straus (Eds.), *The dark side of families: Current family violence research.* Beverly Hills, CA: Sage.

Pelton, L. H. (Ed.). (1981). *The social context of child abuse and neglect.* New York: Human Sciences Press.

Peters, S. D. (1984). *The relationship between childhood sexual victimization and adult depression among Afro-American and white women.* Unpublished doctoral dissertation, University of California at Los Angeles. (University Microfilms No. 84-28, 555).

Plummer, C. (1984, August). *Preventing sexual abuse: What in-school programs teach children.* Paper presented at the Second National Conference for Family Violence Researchers, Durham, NH.

Russell, D. E. H. (1983). The incidence and prevalence of intrafamilial and extrafamilial sexual abuse of female children. *Child Abuse and Neglect, 7*, 133–146.

Russell, D. E. H. (1984a). *Sexual exploitation: Rape, child sexual abuse, sexual harassment.* Beverly Hills, CA: Sage.

Russell, D. E. H. (1984b). The prevalence and seriousness of incestuous abuse: Stepfathers vs. biological fathers. *Child Abuse and Neglect, 8*, 15–22.

Russell, D. E. H. (1986). *The secret trauma: Incest in the lives of girls and women.* New York: Basic Books.

Straus, M. A., Gelles, R., & Steinmetz, S. (1980). *Behind closed doors: Violence in the American family.* Garden City, NY: Doubleday.

Summit, R., & Kryso, J. (1978). Sexual abuse of children: A clinical spectrum. *American Journal of Orthopsychiatry, 48*, 237–251.

Timnick, L. (1985a, August 25). 22% in survey were child abuse victims. *Los Angeles Times*, p. 1.

Timnick, L. (1985b, August 26). Children's abuse reports reliable, most believe. *Los Angeles Times*, p. 1.

Trainor, C. (1984). *Sexual maltreatment in the United States: A five-year perspective.* Paper presented at the International Congress on Child Abuse and Neglect, Montreal.

Wood, S. C., & Dean, K. S. (1984). *Final report: Sexual abuse of males research project* (90 CA/812). Washington, DC: National Center on Child Abuse and Neglect.

Wyatt, G. E. (1985). The sexual abuse of Afro-American and White American women in childhood. *Child Abuse and Neglect, 9*, 507–519.

Chapter 6

Victims of Interpersonal Violence

On Being Mugged: The Event and its Aftermath

Robert Lejeune and Nicholas Alex

AN UNEXPECTED EVENT

Casual conversations with urban citizens or regular reading of the newspapers in recent years would indicate that many, if not most, inner-city residents live with the fatalistic expectation that sooner or later they will be mugged. But closer examination reveals that most of these fear-laden accounts are not associated with a corresponding . . . precautionary behavior. The "street role" of citizens, as it is still enacted most of the time in ordinary public settings in American cities such as elevators, streets, and hallways, involves a minimum of alertness to the contingency of an attack by strangers. . . . The citizen—or at least the middle-class citizen—expects that in "his own territory" he will be relatively free from the threat of attacks by others. . . .

Partly as a result of these expectations and partly as a result of the particular characteristics of the mugging encounter itself, the victim emerges from his mugging as much bewildered as he is morally indignant. . . .

Assumptions of Invulnerability and Trust

Despite the high degree of public awareness of street crime in recent years, the overwhelming majority of victims respond to their mugging as an unexpected event, one whose occurrence surprises as much as it injures. . . . [I]ndividuals may be aware in a general way that some members of society prey upon others without converting this knowledge into suspicion of others in concrete situations of danger. We refer to such mental states, which were typical of most respondents prior to their mugging, as *assumptions of invulnerability and trust*.

How are such assumptions maintained in the face of a barrage of information that would tend to erode them? We suggest that three factors . . . act as brakes on the transformation of unrealistic street-role expectations into expectations more consonant with the realities of present-day urban living.

First, assumptions of invulnerability and trust make it possible for urban citizens to carry out their everyday essential activities with relative psychological ease. To "live with fear," to paraphrase several of the respondents, turns the most elementary activities of urban living—from going out to a play to taking out the garbage—into major "hassles." . . .

Second, many urban residents and some of the respondents . . . still have a residue of commitment to the belief that man is rational and/or basically good. Such Lockeian sentiments are not easily replaced, particularly among the young, educated, liberal respondents, by the Hobbesian view of human nature.[1] Yet the latter view, more functional to the mobilization of urban residents for self-protection, is clearly on the ascendancy, as is suggested, for instance, by the growing use of the jungle metaphor to characterize the city.[2]

Third, most respondents, as most Americans, have lived and continue to live their lives in economically and racially homogeneous enclaves. These segregated experiences have resulted in their mental and emotional—as well as physical—remoteness from the kind of street crime that has always characterized the slums of American cities.[3] It is only as the violence of the ghetto spills over into middle-class neighborhoods that the "other America" takes on emotional meaning for many urban residents.

As a result of these . . . factors, the victims typically report that immediately prior to their mugging they were free of a sense of danger; that they did not perceive any features in themselves, their setting, or the others present that might have increased their likelihood of victimization;[4] and that they were caught off guard.[5] . . .

VULNERABILITY CONVERSION

For the victim, such slogans as "crime in the streets" and "law and order" take on a personal meaning. . . . Whatever the ideological persuasion, however minor the material loss or physical injury, whatever the class or race of the respondent, the psychological impact of having been mugged is traumatic. The effects of this trauma vary depending on the personal characteristics of the victims and the circumstances of the muggings. But uniformly, and without exception in our sample, one effect of the mugging is to raise to a significant degree the victim's sense of vulnerability and mistrust. Although these feelings seem to subside somewhat with the passage of time, all respondents emerge from the mugging with a new sense of their vulnerability to the attacks and demands of strangers. For many, the experience represents a critical benchmark resulting in changes in their own self-perception. Males, for instance, tend to see both the attack on their person and the forceful removal of their property as an attack on their masculinity. For those who did not resist—and all but two of our respondents did not—anger is sometimes mixed with an element of shame. This is evidenced by the great need to explain to others, including the interviewers, the conditions that made resistance impossible or highly dangerous.[6] In this context several respondents—as it happens all male—report spontaneously the heightened awareness of the possibility of their own death, what one sociologist-respondent refers to as a "vulnerability conversion":

> I think that I had a vulnerability conversion. Before the mugging I had been robbed three or four times. Me and my wife's possessions had been taken [in burglaries of our apartment]. But when you have someone holding a knife to your stomach and his hand is shaking and you know he can kill you, well, that's something else.

Such feelings are echoed in other accounts. A young teacher who was seriously injured . . . told us:

> I think the biggest thing that came out of this was the realization of how easy it is to die. And again the doctor pointed this out—if he had hit me on the right spot that could have been it. I had never come close to dying. It wasn't something I thought about.

Accompanying this new sense of vulnerability, an awareness of the self as a potential target, there is the sense that an environment previously perceived as benign has become a jungle. Appearances are no longer "normal," and trust is an inappropriate attitude for survival.[7] This emergent attitude of distrust is also, in varying degrees, a universal psychological effect of the mugging. . . . Combined with a heightened sense of vulnerability, this attitude of distrust leads to a total transformation in the way the environment is perceived:

> Q: Has this changed your outlook on life in any way?
> R: I am just so much more frightened wherever I turn, and it seems as though the entire city has turned into an incredible jungle. . . . Once you pass nine o'clock that's it; it's the middle of the night. It's incredible that I think that way, that I feel that way; it's so unlike me.

Although distrust of one's environment can be generalized to many aspects of the victim's daily rounds, the most severe effects are noted with respect to the specific time, place, and circumstances associated with their own victimization. Thus, a young social worker . . . responds[:] . . .

> Q: Have there been any other changes?
> R: Well, I would like to move out of the area. My perception of it has completely changed. I've been living here for three and a half years, and I've never had any real fear of it. It's like it's my home. I know the block. I recognize people. It's all very familiar to me. Now it's become very unfamiliar, very threatening, very, very much like a jungle. I trust nobody. . . .

The mental frame that provided the victim with a sense of security and predictability and that made the mugging encounter such an unexpected event for the victim is suddenly shattered. . . .

While the reactions, particularly in the few days or weeks after the mugging, tend to be exaggerated, they are for the most part understandable in terms of the characteristics of the mugging encounter, rather than in terms of any particular psychological predisposition to anxiety.[8] The respondents found the victimization traumatic; therefore, they seek ways to avoid further traumatization. . . . [I]f the individual is to avoid being mugged, or at least reduce the likelihood, he must maintain an attitude of distrust toward many situations that are innocuous. [Because] the probability is very low that any given encounter with strangers, even in a high risk area, will develop into a mugging, the level of distrust required to avoid the unusual but highly traumatic situation involves a highly inefficient use of psychic energy for citizens.[9]

> Entirely too much of my thinking goes to devising ways to avoid getting robbed. I turn to see who's behind me. I tend to classify all approaching men as to whether they are or are not aggressors. I take care not to carry anything with me that I won't absolutely need, for who knows, it might be taken from me before I get back. Paranoia? I don't think so, since it all grows out of real-life experiences and is a defensive reaction to my actual environment. I wasn't always like this.[10]

Such an attitude, normal for undercover agents, policemen, criminals, and others involved in dangerous missions, is not usually maintained or prescribed as part of the role of citizen as he carries out the everyday routines of life in areas and at times of day considered "safe." . . .

Insofar as victims are still ambivalent about classifying their own territory as unsafe, their own apprehension and suspicious behavior following the mugging does tend to appear to them as "ridiculous," "sick," "paranoid," or "irrational." But at the same time, they feel that their new sense of vulnerability and the unpredictable and deceptive character of the mugger justify their state of mind and their behavior. . . . The acceptance of this attitude as a normal state of affairs and the emergence of new behavioral patterns associated with it are facilitated by—indeed can probably only be maintained through—the social support provided by the victim's social circle.

THE POSTVICTIMIZATION INTERCHANGE

In the hours, days, and weeks following the mugging the respondents are cast in the role of the victim. They relate to others and others relate to them in terms of their mugging experience. This process frequently begins when reporting the crime to the police. In the case of serious injuries, the first to treat the respondent in his role of victim are the hospital personnel. The police . . . only become involved when the victim chooses to report the crime or when the physical injury is so great that it comes to their attention through other channels. In such instances they are among the first to speak to the respondent. At this moment, the victim is shocked, angry, and bewildered. The police may therefore be singularly crucial in defining the situation for the victim.

As experts in crime, the police view the victim as one more case among many. They are likely to communicate to the victim the ordinariness of his plight, and to inform him that there is little likelihood that he will receive satisfaction for his loss or injury, even if the criminal is apprehended, which happens rarely. These revelations seem to represent a crucial step in the victim's role-taking process. The victim comes to perceive his individual plight as common and unimportant in the light of the enormousness of the crime problem and the inadequacies of the law enforcement and court systems. . . .

[T]he victim, if conscious, . . . relates the incidents to others within minutes of its occurrence. Thus begins the first of many tellings of the victim's story to that vast audience of relatives, neighbors, friends, and co-workers who within days come to share vicariously in the mugging and in turn participate in defining its meaning.

An intensified communication about the self seems to represent a near universal effect of muggings and similar traumas. There is a great psychological need on the part of the injured person to tell others, to relive and thereby perhaps to relieve the anxiety the experience has created.

> I'm talking constantly and incessantly about the problem. It's become an obsession in my life.
> I just had to talk to somebody. I really didn't know what I was doing. In fact for the next few days that's all I was talking about.

The desire of the victim to talk about his mugging is apparently matched by the desire of others to hear about it. A fascination for the victim, as well as for the criminal, is . . . reflected in the media as well as in everyday conversation.[11] Consequently, at least for some, the intrusion of the mugger into their lives is not completely negative.[12] The telling of the story of one's mugging provides some victims with an exciting contrast to their everyday routine. . . . The victim may indeed attain a kind of "star" quality, for within his own social circles he has been "where the action is":

> When someone becomes aware I've been mugged I suddenly take on the aura of a movie star. People do feel sorry for me, but they're intrigued—almost the same way as if they met someone famous. . . .

Sociologically, the functions of the psychological need to tell and hear about the mugging are diverse. One of the most important is that the very intensive communication . . . following the mugging creates a social network of awareness about crime.[13] . . . [M]any intermediaries in the network who have not been victimized have their awareness of crime raised:

> I've never heard that much about muggings. Now everybody keeps telling us stories. It seems that everyone we've met since [my roommate and I] were mugged can tell us similar incidents about someone they know. People come to tell us, you know; we're the mugging celebrities. . . .

A second and related function of intensified communication is the *gleaning* process. The victim carries out a search for information and interpretation that will enable him and those with whom he interacts to reconstruct the social reality that has been shattered or damaged. . . . Through such communication networks, the victim creates little cultures that give character, texture, and context to [his] plight. In this way, others participate with the victim in the recreation of the mugging encounter, give it meaning, and most important, assist in establishing survival patterns to correspond with the new threat that has entered the person's life. . . . Much of the cautionary information comes in the form of crime lore, through which the victim learns to "know the enemy" in his many lurid manifestations and from this, hopefully, draws the proper lesson:

> The girl next door to me said they come to see her about fixing her pipes and she opened the door and let them in. He acts like he was a plumber and she let him in. And he went right to the bathroom and took her bag and started out the door and she grabbed it and he hit her in the mouth and knocked out two teeth. . . .
> You hear stories that make you acutely aware of how to conduct yourself, such as the tricks that thieves use. They disguise themselves as telephone repairmen and ring your bell.

Such stories, as the respondent just quoted observes, "Make you acutely aware of how to conduct yourself." But in addition to providing information, this kind of interchange facilitates the emergence of new norms of behavior in public places.[14] It reinforces the sense of vulnerability, justifies an attitude of distrust as a normal response to an abnormal situation, and . . . drives home the moral that vigilance is not a matter of individual choice. It is the individual's responsibility to prevent his being mugged. Failing this, it is his responsibility to minimize personal injury or financial loss or both.

As the awareness of crime spreads, victims, near victims, and would-be victims become sanctioning agents and the object of sanctions for more vigilant behavior in public places. . . .

> I don't wear my rings. My husband told me to take those rings off your fingers. I'm afraid to wear them. I always carry a couple of dollars just in case. My husband says, "Keep a couple of dollars. If they want, let them have it." I take my keys out and put them in my pocket. I never carry a pocketbook anymore [since an attempted purse snatching]. . . .

Group support for vigilance is not limited to victims—nor is it given only to close friends or relatives. The triggering factor for more vigilant behavior may come from a chance remark from a near stranger[:] . . .

> Believe it or not, I didn't stop carrying pocketbooks until a later time—when a round-eyed young man behind a grocery counter pointed to the bag, a large one I'd been given for my birthday and said, "You carry *that*? They'll kill you!"[15]

Given the prevalent feeling on the part of victims that they cannot depend on other citizens nor on the police for protection, some look to illegal means for their own defense. Indeed, at times the police and others in the postvictimization interchange confirm the powerlessness of the police and provide the victim with the information and rationalizations necessary for illegal modes of defense.

> After my second mugging I told the sergeant: I got mugged twice and I got my apartment robbed twice. And I said, that officer came up and asked me questions like I was the one doing the robbery, but I'm going to get something to protect myself. So he laughed and said, "Don't be too drastic and get a gun." I said, "No, I'm not going to get a gun, but I'm going to get me a knife." So he said, "Get two." If there ain't nobody around and if I do get the advantage of him I would plant the other knife on him. [This respondent bought both a knife and a .22 caliber pistol.]
> Since then I've been more alert in carrying a little gas gun. I was given two by a private detective. And I've talked since with a black lawyer friend of mine in Harlem that I've known for many years. He encouraged me to use it. I said, "It's illegal." "Of course, but don't hesitate to use it," he said. "And your story should be. . . ." Now this is a man whom I respect highly—a highly moral man in many ways. "Of course you use it and if the police say anything about it, or find it, say they used it on you first. And that's your story: You took it away from them. And you stick to it."

Thus, in his own protection the victim may become a "criminal," just as in his own protection the victim becomes adept at evasion and deception. In order to survive, the victim may become as ruthless and as vicious as the victimizer.[16] Under such prevalent conditions of anomie the barrier separating the victim and the victimizer tends to break down. . . .

NOTES

1. The distinction between the Lockeian and Hobbesian views of man is discussed by Parsons (1949: 89–94).
2. For impressionistic accounts of such transformations see Etzioni (1970, 1972) and Hentoff (1973).
3. For discussions and documentations of the extent of violent crime by earlier generations of migrants to American cities see, for example, Koenig (1961) and Stofflet (1941).
4. The factors in the victim's presentation and in the situation that are likely to increase the probability of victimization are discussed by Shafer (1968: 39–103).
5. There are, of course, the exceptions that prove the rule. The one respondent who *reported* that he was *not* surprised by his attacker was a young man with a brown belt in jiujitsu who was able to disarm and capture one of the two men who attacked him. He was also a person raised in a "tough" working class neighborhood, and therefore quite used to street fighting.

   Goffman (1971: 242–243) notes that there is significant variability in the capacity or tendency to be caught off guard. We would add that, to a point, this predisposition is influenced by subcultural norms and location in the social structure. Thus, until recently, and even still today, most middle-class persons define the role of citizen in such way as to increase the likelihood of "surprise." On the other hand, lower-class definitions of the "street role" probably involve greater wariness, and therefore less likelihood of being caught off guard. The ghetto resident has always been and remains more at the mercy of predators. See, for instance, Coombs (1972).

6. This is related to the tendency we find for a few victims to blame themselves in part for their victimization. Such self-blame seems to be encouraged by the explicit or implicit sanctions given by others to whom the account of the victimization has been related: "What were you doing walking there at night?" "Why didn't you scream?" "Why didn't you squirt him in the face with your gas gun?"

7. We use the word "normal" as Goffman (1971: 239) most recently uses it: "When the world immediately around the individual portends nothing out of the ordinary, when the world appears to allow him to continue his routine (being indifferent to his design and neither a major help nor a major hindrance), we can say that he will sense that appearances are 'natural' or 'normal'."

8. There are of course some psychological consequences that have no rational relationship to avoid future victimization:

   And, uh, for about two or three weeks I couldn't sleep at night even though my husband was in the house with me. And when he went to work I'd be afraid to be alone.

   Well, I'll tell you, now I have to have the lights on. I got to have a light on when, you know, I go to bed. I have to have a light on.

9. We speculate that one of the factors involved in "fleeing" to the suburbs is not simply a fear of crime, but the psychological difficulty most people have in maintaining an attitude of distrust.

10. Mooney, 1972: 28.

11. For a discussion of some of the underlying motivational roots, see, for instance, Barton (1969: xiiii).

12. There may be other positive benefits. The mugging tends to create a high degree of mobilization in some individuals. The actions that follow depend on the victim's predispositions. Some head to psychiatrists, others to karate school, while others found or join organizations for self-protection.

13. For journalistic accounts of the emergence of postvictimization interchange networks and its imputed effects, see Etzioni (1970, 1972) and Mooney (1972).

14. For examples of such new norms of behavior as promulgated in the mass media, see *Life* Editors of (1972) and Alexander (1971).

15. Mooney, 1972: 27.

16. Two excerpts from group interviews suggest the depth of anger on the part of citizens who feel powerless. The first quotation is from a woman in her late eighties, the second from a man in his early sixties. Both received a great deal of positive response from their respective groups.

    And you hear so many people. What could be done about it? Like these two policemen that just got killed . . . I'm terrible. I don't want to see a gun. But if they could get these two guys that killed the policemen I could watch on Times Square when they cut them up in pieces. That's how much I'm against them.

    I got held up in Brooklyn. I had a piece of pipe with me. I took a piece of pipe, hit him over the head, sent him to the hospital. Concussion of the brain. He'll never be able to be a normal human being. I went on trial. I laughed at it. I said, "Your honor judge if it came to do it again, I'd do it again." My Bible taught me one thing: if anyone is out to kill you, be quick and kill him.

REFERENCES

Alexander, G. (1971) "The pause in the day's occupation known as the mugging hour." New York 4 (April 26): 35–36.
Barton, A. H. (1969) Communities in Disaster. Garden City, N.Y.: Doubleday.
Bateson, G. (1972) "A theory of play and fantasy," pp. 177–193 in G. Bateson, Steps to an Ecology of Mind. New York: Chandler.
Burgess, A. (1972) "Anthony Burgess meets New York: Cucarachas and exiles, potential death and life enhancement." New York Times Magazine (October 29): 28.
Coombs, O. (1972) "Fear and trembling in black streets." New York 5 (November 20): 47–50.
Etzioni, A. (1972) "Mugging is now the number one topic." Village Voice (October 12): 13.
———(1970) "A swing to the right?" Trans-Action 7 (September): 12.
Goffman, E. (1971) Relations in Public. New York: Harper & Row.
Hentoff, N. (1973) "Growing up mugged." New York Times Magazine (January 28): 35–38.
Koenig, S. (1961) "The immigrant and crime," pp. 138–159 in J. S. Roucek (ed.) Sociology of Crime. New York: Philosophical Library.
Life, Editors of (1972) "Advice from experts on how to foil a mugger." Life 72 (January 28): 34.
Maurer, D. W. (1964) Whiz Mob. New Haven, Conn.: College & University Press.
Mooney, R. (1972) "A dollar for the mugger." Harper's 244 (April): 26–29.
Myrdal, G. (1944) An American Dilemma. New York: Harper.
New York Times (1972) October 12.
Parsons, T. (1949) The Structure of Social Action. New York: Free Press.
Shafer, S. (1968) The Victim and His Criminal. New York: Random House.
Stofflet, E. H. (1941) "The European immigrant and his children." Annals of Amer. Academy of Pol. and Social Sci. 217 (September): 84–92.

The Experiences of Violent and Serious Victimization

Gary D. Gottfredson

INTRODUCTION

. . . The victims' movement has recently dramatized the consequences of being a victim of crime. This social movement has accomplished changes in public attitudes and public policy and has increased professional attention to the consequences of victimization. . . . The objectives sought by victims' advocates vary, but three themes are common: One is a concern that the difficulties some victims experience have been ignored by researchers, practitioners, and the public. Second, these difficulties are exacerbated by other citizens and by the criminal justice system. And finally, the safeguards and arrangements that protect or serve alleged or convicted offenders outweigh the safeguards and arrangements that protect or serve victims.[1] . . .

Divergent Perspectives on Victimization

Contemporary criminal law views a criminal offense as an offense against the state—the state, rather than the victim, prosecutes the offender. In criminal proceedings, victims are often viewed as persons useful in providing evidence rather than as the focus of the prosecutorial exercise (Dussich 1981). This focus on the crime (rather than on the victim) may have drawn attention away from the needs, comfort, and convenience of victims who participate in the system and to the dissatisfaction of many of those participants.

Much criminological research has attended to the ways lifestyle contributes to the likelihood of victimization, the characteristics of victims, and the ways victims contribute to their own victimization (Sparks 1982). Seldom has mainstream criminological research focused on victims' responses to victimization or interventions to help victims.

Current interest in the sequelae of victimization has stemmed mainly from the concerns of citizen-victims, practitioners, and victim assistance organizations about the observed neglect of and insensitivity to victims' problems and the ways in which the callous handling of victims by the criminal justice system exacerbates victims' difficulties. . . .

Criminology

. . . Victimization surveys have been conducted to gauge the extent and costs of crime. . . . Researchers have been concerned with the amount of crime and the numbers of victims (Penick and Owens 1976; Sparks 1982), the social ecology of victimization (Gottfredson and Gottfredson 1985), aspects of lifestyle that increase or decrease the likelihood of victimization (Hindelang, Gottfredson, and Garofalo 1978), victim precipitation (von Hentig 1948; Wolfgang [1958] 1975), and other ways victims or their circumstances make victimization more likely (Sparks 1982).

These topics are important, for research on them helps us to understand and predict who is typically victimized and where; it helps to explain crime; and it can guide the design and estimate the costs of services for victims or efforts to reduce the risk of victimization. . . . Because the information derived from such research is useful in planning services to help victims, an examination of some of the research results . . . is in order. . . .

Different Groups of People—with Different Social Circumstances and Different Lifestyles—are at Different Risks of Victimization. Hindelang, Gottfredson, and Garofalo (1978) developed a list of eighteen groups differing markedly in likelihood of victimization. For example, divorced or separated females age 65 or older had a victimization likelihood of 30 per 1,000 in a six-month reporting period, whereas males ages 16 to 19 who were not in school had a likelihood of 143 per 1,000. Taken together, the evidence about victimization implies that victims tend to be adolescents or young adults, poor, and more often males than females. In many respects, the personal characteristics of victims in aggregate resemble the personal characteristics of offenders in aggregate (see Gottfredson 1984; Singer 1981).

Implication: Victimization is not independent of lifestyle or patterns of association with others; and services to reduce the negative effects of victimization may have to anticipate and cope with these lifestyles and associations to be realistic and helpful.

Some Persons are at an Elevated Risk of Multiple Victimizations. Sparks (1982) summarized results from a 1972 survey conducted in London implying that 6 percent of persons accounted for 40 percent of the victimizations.[2] Similarly, Hindelang, Gottfredson, and Garofalo (1978) showed that victimizations are not independent and, instead, tend to cluster so that some persons are at greater risk than others of multiple victimizations. . . .

Implication: Although there is a random component in victimization, a small proportion of the population is disproportionately victimized, is in need of assistance, and may be reluctant to seek assistance—or may perceive itself as unable to do so.

Victimization Tends to be an Urban Phenomenon. Rates of victimization are higher for residents of central cities than for suburban or rural populations. The 1983 National Crime Survey rate for crimes of violence was almost twice as high for central city dwellers (43.3 per 1,000 persons age 12 and over) as for those living in nonmetropolitan areas (22.4 per 1,000) (Dodge 1985). Furthermore, whereas about 90 percent of central city residents who were robbed, for example, were robbed in their city of residence, only 54 percent of nonmetropolitan robbery victims were robbed in their *county* of residence (26 percent were robbed in a metropolitan area).

Implication: A disproportionate number of persons who might benefit from victim services live or work in central cities. It may be necessary to locate services in central cities and to plan programs that assist victims to cope with urban lifestyles and risks.

The Range of Victim Responses to being Victimized is Broad. Some victims experience transient distress; others experience severe disorientation, long-lasting distress, and severe mental health difficulties. The proportions of victims experiencing postvictimization difficulties of different types and severities are unknown.

Victimization surveys imply that many victims of crime regard some kinds of victimization as trivial or unimportant events. The most frequent reason given for not reporting a personal victimization involving theft or attempted theft and household crimes is that the crime was not viewed as important enough to report (U.S. Department of Justice 1985). This is the second most frequent reason for not reporting violent crimes (following private or personal matter). Victims' views of the importance of the incident vary, of course, with the [seriousness] of the incident. . . .

Victimization surveys also imply that the majority of victims who report crimes do so because they want help of one kind or another. A large proportion (45 percent) of victims of violent crime reported their victimizations to stop the incidents, to keep such incidents from recurring, or because they needed help as a result of injuries. . . .

The U.S. victimization surveys are poor instruments for assessing the psychological effects of victimization. The 1983 British Crime Survey provided a slightly more useful way of assessing the effects of victimization because it asked about victims' reactions. Mayhew (1984) summarized results for . . . 3,000 British victims: 40 percent reported that their victimizations had not affected them or their households at all, whereas 12 percent reported that they had been affected very much. Two-thirds of the victimizations reportedly caused no emotional upset; one-tenth of the victimizations caused anger, frustration, or annoyance; and one-tenth caused worry, fear, or wariness. The percentages reporting being affected "very much" were 24 percent for burglary victims, 20 percent for victims of vehicle theft, and 30 percent for victims of serious assaults or robberies. Other kinds of information . . . imply that for an unknown fraction of victims of both violent and "nonviolent" crimes the trauma induced by the victimization is great.

Implication: Not all victims of crime want or need assistance, but many do want or need help. Among the more important reasons for notifying the police are a desire to stop or prevent the recurrence of incidents, to get help because of an injury, or to assist in the recovery of losses. Crimes often thought of as nonviolent (such as burglary) can be seriously upsetting.

Most Victimization Experiences are not Reported to the Police. Survey data imply that only about 32 percent of personal events . . . perceived to be crimes by the victims are reported to the police (U.S. Department of Justice 1985). . . . The police are more likely to be called when the crime is more serious or involves greater harm for the victim and when the victim and offender are strangers (Hindelang and Gottfredson 1976). Young victims (ages 12–19) are less likely than older victims, home owners are more likely than renters, and affluent households are more likely than low-income households to report crimes to the police (U.S. Department of Justice 1985).

Many victims of violent crimes do not notify the police because they expect the latter to regard the incident as unimportant or to be insensitive or ineffective; many also think a report would entail too much time or trouble. In all, about 12 percent of victimizations go unreported for such reasons. For another 13 percent of unreported victimizations, victims think a report would be useless for protecting their safety or for recovering lost items.[3]

Implication: It is likely that many victims who could benefit from assistance will not come to the attention of the police. Unless special steps are taken to identify victims of nonstranger crimes and adolescent victims and to provide services to less affluent persons, these groups will tend not to avail themselves of services. Some victims do not seek help because they expect police to be insensitive or ineffective in recovering property or securing their safety or to require too much of their time or trouble.

Crimes Generally Involve Some Form of Interaction between Victim and Offender. Victims' displayed or omitted behaviors plausibly increase or decrease the likelihood of their own victimization. Consistent with criminology's focus on the criminal and the causes of crime, criminologists have often examined the contributions of the interaction between the victim and offender with respect to the crime. Von Hentig (1948) discussed the ways a victim's behavior may define an act as a crime or increase the likelihood that the person would be perceived as a potential victim. . . .

Implication: In most cases of victimization, the victim—either through acts of omission or commission or through some personal characteristic, status, or predicament—has in some sense contributed to his/her own victimization. Police, bystanders, health professionals, family, and victims all notice this fact (and some are predisposed by training to focus on it). In the context of victims' tendencies toward self-blame following victimization, the manner in which communications about victims' contributions to their victimization are handled in a sensitive matter that must be broached adroitly by those coming in contact with the victims as well as by the victims themselves. . . .

. . . [C]riminological research has contributed to understanding the causes of victimization in its pursuit of an explanation of crime, but by focusing on the causes of crime, it has directed attention to victims' contributions to their own victimization while focusing relatively little attention on the consequences of victimization for the victims. Nevertheless, much of the information gained is directly relevant to planning services to help victims cope with those consequences. . . .

The Victims' Movement

The perspective on victims provided by the victims' movement diverges from perspectives traditionally adopted by criminology and the operation of the criminal justice system. The core of this movement is a desire for a more explicit recognition of the victims' injured position, accompanied by a desire for better treatment at the hands of the criminal justice and health systems and the public. The primary image of the victim portrayed in the literature associated with this movement is as an innocent victim of crime[4] who is seriously psychologically injured and is repeatedly reinjured by the callous indifference or ineptitude of criminal justice practitioners and others. Quotations from victims accompanying the report of the President's Task Force on Victims of Crime illustrate the perspective:

> To blame victims for crime is like analyzing the cause of World War II and asking, "What was Pearl Harbor doing in the Pacific, anyway?" (1982, 2)

> I will never forget being raped, kidnapped, and robbed at gunpoint. However, my sense of disillusionment [with] the judicial system is many times more painful. I could not in good faith urge anyone to participate in this hellish process. (1982, 5)
> Why didn't anyone consult me? I was the one who was kidnapped, not the State of Virginia? (1982, 9) . . .

We know little about the proportions of victims of various personally intrusive crimes who experience various degrees of disorientation, self-derogation, social isolation, sleeplessness, fear, etc. Nor do we know much about those factors that predispose some persons to experience a victimization as more traumatic than do others exposed to similar incidents. And we know even less about the typical long-term course of adaptation or reintegration after a traumatic victimization experience. There can be no doubt, however, that serious problems are experienced by many victims. The following sections outline some of what we do know.

PSYCHOLOGICAL HARM

The psychological harm[5] consequent to criminal victimization is often substantial and varies with the nature of the incident, the victim's capacity to cope, and [the] resources available to the victim.[6] . . .

Rape

The responses of rape victims are described more thoroughly than those of any other victims. None of the descriptions is based on representative samples of rape victims, however. The accounts that have received the most attention (Burgess and Holmstrom 1974, 1976, 1979; Symonds 1976) have been based on interviews and clinical work with victims.

Symonds described immediate responses to rape victimization as shock and disbelief followed by near-panic fright. . . . [T]he behavior of most women during their contact with rapists displays traumatic psychological infantilism, which may look like cooperative behavior although it has its roots in "profound primal terror" (1976, 30), with the victim submitting to avoid being killed. He noted that the victims' innocent and unsuspecting behavior—which may have made them vulnerable to the rapist—may "lay the groundwork for persistent guilt and shame" (1976, 33) and that society, the family, and the criminal justice system may contribute to these feelings of guilt and shame.

Burgess and Holmstrom (1974, 1979) reported on the short-term (acute) reactions to rape and the longer-term reorganization. They reported that extreme stress leads initially to "rape trauma syndrome." During this disorganized acute phase, victims may display a controlled style of muted affect or an expressive style characterized by anger, anxiety, crying, embarrassment, fear, humiliation, a desire for revenge, self-blame, or tension. . . .

. . . [C]linical impressions of extreme anxiety or disorganization following rape are supported by quantitative assessments using objective psychological instruments. Kilpatrick, Veronen, and Resick (1979) quantified some aspects of rape victims' reactions by assessing forty-six female victims who had sought counseling or advocacy services from a rape crisis center and who agreed to participate (45 percent) with a battery of psychological tests. They compared these assessment results with those for thirty-five nonvictimized volunteers recruited on the basis of proximity to the victims' homes and similarities in race and age.

The two groups differed dramatically when assessed six to ten days after the incident. . . . [T]he assessment results . . . [showed] that the victims experienced anxiety, fear, mood disturbance, and other symptoms. . . .

Kilpatrick, Veronen, and Resick (1979) also assessed rape victims and comparison women one, three, and six months after the incident. By the time of the three-month assessment, mood disturbances had diminished to the point where, on average, the victims resembled the comparison group. . . .

Kilpatrick, Veronen, and Resick's results implied that by three months the victims had usually "regained their psychological equilibrium" (1979, 668); but the measured differences remaining after six months still showed elevated anxiety—general nervousness, trembling, panic attacks, somatic symptoms, irrational or disproportionate fear, and avoidance behavior. For at least some rape victims, there may be even longer-lasting negative effects.[7] . . .

One of the most important studies of recovery from the reactions to rape over time, by Atkeson et al. (1982), examined the predictors of postvictimization adjustment. . . . The best predictors of . . . long-term depressive symptoms were previctimization psychological problems. Women with prior problems of anxiety, obsessive-compulsive behaviors, depression, poor sexual relations or poor physical health had longer-lasting or more severe postvictimization adjustment difficulties. Older women and women of lower socioeconomic status also tended to have more persistent postvictimization difficulties. In contrast, women who had more support from family and friends recovered more swiftly. Some victims may require treatment for psychological problems they had prior to victimization which may exacerbate or confound the effects of their victimization.

Stressful life events prior to a rape may also influence the victims' ability to cope with the rape. Specifically, Ruch, Chandler, and Harter (1980) found that victims with a history of moderately severe stressful events prior to the rape adjusted somewhat better than those victims with no reported stressful life events or with very stressful life events.

Some victims are victimized repeatedly by rape. Silbert (1984) reported on a group of two hundred prostitutes whose . . . responses to an ad hoc questionnaire administered at intake into a treatment program produced a dramatic portrait of powerlessness, passivity, self-deprecation, and hopelessness combined with extreme guilt and shame. The psychological problems of this group of victims were profound.[8]

A special problem of rape victims is the tendency for such victims to blame themselves for the victimization—a tendency shared and often exacerbated by others. Rape victims' lovers or husbands themselves often have negative reactions to the victimization; and interpersonal difficulties associated with the rape may lead to disrupted relations or divorces (Frieze, Hymer, and Greenberg 1984).

Epidemiology and Processes of Harm and Recovery

Victims' responses to criminal victimization are diverse, ranging from mild transient annoyance to profound psychological disorganization. Like those experiencing other stressful events, victims usually achieve some degree of reorganization within four to six weeks after the incident (Atkeson et al. 1982; Caplan 1964; Lindemann 1944). This reorganization is sometimes adaptive and sometimes maladaptive (Burgess and Holmstrom 1979).

On the basis of the available evidence, the following generalizations appear reasonable. Other things being equal: (a) the more intrusive the incident, the greater the psychological and interpersonal disturbance the victim is likely to experience; (b) the more robust a victim's ability to cope with stressful events in general—that is, the less the victim is distressed prior to the victimization and the less the victim has suffered severely stressful events in the recent past—the less severe the disturbance resulting from a victimization; and (c) the more varied and supportive a victim's resources—that is, friends, money, housing, safety—the more easily and rapidly the victim recovers from the victimization.

The available evidence also appears consistent with the following account of the process through which a victimization experience operates. This process is presumably similar to that operating when other stressful life events are experienced.[9] This account is an interpretation or integration of evidence and theory to explain differences and similarities in victims' responses.

1. The initial reaction to an incident often involves a physiological alarm reaction (Hruza and Poupa 1964) experienced in instances of physical trauma or psychological threat. Sensory input leads to the release of adrenal corticotrophic hormone (ACTH) by the pituitary which leads to increased adrenal secretion with a variety of target tissue effects. Large quantities of adrenaline, noradrenaline, or corticosteroids initially lead to being keyed up, may be followed later by feelings of depression (Selye 1956), and may be accompanied by a variety of physiological and psychological effects (see, for example, Ax 1953; Mason 1975). These physiological responses coexist with and influence victims' cognitive and affective responses to victimization.
2. Most experiences of victimization upset an equilibrium. . . . Disequilibrium defines stress, and the degree of disequilibrium determines the degree of stress (cf. Lazarus 1961). The task of a victim experiencing stress is to restore equilibrium.
3. Crimes differ in the extent to which they are stressful: the most intrusive produce the most stress. They upset a victim's balance in ways most

central to the self as well as the victim's sense of autonomy, order, control, or predictability in ordinary activities central to the victim's identity.

4. Individual differences in initial responses to similar experiences are due to differences in the extent to which (a) the crime is regarded by the victim (consciously or unconsciously) as intrusive and (b) the individual has behavioral repertoires and accessible cognitive structures for restoring equilibrium and interpreting the event. Individual differences in personality organization—acquired in a constructive process of learning and organizing experience—help explain why some people have more severe reactions than others to an apparently similar event.
5. Stress persists when the conditions producing it exceed the capacity of a victim to cope with, interpret, or adjust the situation to restore a psychological or physiological equilibrium. . . .
6. Individual differences in the capacity to cope with disequilibrating experiences are due, in part, to previously acquired behavioral repertoires; the assistance of others in helping the victim interpret the event; and the number, intrusiveness, and degree of novelty of such experiences. Among the individual differences of importance in coping with disequilibrating experiences are differences in the propensity to seek help or to experiment with alternative behaviors.
7. Individuals learn that certain cognitions or behaviors reduce stress to some degree. The more successful recovery involves learning that reduces stress to previctimization levels; the less successful recovery involves learning that reduces stress, but not to previctimization levels. . . .

SOME CHALLENGES

The existing knowledge and its limitations present a number of challenges for criminology and related disciplines . . . and for the criminal justice system. These challenges involve (a) developing better knowledge about the definition, measurement, and epidemiology of victim harm; (b) developing and evaluating criminal justice system practices that lead to greater victim satisfaction and less trauma for some victims; and (c) designing and evaluating treatment methods and programs to help victims who are most distressed. . . .

THE DESIGN OF PROGRAMS TO HELP VICTIMS

The first issue . . . is to determine which victims the program is to assist. . . . Consider two contrasting populations of rape victims—one composed of victims accosted by strangers and who are at low actuarial risk of suffering repeat victimization, and the other composed of [a] group of street prostitutes . . . who are at high risk of repeat victimizations. Programs to serve these two groups would have different short-term and long-term aims and would require different program designs. . . . Few victim assistance programs are directed at persons at high risk of repeated victimization (Schneider and Schneider 1981), although some programs for battered women are of this type. . . .

Early Intervention to Help

Victims who need help are in greatest need of it during and immediately following the incident. Safety and medical needs, if they exist, require prompt attention. Some victims are psychologically disorganized during an acute crisis stage shortly after their victimization, may feel powerless and guilty, and are often in need of the assistance of others in restoring their sense of control over events, in defining the event and their own part in it in salutary ways, and in compassionately and nonjudgmentally listening to them (rather than imposing judgments or interpretations, blaming the victim for the crime, or rejecting the person or interaction with him or her). . . .

For those persons experiencing extreme stress, some form of resolution or reorganization is likely within four to six weeks (see, for example, Baldwin 1979); and financial hardship, if it exists, also is often transitory (Shapland 1984). Therefore, significant others, criminal justice personnel, and health and mental health professionals are likely to be most helpful if they intervene early.

Persons in Interaction with the Victim

Victims generally interact with friends, relatives, family members, workmates, and so forth. Some victims interact with agents of the criminal justice system . . . ; and a few interact with health or mental health professionals in connection with their victimization. These interactions can help to restore a sense of equilibrium to those who are experiencing extreme stress. Or they can exacerbate victims' distress if they are rejecting or blaming or if they further undermine the victims' sense of control over events. Changes in public attitudes and the practiced behavior of professionals are called for (Gottfredson, Reiser, and Tsegaye-Spates (1987). . . .

Guidelines for the Development of Programs

Any program to assist victims should be based on both a clear conception of the problems the program is intended to address and a set of ideas (theory) about the nature and causes of those problems. These ideas, together with a definition of the population of victims for whom the program is intended, should determine the content, structure, location, and methods for the program. . . .

Because we cannot forecast confidently the consequences of specific reforms and programs, there is now no alternative to regarding all proposed reforms in this area as experiments. If we do so, both knowledge and more useful reforms may evolve.

NOTES

1. For example, Siegel characterized the imbalance this way: "Vulnerable, angry, insecure, selfless, the victim who survives observes a criminal who is fed, housed, given legal, medical, psychological, and psychiatric aid—even education and vocational training. The victim . . . suffers alone" (1983, 1271).

2. This outcome resembles in some respects the often-cited finding of Wolfgang, Figlio, and Sellin (1972) that about 6 percent of young men account for about half of all criminal acts.

3. Criminologists who have studied victims' reasons for reporting or not reporting incidents to the police have examined a limited range of victims' objectives in decision making. Gottfredson and Gottfredson (1980), in pursuing their reasonable suggestion that decisions be evaluated in light of decision makers' aims, tentatively interpreted victims' decision making in terms of a few aims of the criminal justice system (deterrence, incapacitation) as well as "personal utilitarian" aims. No systematic research has examined victim decision making in terms of any aims suggested by other observations about victims. For example, a victim might report a crime to seek validation of a definition of him/herself as a victim of a crime worthy of official note (Maguire 1980) or might not report a crime to avoid the possibility that the police will blame or shame the victim for contributing to the offense (Frieze, Hymer, and Greenberg 1984).

4. According to Bard, "While instances of victims playing a role in their own victimization do exist, the fact that most victims are innocent of any complicity is hardly ever mentioned by those who focus on victim culpability. The research focus on victim precipitation, often by questionable methods, is suspiciously suggestive of victim blaming" (1980, 2). He did not elaborate on what is questionable about the methods.

5. Research about financial and physical harm is not reviewed here. For some evidence on these matters, see Hindelang, Gottfredson, and Garofalo 1978; Mayhew 1984; U.S. Department of Justice 1985; and Zauberman 1984.

6. The effects of mugging are reviewed by Lejeune and Alex in "On Being Mugged: The Event and its Aftermath," on page 148.

7. Of the eighty-one rape victims studied by Burgess and Holmstrom (1979), nine (11 percent) attempted suicide. Furthermore, of the eleven persons lost from their four-to-six-year longitudinal sample, three had died—one by suicide and two from medical complications of alcoholism.

8. Other groups, such as the homeless ("The Homeless" 1986) and battered women (Browne 1983), also experience special problems and difficulties in obtaining help.

9. For theoretical accounts of responses to crises or stress with which the account in the text is related, see Baldwin 1979; Dohrenwend 1978; and Lazarus 1961. The features of criminal victimization that sometimes distinguish it from other stressful events are (a) moral indignation may be involved, (b) there is sometimes stigma attached to the status of the victim, and (c) the interpersonal nature of a crime may undermine social trust.

REFERENCES

Atkeson, B. M., K. S. Calhoun, P. A. Resick, and E. M. Ellis. 1982. Victims of rape: Repeated assessment of depressive symptoms. *Journal of Consulting and Clinical Psychology* 50:96–102.

Ax, A. F. 1953. The physiological differentiation between fear and anger in humans. *Psychosomatic Medicine* 15:433–42.

Baldwin, B. A. 1979. Crisis intervention: An overview of theory and practice. *Counseling Psychologist* 8:43–52.

Bard, M. 1980. Psychology and the study of crime as a stressful life event. *International Journal of Group Tensions* 10:73–85.

Browne, A. 1983. Battered women, the self-defense plea, and the role of the district attorney. Denver: Walker & Associates. Typescript.

Burgess, A. W., and L. L. Holmstrom. 1974. Rape trauma syndrome. *American Journal of Psychiatry*, 131:981–86.

———. 1976. "Coping Behavior of the Rape Victim." *American Journal of Psychiatry* 133:413–18.

———. 1979. "Adaptive Strategies and Recovery from Rape." *American Journal of Psychiatry* 136:1278–82.

Caplan, G. 1964. *Principles of preventive psychiatry*. New York: Basic Books.

Dodge, R. W. 1985. *Locating city, suburban, and rural crime*. Bureau of Justice Statistics Special Report. Washington, D.C.: U.S. Government Printing Office.

Dohrenwend, B. S. 1978. Social stress and community psychology. *American Journal of Community Psychology* 6:1–14.

Dussich, J. P. 1981. Evolving services for crime victims. In *Perspectives on crime victims*, ed. B. Galaway and J. Hudson, 27–32. St. Louis: Mosby.

Frieze, I. H., S. Hymer, and M. S. Greenberg. 1984. Describing the victims of crime and violence. In *Victims of crime and violence*, ed. A. S. Kahn, 19–78. Final report of the American Psychological Association Task Force on Victims of Crime and Violence. Washington, D.C.: American Psychological Association.

Gottfredson, G. D., and D. C. Gottfredson. 1985. *Victimization in schools*. New York: Plenum Press.

Gottfredson, G. D., M. Reiser, and C. R. Tsegaye-Spates. 1987. Psychological help for victims of crime. *Professional Psychology: Research and Practice* 18:316–25.

Gottfredson, M. R. 1984. *Victims of crime: The dimensions of risk*. Home Office Research Study no. 81. London: Her Majesty's Stationery Office.

Gottfredson, M. R., and D. M. Gottfredson. 1980. *Decision making in criminal justice: Toward the rational exercise of discretion*. Cambridge, Mass.: Ballinger.

Hindelang, M. J., and M. R. Gottfredson. 1976. The victim's decision not to invoke the criminal justice process. In *Criminal justice and the victim*, ed. W. F. McDonald, 57–78. Beverly Hills: Sage.

Hindelang. M. J., M. R. Gottfredson, and J. Garofalo. 1978. *Victims of personal crime: An empirical foundation for a theory of personal victimization*. Cambridge, Mass.: Ballinger.

The homeless: Who are they and why are they on the streets? 1986. *Western City* (Sacramento, Calif.), March, 3–6.

Hruza, Z., and O. Poupa. 1964. Injured man. In *Handbook of physiology*, ed. D. B. Dill, 939–48. Baltimore: Williams & Wilkins.

Kilpatrick, D. G., L. J. Veronen, and P. A. Resick. 1979. The aftermath of rape: Recent empirical findings. *American Journal of Orthopsychiatry* 49:658–69.

Lazarus, R. S. 1961. *Adjustment and personality*. New York: McGraw-Hill.
Lindemann, E. 1944. Symptomatology and management of acute grief. *American Journal of Psychiatry* 101:141–48.
Maguire, M. 1980. The impact of burglary upon victims. *British Journal of Criminology* 20:261–75.
Mason, J. W. 1975. A historical view of the stress field; part 2. *Journal of Human Stress* 1:22–36.
Mayhew, P. 1984. *The effects of crime: Victims, the public and fear*. Strasbourg: Council of Europe, Sixteenth Criminological Research Conference.
Penick, B. K. E., and M. E. B. Owens III. 1976. *Surveying crime*. Report of the National Research Council Panel for the Evaluation of Crime Surveys. Washington, D.C.: National Academy of Sciences.
President's Task Force on Victims of Crime. 1982. *Final report*. Washington, D.C.: President's Task Force on Victims of Crime.
Ruch, L. O., S. M. Chandler, and R. A. Harter. 1980. Life change and rape impact. *Journal of Health and Social Behavior* 21:248–60.
Schneider, A. L., and P. R. Schneider. 1981. Victims assistance programs. In *Perspectives on crime victims*, ed. B. Galaway and J. Hudson, 364–73. St. Louis: Mosby.
Selye, H. 1956. *The stress of life*. New York: McGraw-Hill.
Shapland, J. 1984. Victims, the criminal justice system and compensation. *British Journal of Criminology* 24:131–49.
Siegel, M. 1983. Crime and violence in America: The victims. *American Psychologist* 38:1267–73.
Silbert, M. H. 1984. Treatment of prostitute victims of sexual assault. In *Victims of sexual aggression: Treatment children, women, and men*, ed. I. R. Stuart and J. G. Greer, 251–82. New York: Van Nostrand Reinhold.
Singer, S. I. 1981. "Homogeneous victim–offender populations: A review and some research implications." *Journal of Criminal Law and Criminology* 72:779–88.
Sparks, R. F. 1982. *Research on victims of crime: Accomplishments, issues, and new directions*. Rockville, Md.: U.S. Department of Health and Human Services.
Symonds, M. 1976. The rape victim: Psychological patterns of response. *American Journal of Psychoanalysis* 36:27–34.
U.S. Department of Justice, Bureau of Justice Statistics. 1985. *Criminal victimization in the United States, 1983*. Washington, D.C.: U.S. Government Printing Office.
Von Hentig, H. 1948. *The criminal and his victim: Studies in the sociobiology of crime*. New Haven: Yale University Press.
Wolfgang, M. E. [1958] 1975. *Patterns in criminal homicide*. Reprint. Montclair, N.J.: Patterson Smith.
Wolfgang, M. E., R. M. Figlio, and T. Sellin. 1972. *Delinquency in a birth cohort*. Chicago: University of Chicago Press.
Zauberman, R. 1984. *Sources d'information sur les victimes et problemes methologiques dans ce domaine*. Strasbourg: Council of Europe, Sixteenth Criminological Research Conference.

Part 3

Collective and Political Violence

*C*ompeting social, economic, and political interests have sparked some of the most brutal and divisive disorders experienced by our nation. These divergent and often antagonistic interests have periodically resulted in collective violence.

American Labor Violence

Some of the most protracted violence in American history has centered around the workplace—the rights and responsibilities of employers and employees. Indeed, as Philip Taft and Philip Ross note, in "American Labor Violence: Its Causes, Character, and Outcome," "[t]he United States has had the bloodiest and most violent labor history of any industrial nation in the world."

The history of the American labor movement is strewn with deadly incidents. Taft and Ross observe that "labor violence was not confined to certain industries, geographic areas, or specific groups in the labor force. . . ." Most labor violence erupted as part of limited labor disputes involving specific grievances, often resulting from the refusal of management to recognize a union or attempts by management to destroy a union by discharging its leaders. However, both employers and employees have been parties to violent escalations.

The passage of the Wagner Act in 1935, which legally protected and institutionally legitimized the union movement, significantly decreased the extent and ferocity of labor-management disputes. Since the end of the Second World War, labor violence has greatly subsided despite the onset at that time of the most pronounced strike wave in our nation's history. Potentially explosive incidents were defused by legislation, particularly the Taft-Hartley Act, which established specific rules and procedures that were imposed on all legitimate parties to labor negotiations or disputes. The implementation of formal legal means to resolve labor conflict undercut the causes of the most virulent forms of this conflict. On balance, violence rarely succeeded in resolving labor disputes or in advancing the causes of unions and managements.

Tumultuous racial strife has also punctuated our history. Contemporary racial clashes reached their peak levels in the 1960s, resulting in the appointment of several national commissions with mandates to review the origins and extent of these violent disorders and to recommend ways to avoid their future occurrence: the President's Commission on Law Enforcement and Administration of Justice (the Katzenbach Commission, 1967), the National Advisory Commission on Civil Disorders (the Kerner Commission, 1968), and the U.S. National Commission on the Causes and Prevention of Violence (1969).[1] The convergence of opposition to the Vietnam War and of the civil rights movement produced a national resolve to remedy the roots of collective racial and urban violence.

In general, racial violence was considered to have resulted from long-standing institutional impediments to the rightful and equitable participation of minorities in the social, economic, and political structures of American society. Specific grievances focused on deprivations in housing, employment, and educational opportunities. These conclusions by the national commissions were far different from earlier accounts of racial strife that endorsed psychological explanations rooted in theories of personal and collective "pathology."

Collective Violence and the Redress of Grievances

Sandra J. Ball-Rokeach and James F. Short, Jr., emphasize, in "Collective Violence: The Redress of Grievance and Public Policy," that, since the urban racial upheavals of the 1960s, there has been a decline in the number of these violent incidents, despite the absence of a sustained and substantial redress of major social and political discontents. Indeed, Ball-Rokeach and Short present evidence that racial and ethnic minorities have suffered a worsening of conditions in the economic, political, and educational arenas. These conditions have converged to create a large disenfranchised "underclass" characterized by families that are dependent economically on external agencies for support, by a high crime rate, and by the absence of marketable occupational skills. The authors suggest that the underclass, "like other underclasses throughout history, exhibits a sort of political paralysis born of economic dependency and psychological despair." The underclass may be impotent politically both because its members perceive change in life conditions to be impossible and because of a void in political leadership.

Although the political involvement and violent activity of the urban underclass are now dormant, the potential for incendiary racial conflict will remain rife unless grievances are satisfactorily redressed. Ball-Rokeach and Short indicate several directions that a viable remedial policy might take, including the continuation and expansion of affirmative action programs; the contraction of the underclass through educational programs and opportunities; greater attention by the media to the broad socially corrosive effects of the underclass; capitalizing on some of the noteworthy strengths of impoverished communities, such as extended familial bonds and religious and civic organizations; and encouraging reorientations in the criminal justice system away from its current mainstays of coercion and confinement toward rehabilitative goals.

In the American political arena, violence has rarely been used as an acceptable means to facilitate political change or to assume the reins of political power. Since the Civil War, assassination has certainly taken its toll at the apex of our political structure. However, lethal politics has not won widespread appeal in securing political objectives. Richard Maxwell Brown previously reviewed in this volume incidents of American economic uprisings, the episodic embracement of lynch law, and the bitter violent activities of right-wing and, less often, left-wing political extremists. As bloody as these events have been, America has generally been more immune than other nations to violent strife born of political expediency. However, the potential for modern forms of political violence to be cultivated indigenously or to be introduced into or targeted at the United States is significant. It is essential, therefore, that we come to grips with the chief dimensions of political terrorism—"reign of terror" (terror from above or governmental terror) and "state of siege" (terror from below or civilian terror).

Terrorism

Robert H. Kupperman and Darrell M. Trent focus, in "Terrorism: Threat, Reality, and Response," on the historical roots and character of transnational ("state of siege") terrorism. At the heart of transnational terrorism is the attempt to "seek reversals in the system of authority . . ." through the shocking and random use of force and violence. Terrorists attack democracies fundamentally by attempting to force these nations to curtail freedom in the service of securing law and order and, as a consequence of this progressive contraction in liberty, by producing irreparable political cleavages, antagonisms, and oppression. Violence and fear introduced and instilled through the random selection of targets are the political weapons of transnational terrorists. Capturing world attention through well-staged dramatic events that become the focus of the media is the life blood of the terrorist. Without this media coverage, the influence of delimited acts of force and violence would hardly compel significant political change. However, with the implicit assistance of the media, a small number of terrorists can potentially hold hostage the attention of the nations of the world.

Transnational terrorism has had successes. Note the recognition of the Palestinian Liberation Organization by the United Nations in 1974 culminating in the address by Yasir Arafat. The improved training, organization, and cooperation of terrorists at the international level, in conjunction with the widening technologies of violence—chemical, biological, and nuclear—have made transnational terrorism a major potential threat to every nation, including our own.

Minimanual of the Urban Guerrilla

The fervent sense of mission, the absolute dedication to political ideals and goals, and the unequivocal justification for terrorist actions are conveyed vividly by the Brazilian Communist guerrilla strategist Carlos Marighella in his "Minimanual of the Urban Guerrilla." In this widely distributed and read document, Marighella asserts the sanctity of the urban guerrilla cause: "Today to be an assailant or a terrorist is a quality that ennobles any honorable man because it is an act worthy of a revolutionary engaged in armed struggle against the shameful military dictatorship and its monstrosities." The minimanual, which reviews the techniques, technologies, and tactics that are part of the urban guerrilla repertoire, is a classic primer in the who, what, when, where, how, and why of urban warfare.

The Terror Network

Edward S. Herman's "The Real Terror Network" details the historical growth of the political regimes that Marighella and his comrades so violently opposed. Herman argues that "the really massive and significant growth of terrorism since World War II has been carried out by states" as part of the "reign of terror." This strand of political terrorism can be traced back at least to Nazi brutalities and Stalin's bloody purges. Modern state terrorism, the type Marighella targeted in South America, is characterized by institutionalized violence, usually manifested as torture and murder. State terrorism is organized and designed to permit "an elite, local, and multinational [corporation], to operate without constraint from democratic processes." Within an economic and political setting that Herman refers to as the National Security State (NSS), the elites, mainly comprising and dominated by the military, treat the population as the enemy, as a labor source that must be cowered into submission in order to meet the workforce needs of the NSS. Security threats do not, therefore, originate primarily from external loci but from the internal population itself, particularly when that population seeks social, economic, or political redress. In the NSS, police and military personnel are custodians rather than the legally constrained servants of the population.

Herman argues that this "real terror network" of the NSS is more dominant and destructive than the indigenous and spontaneously born guerrilla terrorist groups, which he calls "retail" terrorists. These terrorists, rather than the "wholesale" terrorists of the NSS, most often command the attention of the world media. Both forms of terrorism pose a significant threat and should stir the conscience and and conduct of democratic institutions to enact self-protective and remedial measures.

The Social Dynamics of Terrorism

The roots of terrorism are diverse and deep. In "The Social Dynamics of Terrorism," Austin T. Turk examines some of the social processes which facilitate political violence in general and terrorist violence in particular. Turk first identifies several core aspects of terrorism, which comprise purposive, randomly targeted violence that is initiated and sponsored by a political organization and is intended to strengthen terrorist group resolve and cohesion and to deter political opposition. Social dynamics and relations associated with heightened risks of terrorism include: the awareness and rejection of existing political coercion and social inequality, the presence of a totalitarian political structure, and the deterioration and replacement of traditional authority structures. Turk concludes his analysis by arguing that justifications for the use of terror cannot be found in research studies because such justifications involve moral and political principles. However, Turk does note that, to the extent that viable and legitimated authority structures require negotiation and compromise to prosper and serve wide constituencies, terrorism undermines these processes and, on this ground, is not justifiable.

NOTE

1. President's Commission on Law Enforcement and Administration of Justice, *The Challenge of Crime in a Free Society; Final Report* (Washington, D.C.: U.S. Government Printing Office, 1967); National Advisory Commission on Civil Disorders, *Report* (Washington, D.C.: U.S. Government Printing Office, 1968); and U.S. National Commission on the Causes and Prevention of Violence, *To Establish Justice, to Ensure Domestic Tranquillity; Final Report* (Washington, D.C.: U.S. Government Printing Office, 1969).

Chapter 7
Labor

American Labor Violence: Its Causes, Character, and Outcome

Philip Taft and Philip Ross

*T*he United States has had the bloodiest and most violent labor history of any industrial nation in the world. Labor violence was not confined to certain industries, geographic areas, or specific groups in the labor force, although it has been more frequent in some industries than in others. . . . Native and foreign workers, whites and blacks have at times sought to prevent strike replacements from taking their jobs, and at other times have themselves been the object of attack. With few exceptions, labor violence in the United States arose in specific situations, usually during a labor dispute. The precipitating causes have been attempts by pickets and sympathizers to prevent a plant on strike from being reopened with strikebreakers,[1] or attempts of company guards, police, or even by National Guardsmen to prevent such interference. At different times employers and workers have played the roles of aggressors and victims. Union violence was directed at limited objectives: the prevention of the entrance of strikebreakers or raw materials to a struck plant, or interference with finished products leaving the premises. While the number of seriously injured and killed was high in some of the more serious encounters, labor violence rarely spilled over to other segments of the community.

Strikers, no matter how violent they might be, would virtually always seek to win the sympathy of the community to their side, and therefore attacks or even incitements against those not connected or aiding the employer would be carefully avoided. Such conduct was especially common in the organized strikes, those which were called and directed by a labor organization. Strike violence can therefore be differentiated from violence that is stimulated by general discontent and a feeling of injustice. Moreover, the unions were normally anxious to avoid violence and limit its impact because, simultaneously with the strike, the organization might also be operating under a contract and negotiating with other employers in an attempt to solve differences and promote common interests. Unions seek and must have at least the grudging cooperation of employers. No major labor organization in American history ever advocated violence as a policy, even though the labor organizations recognized that it might be a fact of industrial life.

Trade unions from the beginning of their existence stressed their desire for peaceful relations with employers. However, minority groups within the labor movement or without direct attachment to it advocated the use of violence against established institutions and also against leaders in government, industry, and society. The union leader might hope to avoid violence, but recognized that in the stress of a labor dispute it might be beyond the ability of the union to prevent clashes of varying seriousness. They might erupt spontaneously without plan or purpose in response to an incident on the picket line or provocation. Those who saw in violence a creative force regarded the problem differently; they had no objectives of immediate gain: they were not concerned with public opinion. They were revolutionaries for whom the radical transformation of the economic and social system was the only and all-consuming passion.

The most virulent form of industrial violence occurred in situations in which efforts were made to destroy a functioning union or to deny to a union recognition.

THE INFLUENCE OF IDEOLOGY

There is only a solitary example in American labor history of the advocacy of violence as a method of political and economic change. In the 1880s a branch of anarchism emerged that claimed a connection with organized and unorganized labor and advocated individual terror and revolution by force. The principle of "propaganda by the deed," first promulgated at the anarchist congress in Berne, Switzerland in 1876, was based upon the assumption that peaceful appeals were inadequate to rouse the masses. This view could be interpreted as a call upon workers to create their own independent institutions, such as trade unions, mutual aid societies, and producer and consumer cooperatives. However, almost from the beginning this doctrine was interpreted to mean engaging in insurrectionary and putschist activities, and in terror directed against the individual.[2] . . .

The anarchists were not all of the same view, but many of them . . . not only advocated the formation of armed societies, but published materials on the making of explosives. *Revolutionary War Science (Revolutionare Kriegswissenschaft)* is a treatise on the use of arms and the making of what we would call "Molotov cocktails." There is little evidence that these suggestions were ever taken seriously by many workers, and the anarchist movement's greatest influence in the United States was in the 1880s. Even at the height of their influence the anarchists had few supporters. . . . In fact, even then it was widely believed that the armed societies were engaging in playing a game, and that they represented little danger to the community. . . .

THE PRACTICE OF VIOLENCE IN THE 1870S[,] . . . 1880S [AND 1890S]

Repudiation of theories did not eliminate the practice of violence from the American labor scene. The pervasiveness of violence in American labor disputes appears paradoxical because the great majority of American workers have never supported views or ideologies that justified the use of force as a means of reform or basic social change, nor have American workers normally engaged in the kind of political activity that calls for demonstrations or for physical confrontation with opponents. Through most of its history, organized labor in the United States has depended largely upon economic organizations—unions—for advancement through collective bargaining, and upon pressure politics and cooperation with the old parties for achieving its political aims. Yet we are continually confronted with examples of violent confrontations between labor and management. Does industrial violence reveal a common characteristic with basic causes and persistent patterns of behavior, or is it a series of incidents linked only by violence? . . .

The riots of 1877 mirrored deeply felt grievances generated by several years of unemployment and wage cuts. . . . [They] were . . . a violent protest against deteriorating conditions and the suffering and misery endured during a great depression. The widespread and ferocious reaction has no parallel in our history, but there are others of lesser magnitude that were important in shaping labor-management relations.[3]

There is no evidence that [these] riots . . . brought reforms in the handling of railroad disputes, which was the initial cause of the disturbances. They did demonstrate that the United States would not escape the trials and tribulations affecting other industrial nations, and that more attention must be given to the problems that industrial societies tend to generate. . . .

Not all violence was inspired by employers. While employer obduracy might lead to rejection of recognition, such conduct was in itself legally permissible. Had workers passively accepted such decisions, the level of violence in American labor disputes would have been reduced. Workers were, however, unwilling to watch their jobs forfeited to local or imported strikebreakers. Employers could shut down their plants and attempt "to starve" their employees out of the union. Such a policy might have worked, but employers cognizant of their rights and costs frequently refused to follow such a self-denying tactic. As a consequence violence initiated from the labor side was also prevalent. In the 1890s violent outbreaks occurred in the North, South, and West, in small communities and metropolitan cities, testifying to the common attitudes of Americans in every part of the United States. While workers might react against the denial of what they regarded as their rights, the outcome of their violent behavior seldom changed the course of events.

In Homestead, Pa., the domineering head of the Carnegie Steel Co., Henry C. Frick, used a difference over wages and a contract expiration date as an excuse for breaking with the union. When the union called a strike against the demands of Frick, the latter was ready to bring in a bargeload of Pinkerton operatives to guard his plant from the harassment of union pickets. Frick's plan became known, and the guards were met by several hundred steelworkers. In the battle to land the guards from the barges, two Pinkertons and two strikers were killed. Another attempt to land also ended in failure. Eventually the Pinkertons were forced to surrender and some were severely mauled by strikers and sympathizers. At the plea of the sheriff, the governor ordered 7,000 troops to Homestead. . . .

While the violence was temporarily successful in holding off the landing attempted on July 4, it was unable to change the outcome of the contest between the union and Frick. Under the cover of the protection given to him by the National Guard, he was able to open his mills. Furnaces were lit on July 15, and the company announced that applications for work would be received until July 21. The following day a large force of nonunion men entered the plant. Ultimately the union was defeated, and according to a leading student of the steel industry of another generation, John A. Fitch, the union never recovered from its defeat in Homestead. . . .

THE DECADE BETWEEN 1900 AND 1910

The first decade of the twentieth century witnessed expansion of union membership, which increased opportunities for conflicts with employers. As in previous periods, strikes were on occasion marked by violence. The prospect of violence was heightened by rising employer resistance to union objectives. . .

. . . Through the 1870s the Pennsylvania anthracite area was dominated by English-speaking workers: Americans, English, Scotch, Irish, and Welsh were the principal sources of labor.[4] By 1900, large numbers of eastern and southern Europeans had come into the area, and the English-speaking ratio in the population had dropped from 94 percent in 1880 to 52 percent in 1900.[5] With the destruction of the Knights of Labor and the Amalgamated Association of Anthracite Miners, no counterweight to the companies' power existed. Absence of checkweighmen, the existence of the company store, and the complete domination of the area by the coal companies were unrestrained evils. Nothing better demonstrates the abuse of power than an attack in 1897 upon miners who had struck against the high prices at the company store and were peacefully marching from Hazleton to Latimer. The sheriff and a force of deputies met the marchers on the road and ordered them to disperse. When they failed to obey instantly, the sheriff ordered his deputies to fire on the unresisting paraders. Eighteen were killed and 40 seriously wounded, and many of the killed and wounded were shot in the back. The sheriff and several deputies were tried for murder, but were acquitted.[6] . . .

The use of force to settle differences was more common in the Western mining camps at the turn of the century than in Eastern manufacturing or even mining communities. In the West there was a tendency for violence to erupt on a larger scale. The tendency for each side to resort to force to settle differences led to a gradual escalation of the level of violence, which reached a point where the Western Federation of Miners faced the combined power of the Mine Operator's Association, aided by the state government and a private employer's group, the militant Citizen's Alliance. It was an unequal struggle in which men were killed and maimed: union miners imprisoned in the bullpen; union halls, newspapers, and cooperatives sacked; and many strikers deported. There is no episode in American labor history in which violence was as systematically used by employers as in the Colorado labor war of 1903 and 1904. The miners fought back with a ferocity born of desperation, but their use of rifles and dynamite did not prevent their utter defeat. . . .

The Chicago teamsters' strike of 1905 was one of the more violent of the decade. Although it lacked the dramatic confrontations typical of the Western mining camps, the strikers' constant clashes with strikebreakers, guards, and police resulted in a number of deaths, hundreds of injuries, and the arrest of 1,108 persons. . . . The entire business community was united against the union, and hundreds of thousands of dollars were raised to fight the walkout. In the end, the union was forced to surrender without attaining any of its demands. . . .

Many disputes in this period took place which failed to attract national attention because of the fewer numbers of employees involved and the smaller economic importance of the firms. The significance of these minor strikes lies not only in their demonstration of the ease with which violence arose in the industrial arena, but in the dispersion of violence in virtually every part of the country. No region or industry can claim a monopoly on violent confrontation, although labor disputes in some industries were more susceptible to the exercise of force. . . .

Despite explicit repudiation of force as an accepted tactic, a number of unions pursued systematic campaigns against opponents. These campaigns were directed against workers who refused to join a given labor organization, against employers, or both. One such campaign was carried on by the Western Federation of Miners against mine managers, company agents, and public officials. Harry Orchard, a member of the federation, confessed to the commission of many crimes, including the murder of Governor Frank Steunenberg of Idaho on December 30, 1905, at the alleged orders of the chief union officers.

The outstanding example of a campaign of force is the one conducted by the International Association of Bridge Structural Iron Workers in the first decade of the century against some employers. When the National Erectors' Association decided in 1906 that it would no longer continue its agreement with the union, the latter turned to terror and dynamite. In the first few years of the open-shop fight, about 100 nonunion ironworkers and company guards were assaulted, three guards being killed. Between 1906 and 1911, about 100 structures were damaged or destroyed by charges of explosives.[7] . . .

INDUSTRIAL VIOLENCE 1911–1916

These six years rank among the most violent in American history, except for the Civil War. Although the origins of violent encounters were not different from those in the past, they frequently attained a virulence seldom equaled in industrial warfare in any nation. This was as true of many small disputes as it was of the major confrontations in Michigan copper and the West Virginia and Colorado coalfields. . . .

The textile strike in Lawrence, Mass., including more than 25,000 workers, was the most important [Industrial Workers of the World]-led strike and made a deep impression on contemporary observers.[8] Refusal of employers to offset the loss of wages that followed the reduction of hours required for women workers by a recently enacted law was the cause of the walkout on January 11, 1912. As the workers belonged to no union, they invited the general organizer of the IWW, Joseph Ettor, to aid them. He succeeded in having specific demands formulated and presented to each employer of the strikers. Troops were sent into the city, and their number was increased as the strike continued. At the same time, the governor of Massachusetts sought to have the state board of arbitration settle the dispute. The strikers were willing, but the American Woolen Co., the largest employer, refused to participate. A number of clashes between pickets and the militia took place, and in one a woman was killed. The strike continued until March 12, and was ended by the offer of a wage increase. Although the strike was a victory for the textile workers, the IWW was unable to gain a permanent foothold in Lawrence or in the textile industry. . . .

. . . The West Virginia and Colorado coal strikes of 1912–1914 were fought with an unrelenting fury that shocked the conscience of the country. Since 1897 the United Mine Workers of America had held contracts for the majority of bituminous coal miners, but union efforts to organize the expanding West Virginia mines failed a number of times after the beginning of the central competitive field agreement in 1898. Conscious that the failure to organize West Virginia constituted a serious threat to the union-held fields, the union sought greater recognition in the Paint Creek district, and a wage increase. Rejection by the operators led to a strike on April 20, 1912. Later the miners in the Cabin Creek district joined the walkout.

Guards provided by the Baldwin-Felts detective agency entered the area in large numbers and began evicting strikers from company-owned houses. On June 5, the first miner was killed, and nine guards were indicted for murder. Miners and Baldwin-Felts guards fought a pitched battle at Mucklow, on July 26, in which twelve men, mostly guards, were killed. The governor sent several companies of militia into the strike area, and arrests of strikers began. The military force was withdrawn at the end of 30 days, but with an increase in violence, it was reimposed on October 12. . . .

. . . The Colorado coal industry was virtually nonunion. A number of efforts to establish collective-bargaining relations had been made, but all failed. In 1913 the United Mine Workers of America tried again, and Frank J. Hayes, vice president of the union, came to Colorado and enlisted the aid of Governor Elias Ammons towards obtaining a conference with the mine operators. The governor tried and failed. Further efforts to gain a conference were made by the union, and when they did not succeed, a strike was called on September 25, 1913. An estimated 8,000 to 10,000 miners left their jobs, and they and their families left their company-owned houses for the tent colonies which the union rented. In the meantime the companies had been preparing for the strike. . . . On October 7, 1913, after an exchange of shots between strikers and guards, the latter attacked the tent colony at Ludlow and killed a miner. . . . Another battle between strikers and guards was fought there without reported casualties. An armored train, the "death special," was outfitted and while on the way to Ludlow, it was shot up by armed miners who killed the engineer. The train was forced back. . . .

While the fighting was going on, Governor Ammons was trying to bring about a settlement. Failing in the attempt, he sent the entire National Guard to the strike zone. . . . At the request of the state federation of labor, the governor appointed an investigating committee, which found that militia men had abused strikers and their wives and daughters. . . .

During February and March of 1914 there were few clashes, but it was believed that the presence of a congressional investigating committee in the state had a moderating influence on behavior. . . . [T]he Colorado labor movement notified President Woodrow Wilson that it had called on the workers of the state to arm themselves and . . . organize . . . to protect the workers of Colorado. . . . In one action, 200 armed strikers left their base near Trinidad and attacked the mining camp at Forbes. Burning buildings, they poured deadly fire into the camp, killing nine guards and one strikebreaker; the strikers lost one man. Twenty-four hours later, federal troops arrived, and the fighting ended. "During the ten days of fighting, at least fifty persons had lost their lives, including twenty-one killed at Ludlow."[9] The Ludlow war ended with a total of 74 dead. Despite the bloodshed, no recognition of the union was granted. . . .

VIOLENCE IN LABOR DISPUTES DURING AND AFTER THE FIRST WORLD WAR (1917–1922)

. . . The number of strikes between 1917 and 1922 was high compared with the following decade. The influence of wartime demand for labor, the dislocations which accompany wartime economic activity, the sharp rise in union membership, and reduced unemployment all exercised an influence on the potential for labor violence. Strikes tended to be shorter during wartime, but with the ending of hostilities the country experienced severe tension in the labor market. Several factors accounted for heightened labor discontent. Union membership rose sharply between 1916 and 1920, from 2,772,000 to 4,881,000. Considerable dissatisfaction existed as a result of rises in the cost of living during wartime and the general malaise that war normally generates. Many employers who had accepted union organization as a wartime necessity or as a result of government fiat were now anxious to rid themselves of labor organizations. The large accretion of union members also brought demands for changes in union policy and for the use of more aggressive tactics in labor disputes. . . .

The Arizona Deportations

During the First World War, strikes in most of the Arizona copper mines were called by the Industrial Workers of the World, or the International Union of Mine, Mill & Smelter Workers, an affiliate of the American Federation of Labor. A common response of employers was to deport the strike leaders and their followers.

Virtually the entire business and mining employer community participated in the deportations of 1,284 men from Bisbee, Ariz., on July 12, 1917. Great discontent with wages and working conditions existed in the Arizona copper county during 1917 and 1918. . . .

A large proportion of the miners in the Bisbee area responded to the strike call. Testimony showed that there was no violence. . . . On the morning of July 12 the streets of Bisbee were filled with nearly 2,000 men wearing white handkerchiefs on their sleeves. They had been deputized. . . . Men on the street were stopped and their business ascertained. Those unable to give satisfactory explanations were seized and taken to the local ball park which served as the assembly point for "undesirables." Homes of known strikers and sympathizers, including some lawyers, tradesmen, businessmen, and property owners, were visited and many were taken into custody. . . .

. . . [T]he prisoners were compelled to march between two lines of armed men and to board a cattle train which the railroad provided. According to Fred W. Brown, a voluntary organizer of the American Federation of Labor, the tracks along the first stop of the train were "lined with gunmen" who had left Bisbee and had overtaken the train. Mounted guns stood on both sides of the track and no one was allowed to leave. The train arrived in Columbus, stayed for an hour, and left for Hermanes, where the men were dumped. . . .

THE PERIOD BETWEEN 1923 AND 1932

Union membership sharply declined between 1920 and 1923, from the high point of 4,881,000 in 1920 to 3,622,000 in 1923. Union activity similarly declined. Even more consequential than the decline in membership was the loss of elan and confidence that overcame the labor organizations as a result of repeated lost strikes. In effect, the removal of government protection made many of the wartime's gains temporary, and numerous employers reverted to a nonunion status. Although membership did not fluctuate sharply through the rest of the decade, the failure to make substantial gains in a generally prosperous period reflected a low level of organizing capacity, which was in turn a sign of loss of confidence.

The number of strikes dropped sharply, and while they varied from year to year, the number in 1928 was below those of any year of record since 1884. The years from 1920 through 1932 reveal the same experience, a moderate number of strikes. One result was a lowering of the level of industrial violence. . . .

THE NEW DEAL

Between 1933 and 1937 the labor movement underwent profound changes internally as well as in its relations to employers. For the first time in peace-time history, union organizations had the attention and approval of the federal government. Influenced by the labor legislation of the first years of the Roosevelt administration, unions began to expand, and by 1937 more members were enrolled in unions than at any time in history. The increases in union membership were reflected in a doubling of strikes between 1932 and 1933, and another doubling from 2,172 in 1936 to 4,740 in 1937. Almost half of the strikes in 1937 were for union recognition. . . .

The 1934 strike that involved the largest number of workers took place in the cotton textile industry after the convention of the United Textile Workers of America had demanded a general wage increase and other improvements in working conditions. When all proposals for meetings were rejected by the industry, a strike was called on August 31, 1934. The workers in Alabama commenced their walkout earlier, on July 15, and an estimated 20,000 in 28 mills were reported on strike. In Alabama, the president of the Decateur local was shot and two of his aides were beaten. The National Guard was sent to Chambers and Lee counties. In Georgia, complaints of roving pickets were made at the beginning of the strike. Clashes between pickets and strike guards led the governor to proclaim martial law, and to set up an internment camp. . . . Throughout the strike, 5,000 state troops were active in New England, and an estimated 2,000 strikers were interned in Georgia. The strike cost 15 lives, and an unestimated number of wounded by gunfire and other means.[10] The textile strike was completely lost. . . .

. . . The most violent walkouts in 1936 were in the coal, steel, and textile industries, at least from the point of view of persons killed, one or two deaths occurring in each of seven strikes in these and other industries. . . .

By 1937, unions had been for four years the beneficiaries of government legislation to protect their rights to organize and to bargain. Despite this, using the index of people killed in labor disputes, this year was one of the more bloody in the history of American labor violence. One dispute, the Little Steel strike, accounted for 16 deaths and many others seriously injured. In addition, an estimated eight other people died in industrial disturbances.[11] . . .

VIOLENCE IN 1940–1946

By 1940, union organizations entered into a new phase of growth and security. Strikes took on more and more their contemporary character of an economic conflict attended with minor violent episodes. This period was one of serious turbulence in the labor market, and the shift to war production was accompanied by widespread dislocations. The subsequent reconversion to a peacetime economy was a challenge to the new industrial relations. The continual increase in union membership and union strength resulted in record-high numbers of strikes over important issues at the end of this period.

In 1940, there were seven deaths in labor disputes. While people were killed in most of the subsequent years, the incidents which generated violence were sporadic clashes and usually involved few workers. . . .

A rising share of violent clashes was caused by jurisdictional disputes. In June 1940, a nonstriking bus driver, who was a member of the Amalgamated Association of Street Railway & Motor Coach Employees, was killed in a jurisdictional dispute with the Brotherhood of Railroad Trainmen. . . .

THE POST-TAFT-HARTLEY ACT PERIOD (1947–1962)

The passage of the Taft-Hartley Act in 1947 had numerous causes, including a continuing resentment by some employers' groups of the Wagner Act, the post-war strike wave, and patent abuses by some unions. Whatever the consequences of the newly imposed legal restraints upon union activities may have been, the Taft-Hartley Act did not in any significant way diminish the protection accorded to unions by the Wagner Act. . . .

Violence . . . was not completely erased from the labor-management scene and several strikes appeared to resemble outwardly the industrial disputes of another day. However, even those in which violence took place lacked the ferocity of the battles of the pre-Wagner Act days. These incidents seem to demonstrate that the potential for violence is always present in industrial disputes in the United States, but they do not, in most instances, show the relentless bitterness of Homestead, Pullman, Ludlow, and many other affrays which desecrated the industrial landscape of earlier periods. Using fatalities as an index of violence, the comparative numbers are very small considering the high number of labor disputes. . . .

CONTEMPORARY VIOLENCE

The most informative source of the extent of contemporary violence is found in the records of the National Labor Relations Board. . . .

An example of present-day violence occurred during a labor conflict between District 50, United Mine Workers, and a manufacturer of iron castings in a small Michigan city. Despite a long history of collective bargaining, a strike of the 85 employees for a new contract that took place on March 13, 1967, lost its peaceful character on March 30 when some pickets were armed with baseball bats. It was alleged that an employer representative and two strike replacements were assaulted by several pickets and formal complaints were made to the police. The employer had been operating the plant at a reduced scale using supervisors and hiring strike replacements from any source. The alleged assailants were not union officers, but the Board imputed agency responsibility to the union on the grounds that this conduct took place under a controlled picket line. . . .

The pattern of illegal activities which constitutes violence and coercion subject to the jurisdiction of the Labor Board rarely varies. Frequently there is some blocking of plant ingress and egress, occasionally the laying of nails "by persons unknown" on the plant driveway, sometimes allegations that sugar or other foreign material is put in the gas tanks of company and nonstriking employees' vehicles, accusations of object throwing which may include rocks, eggs, or paint, some physical scuffling or pushing, and always the making of threats. Damage to company plant is rarely observable in these cases, although vehicles standing in the street appear to be fair game. In very few cases does more violence take place, such as physical assaults or the following and harassing of drivers of company trucks on the highway and at stops. . . .

The diminution of the level of violence is attested to by its relatively scant treatment in congressional hearings since 1947. The essential concern of proponents of labor reform during the Taft-Hartley hearings was to deprive employees guilty of violence, threats, sitdown mass picketing, and other forms of intimidation of their reinstatement rights. . . .

A fundamental purpose of the national labor policy, first enunciated by the Wagner Act and confirmed by its subsequent amendments in the Taft-Hartley and Landrum-Griffin Acts, was the substitution of orderly procedures for trials of combat. But in balancing the public interest in the peaceful settlement of industrial disputes with the freedom of labor and management to work out their problems in light of their needs and experience, the law did not outlaw the exercise of economic force.

. . . Because employer refusal to meet and deal with unions was the major cause of past violent labor strikes, the effective enforcement of the Wagner Act reduced sharply the number of such encounters. This diminution of labor violence was not a temporary phenomenon but endured the strains of major and minor wars, a number of business cycles, and substantial changes in national and local political administrations. Moreover, the social and economic environment in post-New Deal America was scarcely conducive to the pacific resolution of disputes of any kind. The reconversion of American industry after the Second World War brought on the greatest strike wave in our history. Yet, these mammoth strikes were accompanied by virtually no violence, completely at variance with the experience after 1918. . . .

SUMMARY AND CONCLUSIONS

The Persistence of Violence

We are . . . confronted with a paradox in that violence in labor disputes persisted even though it seldom achieved fruitful results. With few exceptions, labor violence was the result of isolated and usually unplanned acts on a picket line, or occurred during a prohibited parade or demonstration protesting employer obduracy or police brutality. It might also start by attempts of pickets to prevent the transportation of strikebreakers or goods, and a clash would follow police intervention. Where the employer refused to deal with the union, the possibility of eventual violence was always high. The desire of the American worker for union representation took place in the teeth of employer opposition that was able to impose heavy sanctions for union activity. The reproduction of conditions in which violence is spawned inevitably was followed by outbreaks of violence. Violence could be successfully repressed by superior forces but it could not be eliminated until its causes were removed.

The Reduction in Violence

The elimination in 1933 of the most important single cause of violence, refusal to recognize the union for purposes of collective bargaining, came about at the time when union membership was lower than it had been for 15 years. The first step taken was the adoption of section (7)(a) in the National Industrial Recovery Act, which guaranteed workers in industries operating under codes of fair competition the right to organize and bargain collectively through their own representatives. . . . Its successor, the National Labor Relations Act, with its amendments, has been on the books and upheld by the Supreme Court for almost a half a century. The sharp decline in the level of industrial violence is one of the great achievements of the National Labor Relations Board.

It may have been a fortunate coincidence that the labor laws guaranteeing the right to organize were enacted at the time the character of business management was changing. The professional business executive, who has increasingly come to dominate management, is not inclined to regard his business in the same sense as the head of a family-developed firm. He is more flexible in his thinking and more responsive to social and political changes. It may not be an accident that some of the bitterest contemporary labor disputes—Kohler and Perfect Circle, for example—took place in family-held businesses. The professional business leader is more detached, more pragmatic in his reactions, and knows that American business has sufficient resilience to adapt itself to free collective bargaining. The performance of American industry since the end of the Second World War demonstrates that union organization and collective bargaining are not incompatible with satisfactory profits and a high rate of technological change. . . .

NOTES

1. For a long period of time strikebreakers were not regarded as replacements.
2. Jean Maitron, *Histoire du Mouvement Anarchiste in France* (Paris: Societe Universitaire D'Editions et de Libraire, 1961), 67–69.
3. See Robert V. Bruce, *1877: Year of Violence* (Indianapolis: Bobbs Merrill, 1959); J.A. Dacus. *Annals of the Great Strikes* (St. Louis: Schammell, 1877); Edward Winslow Martin. *The History of the Great Riots* (Philadelphia: National Publishing Co., 1877).
4. The Molly McGuires, a terrorist organization that operated in the anthracite area at this time, was not a bargaining organization. Made up of Irish miners, it exercised vengeance against arrogant mine bosses of British origin and others who came into its disfavor. It did not direct demands for improvements in working conditions, although it issued warnings against oppressors. Whatever its connection with the labor movement may have been, we know that this group was destroyed and many of its leaders hanged.
5. Frank Julian Warne, *The Coal Mine Workers* (New York: Longmans, 1905).
6. New York *World*, Sept. 11–12, 1897. Also see Edward Pinkowski, *The Latimer Massacre* (Philadelphia: Sunshine Press, 1950).
7. Luke Grant, *The National Erectors' Association and the International Association of Bridge and Structural Iron Workers* (Washington: U.S. Commission on Industrial Relations, 1915), especially 107–148.
8. *Annual Report of the State Board of Conciliation and Arbitration in Massachusetts, 1912*, 31; *Report of Massachusetts Adjutant General for 1912*, 7; *Report on Textile*

Strike in Lawrence, Massachusetts, S. Doc. 870, 62d Cong., 2d session; *Hearings on the Strike at Lawrence, Massachusetts*, H. Doc. 671, 62d Cong., 2d sess.

9. George P. West, *Report on the Colorado Strike* (Washington: U.S. Commission on Industrial Relations, 1915), . . . 135. West was an investigator for the U.S. Commission on Industrial Relations and was acquainted with the facts.

10. *Report of the Adjutant General of the State of North Carolina, January 1, 1933–December 31, 1935*, . . . 447–449. See also *New York Times* through August and September 1934 for detailed coverage of the textile strike situation.

11. President Thomas Girdler, of the Republic Steel Co., testified before the La Follette Committee in August 1938, and stated that his industrial relations policy had succeeded. Senator Robert M. La Follette commented: "Mr. Girdler, in connection with the success of his industrial-relation policy, the record of this investigation shows that the steel strike of 1937 cost the country sixteen lives and 307 persons were injured." *Hearings before a Subcommittee on Education and Labor*, U.S. Senate, 75th Cong., 3d sess., pt. 34, 13889.

Chapter 8

Riots: Urban and Racial

Collective Violence: The Redress of Grievance and Public Policy

Sandra J. Ball-Rokeach and James F. Short, Jr.

CONCLUSIONS AND RECOMMENDATIONS OF THE VIOLENCE, KERNER, AND CRIME COMMISSIONS

The National Commission on the Causes and Prevention of Violence (Violence Commission) was appointed by President Johnson in June 1968 following the assassinations of Martin Luther King and Senator Robert Kennedy. Its charge was broad, encompassing the many individual as well as collective acts of violence in American life. The Violence Commission's inquiry focused on collective violence associated with two phenomena: opposition to the Vietnam War, leading to violence on college campuses . . . and urban violence linked to racial inequality in Cleveland. . . . The history of collective violence in America . . . and the role of the mass media in collective violence . . . were also examined.

After noting that collective violence in this country is a relatively rare outcome of the exercise of the constitutional right of assembly to petition for redress of grievances, the commissioners put forth several conclusions about the causes of collective violence. President Johnson's suspicion at the time that collective violence was caused by an organized group of conspirators who held no allegiance to the democratic process was soundly rejected. To the contrary, the commissioners located the chief cause of both student and urban group violence in failures of the political system that either blocked legitimate expression of grievances or prevented decision makers from recognizing and effectively responding to legitimate grievances. Collective violence, then, was first and foremost a product of breakdown in the democratic process that prevented rightful participation of groups in decisions affecting their lives. Violence as a response to threatened loss of status and position in life was also noted. . . .

More proximate grievances giving rise to collective violence in the ghetto included deprivation in housing, employment, and educational opportunities. Finally, weak or inconsistent social control policies and practices were identified as important factors that could transform peaceful protest in the ghetto and on the campus into collective violence.

The recommendations of the Violence Commission pertaining to the prevention of collective violence were formulated to achieve three basic goals—"controlling disorder, keeping open the channels of protest, and correcting social injustices." . . .

The Commission on Civil Disorders (Kerner Commission), formed one year earlier than the Violence Commission, also was appointed by President Johnson. This commission was charged specifically with the task of determining what had happened in the urban disorders of the 1960s in Detroit, Newark, and other cities, why they happened, and how such civil disorders could be prevented in the future. In the summer of 1967, at least 150 cities reported civil disorders, most of which occurred in the black ghettos of these cities. A mounting wave of "burn, baby, burn" swept the nation, leaving fear in its wake.

The Kerner Commission's hallmark analysis of twenty-four of the most destructive urban disorders produced a startling conclusion: the most basic cause of the disorders was that "our nation is moving toward two societies, one black, one white—separate and unequal." The term *institutionalized racism* captures the central diagnosis of the problem in the Kerner Commission report. Consistent with this diagnosis, the dominant motive attributed to rioters was to have their piece of the American pie—material and political resources that were being denied them by a white society ruled by the ideology and the practices of institutionalized racism. . . . Having thus spoken to the very fabric of American society, the commissioners put forth an equally monumental set of recommendations as to how civil disorders might be prevented from happening again.

Many of the recommendations were directed to problems at the local community level. They focused on (1) the creation or improvement of mechanisms for ghetto residents to communicate effectively their needs and grievances to appropriate government agencies and to ensure their participation in policy formation; (2) improvements in the criminal justice system to remove discriminatory practices and to better provide for the everyday security of ghetto residents and for effective control of ghetto disorders; and (3) increasing the quantity and quality of media coverage of ghetto life and the development of informed guidelines as to how the media might ameliorate, rather than exacerbate, crisis situations. The many recommendations for national action to create "a true union—a single society and a single American identity," were aimed at removing barriers to equal opportunity in jobs, education, and housing, designing efficacious means for ghetto residents to participate in the political process, and creating "a common ground" between whites and blacks for mutual respect and joint efforts to achieve both public order and social justice. . . .

The Commission on Law Enforcement and Administration of Justice (Katzenbach Commission), appointed in 1965, was the first of the 1960s commissions to work in an era when both crime and the law-and-order theme in American politics were on the rise. . . . Its general theme concerning the causes and prevention of crime, however, is similar to the theoretical stance on the causes and prevention of disorder subsequently found in the reports of the Kerner and Violence commissions.

The common theme is that the roots of crime and disorder lie deep in the social fabric of American society, in its traditions, inequalities, and conflicts, and in ineffective governance. This common theme marked a substantial and significant departure from previous commission statements that emphasized psychological deficits and susceptibility to contagious processes in their accounts of the causes of collective violence and other disorders. Taken together, the Violence, Kerner, and Katzenbach reports articulate a fundamental shift in the political and policymaking spheres away from "psychological disorders" to "social disorders" as the primary causal nexus of both individual and collective violence. . . .

COLLECTIVE VIOLENCE IN THE DECADE OF THE SEVENTIES: CONTINUED GRIEVANCE, LITTLE REDRESS

For analysts of collective violence, the most glaring fact of the last decade is the rapid decline of urban disorders after 1968. The seventies were a decade of uneasy quiet when collective protest steadily declined on college campuses and riots virtually ceased in urban ghettos. It would be sheer sophistry to contend that these developments were due to the removal of the major social causes of collective violence identified by the Violence and Kerner commissions. So how can we explain the pattern of declining collective violence? In this section we seek to address, if not solve, this puzzle.

. . . If the common thrusts of the Violence and Kerner commission reports provide a theory that can account for the high incidence of such urban violence in the 1960s *and* its markedly lower incidence in the 1970s, then substantial progress should be apparent in removing or ameliorating the causal conditions identified as responsible for the violence of the sixties. In the broadest sense, we might expect to find a substantial reduction in the institutionalized racism that had split America into two societies of advantaged whites and disadvantaged blacks. More specifically, we should observe steady improvements in the economic, political, familial, educational, and law enforcement conditions of the urban ghetto.

Economic Conditions

Some progress has been made. Sociologist William Wilson . . . notes that the number of blacks in managerial and professional jobs was 1.6 million in 1979, double the number in 1969.[1] However, total black unemployment in April 1982 was 18.4 percent, rising from 8.2 percent in 1970.[2] Overall increases in unemployment do not account for this rise as the comparable figures for whites are 4.5 percent and 8.4 percent, respectively.[3] Thus, the ratio of black to white unemployment rates has deteriorated from 1.8 in 1970 to 2.19 in April 1982.[4] The black unemployed are also more heavily concentrated in urban ghettos than are whites. ... Employment opportunities for low-income blacks have declined as cities have lost the goods-producing jobs that have been occupied by urban blacks in the past. ... Finally, there is the much publicized fact that the unemployment problem is most severe for black teenagers (sixteen to nineteen years old).[5] ... That black poverty is still very much a feature of the urban ghetto is evidenced by the fact that 85.1 percent of all black families with yearly incomes under $4,000 in 1978 were families headed by women living in metropolitan areas.[6] Such concentration of poverty is not so evident for whites. ...

There is ... disturbing evidence that for many in the United States poverty is a permanent condition and that for minorities the likelihood of permanent poverty is far greater than it is for the majority. ... [S]ociologist Lee Rainwater ... finds that over the 1967–76 decade he analyzed, 9.4 percent of the sample were "always poor" and an additional 7.1 percent were "near poor when not poor." Among young people, eighteen to twenty-four years old, "the likelihood of being poor or near poor was eight times greater for minority than for majority youth, and between the ages of twenty-five to fifty-four, the odds were seven times greater for minority people."[7]

Political Conditions

Following passage of the Voting Rights Act of 1965, the number of blacks holding elective office in the United States increased rapidly, from 100 to 1,813 in 1980.[8] Unfortunately, these increases occurred during a period of increasing economic stress and the federal pullback from federal programs designed to aid cities under the Great Society and its War on Poverty. Goods-producing industry, the traditional economic and occupational base of many cities, was in many cases leaving the central city, thus weakening both the economic base of cities and occupational opportunities for ghetto residents. The dismantling of federal programs designed to aid cities has had consequences, not only with respect to services, jobs, and training opportunities for ghetto residents, but for employment of the black middle class as well. This, in turn, removes from the black community many government representatives who might be more sensitive than nonminority government employees to the needs of ghetto residents. ...

On the national level, some of the gains in black political participation, such as the presence of twenty-one blacks in the Ninety-eighth Congress and a rise in voter registration of blacks ... have been threatened by reapportionment and by attempts to undercut the Voting Rights Act. ...

Media

Many hoped that the trend toward concentration of media ownership might be countered by black ownership and operation of cable channels. That hope has not been realized as blacks have lost rights to approximately thirty cable franchises they had acquired in recent years because of insufficient financial resources. The total television station ownership picture is also poor with blacks owning only eight of the approximately one thousand stations nationally.[9] Commission recommendations on vastly increased hiring of blacks in the media have also gone unmet. . . .

Familial Conditions

Sociologist Wilson's analysis notes that the urban family, especially the poor black family, changed for the worse in the decade of the seventies. In 1978, 53 percent of all black births were out of wedlock, and many of the infants were born to teenagers. From 1970 to 1979, the number of households headed by women increased 72.9 percent for blacks and 76.5 percent for Hispanics, compared to 42.1 percent for whites. The proportion of poor black families headed by a female was 74 percent in 1978. More than one-third of all black children under the age of six in 1978 were living in female-headed households with incomes below the poverty level. . . . Finally, the number of black children less than eighteen years old in families receiving aid to families with dependent children went from 35 per thousand in 1960 to 113 per thousand in 1979.[10]

The fact of an astonishing number of female-headed households in the poor areas of cities is literal evidence of family dissolution in the sense that the both-parents-present nuclear family is becoming a rarity for poor urban blacks. . . .

Law Enforcement Conditions

Affirmative action in police hiring became a reality in many cities during the 1970s. A 1969 survey of 254 U.S. cities found the percentage of minority police officers to be 5.1 percent, compared to the minority percentage in the total 1970 population of 16.7 percent in these cities. A 1981 survey of these same cities yielded figures of 11.6 percent minority officers and 27.6 percent minority population. These figures mask much variation, however. The top one-third high-affirmative-action cities in 1981 had increased minority representation on their police forces from an average of 2.6 percent in 1969 to 16.0 percent in 1981. In contrast, the percentage of minority police actually decreased during this period in the one-third low-affirmative-action cities, from 6.2 percent to 5.3 percent. . . .[11]

These figures tell us nothing of the process and the problems associated with integrating police forces or of failing to integrate them. Nor do they reflect changes and problems at other levels of the criminal (and juvenile) justice systems. . . .

The Civil Rights Commission concurred with the Kerner Commission that "racial violence in America almost invariably has occurred when an encounter between law enforcement officers and a member of the black community escalates to physical confrontation."[12] . . .

The commission called for more blacks on the police force, particularly in supervisory positions, and for more black attorneys in the state attorney's office.[13] . . .

Lack of adequate community review of police policies and practices and of procedures for receiving and handling complaints concerning public officials were also noted. . . .

ACCOUNTING FOR THE DECLINE IN COLLECTIVE VIOLENCE

Our analysis of economic, political, familial, and law enforcement conditions in the urban ghetto of the 1970s indicates that the ghetto poor were virtually untouched by the progress that has been made in reducing racial and ethnic discrimination in the economy, in politics, in the media, and in education. We thus face a puzzle of continued, even increasing, grievance and declining attempts to redress grievance through collective protest and violence. We must . . . solve this puzzle by looking to changes in social control, expectations, and economic structure that might account for the decline in collective violence.

Social Control

Of all of the recommendations made by the Violence, Kerner, and Katzenbach reports, those concerning the beefing-up of the arsenal and size of law enforcement agencies received the most extensive financial and political support. . . . [A] tantalizingly straightforward interpretation of the decline in the incidence of collective violence in the 1970s is that enormous federal and local expenditures on law enforcement have had the effect of increasing the *costs* of urban violence. Increased fear of reprisal for collective violence could be one possible factor in the declining incidence of collective violence in the 1970s. But the many indicators of increased crime and other problems in the ghettos suggest that social control per se has done little to alter the internal dynamics or the social fabric of ghetto life. Careful studies by urban ethnographers find that social control in ghetto communities occurs through relationships and institutions quite outside and often in opposition to conventional law enforcement agencies. . . .

Declining Expectations

A common premise in theories of collective violence is that rising expectations in the face of declining resources create the most volatile condition for the emergence of collective violence. We know that the resources of large northern cities have declined, but we do not know whether expectations have also declined, such that residents have become resigned to low-resource conditions. The most obvious change that might have brought about a decline in the expectations is the progressive retreat of federal government policy with respect to problems of cities and minorities. . . .

Economic Structure

Wilson has argued that the poor of the urban ghetto have become an underclass characterized by economic dependency caused by unemployability and community disorganization. . . . The underclass pattern of life is marked by unstable families dependent on external social agencies for economic support, by high crime rates, and by an absence of negotiable occupational skills. . . .

With regard to the question of why collective violence has declined in the urban ghetto of the 1970s, the underclass thesis provides at least two possible insights. One is that the urban ghetto population has become—objectively and subjectively—an underclass that, like other underclasses throughout history, exhibits a sort of political paralysis born of economic dependency and psychological despair. . . . The second and related insight is that the hope that spurs collective action is based on the perception that change is possible, that better conditions can be achieved through collective action. . . . It may be that the urban ghetto has lost much of the organizational infrastructure necessary to sustained collective protest, not only because of the exodus of the black middle class, but also because of the decline of the industrial city as a viable political and economic entity.

Unique Social/Historical Circumstances

[S]ociologist-historian Charles Tilly emphasizes the importance of unique and local political, economic, and social conditions that combine to produce collective actions, including violence.[14] . . . From this perspective, the identification of general causes, such as racial discrimination, necessarily fails to comprehend why collective violence occurs at a particular time and place. Variations in the history and structure of local governments and in police-community conflicts, and their convergence at particular points in time, heighten or lower the probability of collective violence and determine when and how collective action occurs. . . .

VIOLENCE FROM THE RIGHT

Due to a paucity of recent research, we can do little more than draw attention to another potential arena of collective violence—that from the extreme Right of the political spectrum. Conservative theorist Kevin Phillips writes of the "Balkanization of the national spirit" and the "politics of cultural despair" that followed the 1960s and 1970s, a period he (and others) have characterized as two decades of "erosion of American economic productivity, civic commitment and global determination." That period of "breakdown," he suggests, "has left a skittish populace beneath a patina of suburban affluence,"[15] which is likely to be politically unstable and perhaps volatile. While stopping short of predicting the occurrence of increased conflict among interest groups, Phillips points to the similarity of conditions that in the past have led to such conflict. . . .

Ideological rightist movements are apparently suffering from the experience of unmet expectations, expectations that the present federal administration would institute a conservative economics on the one hand and a conservative morality on the other. Insofar as the failure to meet heightened expectations is a condition for the emergence of collective protest and violence, these developments may presage increased activity with the potential for collective violence among far-right groups. . . .

NOTES

1. WIlliam Julius Wilson, *The Declining Significance of Race: Blacks and Changing American Institutions*, 2d ed. (Chicago: University of Chicago Press, 1980).
2. Current Labor Statistics, "Household Data," *Monthly Labor Review*, June 1982.
3. Ibid.
4. Ibid.
5. William Julius Wilson, "The Urban Underclass in Advanced Industrial Society," paper presented at the Future of Our City Conference, University of Chicago, June 1982.
6. Current Labor Statistics, "Household Data."
7. Elizabeth Evanson, "The Dynamics of Poverty," *Focus 5* (Summer 1981).
8. Vernon Jordan, Jr., and John E. Jacob, Introduction to *The State of Black America 1982*, ed. James D. Williams (New York: National Urban League, 1982).
9. Pat Patterson, "Blacks and the Media in the 1980's," in *State of Black America 1982*.
10. Wilson, "The Urban Underclass in Advanced Industrial Society."
11. Nicholas P. Lovrich and Brent S. Steel, "Affirmative Action and Productivity in Law Enforcement Agencies," *Review of Public Personnel Administration*, forthcoming.
12. U.S. Civil Rights Commission, *Confronting Racial Isolation in Miami* (Washington, D.C.: U.S. Government Printing Office, 1982).
13. Other police-related issues include promotion and development policies with respect to minority officers, both of which have been the subject of litigation. Even the actions taken to give more racial balance to police forces sometimes create problems. In 1983, upon achieving an agreed upon level of minority police officers in response to a 1976 court action (*U.S.* v. *City of Miami et al.*, Civil Action #75-3096, U.S. District Court, Southern District of Florida, 1976), the city found itself with a large number of young and relatively inexperienced officers who had great difficulty policing a racially tense city.
14. Charles Tilly, *As Sociology Meets History* (New York: Academic Press, 1981).
15. Kevin Phillips, *Post-Conservative America* (New York: Random House, 1982).

Chapter 9
Terrorism

Terrorism: Threat, Reality, and Response

Robert H. Kupperman and Darrell M. Trent

Terrorism has been correctly described as a strategy of the weak. The relationships of power between a terrorist organization and a sovereign state present a contrast in extremes. Like a muscle-bound giant, a great nation with full military resources can be reduced to impotence. By exploiting legal and cultural traditions that emphasize restraint, fairness, and the sanctity of life, terrorists seek to determine their adversary's response. They play on the inherent tension between freedom and order in all democratic societies.

The strategy of terrorism can be compared with the strategy used in various martial arts: the aim is to turn an opponent's strength against him. Terrorists seek reversals in the system of authority that is the framework of a civilized people—by demanding release for those who have been imprisoned according to due process, by attempting to dictate policy without regard to the structure of democracy, by aspiring to reorder society or determine its direction without consideration of, or in spite of, a majority consensus. A relative handful reject the basis of ordered existence, certain that they are working for something better. In this assumption of superior knowledge, transnational terrorists betray their essentially authoritarian character. . . .

Terrorists have always tried to deliberately provoke tyranny, in the mad hope that this will bring about the necessary preconditions for revolution. But, as in Uruguay, the conditions of tyranny they induce are more likely to stifle than to promote possibilities for change. The West German response to terrorism, while by no means tyrannical, already has been characterized by a diminution of civil liberties. However paradoxical, one of the responses terrorists desire is state tyranny. . . .

Perhaps the most perplexing characteristic of terrorism is the glaring disjunction between terrorist action and terrorist (stated) goals. What possible connection can there be between the cause of the Palestinians and the slaughter of Puerto Rican Christians at an airport in Israel or of New York-bound passengers at an airport in Athens? . . . There are, of course, no satisfactory answers. Terrorist violence is by its nature random. Its immediate victims are of no real consequence to its perpetrators' goals. . . .

By its very nature, terrorism is engaged in the disruption of norms, the violation of generally accepted standards of decency, including the rules of war as they apply to the innocent and the helpless. . . . [T]errorism is staged to call attention to an often unrelated situation through shock—creating situations of horror, doing the unthinkable without apology or remorse. . . . To be effective, terrorism must evoke a severe emotional response.

While contemporary terrorism has an obvious relationship to state terror in its use of fear as a political weapon, it differs in its separation of actions from goals and in its usual indifference to immediate victims. Beginning with Robespierre, state terror has employed fear as a direct means of establishing authority and assuring obedience. It has proven particularly useful during the period in which a new state seeks to consolidate and legitimize its authority. The Soviet Union in its early days and Cambodia today provide examples of what we may expect if terrorists ever do achieve state power, but they tell us little about the contemporary terrorist problem. The real antecedents to contemporary terrorism are the various anarchist movements of the nineteenth century, in which the figure of Bakunin stands central. . . .

In their love of violence for its own sake, their desire to horrify and disrupt the society at large, as well as in the absence of any kind of systematic plan for social organization beyond the revolution, the nineteenth-century anarchists prefigure our contemporary terrorists. There are major differences, and some of them are alarming: the present sophisticated organization of terrorists throughout the world, what one commentator has called "the New International"; the related phenomenon of today's terrorists claiming for themselves a global battleground[;] . . . and finally, the magnitude of damage of which contemporary terrorists are capable—the potential for nationally disruptive acts, including mass destruction. . . . [T]hese characteristics make our terrorist problem an unprecedented challenge.

Does terrorism work? We can find, well before Yasir Arafat's reception at the United Nations in 1974, historical illustrations of terrorism's efficacy. Earlier in this century, some nationalist groups employed terrorist methodology successfully in their struggle against colonialism. But these efforts differed significantly from contemporary terrorism in that much of the violence was directed against a foreign presence, almost always European. The political goal of the violence was independence—departure of the foreign administration and establishment of a new nation. India, Israel, and Algeria, for example, employed varying degrees of terrorist violence in their drive for independence. . . .

CONTEMPORARY TERRORISM

The collapse of the great colonial empires in the wake of World War II engendered a vast and rapid reordering of global relations, carried out under the pressures of burgeoning nationalism in former colonies and protectorates. . . . Many of the terrorist groups committed to separatism or nationalism (the PLO being the best-known example) have operated in the knowledge that the use of limited force may be needed to carve out a niche for one's people. It is a classic application of Clausewitz's famous dictum that warfare is a continuation of diplomacy by other means, invested with a modern understanding of selective violence. Within much of the world community the pervasive anticolonialist sentiment of the postwar period has translated into a sympathetic attitude toward terrorism along these lines. At the same time, the writings of Mao, Guevara, Frantz Fanon, and Carlos Marighella illustrate strategy, foster a quasi-religious faith that history is on the side of the oppressed, and provide a theoretical link to ultraleftist terrorist groups in the advanced industrial societies of Western Europe and Japan. . . .

A . . . concurrent development is the advent of satellite communications, particularly the capability, first realized in 1968, for transmitting television signals around the globe. The social implications of this technological innovation are far-reaching and as yet not fully understood. . . . Instantaneous worldwide television coverage of wars, insurrections, assassinations, and catastrophes contributes to and reinforces the sense of apparent disorder and instability that for many is the chief characteristic of our age, suggesting an environment in which the violent actions of desperate men and women are somehow appropriate. At the same time, television satellites provide a global audience for terrorist histrionics. We may yet see the global village held as hostage by terrorists with, say, a nuclear capability or access to advanced biological weaponry.

We must also consider what may be referred to as the cost-effectiveness of terrorism. A study prepared by the Rand Corporation examined sixty-three major kidnapping and barricade events staged by terrorists between early 1968 and late 1974. The conclusions . . . were striking. . . .

- 87 percent probability of actually seizing hostages;
- 79 percent chance that all members of the terrorist team would escape punishment or death, whether or not they successfully seized hostages;
- 40 percent chance that all or some demands would be met in operations where something more than just safe passage or exit permission was demanded;
- 29 percent chance of full compliance with such demands;
- 83 percent chance of success where safe passage or exit, for the terrorists themselves or for others, was the sole demand;
- 67 percent chance that, if concessions to the principal demands were rejected, all or virtually all members of the terrorist team could still escape alive by going underground, accepting safe passage in lieu of their original demands, or surrendering to a sympathetic government; and
- virtually a 100 percent probability of gaining major publicity whenever that was one of the terrorists' goals.[1]

. . . [O]ne of the most dramatic examples of the efficacy of terrorism has been the emergence of the PLO's Yasir Arafat as the recognized spokesman for the

Palestinian people, a position cemented by his unparalleled address to the UN General Assembly in 1974.

. . . [T]he heavy increase in the number of terrorist incidents as well as in the number of terrorist groups over the last decade is disturbing. So, too, are certain qualitative aspects of the expansion of terrorist activity.

Cooperation

There is evidence of increasing cooperation among national and international terrorist organizations in the form of common financial and technical support. As a result of this cooperation and of the extensive media coverage that terrorist activities have received, procedure techniques and even attitudes of particular groups are apparently being adopted by other groups.[2]

For example, Palestinian terrorist camps in Lebanon, Syria, Libya (and until 1970, Jordan) have trained revolutionaries from Western Europe, Africa, Latin America, Asia, and North America in terrorist techniques. Such groups have included representatives from America's Weathermen and Black Panthers, the Irish Republican Army, the Turkish People's Liberation Army, the Eritrean Liberation Front, Japan's United Red Army (URA), and West Germany's Baader-Meinhof Gruppe.[3] But the Palestinians have not restricted their training to leftists. They have also recruited German neo-Nazis, presumably on the basis of shared anti-Semitism.

This Palestinian connection appears to be the main thread linking a diverse number of terrorist groups and events in what has come to be known as transnational terrorism. To the extent that there is an alliance, it appears to be quite loose, grounded more in common sympathies than in shared experience. . . .

The groups discussed above are responsible for a large measure of the terrorist activities of this decade. They are distinct from organizations like the IRA or the Eritrean or Basque terrorists in a way that is extremely illuminating for an understanding of transnational terrorism. What sets them apart is that they do not claim to be representatives of an oppressed class in their homeland. They are by and large the children of affluent societies, of modern industrial civilization itself. What they have rejected is their bourgeois origins, but not in favor of a downtrodden working class. Instead they have made a powerful identification with the struggles of the Third World, mythicized throughout the 1960s in the personae of such "heroes" as Che and Fidel. The very concept of the urban guerrilla that they embraced as a model was developed in Latin American revolutionary politics. Horst Mahler, a . . . jailed Baader-Meinhof member, put it this way: "We didn't feel German any more, but a kind of fifth column of the Third World." . . .

This rejection of class origin and creation of a new antibourgeois identity on the model of an archetypal Third World revolutionary implies a shared set of values and a shared mode of action among such terrorists, the basis for extensive cooperation in the struggle against the common enemy (Western industrial democracy) on behalf of oppressed peoples of the Third World. . . . Finally, this is a shared perception of the world, defined in terms of struggle, in which alliance with more localized terrorist movements is not only logical but necessary. . . .

The exchange of personnel in domestic and foreign terrorist operations has also been well documented. During a 1970 Palestinian attempt to capture an Israeli airliner in London, Israeli security agents killed a Nicaraguan terrorist carrying three passports, including an American one. A captured member of the Turkish People's Liberation Army informed the Israelis that the killing, in May 1971, of the Israeli Consul General in Istanbul was in payment for a debt owed by the group to the PLO. The May 1972 Lod airport massacre was a joint suicide mission of the URA and the PFLP. . . .

In 1974, revolutionary groups in Argentina, Bolivia, Chile, and Uruguay established a central organization called the Revolutionary Coordinating Junta (JCR). The following year they were joined by Dominican, Colombian, Paraguayan, and Venezuelan revolutionaries at a meeting in Lisbon, where the pact was formalized. Together they have raised a sizable amount of cash, mainly from ransoms paid for kidnapped businessmen. The Argentinians alone are believed to have collected over two hundred million dollars within a recent three-year period.

In mid-October of 1977, *The Times* of London reported that the junta had set up a headquarters in Paris that "has become a kind of clearinghouse for international terrorism," specializing in the publication of revolutionary pamphlets and field manuals.[4]

Summit meetings of the transnational terrorist leadership have occurred at least twice: in Lebanon in 1972 and in Larnaca, Cyprus, in July 1977. These meetings were attended by Germans, Japanese, Iranians, Turks, and the IRA and paid for by the Palestinians.

Government Cooperation and Support

Terrorist groups are known to receive substantial financial and military support from cooperative governments. This is one of the most disturbing aspects of the terrorist problem, and it has a long history. Before World War I, the tsarist government of Russia covertly supported the Serbian Black Hand, a secret organization whose activities in the Balkans were a major factor in the outbreak of war in Europe in 1914. In the 1930s, the Italian government supported the separatist Croatian Ustasha, even providing asylum for several known assassins, while denying any involvement. . . .

There are, of course, many ways a government may support terrorist activities, ranging from the apparently passive provision of safe harbor or use of air space to actively promoting and supporting terrorists with money, arms, or training. The list of nations that are now or have recently been involved in supporting terrorism includes Libya, Cuba, the Soviet Union, China, North Korea, Algeria, the People's Democratic Republic of Yemen (Southern Yemen), Tanzania, Congo, Zaire, Egypt, Syria, Iraq, and Lebanon.

Among the most active has been Libya, which supported and continues to support a wide range of nationalist groups of various ideologies. Much of this backing has been covert, but in the summer of 1972, Colonel Muammur Qaddafi, Libya's dictator, began openly to boast about his contributions to world terrorism.

Qaddafi told an interviewer that, besides establishing training camps for volunteers and providing refuge for Arab hijackers, he was supplying arms to the IRA in Ulster and to Muslims in the Philippines. He added that he would be happy to supply weapons to blacks, "unfurling in the United States the banner of the struggle against American racism." In September 1972, Qaddafi gave Yasir Arafat five million dollars as an "expression of gratitude" for the Fatah-Black September murder of eleven Israeli athletes at the Munich Olympics. . . .

With somewhat more secrecy, the training of terrorists was occurring in Communist countries. In the late 1960s, Mexican guerrillas received training in North Korea and North Vietnam. In the early 1970s, African insurgents fighting the Portuguese were trained in the use of sophisticated weaponry, including ground-to-air missiles, by Soviet officers at bases within the Soviet Union.

Throughout the 1960s, the Soviets underwrote Cuban training programs in which Third World youths were given instruction in guerrilla methods. Similarly, in the 1970s, most of the Soviet support for terrorist groups has been channelled through client states and other intermediaries. . . . There is no question that the Soviets view terrorism as dangerous primarily because of its uncontrollable nature, and their support for it outside the Middle East is highly selective, dictated by strategic considerations. . . .

NOTES

1. For a discussion of the factors cited here, see David Milbank, "International and Transnational Terrorism: Diagnosis and Prognosis," Research Study, PR 76 10030 (Washington, D.C.: Central Intelligence Agency, Office of Political Research, April 1976) [p. 22].
2. See Brian M. Jenkins, "International Terrorism: A New Mode of Conflict," in David Carlton and Carlo Schaerf, eds., *International Terrorism and World Security* (New York: John Wiley and Sons, Halsted Press, 1975), p. 29.
3. For a full, unclassified overview of terrorist trends, see Historical Evaluation and Research Organization, "The Terrorist and Sabotage Threat to United States Nuclear Programs" (Dunn Loring, Va., August 1974).
4. R. W. Apple, "A Loose Alliance of Terrorists Does Seem to Exist," *New York Times*, October 23, 1977, sec. 4, p. 1.

Minimanual of the Urban Guerrilla

Carlos Marighella

The accusation of assault or terrorism no longer has the pejorative meaning it used to have. It has acquired new clothing, a new coloration. It does not factionalize, it does not discredit; on the contrary it represents a focal point of attraction.

Today to be an assailant or a terrorist is a quality that ennobles any honorable man because it is an act worthy of a revolutionary engaged in armed struggle against the shameful military dictatorship and its monstrosities.

A DEFINITION OF THE URBAN GUERRILLA

The chronic structural crisis characteristic of Brazil today, and its resultant political instability, are what have brought about the upsurge of revolutionary war in the country. The revolutionary war manifests itself in the form of urban guerrilla warfare, psychological warfare, or rural guerrilla warfare. Urban guerrilla warfare or psychological warfare in the city depends on the urban guerrilla.

The urban guerrilla is a man who fights the military dictatorship with arms, using unconventional methods. A political revolutionary and an ardent patriot, he is a fighter for his country's liberation, a friend of the people and of freedom. The area in which the urban guerrilla acts is in the large Brazilian cities. There are also bandits, commonly known as outlaws, who work in the big cities. Many times assaults by outlaws are taken as actions by urban guerrillas.

The urban guerrilla, however, differs radically from the outlaw. The outlaw benefits personally from the action, and attacks indiscriminately without distinguishing between the exploited and the exploiters, which is why there are so many ordinary men and women among his victims. The urban guerrilla follows a political goal and only attacks the government, the big capitalists, and the foreign imperialists, particularly North Americans. . . .

. . . The principal task of the urban guerrilla is to distract, to wear out, to demoralize the militarists, the military dictatorship and its repressive forces, and also to attack and destroy the wealth and property of the North Americans, the foreign managers, and the Brazilian upper class. . . .

Money, arms, ammunition and explosives, and automobiles must be expropriated. And the urban guerrilla must rob banks and armories and seize explosives and ammunition wherever he finds them.

None of these operations is undertaken for just one purpose. Even when the assault is for money, the arms that the guards bear must also be taken. . . .

THE TECHNIQUE OF THE URBAN GUERRILLA

In its most general sense, technique is the combination of methods man uses to carry out any activity. The activity of the urban guerrilla consists in waging guerrilla warfare and psychological warfare. . . .

The technique of the urban guerrilla has the following characteristics:

a) it is an aggressive technique, or in other words, it has an offensive character. As is well known, defensive action means death for us. Since we are inferior to the enemy in fire power and have neither his resources nor his power force, we cannot defend ourselves against an offensive or a concentrated attack by the gorillas. And that is the reason why our urban technique can never be permanent, can never defend a fixed base nor remain in any one spot waiting to repel the circle of reaction;

b) it is a technique of attack and retreat by which we preserve our forces;

c) it is a technique that aims at the development of urban guerrilla warfare, whose function will be to wear out, demoralize, and distract the enemy forces. . . .

THE INITIAL ADVANTAGES OF THE URBAN GUERRILLA

The dynamics of urban guerrilla warfare lie in the urban guerrilla's violent clash with the military and police forces of the dictatorship. In this clash, the police have the superiority. The urban guerrilla has inferior forces. The paradox is that the urban guerrilla, although weaker, is nevertheless the attacker. . . . He can only avoid defeat if he counts on the initial advantages he has and knows how to exploit them to the end to compensate for his weaknesses and lack of matériel.

The initial advantages are:

1. he must take the enemy by surprise;
2. he must know the terrain of the encounter better than the enemy;
3. he must have greater mobility and speed than the police and the other repressive forces;
4. his information service must be better than the enemy's;
5. he must be in command of the situation and demonstrate a decisiveness so great that everyone on our side is inspired and never thinks of hesitating, while on the other side the enemy is stunned and incapable of responding. . . .

EXECUTION

Execution is the killing of a North American spy, of an agent of the dictatorship, of a police torturer, of a fascist personality in the government involved in crimes and persecutions against patriots, of a stool pigeon, informer, police agent, or police provocateur. . . .

Execution is a secret action in which the least possible number of urban guerrillas are involved. In many cases, the execution can be carried out by one sniper, patiently, alone and unknown, and operating in absolute secrecy and in cold blood.

KIDNAPPING

Kidnapping is capturing and holding in a secret spot a police agent, a North American spy, a political personality, or a notorious and dangerous enemy of the revolutionary movement.

Kidnapping is used to exchange or liberate imprisoned revolutionary comrades, or to force suspension of torture in the jail cells of the military dictatorship. . . .

The kidnapping of North American residents or visitors in Brazil constitutes a form of protest against the penetration and domination of United States imperialism in our country.

SABOTAGE

Sabotage is a highly destructive type of attack using very few persons and sometimes requiring only one to accomplish the desired result. When the urban guerrilla uses sabotage the first phase is isolated sabotage. Then comes the phase of dispersed and generalized sabotage, carried out by the people.

Well-executed sabotage demands study, planning, and careful execution. A characteristic form of sabotage is explosion using dynamite, fire, and the placing of mines.

A little sand, a trickle of any kind of combustible, a poor lubrication, a screw removed, a short circuit, pieces of wood or of iron, can cause irreparable damage.

The objective of sabotage is to hurt, to damage, to make useless, and to destroy vital enemy points such as the following:

a) the economy of the country;

b) agricultural or industrial production;

c) transport and communication systems;

d) the military and police systems and their establishments and deposits;

e) the repressive military-police system;

f) the firms and properties of North Americans in the country. . . .

TERRORISM

Terrorism is an action, usually involving the placement of a bomb or fire explosion of great destructive power, which is capable of effecting irreparable loss against the enemy.

Terrorism requires that the urban guerrilla should have an adequate theoretical and practical knowledge of how to make explosives.

The terroristic act . . . is an action the urban guerrilla must execute with the greatest cold bloodedness, calmness, and decision. . . .

Terrorism is an arm the revolutionary can never relinquish.

ARMED PROPAGANDA

The coordination of urban guerrilla actions, including each armed action, is the principal way of making armed propaganda.

These actions, carried out with specific and determined objectives, inevitably become propaganda material for the mass communications system. . . .

[T]he urban guerrilla must never fail to install a clandestine press and must be able to turn out mimeographed copies using alcohol or electric plates and other duplicating apparatus, expropriating what he cannot buy in order to produce small clandestine newspapers, pamphlets, flyers, and stamps for propaganda and agitation against the dictatorship. . . .

It is enough to win the support of a part of the people and this can be done by popularizing the following slogan: "Let he who does not wish to do anything for the revolutionaries, do nothing against them."

THE WAR OF NERVES

The war of nerves or psychological war is an aggressive technique, based on the direct or indirect use of mass means of communication and news transmitted orally in order to demoralize the government.

In psychological warfare, the government is always at a disadvantage since it imposes censorship on the mass media and winds up in a defensive position by not allowing anything against it to filter through.

At this point it becomes desperate, is involved in greater contradictions and loss of prestige, and loses time and energy in an exhausting effort at control which is subject to being broken at any moment.

The object of the war of nerves is to misinform, spreading lies among the authorities, in which everyone can participate, thus creating an air of nervousness, discredit, insecurity, uncertainty, and concern on the part of the government. . . .

HOW TO CARRY OUT THE ACTION

The urban guerrilla who correctly carries through his apprenticeship and training must give the greatest importance to his method of carrying out action, for in this he cannot commit the slightest error.

Any carelessness in the assimilation of the method and its use invites certain disaster, as experience teaches every day. . . .

The giant is known by his toe. The same can be said of the guerrilla who is known from afar for his correct methods and his absolute fidelity to principles.

The revolutionary method of carrying out action is strongly and forcefully based on the knowledge and use of the following elements:

a) investigation of information;

b) observation or *paquera*,

c) reconnaissance or exploration of the terrain;

d) study and timing of routes;

e) mapping;

f) mechanization;

g) selection of personnel and relief;

h) selection of firing capacity;
i) study and practice in completion;
j) completion;
k) cover;
l) retreat;
m) dispersal;
n) liberation or transfer of prisoners;
o) elimination of clues;
p) rescue of wounded. . . .

GUERRILLA SECURITY

The urban guerrilla lives in constant danger of the possibility of being discovered or denounced. The chief security problem is to make certain that we are well hidden and well guarded, and that there are secure methods to keep the police from locating us or our whereabouts.

The worst enemy of the urban guerrilla and the major danger we run is infiltration in our organization by a spy or an informer.

The spy trapped within the organization will be punished with death. The same goes for those who desert and inform the police.

A good security is the certainty that the enemy has no spies and agents infiltrated in our midst. . . .

Nor is it permissible for everyone to know everyone and everything else. Each person should know only what relates to his work. . . .

The danger to the urban guerrilla is that he may reveal himself through imprudence or allow himself to be discovered through lack of class vigilance. . . . Annotations in the margins of newspapers, lost documents, calling cards, letters or notes, all these are clues that the police never underestimate.

Address and telephone books must be destroyed and one must not write or hold papers; it is necessary to avoid keeping archives of legal or illegal names, biographical information, maps, and plans. . . .

Guerrilla security must be maintained also and principally in cases of arrest. The arrested guerrilla can reveal nothing to the police that will jeopardize the organization. . . .

THE SEVEN SINS OF THE URBAN GUERRILLA

One of the methods we should use to diminish the margin of error is to know thoroughly the seven sins of the urban guerrilla and try to fight them.

The first sin of the urban guerrilla is inexperience. The urban guerrilla, blinded by this sin, thinks the enemy is stupid, underestimates his intelligence, believes everything is easy and, as a result, leaves clues that can lead to his disaster.

Because of his inexperience, the urban guerrilla can also overestimate the forces of the enemy. . . .

The second sin of the urban guerrilla is to boast about the actions he has completed and broadcast them to the four winds.

The third sin of the urban guerrilla is vanity. The urban guerrilla who suffers from this sin tries to solve the problems of the revolution by actions erupting in the city, but without bothering about the beginnings and the survival of the guerrilla in rural areas. . . .

The fourth sin of the urban guerrilla is to exaggerate his strength and to undertake projects for which he lacks forces and, as yet, does not have the required infrastructure.

The fifth sin of the urban guerrilla is precipitous action. The urban guerrilla who commits this sin loses patience, suffers an attack of nerves, does not wait for anything, and impetuously throws himself into action, suffering untold reverses.

The sixth sin of the urban guerrilla is to attack the enemy when he is most angry.

The seventh sin of the urban guerrilla is to fail to plan things and to act out of improvisation.

POPULAR SUPPORT

One of the permanent concerns of the urban guerrilla is his identification with popular causes to win public support.

Where government actions become inept and corrupt, the urban guerrilla should not hesitate to step in to show that he opposes the government and to gain mass sympathy. . . .

The rebellion of the urban guerrilla and his persistence in intervening in public questions is the best way of insuring public support of the cause we defend. We repeat and insist on repeating: *it is the best way of insuring public support.* As soon as a reasonable section of the population begins to take seriously the action of the urban guerrilla, his success is guaranteed. . . .

When [the people] see the militarists and the dictatorship on the brink of the abyss and fearing the consequences of a revolutionary war which is already at a fairly advanced and irreversible level, the pacifiers, always to be found within the ruling classes, and the right-wing opportunists, partisans of nonviolent struggle, join hands and circulate rumors behind the scenes, begging the hangmen for elections, "redemocratization," constitutional reforms, and other tripe designed to fool the masses and make them stop the revolutionary rebellion in the cities and the rural areas of the country. . . .

URBAN GUERRILLA WARFARE, SCHOOL FOR SELECTING THE GUERRILLA

Revolution is a social phenomenon that depends on men, arms, and resources. Arms and resources exist in the country and can be taken and used, but to do this it is necessary to count on men. Without them, the arms and the resources have no use and no value. For their part, the men must have two basic and indispensable obligatory qualities:

a) they must have a politico-revolutionary motivation;

b) they must have the necessary technical-revolutionary preparation. . . .

As of now, the men and women chosen for urban guerrilla warfare are workers; peasants whom the city has attracted as a market for manpower and who return to the countryside indoctrinated and politically and technically prepared: students, intellectuals, priests. This is the material with which we are building—starting with urban guerrilla warfare—the armed alliance of workers and peasants, with students, intellectuals, priests.

The Real Terror Network

Edward S. Herman

. . . **T**he really massive and significant growth of terrorism since World War II has been that carried out by states. And among states, the emergence and spread of the National Security State (NSS) has been the most important development contributing to state terrorism and thus to the growth of overall world terrorism, using the word in its basic sense—intimidation by violence or the threat of violence. . . . [T]he power of even small states to intimidate is much greater than that of non-state terrorists. Only states use torture extensively as a means of intimidation, and if we use as our measure of the scale of terrorist violence either political murders or incarceration accompanied by torture, retail terrorism [the terrorism of selected individuals and small groups on the left—as opposed to "wholesale" state terrorism] pales into relative insignificance. State terrorism is also much more important than non-state violence because it is rooted in relatively permanent structures that allow terror to be institutionalized. . . . Retail terrorists are frequently transitory, and they are often produced by the very abuses that state terror is designed to protect. . . .

If state terrorism *is* designed to protect systems of injustice, to allow them to persist and perhaps even to be extended in scope, this suggests a further aspect of wholesale terror that greatly enhances its potential for evil. . . .

. . . [T]he NSS is an instrument of class warfare, organized and designed to permit an elite . . . to operate without any constraint from democratic processes. . . . Retail terrorists do not deprive large numbers of their subsistence and produce hunger, malnutrition, high infant mortality rates, chronic diseases of poverty and neglect, and illiteracy. This is all done by state terrorists. . . .

In the real terror network that is to be discussed here, it is the *function* of state terrorism to keep popular participation down, to limit services to the lower classes, and to freeze the structures that have generated this very critical situation.

. . . [T]he NSS rests on the primacy of "National Security," which is to be imposed by military force to contain forces of "Communism" and "Subversion." "National Security," "Communism," and "Subversion" are coordinate terms, all defined in the NSSs with a generous scope that conveniently reaches anything that would threaten elite privilege and power. . . .

The military elites, who are the direct rulers of the NSSs, have produced an ideology that puts decisive weight on power and military security and explicitly shunts into the background the well-being of the masses. It rests on an alleged "new dilemma—Welfare or Security—previously pointed out by Goering in less just but highly suggestive terms: 'more guns, less butter.' In fact there is no getting around the necessity of sacrificing Welfare to the benefit of Security when the latter is actually endangered."[1] . . . In the NSSs there is no external security threat; the "enemy" is the people within the country who are trying to assert basic rights—the "security threat" is that posed by unionism and majority rule. . . .

The nominal ideology of the NSS, and even more clearly its real purpose . . . involves a denial of the worth and rights of most human beings and constitutes a throwback to pre-Enlightenment ideas of hierarchy and structured and permanent inequality (including inequality of opportunity). . . .

It cannot be too strongly emphasized that terror is a built-in feature of the NSS, firmly grounded in its ends and in the objective situation with which it was designed to cope. . . . [I]ts objectives are those of a small elite minority, who need and use the NSS to implement a system of permanent class warfare. The economic model of Third World development favored by the west does not say "use terror," but the policies that are favored, which would encourage foreign investment and keep wages and welfare outlays under close control, could often not be put into place without it. Privilege cannot be maintained and enlarged from already high levels if "the people" are allowed to organize, vote, and exercise any substantial power. . . .

With undeviating regularity, the imposition of an NSS is accompanied by a rapid dismantling, or other mode of neutralization—frequently by killing, imprisoning or exiling the leadership—of working class and peasant organizations, like unions, cooperatives, leagues, and political groupings. . . .

A primary characteristic of the NSS is . . . exceptional numbers, activities, power and rewards of the military and police establishments. . . .

In performing their function of returning the majority to a state of apathy, and keeping them there, it is possible that once the leadership of popular organizations is decimated and an environment of fear and hopelessness is created through years of direct violence, that tacit threats alone will suffice. If, however, the very logic of the system is to depress the masses—politically and economically—to allow unconstrained pursuit of elite benefits, to protect an increasing income gap, and to keep costs down in a competitive world, permanent immiseration and permanent repression may be required. . . .

Human torture . . . only came into widespread and *institutionalized* use as the NSSs emerged and matured in the 1960s and 1970s. By institutionalized I mean employed as standard operating procedure in multiple detention centers . . . applicable to hundreds of detainees, and used with the approval and intent of the highest authorities. By my calculation, 14 countries in Latin America and the Caribbean, as well as a dozen other countries in the U.S. sphere of influence, were using torture as a mode of governance, on an institutionalized and administrative basis, in the early 1970s.[2] . . . As torture spread through the NSS system a fairly standardized core of electronic and medical technology was used that allowed the victims to be carried to a more severe state of pain and dehumanization just short of death. The fearfulness of the violence imposed on the tortured thousands in the NSSs has been documented extensively. . . .

I give here only the following brief summary of processes in Chile and one witness's statement of torture procedures in Argentina. According to AI's [Amnesty International's] *Report on Torture*, in Chile:

> The most common forms of physical torture have been prolonged beating (with truncheons, fists or bags of moist material), electricity to all parts of the body, and burning with cigarettes or acid. Such physical tortures have been accompanied by the deprivation of food, drink and sleep. More primitive and brutal methods have continued to be used.[3] . . .

A long term resident of Argentina's detention centers gives the following description of his experiences:

> As regards physical torture, we were all treated alike, the only differences being in intensity and duration. Naked, we were bound hand and foot with thick chains or straps to a metal table. Then an earthing cable was attached to one of our toes and torture began.
>
> For the first hour they would apply the "picana" (cattle prod) to us, without asking any questions. The purpose of this was, as they put it, "to soften you up, and so that we'll understand one another." They went on like this for hours. They applied it to the head, armpits, sexual organs, anus, groin, mouth and all the sensitive parts of the body. From time to time they threw water over us or washed us, "to cool your body down so that you'll be sensitive again."
>
> Between sessions of the "picana", they would use the "submarino", (holding our heads under water), hang us up by our feet, hit us on the sexual organs, beat us with chains, put salt on our wounds and use any other method that occurred to them. They would also apply 220-volt direct current to us, and we know that sometimes . . . they used what they called the "piripipi", a type of noise torture.
>
> There was no limit to the torture. It could last for one, two, five or ten days. Everything done under the supervision of a doctor, who checked our blood-pressure and reflexes: "We're not going to let you die before time." That is exactly how it was, because when we were on the verge of death they would stop and let us be revived. . . .
>
> Many of the prisoners could not endure this terrible treatment and fell into a coma. When this happened, they either left them to die or else "took them off to the military hospital." We never heard of any of these prisoners again.[4] . . .

This is terrorism in a form that retail terrorists cannot duplicate. . . . [I]t is an important part of a *real* terror network that the Free Press pretends does not exist.

The "death squad" has been an equally noteworthy aspect of NSS terror, complementing the seizure, torture and killing activities by the regular police, army and security forces. . . . [D]eath squads came into existence in ten separate states of Latin America during the past two decades. Usually they are composed of regular military, police and intelligence personnel working in "off-duty" functions. . . .

In other NSSs, while the death squads are often official personnel working secretly, sometimes they are made up of former police or military personnel; or they may be mainly civilian paramilitary rightwing groups who kill people the NSS wants, or doesn't mind being, killed. In almost all cases the activities of death squads are under the direct supervision of the authorities in their political kidnapping and murder activities. . . .

Important characteristics of death squad activities in Latin America, which bear on the nature and purposes of the NSS, have been their sadism and their tie-in with ordinary illegal activities like theft, kidnappings for ransom and the drug trade. They are served by thugs. In Argentina, Brazil, Chile, El Salvador and Guatemala death squads rarely just kill; they rape, torture and mutilate. AI mentions the fact that the security operations of Paraguay are "carried out by teams whose members include the mentally deficient and the sexually disturbed."[5] And fanaticism and pathology are evident throughout the NSS system in the cigarette burnings, amputations, and sexual violence and mutilations. . . .

The thugs have a role to play in the NSS—they eliminate "subversives" and intimidate and create anxiety in the rest of the population, all potential subversives. . . .

. . . The linkages between the United States and the NSSs are clear and powerful—one can show interest and purpose on the part of the superpower, ideological harmony, and a flow of training and material aid that is both massive and purposeful. It is, once again, a testimonial to the power and patriotism of the Free Press that, not only is the terrorism of the NSSs underrated, but the role of the United States as the sponsor—the Godfather—of this real terror network is hidden from view. . . .

. . . U.S. links to this terror network are not only very extensive but . . . this network is also in significant measure a product of U.S. interest, intent, initiatives, and material and moral support.

1. *U.S. interest in the NSS.* . . . The U.S. military and political establishment also prefers highly reliable allies who escape the local tides of nationalism and reformism and look abroad for ideals and material support. . . .

   A . . . measure of U.S. interest in the NSS is the economic stake of U.S. business, which is large and has been growing by leaps and bounds over the past decade. U.S. merchandise exports to Latin America amounted to $38.8 billion in 1980, imports $37.5 billion—both totals larger than the comparable trade volumes with Japan. U.S. direct investment in Latin America grew from $12.2 billion in 1970 to $38.3 billion in 1980, with earnings from these direct investments rising from $1 billion to $4.6 billion. These investments have been highly profitable, with nominal rates of return in recent years averaging between 15 and 20 percent. . . . The most notable recent development in the growing U.S. stake in the

NSS has been the enormous rise in multinational bank lending and profitability, a response to the oil price increases, to the development strategies of the NSSs, and to banker perceptions of their "creditworthiness." Total U.S. cross-border bank claims on Latin American countries reached a staggering $77.3 billion in June 1981. . . .

2. *U.S. intent and the emergence of the NSS.* [T]he wide-ranging U.S. complicity in the Brazilian coup of 1964 and the Chilean coup of 1973 were of outstanding importance. In both cases, U.S. efforts at subversion were of long duration, multidimensional, extensive at each level, and brazen. They included economic and political destabilization efforts, propaganda, and large scale funding of and conspiracy with Brazilian and Chilean politicians, journalists and editors, military and security personnel, intellectuals and labor leaders. The military establishments of both countries were encouraged to carry out the coups and the outcomes were greeted with great warmth and protectiveness by Washington. In the immediate wake of both the Brazilian and Chilean coups, U.S. personnel actually helped in the writing of White Papers justifying and explaining these constructive developments. . . .
   . . . U.S. intervention has tended either to bring NSSs into existence directly, as in Brazil, Chile or Guatemala, or to create a balance of forces that made the NSS probable. . . .
   The other set of *deeds* that reveal a U.S. intent to create the NSS is the greatly enlarged training and supply of the military and police establishments of U.S. clients and the deliberate attempt to cultivate personal relationships with them and to make them dependents. This was done with many accompanying statements that stressed the usefulness—the wisdom in our own interest—of an investment in building up, winning over, and "educating" these police and military forces. They were viewed as already conservative and anticommunist, and capable of being reinforced in the needed ideology and tied to us by training, personal linkages and arms. They would then serve as a force for "stability" and "nation-building" in ways consistent with our interests.

3. *U.S. aid and training.* . . . [T]he volume of these arms and training flows has been of staggering dimension over an extended time period, which strengthens the case for domination or substantial influence by the United States. . . . U.S. training and supply have tended to encourage human torture and . . . there are significant positive relationships between U.S. flows of aid and *negative* human rights developments (the rise of torture, death squads and the overturn of constitutional governments). This is a result, not of any U.S. elite attraction to human torture, but rather of the demands of the higher priorities (favorable investment climate, worker and peasant atomization) that regrettably necessitate the support of torturers. . . .
   . . . [T]here is a great deal of evidence of U.S. provision of torture technology and training, which have been diffused among a great

variety of client states. Electronic methods of torture, used extensively in the field and in the Provincial Interrogation Centers in South Vietnam, have spread throughout the system of U.S. clients. A. J. Langguth claims that the CIA advised Brazilian torturers using field telephones as to the permissible limits that would avoid premature death.[6] Klare and Arnson show that U.S. firms and agencies are providing CN and CS gas grenades, anti-riot gear, fingerprint computers, thumbscrews, leg-irons and electronic "Shok-Batons" among a huge flow of "equipment, training and technical support to the police and paramilitary forces *most directly involved in the torture, assassination, and abuse of civilian dissidents.*"[7] . . .

. . . [T]he NSS in Latin America, and all of its ugly terroristic and exploitative qualities, came into existence in accord with U.S. desires and plans. This is a region of preeminent U.S. influence, and it has gone to great lengths to assure that political economies are in place that suit its desires. There can be little doubt that, while U.S. efforts have not been uniformly successful, the main drift has been in accord with U.S. preferences.

NOTES

1. Quoted in *IDOC* [*Monthly Bulletin*], Jan.–Feb. 1977, p. 6.
2. See Noam Chomsky and Edward S. Herman, *The Washington Connection and Third World Fascism*, South End Press, Boston, 1979, Frontispiece and associated footnotes.
3. AI, *International Report 1975–1976*, p. [205].
4. AI, *Testimony on Secret Detention Camps in Argentina*, 1980, pp. 18–19.
5. AI, *Report on Torture*, p. 216.
6. *Hidden Terrors*, p. 139.
7. Klare and Arnson, *Supplying Repression*, p. 6.

Social Dynamics of Terrorism

Austin T. Turk

. . . *[F]*or a great many people the legitimacy and efficacy of political and economic institutions are increasingly questionable. Despite promises and expectations, the vast majority of the many millions of "old poor" have found their life chances not only not improving but deteriorating even further. Other millions, the "new poor," are increasingly threatened and have begun to experience the loss of resources, status, security, and hope familiar in the lives of the old poor. There is, then, reason to expect that the coming struggles will be more politically focused, determined, and violent than in the recent past, specifically the turbulent 1960s. . . .

. . . Strategic, and eventually tactical, success depends on acquiring and applying empirically grounded knowledge of those processes. The task for sociologists is to help produce such knowledge—by doing whatever we can to clarify and resolve the issues of definition, causation, and justification with respect to political violence.

ON DEFINING TERRORISM

Laqueur[1] has rightly observed that consensus on a definition of terrorism is most unlikely. The basic problem is that the word has been used more as an ideological weapon than as an analytical tool. At best, it has served little purpose other than to allude to some mode or level of politically consequential violence other than spontaneous uprisings or rioting and short of conventional warfare. Within this broad conceptual range, "terrorism" has connoted deliberate, shocking, unjustifiable violence against non-combatants as well as combatants. Moreover, subjectivity has extended to partisanship: the distinction between "terror from below" and "terror from above" has been more verbal than real. To nearly everyone, terrorism connotes violence against, not by or on behalf of, governments and other establishments. A necessary step toward a theory of terrorism as a mode of political violence is to find a more specific, less subjective, and nonpartisan way of defining the object of inquiry.

To understand political violence, it is essential to distinguish the politics of an act from the act itself. The search for an analytically useful definition of terrorism—and of political violence in general—has foundered in part because the political meaning of violent acts tends to be more often inferred than investigated. In common usage, terrorism will undoubtedly continue to encompass and confuse acts and meanings. Even so, in research, acts of terror have to be distinguished from the politics of terrorism. Hereafter "terrorism" will mean an ideology justifying acts of terror or a strategy giving priority to such acts. "Terror" will refer to violence expressing such an ideology or implementing such a strategy. For the tautology to be useful, terror must be distinguished from other violence, which here means behavior proximately causing personal injury or property destruction.

Intentionality

Political violence —violence associated with political efforts—may be the product of a scarcely articulate resentment of felt obstructions and sensed antagonists, or of a highly developed consciousness and analysis of political relationships.

Terrible acts can be committed without deliberation but at least since the French Revolution, acts of terror have been assumed to involve some calculation, some conception of means-end linkages. Terror is intended violence.

Objectives

The goals of calculated violence are both expressive and instrumental. Violent acts serve such expressive purposes as strengthening resolve and group cohesion, symbolizing determination, venting frustrations, and assuring the actors of their potency. Whatever they may be, the strategic instrumental aims of political effort are transformed and narrowed through violence into the tactical options of neutralizing known enemies or deterring potential ones. To terrorize people means not only, or even necessarily, to neutralize specific opponents but also to show that the cost of opposition is too high even to be risked. Terror is violence intended to deter opposition.

Targeting

Targeting decisions are a function of tactical emphasis. If neutralization, then the personnel and matériel of the enemy are the prime targets of political violence. If general deterrence, targets are selected to maximize the impact of death, destruction, or disruption. A common belief inside and outside governments is that the deterrent impact of political violence increases with the subjective probability of victimization. That is, the more vulnerable people can be made to feel, the less inclined they are to contest one's political demands. One way to increase the fear of victimization is to randomize targeting—which may well be the hallmark of political terror. Randomization can be accomplished in two ways: first, by the largely indiscriminate selection—analogous to quota sampling—of one or more persons representing a social category viewed as somehow a "problem," such as an enemy, obstacle, or irritant; second, by creating a generalized risk of injury or property loss for anyone who happens to be in, or to have property in, a targeted site. Terror is random violence.

Organization

Political violence may be the work of individuals or of groups varying from small, ephemeral, and/or minimally organized to large, enduring, and/or highly organized. The more calculated the violence, the more likely it is to be a group rather than an individual act. Truly lone individuals are rare, and are much more likely to be expressive reactors to a climate of political conflict and vilification than to be political actors in the sense of using violent means to further reasoned political ends. Because any group may adopt terror tactics, it is misleading to assume either that "terrorism is the weapon of the weak" or that terrorists are always small groups of outsiders—or at most the "lunatic fringe"—in relation to large, enduring, and highly organized political groups, including governments.

Therefore we cannot assume, but must leave empirically open, whether and how the use of terror varies with the scale, duration, tightness, or other aspects of political organization. Terror is organized violence, but the nature of the organization cannot be specified in defining terror.

Summary

The foregoing discussion points to a summary definition of terror as organized political violence, lethal or nonlethal, designed to deter opposition by maximizing fear, specifically by random targeting of people or sites. Fear may also be promoted by adding repugnant, shocking elements to the violence, for example, mutilation of bodies, torture, maiming, degradation, and destruction of pets and toys. However, such elements are common in violent behavior of all kinds. The defining element of terror is the randomness, not the horror, of the violence. . . .

ON CAUSATION

How one approaches the problem of explaining terrorism depends on one's postulates about the nature of social order. One view is that the basic social reality comprises durable, complementary relationships sustained by cooperative interaction. Disputes are resolved by consensual methods, violence is an aberration, and social change occurs by evolution. The contrary view is that the basic social reality comprises tenuous, antagonistic relationships sustained by exploitative interaction. Conflicts are suppressed by deception and force, violence is normal, and social change occurs by revolution.

A growing number of sociologists eschew both extremes and are working from and toward a model of social reality as variable and dialectical. In this view, the relationships constituting social structures are not either/or, but more or less durable and tenuous, complementary and antagonistic, cooperative and exploitative. Disputes and conflicts may be resolved, or perhaps are not resolvable, by consensual methods as well as by deception and force. Violence is neither aberrant nor normal, but merely a resource whose use may be frequent or rare, effective or ineffective. Social change is the product of both evolution and revolution. In sum, the mutually exclusive attributes posited by the two extreme models of social order become "pair variables" linked by the ongoing dialectical process of political organization and reorganization.

From what may be dubbed the "structural/dialectical" perspective, terrorism is to be approached as neither an aberration nor a normal feature of social life, but instead as one of a range of ideological and strategic options that politically active groups may adopt. Explaining terrorism means indicating when and how the social dynamics of political relationships encourage or discourage the adoption of the terrorist option. . . .

Differences in the propensity to adopt terrorism are associated with variation in the dynamics of such relationships. Variation in relational dynamics is associated with variation in authority structures, as a product of reciprocal causation. . . .

Relational Dynamics and Terrorism

Authority structures are built out of two kinds of social relationships: functional and interactive. Functional relationships are those of economic, legal, and other forms of interdependency among groups who may have no direct contact with one another. Interactive relationships are the patterns of dealing with one another that emerge in the course of direct contact among groups. The interactive process of political organization involves conflicts and coalitions, negotiation and cooperation, resulting over time in a hierarchical structure of functional relationships marked by the differential allocation of resources—inevitably favoring winners and their heirs at the expense of losers and their successors.

Institutions of social control are more or less deliberately created to perpetuate authority structures. In fact, authority—as distinguished from sheer power—is the anticipated product of such institutions. Varying blends of persuasion, deception, and violence are employed to promote acceptance of the structure of inequality among groups. . . .

The dialectic control and resistance can be observed in any authority structure, not just in political systems as usually defined. . . . At least for the present, the focus for research on terrorism remains the state. But our studies can be informed by research on conflict over authority in subsidiary or adjunct structures. For example, the considerable work done on labor relations and on race and ethnic relations may tell us a great deal about which kinds of groups resort to terrorism under particular conditions. . . .

Class conflicts and racial or ethnic conflicts may be either inhibited or exacerbated by state control efforts. The institutions of state control exacerbate such conflicts by supporting or permitting exploitation, racism, ethnocentrism, collective violence, and resistance to accommodation. Apart from or in addition to contributing to intergroup violence, state control efforts increase the probability of terrorism—though not necessarily terror, as discussed later—insofar as authorities adopt control strategies emphasizing violent over nonviolent tactics in neutralizing and deterring resistance. But even when authorities try to give priority to nonviolent tactics aiming at persuasion and/or deception, some violence is occasionally necessary, and both violent and nonviolent control efforts tend to produce increased awareness and resentment of political and other inequalities. . . .

Awareness and resentment of political coercion and social inequality do not usually lead to terrorism. Even where the prerequisites for organized group violence are met, most subordinate people do not readily move from resentment to resistance, from nonviolent to violent resistance, or from other forms of political violence to terror. . . .

Research on political deviance indicates that social class and youthfulness are significantly related to the process of moving from resentment to the adoption of a terrorist ideology or strategy. Specifically, lower-class socialization reflects experiences of material and cultural deprivation and defeat, while higher-class socialization reflects experiences of privilege and success. It follows that lower-class people are more likely to be resentful without actively resisting, to avoid rather than confront authorities, to resist in spontaneous instead of calculated ways, and consequently to be wary of committing themselves to terrorism.

In contrast, higher-class people are more inclined to take decisive action, to challenge authorities openly if displeased by social arrangements or policies, to intellectualize and plan resistance, and consequently to view terrorism as either a last resort or as the most decisive expression of political commitment.[2]

Although old as well as young people may "reflect on violence," the simplistic imagery of terrorism is more likely to attract the politically inexperienced. Beyond theorizing and rhetoric, putting terrorism into practice is, like other violence, nearly always the work of the young. With experience tend to come the accommodations of dominance and deference that characterize well-established authority structures. . . .

Terrorism and Authority Structures

Typologies of societies, cultures, social institutions, political systems, and legal orders are legion, but no really usable typology of authority structures has yet been devised.[3] So far, two main dimensions of variation appear to be related to terrorism and terror. The first is the continuum from democracy to totalitarianism; the second is that from traditionalism to modernity.

To the extent that relatively democratic structures offer more options to violence in political struggles, the relational dynamics conducive to terrorism are less likely to be found. Terrorism is more likely to appear in relatively totalitarian structures, as an ideology and strategy of governance as well as of resistance and intergroup conflict. But somewhat paradoxically, the more ruthless the authorities in adopting terrorist and other repressive measures, the lower the incidence of "private" terror and other political violence. Moreover, totalitarian states contribute to the higher incidence of terror in more democratic, open authority structures in three ways. First, they provoke the creation of terrorist ideologies that may then become models for political struggle elsewhere. Second, insofar as resistance and intergroup conflicts are repressed instead of resolved, they are likely to be "exported" through emigration, exile, and escape. Groups may be freer to fight one another or the government abroad than in their home country. Finally, the rulers of totalitarian structures are more likely than those of democratic ones to sponsor terror within other authority structures.[4]

Terrorism and terror are associated with the breakdown of traditional authority structures and with efforts to create modern ones. Terrorism is improbable in traditional structures because the ideological and logistical prerequisites for political violence are usually lacking. Changes resulting from internal dynamics and external pressures—especially modernization in all forms—destroy such structures. . . . [M]odernization tends to weaken established accommodations inhibiting intergroup violence and to promote consciousness and resentment of unequal life chances.[5]

The combination of deteriorating traditional authority structures and conflict in the process of creating replacements is likely to promote terrorism and terror among both conservative (opposing change) and progressive (favoring change) groups. This makes justifying or rejecting the terrorist option an increasingly crucial issue in political conflict.

ON JUSTIFICATION

Empirically, violence is amoral. Acts of violence may effectively neutralize or deter opposition, may have no significant impact upon the success or failure of political efforts, or may be counterproductive. From the historical and operational record, one may conclude that the onus of proof is on those who claim that terrorism—from below or above—is an effective political strategy. Terror is likely to provoke counterterror instead of conformity, and to deter potential support more than potential opposition. Where terror seems to have contributed to political success, it has been impossible to separate its net contribution from the effects of other forms of violent and nonviolent political efforts.

Ideologies of terrorism fare no better. Most people find them intellectually unconvincing or ethically unappealing. To the extent that the "philosophy of the bomb" convinces anyone, it is most likely to convince only terrorists and a minority of people already sharing their political objectives.

Terrorist or not, zero-sum conceptions of political conflict lead more often to further conflict than to improvement in the life chances of groups animated by such fundamentally anti-political notions. To function at all, authority structures depend on negotiation and compromise recognizing factual differences in the interests and power of groups. To be viable, authority structures depend on common acceptance of the basic right of any group to survival as long as its political efforts do not demonstrably threaten the survival of other groups—or obstruct the quest for more viable structures. On such grounds, terrorism and terror are not empirically justifiable.

NOTES

1. Walter Laqueur, *Terrorism* (Boston: Little, Brown, 1977), pp. 5–7.
2. Claus Mueller, *The Politics of Communication: A Study in the Political Sociology of Language, Socialization and Legitimation* (New York: Oxford University Press, 1973). See also Austin T. Turk, *Political Criminality: The Defiance and Defense of Authority* (Beverly Hills, CA: Sage, 1982), pp. 81–108.
3. By far the most promising attempt is that by Harry Eckstein and Ted Robert Gurr, *Patterns of Authority: A Structural Basis for Political Inquiry* (New York: John Wiley, 1975), pp. 351–88.
4. The necessity of controlling terror from above in order to curtail the production and export of terror from below has been clearly indicated by Louk Hulsman, "Terrorism and Victims: Reactions to Jaszi's Paper," in *Dimensions of Victimization in the Context of Terroristic Acts*, ed. Ronald D. Crelinsten (Montreal: International Centre for Comparative Criminology, 1977), pp. 158–63. But little research has yet been done on governmental terrorism, and efforts to curtail the export and sponsorship of terrorism and terror have had very limited success.
5. Austin T. Turk, "Social Control and Social Conflict," in *The Future of Social Control*, ed. Jack P. Gibbs (Beverly Hills, CA: Sage, 1982).

Part 4

Organizational Structures and Violence

The preceding parts have described violence that can permeate households and ordinary streets. Yet violence is not confined to these locations. Violence also can take place within organizational settings that are diverse in goals, operating procedures, and environments.

Some organizational violence represents an adaptation to occupational risks and rewards. Police departments and prisons were created, in part, to deal with violent persons and, on occasion, must maintain and protect themselves through violent exchanges. Police officers and prison guards learn routines of conduct that minimize danger to themselves, ease the performance of their roles, and win the respect and recognition of colleagues. The desire to control and neutralize potential violence can translate into the excessive exercise of force.

The police recruit is taught by fellow officers to expect dangerous confrontations and to remain ever mindful of their potential for lethal eruption. The number of police deaths in performance of duty has been fairly stable over the last decade at approximately 100 annually. However, high-stakes drug trafficking and the associated escalation in armaments can be expected to increase the rate of police casualties. More than ever, police officers must learn to take self-protective measures, yet avoid overreactions that contribute to an already lethal environment.

Prison populations are growing at unprecedented rates, and the character of their clientele has been changing. Twenty years ago, approximately 40 percent of all prison inmates were incarcerated for violent offenses. In 1982 that figure increased almost one and one half times to 57.5 percent.[1] These violent prisoners represent a serious custodial problem for prison administrators. Most prison violence involves inmate-to-inmate encounters, the result of sporadic personal confrontations. Prison riots, a much different order of confrontation, often indicate a severe breakdown of routines that once accommodated and sustained nonconflictual relations among inmates and between jailer and jailed.

Schools were created for teaching and learning, and the violence that strikes within is an unanticipated and shocking lesson. School routines, with their emphasis on orderliness and disciplined instruction, may frustrate youngsters who have not mastered skills appropriate to the learning task. This can result in impulsive, even violent responses in the classroom. Schools may also be the convenient custodians of children whom other institutions have failed. Sometimes teachers and students are simply the convenient targets of youthful intruders engaging in violence for fun and profit.

Violence in the presumably staid corporate world also appears incongruous. Yet scholarly journals and the media are increasingly directing our attention to many corporate practices that place individuals, and even whole communities, at risk. A "bottom-line" philosophy in executive suites may lead to cost-cutting that imperils clean air and water, undermines safety in product-design systems, and results in injury and even death to an unwary public.

Violence and the Police

Hans Toch, in discussing the many dimensions of "The Shape of Police Violence," observes that when force is directed against a police officer, the criminal justice system immediately marshalls its resources to apprehend the offender. For example, of 343 persons known to have killed law enforcement officers between 1968 and 1970, only 5 remained at large by the end of 1971. In contrast, when police use excessive force against a civilian, their codes of silence and in-group loyalty can result in the absence of a correspondingly proportionate response. In day-to-day confrontations leading to violence, Toch describes a typical pattern whereby a police officer and suspect engage in a "test of respect," probing each other for vulnerabilities and watching for signs of compliance. Backed by massive institutional power, the officer is more likely to prevail.

Police Shootings

James J. Fyfe, in "Blind Justice: Police Shootings in Memphis," discusses the controversy surrounding complaints by the black community that blacks are victims of police shootings far in excess of their proportion in the population. Studies confirm this disparity, along with the finding that some jurisdictions display unusually high rates in police use of deadly force. Fyfe studied the problems of black overrepresentation and jurisdictional variation, comparing police shootings in Memphis, Tennessee and New York City. He analyzed shooting incidents that could be justified within police department guidelines and incidents that resulted when officers improperly perceived black suspects as more threatening than whites in similar circumstances. Fyfe concludes that one cannot generalize across jurisdictions. The higher rates of police shooting in some communities are an expected response to the higher felony rates in those communities. However, departmental practices, such as special training programs and explicit directives, have been shown to decrease shooting rates in some jurisdictions. Consequently, Fyfe recommends that police departments give their strong support to guidelines that clarify when deadly force is permissible.

Since Fyfe's article was first published in 1982, the Supreme Court enunciated a standard that should further curtail "elective" police shootings. In *Tennessee* v. *Garner* 471 U.S. 1 (1985), the Supreme Court restricted the use of deadly force to suspects who threaten an officer with a weapon, or where there is probable cause to believe that the suspect has committed a crime involving serious physical harm. Previously, many states had permitted officers to shoot a fleeing felon regardless of the degree of danger to the officer or community.

Prison Violence

While most police violence takes place on the streets and is sometimes visible to the public and media, violence within prisons is markedly less visible. Attacks within prison walls typically involve inmate-to-inmate confrontations. However, it is the dramatic escalation of violence associated with the prison riot—the massive threat to formal authority—that usually commands public attention. Israel L. Barak-Glantz reviews the waves of prison disorders in twentieth-century America in "Prison Revolt: A Brief History." Some riots have centered on demands to establish inmate programs, such as educational and counseling; others on facilitating contact with the outside world through extending visiting privileges or the right to possess radios. Barak-Glantz notes that while prison riots certainly are not a new phenomenon, the current wave of flare-ups represents a striking increase in levels of injury and property damage.

The 1980 New Mexico Prison Riot

Prison disorders at Attica, New York in 1971 and Santa Fe, New Mexico in 1980 were similar to one another only in the enormity of their destruction and bloodshed. Mark Colvin compares and contrasts the two catastrophes, but his primary focus is on the New Mexico disaster. Reviewing possible explanations, Colvin gives particular weight to the quality of prison administrations and the nature of inmate social structures in "The 1980 New Mexico Prison Riot." Abrupt changes in administrative practices, regulatory crackdowns, and curtailments of inmate privileges and power contributed to igniting prison animosities and passions. The author concludes by recommending strategies for riot prevention, some of which may appear controversial because they aim to increase rather than decrease cohesion and solidarity among prison inmates.

Violence in School

Jackson Toby assesses the extent of "Violence in School" using two surveys, one national in scope, the other limited to twenty-six of our nation's largest cities. Nonviolent theft is more common in schools than violence against students and teachers. At the national level, when violent crimes such as robbery and assault do occur, students are the primary victims as well as offenders. However, in our largest cities, outside "intruders" most frequently commit these violent crimes.

Toby urges schools to enforce strict behavioral standards to control and reduce violence. He also recommends that the age of compulsory attendance be lowered in order to rid classrooms of reluctant and disorderly students. However, even if these recommendations were to be enacted, the problem of trespassers in the larger city schools would remain. Toby advocates that these urban schools must develop adequate security programs that deny access to invading predators. He suggests that only after sharp lines are drawn between educational institutions and the streets will it be possible to determine whether increased voluntary attendance can measurably reduce school violence.

School administrators also have the capability for violence because they generally possess the authority to employ corporal punishment for purposes of student control. While there are occasional newspaper reports of its use, there are no definitive studies on corporal punishment in school systems. At the present time, the general public does not appear to be concerned about this potential for the application of force.

Corporate Homicide

Corporations, like other organizations, may be both victims and initiators of violence. Some executive decisions yield violent consequences along with hefty profits. Management may ignore, or even encourage, practices such as toxic dumping, unsafe working conditions, adulterated food ingredients, or faulty product designs. The National Product Safety Commission has estimated that each year 30,000 deaths and 20 million serious injuries are caused by unsafe consumer products.[2]

Victoria Lynn Swigert and Ronald A. Farrell, in "Corporate Homicide: Definitional Processes in the Creation of Deviance," discuss the development of corporate criminal responsibility, particularly as it pertains to the concept of criminal homicide. They review the important legal precedent of securing an indictment for reckless homicide against the Ford Motor Company. Although the 1980 Ford Pinto case resulted in acquittal, prosecutions for reckless homicide in other cases were subsequently sustained: in 1981, Wisconsin successfully prosecuted a nursing-home corporation.[3] In 1985, Illinois prosecuted and won a case involving an employee death due to unsafe working conditions at a film reprocessing company; three top executives received sentences of twenty-five years in prison and fines of $10,000.[4] Corporate homicide has evolved into a legal concept of consequence.

NOTES

1. George F. Cole, *The American System of Criminal Justice* (Monterey: Brooks/Cole Publishing Company, 1986), 518.
2. James W. Coleman, *The Criminal Elite* (New York: St. Martin's Press, 1985), 7.
3. Ellen Hochstedler, *Corporations as Criminals* (Beverly Hills: Sage Publications, 1984).
4. "July 5, 1985," *Facts on File* (New York: Facts on File, Inc., 1985), 495–96.

Chapter 10
Police

The Shape of Police Violence

Hans Toch

For the police, violence is an occupational risk, and force is an occupational tool. The public is most aware of the fact as it relates to the use of *extreme* violence by—and against—the police. . . . Men who start their working day or night sensitized to the possibility, however remote, of death or serious injury must face the management of their fear, and suspects who view police as sources of serious victimization are apt to be apprehensive of encounters with officers. When fears are played out against a backdrop of ethnic feelings—since most police officers are white, and many suspects nonwhite—violent incidents can lead to an ethnic "warfare model."

Symptomatic of the impact of extreme violence is the impetus it provides to the escalation of police armament. . . . Even where police organizations stand fast against such a call to arms, rank-and-file feelings can produce informal changes in conduct. Do-it-yourself measures can include the carrying of unauthorized weapons and heavy duty ammunition. Given strong fear among officers, such practices can become prevalent in the face of explicit prohibitions. In the words of one New York patrolman,

> we have been told that if we get caught in the car with anything other than a .38, we'll have charges brought against us. But it's better to be judged by 12 men than to be carried by six. That's the motto around here (*New York Times* Jan. 31, 1973).

Violence-inspired responses may not only create new violence for the police and the community, but for individual officers and citizens. Officers may be more likely to kill suspects who make "furtive movements" towards guns that never materialize. If a stimulus is ambiguous, an officer is more likely to infer the possibility of danger if his perceptions are conditioned by fear. Reactions to low probability violence (if it is extreme enough) can increase the chances of violent reactions, which in turn create occasions for fear. Riots illustrate this process, because they often break out when police incidents are viewed by hostile spectators against a backdrop of past police-citizen confrontations (U.S. Riot Commission 1968).

Ethnicity is a contributing variable to violence, because a disproportionate number of civilians involved in police violence are nonwhite. Of persons who were killed by police officers, 468 out of 975 identified between 1962 and 1971 were black. Nationally, 60 percent of persons shot by officers are nonwhite (U.S. Dept. of HEW 1972). In New York City, where blacks make up 19 percent of the population, they account for 59 percent of fatal police victims (*New York Times* Aug. 26, 1973).

Such data are sometimes translated into inferences about discrimination. This conclusion is not fair, because most persons who are shot by police are involved in serious offenses at the time of the incident (Robin 1963). Distributions of known offenses and of arrests show ethnic disproportions similar to those of shootings. . . .

As for public outrage, no instance is known where the occasion for public concern rested on statistical distributions. Fear and anger are stimulated by dramatic encounters in which an officer's misjudgement is at issue, where the offense is minor, where the suspect is young, or where some combination of these factors is present.

The point holds also for police reactions to police fatalities. The concern here is often couched in terms of snipings or premeditated ambushes, which account for some 10 percent of police deaths. Such acts have the most substantial claim to impact, because they are hardest to anticipate, and because they raise the specter of a mysterious conspiracy aimed at the lives of officers.

Every police death, on the other hand, is apt to mobilize both fear and anger. Police funerals are the occasion for well-publicized ceremonials and the subject of emotion-laden interest. The facts of the specific incident (including possible negligence) figure insignificantly in its perception by officers. The point at issue appears to center around feelings of vulnerability, and around group identification with the victim.

Although police violence that results in death may spark feelings of impotence, the criminal justice machinery is comparatively well equipped to react to these events. Discharges of police guns are subject to tight monitoring and review; questionable killings by officers are reacted to as criminal and civil matters, and as departmental problems. Killers of policemen rarely escape conviction or death. Out of 343 known offenders between 1968 and 1970, only 5 remained fugitives by the end of 1971 (U.S. Dept. of Justice 1972).

Police who kill citizens are not as vulnerable. One reviewer of the situation notes that "of 1500 incidents (of fatal shootings by police) I have been able to discover only three in which criminal prosecution resulted" (Kobler 1975, 164). The same reviewer points out that the information that is available about police deaths is not matched by diligent inquiries into police killing. "Information about incidents where policemen are killed," he tells us, "is easily available (for instance, in the annual reports-issued by the FBI); however, even simple data on police killings are hard to find, and details of these homicidal encounters are extremely difficult to locate" (Kobler 1975, 164). The fact remains that police departments are well informed about shootings by their own men, including off-duty shootings and firearms discharges.

NONLETHAL POLICE VIOLENCE

Violence involving injury, but no fatality, occurs frequently between police and public.[1] This kind of violence is hard to control, because it is hard to establish and is difficult to define. Its physical cost is minor, compared to its corrupting and corrosive influence, which is subsurface. In fact, its visibility is generally minimal. Although police assaults involve thousands of daily confrontations, these incidents rarely make news. . . .

The social science literature relating to police violence is most intensively concerned with . . . the police role in promoting it. Questions of the most practical concern have been sparked by the suspicion that officers sometimes polarize conflict, or use force in excess of that dictated by circumstances or by law. . . . [M]ost available data show that few officers are in fact confrontation prone. But the data also suggest that a great many officers tend to protect and support those few officers who often are involved in violence. This latter observation makes the problem of police violence a difficult and challenging one.

Several sources of information have been used to generate data about police violence. One such source is the civilian observer who rides with police, and views police conduct directly. A related strategy is that of interviewing officers about incidents in which police violence was employed. These data sources have been very rich, which suggests that the officers may tend to view their violence as relatively justifiable (Reiss 1970, 1971).

Another source of data has been the civilian participant in violent incidents. Police assaulters and assaultees have been interviewed by researchers, and attorneys for such men have provided accounts of civilian versions of police violence. . . . [T]hese data . . . supplement the police version with a totally different perspective.

Other data sources are arrest reports and civilian complaints about police. The availability of such data stems from the legal context of police confrontations. For one, assaulting an officer is a clear-cut offense, often more serious than the grounds for arrest—if any—that spark confrontations. When an officer uses violence he is also on more secure grounds (in court, and in his own department) if he can establish that he was subject to a prior attack. This fact is persuasive enough for officers to continue to file charges such as resisting arrest even when their supervisors suspect that a man who frequently arrests people on such grounds may have problems. Similarly, police assaulters sometimes file brutality charges to buttress a case, otherwise tenuous, in court.

THE SEMINAL STUDY OF POLICE VIOLENCE

William Westley ranks as a pioneer among students of the police. His work [has] been confirmed in more recent investigations. . . . [He] emphasizes that the policeman's workaday reality—the circumstances under which he encounters the public—is such that it forces the officer to derive a jaundiced view of segments of the public. This outlook has nothing to do with personal motives and attitudes; it arises instead out of the adversary nature of police–citizen interactions. The officer's enforcement role defines him as an unwelcome intruder who is apt to meet hostility from people:

> The fight in the bar, the driver in a hurry, the bickering mates, the overtime parker, the cutters of edges and finders of angles; the underworld—bitter, sarcastic, afraid; none of these find the policeman a pleasant sight. To them he is the law, the interfering one, dangerous and a source of fear. He is the disciplinarian, a symbol in brass and blue, irritating, a personal challenge, an imminent defeat and punishment. To him they are the public, an unpleasant job, a threat, the bad ones, unpleasant and whining, self-concerned, uncooperative, and unjust (Westley 1970, 49).

Westley tells us that when the officer is on the job, he cannot draw subtle distinctions between his role and his feelings as a human being who is disliked and disrespected by other human beings. This contamination can work both ways. The officer invokes his badge where the law is not at issue, or becomes personally involved in matters that call for dispassionate reactions. He may come down hard on men he finds uncongenial or distasteful. He may react to challenges; he may see the police role compromised where he is not shown as much deference or cooperation as he would like. Persons who treat the officer with disdain become classed as "wise guys." . . . Other things being equal, the officer is more likely to arrest the man who is disrespectful to him. . . .

Because all police activity is ostensibly exercised on behalf of law, there is need to maintain a pretense of objectivity and legality vis-à-vis the . . . non-police world. This is especially the case when violence is deployed. When violence is used by some officers to punish "wise guys," other officers tend to keep silent about such incidents, even when it is known that the officers involved acted extralegally. Westley maintains that

> Secrecy and silence are among the first rules impressed on the rookie. "Keep your mouth shut, never squeal on a fellow officer, don't be a stool pigeon," is what the rookie has dinned into his ears; it is one of the first things he learns (Westley 1970).

Westley also argued that since police officers find the public unappreciative, they look to each other for protection, esteem, and understanding. . . . [His] contribution to the police violence literature is a two-fold one. He showed that there were relatively few police officers who were inclined to excessive and repeated use of violence, and that these were men concerned with problems of respect and self-esteem. He described a generous support system for the violence-prone officer in the shape of in-group loyalty, and through norms of secrecy and mutual support. Westley tells us that the police violence problem rests among officers who feel strongly about disrespect and evil, and with the police solidarity that makes the problem officer difficult to identify and to discipline.

In a . . . preface to his study, Westley draws a practical inference. Violence, he tells us, must be addressed by involving the police more positively in society, so as to decrease the adversary (in-group, out-group) relationship between most officers and the public they serve. He states that:

> Means must be found for integrating the police with the community and for de-escalating their adversarial role. To do this, police organizations must be democratized by involving as many policemen as possible in decision making on all aspects of the department's jobs. Policemen must also be integrated with the community through increased police participation in decision-making bodies, and through public participation in a wide range of police activities (Westley 1970, xvii). . . .

THE POLICE PERSPECTIVE

Westley postulates a support system for violence in the shape of locker-room norms. Some of these norms, such as the premise that disrespect must be curbed because it makes you look weak, translate into violence when they are taken literally. Other norms, such as the premise that a brother-officer can do no wrong, do not promote violence, but help to protect it. Both sets of norms are impressed on a man by his fellow officers through a process of informal socialization.

Niederhoffer, a sociologist with 20 years service as a police officer, has confirmed and elaborated this point. Like Westley, Niederhoffer maintains that police come to see the law as a tool, and that they often view it very pragmatically. If police meet special circumstances about which they feel strongly, they are especially apt to bend the law to accommodate their aims[:] . . .

> The rookie begins with faith in the system. He tries to follow the book of rules and regulations. Then, he discovers that many cases have repercussions of which the book seems wholly ignorant. He is chastised by his colleagues for being naive enough to follow the book. Gradually he learns to neglect the formal rules and norms and turns elsewhere for direction. Individual interpretation replaces the formal authoritative dictum of the official book and the young policeman is an easy prey to cynicism (Niederhoffer 1969, 52–53).

Cynicism may take the form of underenforcement—the norm of leaving well enough alone—or overenforcement—the tradition of acting without basis in law. Overenforcement sometimes features violence, but so does underenforcement. When potentially troublesome situations are avoided, this reduces the chances of a then-and-there confrontation. But unresolved problems may contribute to violence in the community, and may reinvolve the police at a later (more advanced) stage.

Niederhoffer adds a new dimension to Westley's thesis by calling attention to the fact that socialization within the police does not take uniform hold. Whereas some officers become "hard-nosed," others become service oriented. Assignment may accentuate the differences between groups; it may even polarize them. The "tougher" officers may find themselves in "tougher" situations, which cement and reinforce their outlook.

Documentation for the violence-related impact of police socialization also has been provided by John McNamara (1967), who conducted a study of training and its impact on police practices and beliefs.

One unusual feature of the McNamara study is that it not only explores violence-promotive norms, but also describes ways in which police can contribute to violence through lack of social skills. Recruits can become participants in conflicts if they have skill deficits in areas such as

> (1) the gathering of an adequate amount of relevant information about a situation and the citizens in it both prior to and during the interaction between the officer and the citizen(s); (2) the clarification of police expectations for the citizen; (3) the exploitation or utilization of the values of the citizen(s) (McNamara 1967, 169).

McNamara tells us that officers often provide a citizen with overly restricted alternatives. A suspect may be given no choice other than complying with unacceptable demands or attempting to escape. Where incidents involve spectators, such as friends or relatives of the suspect, officers may take insufficient cognizance of threats they pose to the suspect's reputation or "position of authority." Police may also reinforce a man's feelings of victimization by demonstrating disinterest in him as a person. . . .

THE SUSPECT'S VIEW OF POLICE VIOLENCE

Paul Chevigny and an ACLU project he headed offered legal representation to men and women who claimed that they had been assaulted by police. From intensive investigation of numerous such cases, Chevigny tells us that:

> Complaints . . . bear out the hypothesis that most such acts arise out of defiance of authority, or what the police take to be such defiance. A majority of the complaints about force (55 percent), whether authenticated or not, appeared on their face to involve defiance, and the overwhelming majority of the authenticated complaints were shown to involve such defiance (71 percent) (Chevigny 1969, 70).

Like Westley, Chevigny feels that . . . police operate on the premise that they must act to redress disrespect, because failure to do so weakens their authority. . . .

Perceived defiance of authority can take many forms. Some, such as wrestling the officer for his nightstick, are extreme, while others (such as refusing to move) are minor. A spectator who criticizes an officer at work may be viewed as an agitator; a person who quotes the Bill of Rights may be seen—in context—as a cop hater. Some challenges are verbal, and others are gestures; some are intended, and others, such as a drunk urinating on the station room floor, may not be addressed to the police. . . .

Chevigny contends that police departments provide support for violence, by emphasizing arrest criteria of productivity. Although violence may be undesirable, the violent officer is an active officer; it is to the department's interest to help him be productive. It must try not to discourage such a man, even if he is "a bit rough":

> The Department seems to have made a decision, poorly articulated to be sure, that an officer is not to be disciplined for acts performed in the line of duty if those acts

> show initiative and an effort to maintain order. . . . The officer is at least showing initiative and the will to make arrests and obtain convictions—as far as the Department is concerned, virtues of a "good cop" (Chevigny 1969, 67).

Chevigny feels the criminal justice system is generally less concerned about curbing police violence than it may pretend. Judges and prosecutors are reluctant to intervene, in part because the system relegates the dirty work of crime fighting to the police, while preserving its formal legality elsewhere. The public has a similar interest, a similar subconscious view. Its concern for fairness goes hand in hand with a desire for "efficiency," with few questions asked. Police norms do not evolve in vacuity; they have supports outside the police system. . . .

THE OFFICER-SUSPECT TRANSACTION

In police files, police violence is invariably assault on the police. But even as the police assault is officially described it is rarely a one-sided event. The most frequent motive for assaulting an officer that one finds in police reports is the suspect's indignation at having been tampered with on unconvincing grounds. In most cases, the suspect serves notice of his resentment, but the officer perseveres in approaching him. Fully half of the violent police incidents reviewed in one study showed

> the type of sequence where, in the first step, the officer starts an interaction with a civilian by means of an order, a demand, a suggestion, a question, a request, or some other communication. Usually, no serious offense has been committed by the civilian (where there is a formal infraction, the most common is a traffic violation) and the contact is classifiable either as preventive police work or as an effort to cope with a nuisance act. A group of boys is "told to move" or "questioned as to what they are doing"; an errant driver is "told to stop" or "notified" of his violation; a person who is engaged in an altercation is queried as to "what the problem was" or is "instructed to be quiet" or "told to go home." A request for name, address, or identification may also provide the opening spark of the sequence (Robin 1969, 41).

[Robin, 1969] suggests that chronically violent men—whether officers or civilians—contribute to their violence in a patterned way. They are not only involved often, but are also involved in similar ways on different occasions. This fact holds in situations where an aggressive man encounters a man who is not violently inclined, but also where two violent men interact. In such instances, each of the two parties tends to play an assigned role in his opponent's habitual game. . . .

Preferred activity patterns of officers are related to their involvement in violence. A gruff officer is a problem, but a gruff officer who looks for action is a disaster. And not the least reason for concern is that such an officer, as he goes about his personal crusade, is apt to find targets in the shape of civilian counterparts. Once such a meeting occurs, the stage is set for the operationalizing of norms such as "respect."

Violent officers are visible in police records and responsible for much of police violence. They are also, however, systemic products. Although they court trouble, trouble is tied to productivity, which is esteemed. The act of violence itself ("interference" or "assault on a peace officer") thus turns into an arrest, which is a unit of police production.[2] And even where an officer's act is flagrant, it is still entitled—because it is police business—to protective measures.

It follows that the violence-prone officer cannot be dealt with as an individual problem. To target such an officer for attention calls into question organizational goals, such as wide discretion and high productivity. . . . Even if the accusations are deemed meritorious (for instance, if Officer Smith is seen as a Dangerous Nut), there is always the concern with autonomy. If administrators can monkey with Smith—however unsavory he may be—they may be tempted to encroach on others. . . .

The difference between the officer and the [police] assaulter is that the assaulter's subculture is not available to him where it counts. While the officer may obtain evasive testimony from his partner, the suspect's peers may make poor witnesses. The fact that a citizen does not have others rise to his defense may make him more vulnerable than the officer.

TYPES OF POLICE VIOLENCE

Putting aside the issue of change implications, . . . what can we say so far? What is "police violence?" What defines it? Nurtures it? Gives it shape?

The literature, from Westley down, centers on police–citizen confrontations that end in assaults. It probably takes this turn because sheer prevalence permits inquiry yielding inferences backed by data. The . . . portrait traced by research holds over time, over place, over types of data. . . .

Westley's view shows that violence, when used by police, responds often to taunts. It does so because the officer's self-love is gauged by "respect" from others. "Respect" for law, when a man feels he embodies law, inspires private wars under color of law. Few officers may be violent, but these are backed by others—by peers who see police bonds as links to survival. . . .

We have seen that violent suspects often tend to be counterparts of violent officers. These suspects also prize respect, and view it as a measure of self-esteem. This suggests that much police violence comes about when either party to a confrontation engages the other in a test of respect. Violence becomes probable where issues of self-esteem are mobilized for both contenders. . . .

It is also clear that the "cop and robber" game is sometimes at play. An officer faced with an on-view burglar is reluctant to let the suspect escape. Similarly, suspects faced with detention may take a short-range view of their fate, and attempt to shoot their way out. This may occur particularly in incidents where the suspect feels vulnerable, although the officer is unaware of the man's vulnerability.

There may also be suspects or officers disturbed enough to use weapons without realizing the full gravity of their acts. Guns are sufficiently available in our society, and sufficiently in use, for some persons to deploy them casually. The presence of alcohol or strong feelings may create such casualness in individuals who are otherwise normal.

. . . [F]ear [also] plays [a] role. This is particularly true where acts viewed through fear spawn "preventive" violence. The youngster who flees because police spell danger may be gunned down by an officer who feels threatened by the youngster's running. Such occasions are doubly tragic, because the two parties are victims of reciprocal errors.

It is worth repeating that violence arises out of violence and brings about more violence. A police obsessed with danger, a public in fear of police, produce polarization and distance. Fear increases in-grouping among police, which leads to isolation and cynicism, and breeds police violence.

NOTES

1. Assaults on police officers, as reported to the FBI, have steadily averaged 1 for every 5 officers, per annum. Assaults with bodily injury to the officer occur at an average rate of 7 per 100 officers per annum.
2. Actually, this is true in a very narrow sense only. The San Francisco Police Department [1964] once found, for example, that fully half its interference and resistance arrests were dismissed, and an average of only 13 percent of arrestees were jailed. . . .

REFERENCES

Chevigny, P., *Police Power: Police Abuses in New York City*. New York: Pantheon, 1969.

Kobler, A.L., "Police Homicide in a Democracy," *Journal of Social Issues*, 1975, *31*, 163–184.

McNamara, J.H., "Uncertainties of Police Work: The Relevance of Police Recruits' Background and Training," in Bordua, D.J., ed., *The Police: Six Sociological Essays*. New York: Wiley, 1967.

New York Times, January 31, 1973.

———, August 26, 1973.

Niederhoffer, A., *Behind the Shield: The Police in Urban Society*. New York: Doubleday, Anchor, 1969.

Reiss, A.J., "Police Brutality: Answers to Key Questions," in Lipsky, M., ed., *Law and Order: Police Encounters*. Chicago: Aldine, 1970.

———, *The Police and the Public*. New Haven: Yale, 1971.

Robin, G.D., "Justifiable Homicide by Police Officers," *Journal of Criminal Law, Criminology and Police Science*, 1963, *54*, 225–231.

San Francisco Police Department, Internal Memorandum, 1959–1963, dated 10-12-64, memo.

Toch, H., *Violent Men: An Inquiry into the Psychology of Violence*. Chicago: Aldine, 1969.

U.S. Department of HEW, National Center for Health Statistics, *Vital Statistics of the U.S., 1968*, Vol. 2, *Mortality*, Part A, 1972.

U.S. Department of Justice, Federal Bureau of Investigation, *Uniform Crime Reports*, 1971, August 1972.

U.S. Riot Commission, *Report of the National Advisory Commission on Civil Disorders*. New York: Bantam Books, 1968.

Westley, W.A., *Violence and the Police: A Sociological Study of Law, Custom, and Morality*. Boston: The M.I.T. Press, 1970.

Blind Justice: Police Shootings in Memphis

James J. Fyfe

The literature on police use of deadly force[1] has produced two major findings. First, researchers report extreme variation in rates of police shooting among American jurisdictions.[2] Second, regardless of its geographic scope, the research invariably reports that the percentage of police shootings involving black victims far exceeds the percentage of blacks in the population.[3] . . .

I. INTERJURISDICTIONAL VARIATIONS

Attempts to identify sources of interjurisdictional shooting rate variation have produced mixed results. Milton suggests that differences among shooting rates are associated with differences in levels of community violence and risk to officers.[4] Kania and Mackey . . . report strong associations between fatal police shooting rates and public homicide and arrest rates over the 50 states.[5] . . . [T]heir thesis, that shootings are associated with community violence and risk to officers, is supported by Fyfe. He reports close associations between police shooting rates and arrest and homicide rates across the geographic subdivisions of a single large police jurisdiction, where internal organizational policies and practices which might influence shooting rates are presumably constant.[6] . . .

. . . Uelman . . . reports that the major determinants of the levels of police shooting in the California agencies he studied were the "personal philosophies" of police chiefs and the administrative controls they devised.[7] . . . [V]ariations in the shooting rates of American police jurisdictions apparently are associated both with "external" variables (*e.g.*, community violence; threats to officer safety) and with "internal" variables (*e.g.*, administrative philosophies; adequacy of training; restrictiveness of police shooting policies; intensity of shooting incident review).

II. BLACK DISPROPORTION

Goldkamp's survey of the literature of police deadly force offers a similar and useful construct of . . . theories regarding minority disproportion among those shot and shot at by police.[8] Those who have studied deadly force, he states, subscribe to one of two "Belief Perspectives." Belief Perspective I . . . attributes black disproportion among shooting victims to variables *internal* to police organizations (*e.g.* racism by officers and by the administrators who encourage or allow them to express it by shooting blacks in situations in which they would refrain from shooting whites). Belief Perspective II views black shooting victim disproportion as a consequence of variables *external* to police organizations [(*e.g.*, a consequence of justifiable police responses to the relatively great involvement of blacks in violent crime and other activities likely to precipitate shooting[)].[9] . . .

. . . Fyfe found that black disproportion among New York City police shooting victims was closely associated with the representation of blacks among violent crime arrestees and among homicide victims.[10] Belief Perspective II is also supported by Blumberg's study of police shootings in Atlanta and Kansas City, which, like Fyfe's work, reports little variation in the degree of danger confronted by police officers involved in shootings of citizens of different racial groups.[11]

Despite these apparent confirmations of Belief Perspective II, it is possible that the relationships between high rates of police shooting victimization and indications of black violence are artifacts of differential police enforcement and reporting practices. In other words, it may be that the relationship between black shooting rates and black arrest rates is a result of arbitrariness in arrest and crime reporting practices, as well as in shooting practices. Further, given great inter-jurisdictional variation in police shooting rates, it is also possible that the validity of either of Goldkamp's two Belief Perspectives is place dependent.

In jurisdictions where police shooting is infrequent and closely controlled by stringent policies and incident review procedures conducted by administrators whose personal philosophies mitigate against arbitrary shootings, black disproportion may be explained by Belief Perspective II. In such places, it may be that internal organizational strategies have minimized officer arbitrariness, and that external variables (*e.g.*, crime rate differentials among the races) do account for black shooting victim disproportion. Conversely, in jurisdictions characterized by high police shooting rates and loose or non-existent training, shooting policies and review procedures, it may be that officers are exercising their broad discretion in a manner that validates Belief Perspective I. In such places, it may be true that officers shoot blacks in situations in which they would refrain from shooting whites, and that their actions are congruent with the personal philosophies of their supervisors. In view of the wide range in restrictiveness of police shooting policies and other internal organizational variables across jurisdictions,[12] therefore, it would be surprising if either Belief Perspective I or Belief Perspective II was universally valid among American police agencies. Indeed, it may be that the empirical support for Belief Perspective II exists because research access has been granted by only those police agencies that have attempted to control shooting discretion in a manner that minimizes the opportunity for officers to exercise "differential trigger fingers," and which, consequently, have little fear that researchers will publish embarrassing findings.

III. A MODEL FOR ANALYSIS

At the most basic level, police shootings may be dichotomized into "elective" shootings (those in which the officer involved may elect to shoot or not to shoot at little or no risk to himself or others), and "nonelective" shootings (those in which the officer has little real choice but to shoot or to risk death or serious injury to himself or others). Like elective surgery, elective shootings—those involving unarmed fleeing property criminals, for example—are real exercises in discretion. Thus, they are subject to reduction by internal police policies and practices designed to limit officer discretion. . . . Nonelective shootings, by contrast, are largely a consequence of influences external to the police agency [involving] . . . life-threatening circumstances.

Stated most simply, elective shooting rates are most greatly influenced by factors internal to police organizations, and nonelective shooting rates are most greatly influenced by factors external to police organizations. . . .

. . . To know whether police differentiate along racial lines with their trigger fingers, one must know something about the situations in which police shoot at members of different racial groups. . . . [Fyfe] suggested the utility of a typology of police shooting based on a "scale of immediate hazard" to the officer. Using "degree of officer injury" as a criterion, such a scale . . . was constructed and used in [Fyfe's] analysis of New York City police shootings; it was found that the situations in which officers shot blacks threatened life relatively more often and more seriously (and, thus were more often nonelective) than those in which they shot whites.[13] . . .

Data Sources

The New York City shooting data used in this research are part of a data set which includes all reported incidents in which members of that agency discharged firearms and/or were seriously assaulted or killed between January 1, 1971, and December 31, 1975. . . .

The Memphis shooting data employed herein cover slightly different time periods and . . . consist of a Memphis Police Department condensation of the circumstances in which officers in that agency employed deadly force against property crime suspects, as well as summary data on other uses of firearms during the years 1969–74. In addition, this research employs data on all fatal police shootings in Memphis during 1969–76, except for those occurring between January 16 and December 31, 1972, a period for which no information is available.[14] In neither city was any attempt made to reconcile these official versions of shootings with other accounts.

IV. ANALYSIS

A. Interjurisdictional Variations: Memphis and New York City

. . . [A]ggregate rates indicate that Memphis police use their guns considerably more often than their New York City counterparts. They tell us little, however, of the variations in violence and police hazard generally in those cities. Nor are they informative on the questions of percentages or rates of elective and nonelective shootings in Memphis and New York. [Moreover], . . . not all of the shootings . . . involve shootings at other persons.

Table 10-1 presents surrogate measures of general police hazard in Memphis and New York City [and] . . . suggests . . . that these external influences are not associated with the differences in shooting rates between Memphis and New York. The table indicates that F.B.I. Uniform Crime Reports derived murder rates per 100,000 population were relatively similar in those cities during the periods studied . . . , and that New York City police annually effected approximately twice as many violent felony arrests per 1,000 officers . . . as Memphis officers (587.12). Further, the table's rates of police shootings per 1,000 violent felony arrests effected indicate that Memphis officers were more than three times as likely to have used their guns in relation to this measure of police hazard than were New York officers (rates = 56.98 and 16.71, respectively).

The absence of association between variations in these measures and variations in Memphis and New York City police shooting rates suggests that varying internal police organizational influences may be operative. In Table 10-2, the reasons for shooting given by the officers involved in the incidents in each city are presented. . . .

[T]he table shows great differences in the reasons given for shooting by officers in Memphis and New York City. . . . Three fifths (60.2%) of the New York City shootings reportedly occurred in defense of the lives of officers or others, while only slightly more than one fourth of the Memphis shootings involved either the defense of life *or* the apprehension of persons suspected of crimes of violence. Conversely, half (50.7%) of the Memphis shootings involved apprehensions of property crime suspects, while only one in seventeen (6.1%) of the New York shootings was precipitated by attempts to apprehend persons suspected of either property crimes or crimes of violence. . . .

. . . [T]able 10-2 provides strong evidence that the variation in shooting rates between Memphis and New York is largely attributable to the great frequency with which Memphis officers engaged in elective shootings of fleeing property crime suspects. . . . [S]uch relatively unrestrained use of firearms in elective shootings at fleeing property crime suspects suggests that internal agency controls in policy shooting are loose or nonexistent. . . . [Fyfe] has reported that the 1972 imposition of restrictive shooting policy guidelines and accompanying

Table 10-1.
Measures of Public Violence, Police Hazard and Police Shooting in Memphis and New York City

Measure	Memphis 1969–74	New York City 1971–75
Mean Annual Murder/Nonnegligent Manslaughter Rate per 100,000 Population	2.97	2.75
Mean Annual Violent Felony Arrest Rate per 1,000 Officers[a]	587.12	1172.95
Police Shooting Rate per 1,000 Violent Felony Arrests	56.98	16.71

[a]Includes arrests for murder/nonnegligent manslaughter, rape, robbery, aggravated assault.

Table 10-2.
Officer's Reason for Shooting in Memphis and New York City

Measure	Memphis 1969–74		New York City 1971–75	
Defend Life[a]	28.0%	(n = 63)	60.2%	(1760)
rate[b]	9.4		11.8	
Apprehend Suspects[c]	50.7%	(114)	6.1%	(179)
rate	16.9		1.2	
Accidental	4.9%	(11)	8.5%	(249)
rate	1.6		1.7	
Destroy Animal	5.8%	(13)	9.2%	(270)
rate	1.9		1.8	
Warning Shots	4.4%	(10)	11.1%	(326)
rate	2.1		2.2	
Miscellaneous[d]	4.4%	(10)	4.9%	(142)
rate	1.5		1.0	
TOTAL	100.0%	(225)	100.0%	(2926)
RATE	33.5[e]		19.6	

chi-square = 414.18, df = 5
$p < .001$

[a]Memphis "Defend Life" includes [shootings to "apprehend violent suspects" regardless of whether the officer was in imminent danger at the time shots were fired or whether the "violent suspect" was fleeing from a completed violent crime. Thus, Memphis "Defend Life" includes elective and nonelective shootings. New York includes only nonelective shootings].

[b]Rate = mean annual rate per 1,000 officers.

[c]Memphis "Apprehend Suspects" includes only apprehensions of property crime suspects; New York includes apprehensions of property crime and personal violence crime suspects.

[d]Memphis = non ascertained; New York = suicides, criminal shootings, etc.

[e]Subcell rates may not equal totals due to rounding.

internal review procedures were associated with a 75 percent decrease in New York City shootings at fleeing suspects.[15] Those guidelines describe the . . . officer's weapon as an instrument to be carried "for personal protection against persons feloniously attacking an officer or another at close range,"[16] and are enforced stringently. . . . [In contrast, the] 1975 Memphis Police department regulations . . . state[:]

> ["]Officers are permitted to use whatever force is reasonable and necessary to protect others or themselves from bodily harm[."[17] And] . . . "*Under certain specified conditions*, deadly force may be exercised against a fleeing felon[."[18] However, "] Nowhere in the department's *Policies and Regulations* are those "certain specified conditions" written.["[18]]

Thus, [it has been] suggest[ed] that black disproportion among Memphis police shooting victims is a consequence of the absence of clear shooting guidelines. If that assertion is correct, it may also be true that Goldkamp's Belief Perspective I—that police shoot blacks in situations less threatening than those in which they shoot whites[19]—was also valid in Memphis during 1969–74.

B. Black Disproportion in Memphis

. . . [I]t is useful to examine black shooting victim disproportion in Memphis, a city in which police shooting guidelines were very loose. . . . [Data were analyzed regardless] of the races and injuries of property crime suspects shot at by Memphis police during 1969–74. . . . [They revealed] that 85.7% of those shot at were black, and that 14.3% were white, with similar racial distributions among [the] injury categories [no injuries, wounded, killed].

[Using] the rate per 1,000 officers . . . , between 1969 and 1974, Memphis police were six times as likely to have shot at and missed black property crime suspects as they were for whites (noninjured rates = 10.4 and 1.6 per 1,000 officers annually). . . . [T]hey were 13 times more likely to have wounded blacks than whites under such circumstances (. . . black rate = 1.9; . . . white rate = 0.1). . . . [And] they were three times more likely to have killed blacks than whites at scenes of property crime (rates = 1.9 and 0.6).

[A] second set of rates shows that black Memphians were nearly ten times as likely as whites to have been shot at in such circumstances (rates per 100,000 population = 39.6 and 4.2). . . . [B]lacks were 18 times more likely to have been wounded (black wounded rate = 5.4; white = 0.3), and more than five times as likely to have been killed in these situations than were their fellow white citizens (black killed rate = 5.4; white = 1.0).

Neither of these rates . . . gives a precise measure of the degree to which blacks disproportionately may expose themselves to the risk of being shot while fleeing from officers at scenes of property crimes.

. . . [A] third set of rates presents the number of persons shot at for each category per 1,000 property criminals of that same category arrested by Memphis police. Here again, one finds great disproportion. During the years studied, 4.3 black property crime suspects were shot at for each 1,000 black property crime arrestees; the comparable white rate is 1.8. . . .

. . . [The data strongly] suggest that Memphis blacks were in far greater risk of being shot or shot at in these circumstances than can be explained by either their presence in the general population or the arrestee population.

Similar inferences may be drawn from [other data] which [link] . . . the actions and races of persons fatally shot by Memphis police during 1969–76. . . . The[se data] [reveal] that more than three fourths (26) of the 34 persons whose race is known were black. Half of these blacks (13) were reportedly unarmed and nonassaultive at the time of their death. Only one of the eight whites shot and killed died in such an elective event. This disparity yields a black death rate from police shootings while unarmed and nonassaultive (5.4 per 100,000) that is 18 times higher than the comparable white rate (0.3). Looking into shootings involving situations which are more life threatening, we find assaultive blacks not armed with guns dying at a rate (2.5) five times higher than whites (0.5). Finally, black representation among those reportedly armed with guns and presumably leaving officers few alternatives to shooting (2.9 per 100,000) is slightly more than twice as high as the comparable white rate (1.3).

V. CONCLUSIONS

. . . [The analysis] clearly indicate[s] [a] black disproportion among shooting victims [but] that this disproportion is greatest where elective shootings of nonassaultive, unarmed people are concerned. Unless Memphis officers differentially *reported* the circumstances of shootings of black and white citizens during the period studied, the data suggest also that the difference between the shooting rates of Memphis and New York was not an artifact of reporting practices, but was, in fact, a reflection of the great frequency with which Memphis police shot unarmed blacks. [The data further suggest] . . . the negative impact upon Memphis blacks of the absence of clear shooting guidelines . . . [and] strongly support the assertion that police there did differentiate racially with their trigger fingers, by shooting blacks in circumstances less threatening than those in which they shot whites.

This analysis has demonstrated that one cannot generalize readily about police shooting rate disparities. . . . Hopefully, it also provides some direction for future examinations of shooting rate variation among jurisdictions and among races. Intensive analyses of those phenomena are required so that policing in this democratic society can occur with minimal bloodshed. Police shootings *are* a consequence of violence in the community and the number of times members of various population subgroups expose themselves to the danger of being shot at by police; but levels of police shootings are also greatly affected by organizational variables. Thus, analysis of the circumstances under which shootings occur can point the way to police administrative action to reduce elective shootings. It may also suggest broader social action to change the conditions which spawn the nonelective shootings over which police chiefs and police officers have very limited direct control.

Administrative action to reduce elective shootings in Memphis has occurred since the end of the period studied in this report. In 1979, . . . that department instituted a more stringent shooting policy and incident review procedure than had existed.[20] It has also initiated an "officer survival" training program designed to help police more safely respond to the potentially violent situations which often precipitate nonelective shootings. . . .

NOTES

1. "Deadly Force" generally is defined as force likely to kill or capable of killing. Since police deadly force most often occurs when police point and fire their guns at other human beings, and since such actions do not always result in death, "police deadly force" will be defined in this paper to include all police shootings at others.
2. *See* C. Milton, Police Use of Deadly Force (1977); Kania & Mackey, *Police Violence as a Function of Community Characteristics*, 15 Criminology 27 (1977); Kiernan, *Shooting by Policemen in District Declines*, Wash. Star, Sept. 2, 1979, § B, at 1, col. 2; Sherman & Langworthy, *Measuring Homicide by Police Officers*, 70 J. Crim. L. & C. 546 (1979).

3. *See* C. Milton, *supra* note 2, at 22; Fyfe, *Race and Extreme Police-Citizen Violence*, in Race, Crime, and Criminal Justice 89 (C.E. Pope & R. McNeely eds. 1981); Harding & Fahey, *Killings by Chicago Police, 1969–70: An Empirical Study*, 46 S. Cal. L. Rev. 284 (1973); Kobler, *Police Homicide in a Democracy*, 31 J. Soc. Issues 163 (1975); Meyer, *Police Shootings at Minorities: The Case of Los Angeles*, in 452 Annals 98 (1980); Takagi, *A Garrison State in "Democratic" Society*, in Police–Community Relations 357–71 (A. Cohn & E. Viano eds. 1976).

4. C. Milton, *supra* note 2, at 144.

5. Kania & Mackey, *supra* note 2. [They] . . . necessarily included in their analysis only data on *fatal* police shootings, thus excluding many nonfatal exercises of police deadly force. Further, their data on fatal shootings were obtained from the United States Vital Statistics' annual reports on Causes of Mortality, a source subsequently found highly unreliable by Sherman & Langworthy, *supra* note 2, at 559.

6. Fyfe, *Geographic Correlates of Police Shooting: A Microanalysis*, 17 J. Research Crime & Delinquency 101 (1980).

7. Uelman, *Varieties of Police Policy: A Study of Police Policy Regarding the Use of Deadly Force in Los Angeles County*, 6 Loy. L.A. L. Rev. 1 (1973). *See also* Fyfe, *Administrative Interventions on Police Shooting Discretion: An Empirical Examination*, 7 J. Crim. Just. 309 (1979); Sherman & Langworthy, *supra* note 2.

8. Goldkamp, *Minorities as Victims of Police Shootings: Interpretations of Racial Disproportionality and Police Use of Deadly Force*, 2 Just. Sys. J. 169 (1976).

9. *Id.* at 173.

10. Fyfe, *supra* note 3, at 93–94.

11. M. Blumberg, Race and Police Shootings: An Analysis in Two Cities (1980) (paper presented to the Annual Meeting of the American Society of Criminology). *See also* W. Geller & K. Karales, Split Second Decision: Shootings Of and By Chicago Police (1981).

12. *See* Uelman, *supra* note 7.

13. Fyfe, Shots Fired: An Examination of New York City Police Firearms Discharges 921 (1978) (unpublished Ph.D. dissertation, State University of New York at Albany).

14. Tennessee Advisory Committee to the U.S. Comm. on Civil Rights, Civil Crisis—Civic Challenge: Police Community Relations in Memphis (1978) [hereinafter cited as Tennessee Advisory Committee].

15. Fyfe, *supra* note 7 at 318.

16. New York City Police Department, *Temporary Operating Procedure 237* (1972).

17. Memphis Police Department, *Policies and Regulations* 5[, 9] (1975) [emphasis added].

18. Tennessee Advisory Committee, *supra* note 14, at 80.

19. *See* Goldkamp, *supra* note 8.

20. Memphis Police Department, Training Academy, *General Order #5-79, Deadly Force Policy* 1–2 (1979), states that officers may use deadly force in arrest situations

only as a last resort in order "(t)o apprehend a suspect fleeing from the commission of a dangerous felony when an officer has witnessed the offense or has sufficient information to know as a virtual certainty that the suspect committed the offense." *General Order #5-79* defines as "dangerous felonies" kidnapping, murder in the 1st or 2nd degree, manslaughter, arson, criminal sexual assault, 1st, 2nd, or 3rd degree (rape and attempted rape), aggravated assault, robbery, burglary 1st, 2nd or 3rd degree, or any attempt to commit these crimes. The order also establishes an internal shooting review procedure.

Chapter 11

Prisons

Prison Revolt: A Brief History

Israel L. Barak-Glantz

*I*nterpersonal, one-to-one violence is endemic to prison life. However, group action precipitated chiefly by internal changes in prison structure and organization and by the intrusion of outside conflicts beyond the walls is much more spectacular, deadly, [and] destructive. . . . It is not surprising that there has been at least one major prison riot in the United States each year. These riots occur coast to coast and, more often than not, involve the taking of guards as hostages, and nearly always include arson and vandalism (DesRoches, 1974). Ironically, the usual targets of destruction have been prison schools, shops, infirmaries, counseling centers, chapels, and recreational facilities—the very programs and institutions designed to aid inmates during their period of confinement. Another irony has been pointed out by Huff (1982) who argues that the penitentiary, an American invention, was conceived as an alternative to violence. He argues, like Rothman (1971), that the prison was originally introduced to substitute executing the offender. In advancing the new ideology of the penitentiary, the Quakers attempted to establish a place where the criminal could be penitent, remorseful, and have an environment where he could reflect on his sins. The intention was to build institutions which would transform and reform these wayward transgressors. . . . In reality, however, institutions soon became overcrowded, the unqualified personnel became overworked, and the institutional resources gradually diminished to a point where adequate care and humane living conditions were impossible to provide. Thus, the institution which was invented as an alternative to violent punishment became the context within which individual violence became a way of life.

An examination of institutional disorders and disturbances reveals not only a cyclical pattern of periodic flare-ups every decade or so, but also a steady increase in occurrences of disruptive behavior and a change in the seriousness of the riots in terms of injuries and damage to property. Prisoner revolt historians identify several major waves of riots and disorders in the twentieth century. The first one coincided with the First World War. Although information on these earlier prison riots is relatively sketchy, we know that violence was usually brief, it cost few lives, and involved a relatively small number of hostages. This first riot lasted some 24 months and led to the introduction of some of the proposals which were originally set forth in the American Prison Congress meeting in Cincinnati in 1870. These programs included education, the introduction of counseling services, declining emphasis on regimentation, and harsh disciplinary approach to management, as well as some improvements in prisoners' living conditions. This wave ended in 1915 (Garson, 1972:535).

Another wave of prison disorders and disturbances came in America in 1929 and lasted for about two years (Garson, 1972:536; Dinitz, 1980:8). This wave of riots coincided with the old "new criminology." This brand of criminology was associated with the doctrines of the rehabilitation model and all its derivatives, i.e., diagnosis, testing, differential psychiatric treatment and counseling, indeterminate sentencing, and parole. This philosophy was clearly therapeutic in nature and thus undermined the existing *modus vivendi* which existed in American prisons at that time. Some students of prison riots (Dinitz, 1980; Huff, 1982) feel that this state of affairs may have served as a trigger for the coast-to-coast prison revolts of the early years of the great depression. This second wave of riots produced an atmosphere within which prison reforms, such as the right to possess radios, extended inmate interaction with the world outside the prison, and visiting privileges were implemented. It can be argued that these prison disorders created the first fissures in the walls around many American prisons, thus paving the way for outsiders to become more involved with prisoners.

The next series of serious riots came after 20 years, with the Korean War in 1951. This wave began in Utah (May and August 1951) involving the usual complaints of poor food, brutal treatment by guards, inhumane sanitary conditions, and capricious parole board decisions. Like epidemics of any kind, destruction spread to West Virginia, Illinois, Kentucky, Michigan (April 1952), New Jersey (April and October 1952), Pennsylvania, Washington, and Oregon, before it subsided. The years 1952 and 1953 saw more than 45 riots involving over 21 states. Most of these prison riots were specifically directed and motivated by dissatisfaction with the way in which the rehabilitation was implemented (*Prison Riots and Disturbances*, 1953; *Riots and Disturbances*, 1970; Carter, McGee and Nelson, 1975; Flynn, 1980).

Since 1953, the number of outbreaks has declined—until 1968 when violence and injuries increased in severity with each consecutive year. Dinitz holds that the 1960's in the United States were "the most riotous years of the century." . . .

. . . [T]he revolution in the streets rapidly penetrated behind prison walls, and "burn, baby burn," and "down the pigs," were slogans imported into prison lingo, and another wave of unrest in prisons was ushered in (Dinitz, 1980:10). This wave began at the Oregon Penitentiary with 22 hostages taken, five prisoners killed, 61 wounded persons, seven destroyed buildings, more than $1 million in property damage, and one warden fired. . . .

Of all years, 1971 led to the bloodiest riot wave in the history of prison unrest and disorders, culminating at the State Prison at Attica, New York, which exploded late that year. After the prison at Attica was taken over, 32 inmates and 11 guards were dead. All but three were killed by the state forces (*The Official Report of the New York State's Special Commission on Attica*, 1972). . . .[1] [T]he Attica riot would stand out in the eyes of American citizens as the worst riot in American prison history, particularly because it was televised daily across the United States. This wave of riots did not completely end in 1971. . . .

Perhaps the most serious of all prison riots, in terms of its level of violence and brutality, is the one which took place at the New Mexico State Penitentiary in 1980. Students of the prison, its critics, journalists, and others tend to compare the New Mexico riot with the one at Attica.

However, there are several fronts in which these two major prison riots are distinguishable (Huff, 1982), and these must be considered before comparison becomes useful.

First, demands in the case of the Attica situation were presented to the management and specifically to New York's Commissioner of Correctional Services, Russell G. Oswald, before the riot began (Wicker, 1975:311). By contrast, in the New Mexico State Prison situation, it was clear that the riot occurred in a prison where "inmates certainly had serious grievances but the riots seemed to take place within an overall *context* of poor conditions, rather than as a protest directed against those conditions" (Huff, 1982:8). . . .

Second, from an examination of the events in these prison riots, it is evident that, in the case of Attica, force and revolt [were] used as a means to other ends, rendering the Attica riot instrumental in nature. One might argue that it was designed to achieve specific goals. . . . In the case of the New Mexico situation, however, force and rebellion were clearly used in a rather hedonistic fashion.

It is obvious from this account that prison violence is not a relatively recent phenomenon. Rather, it has always been with us, even though some of its elements and characteristics have undergone considerable change (*Prison Riots and Disturbances*, 1953; *Riots and Disturbances*, 1970; Flynn, 1980). . . .

NOTE

1. *The Official Report of the New York State Special Commission on Attica* found that in the course of ending the riot, state police killed 29 inmates and 10 officer hostages; 3 hostages and 85 inmates were wounded. No hostages were killed by inmates.

REFERENCES

Carter, Robert M.; McGee, Richard A.; and Nelson, E. Kim. *Corrections in America*. Philadelphia: J. B. Lippincott Co., 1975.

DesRoches, Fred. "Patterns of Prison Riots." *Canadian Journal of Criminology and Corrections* 16 (1974):332–351.

Dinitz, Simon. "Are Safe and Humane Prisons Possible?" The John Vincent Barry Memorial Lecture, University of Melbourne, Australia, October, 1980.

Flynn, Edith S. "From Conflict Theory to Conflict Resolution: Controlling Collective Violence in Prisons." *American Behavioral Scientist* 23 (May–June 1980):745–776.

Garson, David G. "Force Versus Restraint in Prison Riots." *Crime and Delinquency* 18 (October 1972):411–421.
Huff, Ronald C. "Prison Violence: Sociological and Public Policy Implications." Paper presented at the Annual Meeting of the Israeli Criminological Society, Hebrew University Law School, Jerusalem, Israel, April 1982.
Prison Riots and Disturbances. New York: American Prison Association, 1953.
Riots and Disturbances. Washington, D.C.: American Correctional Association, 1970.
Rothman, David J. *The Discovery of the Asylum: Social Order and Disorder in the Republic*. Boston: Little, Brown, and Co., 1971.
The Official Report of the New York State's Special Commission on Attica. New York: Bantam Books, 1972.
Wicker, Tom. *A Time to Die*. New York: Quadrangle, 1975.

The 1980 New Mexico Prison Riot

Mark Colvin

The riot that began at the Penitentiary of New Mexico in Santa Fe at 1:40 a.m. on February 2, 1980, is without parallel in the penal history of the United States for its brutality, destruction, and disorganization among the rioters. In the 36 hours before order was forcefully restored by the New Mexico State Police and National Guard, 33 inmates were killed by other inmates; 12 were first tortured and mutilated. The exact number of inmates injured during the riot is not known. Serrill and Katel (1980:6) report that as many as 200 inmates were beaten and raped; the New Mexico attorney general reports that at least 90 inmates were treated at local hospitals for overdoses of prison pharmacy drugs and for injuries sustained in fighting among inmates (Office of the Attorney General, 1980a:1). Seven of the 12 correctional officers who were taken hostage were beaten, stabbed, or sodomized, though none were killed. No inmates or hostages were killed or injured during the retaking of the institution by authorities.[1]

Unlike the 1971 inmate revolt at Attica, New York, in which a high degree of inmate organization, solidarity, and political consciousness was evident, the New Mexico riot is notable for the fragmentation, lack of effective leadership, and disorganization apparent among the inmates. As Garson's (1972) historical survey of prison riots makes clear, it is important to place prison disturbances within their historical context. The Attica revolt was the ultimate expression of the politicization and solidarity among inmates in the United States in the late 1960s and early 1970s. . . . The 1980 New Mexico riot revealed the extent to which relations between inmates had become fragmented during the 1970s and early 1980s:

political apathy and infighting had replaced the politicization and solidarity of a decade earlier (. . . Cohen *et al.*, 1976; Colvin, 1981; Fox, 1982; Irwin, 1980; Jacobs, 1977 . . .). . . .

. . . Both an official control structure and an inmate social structure contribute to the organization of prisons. The official control structure is comprised of those formal and informal relations of power and authority instituted and maintained by the administration and staff to control inmate behavior. The inmate social structure involves relations of power, status, and economic exchange between inmates (Clemmer, 1940; Davidson, 1974; Sykes, 1958; Sykes and Messinger, 1960). These two structures are closely linked: they can either accommodate or challenge one another. Prisons are relatively calm and orderly when the staff and administration use the cohesive economic and power relationships within the inmate social structure to secure compliance from inmates (Sykes, 1958).

Previous studies of prison riots have focused on the consequences of administrative actions which disrupt the patterns of accommodation and thus disrupt the cohesive forces in the inmate social structure (Fox, 1971; Hartung and Floch, 1956; McCleery, 1968; Ohlin, 1956, 1960; Sykes, 1958). Such administrative actions may result from: (1) the discovery and exposure of "corruption of authority" (Sykes, 1958); (2) policy conflicts between competing interests associated with the prison organization (Jacobs, 1977; Ohlin, 1960); or (3) a change in policies associated with changes in the prison administration (Grusky, 1968; Jacobs, 1977; McCleery, 1968). When all three conditions occur simultaneously, the disruption of cohesive forces in the inmate social structure becomes acute and results in a prolonged period of conflict between the administration's control structure and the inmates' social structure. Inmates often organize protests such as strikes to restore the privileges and rights lost with the removal of the accommodations. When a prison administration bows to pressure and grants formal or informal concessions—in effect re-establishing accommodations—order is restored. Sykes (1958) argues that this cycle of conflict and accommodation is normal in prisons.

Sometimes, however, political events and ideological commitments may compel a prison's administration to respond to an organized inmate protest with increased restrictions, coercion, and a "tightening up" of security—all in an attempt to re-establish control (Ohlin, 1956). When this happens, a cycle of increasing inmate disorder and increasing reliance on coercion by the administration may develop. . . . As the cohesive relations between inmates are steadily eroded, it becomes increasingly difficult to re-establish a base upon which accommodations that might restore order can be built. The process is complicated by growing resentment and an escalation of mutual harassment between guards and inmates. . . . [T]he inmate social structure fragments into small, self-protective cliques as the cohesive forces between inmates continue to dissolve. If patterns of accommodation are not reinstituted, full-scale rioting eventually erupts. The riot is characterized not by inmate solidarity but by fragmentation and fighting among the inmates. This, I submit, is precisely what happened at New Mexico. . . .

PREDISPOSING FACTORS OF THE NEW MEXICO PRISON RIOT

The 1980 New Mexico riot was preceded by five years of relative calm followed by five years of increasing disorder. From 1970 to late 1975, there were three successful and three unsuccessful over-the-fence escapes from the prison; from late 1975 to 1980, there were 36 successful and 18 unsuccessful over-the-fence escapes (Office of the Attorney General, 1980b:5). Violence between inmates, including fist fights, sexual assaults, and stabbings, was rare at New Mexico in the early 1970s. In the late 1970s, however, inmate violence became commonplace.[2] The reasons for this dramatic change in relations among inmates are the key to understanding the predisposing factors of the riot.

Alternative Explanations of Growing Disorder . . .

1. *Security lapses:* According to correctional staff and inmates, the level and quality of security remained relatively constant during the two periods of order and disorder. Security lapses such as open doors and grills, which allowed the riot to spread, were so common over the previous 10 years that guards described them as virtually "standard operating procedures" (Office of the Attorney General, 1980b:10). The ratio of guards to inmates was unchanged during the two periods. Measures designed to tighten security were actually instituted in 1976, including formal training programs, a pass system to control inmate movement, and the placing of concertina wire on perimeter fences. None of these measures curtailed the sharp increase in violence and escapes. A relaxation in security does not seem to have occurred and, therefore, is not a plausible explanation for growing disorder.
2. *Food and services:* The inmates found the food and other basic services equally unsatisfactory during the periods of order and disorder. . . . Some services, such as medical care, reportedly improved in the latter period, while others such as recreation, deteriorated. . . .
3. *Overcrowding:* The inmate population fluctuated during the two periods of order and disorder. Designed to hold 950 inmates, the prison housed 1,272 inmates at one point in 1978. Yet the highest population in the prison's history, 1,294, was recorded in 1963 with no increase in disorder. In 1979, the year before the riot, the population stayed near the capacity figure of 950. . . . [O]vercrowding cannot be completely discounted as a contributing factor of the New Mexico riot: it exacerbated other trends, especially in the three months prior to the riot, when inmate population suddenly increased by 200.
4. *Conspiracies:* Another possible factor . . . was the presence of an entrenched administrative clique alleged to have been conspiring in corruption, brutality, arbitrary discipline, and cover-ups. This argument infers that growing disorder and, eventually, the riot were a *direct* result of this group's miscreant behavior. However, the press reported

allegations of brutality in both periods . . . ; and corruption associated with heroin trafficking was more pronounced in the early 1970s when the prison was relatively calm (Office of the Attorney General, 1980b:17). In addition, the administrative clique, whose most important members were Warden Felix Rodriguez and Deputy Warden Horatio Herrera, also had greater power in the prison organization in the early 1970s. . . .

5. *"New breed" theory:* Some New Mexico correctional administrators argued that a "new breed" of violent, disruptive, and aggressive inmate was to blame for the riot. These inmates were described . . . as "psychopathic personality types;" a few administrators even spoke of them as a new "genetic type" with violent propensities. These allegedly hard-to-control inmates were said to have begun entering the prison around 1975 and 1976. But this argument is weakened by the fact that crimes for which inmates were sent to the New Mexico prison became proportionately less violent as the prison itself became more violent. In 1970, 45 percent of all crimes for which New Mexico prisoners were convicted were violent crimes. By 1975, the figure had dropped to 38 percent, and by 1979 it was 33 percent.[3] (Department of Corrections, 1971, 1976, 1980a). In addition, inmate leaders who, in the early 1970s, helped maintain order (the "old breed") were almost all in prison for violent crimes (Office of the Attorney General, 1980b:29). Other studies also indicate a lack of correlation between prison violence and the entry of "violence-prone" inmates into prisons (Bennett, 1976:151; Ellis *et al.*, 1974:38; Garson, 1972:551; Jacobs, 1977:160).

   These facts suggest that the so-called "new breed" is better understood as a product of internal changes within the prison itself. While a new type of inmate who behaved more violently was certainly emerging in the late 1970s, this fact alone does not adequately explain the long-term build-up to the riot. The emergence of the "new breed" itself needs to be explained. How the "new breed" was produced by the changing control structure and inmate social structure is the key to explaining the New Mexico riot.

Structure of Control and the Inmate Social Structure: 1970–1975

The structure of control in the early 1970s was vastly different than that of the late 1970s. During the period of relative order inmate power was accommodated by the administration. Strong inmates were induced into maintaining order because their sources of power over other inmates were connected to formally established programs and informally tolerated drug trafficking.

Two powerful groups of inmates emerged. The first group included the inmate administrators of several programs initiated in 1968. These included a college program through the College of Santa Fe, a computer key punch shop, a "college prep" program (Project Newgate), an adult basic education program, and several "outside contact" programs. The inmate administrators formally and informally influenced the staff's selection of other inmates for participation in the programs. Participation in these programs greatly enhanced chances of parole; thus, the inmate administrators held considerable power. The inmate administrators were an important element of "self-policing" within the inmate society (Office of the Attorney General, 1980b:15). They had a strong self-interest in maintaining order to protect programs and, consequently, their sources of power. Most of the inmate leaders associated with programs had entered prison with convictions for violent crimes, but they exercised power non-violently.

A second group of inmates controlled trafficking of heroin and other drugs within the prison. Drug consumption increased dramatically at New Mexico from about 1971 to 1976, as did the number of inmate sub-groups involved in trafficking (Office of the Attorney General, 1980b:17). The toleration of, and in some cases collusion with, drug trafficking by prison staff members became an important feature of accommodation and the growing "corruption of authority" during the early 1970s. . . .

That order was maintained from 1970 to 1975 is reflected in the low level of escapes and violence, the large number of "voluntary" (unsolicited) informants, and the fact that less than five percent of the inmate population was in solitary confinement[4] (Office of the Attorney General, 1980b:18). . . .

Structure of Control and the Inmate Social Structure: 1975–1980

In late 1975, the control structure at the prison underwent a dramatic change which disrupted the non-violent relations within the inmate society. The deputy warden was fired and the warden was transferred out of the prison to a "do-nothing" job in [the] central office after New Mexico Attorney General Anaya accused them of mismanagement and corruption. . . . In October, 1975, Governor Apodaca appointed a new prison administration which supported a stricter custodial philosophy. Four other key members of the old administration . . . were soon transferred out of the prison. . . .

In an attempt to wrest control of the prison from the inmates, the new administration removed all inmates from administrative positions in programs, tightened restrictions on inmate movement, stopped "outside contact" programs, increased drug searches, and clamped down on possible conduits for drugs. The curtailment of drugs and many programs . . . disrupted important sources of inmate power than had been connected to these incentives. . . .

. . . Organized protests from inmates quickly erupted. In June, 1976, the inmates organized and staged a work strike to protest the new administration's changes. . . . Given the administration's ideological commitment to tighter custodial policies, public criticism of the former administration, continuing media interest in the prison, and the need for the new administration to establish its credibility with a guard force that resented the power inmates had gained, the administration felt it could not grant any concessions to the strikers.

Instead, force was used to end the strike. . . . Organized inmate opposition was thus suppressed. . . .

The breaking of the strike inaugurated a new era, characterized by a greater reliance by the administration on more coercive control measures. The removal of incentives associated with the previous administration reduced the number of "voluntary" inmate informants and forced staff members (under pressure from supervisors to obtain information) to rely increasingly on direct solicitation of information through threats and promises. The coercive "snitch game" included such tactics as threatening to label an inmate a "snitch" in front of other inmates if the inmate refused to inform (Office of the Attorney General, 1980b:24).

The increased use of solitary confinement further escalated coercion. . . . Use of disciplinary segregation, the most severe *legal* sanction, also increased dramatically. Population in disciplinary segregation, Cell Block 3, designed to hold 86, rose from an average of about 50 in the early 1970s to an average of about 150 for most of the late 1970s. In 1978, it held a record 200 inmates (Office of the Attorney General, 1980b:27).

In late 1977, two inmates in disciplinary segregation—both of whom were among the alleged leaders of the June, 1976 work strike—filed on behalf of several other inmates a class-action suit in federal court against the State of New Mexico, seeking an improvement in conditions at the prison (Serrill and Katel, 1980:16). This suit and its subsequent negotiations, which dragged on until after the riot, represented the last effort at collective opposition to the administration by inmates.

The increased use of coercive controls became inevitable after formal and informal incentives were removed in late 1975 and 1976. This alteration in the structure of control had a devastating impact upon the inmate social structure. The removal of incentives disrupted inmate sources of non-violent power, and the segregation and transfer of many inmate leaders implicated in the 1976 strike removed the agents of political cohesion from the inmate social structure. A power vacuum developed, triggering a struggle for power among the inmates. Power became increasingly based on violence as alternative sources of non-violent power diminished. . . .

The competition to establish a violent reputation in turn generated more violence. Inmates found that a willingness and ability to engage in violence was the best protection against other inmates. . . .

Some staff members and inmates have inferred that inmates who were caught up in this violent competition began to develop an ideology of "moral weakness versus moral strength," based on the "will" to engage in violence, confront guards, and "tough it out" in disciplinary segregation. . . . These inmates were *not* a cohesive group, but constituted several uncoordinated and unstable cliques, each composed of a few inmates.[5] . . .

Under these circumstances, it is not surprising that New Mexico prison administrators began to notice, about 1976, a "new breed" of violent and disruptive inmate emerging in the New Mexico prison. Clearly a sociological phenomenon, the "new breed" becomes inexplicable only when viewed primarily as a psychological or supposedly "genetic" aberration.

Cloward (1960:45) connects the emergence of a similar disruptive inmate role (known as the "hero," "martyr," or "screwball" in correctional literature) with the differential opportunity structure of prisons. . . . [V]iolent, disruptive inmates are engendered through failure to establish themselves in either the legitimate or illegitimate opportunity structures within prisons, and ultimately become "double failures."

Applying Cloward's argument to New Mexico, the change in the prison's control structure in 1975 and 1976 dramatically altered the legitimate and illegitimate opportunity structures upon which non-violent inmate power had been based. Removal of legitimate (program) and illegitimate (drug trafficking) opportunities in the prison created a new opportunity structure that produced the "hero" or "new breed" role. A self-reinforcing structure of violent competition emerged which further incited inmate violence. . . . [G]rowing violence and disorder are . . . understood as responses to a new set of structural imperatives.

With these changes in the organizational structure at the New Mexico prison, inmate society became increasingly fragmented into small and unstable self-protection cliques. While most cliques were racially segregated, they were not organized around race or ethnicity. Many cliques of similar ethnic composition vied with each other as well as with cliques and individuals of different races. Violence between inmates was reported by staff and inmates to be both inter- and intra-racial, with no apparent pattern (Office of the Attorney General, 1980b:8). Nor was race an apparent factor in the killings during the riot. . . . The disorder and fragmentation certainly added to racial tension in the prison, but were not caused by it.

A more important factor in this fragmentation was the coercive pattern of communication (the "snitch game") between staff and inmates which created a growing class of solicited informants and thus convenient and (from the perspective of most inmates) legitimate targets for those seeking a reputation for violence. The coercive tactics for gaining information (and carelessness by staff members in protecting identities of informants) contributed to a growing isolation and mutual suspicion among inmates. Suspected informants were a major target for violence during the riot (Office of the Attorney General, 1980b:25). . . . By the late 1970s, any basis for solidarity between inmates had dissolved.

Fragmentation of the Corrections Administration

While the New Mexico inmate society was fragmenting in the late 1970s, the administration of the prison and the state corrections department was becoming increasingly disorganized as a result of the steady turnover in administrators.[6] . . . The rapid administrative turnover and resulting confusion in policies contributed to the growing disorder at the prison that left both guards and inmates in a state of uncertainty. Guards complained of arbitrary and confused directives from supervisors; inmates complained of arbitrary and conflicting orders from guards. "Mutual harassment" between guards and inmates increased, and the turnover rate for guards at the prison doubled in the late 1970s (Office of the Attorney General, 1980b:21).

The control structure at New Mexico in the late 1970s mirrored the inmate social structure: both depended upon coercion and resulted in fragmentation into cliques. These gradual structural changes within the organization set the stage for the riot.

PRECIPITATING FACTORS OF THE NEW MEXICO PRISON RIOT

Seven events hastened the disintegration of order that finally culminated in the riot:

1. A new warden, the fourth since 1975, began removing inmates from segregation in June 1979, as part of an attempt to receive accreditation for the prison from the American Correctional Association.[7] This brought the unit down to a near capacity population prior to the riot, but the easing of segregation policies without a concurrent increase in positive incentives and other controls removed a level of containment by placing many of the "new breed" inmates in the general prison population. It also transferred overcrowding from cell blocks to less secure dormitories (Office of the Attorney General, 1980a:C3). . . .
2. The administration eliminated one of the last remaining formal incentives, transfer to a minimum security prison, in November 1979, after an inmate killed another inmate during an escape at Camp Sierra Blanca. . . .
3. Inmates became frustrated in late 1979 when federal court orders to improve conditions at the prison, a response to the inmates' 1977 class action suit, were sporadically implemented or ignored by administrators (Office of the Attorney General, 1980b:31).[8]
4. Cell Block 5, which housed the so-called "new breed" inmates, was closed for renovation in November 1979. Most of these inmates were transferred to a less secure dormitory, E-2. This removed yet another level of containment within the prison. . . .
5. On December 9, 1979, 11 inmates escaped. Most were identified as belonging to the violent "new breed" cliques. Though all but one were captured and placed in Cell Block 3 prior to the riot, a sudden increase in searches and restrictions on movement heightened inmate frustration.
6. While the security lapses that allowed inmates to take over the prison had been commonplace for at least 10 years, an important change in a security apparatus occurred in mid-January, 1980. Bullet-proof glass was installed in the control center, replacing steel bars which had blocked visibility from the control center into the main corridor. The control center houses keys and controls access to the entire prison. Security personnel expressed their fears about the vulnerability of the glass to their supervisors. . . . On the morning of the riot, inmates quickly broke through the glass, allowing them to spread the riot through the entire prison.

7. There were a number of forewarnings that a major disturbance was imminent (Office of the Attorney General, 1980a:14; Serrill and Katel, 1980:8). . . . Officials had no way to distinguish reliable from unreliable intelligence, a legacy of the coercive "snitch game" which often resulted in inmates telling officials anything to escape punishment. The forewarnings about a possible disturbance in Dormitory E-2 were unknown to officers and their supervisors who were on duty the morning of the riot (Office of the Attorney General, 1980a:15).

CHARACTERISTICS OF THE RIOT

At 1:40 a.m. on February 2, 1980, several so-called "new breed" inmates in Dormitory E-2 overpowered four guards after hasty planning and several drinks of home-made alcohol. The inmates quickly captured guards stationed at other dormitories in the south wing of the prison. Without any apparent plan, the inmates took over the prison, improvising as they stumbled upon an open dormitory door, an open security grill separating the south wing from the rest of the prison, the glass in the control center, and blow torches left behind by renovation crews.

A group of inmates, allegedly led by one of the inmates from Dormitory E-2, proceeded to the north wing of the prison and opened Cell Block 3 with keys seized from the control center, freeing what were considered to be the most disruptive inmates in the prison. Keys to the protective custody unit, Cell Block 4, were lost during the siege of the control center, but blow torches were used to cut through doors and gain access to vulnerable inmates.

Seventeen of the 33 inmates killed were housed in Cell Block 3 and Cell Block 4. Twelve of these inmates were tortured with blow torches, set afire, and mutilated; one was beheaded with a shovel. The victims included suspected "snitches," a child rapist, and "mentally disturbed" inmates whose screaming had kept other inmates in segregation awake at night. There does not seem to have been any motive for these uncoordinated killings beyond the fact that the victims were vulnerable inmates whose deaths would not be revenged. Killings occurred in other parts of the prison too. . . .

During the riot, inmates involved in the class action suit made a futile attempt to organize the disturbance into a collective protest. They presented a list of demands to the prison administration and attempted to gather hostages in one place for effective negotiation. Their small band of followers were unable to pry hostages away from inmates until near the end of the riot, when two hostages who had been badly beaten were handed over to these inmates for release. . . . [O]nly two of the 12 hostages were released through negotiation—one in exchange for allowing a TV cameraman into the prison; the other for a promise of transfers out of state for certain inmates. . . . The "negotiations" had practically no impact on the outcome of the riot. There was simply no cohesive group of inmates with whom the administration could realistically negotiate.

Most of the hostages were released sporadically by the various groups who held them; a few actually escaped during the mayhem. Thirty-six hours after the riot began it exhausted itself. Barbiturates, stolen from the prison pharmacy and ingested by hundreds of inmates, are cited as one factor for the deceleration of the riot (Office of the Attorney General, 1980a:25; Serrill and Katel, 180:14). An anti-climactic armed assault on the prison officially ended the riot, but no resistance was offered by any of the inmates.

The riot itself was clearly distinguished by three characteristics which reflect changes in the control structure and inmate social structure of the preceding five years. These characteristics are:

1. The rapid and spontaneous takeover of the prison by inmates associated with the violent "new breed" cliques produced by structural changes within the prison organization.
2. The most extreme and apparently uncoordinated brutality by inmates in U.S. penal history. The riot was clearly an occasion to enhance or build reputations for violence and represents an escalation of the relations that had evolved in the inmate social structure prior to the riot. . . .
3. Fragmentation and a lack of solidarity among inmates that contrasts starkly with the 1971 Attica uprising and previous inmate rebellions at New Mexico in 1971 and 1976.

CONCLUSION

Prison riots open to view the grim realities that underlie the U.S. penal system. . . . [P]ositive steps toward reform must be initiated. Thomas *et al.* (1981) offer six strategies to alleviate the current crisis in prisons:

1. Redirect funding toward viable rehabilitation and create positive incentives for inmates to organize themselves around mutually beneficial and non-violent activities.
2. Expand existing citizen prison committees, such as the Fortune Society and the American Civil Liberties Union, to provide monitoring and publicizing of prison conditions.
3. Reform the organizational structure of prisons to enhance the flexibility of administrative policies, remove the rigid hierarchical division of labor, and improve accountability of line personnel. These steps will require an administrative structure that seeks input from, and is responsive to, both inmates and line staff.
4. Seek legislative reforms that shorten prison sentences, remove discriminatory sentencing practices, and remove the prison from disputes between state politicians.
5. Enhance political collectivism among inmates through education and political self-development.
6. Focus research on the *empirical* problems in prisons; move away from mere theoretical speculation and political rhetoric. . . .

None of these steps will be successful without an informed public that is ready to form political alliances with the other victims of our current penal system: the inmates and the guards. . . .

NOTES

1. For complete descriptions of the riot see Office of the Attorney General (1980a) and Serrill and Katel (1980).
2. Exact figures on the number of violent incidents are unavailable because all inmate records were destroyed in the riot. The assertion of increasing violence after 1975 is based primarily on interviews with inmates and staff. Press reports . . . and minutes of the New Mexico Corrections Commission hearings (Department of Corrections, 1980b) also corroborate the trend toward disorder.
3. Included as violent crimes are homicides, kidnappings, rapes, assaults, and armed robberies. It should be stressed that this figure refers to crimes and not individuals. In addition, these figures refer to all New Mexico prisoners, including those in minimum security camps. The minimum security camps housed about 10 percent of all prisoners throughout the ten-year period, and were filled only through transfer from the prison. . . .
4. Solitary confinement includes both disciplinary and protective custody cases.
5. Some of these inmates tried to model themselves after members of California prison gangs, known as the Aryan Brotherhood and La Nuestra Familia (Irwin, 1980). But this level of gang organization, observed in California prisons, did not exist at New Mexico.
6. See Colvin (1981) for details of this bureaucratic conflict and the political and historical context in which it occurred.
7. The American Correctional Association standards call for one man per cell (Gettinger, 1982).
8. The law suit, which was handled by the American Civil Liberties Union, was finally settled five months after the riot. The State of New Mexico consented to each of the issues prior to an actual ruling from the federal court. A monitor, Daniel R. Cron, was appointed to oversee implementation of federal court orders arising from the suit. In May 1981, Cron cited the corrections department with "across the board disobedience of the standards mandated for maximum security inmates" (*Denver Post*, 1981:8).

REFERENCES

Bennett, Lawrence A.
1976 "The study of violence in California prisons: A review with policy implications." Pp. 149–168 in Albert K. Cohen, George F. Cole, and Robert G. Bailey (eds). Prison Violence. Lexington, Mass.: D.C. Heath.

Clemmer, Donald
1940 The Prison Community. Boston: Christopher.

Cloward, Richard A.
1960 "Social control in the prison." Pp. 20–48 in Richard A. Cloward, Donald R. Cressey, George H. Grosser, Richard McCleery, Lloyd E. Ohlin, Gresham M. Sykes, and Sheldon L. Messinger (eds.), Theoretical Studies in Social Organization of the Prison. New York: Social Science Research Council.
Cohen, Albert K., George F. Cole, and Robert G. Bailey (eds.)
1976 Prison Violence. Lexington, Mass.: D.C. Heath.
Colvin, Mark
1981 "The contradictions of control: Prisons in class society." The Insurgent Sociologist 10(4) and 11(1): 33–45 (combined issue).
Davidson, R. Theodore
1974 Chicano Prisoners: The Key to San Quintin. New York: Holt, Rinehart and Winston.
Denver Post
1981 "Santa Fe prison strife continues." Sept. 14: sec.A, pp. 1, 8–9.
Department of Corrections
1971 Annual Report, 1970–1971. State of New Mexico: unpublished document.
1972 Annual Report, 1971–1972. State of New Mexico: unpublished document.
1973 Annual Report, 1972–1973. State of New Mexico: unpublished document.
1974 Annual Report, 1973–1974. State of New Mexico: unpublished document.
1975 Annual Report, 1974–1975. State of New Mexico: unpublished document.
1976 Annual Report, 1975–1976. State of New Mexico: unpublished document.
1977 Annual Report, 1976–1977. State of New Mexico: unpublished document.
1978 Annual Report, 1977–1978. State of New Mexico: unpublished document.
1979 Annual Report, 1978–1979. State of New Mexico: unpublished document.
1980a Annual Report, 1979–1980. State of New Mexico: unpublished document.
1980b Minutes of the New Mexico Corrections Commission. State of New Mexico: unpublished document.
Ellis, Desmond, Harold G. Grasmick, and Bernard Gilman
1974 "Violence in prisons: A sociological analysis." American Journal of Sociology 80(1):16–43.
Fox, James G.
1982 Organizational and Racial Conflict in Maximum-Security Prisons. Lexington, Mass.: D.C. Heath.
Fox, Vernon
1971 "Why prisoners riot." Federal Probation 35(1):9–14.
Garson, G. David
1972 "The disruption of prison administration: An investigation of alternative theories of the relationship among administrators, reformers, and involuntary social service clients." Law and Society Review 6(2):531–561.
Gettinger, Stephen
1982 "Accreditation on trial." Corrections Magazine 8(1):6–19.
Grusky, Oscar
1968 "Role conflict in organizations: A study of prison camp officials." Pp. 455–476 in Lawrence Hazelrigg (ed.), Prison Within Society. Garden City, N.Y.: Doubleday.
Hart, William
1976 "Profile: New Mexico." Corrections Magazine 2(3):27–36, 45–50.
Hartung, Frank E., and Maurice Floch
1956 "A social-psychological analysis of prison riots: An hypothesis." Journal of Criminal Law, Criminology and Police Science 47(1):51–57.

Irwin, John
1980 Prisons in Turmoil. Boston: Little, Brown.
Jackson, George
1970 Soledad Brother. New York: Bantam.
Jacobs, James B.
1977 Stateville: The Penitentiary in Mass Society. Chicago: University of Chicago Press.
Jankovic, Ivan
1977 "Labor market and imprisonment." Crime and Social Justice 8 (Fall–Winter): 17–31.
Lieber, James
1981 "The American prison: A tinderbox." New York Times Magazine, March 8:26–35, 56–61.
McCleery, Richard
1968 "Correctional administration and political change." Pp. 113–149 in Lawrence Hazelrigg (ed.), Prison Within Society. Garden City, N.Y.: Doubleday.
Office of the Attorney General
1975 Penitentiary Investigation. State of New Mexico: unpublished document.
1980a Report of the Attorney General on the February 2 and 3, 1980 Riot at the Penitentiary of New Mexico, Part One. State of New Mexico: unpublished document.
1980b Report of the Attorney General on the February 2 and 3, 1980 Riot at the Penitentiary of New Mexico, Part Two. State of New Mexico: unpublished document.
Ohlin, Lloyd E.
1956 Sociology and the Field of Corrections. New York: Russell Sage.
1960 "Conflicting interests in correctional objectives." Pp. 111–129 in Richard A. Cloward, Donald R. Cressey, George H. Grosser, Richard McCleery, Lloyd E. Ohlin, Gresham M. Sykes, and Sheldon Messinger (eds.), Theoretical Studies in Social Organization of the Prison. New York: Social Science Research Council.
Serrill, Michael S., and Peter Katel
1980 "New Mexico: The anatomy of a riot." Corrections Magazine 6(2):6–24.
Silberman, Charles E.
1978 Criminal Justice, Criminal Violence. New York: Random House.
Sykes, Gresham M.
1958 The Society of Captives. Princeton, N.J.: Princeton University Press.
Sykes, Gresham M., and Sheldon L. Messinger
1960 "The inmate social system." Pp. 5–19 in Richard A. Cloward, Donald R. Cressey, George H. Grosser, Richard McCleery, Lloyd E. Ohlin, Gresham M. Sykes, and Sheldon L. Messinger (eds.), Theoretical Studies in Social Organization of the Prison. New York: Social Science Research Council.
Thomas, Jim, David Stribling, Ra Rabb Chaka, Edmond Clemons, Charlie Secret, and Alex Neal
1981 "Prison conditions and penal trends." Crime and Social Justice 15 (Summer): 49–55.

Chapter 12
Schools

Violence in School

Jackson Toby

*I*n most schools violent crimes are unusual enough to be regarded the way pedestrians regard the possibility of being struck by an automobile: as wholly unpredictable acts of God. But the traditional expectation that schools are safe places for children is changing, not just in the United States, but in many industrialized countries. School violence has been reported on the increase in Great Britain, Sweden, France, Israel, mainland China, and even authority-conscious Japan. . . . School-violence data from outside the United States are mostly anecdotal press and television accounts. In the United States, on the other hand, quantitative studies exist. . . .

THE FACTS ABOUT VICTIMIZATION AT SCHOOL AND THEIR INTERPRETATION

[S]ystematic data concerning victimization [are] based primarily on two large national surveys. . . . The National Institute of Education survey had the advantage that it was specifically designed to describe the school-crime problem in the United States. It attempted to question students and teachers in a random sample of public secondary schools in different types of American communities: rural areas, suburbs, small cities, and large cities. . . . [However] . . . the 31,373 students and the 23,895 teachers who filled out questionnaires were not a random sample of American students and teachers . . . :

1. School systems, being under local control, had to be persuaded to cooperate with the survey; they could not be compelled. . . .

2. The cooperation of [students and] teachers varied from one school to another. . . .

. . . [T]he National Crime Survey tabulated victimizations reported to Census Bureau interviewers [in 1974 and 1975,] whether or not they were previously reported to the police, thereby making possible estimates of unreported crime. One component of the National Crime Survey is a countrywide survey of 72,000 households, conducted every six months, and yielding victimization data on a sample of approximately 136,000 persons 12 years of age and over. . . . One question in . . . the survey asks where the incident occurred, and one response category is "inside school." Thus, separating out all the victimization reports of crimes that occurred in school from all other victimizations made possible a special report on school crime. This was [also] done for . . . the data from the twenty- six city-level surveys [that were conducted in addition to the national survey]. . . .

The Prevalence of School Violence

Table 12-1 presents quantitative victimization reports from the 1976 National Institute of Education survey; it compares the rate of nonviolent theft from teachers with the rates of two violent offenses, assault and robbery. . . . [A]ssault and robbery of teachers were rare compared with nonviolent theft of their money or property. Even in the secondary schools of large cities, which had rates of teacher robbery and assault several times the rates in small communities, assault and robbery rates were small fractions of the rate for larceny.

A similar pattern emerges in table 12-2, which presents the reports of personal victimization of students from the same survey. However, the percentage of *students* claiming that they were assaulted or robbed was much greater than

Table 12-1.
Percentage of Teachers Victimized in Public Schools over a Two-Month Period in 1976

	By Larcenies		By Assaults		By Robberies	
Size of Community	In Junior High Schools	In Senior High Schools	In Junior High Schools	In Senior High Schools	In Junior High Schools	In Senior High Schools
500,000 or more	31.4% (56)	21.6% (59)	2.1% (56)	1.4% (59)	1.4% (56)	1.1% (59)
100,000–499,999	24.5 (45)	22.8 (36)	1.1 (45)	1.0 (36)	0.7 (45)	0.9 (36)
50,000–99,999	21.0 (23)	19.3 (31)	0.2 (23)	0.3 (31)	0.3 (23)	0.4 (31)
10,000–49,999	20.8 (94)	16.5 (75)	0.6 (94)	0.3 (75)	0.5 (94)	0.4 (75)
2,500–9,999	16.9 (41)	19.1 (47)	0.3 (41)	0.2 (47)	0.4 (41)	0.4 (47)
Under 2,500	15.9 (42)	18.5 (53)	0.2 (42)	0.2 (53)	0.0 (42)	0.4 (53)
All communities	22.1 (301)	19.3 (301)	0.8 (301)	0.5 (301)	0.6 (301)	0.6 (301)

Note: Numbers in parentheses refer to the number of schools on the basis of which the average percentage of personal victimization was calculated for each cell.
Source: Special tabulation of data from U.S. Department of Health, Education, and Welfare 1978.

Table 12-2.
Percentage of Students Victimized in Public Schools over a One-Month Period in 1976

Size of Community	By Larcenies: In Junior High Schools	By Larcenies: In Senior High Schools	By Assaults: In Junior High Schools	By Assaults: In Senior High Schools	By Robberies: In Junior High Schools	By Robberies: In Senior High Schools
500,000 or more	14.8%	14.9%	8.5%	3.7%	5.7%	2.8%
	(56)	(59)	(56)	(59)	(56)	(59)
100,000–499,999	18.0	16.8	7.8	2.7	3.6	1.9
	(45)	(36)	(45)	(36)	(45)	(36)
50,000–99,999	18.0	15.3	7.7	2.9	3.8	1.3
	(23)	(31)	(23)	(31)	(23)	(31)
10,000–49,999	15.5	15.8	6.8	2.7	3.3	1.4
	(94)	(74)	(94)	(74)	(94)	(74)
2,500–9,999	16.1	14.6	7.4	3.1	3.5	1.4
	(41)	(47)	(41)	(47)	(41)	(47)
Under 2,500	15.8	14.2	6.2	3.5	3.8	2.0
	(42)	(53)	(42)	(53)	(42)	(53)
All communities	16.0	15.2	7.3	3.1	3.9	1.8
	(301)	(300)	(301)	(300)	(301)	(300)

Note: Numbers in parentheses refer to the number of schools on the basis of which the average percentage of personal victimization was calculated for each cell.
Source: Special tabulation of data from U.S. Department of Health, Education, and Welfare 1978.

the rate of *teachers* reporting such violent victimizations—despite the fact that the student data covered a *one*-month period and the teacher data a *two*-month period. . . . Another difference between table 12-1 and table 12-2 is that assaults and robberies of *students* occurred twice as often in junior high schools as in senior high schools, whereas assaults and robberies of *teachers* occurred at more nearly the same rate in junior and senior high schools except in schools in the very largest cities. Either junior high schools were more dangerous than senior high schools for students but not for teachers, or perhaps junior high school students were more likely than senior high school students to engage in minor attacks and petty extortions. . . .

Fear of School Violence

Before turning to data on the characteristics of victims and perpetrators, let us try to place school violence in a broader perspective. We have already seen that violent school crime is quantitatively small compared with nonviolent school crime. However, there is evidence that violent school crime, though infrequent, arouses destructive fears among students and teachers. According to the National Institute of Education study, students and teachers reacted to the danger of violence by avoiding certain places in the more violent schools, such as restrooms, stairways, and corridors. Some students avoided school altogether. Four percent of all secondary school students in public schools said they stayed home out of fear at least once a month; but 7 percent of the senior high school students in the largest cities said this, as did 8 percent of the junior high school students (U.S. Department of Health, Education, and Welfare 1978, pp. 63–64). Students were more fearful in the big-city schools, where violence was more prevalent. Teachers were fearful too. Twelve percent of the public school teachers nationwide said that *within the month previous to the survey* they had hesitated to confront misbehaving students out of fear for their own safety. Twenty-eight percent of the teachers in large cities said so. . . .

Perpetrators of School Violence: Students and Intruders

The two main groups contributing to school violence are trespassers from the community and enrolled students. Neither of the victimization studies provided conclusive evidence on the relative proportions of trespassers and students among the perpetrators of school violence. . . .

[The National Crime Survey data for the twenty-six cities show that] [f]or rape and robbery, the perpetrators were largely unknown to the victims. Aggravated and simple assaults were less likely to be committed by strangers than were robbery and rape, as might be expected for offenses that often develop outside school as a result of arguments between friends or relatives. However, in a *majority* of all offenses where the victim had an opportunity to recognize the perpetrator, the victim could not do so. . . . Some big-city high schools are enormous—enrolling two to four thousand students. . . . The resulting anonymity makes it difficult for a victim of assault or robbery to identify even a perpetrator who is an enrolled student. . . . [However, the data] suggest . . . that intruders are an important factor in the crime problem of big-city schools.

. . . [But] intruders are not a homogeneous group. The term "intruder" refers to persons who enter school buildings without legitimate business. One type of intruder is the stereotypical predator—completely alien to the school, perhaps not even a resident of the surrounding neighborhood. Such intruders are criminals who consider schools more vulnerable than stores or banks or private homes. . . . The other type of intruder is no stranger to the school, although he or she may not currently be enrolled. This type of intruder may include an angry parent intent on beating up a child's teacher; friends of enrolled students who have come to visit; suspended students who prefer a warm, dry school building to the streets; or dropouts who are unemployed and bored. They may even be graduates from a few years back. . . .

. . . [T]he pattern of offenses was different for intruders and for enrolled students. Intruders tended to commit robberies and larceny with contact (e.g., purse snatching), whereas enrolled students were more likely to be assaultive. On the assumption that unknown perpetrators were mainly intruders, half of the crimes intruders committed against students and nearly a third of the offenses against staff members were either robbery or larceny with contact. Only a quarter of the offenses students committed against other students and only a tenth of the offenses they committed against staff members were these predatory crimes. On the other hand, nearly three-quarters of the offenses that students committed against other students and two-thirds of the offenses they committed against staff members were simple or aggravated assaults. . . .

[Group Violence]

[R]oughly a quarter of the robberies and assaults—of both students and staff members—involved three or more perpetrators. Close to half of the robberies of students involved two or more perpetrators. . . . [V]iolent crime *outside* schools also tends to involve groups of offenders (McDermott and Hindelang 1981, pp. 19–20). . . .

Age Specificity. . . . [I]ntruders were seven times more likely to rob students than to rob staff. . . . Students tended to be victimized by persons the same age or slightly older, not by persons a great deal older. . . . By contrast, about a quarter of the victimized staff members 20 years of age or more perceived the perpetrators as 21 or older. . . . [I]t was found that older intruders specialized in *robbing* staff persons rather than in assaultive offenses.[1] Perhaps older intruders preferred staff victims because teachers and secretaries were more likely than students to have something worth stealing. Intruders eighteen years old or older committed three-quarters of the robberies of teachers and other nonstudents, but only 21 percent of the robberies of students.

Gender Specificity. . . . The overwhelming majority of those perpetrating offenses against male students and male staff members were males. Two-thirds of the offenders who victimized female teachers and other female staff members were also perceived as males. But 60 percent of the large number of victimizations of female students were committed by females. . . . Known males were also more likely than known females to assault, rob, and steal from female teachers.

Racial Specificity. Overall, about 80 percent of all victimizations involved black offenders—although blacks constituted only 29 percent of the population of the twenty-six cities in which the National Crime Survey was conducted. Blacks constituted 88 percent of the offenders in cases involving black students. . . .

. . . [G]enerally, white offenders victimized *white* students, teachers, and other staff members. If these white offenders were students rather than intruders, the offenses they engaged in were probably assaults rather than robberies. The exception to the rule of white perpetrators victimizing fellow whites is the report from black teachers of 20 percent white perpetrators. These probably reflect the experiences of black teachers in schools with considerable white enrollment and where the teachers were victimized by enrolled students.

To sum up . . . : Intruders are an appreciable factor in big-city school crime, especially predatory crimes of violence against teachers and nonteaching staff. Intruders are likely to invade schools in groups rather than as lone individuals; they tend to be black males; and they are mostly in their late teens or early twenties. . . .

Victims of School Crime

A comparison of the rate of violence against teachers and students shows that a much higher proportion of students than of teachers were robbed and assaulted, according to tables [12-1 and 12-2], which came from the 1976 survey of the National Institute of Education. But it is likely that the meanings of assault and of robbery were different for teachers and students. For students, robbery meant extortion of lunch money, bus passes, or articles of clothing. Students in Hawaiian public schools called this type of robbery "hijacking" (Hawaii Crime Commission 1980). For students, assault frequently meant fights in which it was difficult to disentangle victims from instigators. For teachers, robbery meant victimization by intruders, and intruders were neighborhood criminals who were more intimidating than students. For teachers, assault meant one of two seriously unpleasant experiences. Sometimes assault was a gratuitous accompaniment to a robbery, perhaps to discourage pursuit or outcry. More often, assault was the angry response of an enrolled student after being admonished for disruptive behavior in the lunchroom, for loitering in the hallway without a pass, for fighting with other students, or for some other violation of school rules. What made a student attack on a teacher different from a student attack on another student was that this was not a quarrel between status equals. It represented a flouting of the authority system of the school as well as a prohibited act of violence. Teachers who were assaulted by students—or, even worse, their own students in their own classrooms—felt defiled as well as injured. . . .

. . . *Male* students reported being assaulted or robbed twice as often as *female* students, and male teachers were somewhat more likely to be attacked than female teachers, although less likely to be robbed. If we assume that the robbery of teachers was in good part the work of intruders, the greater victimization of female teachers reflected their greater vulnerability to violent theft. Greater vulnerability may also explain other findings of the survey: younger students and the youngest, least-experienced teachers were more likely to report being robbed or attacked. But the explanation for the higher rate of violence directed at male students than at female students is obviously not vulnerability. It is, however, exactly what has been found in victimization studies in American society outside school buildings; males are more likely to be victimized than females. . . . It should not be forgotten that males are the main perpetrators of violent crimes, both in schools and out. . . .

[Places of Victimization]

Where violent victimizations occurred was investigated in the National Institute of Education study. But only *student* victims were asked where the robbery or assault occurred. . . . [Eighteen] percent of the attacks and robberies occurred in classrooms, and some of these violent acts may have taken place in *empty* classrooms. Since schoolchildren spend a large part of their school day in class, 18 percent seems low for classroom violence. Maybe the presence of teachers protected students from the violence of their classmates. Apparently, hallways and stairs (where teacher supervision was weak) were the sites for about a third of the violent acts, and other poorly supervised places—toilets, cafeterias, and locker rooms—the sites for another third.

Poor as adult supervision is in hallways, stairs, toilets, cafeterias, and locker rooms, it is better than on the streets approaching the school or on buses carrying children to and from school. School officials do not have responsibility for children while they are on *public* buses. Even in places where children ride *school* buses, maintenance of close discipline is often difficult. The drivers, preoccupied with driving, can respond only to the most flagrant acts of violence, vandalism, or disorderly behavior. . . . Neither the National Institute of Education survey nor the National Crime Survey data provided the information necessary to compare violent victimization within school buildings with victimization while traveling to and from school. Depending on how serious this problem is, especially in the largest cities, safe schools might be a practical impossibility. If getting to and from school were sufficiently dangerous in the largest cities, neither success in keeping intruders at bay nor better control over students within school buildings would be enough to change the perception of public secondary schools. Unfortunately, one study in Philadelphia showed that both black and white schoolboys regarded the streets to and from school as presenting a greater risk of being beaten or robbed than schoolyards, hallways, or classrooms (Savitz, Lalli, and Rosen 1977, p. 34). . . .

THE SOCIOCULTURAL CAUSES OF SCHOOL VIOLENCE

. . . [S]chool violence is not simply the result of emotional disturbance on the part of intruders or enrolled students. Whatever the aggressive or predatory impulses of youngsters, social conditions can promote or impede their expression in behavior (Toby 1974). On one level, therefore, explaining school violence in modern societies requires explaining the sociocultural circumstances that make social control over such violence difficult. To do this, controlling school violence must be considered in the wider context of controlling deviant behavior and criminality. . . . There are inherent difficulties in controlling deviant behavior in urbanized societies that emanate from the anonymity and mobility of urban life and the difficulty of identifying the ownership of property (Toby 1979, p. 118). . . .

. . . Larger schools have a significantly higher incidence of student behavior problems, even when student background characteristics are controlled (McPartland and McDill 1976, pp. 20, 30, 32). Social changes in American society have tended to reduce control generally over students in the public schools. Some of these developments [are discussed below.[2]] . . .

Professional-Bureaucratic Differentiation of School and Neighborhood

Historically, the development of American public education increasingly separated the school from students' families and neighborhoods. Even the one-room schoolhouse of rural America represented separation of the educational process from the family. But the consolidated school districts in nonmetropolitan areas and the jumbo schools of the inner city carried separation much further. . . . [T]he unintended consequence of large schools that operated efficiently by bureaucratic and professional standards was to make them relatively autonomous of the local community. . . .

Until the 1960s and 1970s school administrators did not sufficiently appreciate the potential for disorder when many hundreds of young people come together for congregate education. Principals did not like to call in police, preferring to organize their own disciplinary procedures. They did not believe in security guards, preferring to use teachers to monitor behavior in the halls and lunchrooms. They did not tell school architects about the need for what has come to be called "defensible space," and as a result schools were built with too many ways to gain entrance from the outside and too many rooms and corridors where surveillance was difficult. Above all, they did not consider that they had lost control over potential student misbehavior when parents were kept far away, not knowing how their children were behaving. The focus of PTAs was the curriculum, and it was the better-educated, middle-class parents who tended to join such groups. In short, the isolation of the school from the local community always meant that, if a large enough proportion of students misbehaved, teachers and principals could not maintain order.

Rising Expectations for Secondary and Postsecondary Education

Another trend helping to explain how a less orderly school environment developed was the pressure to keep children in school longer—on the assumption that children needed all the education they could get to cope with a complicated urban industrial society. The positive side of this development was rising educational levels. Greater proportions of the age cohort graduated from high school and went on to postsecondary education than ever before. The negative aspect of compulsory school attendance laws and of informal pressure to stay in school longer was that youngsters who did not want further education were compelled to remain enrolled. . . . In reality, compulsory education laws are successful only in keeping children *enrolled*. . . .

. . . The existence of a large population of enrolled nonattenders blurs the line between intruders and students. School officials understand this all too well, but the compulsory school attendance laws prevent them from doing much about it. Thus the attempt to force education on unwilling students produced a downward slide in academic and behavioral standards. . . .

The Extension of Civil Rights to Children

A third trend indirectly affecting school violence was the increasing sensitivity of public schools to the rights of children. A generation ago it was possible for principals to rule schools autocratically, to suspend or expel students without much regard for procedural niceties. Injustices occurred; children were "pushed out" of schools because they antagonized teachers and principals. But this arbitrariness enabled school administrators to control the situation when serious misbehavior occurred. Student assaults on teachers were punished so swiftly that they were almost unthinkable. Even disrespectful language was unusual. Today, as a result of greater concern for the rights of children, school officials are required to observe due process in handling student discipline. . . . Hearings are necessary. Charges must be specified. Witnesses must confirm suspicions. Appeals are provided for. Greater due process for students accused of misbehavior gives unruly students better protection against teachers and principals and well-behaved students worse protection from their classmates. . . .

The Erosion of the Authority of Teachers

. . . There have also been *cultural* changes undermining the authority of teachers. We have come a long way from the time when teachers were considered godlike. Doubtless, reduced respect for teachers is part of fundamental cultural changes by which many authority figures—parents, police, government officials, employers—have come to have less prestige. In the case of teachers, the general demythologizing was amplified by special ideological criticism. Best-selling books of the 1960s portrayed teachers, especially white middle-class teachers, as the villains of education, insensitive, authoritarian, and even racist (Herndon 1968; Holt 1964; Kohl 1967; Kozol 1967). . . .

. . . Many teachers felt they lacked authority to induce students to do *anything* they did not want to do: to attend classes regularly, to keep quiet so orderly recitation could proceed, to refrain from annoying a disliked classmate. . . . What has changed is that the *role* of teacher no longer has the authority it once did for students and their parents; this means that less forceful, less experienced, or less effective teachers cannot rely on the authority of the role to help them maintain control. They are on their own in a sense that the previous generation was not (Rubel 1977).

Sociocultural Differentiation of Schools within School Systems

School violence occurs in all kinds of schools. However, school violence is harder to control in large urban school systems than in rural or suburban schools for two reasons. One is the intruder problem, which springs from the general weakness of social control in big cities. The other is that certain big-city public high schools are more likely to develop a critical mass of rebellious students than are high schools in smaller school systems. Large school systems tend to become differentiated into better and worse schools. . . . As a result of natural processes of social competition in big-city school systems, the least troublesome students with the best academic skills, the more stimulating teachers, and the more competent principals gravitate to one group of high schools, and badly behaved students, demoralized teachers, and administrative hacks gravitate to another. . . .

. . . Individual high schools within a large urban school system can be selective even though the school system as a whole is not permitted to give up on any student, no matter how unmotivated, rebellious, or handicapped he or she may be. Paradoxically, the more numerous the selective high schools within an urban school system, the more likely it is that other schools within the system will have a high concentration of troublesome students. They are attended by students not admitted to selective schools and by the failures and disciplinary problems rejected from parochial and private schools. Even in the absence of an ethnically diverse population, the differentiation process tends to be fueled by socioeconomic differences; schools containing a large proportion of middle-class children are more oriented to educational achievement and less violent than schools with many lower-class children. But ethnic diversity reinforces this socioeconomic basis for differentiation. . . .

THE INDIVIDUAL CAUSES OF SCHOOL VIOLENCE

Whatever the sociocultural roots of school violence, some students are more prone to violence than others. Sociocultural variables operate through family and neighborhood socialization experiences to produce some violent students in middle-class suburban schools and some high academic achievers from the black ghetto of Chicago's South Side. . . . , [H]owever they are produced, the personalities of some students are more violent than others and are more likely to lead to violent behavior. In addition, some students, because of their attitudes and interests, are less responsive to the informal controls consisting of the approval and disapproval of teachers and other authority figures in the school. Having less stake in conformity (Toby 1957), they are freer to engage in deviant behavior of all kinds, including violence. . . .

. . . [P]sychiatric experts have a difficult time putting adolescent misbehavior into clear-cut diagnostic categories because personality disturbances in young people are more amorphous than in older people. And the rules governing "special education" in the public schools have compounded the confusion between compulsive violence and violence that may be deliberate. . . . The ordinary student and the "emotionally disturbed" special education student may be misbehaving in similar ways in the same classroom, yet different rules apply to them. [T]he better strategy from a social control point of view is to assume that self-control is possible for an emotionally disturbed youngster. Failure to make this assumption undercuts the effectiveness of social control. . . . It seems unjust to hold a child responsible for violent behavior that he cannot help. Yet failure to hold children responsible means that they are more likely to engage in violence than they would otherwise be.

ALTERNATIVE STRATEGIES FOR RESTORING ORDER IN VIOLENT SCHOOLS

Most public schools are reasonably orderly. Even in the largest cities, where school violence is statistically most frequent, the number of schools that are truly dangerous is small. But though only a minority of big-city schools are chaotic, chaotic schools are highly visible through mass-media reports. They give all public schools a bad name and thereby promote the flight of educationally oriented students to private and parochial schools. One reason the descent into violence is difficult to reverse is that, from the point of view of nonviolent students and their parents, it seems simpler to transfer to a safer school than to wait and see whether the downward slide can be reversed. Of course this is not a solution from the point of view of the community.... Most parents are not affluent enough, cunning enough, or concerned enough to transfer their children out of violent schools.

From the point of view of American society . . . , the solution is to upgrade the disorderly schools, not only so that the children attending them feel safe, but also so that intellectually able students can use them as stepping-stones to further educational and occupational opportunities. At least three strategies are possible.

Charismatic Administrative Leadership

A charismatic principal can maintain order in a difficult urban school, but it requires enormous energy. The principal must be everywhere, talking with students in halls and classrooms, explaining to teachers why due-process requirements mandated by the courts make it difficult to back them up in disciplinary cases, watching for intruders, mollifying parents, controlling by effort what was possible by decree a generation ago. Such dedication is rare. The personal cost is great. Principals burn out too. . . .

Redistribution of Behavior Problems within Large School Systems

One aspect of the problem of disorderly schools is the concentration of educationally uninterested, violence-prone students in certain schools of large school systems. Redistributing these difficult cases uniformly through the system instead of permitting them to pile up in a few schools might at least improve the most troublesome schools. This strategy is in fact attempted. Central administrations set quotas of emotionally disturbed "special education" students for high schools whether the principals want them or not. Disciplinary transfers of students are made, partly to give problem students a fresh start in a new milieu but also to help principals cope with a high concentration of violence problems. Students are also transported into schools they have not selected and that are not near their homes in order to achieve racial balance in the school system as a whole. . . . Nevertheless, no school system has come close to equalizing behavior problems within its constituent schools.

There are several reasons for this failure. In the first place, school boards are not insulated from political pressure[,] . . . where education is primarily a local responsibility. Parents strenuously resist the introduction of large numbers of problem students into a tranquil school that their children attend—and resist even more strenuously the transfer of their children into a violent school. Second, big-city school systems are unwilling or unable to do away with selective high schools, probably because powerful constituencies demand such educational resources. These constituencies tend to oppose allocating a fair share of problem students to such schools as the Bronx High School of Science. In short, it is difficult to impose a political solution in a pluralistic society with a strong tradition of individual choice. Students cannot readily be forced to attend schools they or their parents consider unsafe, because alternatives exist: not only private and parochial schools but illegal evasions of official assignments. . . .

Perhaps this is just as well. An equitable distribution of behavior problems throughout an urban school system might well spread violence into more schools and accelerate the decline of the public school system as a whole. Historically, the opposite distributive strategy has proved more feasible; allow some schools to become excellent and others terrible, and at the same time track students within schools so that even bad schools have islands of academic achievement and safety. . . .

Establishing Minimum Behavioral Standards for Continuing Enrollment

A third strategy is to establish minimum behavioral standards for students in public schools that are enforceable by credible threats, including possible termination of enrollment. Such a strategy is an affront to the ideological tradition that children need an education whether they want one or not. Terminating enrollment for failure to meet minimum behavioral standards violates the philosophy of the compulsory attendance laws. Note that minimum behavioral standards are what make private schools successful. . . .

An obstacle preventing public schools from imitating private schools in insisting on nonviolent behavior from students is the lack of integration between laws defining juvenile delinquency and laws compelling school attendance. Unless a juvenile court judge decides to send a juvenile offender to a correctional institution, thereby removing him or her from the public schools, the youngster is still required to attend school. . . . For example, a boy who has slapped his teacher or extorted money from his classmates may be treated by a juvenile court judge in terms of his own needs and the protection of the larger society but not in terms of the school as an important social institution. . . .

Compulsory attendance is treated, at least implicitly, as more important than promoting an orderly classroom environment. . . . In order to require studious behavior on the part of students[,] . . . the assumption that enrollment guarantees education would have to be changed. Youngsters would have to do certain things and refrain from doing others to remain students in good standing. . . .

. . . [C]onsideration might be given to lowering the age of compulsory attendance to [15 or even 14 years]. . . . Most youngsters presented with a choice between going to a real school, which involves educational effort and self-control, and becoming a nonstudent, with the attendant stigma resulting from not being employed and not attending school, opt for education. Even in neighborhoods where the drop-out rate is already high, parental pressure works in favor of continued school enrollment. . . .

To be sure, insisting that enrolled students meet minimum behavioral standards instead of requiring all youngsters to attend school, no matter what they do and how little they learn, represents a shift in educational philosophy. It would mean that schools would no longer be multipurpose institutions, part educational, part recreational, part incarcerative. The paramount orientation of the school would be educational. Youngsters not interested in education would temporarily lose their enrollment—on the understanding that, as soon as they felt ready to use the school for its proper purpose, they should hasten to return. . . .

It would be useless to redefine the mission of the school and to insist that enrolled students be committed to education if those who choose not to remain enrolled can infiltrate school buildings at will. It will be even more necessary than at present to be vigilant about intruders so that street youths are prevented from making disruptive forays into school buildings. . . . Only when the lines are sharply drawn between education and the streets will it be possible to tell whether increasing the voluntariness of public education can reduce school violence appreciably. . . .

The genie cannot be stuffed back into the bottle. Now that school violence has become a national concern and the public schools are in danger of losing the universal educational appeal that was their virtue, it is difficult to accept violent schools with fatalistic resignation. . . . Eventually, solutions to the problem of school violence will be discovered. The alternative would be the erosion of public secondary education.

NOTES

1. This conclusion is based on an unpublished tabulation made for this essay by the staff of the Criminal Justice Center, Albany, New York.
2. The section that follows draws extensively on Toby 1980a, pp.26–32.

REFERENCES

Herndon, James. 1968. *The Way It Spozed to Be*. New York: Simon and Schuster.

Holt, John. 1964. *How Children Fail*. New York: Pittman.

Kihss, Peter. 1981. "Student, 16, Is Charged in Death of Teacher Trying to Halt a Fight." *New York Times*, 7 April.

Kohl, Herbert. 1967. *Thirty-six Children*. New York: New American Library.

Kozol, Jonathan. 1967. *Death at an Early Age: The Destruction of the Minds and Hearts of Negro Children in the Boston Public Schools*. Boston: Houghton Mifflin.

McDermott, N. Joan, and Michael J. Hindelang. 1981. *Juvenile Criminal Behavior in United States: Its Trends and Patterns*. Washington, D.C.: U.S. Government Printing Office.

McPartland, James M., and Edward L. McDill. 1976. *Violence in Schools: Perspectives, Programs, and Positions*. Lexington, Mass.: D.C. Heath.

Rubel, Robert J. 1977. *The Unruly School: Disorders, Disruptions, and Crime*. Lexington, Mass.: D.C. Heath.

Chapter 13

Corporations

Corporate Homicide: Definitional Processes in the Creation of Deviance

Victoria Lynn Swigert and Ronald A. Farrell

*C*oncern with the criminal activities of corporations coincided with the emergence of corporate capitalism during the late nineteenth century. Both legal scholars (e.g., Edgerton, 1927) and social reformers (e.g., Sinclair, 1905) argued that corporations were capable of committing crimes and should be held responsible for such actions. Social scientific attention was soon to follow. In his presidential address to the American Sociological Society in 1939, Edwin H. Sutherland (1940) called for the systematic study of corporate criminality. He . . . went on to document the widespread existence of corporate offenses in his study of white-collar crime (1945; 1949), a work that brought attention to the phenomenon as a legitimate area of social scientific research. . . .

Many activities are already subject to legal sanction. Unsafe work conditions, defective products, air and water pollution, food and drug adulteration are illegal. Regulatory agencies are charged with the control of such offenses, and civil protections compensate personal loss. Increasingly, however, the vocabulary has turned from regulatory and civil liability to criminal liability. A conception of corporate behavior as criminal has entered the scientific and popular vocabulary.

I. THE PARAMETERS OF CRIMINAL LAW

A fatal argument between friends following a Saturday evening of drinking, for example, would leave little doubt as to the applicability of criminal statutes. Fatal bodily harm, however, may just as easily be a product of dangerous factory conditions, polluted air, or unsafe motor vehicles as it is of bullet wounds, knifings, or beatings. The latter fall clearly within the cultural meaning of homicide; the former do not. The distinction is an implicit one. There are no statutory exemptions from criminal responsibility accorded those whose damages to human life occur within the context of the manufacture and sale of consumables. Rather, they have enjoyed a de facto exemption which has become institutionalized in the law.

Cultural definitions of crime do undergo change. Parameters are expanded or contracted, and behaviors are realigned relative to the new definitional limits. The impact of the *Carrier's Case* of 1473 on contemporary conceptions of theft is a case in point (Hall, 1952). Legal proscriptions against unlawful taking predate the *Carrier's Case* by centuries. The confiscation of goods by someone temporarily entrusted with the property, however, fell outside the culturally defined limits. Loss of private possessions to a burglar was a crime; their loss to a hired transporter was only indicative of the owner's poor judgment of character. The fifteenth-century indictment and conviction of an errant carrier altered traditional definitions of unlawful taking. There was no new legislation, only a judicial decision to recognize a new form of property crime.

A similar event may alter the current parameters of criminal homicide. On September 13, 1978, a county grand jury in Elkhart, Indiana, indicted the Ford Motor Company on three counts of reckless homicide and one count of criminal recklessness.[1] The charges stemmed from the death of three teenage girls who suffered fatal burns when their Ford Pinto burst into flames following a low-speed rear-end collision. As with theft in the *Carrier's Case*, the new homicide has emerged because of the application of extant statutes to formerly exempt behaviors.

Although Ford was subsequently acquitted on the merits of the case (March 13, 1980), the trial of a corporation for criminal homicide is a precedent-setting event in American jurisprudence. The Ford trial, moreover, appears to be the culmination of a series of definitional changes that have occurred in the eight-year period following the Pinto's introduction to the automotive market. An analysis of the events preceding this action provide insight into the process by which deviance is created.

II. THE CORPORATION AND THE LAW

The indictment and trial of Ford Motor Company was a contemporary effort to establish the position of the corporation before the law. The issue of corporate liability has been ambiguous throughout history. The problem has been one of reconciling a legal commitment to individual responsibility with the emergence of a social entity capable of actions independent of readily identifiable human agents. Since the middle ages, the law has attempted to resolve the dilemma by defining the corporation as a person (Coleman, 1974: 13–18; Stone, 1975: 11–12). Until the seventeenth century, legal decisions based on this definition posed little problem. Given the limited size and complexity of organizations, individuals could usually be identified to bear responsibility for corporate actions. The law could thus recognize the corporation while maintaining its individualistic orientation. . . .

The dominant precedent . . . , first established in 1909 in *People* v. *Rochester Railway and Light Company*, has been that corporations are incapable of forming intent and, therefore, cannot be held liable for crimes against persons (19 American Jurisprudence § 1436 et seq.; see also Stone, 1975).

While the issue of locating *mens rea* in the corporate structure has been and continues to be the object of legal debate (Edgerton, 1927; Epstein, 1980), the force of the *Rochester* decision has been weakened within recent years. Courts have held that the "killing of a human being by a corporation is an act that *can be proscribed* by the Legislature" (*People* v. *Ebasco Services, Inc.*, 1974; emphasis added). Failure to sustain indictments against corporations lies less in the logic of corporations as potential offenders and more in the language of particular state and federal statutes. Most typically, homicide is defined in these codes as the criminal slaying of "another human being," with "another" referring to the same class of beings as the victim (Clark, 1979).[2] The developing trend within the courts which recognizes the possibility of corporate homicide has come to be reflected in the rewording of state and federal model penal codes to include corporation in the definition of criminally liable persons (Clark, 1979).

The state of Indiana adopted the definition of corporations as criminally liable in 1976. This statutory revision formed the basis for the September 13, 1978, indictment of Ford Motor Company on charges of reckless homicide. After three days of deliberation, the grand jury determined that a crime had been committed and that Ford was to be tried as the responsible party. The applicability of the criminal definition was based on evidence that the manufacturer had known that the fuel tank on its subcompact Pinto was defectively designed and had consciously decided to proceed with production in spite of the potential hazards. This decision, the grand jury found, was predicated on a cost-benefit analysis. Officials at Ford allegedly predicted the number of severe burn injuries and deaths that would result from the defect, and estimated that the cost of repairing the car would exceed anticipated court settlements. . . .

What is unique in the case of Ford is the definition attached by the Indiana grand jury to such a profit strategy. A calculation of the costs of reducing the number of injuries and deaths became evidence of the willfulness and intentionality of the corporate action. Once the company policy had been defined in these terms, the indictment became possible. . . .

The emergence of a vocabulary of criminal liability depends upon the extent to which the harm produced by the corporation is, in fact, *like* the harm already associated with conventional criminality. Traditionally, the illegal activities of corporations and those of conventional criminals have been defined as involving very different consequences. Corporate misbehavior has been viewed as entailing a diffuse, impersonal cost to society. The harms produced by price fixing, false advertising, or mislabeling, for example, have been perceived as increased financial burdens on the consumer. This differs dramatically from the imagery of personal threat or injury suffered at the hands of the robber, rapist, or murderer. These social definitions of harm provide important distinctions between air and water pollution, on the one hand, and assault and battery, on the other; or false advertising and theft, or unsafe product liability and homicide. Before the activities of corporations can be recognized as instances of conventional crime, the social harms produced by those activities must be recognized as conventional harms. In the case of the Pinto, this seems to have been accomplished through a personalization of harm. Throughout the period of investigation, we found increased attention to the injuries and deaths of Pinto burn victims, and a relative decrease in attention to the consumer issue of product defect. This public recognition of personal harm, we might suggest, was ultimately reflected in the grand jury decision that the Pinto-related deaths of three Indiana teenagers were *like* homicide.

A similar process of personalized injury may be seen in other spheres of corporate activity. Particularly illustrative are the recent concerns with chemical disposal, industrial use of asbestos, and "windfall profits" by oil companies. The social harms associated with these behaviors have been depicted in terms of the loss of homes and property by Love Canal victims, the fatal lung diseases of shipbuilders, and exposure deaths [of] those who could not afford heating fuel. To the extent that the victims of these activities are perceived as similar to the victims of theft, assault, and homicide, we might expect legal definitions to follow accordingly.[3]

Finally, the indictment against Ford may be viewed as an attempt on the part of the state to assert moral integrity in the face of enemy deviation. In its decision to contest civil suits, the corporation refused to recognize that moral boundaries had been transgressed. This opened the way to a definition of the manufacturer as a force against whom the power of the law must be directed. In light of National Traffic Highway Safety Administration findings that other subcompacts also had improperly designed fuel tanks, regulatory actions against Ford, in the form of governmental investigations and the threat of recall, may have led corporate officials to feel unfairly singled out. Consequently, the company may have intensified its efforts to fight openly the charges from both public and private sectors. These maneuvers, however, appear to have reinforced the public's perception of the enemy nature of the corporation. The emerging public imagery of the manufacturer was confirmed in media accounts of its production policies. Newspapers reported that the company was aware of the defectively constructed fuel tank and of the death and injury that it produced. Based on a cost-benefit analysis, however, Ford chose to continue production and sale of the vehicle. This depiction of the corporation, along with the application of a vocabulary of deviance and the personalization of harm, had the effect of transforming a consumer problem into a crime. At issue was no longer bad-faith sales to unwitting consumers, but reckless violence against individuals in exchange for corporate profit.

NOTES

1. At the prosecutor's request, the charge of criminal recklessness later was dropped.
2. In its motion to dismiss the indictment, Ford Motor Company urged that a strict interpretation of "another" as referring to a human being be adopted. The trial judge, however, ruled that corporations can be indicted under the Indiana Statute (Clark, 1979: 919–920).
3. It must be acknowledged that efforts to control corporate activities may be rendered ineffective if stringent regulations are construed as responsible for the economic failures of the corporation. That is, as layoffs and plant closings increase, ostensibly as a result of the cost of complying with the new standards, popular demands for official sanctions may diminish.

REFERENCES

Clark, Glenn A. (1979) "Corporate Homicide: A New Assault on Corporate Decision-Making," 54 *Notre Dame Lawyer* 911.
Coleman, James S. (1974) *Power and the Structure of Society*. New York: Norton.
Edgerton, Henry W. (1927) "Corporate Criminal Responsibility," 36 *Yale Law Journal* 827.
Epstein, Richard A. (1980) "Is Pinto a Criminal?" 4 *Regulation* 15.
Hall, Jerome (1952) *Theft, Law and Society*. Indianapolis: Bobbs-Merrill.
Sinclair, Upton Beall (1905) *The Jungle*. N.Y.: Vanguard.
Stone, Christopher D. (1975) *Where the Law Ends: The Social Control of Corporate Behavior*. N.Y.: Harper and Row.
Stuart, Reginald (1978) "Pintos Withdrawn in Oregon in Dispute Over Tank Safety," *The New York Times*, April 21, 1978: D3.
Sutherland, Edwin H. (1940) "White-Collar Criminality," 5 *American Sociological Review* 1.
——— (1945) "Is 'White Collar Crime' Crime?" 10 *American Sociological Review* 132.
——— (1949) *White Collar Crime*. N.Y.: Dryden Press.

CASES CITED

People v. *Ebasco Services, Inc.*, 77 Misc. 2d 784, 354 NYS 2d, 1974.
People v. *Rochester Railway and Light Company*, 195 NY 102, 107, 1909.
State v. *Lehigh Valley Railroad Company*, 90 NJL 372, 103 A 685, 1917.
U.S. v. *Van Schaick*, 134 F 592, 1904.

Part 5

Causes, Correlates, and Contexts

Explaining Violent Behavior

This part deals with the origins of violence and the factors which maintain or escalate such behavior. Neil Alan Weiner and Marvin E. Wolfgang, in "Explaining Violent Behavior," review research in several disciplines on the causes and correlates of interpersonal violence.

The disciplines of biology, ethology, psychology, and sociology all have investigated causes using diverse methodologies, including ethnography, statistical analysis, and experimental and quasi-experimental designs. Biological investigations, for instance, have focused on genetic evidence; psychophysiological, neurophysiological, and neuropsychological factors; hormonal influences; drug consumption; prenatal and perinatal factors; minimal brain disorder and hyperactivity; and diet and nutrition. Strong substantive relationships or promising explanatory leads have been reported in many of these areas. The kindred fields of psychiatry, psychoanalysis, and psychology also have formulated explanations of violence and aggression, asserting proposals of mental pathology, intrapsychic conflict, and behavioral learning dynamics, respectively. Sociological perspectives focus on socialization processes, for example, child-rearing; the formation of subcultures which support violent activity through normative regulation; social structural impediments to legitimate and illegitimate opportunities, including education and work; and interpersonal dynamics of face-to-face interaction centering on reciprocal sequences of actions and reactions that can precipitate, provoke, and escalate violence.

Unfortunately, the extensive theoretical and research literature on violent interpersonal behavior is inconclusive and lacks interdisciplinary integration, providing no general, unitary explanation of interpersonal violence.

Drugs and Violent Crime

Continuing heated debates about the influence of drugs on violent crime make the detailed discussion by Paul J. Goldstein in "Drugs and Violent Crime" especially timely. As Goldstein underscores, this relationship is complex. Much of the public's attention has been directed at biological and physiological effects of substances such as alcohol, stimulants, and barbiturates. However, the precise ways in which they biologically stimulate aggression is still not fully understood.

Probably the least systematically considered components of the relationship between drugs and violence are its economic aspects. Drug users must acquire money to purchase drugs and, to do so, may engage in violent crimes such as robbery. Furthermore, drug distribution and use can involve confrontations centering on territorial disputes, product distributional rights, and price. Interventions into the drugs-violence relationship will surely require a multipronged strategy which acknowledges various dynamic relationships.

The Armed Criminal in America

One of the main features of both interpersonal and collective violence in America has been the weaponry used in these incidents. James Wright and Peter Rossi, in "The Armed Criminal in America: A Survey of Incarcerated Felons," examine patterns in weapons ownership and use in criminal and noncriminal activities. Wright and Rossi distinguish various types of persons who use weapons, ranging from "unarmed criminals" to those felons who repeatedly use the most lethal weapons in the pursuit of crime—the "handgun" and "shotgun" predators. The two predator groups account for a disproportionate amount of the total serious crimes among the men surveyed. Controlling violent and other serious crime in America centers on restraining the behavior of these criminal predators.

Those felons who carried guns all the time, and thereby had the weapon available whenever a criminal opportunity arose, were most likely to belong to family or peer groups in which similar "carrying" behavior occurred. Friends and acquaintances, rather than family, seem to be centrally involved in the dynamics of gun ownership which later lead to their criminal use. Family and friends are the main source, through purchases, of firearms. This kind of information will figure prominently in policies to modify the etiology of criminal armament. The authors also discuss characteristics of weapons that make them criminally attractive, such as their accuracy, untraceability, and the quality of their construction.

Violent Crime and Mental Illness

Joseph J. Cocozza, Mary Evans Melick, and Henry J. Steadman, in "Trends in Violent Crime among Ex-Mental Patients," debunk the widespread belief that the mentally ill are overwhelmingly dangerous, that the psychopathologies associated with mental illnesses substantially heighten the risk that the mentally ill will engage in violent criminal behavior. Their careful investigation reveals that murder, manslaughter, assault, robbery, and sexual crimes did not appear to occur more often in a group of released mental patients than in the general population. Few released patients were later arrested for these violent crimes.

The one characteristic found to be related to a subsequent arrest for violence was the total number of prior arrests: former patients with more prior arrests were more likely to be arrested at a later time; and those patients with no prior arrests had a lower chance than the general population of later arrest for violence. Apparently, recent residents in mental hospitals in some states tend to have longer arrest records than in earlier years because more offenders are now confined in mental facilities. This increase in offender populations in mental hospitals has occurred at the same time that many more mental patients have been placed residentially in their native communities. The result has been the progressively larger proportionate representation of offenders in mental hospitals. These two convergent trends may have created the appearance that an increasing number of mental patients commit violent crimes after their release. However, these ex-patients are violently involved because of their criminal backgrounds rather than because of their mental disorders. These findings do not mean that mental illness is unrelated to violent activity. Serial murderers and persons who commit brutal mutilation and sexual homicides often exhibit symptoms of severe mental illness. However, overall, very little violent crime appears to be primarily a product of mental disorders.

Violent Crime and the Mass Media

Violent behavior is partly a function of dynamics pertaining to child-rearing and, more generally, socialization. One of the most significant contemporary mechanisms of "rearing" Americans is the mass media, specifically television. James Garofalo, in "Violent Crime and the Mass Media: A Selective Review of Research," concludes that "social science evidence indicates a causal link between viewing television violence and aggression, and the evidence of this has been increasing rather than diminishing since the 1960s." The dynamics of media socialization involve three main components: modeling or imitation (the learning of new behavior), disinhibition (the weakening of internal controls over violent and aggressive behavior), and desensitization (violent behavior is viewed as less morally repugnant).

The Violent Face of Television

George Gerbner and Larry Gross place the influence of television on violence within a much broader analytical context than many other researchers. In "The Violent Face of Television and Its Lessons," Gerbner and Gross argue that "what children and other viewers learn about violence from television is not necessarily learned from just seeing acts of violence." Television functions to teach, maintain, stabilize, and reinforce conventional values, beliefs, and behaviors. Only certain persons are depicted as able to engage justifiably in violence. Conversely, only certain people are viewed as legitimate targets of violence. In short, television communicates information about the distribution of power and violence and about fear of the same. The few real-life instances of violence that television might promote are simply the modest costs of the larger function that television plays in preserving and perpetuating the American social order. Responding to television as a direct cause or facilitator of violence is not perhaps as important as critically examining the implicit conservative function of television, which is to maintain certain forms of public order and interrelationships through violent programming.

Chapter 14
Explanations

Explaining Violent Behavior

Neil Alan Weiner and Marvin E. Wolfgang

. . . *[D]*ialogue and debate about the causes of violence have often turned into heated controversy, with passions inflamed more by philosophical or political ideology than by scientific principles and convictions. To cite what might be the clearest example . . . biological explanations have been periodically rejected by sociologists as deterministic—as implying a set of organic factors which exclusively drive or control the onset and course of violent behavior. Concern has arisen that such a stance might lead to "predatory ethics" embracing medical techniques (e.g., eugenics, psychosurgery, etc.) as part of a general strategy of violence prevention and control (Shah and Roth, 1974: 102–103).

At present, however, a more moderate and reasonable position prevails. Biological and sociological, as well as other nonorganic and environmental factors are thought to interact with one another to make violent behavior more or less likely to occur. Biological endowments, for example, present the organism with a behavioral range or potential and not with immutable behavioral traits or realizations. These innate somatic attributes interact with social influences in a developmental (maturational) process which results in behavioral performance, one form of which may be violent conduct. Within the biologically established bounds of potential behavior, a wide array of conduct may be selected and pursued based upon various kinds of considerations, including moral convictions or pragmatic concerns.

We take the position . . . that . . . factors hypothesized to influence violence interact in the manner just described. Biological, psychological, sociological and other factors set behavioral bounds and options: The likelihood that violent conduct will occur depends upon the substance and strength of the factors involved in any particular case. . . .

BIOLOGICAL HYPOTHESES

Considerable and strong evidence has . . . mounted that establishes the relationship of biological factors to aggression and violence. Shah and Roth (1974), in a major contemporary overview of these links, divided biological influences into two groups: those that are "more directly related" and those that are "more indirectly related" to violent behavior (p. 110). In the former, the authors included tumors and other destructive or inflammatory processes of the limbic system of the brain, the continuum of epileptic cases ([violence] occurring during, just after, and between seizures) and endocrine abnormalities. Factors "more indirectly related" to violence are birth complications (i.e., perinatal difficulties), minimal brain dysfunction (MBD) and related neurological abnormalities, hyperactivity, genetic structures, chromosomal abnormalities, body or constitutional type, and psychophysiological functions related both to learning and psychopathic disorders (pp. 110–111). Mednick et al. (1982) have partitioned the literature on biology and criminal violence into the following areas: genetic studies, sex differences in aggression, autonomic nervous system research, neurophysiological and neuropsychological evidence, and pharmacological and biochemical factors. . . .

Biological treatments of human aggression and violence often begin with discussions of genetic factors. Evidence indicating such a linkage has been drawn from experimental and ethological studies of animals, from human family, twin and adoption studies and from research on human chromosomal abnormalities. It is well-known, for example, that selective breeding of certain strains of animals (such as mice) can increase their aggressive traits relative to other selectively bred strains. These results are consistent with work done by several ethologists (e.g., Lorenz, 1966; Tinbergen, 1951) who have conducted elaborate observational studies of animals to assess the evolution and functions of species-specific behavior such as aggression. These studies assert that aggressive animal behavior is instinctive (i.e., heritable through genetic transmission) because it appears to be unlearned, resistant to change and similar in all members of a species (Schuster, 1978). One of the better-known and more debated ethological theories was developed by Lorenz (1966), who argued . . . that aggression is adaptive in animal populations (for instance, it functions to disperse members more evenly over sustaining territories, to control sexual rivalry and mating, and to produce a stable "social" organization), that aggression is ritualized (stereotyped) in such a way as to minimize injurious and lethal conflict among the members of a species (such as through appeasement postures), and that aggression is propelled by the build-up of aggressive motivation (drives) which presses to be released periodically (Schuster, 1978). Viewed in this way, animal aggression is not uncontrolled attack behavior but is well-defined activity within the specific contexts which trigger it. The aggressive drive and its corresponding behavior are, then, eminently functional.

Although animal research on the heritability of aggression and violence cannot be accepted uncritically as applicable to human conduct (to do so ignores important species differences), such efforts have nevertheless provided important and suggestive evidence in this regard. These hypotheses have received support from several quarters, specifically from human family, twin, and adoption studies and from investigations of human chromosomal abnormalities.

Family, twin, and adoption studies use the aggressive and violent behaviors of biological relatives as indicators of genetic transmission. When biological relatives (e.g., twins) exhibit the same behavior (e.g., violence), they are said to be concordant in that behavior and, conversely, when biological relatives show dissimilar behavior, they are said to be behaviorally discordant. If genetic factors indeed play a part in shaping violent and antisocial behavior, then biological relatives (for instance, biological parents and their offspring) should be concordant more often than nonbiological relatives (for instance, adoptive parents and their adopted children). Alternatively stated: Persons who are most alike genetically should be most alike behaviorally (under similar environmental conditions) if genetic components are causal contributors. Identical twins (developed from the same ovum), for example, would be expected to have a higher concordance rate than fraternal twins (matured from different ova).

Christiansen's (1977b) review of eight major twin studies showed that nearly two-thirds of the identical twins were concordant for officially designated criminal and delinquent behavior, whereas less than one-third of the fraternal twins were concordant. Christiansen's (1977a) own study of twins born in Denmark between 1881 and 1910 indicated that identical twins had a criminal concordance rate 2.7 times higher than that of fraternal twins. Other research has confirmed these results (Dalgaard and Kringlen, 1976).

One problem with twin studies, however, is that genetic and environmental influences cannot be disentangled easily. The high concordance rate for identical twins, for example, may be due to the fact that they are treated very similarly by other people.

Adoption studies have proven useful in sorting out biological and social influences. If biological influences, such as genetically heritable factors, to some extent produce violent behavior, then persons who have been adopted at birth should exhibit behaviors more like their biological relatives (parents, for example) than their adoptive relatives. Research supports this position. Hutchings and Mednick's (1977) study of male adoptees showed that the highest proportion of adopted sons had official criminal records if the biological fathers were also criminals. Studies in antisocial personality and other psychiatric disorders are in accord with these findings. . . .

Chromosomal abnormalities have been implicated as a possible cause of violent behavior. Normal human cells have forty-six chromosomes which carry genetic material (genes). Forty-four of these chromosomes are related to bodily structures and processes. The remaining two determine the sex of the individual. (The male chromosome has been designated by the symbol Y and the female analogue by X. Females have an XX configuration, whereas males exhibit an XY pair.)

Two sex-related irregularities have received especially widespread attention over the last several decades—the XYY anomaly (the "super-male") and the

XXY syndrome (Klinefelter's syndrome). In the former case, it has been suggested that the extra Y (male) chromosome might predispose a person to heightened aggressivity. A number of surveys of men . . . in institutions for the mentally ill and subnormal and for offenders have shown a higher prevalence rate than noninstitutionalized populations. [However,] contradictory evidence has also been found. . . .

Work conducted on the XXY syndrome has shown that, in addition to the physical irregularities exhibited by these males (sterility, diminished facial hair, enlarged breasts, etc.), they also have a high vulnerability to mental disorders, especially sexual disturbances (e.g., homosexuality, pedophilia and transsexualism). Higher rates of criminal and antisocial behavior have also been indicated. Despite this suggestive evidence, Klinefelter's syndrome has not been demonstrably related to male violence.

Antisocial behavior has been linked to autonomic nervous system (ANS) functioning. One aspect of the ANS is that it mediates physiological activity associated with emotions. Peripheral (i.e., nonbrain or central nervous system) signs of ANS activity include cardiovascular activity (e.g., heart rate and blood pressure), electrodermal activity (e.g., galvanic skin response—GSR—or electrical activity of the skin), respiration rate, muscle tension, pupillary size, and so on.

Several indices (especially the GSR) of ANS activity have been used to investigate the relationship between emotional arousal (timing, degree, and types) and the ability to anticipate and learn from punishment. Particularly important in this regard have been studies of psychopaths, for they show a relative lack of emotion (incapacity to love, lack of remorse or shame, absence of nervousness or other psychoneurotic traits, and the inability to learn from punishment, to foresee negative consequences or to be socialized) (Cleckley, 1964; McCord and McCord, 1964). . . . While results are not conclusive, findings indicate that psychopaths, delinquents, and prisoners show less or no physiological (ANS) apprehension of punishment to themselves or others when compared to nonpsychopaths, nondelinquents, and noncriminals (Mednick et al., 1982: 33, 36–38). Few studies have focused on violence, but those that have done so show lower ANS activity among persons exhibiting the more serious behavioral disorders (Mednick et al., 1982: 44).

Central nervous system (CNS) structures (particularly the limbic or "visceral" areas of the brain) and processes (i.e., neurophysiological activity) are known to influence emotion (fear, anger, rage), aggression, sexual activity and other related behaviors. Limbic regions of special importance are portions of the thalamus and hypothalamus, upper parts of the brain stem and contiguous areas. When it is functioning normally, the limbic area is integrated with those brain structures which inhibit behavior (Shah and Roth, 1974: 112). Disease, injury, and other insults to these CNS locations can, however, reduce the threshold (i.e., increase the readiness) at which sexual or aggressive responses are activated (Shah and Roth, 1974: 115). . . . Experimental stimulation and surgical alteration of selected areas of the limbic structure have been shown to induce or modify emotional activity related to aggression (Shah and Roth, 1974: 114–116).

A high prevalence of epileptic disorders, which involve an unusually high neuronal discharge within the CNS (resulting in a seizure or "fit"), have been found among repeatedly assaultive offenders and psychopaths (Shah and Roth, 1974: 118–119; Mednick et al., 1982: 49). Evidence has not shown conclusively that assaultive activity occurred during the epileptic episode. . . .

One approach to studying epileptic disorders is to perform electroencephalographic (EEG) tests on various populations. This procedure traces the minute electrical oscillations (brain waves) emitted by the cerebral cortex. Although the research using this technique has had serious methodological flaws (Wolfgang et al., 1983: 60), some studies have found evidence of a disproportionate number of seriously violent offenders (murderers and assaulters) and repeat offenders with various kinds of EEG abnormalities, such as an excess of either fast or slow activity and temporal lobe epilepsy (pp. 60–62; Mednick et al., 1982: 47–48). . . .

Several chemical substances produced by or ingested into the body have been related to aggression and violence. . . . Important in this regard among the internally produced substances are testosterone (the male hormone) and glucose (blood sugar). Significant externally produced substances are alcohol, amphetamines and barbiturates. Research indicates that males are usually more aggressive than females, even before the school years (up to age 6), indicating that biological rather than gender-related childrearing practices may be the more influential determinants of aggression during the earliest years (Wolfgang et al., 1983: 74).

These results and others point to the influence of the male hormone, testosterone, on aggression. Studies of violent male offenders, for example, have shown that these men have higher testosterone levels than nonoffenders and, further, that the more seriously violent subgroups have the higher testosterone levels (Mednick et al., 1982: 30–31, 63).

Low blood sugar (hypoglycemia) has been well-established as related to CNS functioning, particularly to impaired cerebral functioning (Mednick, et al., 1982: 63–64; Shah and Roth, 1974: 125–126). Fatigue, irritability, aggression and, occasionally, rage are initial concommitants of reduced blood sugar. Despite the suspected and often asserted relationship between hypoglycemia and violence, research is still tentative in this regard.

Researchers agree that nonmedical drug consumption is implicated in violent behavior, though not in a simple causal fashion. The influences of alcohol on violence have been most widely documented. A high proportion of criminal homicides, forcible rapes and assaults involve at least one participant who has ingested some kind of alcoholic beverage (Mednick, et al., 1982: 58–60; Wolfgang, et al., 1983: 46). The depressant and disinhibitory effects of alcohol in combination with social setting factors facilitate aggressive exchanges. Accumulating research has also begun to link barbiturate and amphetamine abuse to assaultive behavior. . . .

Analyses of the relationships between constitutional (body structure or physique) factors and violent and antisocial behavior have had a long tradition.

Deficient physical growth has been associated with prenatal deficits such as premature birth and low birth weight (Wolfgang, et al., 1983: 79). Reports also have shown a higher incidence of short stature and obesity in children exhibiting MBD symptoms. These growth and CNS deficits have, in turn, been related to other physical disorders and to behavioral problems and delinquency (pp. 80–81).

[Alternative] . . . suggestive work on body structure and criminality has appeared. Findings have tended to indicate that delinquents and criminals are physically superior to nondelinquent comparison groups. The "delinquent" body type is generally more muscular, athletic and bony than the "nondelinquent" body type (Shah and Roth, 1974: 141). [However,] the mechanism by which physique might affect serious and assaultive delinquency and crime is not well understood. . . . Hypotheses range from direct effects of biological processes on behavior to indirect effects of societal responses to and the socialization of persons having particular physiques (Shah and Roth, 1974: 139–141). . . . Methodological problems with research on constitution and antisocial behavior make conclusions in these regards tentative and suggestive.

PSYCHIATRIC, PSYCHOANALYTICAL AND PSYCHOLOGICAL FORMULATIONS

Theories and studies of human mental functioning have provided some of the most long-standing, dominant, and controversial approaches to understanding behavior, most notably the more physically and socially harmful forms of deviant and unlawful conduct. Psychiatry is perhaps the oldest of those approaches concerned with mental analyses. As a specialty of medicine, psychiatry views the causes and courses of behavior and its related mental processes in terms of medical concepts and metaphors, most importantly, the illness-health continuum. . . . Central to this perspective is the identification of psychological abnormality and pathology.

The psychiatric literature on violence is substantial. Much of it has been reviewed by Wolfgang and Ferracuti (1982), who have focused on homicide. Much work has appeared as clinical case studies that detail and explain individual psychological dynamics and pathological developments. Recent studies have been broader in scope and have examined either psychological disorders in criminal (generally prison) populations, often focusing on violent prisoners, or violent (criminal and noncriminal) behavior among released mental patients (Guze, 1976; Monahan, 1981; Monahan and Splane, 1980; Monahan and Steadman, 1983).

Psychiatry does not have an integrated conception of the psychopathology of violence. . . . Though psychological perspectives on the psychopathological roots of violence are many, one theme which often emerges is that of psychological conflict or stress (Halleck, 1967: 51–53). . . . Substantial, intense and enduring conflictual demands can result, depending upon the specific features of the case, in psychopathology, including functional psychoses, psychoneuroses, psychosomatic disabilities, personality disorders, manic and depressive states, behavioral disturbances and the like. These disorders often involve irrational or inappropriate thought or behavior as well as psychological distress or discomfort (anxiety). Cognitive, emotional and behavioral outcomes like these can impede in varying degrees the person's ability to function in what might be considered, for that person, routine personal and social activities. . . . Each pathological posture exhibits its distinctive causal and developmental path which, in conjunction with special constellations of external factors and contingencies, can result in varying degrees of violent behavior.

. . . [P]sychiatric hypotheses of violence do not argue that mental malfunctions necessarily or even usually entail such extreme behavioral components. (Psychopathology most likely accounts for a small portion of all violence, although no firm evidence currently exists in this regard.) Psychiatry does propose, however, that some portion of violent conduct is related to psychopathology and that certain kinds of violence are more likely to be so related than are others. For example, certain kinds of brutal homicides or sexual offenses may involve a disproportionately large number of psychopathological individuals. A . . . report by the U.S. President['s] Commission on Mental Health (1978) concluded in its overview of violence that although some mentally ill people are violent, the image of the mentally ill person as violent is incorrect (p. 56).

Psychoanalysis is perhaps the most widely and popularly known psychiatric approach. The theory postulates that all psychological and behavioral activity is motivated to reach some goal and that the nature of the motivation may be either consciously or unconsciously known to the person. These goals stem from three internal (organic or psychological) sources: innate drives ("instincts") such as sex and aggression ("id" functions); rational considerations of self-interest and self-preservation based upon the recognition of internal and external limitations, prohibitions, opportunities, dangers and the like ("ego" functions); and moral restrictions instilled through social contacts and affiliations ("super-ego" and "conscience" functions).

Psychoanalysis interprets the origin and development of aggression and violence from several angles, depending upon the dynamic interplay among the three internal sources. . . . Because of the disruptive and destructive aspects of assaultive behavior, all societies have developed rules which prohibit or regulate the external expression of innate aggressive processes. . . . When violence is initiated, the behavior is likely to comprise . . . a moral violation (unless exempted due to socially stipulated mitigations. . .).

Viewed in this way, the innate drive propelling the individual toward aggressive conduct is realized as violent behavior because of an improper or defective moral education (socialization). . . . [T]he psychological balance of power between biological drives and moral considerations has evolved in such a way that a primary aggressive drive overpowers internal moral restrictions.

Depending upon the particulars of the case, the psychological processes leading to violent displays may be either normal or abnormal (psychopathological). From a psychoanalytical standpoint, the boundaries between psychologically healthy and unhealthy forms of violence depend crucially upon such factors as whether the individual is consciously aware and accepting of the character and intent of the behavior or whether these thought processes and motivations are mostly unconscious and cause anxiety, discomfort, psychological and behavioral impairment, and associated complexes of irrational symptoms.

As psychoanalytic theory evolved, innate processes began to play a less central role in explanatory and interpretative contexts. . . . In addition to explaining violence as the overpowering expression of innate propulsions pitted against opposing moral forces, violence in its many guises became increasingly acknowledged as the resultant of both rational and moral influences, for clearly innate aggressive potentials can be channeled to promote both self-interest and moral concerns. . . .

In addition to the psychiatric approaches, several psychological theories have been developed and applied to aggressive and violent behavior: frustration-aggression hypotheses, social learning theory, and, more recently, stress formulations. According to the classical version of frustration-aggression theory, aggression (i.e., real or fantasized behavior that is intended to injure or destroy persons or objects to which it is directed) is always a consequence of frustration (i.e., the interruption of behavior organized to obtain some goal) (Berkowitz, 1962: 26, 28; Dollard et al., 1939: 1). [One] important feature of frustration is that it can remain active (a driving force) over time, resulting in delayed and potentially extreme aggressive displays (Dollard et al., 1939: 31). Other factors affecting the level of aggression are the strength of the frustrated behavior and the degree of interference with the goal-directed activity.

Several reservations have been raised about the theory. . . . For example, it would appear that frustration does not always culminate in aggression and, further, that not all aggression is preceded by frustration (Berkowitz, 1962: 29–50; Megargee, 1969: 1059–1063). As a result of these and other objections, the theory was modified somewhat to [hypothesize] that frustration produces the instigation (drive or readiness) to engage in various types of responses, one of which may be aggression (Miller, 1941: 338).

An important modification and extension of the frustration-aggression thesis has been made by Berkowitz (1962) who hypothesized that frustration produces anger (i.e., the predisposition to initiate hostile behavior) which, in turn, may result in aggression. Whether aggression in fact occurs depends upon past experiences (learning), cognitive interpretation of the frustrating situation (e.g., [whether] the frustration [is] accidental or intentionally imposed) and immediate situational factors (e.g., presence of weapons, bystanders . . .) (pp. 32–36, 46). This posture represents an important conceptual shift, for it argues that factors other than frustration can influence the likelihood of aggressive and violent outcomes [including] . . . social processes. . . .

Perhaps the most influential contemporary psychological formulation of aggression is social learning or conditioning theory. (See, for example, Bandura, 1973; Bandura, 1979; and Bandura and Walters, 1959[;] . . . Monahan and Splane, 1980; and Wolfgang and Ferracuti, 1982.) Central to social learning theory is the thesis that much behavior, including violent forms, develops from the ongoing and sequential processes of social rewards and punishments that follow from the completion of behavior. . . . Several other processes also operate, including (but not exhausted by) observational learning (the imitation by observation of previously unlearned [violent] behavior), disinhibition (the dissipation of internal prohibitions to engage in previously learned [violent] behaviors) and social facilitation (the activation by observation of previously learned [violent] behavior that has not been subjected to internal prohibitions).

Megargee (1969, 1982) has reviewed the research and theoretical literature on social learning and has shown its links to the broader conditioning or behavioristic learning perspective. Behaviorist formulations generally posit five interlocking processes which, depending upon their respective strengths and substance, may lead to aggression and violence. These dynamics include the instigation to aggression (the sum of all internal factors which motivate a person to commit an aggressive act), habit strength (learned preferences for using aggression based on past rewards for having done so), inhibition (the sum of all internal factors which motivate a person not to engage in aggressive conduct), stimulus factors (immediate situational influences which facilitate or impede aggression and violence), and response competition (patterns of nonaggressive and nonviolent behaviors which may be selected in place of the hostile forms). Violent activity is most likely to erupt when instigations to aggression, aggressive habit strength and facilitating stimulus factors are more pronounced relative to inhibitions and nonviolent behavioral [alternatives]. . . . (. . . [C]onditioning hypotheses distinguish between those processes and conditions under which violence is learned and those under which it is maintained, regulated and performed.)

One of the more recent psychological approaches to violence involves the idea of stress, which has been defined as a state of substantial imbalance between environmental demands made upon a person and the capacity of the person to respond to these demands (McGrath, 1970: 17). Responses to correct the imbalance can be either adaptive or maladaptive. Violence is often maladaptive for it may not establish the desired equilibrium. Indeed, such behavior may create an even greater imbalance. Several important stressors (. . . "life events" . . .) have been identified, including illness, difficulties at work, residential relocation, accidents [and] changes in employment, marital, and educational statuses. . . . [P]ersons subjected to high stress may be more prone to engage in dangerous behavior (Wolfgang, et al., 1983: 42–45). Family violence has also been consistently related to increased levels of stress. . . .

SOCIOLOGICAL AND CULTURAL PERSPECTIVES

Sociological [approaches] have included the influences of socialization processes (collective teaching and learning of social rules), subcultural formation and maintenance (creation, dissemination and perpetuation of social rules in delimited populations), social structural effects (status and class position in the social hierarchy), and social interaction dynamics (situational actions and reactions based upon the mutual interpretations and expectations of social participants). . . .

According to the subcultural approach, violence is commonly used in those segments of the population (culture) which are characterized by clusters of values, rules of conduct (norms), and attitudes which encourage or tolerate assaultive behavior as the acceptable and often preferred means to resolve certain kinds of interpersonal disputes or to achieve or consolidate status (Wolfgang and Ferracuti, 1982). Socialization and continuing subcultural support for violence promote not only the utilization of such extreme and potentially lethal behavior but also reduce whatever guilt the individual might otherwise experience in the contemplation and performance of these activities. Firearms, knives and other technologies of violence, often available to subcultural members, both express and enhance the collective willingness and readiness to participate in assaultive conduct. In general, subcultural themes like that of violence develop and are transmitted from generation to generation. . . .

Although confrontation and assault are permitted and expected within subcultures of violence, such activity is subject to rules and regulations which stipulate who may legitimately use violence, who may be the proper targets of violent acts, what nonviolent options exist, and so on. Violence is not, then, a part of all or even most interactions, nor is it likely to be used in equal proportions by all subcultural members. . . .

Other work in the area of subcultural analysis has focused on the disadvantaged social classes and on the formation of youth (primarily male) gangs in these populations. One version of this approach argues that violence and other deviant or illegal conduct may be promoted by typical structures of social relations in the lower classes, particularly by youthful male groups (Miller, 1958). Disadvantaged social classes are characterized by widespread and persistent norms and values which highlight and encourage certain behavioral patterns such as toughness, getting into trouble, and excitement. . . . Conformity to these norms, especially those encouraging toughness, often results in aggressive and violent attacks.

Another subcultural approach has focused on the lower-class delinquent male group (Cohen, 1955). These youths, it has been suggested, have adopted middle-class values such as striving for economic success and its exhibition in material consumption. . . . [B]ecause of the impoverished socialization patterns in lower-class families, youngsters at these more depressed social levels are unable to compete successfully with their middle-class counterparts. Frustration and anxiety result which culminate in a "reaction-formation"—the forceful rejection and replacement of middle-class values with values that are in opposition to those that have been rejected. Nonutilitarian (hedonistic), malicious, and negativistic behavior are hallmarks of this subcultural inversion, with violence representing one of the more notable behavioral forms. . . .

Structural (strain) theories postulate that diverse forms of unconventional behavior, such as violence, are generated by discontinuities between commonly extolled and shared goals (e.g., the accumulation of wealth) and the socially approved means ("opportunities") that are available to reach these goals (Cloward and Ohlin, 1960; Merton, 1938). Limitations on legitimate means are most acute in the lower social classes, and it is at these points in the social structure that antisocial solutions to the problem of restricted conventional opportunities [are] most likely to occur. Lower-class members, particularly the youth, tend to view these restrictions as unjust. Legitimacy is progressively withdrawn from those conventional norms which regulate the selection of goals and means. In their place, norms are adopted which encourage, approve or tolerate employing unconventional means to reach goals. One strategy for attaining goals, such as acquiring status among one's peers and associates, is the "conflict" solution: youngsters coalesce into groups and gangs in which violence becomes the favored behavioral technology by which to secure prestige, honor, and other socially valued objectives. . . .

Several researchers have suggested that some violent, antisocial and criminal activities are consequences of the perception of discrepancies between the level of goal attainment that people believe should be rightfully theirs and the level of attainment that they have actually reached (Davies, 1979; Eberts and Schwirian, 1968; Gurr, 1968; Toby, 1967). Monetary, educational, occupational and civil liberty goals have all been explored with this line of thought. Violent behavior is one means to redress what the individual considers to be illegitimate disparity ("relative deprivation"). Violence may be used as an acquisitive technique (e.g., robbery) or [may] represent emotional discharges driven by the frustrations of deprivation.

Interactionist (situational) analyses, based mainly on work done in social and environmental psychology, [are] concerned with the dynamic relationship between persons and between persons and their immediate physical setting (Magnusson, 1981; Monahan and Klassen, 1982; Moos, 1973). Central to this perspective is the idea that the immediate social and physical features of settings can have an important influence on the course and outcome of social interactions. These effects are broadly conceived as either facilitating or inhibiting violent and aggressive exchanges. Some of the more important situational features examined have been the reciprocal sequence of action and reaction by those who commit and those who are victims of violent acts (e.g., victim-initiated violence, intimidating behavior by the primary aggressor, victim resistance to intimidation, and responses to the victim's resistance), the social relationship between the victim and the violent assailant (family members, friends, strangers, etc.), the presence of weapons and drugs, and the time and location of the incident [and the presence of bystanders]. . . .

CONCLUSION

The diversity of perspectives and methods utilized in mounting the many analytical assaults on violent behavior have resulted in the rich and extensive knowledge treated here. Perhaps most striking about the results of these efforts, however, is the relative lack of interdisciplinary and integrative approaches: Theories and empirical findings within and across disciplines tend to be disconnected.

To check analytical discontinuity, communication and collaboration should be encouraged and underscored, for such exchanges can establish a common theoretical and research ground of interlocking propositions, hypotheses and empirical evidence. Emphasizing the need for interdisciplinary initiatives is not recent (Wolfgang and Ferracuti, 1982: 1–13)[;] yet the results of empirical eclecticism and theoretical pluralism have generally not found their way into integrative schemes. The future of integrative, interdisciplinary analyses of violent behavior lies ahead.

REFERENCES

Bandura, Albert. *Aggression: A Social Learning Analysis*. Englewood Cliffs, N.J.: Prentice-Hall, 1973.

———. "The Social Learning Perspective: Mechanisms of Aggression." In *The Psychology of Crime and Criminal Justice*, edited by Hans Toch, 198–236. New York: Holt, Rinehart and Winston, 1979.

———, and Richard H. Walters. *Adolescent Aggression*. New York: Ronald Press, 1959.

Berkowitz, Leonard. *Aggression*. New York: McGraw Hill, 1962.

Christiansen, Karl O. "A Preliminary Study of Criminality among Twins." In *Biosocial Bases of Criminal Behavior*, edited by Sarnoff A. Mednick and Karl O. Christiansen, 89–108. New York: Gardner Press, 1977a.

———. "A Review of Studies of Criminality among Twins." In *Biosocial Bases of Criminal Behavior*, edited by Sarnoff A. Mednick and Karl O. Christiansen, 45–88. New York: Gardner Press, 1977b.

Cleckley, Harvey M. *The Mask of Sanity*. St. Louis, Missouri: C. V. Mosby Co., 1964.

Cloward, Richard A., and Lloyd E. Ohlin. *Delinquency and Opportunity: A Theory of Delinquent Gangs*. New York: The Free Press, 1960.

Cohen, Albert K. *Delinquent Boys: The Culture of the Gang*. New York: The Free Press, 1955.

Dalgaard, Odd S., and Einar A. Kringlen. "A Norwegian Twin Study of Criminality." *British Journal of Criminology* 16 (1976): 213–232.

Davies, James C. "The J-Curve of Rising and Declining Satisfactions as a Cause of Some Great Revolutions and a Contained Rebellion." In *Violence in America: Historical and Comparative Perspectives*, rev. ed., edited by Hugh Davis Graham and Ted Robert Gurr, 415–436. Beverly Hills, Calif.: Sage Publications, 1979.

Dollard, John, Leonard W. Doob, Neal E. Miller, O. H. Mowrer, and Robert R. Sears. *Frustration and Aggression*. New Haven, Conn.: Yale University Press, 1939.

Eberts, Paul, and Kent P. Schwirian. "Metropolitan Crime Rates and Relative Deprivation." *Criminologica* 5 (1968): 43–52.

Eysenck, Hans J. *Criminal Personality*. London: Routledge and Kegan Paul, 1970.

Gurr, Ted R. "A Causal Model of Civil Strife." *American Political Science Review* 62 (1968): 11–24.

Guze, Samuel. *Criminal and Psychiatric Disorders*. New York: Oxford University Press, 1976.

Halleck, Seymour L. *Psychiatry and the Dilemma of Crime: A Study of Causes, Punishment, and Treatment*. Berkeley, Calif.: University of California Press, 1967.

Hutchings, Barry, and Sarnoff A. Mednick. "Criminality in Adoptees and Their Adoptive and Biological Parents: A Pilot Study." In *Biosocial Bases of Criminal Behavior*, edited by Sarnoff A. Mednick and Karl O. Christiansen, 127–141. New York: Gardner Press, 1977.

Lorenz, Konrad. *On Aggression*. New York: Harcourt, Brace and Jovanovich, 1966.

McCord, William, and Joan McCord. *The Psychopath: An Essay on the Criminal Mind*. Princeton, N.J.: Van Nostrand, 1964.

McGrath, Joseph E., ed. *Social and Psychological Factors in Stress*. New York: Holt, Rinehart, and Winston, 1970.

Magnusson, David. "Wanted: A Psychology of Situations." In *Toward a Psychology of Situations: An International Perspective*, edited by David Magnusson, 9–35. Hillsdale, N.J.: Lawrence, Erlbaum Associates, 1981.

Mednick, Sarnoff, A., Vicki Pollock, Jan Volavka, and William F. Gabrielli, Jr. "Biology and Violence." In *Criminal Violence*, edited by Marvin E. Wolfgang and Neil A. Weiner, 21–80. Beverly Hills, Calif.: Sage Publications, 1982.

Megargee, Edwin I. "Psychological Determinants and Correlates of Criminal Violence." In *Criminal Violence*, edited by Marvin E. Wolfgang and Neil A. Weiner, 81–170. Beverly Hills, Calif.: Sage Publications, 1982.

———. "The Psychology of Violence: A Critical Review of Theories of Violence." In *Crimes of Violence: A Staff Report to the National Commission of the Causes and Preventions of Violence*, Vol. 13, edited by Donald J. Mulvihill, Melvin M. Tumin and Lynn A. Curtis, 1037–1115. Washington, D.C.: U.S. Government Printing Office, 1969.

Merton, Robert K. "Social Structure and Anomie." *American Sociological Review* 3 (1938): 672–682.

Miller, Neal E. "The Frustration Aggression Hypothesis." *Psychological Review* 48 (1941): 337–342.

Miller, Walter. "Lower-Class Culture as a Generating Milieu of Gang Delinquency." *Journal of Social Issues* 14 (1958): 5–19.

Monahan, John. *Predicting Violent Behavior: An Assessment of Clinical Techniques*. Beverly Hills, Calif.: Sage Publications, 1981.

———, and Deidre Klassen. "Situational Approaches to Understanding and Predicting Criminal Violence." In *Criminal Violence*, edited by Marvin E. Wolfgang and Neil A. Weiner, 292–319. Beverly Hills, Calif.: Sage Publications, 1982.

———, and Stephanie Splane. "Psychological Approaches to Criminal Behavior." In *Criminology Review Yearbook*, Vol. 2, edited by Egon Bittner and Sheldon L. Messinger, 17–47. Beverly Hills, Calif.: Sage Publications, 1980.

———, and Henry J. Steadman. "Crime and Mental Disorder: An Epidemiological Approach." In *Crime and Justice: An Annual Review of Research*, Vol. 4, edited by Michael Tonry and Norval Morris, 145–188. Chicago: University of Chicago Press, 1983.

Moos, Rudolf H. "Conceptualizations of Human Environments." *American Psychologist* 28 (1973): 652–665.

Schuster, Richard A. "Ethological Theories of Aggression." In *Violence: Perspectives on Murder and Aggression*, edited by Irwin L. Kutash, Samuel B. Kutash, Louis B. Schlesinger, and Associates. San Francisco, Calif.: Jossey-Bass Publishers, 1978.

Shah, Saleem A., and Loren H. Roth. "Biological and Psychophysiological Factors in Criminality." In *Handbook of Criminology*, edited by Daniel Glaser, 101–173. Chicago: Rand McNally Company, 1974.

Tinbergen, Nikolaas. *The Study of Instinct*. Oxford, England: Clarendon Press, 1951.

Toby, Jackson. "Affluence and Adolescent Crime." In President's Commission on Law Enforcement and Administration of Justice, *Task Force Report: Juvenile Delinquency and Youth Crime*, 132–144. Washington, D.C.: U.S. Government Printing Office, 1967.

U.S. President's Commission on Mental Health. *Report to the President*. Washington, D.C.: U.S. Government Printing Office, 1978.

Wolfgang, Marvin E., and Franco Ferracuti. *The Subculture of Violence*. 1967. Reprint. Beverly Hills, Calif.: Sage Publications, 1982.

———, Deborah J. Denno, Robert M. Figlio, Paul E. Tracy, and Neil A. Weiner. "A Longitudinal Study of the Theoretical and Empirical Bases of High-Risk Delinquent and Criminal Behavior: A Multi-Cohort Multi-Wave Design." Proposal and literature review submitted to the John. A. and Catherine T. MacArthur Foundation, Chicago, May 18, 1983. Philadelphia, Pa.: Center for Studies in Criminology and Criminal Law, University of Pennsylvania, 1983.

Chapter 15
Drug Abuse

Drugs and Violent Crime

Paul J. Goldstein

TRIPARTITE CONCEPTUAL FRAMEWORK

. . . [**D**]rugs and violence [are] related to each other in three different ways: psychopharmacologically, economically compulsive, and systemically. This conceptualization is intended to provide a structure within which data may be analyzed most fruitfully. . . .

Psychopharmacological Violence

The psychopharmacological model suggests that some individuals, as a result of short- or long-term ingestion of specific substances, may become excitable and/or irrational and may exhibit violent behavior. The most relevant substances in this regard are probably alcohol, stimulants, barbiturates, and PCP. A lengthy literature exists examining the relationship between these substances and violence.

Barbiturates appear most likely, on a per ingestion basis, to lead to violence. Fortunately, the number of drug users who report barbiturate abuse is relatively small. In three separate studies of incarcerated delinquents, a barbiturate (secobarbital) was identified as the single substance most likely to enhance assaultiveness (Tinklenberg et al. 1974, 1976, and 1981). Collins (1982), studying self-reports of aggravated assaults and robberies by nearly 8,000 drug treatment program new admissions . . . , found that the highest proportions of persons committing one or more aggravated assaults or robberies were those who identified their primary drug problem as barbiturate use. Barbiturates, followed by alcohol and amphetamines, were most strongly correlated with assault. Barbiturates, followed by heroin, were most clearly correlated with robbery.

Early reports, which sought to employ a psychopharmacological model to attribute violent behavior to the use of opiates and marijuana, have now been largely discredited.[1] However, the irritability associated with the withdrawal-from-opiates syndrome may indeed lead to violence. Mednick et al. noted that workers in drug treatment programs are familiar with irritable, hostile, and sometimes aggressive clients in withdrawal (1982, 62).

According to Goldstein (1979), heroin-using prostitutes often linked robbing and/or assaulting clients with the withdrawal experience. These women reported that they preferred to talk a "trick" out of his money, but if they were feeling "sick," that is, experiencing withdrawal symptoms, that they would be too irritable to engage in gentle conning. In such cases they might attack the client, take his money, purchase sufficient heroin to "get straight," and then go back out on the street. . . .

A somewhat similar process has been reported with regard to cocaine. Users characterize being high on cocaine as a positive and "mellow" experience. However, the cocaine "crash"—that is, coming down from the high—has been described as a period of anxiety and depression in which external stimuli may be reacted to in a violent fashion. A cocaine user . . . reported beating his infant child to death because the baby would not stop crying during such a "crash."

A study of institutionalized delinquent boys revealed that about 43 percent took a drug within twenty-four hours of committing an offense against a person.

> Many of these boys stated that they took the drugs to give themselves courage to commit an act of violence. Sometimes an act of violence against a person was not intended since the boys initially wanted to steal goods or money to support a drug habit. Each of the 25 subjects who took drugs prior to an act of violence considered the dose taken to be significant and to have contributed substantially to their commission of the crime. In fact, they speculated that the crimes would not have occurred if they had not taken the drugs in question. . . . (Simonds and Kashani 1980, 308)

The drug scores most significantly correlated with the number of offenses against persons were barbiturates, PCP, cocaine, and, to a somewhat lesser extent, valium and amphetamines. . . .

Drug use may also have a reverse psychopharmacological effect and ameliorate violent tendencies. In such cases persons who are prone to acting violently may engage in self-medication to control their violent impulses. The drugs serving this function are typically heroin, tranquilizers, and . . . marijuana.

Psychopharmacological violence may involve drug use by either the offender or the victim. In other words, drug use may contribute to a person behaving violently, or it may alter a person's behavior in such a manner as to bring about that person's violent victimization. Previous research indicates relatively high frequencies of alcohol consumption in rape (Amir 1971; Rada 1975) and homicide victims (Shupe 1954; Wolfgang [1958] 1975). Public intoxication may invite a robbery or mugging. . . . One study found that in rapes, where only the victim was intoxicated, she was significantly more likely to be physically injured (Johnson, Gibson, and Linden 1976). . . .

An important issue that remains unresolved with regard to psychopharmacological violence concerns our ability to distinguish between what is a direct effect of drug use and what may be a "self-fulfilling prophecy" and/or a "technique of neutralization." Certain drugs acquire a reputation for stimulating aggressiveness. Barbiturates, for example, are referred to as "gorilla pills" by users. Though the reputation of a drug may be deserved, in some cases users may act out violently simply because they have learned that the drug has that effect.

Certain substances may be used in a psychopharmacologically functional manner. In this regard, drugs are ingested purposively because the user is familiar with specific effects and perceives them as positive for the perpetration of criminal acts. Examples of such functional drug use include tranquilizer and marijuana use to control nervousness or barbiturate and alcohol use to give courage. In a similar fashion, users may wish to engage in a violent act, feel deterred by scruples, and ingest the substance in order to be freed from personal responsibility for the act. This entitles them to claim that "the drug drove me to do it!" . . .

Economically Compulsive Violence

The economically compulsive model suggests that some drug users engage in economically oriented violent crime—for example, robbery—in order to support costly drug use. Heroin and cocaine, because they are expensive drugs typified by compulsive patterns of use, are the most relevant substances in this category. Economically compulsive actors are not primarily motivated by impulses to act out violently. Rather their primary motivation is to obtain money to purchase drugs. Violence generally results from some factor in the social context in which the economic crime is perpetrated. Such factors include the perpetrator's own nervousness, the victim's reaction, weaponry (or lack thereof) carried by either the offender or victim, the intercession of bystanders, and so on.

Research indicates that most heroin users avoid violent acquisitive crimes if viable nonviolent alternatives exist because violent crime is more dangerous, embodies a greater threat of prison if one is apprehended, and because perpetrators may lack a basic orientation toward violent behavior (Cushman 1974; Goldstein 1981; Goldstein and Duchaine 1980; Gould 1974; Johnson et al. 1985; Preble and Casey 1969; Swezey 1973).

While research does indicate that most crimes committed by most drug users are of the nonviolent variety—for example, shoplifting, prostitution, and drug selling—there are few data that indicate the proportion of violent economic crimes committed for drug-related reasons. . . .

A report issued by the American Bar Association stated that "to a large extent, the problem of urban crime is the problem of heroin addiction" (1972, 8). This report estimated that between one-third and one-half of the robberies committed in major urban areas are committed by heroin addicts. A 1978 report on bank robbery, issued by the U.S. General Accounting Office, estimated that at least 42 percent of the 237 bank robbers surveyed were drug users.

Voss and Stephens (1973), in studying a sample of 990 patients committed to the federal drug treatment facility in Lexington, Kentucky, found that only 2 percent reported committing armed robbery prior to beginning drug use; however,

18 percent reported committing armed robberies after having begun using drugs. . . .

Wish et al. (1981) analyzed 17,745 arrests in Washington, D.C., in which a urine specimen was obtained from the arrestees. Twenty-two percent of the male robbery arrestees (N = 2,209) and 29 percent of the female robbery arrestees (N = 149) had drug-positive test results, mainly for opiates. In only four other offense categories from among the sixteen surveyed was there a higher proportion of drug-positivity among arrestees: bail violations, larceny, drug offenses, and weapons offenses. . . . Chaiken and Chaiken (1982) showed that, among inmates in Texas, California, and Michigan entering prisons and jails, the robbery rate was generally higher among daily heroin users than among less frequent users or nonusers.

Johnson et al. (1985) studied the economic behavior of 201 active street opiate users in Harlem. . . . During the study period, 72 percent of the respondents committed no robberies; 23 percent committed robberies on an occasional and irregular basis. Ten subjects—5 percent of the sample—were classified as high-rate robbers; they committed 45 percent of all reported robberies, averaging one robbery every 6.6 days. High-rate robbers were more likely to use heroin—and to use a larger amount per day—than low-rate robbers or nonrobbers.

An additional caveat should be offered. . . . Not all studies are able to claim that robberies are, in fact, motivated by the compulsion to obtain money to purchase drugs. In some cases the perpetrator may be under the influence of drugs, such as barbiturates, and the robbery may have more of a psychopharmacological motivation than an economically compulsive one. In other cases robbers may celebrate a successful score by "partying" with drugs such as cocaine. This need not imply that the robbery is committed for the sole purpose of purchasing cocaine.

. . . [T]he mere fact that robbers are also drug users does not necessarily imply an economically compulsive motivation for committing robberies. Research involving intensive interviewing of robbers is necessary to fully unravel their complex motivations and the drug relatedness of their robberies.

Systemic Violence

In the systemic model, violence is intrinsic to involvement with any illicit substance. Systemic violence, which refers to the traditionally aggressive patterns of interaction within the system of drug distribution and use, includes disputes over territory between rival drug dealers, assaults and homicides committed within dealing hierarchies as a means of enforcing normative codes, robberies of drug dealers and the usually violent retaliation by the dealer or his/her bosses, elimination of informers, disputes over drugs and/or drug paraphernalia, punishment for selling adulterated or phony drugs, punishment for failing to pay one's debts, and robbery violence related to the social ecology of copping areas. . . .

There are two rather distinct dimensions of systemic violence: one related to the system of distribution and one related to the system of use. Drug distribution refers to cultivation and/or manufacture, processing, packaging, smuggling, and both the wholesale and retail trade. Violence may occur at any level of this system. . . .

Within the system of distribution, it is possible to differentiate between macrosystem and microsystem violence. A good example of the former was reported in a recent *Wall Street Journal* article on the cocaine business. Discussing Florida's "cocaine wars," Ricks (1986) stated that "the U.S. demand for cocaine and the Miami-area drug-related homicide rate grew at about the same frenzied pace, with Miami's drug murders peaking in 1981 at 101":

> Everyone who fought in or witnessed the war seems to have a different explanation of its causes. . . . What is clear is that certain Colombian organizations emerged from the war in command of the wholesale level. . . . In business school terms, those Colombian organizations, by installing their own middlemen in Miami, "forward integrated" to capture an additional level of profit. (16)

An example of microsystem distributional violence is provided by a subject from [a study that is now in progress]:

> I copped twenty dollars of heroin from this girl. I left and checked the first bag. It was baby powder. I checked the second bag. It was baby powder also. I got my knife, went back, and put it to her throat and took sixteen dollars off her. That's all she had. I don't know what happened to my twenty. She had the sixteen in her bra. We were in a vacant lot and I could have been seen by the cops. That's the only reason I didn't cut her up.

Microsystem violent events occur within the system of drug use as well as that of drug distribution. The system of drug use refers to the norms and values that have emerged to structure interactions around drugs and drug paraphernalia. Violence associated with disputes over drugs have long been endemic in the drug world. Friends come to blows because one refuses to give the other a "taste." A husband beats his wife because she raided his "stash."

The AIDS epidemic . . . has led to an increasing amount of violence because of intravenous drug users' fears of contracting this fatal disease from contaminated "works." This violence has appeared at both the distribution and consumption levels. With regard to distribution, some sellers of needles and syringes claim that the used "works" they are trying to sell are actually new and unused. In some cases, where the ruse was discovered by purchasers, violence has ensued.

At the consumption level, the AIDS epidemic has caused a strain in the social etiquette of the drug world. Users are prone to share "works" for a variety of reasons, including economics, convenience, and fear of arrest. However, fear of AIDS has pressured at least some users to be very selective about the people with whom they will share. This has led to ruffled feelings, verbal disputes, fights, stabbings, and homicides. Violence has erupted when persons have used another's "works" without permission. . . .

Much of the heroin in New York City is being distinctively packaged and sold under "brand names" (Goldstein et al. 1984). These labeling practices are frequently abused, and this abuse has led to violence. Among the more common abuses are the following: Dealers mark an inferior quality of heroin with a currently popular brand name; users purchase the good heroin, use it, and then repackage the bag with milk sugar for resale; the popular brand is purchased, and the bag is "tapped" and further diluted for resale. Such practices have led to threats, assaults, and homicides.

A common form of norm violation in the drug trade in known as "messing up the money." This involves a subordinate returning less money to his superior than is expected. For example, a street dealer is given a consignment of drugs to sell and is expected to return to his supplier, manager, or lieutenant with a specific amount of money. However, for any of a variety of reasons, he returns with too little money or fails to return at all.

When a street dealer fails to return sufficient money, his superior has several options. If only a small amount of money is involved and the street dealer has few prior transgressions and a convincing justification for the current shortage, his superior is likely to give him another consignment and allow him to make up the shortage from his share of the new consignment. Other options include firing the street dealer, having him beaten up, or having him killed.

Fear of becoming a victim of systemic violence has led to involvement in economically compulsive violence. Street dealers who have "messed up the money" may be terrified of what their superiors will do to them. Persons in this situation commit robberies as a quick way to obtain the money they owe. . . .

The social ecology of copping areas is generally well-suited for the perpetration of robbery violence. Major copping areas are frequently located in poor ghetto neighborhoods, such as Harlem in New York City. In these neighborhoods, drug users and dealers are frequent targets for robberies because they are known to be carrying something of value and because they are unlikely to report their victimization. . . .

A number of important issues pertaining to systemic violence remain unresolved. There is no doubt that participation in the drug business increases the probability for participation in violent events, both as victim and as perpetrator. What is not so clear is the extent to which the drug business itself makes people violent or whether violence-prone individuals may self-select themselves for violent roles in the drug business. . . .

Victims of systemic violence are very difficult to identify in official records because they frequently lie to the police about the circumstances of their victimization. Not a single research subject whom I have interviewed, who was the victim of systemic violence and who was forced to give an account of his/her victimization to the police, admitted that he/she had been assaulted because of owing a drug supplier money or selling somebody phony or adulterated drugs. All such victims claimed to have been robbed. . . .

CONCLUSIONS

Clearly, drugs and violent crime are related. Further, they are related in different ways. The tripartite conceptual framework suggests three models of that relationship: psychopharmacological, economically compulsive, and systemic. Different drugs differentially promote violence depending upon which model is operant. Barbiturates, amphetamines, and alcohol are most often associated with psychopharmacological violence. Heroin and cocaine are most often associated with economically compulsive violence. Any illicit drug may be associated with systemic violence. . . .

It should be noted that times change, and relationships between specific substances and types of violence are not immutable. Alcohol is an interesting case in point. During the prohibition years there was a great deal of violence surrounding the illicit liquor trade. Images of Al Capone, Elliot Ness, and the St. Valentine's Day massacre entered into American folklore. But the repeal of prohibition virtually eliminated alcohol-related systemic violence. The current availability and widespread use of alcohol have made it a major contributor to psychopharmacological violence. Ultimately, society must decide through the political process what sorts and levels of violence it is willing to tolerate. The study of alcohol's transition may have important implications for the current debate over how to handle marijuana, cocaine, and other substances. *The Untouchables* may instruct *Miami Vice*.

NOTE

1. See, for example, Dai (1937) 1970; Finestone 1976; Greenberg and Adler 1974; Inciardi and Chambers 1972; Kolb 1925; Kosel, Dupont, and Brown 1972; Kramer 1976; Schatzman 1975.

REFERENCES

American Bar Association. 1972. *New perspectives on urban crime*. Washington, D.C.: American Bar Association.

Amir, M. 1971. *Patterns in forcible rape*. Chicago: University of Chicago Press.

Chaiken, J., and M. Chaiken. 1982. *Varieties of criminal behavior*. Santa Monica: Rand Corporation.

Collins, J. J. 1982. "Drugs and violence: The relationship of selected psychoactive substance use to assault and robbery." Paper presented at the annual meeting of the American Society of Criminology.

Cushman, P. 1974. "Relationship between narcotic addiction and crime." *Federal Probation* 38:38–43.

Dai, B. 1970. *Opium addiction in Chicago*. 1937. Reprint. Montclair, N.J.: Patterson Smith.

Finestone, H. 1967. "Narcotics and criminality." *Law and Contemporary Problems* 22: 60–85.

Goldstein, P. J. 1979. *Prostitution and drugs*. Lexington, Mass.: Lexington Books, 1979.

———. 1981. "Getting over: Economic alternatives to predatory crime among street drug users." In *The drugs/crime connection*, ed. J. A. Inciardi, 67–84. Beverly Hills: Sage.

———. 1985. "The drugs/violence nexus: A tripartite conceptual framework." *Journal of Drug Issues* 15:493–506.

Goldstein, P. J., and N. Duchaine. 1980. "Daily criminal activities of street drug users." Paper presented at the annual meeting of the American Society of Criminology.

Goldstein, P. J., D. Lipton, E. Preble, I. Sobel, T. Miller, W. Abbott, W. Paige, and F. Soto. 1984. "The marketing of street heroin in New York City." *Journal of Drug Issues* 14:553–66.

Gould, L. 1974. "Crime and the addict: Beyond common sense." In *Drugs and the criminal justice system*, ed. J. Inciardi and C. Chambers, 57–75. Beverly Hills: Sage.

Greenberg, S., and F. Adler. 1974. "Crime and addiction: An empirical analysis of the literature." *Contemporary Drug Problems* 3:221–70.

Inciardi, J. A., and C. Chambers. 1972. "Unreported criminal involvement of narcotic addicts." *Journal of Drug Issues* 2:57–64.

Johnson, B., P. J. Goldstein, E. Preble, J. Schmeidler, D. S. Lipton, B. Spunt, and T. Miller. 1985. *Taking care of business: The economics of crime by heroin abusers*. Lexington, Mass.: Lexington Books.

Johnson, S., L. Gibson, and R. Linden. 1976. "Alcohol and rape in Winnipeg: 1966–1975." *Journal of Studies on Alcohol* 39:1887–94.

Kolb, L. 1925. "Drug addiction and its relation to crime." *Mental Hygiene* 9:74–89.

Kozel, N., R. Dupont, and B. Brown. 1972. "A study of narcotic involvement in an offender population." *International Journal of the Addictions* 7:443–50.

Kramer, J. C. 1976. "From demon to ally—How mythology has and may yet alter national drug policy." *Journal of Drug Issues* 6:390–406.

Preble, E., and J. Casey. 1969. "Taking care of business: The heroin user's life on the street." *International Journal of the Addictions* 4:1–24.

Rada, R. 1975. "Alcoholism and forcible rape." *American Journal of Psychiatry* 132: 444–46.

Ricks, T. E. 1986. "The cocaine business." *Wall Street Journal*, June 30, 1, 16.

Schatzman, M. 1975. "Cocaine and the drug problem." *Journal of Psychedelic Drugs* 7: 7–18.

Shupe, L. M. 1954. "Alcohol and crime: A study of the urine alcohol concentration found in 882 persons arrested during or immediately after the commission of a felony." *Journal of Criminal Law, Criminology, and Police Science* 44:661–64.

Simonds, J. F., and J. Kashani. 1980. "Specific drug use and violence in delinquent boys." *American Journal of Drug and Alcohol Abuse* 7:305–22.

Swezey, R. 1973. "Estimating drug-crime relationships. *International Journal of the Addictions* 8:701–21.

Tinklenberg, J., P. Murphy, C. Darley, W. Roth, and B. Kopell. 1974. "Drug involvement in criminal assaults by adolescents." *Archives of General Psychiatry* 30:685–89.

Tinklenberg, J., P. Murphy, P. L. Murphy, and A. Pfefferbaum. 1981. "Drugs and criminal assaults by adolescents: A replication study." *Journal of Psychoactive Drugs* 13:277–87.

Tinklenberg, J., W. Roth, B. Kopell, and P. Murphy. 1976. "Cannabis and alcohol effects on assaultiveness in adolescent delinquents." *Annals of the New York Academy of Sciences* 282:85–94.

U.S. General Accounting Office. 1978. "Bank robberies and addicts." *Addiction and Substance Use Report* 9.

Voss, H. L., and R. C. Stephens. 1973. "Criminal history of narcotic addicts." *Drug Forum* 2:191–202.

Wish, E. D., K. A. Klumpp, A. H. Moorer, E. Brady, and K.M. Williams. 1981. *An analysis of drugs and crime among arrestees in the District of Columbia*. Springfield, Va.: National Technical Information Service.

Wolfgang, M. E. 1975. *Patterns in criminal homicide*. 1958. Reprint. Montclair, N.J.: Patterson Smith.

ter 16

Weapons Use

The Armed Criminal in America: A Survey of Incarcerated Felons

James D. Wright and Peter H. Rossi

Violent crime that threatens or abuses the physical safety of its victims lies at the heart of the crime problem in America today. In turn, the use of firearms to commit crime constitutes a major portion of the violent crime problem. Each year, some 30,000 American citizens die through the suicidal, homicidal, or accidental abuse of guns; several hundreds of thousands are injured; hundreds of thousands more are victimized by gun crime (Wright et al., 1983). . . .

[This research is designed to contribute] to the formation of policy in this area by providing basic information on violent crime and, in particular, on violent criminals. To this end, we have attempted to provide answers to two basic questions: First, *what roles do firearms play in the lives of violent criminals*? What motivates them to acquire, carry, and use guns? And secondly, *how do criminals obtain the firearms that they use to commit their crimes*? . . .

To fill the apparent gaps in our knowledge about how and why criminals obtain guns, we . . . conducted a survey of prisoners who had been incarcerated for felony offenses and were serving time in . . . state prisons all around the country. We questioned them about their acquisition and use of guns in the period of time before their imprisonment. Self-administered questionnaires were filled out by 1,874 felons in a total of eleven state prisons located in Michigan, Missouri, Oklahoma, Minnesota, Nevada, Arizona, Florida, Georgia, Maryland, and Massachusetts. . . .

The principal limitation of the survey data we have gathered lies . . . in making inferences about *criminal* firearms behavior on the basis of data obtained from a very selected subset of criminals, namely, the state prison population. . . . All told, our sample of incarcerated felons probably differs from the total population of criminals in the following ways: Our sample is probably older and has a longer and more sustained involvement in criminality and in the criminal justice system. The sample is also likely to have been more violent in their crime than typical criminals and to have committed more serious offenses. Moreover, the sample may be less skillful (or careful) in committing their crimes and hence more likely to be imprisoned. Finally, our sample may be less responsive to the risks encountered in a criminal career since they were *not* deterred by the risks of imprisonment. Hence our sample probably over-represents the "hard-core" persistent criminals. . . .

A TYPOLOGY OF ARMED CRIMINALS

. . . [T]he men in our sample . . . [varied] considerably among themselves in the kind and amount of their criminal activities, and, most importantly for present purposes, in their patterns of weapons use. To capture this variability, we have developed a typology of armed criminals that figures prominently in all subsequent analyses[:] . . .

> *Unarmed Criminals* (N = 725 or 39%) . . . prisoners for whom we could find no positive evidence . . . that they had ever used any weapons of any sort in committing their crimes.
>
> *Improvisors* (N = 79 or 4%) . . . men who had used weapons, but not guns or knives, in their crimes, usually a variety of ready-to-hand weapons.
>
> *Knife Criminals* (N = 134 or 7%) . . . men who used predominately knives and never firearms in committing their crimes.
>
> *One-Time Firearms Users* (N = 257 or 14%) . . . men who had committed one and only one gun crime (whatever the type of gun they used).
>
> *Sporadic Handgun Users* (N = 257 or 14%) . . . men who have used a handgun "a few times" in committing crimes, but never a rifle or shotgun.
>
> *Handgun Predators* (N = 321 or 17%) . . . men who have used handguns "many," "most," or "all" of the time in committing their crimes.
>
> *Shotgun Predators* (N = 101 or 5%) . . . men who claimed shoulder weapons as their most frequently used weapons and who committed more than one crime with such weapons. Since most of these persons specialized in the use of sawed off shotguns, we use the term Shotgun Predators for this group. . . .

It must be stressed that these typological categories do not represent "pure" types, in that many felons appear to carry several weapons, a handgun and a knife being the most common combination. . . .

The Unarmed Criminals amounted to about 39% of the total sample, but accounted for only 17% of the total crime this sample has committed. The Predators (handgun and shotgun combined), in contrast, amount to about 22% of the sample and yet accounted for 51% of the total crime. If one adds the Sporadics in, we are dealing with just over a third of the total sample and just under two-thirds of the total crime. Thus, when we talk about "controlling crime" in the United States today, we are talking largely about controlling the behavior of these men. . . .

Overall Patterns

. . . [T]hree quarters of the men had owned one or more firearms at some time in their lives. . . . A little more than half (57%) owned a gun at the time of their last arrest; of these, most (78%) owned a handgun, 34% owned a rifle, and 44% owned a shotgun.

Men in the sample who had ever owned guns tended to have owned them in what appear to be fairly large numbers. Indeed, the modal number of guns of all types ever owned was "more than ten," and the average (mean) number ever owned among those having owned at least one was 6.6 firearms. This can be loosely contrasted with the average number of guns owned among all US families owning at least one gun, which is about 3.2 firearms. . . .

Gun-owning criminals were also much more likely ever to have owned handguns than gun-owning families at large appear to be. Available data suggest that about a quarter of all US families, and thus about half of all gun-owning families, possess at least one handgun . . . ; among the men in our sample who had ever owned any firearm, 87% had owned at least one handgun.

As with firearms in general, these men also tended to have owned handguns in large numbers: . . . the mean number owned among those ever owning at least one was 6.2 handguns. More than three quarters of those ever owning any firearm had also owned at least one shotgun and a similar proportion had owned at least one rifle.

Men who had ever owned a gun were asked whether they had ever registered any of their guns with police or other authorities, and also whether they had ever applied for a permit to purchase or carry their guns. The strong majority response was "no" in both cases. . . .

Interestingly, only 28% of our gun owners said that they had ever acquired a gun specifically for use in crime. Since at least half of our respondents had committed at least one gun crime at some point in their lives, it follows directly that many of the firearms that are ultimately used in crime are *not* acquired specifically for that purpose.

Regarding the actual uses of guns, almost half . . . of the gun owners admitted to having *threatened* to shoot someone at some time. Apparently, these were not idle threats: half of the sample also claimed to have *actually fired* their guns at human targets. . . . [A]mong those who had ever threatened to shoot someone, 75% actually did.

Men who indicated that they had actually fired a gun at somebody (military service excluded) were asked about the circumstances. . . . The most common circumstance by far, mentioned by 66%, was one in which the felon felt the need "to protect myself." The next most common circumstance mentioned for firing a gun at somebody was "while committing a crime" (noted by 39%), followed by "during a gang fight" (32%), while leaving the scene of a crime (29%), during a drug deal (29%), and "in a bar or tavern" (27%). . . .

Men who indicated that they had fired a gun at someone were asked whether they had managed to inflict a wound in the process; most (69%) reported that they had. And of those who managed to inflict a wound, 80% said they had intended to do so; accidental woundings were indicated in only 20% of the relevant cases. . . .

Like other men of similar age and circumstances, these men . . . used firearms rather frequently in sport and recreational applications; unlike other men, they also sometimes used them for illicit criminal purposes as well, to which we now turn attention.

Patterns of Weapons Use: The Conviction Offense

. . . [O]ur study asked for considerable details concerning the weapons these men carried during their conviction offense. . . . The handgun was, by far, the weapon of choice among those who were armed during the conviction offense. All told, 60% of these men . . . were armed with a handgun at the time. About 15% were armed with sawed-off equipment; 11% were armed with unmodified shoulder weapons. About 40% carried a knife during the conviction offense; another 16% were armed with some other weapon (e.g., straight razor, brass knuckles, explosives, martial arts weapons, etc.).

As is obvious from the total of these percentages, the carrying of multiple weapons during the conviction offense was fairly common. Of the 789 men who answered all the questions about the kinds of weapons carried during the conviction crime, 25% reported carrying more than one weapon, a handgun and a knife being the most common combination. . . .

Men who had been armed with a firearm during the conviction offense were asked whether the gun was actually fired during the crime. Surprisingly, nearly two-fifths (39%) responded *yes*, which implies a notable readiness to use the weapon(s). . . .

Another question . . . asked whether the felon brought his weapon(s) with him to the scene of the crime, or whether the weapon(s) had been acquired at the scene. The large majority . . . brought their weapons with them. . . . Thus, most armed crime (whatever the type of weapon) apparently involves at least some minimal degree of premeditation—enough advance thought, at least, to bring one's weapons along.

To have carried a weapon during the conviction offense is not necessarily the same as actually using the weapon to commit the offense. We asked the sample whether they had actually used their weapon in committing the crime, or whether they just had it with them. . . . [The majority] reported that they actually used the weapon in some way, but the majority was considerably larger (76%) among those armed with a gun than among those armed with "other" weapons (58%). Judging from these results, some three-quarters of the men who committed crimes while armed with a gun actually used the gun in some fashion in the course of that crime.

Felons who indicated that they had in fact used the weapon in some way were then asked, "How did you use the weapon?" "To scare the victim" was by far the most common usage. . . . A principal motive for the use of weapons in crime, and especially for the use of guns in crime, is apparently to intimidate the victim into quick and ready capitulation to the offender's demands. "To protect myself" was the next most frequent response. . . .

The use of weapons to injure or kill the victim was predictably much less common than the use of weapons for purposes of intimidation; still, 18% of those armed with a gun, and 16% of those armed with something else, said they used the weapon to kill the victim during their conviction offense. . . .

Interestingly, the use of the weapon to injure the victim was somewhat more frequent among those armed with something else (26%) than among those armed with a gun (16%) . . . (presumably because people who are being robbed at gunpoint are less likely to resist.)

The final question . . . asked those who had used their weapon in some way to commit the crime whether they had planned to use the weapon, or whether it "just happened." Advance planning for the use of the weapon was the minority report in both cases. Still, among those armed with a gun, some 44% indicated that they had planned to use the gun in the way that they did. . . .

All told, there were 156 men in the sample who were armed with a gun during the conviction offense, who also used the gun in some way in committing that offense, and who, finally, indicated that they had planned on using the gun in the way that they did. As one might anticipate, most of these . . . men (73%, to be precise) were in prison on a robbery charge. . . . [U]nsurprisingly, 57% of them fell into the two predatory categories of our typology.

Interestingly, among those who were armed with a gun during the conviction offense and who actually used the gun in committing the offense, the tendency to have fired the weapon was much *lower* among those who planned on using the gun than among those who did not.

The strong implication of these findings is that most firings of guns in criminal situations are unplanned. The "plan," to the extent that there was one, was presumably to intimidate the victim and to use the weapon to that end. The actual firing of the weapon was, one senses, a rather unwanted by-product of a situation that "goes sour" for whatever reason: the victim resisted rather than capitulated, the police arrived at the scene, or the offender encountered some difficulty in effectuating his escape. Whatever the reason, however, the finding is reasonably clear: *most of the men who actually fired guns in criminal situations claimed to have had no prior intention of so doing.*

As would be expected, how the gun was in fact used in a crime situation varied rather sharply depending on whether or not it was fired. . . . By far the most common use in the case of unfired weapons was to intimidate the victim . . . ; in contrast, the most common use in the case of fired weapons was "to protect myself." . . . Injury to the victim was predictably much more common in cases when the gun was fired . . . than when it was not . . . , as was the victim's death. . . .

PATTERNS OF WEAPONS USE: OTHER OFFENSES

For most of our sample, the conviction crime is only the most recent in a fairly long series of criminal activities. Many of the questions that we asked about the conviction offenses were also asked about the more general use of weapons in committing crimes. . . .

As in the conviction offense data, handguns are by far the preferred weapon among gun criminals. Among those who had ever committed a gun crime, 90% had used a handgun for at least one of them; 85% stated that the handgun was the weapon they used most frequently. Next in popularity was the justly infamous sawed off shotgun, indicated as a crime weapon by 27% of the gun criminals and as the most frequent crime weapon by 9%. . . .

Men who had committed armed crime, but not with a gun, used mainly knives and a motley assortment of other weaponry. Among this group (N = 177), 38% had used a buck knife at least once and 24% indicated the buck knife as the weapon used most frequently. Next in popularity [were] the pocket knife . . . and the club. . . .

[The] armed criminals were asked how often they were armed when they did their crimes. . . . Among the gun criminals, 26% claimed to have been armed only once . . . among the armed—not with a gun—group, the corresponding percentage is 38%. . . .

In by far the largest majority of cases . . . weapons were available for use in crimes either because of a tendency to carry weapons all the time or through a practice of carrying weapons in particular situations. The follow-up questions concerned these "situations." . . . [T]he single most important reason why a felon might decide to carry a gun more or less all the time is that he associates with other men who carry guns routinely. . . .

By far the most common *usage* of weapons in committing crime was intimidation of the victim, as in the conviction offense data. The second most frequent use in both cases was for "self- protection," mentioned by 50% of the gun criminals and by 44% of those armed—not with a gun. "To get away" was third.

Growing Up with Guns

It has been widely reported that the single best predictor of adult firearms ownership in a "normal" (that is, non-criminal) population is whether one's father had owned a gun. It is a pertinent and, so far as we know, largely unresearched question whether the ownership and use of firearms among felons is similarly influenced by the effects of early socialization. . . . [M]ost of these men were exposed to firearms at a relatively early age and have owned and used guns throughout their lives.

The survey asked about firearms ownership and carrying practices among four groups of potential "socialization agents": fathers, siblings, "the people you hung around with before you came to this prison" (hereafter, simply "friends"), and "the men in your family" (fathers, brothers, uncles, cousins). We also asked about seven "firearms socialization experiences" that many men encounter in their youth (here taken to mean prior to age 14). . . . [A]bout 70% of the fathers of the men in the sample are reported to have owned a rifle or shotgun; more than half owned a handgun. . . . Among handgun owning fathers, about three-fifths carried handguns outside the home. Likewise, about half the fathers . . . showed their son(s) how to shoot guns, and roughly the same proportion . . . gave their son(s) firearms as gifts.

Perhaps the most significant data . . . concern patterns of ownership among the felons' friends. A mere 12 % of the sample reported that *none* of their friends owned a gun; more than two-fifths reported that *most* or *all* of them did. Figures for handgun ownership among the felons' friends were similar although somewhat lower. About 20% reported that most or all of their friends carried handguns. . . . In short, virtually all of these men had at least *some* exposure to firearms early in their lives. . . .

. . . [W]e witness in these data a rather intriguing pattern. When considering the more normal or legitimate aspects of firearms behavior (whether the felon ever owned a gun, how many he has owned, how old he was when he first fired or acquired one, etc.), fathers appeared to be the predominant influence (reinforced, to be sure, by all the other agents of socialization as well). When considering the clearly criminal aspects of firearms behavior, however, the influence of fathers (and other family agents) paled considerably and the effects of one's peer group came to dominate.

The key "turning point" in the lives of most of these men, we suggest, was not that fine sunny day in their early adolescence when their fathers took them out to teach them the manly art of firing guns. Rather, it was when they realized that most of the people they hung around with were themselves carrying guns. Some adolescent males, of course, would respond to this information by finding new people to hang around with. Others might respond by obtaining a gun themselves, and these, it appears, were often the ones who ended up in prison.

THE MOTIVATIONS TO GO ARMED

Why do felons acquire and carry weapons in the first place? Many previous discussions of this question have tended to depict the behavior as mainly the carrying of instruments of the trade, in short, a view of the felon as a rational economic calculator. Cook's (1976) "strategic choice analysis" of robbery, for example, suggests that robbers carry guns (vs. other weapons or no weapons) because it allows them to rob more lucrative targets and thus to maximize their take. Others suggest that it is more a matter of simple convenience: a gun is a very intimidating weapon, and it is just easier to commit crimes (less resistance from the victim, for example) if one is armed with a gun. . . .

On the other hand, some of the results so far presented point as much to habit as to rational calculation as an important, if not predominant, motive. Earlier, for example, we reported that about 30% of the weapons users in the sample carried weapons almost all of the time, whether planning a crime or not; weapons also enhanced some felons' sense of security. . . . Only about one armed felon in five said that he had carried [a weapon] only when he had been planning to do a crime. From these findings alone, one can safely infer that the crime-facilitative aspects of a weapon did not represent the only, or even the major, motive for carrying one[;] . . . habit or fear were of at least equivalent importance.

It would, of course, be mistaken to formulate the issue as one of "rational calculation" or "crime facilitation" *versus* habit, fear, or "self defense," since in fundamental ways these are false opposites. A felon who carried a gun mainly because he feared encounters with armed victims (and many did, as we see later) could be said to carry out of fear, out of a sensed need for self-defense, or as a means of more efficiently robbing potentially armed victims. In the abstract, these seem like separate classes of motives, but in reality they are inextricably related.

Most of the information we have on the motivations to acquire and carry weapons was obtained by directing pointed questions to respondents according to their special circumstances. . . .

We focus first on the responses of the "Gun Criminals" (men who had done at least one gun crime). As these men told it, the single most important reason why they decided to carry a gun while doing crime was, "if you carry a gun your victim doesn't put up a fight, and that way you don't have to hurt them." . . . Likewise, the second most important reason cited was, "There's always a chance my victim would be armed." . . . It is of considerable interest that both the first and second most important motives relate to victims; half the men who had committed gun crimes said that one "very important" reason to carry a gun during crime was the prospect that the intended victim would be armed.

Intimidation of the victim, and defense against an armed victim, are the only motives of the fourteen we asked about that were said to be very important by half or more of the Gun Criminals portion of the sample. Other motives of nearly equal weight included, "when you have a gun, you are prepared for anything that might happen" . . . and "a guy like me has to be ready to defend himself." . . . Self-preservation was clearly the common theme in both these responses.

That "it is easier to do crime if you are armed with a gun" was the fifth (but only the fifth) most commonly cited motive. . . . This plus the first-place result make it clear that the increased ease with which crime can be committed if armed with a gun was one important motive for carrying one; the other results also suggest, however, that self-preservation was a motive of equivalent importance. The twin *motif* of efficiency and self-preservation recurs throughout the results. . . .

As among the gun criminals, the most important reason for carrying a weapon among the Armed-Not-with-a-Gun group was so that the victim would not put up a fight. Indeed, the two groups were agreed on four of the top five motives. Men who carried weapons other than guns, that is, appeared to do so for pretty much the same reasons that gun-carrying felons carried firearms—a combination of efficiency and protection. . . .

The Armed-Not-with-a-Gun group was also asked why they had opted not to carry firearms; the Unarmed Criminals were asked why they had opted not to carry any weapons. Remarkably, there was virtually perfect agreement between the two groups through the first six motives on the list. In both cases, the most important reason for not carrying was "the guy who carries a gun or a weapon is just asking for trouble[,"] . . . followed by "you get a stiffer sentence if you get caught with a gun or a weapon." . . .

Interestingly, then, it appears that the Armed-Not-with-a-Gun criminals carried *weapons* for much the same reasons that the Gun Criminals carried guns, but chose not to carry *guns* for much the same reasons that the Unarmed opted not to carry anything. . . .

. . . [I]t is of some relevance to note that the decision not to carry had little, if anything, to do with availability, knowledge, or price. The least important of all factors asked about was, "A good gun or weapon just costs too much money"; this factor was said to be not at all important by about three-quarters of both relevant groups. "It is too much trouble to get a gun or weapon" and "I wouldn't know how to use a gun or weapon if I had one" were also not at all important to the large majority. As noted earlier, a substantial majority of the Unarmed Criminals in the sample had in fact owned guns. That these men did not use guns to commit crimes is therefore not the result of inadequate knowledge about or exposure to them.

WHAT FELONS LOOK FOR IN FIREARMS

What do felons look for in a handgun? What characteristics are important to them? What kinds of handguns do they actually own and carry?

It is often assumed that criminals prefer small, cheap handguns, the so-called Saturday Night Specials (SNS), or, the currently preferred phrase, the "snubbies," the light-weight, short-barrelled, typically smaller-caliber weapons that are easily obtained, readily concealable, and serve the purpose of intimidation as well as any other. . . .

To assess the traits that our felons looked for in a handgun, every man in the sample (whether a gun owner or not) was given a list of handgun characteristics (e.g., "that it is cheap," "that it is big caliber," etc.) and was asked to state how important each characteristic "would be to you in looking for a suitable handgun." In all, thirteen handgun traits were used for this analysis; each man was also asked to pick from the list of thirteen the single most important factor he "would look for in a handgun."

Judging first from the fraction rating each trait as "very important," the three most desirable handgun characteristics were accuracy (62% rating this as very important), untraceability (60%), and the quality of the construction (that it was "a well-made gun," 58%). That it was "easy to shoot" was very important to 54%; that it was "easily concealed" was very important to 50%. "Easy to get" and "has a lot of firepower" were also relatively important (48% and 42%, respectively). In contrast, the characteristics usually associated with criminal handguns did *not* seem particularly important to these men: "that it is cheap" was very important to only 21%; "that it is small caliber," to only 11%. These data clearly do not suggest a strong preference for SNS-style handguns.

Results for the "single most important" question were generally similar: based on these results, the ideal handgun from the felon's viewpoint was one that had a lot of firepower (22%), was well-made (17%), could not be traced (13%), and was easily concealed (13%). Price, in contrast, was the single most important factor to only 6%; small caliber, to only 3%. In both cases, the importance of concealability was apparent, but beyond that, the traits characteristic of heavier-duty handguns seemed far more important to these men than did the traits of snubbies or the Saturday Night Specials.

The thirteen handgun traits asked about . . . can be roughly grouped into four categories. . . . First are the traits that, for our purposes, define the Saturday Night Special: cheap and small caliber. Second are the traits that, for want of a better term, we will refer to as the "serious handgun" traits: accuracy, firepower, big caliber, well-made gun. Third are a set of three traits that would normally matter only to a felon who intended to use the handgun for criminal or illicit purposes—that it is concealable, a scary looking gun, and cannot be traced—to which we will refer as the "criminal use" traits. Finally, there are four "convenience" traits—easy to shoot, easy to get, ammunition is cheap, ammunition is easy to get—which might be of some importance to a handgun consumer regardless of the intended use. . . .

The distributions on these [four] variables suggest rather strongly that the "serious handgun" traits taken as a whole were the most important factors felons looked for in a handgun. . . . Next in importance were the criminal use and convenience traits, with means of 2.8 in both cases. By far the least important were the Saturday Night Special traits. . . .

The relationship of the [four] preference variables with the criminal typology proved instructive. The preference for SNS characteristics was generally *highest* among the non-gun-using criminals, especially among the Un-armed and Knife Criminals, and *lowest* among the Predator categories. Likewise, preference for the serious handgun traits was *lowest* among the non-users and *highest* among the Predators, as was the preference for the criminal use traits. . . . In short, serious criminals preferred serious equipment.

The preceding describes the characteristics of the "ideal handgun" from the criminal viewpoint. It is a useful question whether the traits they preferred in a handgun were to be found among the handguns they actually carried.

To this end, each handgun owner . . . was asked a series of questions about the most recent handgun he had owned: approximate retail value, manufacturer, caliber, and barrel length. The apparent preference for serious equipment suggested above is amply evident in the handguns these men actually owned. . . .

In sum, these data are *not* consistent with the argument that felons prefer small, cheap, SNS-style handguns. The stated preferences . . . and the equipment they actually carried, suggest, in contrast, a marked preference for larger and better made guns.

PATTERNS OF FIREARMS ACQUISITION

We attempted to obtain fairly comprehensive information . . . as to where and how [our sample] had obtained their guns. Since our respondents tended to have owned guns in fairly large numbers, it was impractical to ask where and how they had obtained every gun they had ever owned. Thus, all our questions refer specifically to their most recent firearms acquisitions. Absent any evidence to suggest otherwise, we assume that patterns of acquisition for these *"most recent"* guns were typical of all the firearms transactions these men undertook.

Each man . . . was asked whether he had ever owned a *handgun*; 1,032 said yes. This amounts to 55% of the total sample and to 79% of those who had ever owned any kind of gun. Each of the handgun owners was asked where and how his most recent handgun had been obtained (Table 16-1).

Concerning "how," outright cash purchase was the most common means of acquiring a handgun . . . about 43%. The only other fairly common means of acquisition was theft. . . . Small but roughly equal proportions obtained their most recent handgun as gifts . . . , by borrowing . . . , or through trades. . . .

Concerning "where," . . . we find that family and friends were by far the most common source for the felons' most recent handguns . . . , followed by various gray and black market sources (fences, drug dealers, off the street, etc., . . .), followed finally by customary retail outlets (gun shops, pawn shops, hardware and department stores, . . .). The remaining . . . were acquired from a variety of other sources. . . .

As one might anticipate, there were fairly sizable differences in the means and sources of handgun acquisitions across the categories of our typology. In the less predatory categories, cash purchase was clearly the most common means of acquisition, and in the more predatory categories, it was theft. One-timers and Sporadics were noticeably more likely to have borrowed (or rented) their most recent handguns than were the other types; knife criminals, noticeably more likely to have received their weapons as gifts.

. . . [F]amily and friends were the major suppliers in all cases but one; among Shotgun Predators, black market sources were slightly more common. Normal retail outlets were exploited by about a third of the Unarmed Criminals and the

Table 16-1.
Means and Sources of Handgun Acquisitions

Means	
Theft	32
Rent/Borrow	9
Trade	7
Purchase	43
Gift	8
% =	99%
N =	970
Sources	
Family/Friends	44
Black Market	26
Retail Outlet	21
All Other	9
% =	100%
N =	943

Improvisors, and by about a fifth or less of everyone else. Fractions who obtained their most recent handgun through purchase from a normal retail outlet varied from 30% of the Unarmed Criminals to 7% of the Handgun Predators. Thus, felons in general avoided usual retail outlets, and the more predatory felons were especially likely to do so.

The presence of sizable numbers of handgun owners in all categories of the typology presents a convenient occasion in which to stress that not all of the handguns acquired by these men were in fact crime guns; what we have said so far pertains to the acquisition of guns by criminals in general, and not specifically the acquisition of guns to *use in crime*. We can, however, provide at least some data on this latter topic as well.

Men who indicated that they owned a handgun were asked about the reasons why they had acquired it. One of the options was, "to use in my crimes." . . . [J]ust over half the men . . . said that use in crime was not at all important; 20% indicated that it was "somewhat important," and 29% said that it was very important. . . .

REFERENCES

Cook, Philip J.
1976 "A strategic choice analysis of robbery." Pp. 173–187 in Wesley Skogan (ed.), *Sample Surveys of the Victims of Crime*. Cambridge, MA: Ballinger.
Wright, James D., Peter H. Rossi, and Kathleen Daly
1983 *Under the Gun: Weapons, Crime, and Violence in America*. Hawthorne, NY: Aldine.

Chapter 17
Mental Disorder

Trends in Violent Crime among Ex-Mental Patients

Joseph J. Cocozza, Mary Evans Melick, and Henry J. Steadman

A core belief of the American public is that the mentally ill are dangerous (Nunnally, 1961; Rabkin, 1972; Steadman and Cocozza, 1978). Reciprocally, it has been argued (Hafner and Boker, 1973; Paull and Malek, 1974) that a major factor in the incidence of violent crime is mental illness. Indeed, one author (Bauer, 1970) has called mental illness and criminality "two sides of the same coin."

Actually, there is little . . . data dealing with the relationships between mental illness and violent crime. Those studies available on the incidence of various types of psychiatric disorders in offender populations convincingly show that mental disorder is no more frequent among offenders than the general population (Muller, 1968; Guze et al., 1969; Rollins, 1972; Rubin, 1972). Rubin (1972: 400), for example, concluded that "the major mental illness rates are not comparable to violence rates." Such findings are not to say that incarceration cannot produce substantial levels of symptomatology among inmates which may exceed those in the general population, since this appears to be the case (Roth and Ervin, 1971; Kaufman, 1973; Dy, 1974). It is to say that among populations of violent offenders there is little to suggest that mental illness is a primary cause.

Another manner in which the relationships between mental illness and violent crime have been examined is by comparing the arrest rates of former patients with those of the general population. . . .

Through the early 1970s, it was assumed that former patients were more dangerous, as indicated by arrests, than the general population. At about this time . . . the studies that had been compiled from 1922 through 1954 (Ashley, 1922; Pollock, 1938; Cohen and Freeman, 1945; Brill and Malzberg, 1954), showing that former patients were less often arrested than the general population, were gaining some currency. This awareness occurred while a series of other studies published from 1965 through 1977 (Rappeport and Lassen, 1965, 1966; Giovannoni and Gurel, 1967; Zitrin et al., 1976; Durbin et al., 1977) were reporting more recent data that consistently found former patients more often arrested for certain offenses than the general population. There were some differences among these post-1965 studies in which offense categories the higher rates occurred, but most often they were for assault, robbery, and rape.

Drawing any inferences from these studies concerning changing rates of violent crime among former mental patients is problematic due to limited samples from a single catchment area, atypical locations, and single study groups followed for varying periods of time. The implication of the consistent trend in the most recent studies—that during a period of heavy deinstitutionalization in many states there was an increase in violent crimes among former mental patients—is tentative given the absence of more generalizable work with multiple study groups within the same jurisdiction. It is to this point that the research reported here was undertaken. By drawing statewide samples of former patients at two . . . points in the well-publicized deinstitutionalization of New York State Psychiatric Centers, comparative data and data which were current enough for contemporary policy issues were generated. Further, because the Brill and Malzberg (1954) study, which found mental patients substantially less often arrested than the general population, utilized data from a sample of patients released in 1947 in New York State, we had a third data point that permitted analyses of the rates of violent crime among former mental patients over a thirty-year period throughout New York. From such trend data it was clear that while the rate of violent crime among former patients had increased, there were significant differences in the rates among certain groups of former patients. These findings suggest that changes in the relationships between the mental health and criminal justice systems may be more responsible for the increasing rates of violent crimes among ex-patients than the trend toward deinstitutionalization.

DESIGN

The research strategy was to select two samples of former patients. One sample was to be as recent as possible while at the same time providing a follow-up period within which a reasonably high percentage of those patients who would be arrested could be expected to have been arrested. The second sample was selected to be representative of those patients released before major deinstitutionalization occurred. The recent group was defined as those patients released in . . . 1975. . . . To obtain approximately 2,000 . . . , a systematic random sample was drawn which included every eighteenth person eighteen years of age or older released from state psychiatric centers in . . . 1975. This produced a sample of 1,938. Of these, 1088 . . . were male and 850 . . . female. The median age of the sample was 41. The majority were white, 71%, with 22% Black, and 7% Hispanic.

An examination of the patient census figures in New York State (N.Y.S.) Psychiatric Centers and discussions with Department of Mental Hygiene (DMH) administrators made it clear that the major shift to community-oriented programs occurred in the late 1960s. . . . [T]he year for which complete data were available and which was closest to the beginning of the community treatment period was . . . 1968. Accordingly, every fourteenth person 18 years of age or older released from psychiatric centers in 1968 was chosen. This produced a study group of 1,920 ex-patients. Of these, 1,075 . . . were males and 844 . . . were females. Their median age, 49, was substantially higher than that of the 1975 group, although the racial distribution was exactly the same: 71% white, 22% Black, and 7% Hispanic.

For all persons in the two study groups hospitalization records were obtained from the N.Y.S. DMH and criminal records from the N.Y.S. Division of Criminal Justice Services (DCJS). [There was a nineteen-month follow-up period for both samples.]

The data to be included from the work of Brill and Malzberg (1954) are for 5,354 males released from N.Y.S. hospitals in . . . 1947 and 1948. . . .

FINDINGS

. . . The data . . . clearly demonstrate that very few former mental patients are arrested and even fewer are arrested for violent, potentially violent, and sex crimes. Only 6.9% of the 1968 sample and 9.4% of the 1975 sample were arrested during their first year and one-half in the community. More remarkable, given public perceptions of the mentally ill, only 17 of the 1,920 (0.9%) 1968 former patients, and 33 of the 1,938 (1.7%) in the 1975 sample were arrested for a violent crime. From 1968 to 1975 there was a 36% increase in the percentage of patients arrested. However, very little of the increase occurred in violent, potentially violent, and sex crimes. The major increases were in property and minor crimes. It is quite apparent that a very small percentage of former mental patients are arrested for violent crime after their release.

These absolute numbers are important to counteract the attitudes and beliefs developed from the media which would suggest that the vast majority of mental patients are dangerous as shown by their frequent arrests for violent crimes and that much of the violent crime that occurs is committed by deranged persons. In fact, extrapolating from our 1975 sample in which 33 persons were arrested over 19 months for murder, manslaughter or assault, only 375 (0.6%) of the 62,151 arrests statewide during 1975 involved patients released from state psychiatric centers during that year. . . .

Regardless of the rarity of arrest for violent crime in any group of former patients, what is often seen as more important than the absolute frequencies . . . are the rates of arrest relative to those of the general population. . . . In examining the rate of arrest for the 1968 and 1975 study groups, it is evident that, while their absolute frequency is lower than the public might think, former patients are much more often arrested in every offense category than the general population.

Overall, in 1968 the former patients were arrested 2.7 times as often as the general population. . . . A similar ratio to the general population, 3 to 1, occurred in 1975. . . . These differences in the overall arrest rate are quite similar to those for violent and potentially violent offenses. The former patients in both the 1968 and 1975 study groups were two to three times more often arrested for the offenses than the general population. . . .

In comparing the 1968 and 1975 rates in the various categories, there is a slight increase in every one. While the general population rate increased from 27.53 per thousand to 32.51, an 18% increase, the rate of arrest for former patients went from 73.50 to 98.50 per thousand, a 34% increase. Likewise, while the population rate for violent crimes rose from 2.29 to 3.62 per thousand, a 58% increase, that of the former patients rose to 12.03 per thousand from 5.58, a 115% increase. Thus, there was a substantial increase in the rate of arrest for violent crime among former patients in the time period in which treatment practices in state mental hospitals became more community oriented resulting in the community placement of tens of thousands of people who by previous standards would have remained institutionalized.

In order to determine what factors might be associated with subsequent arrest for violent crime, we examined 23 variables that were available to us from the DMH and DCJS records. . . .

The single variable in both the 1968 and the 1975 groups that showed the most consistent relationship to subsequent arrest for violent crimes was total prior arrests. . . . It is readily apparent from the subgroup rates . . . that the comparisons of the arrest rates of all the released patients to those of the general population are grossly misleading. *In every offense category for both 1975 and 1968 samples, former patients with no prior criminal records are less often arrested than the general population*. Looking specifically at violent crimes, the rate per thousand for the general population in 1975 was 3.62 while it was 2.21 for ex-patients with no prior arrests. Likewise, in 1968 the general population rates for violent crimes was 2.29 and for former patients without prior records it was 2.03.

The reasons for the overall higher rates of arrest of former patients compared to the general population is explained by looking at those released patients with one prior arrest and those with two or more prior arrests. While these patterns are somewhat different in the 1975 and 1968 samples, generally those with one prior arrest are somewhat more likely than the general population to be arrested, but for those with two or more prior arrests the rate of arrest of former patients is drastically higher. . . .

It would seem that rather than clinical factors associated with mental illness . . . , the primary factors related to the rates of arrest for violent crime among former mental patients are the same types of factors associated with arrest for violent crime among offenders, i.e., a record of multiple prior arrests (England, 1955; Wilkins and Smith, 1964; Wenke et al., 1972). This line of argument becomes clearer and more convincing when these data from 1968 and 1975 are compared with those from 1947 to 1952 reported by Brill and Malzberg (1954). . . . Their work is always included among those studies in which former patients were found less often arrested than the general population. . . .

. . . [I]n five of the six offense categories [they analyzed], released patients taken together are *more* often arrested than the general population. It is only because of the vast difference in the minor category that the overall rates are lower for the ex-patients. The rate for violent crimes by the former patient is nearly twice that of the general population. Similarly for potentially violent and sex crimes the rates are somewhat higher. Like our more recent data, however, the overall rates are most deceptive. In all offense categories, those patients released in 1947 and 1948 who had no prior arrests were less often arrested than the general population. Those ex-patients with prior records . . . are substantially more likely than the general population and other released patients to be arrested. For violent crimes those patients with prior records are 8.5 times more often arrested than patients with no prior records.

Thus, from 1947 to 1968 to 1975 there is unequivocal consistency in the arrest rates of former mental patients in New York State. Overall, mental patients are more often arrested for violent crimes than the general population. The higher overall rate results from the extremely high rates of subsequent arrest by those persons with multiple prior arrests. . . .

. . . [I]t does seem apparent that the rates of arrest for violent crime by ex-mental patients has risen steadily through the thirty-year period, 1947–1977. A further examination of the Brill and Malzberg (1954) data suggests an explanation that takes exception to the theories of increased community care of mental patients as the reason for the increasing rates. In their data, 15% of the males released had prior arrest records. In our 1968 sample, fully 32% of the released males had arrests prior to their current mental hospitalization, and by 1975 this figure had risen to 40%. Rather than more mentally ill persons irrationally becoming involved in violent crimes, it appears that there are more persons admitted to state hospitals who continue their patterns of crime after hospitalization, just as would be expected in any offender group.

DISCUSSION

Based on the data presented here, the public has little to fear from the mentally ill. Few people released from state mental hospitals are involved in violent crime, and very little of the violent crime that occurs results from such persons. Those individuals released from state mental hospitals who are most apt to be arrested for violent crimes are those with characteristics similar to those in offender populations—younger individuals with lengthy prior criminal records. There appears to be little in the clinical constellation of factors associated with mental illness that produces large groups of particularly dangerous individuals. Nevertheless, the media's propensities to highlight the bizarre, distorting the actual relationships between mental illness and violent crime (Steadman and Cocozza, 1978), and legislators' search for crime control strategies that are politically attractive to their constituencies, regardless of their basis in empirical fact, still result in inappropriate policies for secure detention facilities for the mentally ill and poorly conceived mental health diversion programs for some persons in the criminal justice system. . . .

The data from New York State over a thirty-year period display amazing consistency in the relationship between prior criminality and subsequent arrest for violent crime among former patients. In all three samples analyzed, clear differences in the arrest rates of former patients were present. What may be even more remarkable, however, is the very substantial increase in the proportion of male residents in state mental hospitals who have prior arrests. As this percentage has gone from 15% in 1947, to 32% in 1968, to 40% in 1975, it is clear why the rates of arrest for violent crime have increased among released mental patients. This is to suggest that as major medical breakthroughs in psychoactive drugs occurred in the 1950s and as shifts toward community treatment ideologies replete with unfulfilled promises for accompanying programs have influenced state mental hospitals throughout the United States, there may have been major changes in the responsibilities given the mental health system. . . .

. . . It would seem that more persons who might have formerly been in jails or prisons are now housed in New York State mental hospitals. As inappropriate geriatric admissions have been slowed (Kobrynski and Cumming, 1971) and while more intervention occurs in community mental health centers avoiding mental hospitalization, those beds that do remain are more and more being filled by persons with criminal records who are younger than the chronic geriatric patients who made up the largest portions of traditional state hospital populations in the 1960s. Further, as prisons have become overcrowded, other alternatives for detention have been sought with the state mental hospitals apparently being one solution. Thus, there has been a steadily increasing pool of individuals who are identifiable by well-accepted criteria as having a greater risk of arrest for subsequent violent crime.

That such developments and the data reported here would suggest that the mentally ill are becoming more dangerous is incorrect. Mental illness is not an increasingly common factor in violent crime. Rather, mental hospitalization is an ever-increasing occurrence for those with histories of criminal activity. These individuals with criminal histories are more apt to continue such activity than were the chronic geriatric residents of the traditional state hospital, and more than the other residents without prior criminal records currently in state hospitals. Recidivism is not identified by a psychiatric diagnosis and successfully treated by psychotherapy and drugs. Mental illness and violent crime are most often independent, not interactive, despite the movement of criminal justice programs in the opposite direction.

REFERENCES

Abramson, M. (1972) "The criminalization of mentally disordered behavior: possible side-effect of a new mental health law." Hospital and Community Psychiatry 23 (April) 101–105.

Ashley, M. C. (1922) "Outcome of 1,000 cases paroled from the Middletown State Homeopathic Hospital." State Hospital Q. (New York) 8 (November): 64–70.

Bauer, W. (1970) "The other side of the coin." Illinois Medical J. 137 (February): 158–161.

Brill, H. and B. Malzberg (1954) Statistical Report on the Arrest Record of Male Ex-Patients, Age 16 or Over, Released from New York State Mental Hospitals During the Period 1946–48. American Psychiatric Association Mental Hospital Service Supplementary Mailing 153, August 1962. Albany: New York State Department of Mental Hygiene.

Cohen, L. H. and H. Freeman (1945) "How dangerous to the community are state hospital patients?" Connecticut State Medical J. 9 (September): 697–700.

Durbin, J. R., R. A. Pasewark, and D. Albers (1977) "Criminality and mental illness: a study of arrest rates in a rural state." Amer. J. of Psychiatry 134 (January): 80–83.

Dy, A. (1974) "Correctional psychiatry and phase psychotherapy." Amer. J. of Psychiatry 131 (October): 1150–1152.

England, R. (1955) "Postprobation Recidivism," pp. 684–692 in N. Johnston, L. Savitz, and M. Wolfgang (eds.) The Sociology of Punishment and Correction. New York: John Wiley.

Giovannoni, J. M. and L. Gurel (1967) "Socially disruptive behavior of ex-mental patients." Archives of General Psychiatry 17 (August): 146–153.

Guze, S. B., D. W. Goodwin, and J. B. Crane (1969) "Criminal recidivism and psychiatric illness." Archives of General Psychiatry 20 (May): 583–591.

Hafner, H. and W. Boker (1973) "Mentally disordered violent offenders." Social Psychiatry 8 (November): 220–229.

Kaufman, E. (1973) "Can comprehensive mental health care be provided in an overcrowded prison system?" J. of Psychiatry and Law 1 (Summer): 243–262.

Lobrynski, B. and E. Cumming (1971) "The mobile geriatric team in the State of New York." Prepared for the 5th World Congress of Psychiatry, Mexico City.

Muller, D. J. (1968) "Involuntary mental hospitalization." Comprehensive Psychiatry 9 (May): 187–193.

Nunnally, J. D., Jr. (1961) Popular Conceptions of Mental Health. New York: Holt, Rinehart & Winston.

Paull, D. and R. A. Malek (1974) "Psychiatric disorders and criminality." J. of the Amer. Medical Association 228 (June 10): 1369.

Pollock, H. M. (1938) "Is the paroled patient a menace to the community?" Psychiatric Q. 12 (April): 236–244.

Rabkin, J. G. (1972) "Opinions about mental illness: a review of the literature." Psych. Bull. 77 (March): 153–171.

Rappeport, J. R. and G. Lassen (1966) "The dangerousness of female patients: a comparison of the arrest rate of discharged psychiatric patients and the general population." Amer. J. of Psychiatry 123 (October): 413–419.

——— (1965) "Dangerousness-arrest rate comparisons of discharged patients and the general population." Amer. J. of Psychiatry 121 (February): 776–783.

Rollins, B. (1972) "Crime and mental illness viewed as deviant behavior." North Carolina J. of Mental Health 6 (Winter): 18–25.

Roth, L. H. and F. R. Ervin (1971) "Psychiatric care of federal prisoners." Amer. J. of Psychiatry 128 (October): 56–62.

Rubin, B. (1972) "The prediction of dangerousness in mentally ill criminals." Archives of General Psychiatry 77 (September): 397–407.

Steadman, H. J. and J. J. Cocozza (1978) "Selective reporting and the public's misconceptions of the criminally insane." Public Opinion Q. 41 (Winter): 523–533.

Wenke, E., J. O. Robinson, and G. W. Smith (1972) "Can violence be predicted?" Crime and Delinquency 18 (October): 393–402.

Wilkins, L. T. and P. M. Smith (1964) "Predictive attribute analysis," pp. 814–827 in N. Johnston, L. Savitz, and M. Wolfgang (eds.) The Sociology of Punishment and Correction. New York: John Wiley.

Zitrin, A., A. S. Hardesty, E. I. Burdock, and A. K. Drosaman (1976) "Crime and violence among mental patients." Amer. J. of Psychiatry 133 (February): 142–149.

Chapter 18

Mass Media

Crime and the Mass Media: A Selective Review of Research

James Garofalo

TELEVISION AND AGGRESSION

At one time or another, every mass communication medium has been criticized for violent content that stimulates aggressive or other antisocial acts among its audience (DeFleur, 1970:137). In recent decades, television has received the greatest attention because it has become the most extensively used medium, especially among children.

In the late 1960s, Goranson reviewed the literature on the psychological effects of media violence for the National Commission on the Causes and Prevention of Violence. Even then, he was able to conclude that the evidence, although tentative, supported the position that violent media presentations can stimulate the learning and performance of aggressive acts and that frequent exposure to such presentations can produce "emotional habituation" to violence (Goranson, 1969:409–410). Since that time, the amount of relevant research has been growing rapidly, much of it stimulated by the Surgeon General's Scientific Advisory Committee on Television and Social Behavior, which began work in 1969. For example, Andison (1977) reviewed the results of sixty-seven reports of original research on television and aggression that appeared between 1956 and 1975; more than half the reports appeared during the period 1971–75—and the pace of research does not seem to have slackened since 1975.

Because of the extent of research activity in this area, there are findings available on many of the details of the link between viewing violence and behaving aggressively, details involving the context in which the viewing occurs, the specific contents of the portrayals, the variation of effects among viewers with differing characteristics, and so forth. The research has also been conducted with a variety of methodologies. . . .

Three types of effects of media violence have been studied: learning of new behaviors (modeling or imitation), disinhibition (the weakening of internal or external controls on aggressive behavior), and desensitization (weakening of emotional reactions to violence). . . .

Most of the research on imitation/modeling consists of laboratory experiments conducted with child subjects. The experiments have investigated a number of potentially relevant variables: the mode of presentation (e.g., live, film, cartoon), whether the aggressive model is rewarded or punished in the portrayal, whether the subjects are offered rewards as inducements to imitate the model, how much the learning persists over time, use of human or inanimate targets against which the subjects may exhibit aggression, and so forth (e.g., Bandura, Ross, and Ross, 1963; Bandura, 1965; Hicks, 1968; Kniveton, 1973; Savitsky et al., 1971). The numerous experiments have helped to identify the ways in which the learning of aggressive behaviors from the media occurs and the conditions that promote or inhibit subsequent performance of such behaviors. Although all possibilities have not been exhausted in this line of research, the evidence so far strongly indicates that children can and do acquire, retain, and perform at least some of the aggressive and violent behaviors that they observe in the media.

Milgram and Shotland (1973) have reported a series of field experiments designed to test whether older subjects (some teenagers, but mostly adults) would imitate an antisocial act (stealing from a charity display) emphasized in a television show. They used control groups that saw neutral shows and experimental groups that saw versions of the show in which the thief was punished or not punished; they also exposed their subjects to varying levels of frustration and were able to determine whether imitation was affected by the amount of time that elapsed between the viewing and the opportunity to imitate. Subjects did steal from the charity box during the postviewing situation, but the type of television program viewed had no effect on theft rates. Perhaps it was too much to expect that variations of one television program would have enough effect to create differences among older subjects who, presumably, have viewed a very large number of television shows during their lives and who have been equally exposed to the social norm that one does not steal, especially from charity.

Research on disinhibition has shown that exposure to media violence can enhance general tendencies to engage in violent or aggressive behaviors. The research has been conducted with both children and adults, in laboratory and field settings. Again, a number of contingencies have been investigated, particularly in the laboratory experiments: the degree of justification for and the consequences of the violence depicted, whether the subjects are angered (or frustrated) before being given the opportunity to act aggressively, the similarity of the potential subsequent target to the victim in the portrayal, and so forth (e.g., Meyer, 1972; Collins, Berndt, and Hess, 1974; Hoyt, 1970; Berkowitz and Geen, 1966; Geen and Berkowitz, 1967).

A good example of experimental research on disinhibition is a study by Berkowitz et al. (1974) which used institutionalized delinquent boys. Half the subjects were insulted by another boy (a confederate of the experimenter) about their performance on a test; the other half received neutral feedback. Within each of the two groups, two-thirds of the subjects saw an excerpt from a movie in which a boxer receives a severe beating, and one-third saw no movie. For those who saw the movie, the experimenter gave a summary of what had happened in the story before the fight; half the subjects who saw the movie heard a summary that portrayed the beaten boxer as deserving his punishment, while the other half heard a summary that was more sympathetic to the beaten man. Afterward, the subjects were given opportunities to administer what they thought were shocks to the experimenter's confederate, and they were free to select the intensity of the shocks. Overall, subjects who saw the film gave shocks of significantly higher intensity than did those who saw no film, but depicting the film violence as justified made a difference only among subjects who had been insulted. The subjects who had been insulted and had viewed the justified violence administered the most severe shocks.

Field research on disinhibition has tended to support the findings from laboratory studies. There have been a few field experiments in which random assignment of subjects to viewing conditions was possible. In the first of these, Feshbach and Singer (1971) did not find the expected difference in subsequent aggression between groups of boys assigned to schedules of violent versus nonviolent programs. However, evidence from subsequent field experiments has supported the link between the viewing of violence and later aggression (see Eysenck and Nias, 1978: 123–133).

In most field research, random assignment of subjects to violence and nonviolence viewing groups is not possible, so the issue of causal ordering is unclear: Does viewing violence produce aggressive behavior or do people who are aggressive (for reasons other than media exposure) simply prefer to view violent material? Several cross-sectional studies show associations among adolescents between aggressive behavior (or predispositions) and the amount of violent television viewed (or preferences for violent television shows) (McLeod, Atkin, and Chaffee, 1972a; Dominick and Greenberg, 1972; Robinson and Bachman, 1972; McIntyre, Teevan, and Hartnagel, 1972). The latter two studies also contain evidence about self-reported delinquency and viewing violence. Both found that the amount of violence in the subjects' favorite television programs was virtually unrelated to petty delinquency (e.g., trespassing, vandalism), but that it was related to self-reports of contacts with the juvenile justice system. Robinson and Bachman also found that preference for violent programs was related to major theft. . . .

Several efforts have been made to untangle the causal issue that plagues survey research in this area. One approach, which has supported the hypothesized link between viewing violence and behaving aggressively, involves measuring exposure to violent programs retrospectively (McLeod, Atkin, and Chaffee, 1972b; Belson, 1978). Belson's study is the most comprehensive of the two. Belson's team interviewed 1,565 adolescent boys in London to determine amount of exposure to sixty-eight violent television series broadcast during the preceding twelve years and extent of involvement in violent behavior during the past six months. The results indicate that serious violent behavior is related to high levels of prior exposure to some types of television violence (e.g., gratuitous violence and violence depicted as being for a good cause) but not others (e.g., sporting events and cartoons).

Another approach relies on knowledge about the subjects' prior aggressive behaviors. Menzies (1971), for example, presented incarcerated young offenders with choices of violent or nonviolent programs; prisoners with histories of overt aggression were no more likely than were prisoners without such histories to choose violent programs. However, Robinson and Bachman (1972) discovered that the cross-sectional association between aggressive delinquent behavior and preference for violent television in their data was modified when they controlled for amount of aggressive behavior in the prior year; the association was evident only among boys who were most aggressive in the earlier measurement period.

Finally, a few full-fledged longitudinal field studies have been conducted. The first consisted of a ten-year follow-up study of subjects who were studied initially as third graders in a rural upstate New York county (Lefkowitz et al., 1972). Peer ratings of the subjects' aggression and violence ratings of the subjects' favorite television programs were available for both points in time. Although the data have some limitations, the results support the conclusion that early exposure to television violence is related to aggressive behavior later in life, at least among males. The study's findings are especially compelling in light of the complementary findings from the laboratory experiments mentioned above and the confirmatory, although preliminary, findings that are beginning to find their way into print from more recent longitudinal studies (Eron and Huesmann, 1980; Singer and Singer, 1980).

There are several caveats that must be added to this review of the evidence concerning television and aggression. First, the research deals almost exclusively with children and adolescents. Even laboratory experiments, which often rely on college students, rarely involve subjects beyond young adulthood. On the other hand, it is not unreasonable to argue that younger people, who are still learning and changing rapidly, are the most appropriate targets for this research. Second, there are indications that the relationship between violence viewing and aggression differs among categories of people; gender (Eron and Huesmann, 1980) and personality characteristics (Eysenck and Nias, 1978) appear to be particularly important. Third, although the evidence supports the causal inference that viewing television violence produces aggression, there is also evidence of self-selection of violent programming by aggressive individuals, so a model incorporating reciprocal causality appears to be appropriate (Atkin et al., 1979; Fenigstein, 1979). Fourth, and most important for criminologists, the research deals with interpersonal aggression that falls far short of serious criminal violence, such as homicide or rape. These caveats are not criticisms of what has been done; rather, they point to where more research is needed. . . .

The final issue taken up in this section is whether viewing violence in the media tends to make people less sensitive to the violence about them in the real world. A number of laboratory studies provide convincing evidence of desensitization. After viewing violent presentations, indicators of sensitivity to subsequent violence are dulled, whether these indicators are based on physiological measures, tolerance of aggression between other people, or the proneness to perceive violence in ambiguous portrayals (see Eysenck and Nias, 1978: 178–184, for a review). As Eysenck and Nias (1978:184) have pointed out, the theory and evidence supporting the desensitization position are at least in apparent conflict with the theory and evidence behind the enculturation position of Gerbner and his colleagues. If viewing media violence tends to make people less sensitive to violence in their real environments, how can television viewing increase the fear of crime and the perception of the world as a violent place? An important task for future research is to reconcile these notions about the effects of media violence. . . .

In sum, social science evidence indicates a causal link between viewing television violence and aggression, and the evidence of this has been increasing rather than diminishing since the 1960s. . . .

REFERENCES

Andison, F. S.
1977 "TV Violence and Viewer Aggression: A Cumulation of Study Results, 1956–1976." *Public Opinion Quarterly* 41 (3): 314–331.
Atkin, C., et al.
1979 "Selective Exposure to Televised Violence." *Journal of Broadcasting* 23 (1): 5–13.
Bandura, A.
1965 "Influence of Models' Reinforcement Contingencies on the Acquisition of Imitative Responses." *Journal of Personality and Social Psychology* 1 (6): 589–595.
1973 *Aggression: A Social Learning Analysis*. Englewood Cliffs, N.J.: Prentice-Hall.
Bandura, A., D. Ross, and S. Ross
1963 "Imitation of Film-Mediated Aggressive Models." *Journal of Abnormal and Social Psychology* 66 (1): 3–11.
Belson, W. A.
1978 *Television Violence and the Adolescent Boy*. Westmead, England: Saxon House.
Berkowitz, L., and R. G. Geen
1966 "Film Violence and the Cue Properties of Available Targets." *Journal of Personality and Social Psychology* 3 (5): 525–530.
Berkowitz, L., et al.
1974 "Reactions of Juvenile Delinquents to 'Justified' and 'Less Justified' Movie Violence." *Journal of Research in Crime and Delinquency* 11 (1): 16–24.
Collins, W. A., T. J. Berndt, and V. L. Hess
1974 "Observational Learning of Motives and Consequences for Television Aggression: A Developmental Study." *Child Development* 45: 799–802.
DeFleur, M. L.
1970 *Theories of Mass Communication*, 2d ed. New York: McKay.
Dominick, J. R., and B. S. Greenberg
1972 "Attitudes toward Violence: The Interaction of Television Exposure, Family Attitudes, and Social Class." In *Television and Social Behavior*, G. A. Comstock and E. A. Rubinstein, eds. Vol. 3. Pp. 314–335.
Eron, L. D., and L. R. Huesmann
1980 "Adolescent Aggression and Television." In *Forensic Psychology and Psychiatry*, F. Wright, C. Bahn, and R. W. Rieber, eds. New York: New York Academy of Sciences. Pp. 319–331.
Eysenck, H. J., and D. K. B. Nias
1978 *Sex, Violence and the Media*. New York: Harper & Row.
Fenigstein, A.
1979 "Does Aggression Cause a Preference for Viewing Media Violence?" *Journal of Personality and Social Psychology* 37 (12): 2307–2317.

Feshbach, S., and R. D. Singer

1971 *Television and Aggression*. San Francisco: Jossey-Bass.

Geen, R. G., and L. Berkowitz

1967 "Some Conditions Facilitating the Occurrence of Aggression after the Observation of Violence." *Journal of Personality* 35: 666–676.

Goranson, R. E.

1969 "A Review of Recent Literature on Psychological Effects of Media Portrayals of Violence." In *Mass Media and Violence*, R. K. Baker and S. J. Ball, eds. Pp. 395–413.

Hicks, D. J.

1968 "Effects of Co-Observer's Sanctions and Adult Presence on Imitative Aggression." *Child Development* 38 (1): 303–309.

Hoyt, J. L.

1970 "Effect of Media Violence 'Justification' on Aggression." *Journal of Broadcasting* 14: 455–464.

Kniveton, B. H.

1973 "The Effects of Rehearsal Delay on Long-Term Imitation of Filmed Aggression." *British Journal of Psychology* 64: 259–265.

Lefkowitz, M. M., et al.

1972 "Television Violence and Child Aggression: A Followup Study." In *Television and Social Behavior*, G. A. Comstock and E. A. Rubinstein, eds. Vol. 3. Pp. 35–140.

McCleod, J. M., C. K. Atkin, and S. H. Chaffee

1972a "Adolescents, Parents, and Television Use: Adolescent Self-Report Measures from Maryland and Wisconsin Samples." In *Television and Social Behavior*, G. A. Comstock and E. A. Rubinstein, eds. Vol. 3. Pp 173–238.

1972b "Adolescents, Parents, and Television Use: Self-Report and Other Report Measures from the Wisconsin Sample." In *Television and Social Behavior*, G. A. Comstock and E. A. Rubinstein, eds. Vol. 3. Pp. 239–313.

McIntyre, J. J., J. J. Teevan, Jr., and T. Hartnagel

1972 "Television Violence and Deviant Behavior." In *Television and Social Behavior*, G. A. Comstock and E. A. Rubinstein, eds. Vol. 3. Pp. 383–435.

Menzies, E. S.

1971 "Preferences in Television Content Among Violent Prisoners." *FCI Research Reports* 3 (1).

Meyer, T. P.

1972 "Effects of Viewing Justified and Unjustified Real Film Violence on Aggressive Behavior." *Journal of Personality and Social Psychology* 23 (1): 21–29.

Milgram, S., and R. L. Shotland

1973 *Television and Antisocial Behavior*. New York: Academic Press.

Robinson, J. P., and J. G. Bachman

1972 "Television Viewing Habits and Aggression." In *Television and Social Behavior*, G. A. Comstock and E. A. Rubinstein, eds. Vol. 3. Pp. 372–382.

Savitsky, J. C., et al.

1971 "Role of Frustration and Anger in the Imitation of Filmed Aggression against a Human Victim." *Psychological Reports* 29: 807–810.

Singer, D. G., and J. L. Singer

1980 "Television Viewing and Aggressive Behavior in Preschool Children: A Field Study." In *Forensic Psychology and Psychiatry*, F. Wright, C. Bahn, and R. W. Rieber, eds. New York: New York Academy of Sciences. Pp. 289–303.

The Violent Face of Television and Its Lessons

George Gerbner and Larry Gross

What children and other viewers learn about violence from television is not necessarily learned from just seeing acts of violence. To understand the full scope of its lessons we need to look at television as a social institution.

TELEVISION AND SOCIETY

Television comes to us as a combination of radio, movies, the pulps, games, circuses, comics and cartoons, and a dash of journalism, but it is none of these. It is the first mass-produced and organically composed symbolic environment into which all children are born and in which they will live from cradle to grave. No other medium or institution since pre-industrial religion has had a comparable influence on what people of a tribe, community, or nation have learned, thought, or done in common. . . .

Cyclical and Repetitive Programming

Most regular viewers of television are immersed in a vivid and illuminating world which has certain repetitive and pervasive patterns. At the center of this coherently constructed world is network drama. Drama is where the bulk of audience viewing time is. Drama is where total human problems and situations, rather than abstracted topics and fragments, are illuminated. . . .

Characters. In one week the typical evening (8–11 P.M.) viewer of a single network station will encounter about 300 dramatic characters playing speaking roles. . . . Of these 300 characters, 217 are males, 80 are females, and 3 are animals or robots of no clear gender. The racial composition of this typical slice of the world of primetime dramatic television is 262 whites, 35 members of other races, and 3 whose race is hard to tell. . . . Overall, the world of television is three-fourths American, three-fourths between ages 30 [and] 60 (compared to one-third of the real population), and three-fourths male.

Clearly the world of television is not like the real world. Looking at it through the prism of age reveals a population curve that, unlike the real world but much like the curve of consumer spending, bulges in the middle years of life. . . .

Violent Action. In this world where men outnumber women four to one, it is not surprising that much of the action revolves around questions of power: how to manage and maintain the social order. Violence, which we have defined as the overt expression of physical force compelling action against one's will on pain of being hurt or killed or actually hurting or killing, is the key to the rule of power. It is the cheapest and quickest dramatic demonstration of who can and who cannot get away with what against whom. It is an exercise in norm-setting and social typing. It occupies about one-third of all male major characters (but very few women) in depicting violations and enforcement of the rules of society.

Violence is thus a scenario of social relationships. Its calculus of opportunities and risks demonstrates one's odds upon entering the arena. In the world of television, four-fifths of all primetime and weekend daytime programs contain violence, and two-thirds of all major characters get involved. The exercise of power through violence is clearly a central feature of that world.... Men are more likely to encounter it than are women, and adults are more involved than are children, although about half of all women and children still get involved in violence. The question is who comes out of it and how. A character's chances to be a violent or a victim (or both) suggest degrees of vulnerability and probable fate.

Therefore, violence as a scenario of power has a built-in index of risk: It is the numerical relationship of violents to victims within each social group compared to other groups. That index, called the risk ratio, shows the chances of men and women, blacks and whites, young and old, and so on, to come out of a violent encounter on top instead of on the bottom.

In the world of dramatic television, 46% of all major characters commit violence and 55% suffer it (with many being both violents and victims). Thus, the overall risk ratio is − 1.2; meaning that there are 12 victims for each 10 violents.... [I]f and when involved, women, nonwhite women, and older women characters bear a higher burden of relative risk and danger than do the majority types. . . .

CONCERNS ABOUT VIOLENCE

The televised stories that generate the most concern . . . seem to be those that contain scenes of violence. Why should this be? First, it is because, even when committed in the name of law and order, acts of physical aggression are suspected of inciting impressionable viewers to commit similar acts. This is an invariable reaction of "established classes" (adults in this case) when members of "subservient classes" (children, here) are exposed to mass-mediated stories.

A second reason for concern about television violence is the frequency of aggressive acts depicted in television drama, particularly in programs aimed specifically at children. It has often been noted that by the time the average American child graduates from high school, he or she will have seen more than 13,000 violent deaths on television. Given the sheer amount of children's potential exposure to televised violence, we worry that children will become jaded, desensitized, and inured to violence not only on television, but in real life as well.

It appears to be a justifiable fear that viewing televised violence will make people, children in particular, somewhat more likely to commit acts of violence themselves.... Our own research (Gerbner *et al.*, 1978) also has found that young viewers who watch a lot of television are more likely to agree that it is "almost always all right" to hit someone "if you are mad at them for a good reason."

Yet, if the most consistent effect of viewing television violence were that it incited real acts of violence, we would not need elaborate research studies. The average sibling, parent, and teacher would be reeling from the blows of television-stimulated aggression. Clearly this is not the case. Imitative aggression among children may be frequent, but it is relatively low-level. Widely publicized cases of serious violence which seem to be influenced by television programs or movies are rare. At any rate, spectacular cases of individual violence threatening the social order (unlike those enforcing it) have always been "blamed" on some corrupter of youth—from Socrates through pulps, comics, and movies, to television. Are there no other grounds for concern?

Yes! Violence plays an important role in communicating the social order. It provides a calculus of life chances in conflict and shows the rules by which the game is played. It demonstrates the relative distributions of power and of the fear of power. . . . The scenario needs both violents and victims; both roles are there to be learned by viewers. The patterns show the power of dominant types to come out on top. They tend to cultivate acquiescence to and dependence on their rule. If at times (though very rarely) television also incites violence by the ruled against the rulers, that may be the price paid for the tranquilization of the vast majority. . . . Television violence is by and large a cheap industrial ingredient whose patterns tend to support rather than to subvert the established order. In generating among the many a fear of the power of the few, television violence may achieve its greatest effect.

TEACHING THE SOCIAL ORDER

We have addressed this hypothesis . . . by determining the extent to which exposure to the *symbolic* world of television cultivates conceptions about the *real* world among viewers. . . .

The Findings of Research

The results of our previous adult and child surveys (Gerbner & Gross 1976; Gerbner *et al.*, 1978, 1980) showed consistent learning and children's particular vulnerability. They confirmed that violence-laden television not only cultivates aggressive tendencies in a minority but, perhaps more importantly, also generates a pervasive and exaggerated sense of danger and mistrust. Heavy viewers revealed a significantly higher sense of personal risk and suspicion than did light viewers in the same demographic groups who were exposed to the same real risks of life. They more often responded in terms more characteristic of the television world than of the real world when asked about their chances of being involved in some kind of violence, . . . and the percentage of crimes that are violent. . . .

The analysis showed a significant tendency for heavy viewers to overestimate the prevalence of violence and its concomitants compared to the estimates of the light viewers. The analysis also demonstrated that these presumed effects of television cannot be accounted for in terms of the major demographic variables of age, sex, education, or even, in the case of our children's sample, IQ. The effects were consistent and robust for both children and adults across a range of undoubtedly powerful control comparisons.

Surveys of adolescents extended these findings in important new directions (Gerbner *et al.*, 1979). . . . Heavy viewers in both . . . New York and New Jersey schools were more likely than were light viewers to overestimate the number of people involved in violence and the proportion of people who commit serious crimes. . . .

Television viewing also seems to contribute to adolescents' images and assumptions about law enforcement procedures and activities. Among the New Jersey students, more heavy than light viewers in every subgroup believed that police must often use force and violence at a scene of violence. Among the New York students, there was a consistent positive relationship between amount of viewing and the perception of how many times a day a policeman pulls out a gun. . . .

These findings provide considerable support for the conclusion that heavy television viewers perceive social reality differently from light television viewers, even when other factors are held constant. . . . We may conclude, then, that viewers' expressions of fear and interpersonal mistrust, assumptions about the chances of encountering violence, and images of police activities can be traced in part to television portrayals.

COPING WITH POWER

Given these findings that heavy television viewing cultivates a pervasive fear of violence, as well as its occasional perpetration, why is the most vocal concern about television-incited violence? The answer rests in the complex nature of the social scenario called violence and its multiple functions. As action, violence hurts, kills, and scares. The last is its most important social function because that is what maintains power and compels acquiescence to power. Therefore, it is important who scares whom and who is "trained" to be the victim.

The privileges of power most jealously guarded are those of violence and sex. In the public realm it is government that claims the legal prerogatives to commit violence (in defense of law, order, and national security) and to regulate the commission and depiction of sexual acts (in defense of "decency"). In the private realm, parents assert the same prerogatives over their children—the power to determine the range of permissible and forbidden behavior. It would stand to reason, therefore, that the representatives of established order would be more worried about television violence as a threat to their monopoly over physical coercion, however limited that threat might be, than about insecurities that drive people to seek protection and to accept control.

The violence scenario thus serves a double function. By demonstrating the realities of social power, it generates insecurity and dependence and serves as an instrument of social control. This objective is achieved at a great human price. The price is the inciting of a few to destructive violence, the cultivating of aggressive tendencies among some children and adults, and the generating of a sense of danger and risk in a mean and selfish world. . . .

. . . [T]he frequency of violence has not even changed more than 10 percent from the norm of 10 years. To alter it and to provide a freer, fairer, and more equitable experience for children and adult viewers alike, far-reaching measures will be necessary.

First, the education of creative resources and critical viewing skills will have to become a primary task of schooling. . . . Today's fresh approach to the liberal arts demands liberation from unwitting dependence on the mass-produced cultural environment that involves everyone every day. We need education for the age of television.

Second, the imperatives of television as a social institution will have to give way to a freer market in television production. The iron censorship of "cost per thousand" viewers makes violence the cheapest . . . industrial ingredient in the present system of dramatic mass production. The resource base for television will have to be broadened to liberate the institution from total dependence on advertising monies and purposes. . . .

Third, a high-level national commission is needed to examine the ways in which democratic countries around the world manage their television systems in the interest of children and minorities, as well as in the interest of the big middle-consumer majority. The commission should recommend a mechanism that will finance a freer and more democratic system, one that can present a fairer and more democratic world on television. . . .

Finally, television service should become at least as much a part of the process of self-government, overcoming its present policy insulation from the citizenry, as is energy, education, or health. A broad advisory group composed of prominent citizens . . . will have to come into being to offset the pressures of private interest groups and to protect the freedom of creative professionals from both governmental and corporate dictation. . . .

Our review of research on the violent face of television and its lessons has led us into a deeper examination of the institution of television, its role in society, and the conditions for altering that role as the prerequisite for dealing with violence. There is obviously no simple or easy way to transform the mass-produced dreams that hurt our children into the dreams that would heal them.

REFERENCES

Gerbner, G., & Gross, L. Living with television: The violence profile. *Journal of Communication*, 1976, *26*(2), 173–199.

Gerbner, G., Gross L., Jackson-Beeck, M., Jeffries-Fox, S., & Signorielli, N. Cultural indicators: Violence profile no. 9. *Journal of Communication*, 1978, *28*(3), 176–207.

Gerbner, G., Gross, L., Morgan, M., and Signorielli, N. The mainstreaming of America. *Journal of Communication*, 1980, *30*(3), 12–29.

Gerbner, G., Gross, L., Signorielli, N., Morgan, M., & Jackson-Beeck, M. The demonstration of power: Violence profile no. 10. *Journal of Communication*, 1979, *29*(3), 177–196.

Gross, L. Television and violence. In K. Moody & B. Logan (Eds.), *Television awareness training* (2nd ed.). Nashville: Parthenon, 1979.

Part 6

Prevention, Treatment, and Public Policy

The unpredictability and gravity of violence induce fear, loathing, and public demands for increased security. Policymakers, frequently armed only with good intentions, modest budgets, and imperfect knowledge, are besieged to devise strategies of control. Responding to the size and scope of the violence problem, as well as to political constraints, policy initiatives range from the punitive and corrective to the palliative. The selections in this part constitute a wide sampling of policy options proposed by noted scientists. They examine selective incapacitation, gun control, capital punishment, rape prevention, and general social and economic programs aimed at reducing interpersonal and collective violence.

Violent Offenders and the Criminal Justice System

In "The Violent Offender in the Criminal Justice System," Peter W. Greenwood discusses three major strategies by which the criminal justice system attempts to reduce violent crime: deterrence, rehabilitation, and incapacitation. Researchers generally agree that violence reduction is most likely to occur through incapacitation, the prevention of crime during the period an offender is incarcerated. However, with prison space at a premium, policy analysts hope to refine this strategy. Studies of criminal career patterns have revealed that most offenders commit violent crimes at low rates, while only a few exhibit high violence rates. Greenwood argues that by selectively incapacitating the few high-rate offenders, the criminal justice system can minimize prison overcrowding while maximizing civil peace. However, selective incapacitation requires the ability to identify accurately the high-rate offenders. Studies of convicted offenders have yielded some criteria for distinguishing between these two groups. Despite these study results, prospective identification is known to be impaired by prediction errors. Greenwood believes that further prospective studies will reduce the frequency of these errors. While caution is warranted, Greenwood nevertheless concludes that a sentencing policy based on selective incapacitation remains an attractive option.

Offender Types and Public Policy

Marcia Chaiken and Jan Chaiken also focus on distinguishing high-rate from low-rate offending groups in "Offender Types and Public Policy." Their studies found that self-reports of criminal behavior, obtained from inmate interviews, are better than official records in differentiating the two groups. However, the use of self-reports calls into question the ethics of eliciting and using information about crimes that were not formally adjudicated. Another important issue relates to predictive accuracy. The authors reported less success in identifying high-rate offenders than low-rate offenders. Because predictive accuracy remains a serious problem, the Chaikens are not as optimistic as Greenwood that selective incapacitation is a feasible strategy. Rather, they recommend expanding diversion programs for low-rate offenders, who are more precisely identified. This alternative approach serves the same policy goal as selective incapacitation: the efficient use of scarce prison space.

Neighborhood, Family, and Employment

Lynn A. Curtis, in "Neighborhood, Family, and Employment: Toward a New Public Policy against Violence," rejects the prevailing emphasis on deterrence and increased law enforcement hardware as remedies for reducing violent crime. He advocates that we concentrate our efforts on social and economic programs designed to reduce the size of the "underclass." Curtis argues that some broad social policies can be both efficient and effective. As evidence of this, he describes selected programs that he believes have been successful. These programs were designed to develop neighborhoods economically, to enhance social networks, and to mobilize adequate supports for families in high crime areas. "Redevelopment" plans encompassed by these programs were not limited only to new economic enterprises. These plans also entailed educating and encouraging community members to assume leadership roles in their families and neighborhoods. Curtis addresses what he considers to be the "causes of crime," supporting a strong national effort to meet this challenge.

Intervention Strategies and Homicide

Margaret A. Zahn's selection, "Intervention Strategies to Reduce Homicide," favors diverse response strategies. She formulates three categories of homicide which are related to social-structural, cultural, and social-interactional influences and then tailors intervention proposals to the causal processes that characterize each type of homicide. Zahn also discusses broad-based remedies for social inequalities that could result, as their byproducts, in reduced homicide rates. Her formulations are consistent with the public-health approach that views homicide in epidemiological terms: a disease that can "infect" vulnerable populations, yet amenable to remedy. Zahn acknowledges that some policy prescriptions would require massive efforts and commitments because they advocate restructuring some basic social institutions and reshaping long-held beliefs that have nourished cultures of violence.

National Profile of Capital Punishment

From 1967 to 1976 there was a moratorium on capital punishment in the United States while questions about its constitutionality were argued before the Supreme Court. In the 1976 decision of *Gregg* v. *Georgia*, the Supreme Court upheld state death penalty statutes that specified guidelines for determining whether the death sentence was appropriate in a particular case. The Bureau of Justice Statistics's Bulletin, "Capital Punishment, 1986," presents a national profile of prisoners under sentence of death. The Bulletin reports that sixty-eight persons were executed since the moratorium on executions was lifted in 1976. The pace of executions has recently accelerated; and, as of June 1988, twelve of the thirty-seven states with death penalty statutes had executed one hundred death-row prisoners.

Comparative Perspective of Capital Punishment

Capital punishment continues to be supported by those who believe it serves the goals of retribution and deterrence. William J. Bowers is not such an advocate. In "Capital Punishment in Perspective," he counters that retribution, regardless of how it is justified, is merely a disguise for minority group oppression and that deterrence is more myth than reality. Bowers reviews the history of the adoption and abolition of the death penalty in Western societies. Employing a comparative perspective, he discusses five factors that tend to characterize countries that continue to embrace capital punishment. We should consider which of these factors apply to the United States, one of the few Western nations still enforcing capital statutes.

Death Penalty Debate

Issues pertaining to capital punishment are presented in the selection "The Death Penalty: A Debate." Featured in this selection are two articles which argue two opposing viewpoints: John P. Conrad, in "The Abolitionist Rests," details criticisms of a policy that he believes is ineffective and "distracts public attention from the expensive requirements of more police, more courts and more prisons. . . ." Conrad maintains that the life sentence is just as adequate a deterrent as the death sentence. Ernest van den Haag, in "The Advocate Advocates," considers the death penalty a deserved punishment for particularly heinous crimes. He argues that even if only a few murderers are deterred, "[t]he lives of innocents that will or may be spared . . . are more valuable . . . than the lives of murderers."

Stopping Rape

Rape can be a devastating experience to women of all ages and backgrounds. In "Stopping Rape: Effective Avoidance Strategies," Pauline B. Bart and Patricia H. O'Brien report on interviews with women who were victims of both attempted and completed rapes. Based on the interviews, the authors identify a number of strategies that distinguish rape victims from women who were able to avoid rape.

Their preliminary findings suggest that the most successful prevention tactic involved a combination of responses: yelling and using force. However, the authors suggest that while using force to resist an assailant increases a woman's chances of avoiding rape, it "somewhat increases her chance of rough treatment."

Hormonal Treatment for Sex Offenders

Controversy still surrounds the issue of the best approach to prevent rape. Some law enforcement officers have expressed reservations about the "fight back" tactic because it can lead to serious injury. An even more controversial approach is the use of chemical therapies to treat sex offenders. Sexual disorders have been subject to diverse treatments, such as traditional psychotherapy, behavior modification, surgery, and medications. In "Treatment of Sex Offenders with Antiandrogenic Medication: Conceptualization, Review of Treatment Modalities, and Preliminary Findings," Fred S. Berlin and Carl F. Meinecke report on a hormonal treatment program that appears to reduce deviant sexual drives. However, the success of this therapy depends upon continued use of the hormone which, the authors note, raises compliance problems once the offender-patient is released into the community. While the authors briefly mention side-effects, there is currently greater concern over possible cancer risks associated with long-term hormonal use. The public has periodically supported intrusive therapies to curb repugnant deviant behavior. The Berlin and Meinecke article reminds us of the fine line that exists between individual rights and the protection of society when assessing strategies of social control.

Deterrence of Domestic Assault

A recent revision of Minnesota criminal law permits police to make warrantless arrests, based on probable cause, in misdemeanor (simple) assault cases, without requiring that the officer personally observe the violent act. This statutory change provided the opportunity for Lawrence W. Sherman and Richard A. Berk, with the cooperation of the Minneapolis Police Department, to study "The Specific Deterrent Effects of Arrest for Domestic Assault." The authors randomly assigned police calls to one of three types of responses: arrest, advice, and separation. Despite some research limitations, which the authors address, the study found that suspects who are arrested have lower recurrence rates for domestic violence than do suspects who are advised by the police about how to handle their disputes or who are directed to leave their residence for a limited number of hours.

Criminal justice research seldom translates into instant policy implementation. However, soon after the authors published their article on the deterrent effect of arrest, several jurisdictions initiated policy changes in line with this research. In 1984, only fourteen cities permitted arrests in misdemeanor assault cases; by 1985, just one year after the study's publication, forty-four of our nation's largest cities had such policies.[1]

Alternatives to Violence

No society is immune to collective violence, not even a democratic one like the United States. Ted Robert Gurr chronicles, in "Alternatives to [Collective] Violence in a Democratic Society," the history of some of our nation's most disturbing violent events and examines how we might reduce or avoid these conflicts. Alternatives to violence, he suggests, depend "fundamentally on who is seeking what from whom." Governmental responses have generally involved three strategies: acquiescence, control, and reform. There is no single ideal strategy; each alternative must suit the circumstances of group discontent. Drawing upon examples from American history, Gurr identifies the strengths and weaknesses of each option, analyzing its capacity for restoring civil peace or continuing conflict. Despite recurring outbursts of collective violence, Gurr does not view the American record with great pessimism. Rather, he reminds us that our history is also one of accommodation after conflict. Dominant and victorious groups have provided, if at times reluctantly, "seats at the American feast of freedom and plenty."

Gun Legislation and Crime

Massachusetts' Bartley-Fox gun law, mandating a one-year minimum sentence for the unlicensed carrying of a firearm, was one state's response to concerns about gun-related crimes. Glenn L. Pierce and William J. Bowers review "The Bartley-Fox Gun Law's Short-Term Impact on Crime in Boston" and provide comparison data for selected jurisdictions. It appears that the legislation resulted in both deterrent effects (reduced violent crimes) and displacement effects (shifted locations of these crimes), depending upon the type of crime. Because considerable media coverage preceded the law's implementation, Pierce and Bowers cautiously speculate that the results may be due more to publicity than to the law's mandatory requirements and enforcement efforts.

Dangerousness, Mental Illness, and Policy Dilemmas

Long-standing stereotypes may predispose us to overestimate the number of mentally ill persons who are dangerous, despite studies to the contrary. Saleem A. Shah argues, in "Dangerousness and Mental Illness: Some Conceptual, Prediction, and Policy Dilemmas," that we need to conceptualize more precisely those behaviors we label "sick" or "deviant" because these emotionally charged terms can have dire consequences for the persons so designated. Clearly, some mentally ill persons can pose a threat to society. However, the ability to predict accurately who among this group will commit violent crimes is limited. This is especially so when predictions are based on a conception of the individual as merely a collection of personality traits. Shah believes that predictive accuracy will increase if behavior is viewed as the result of the interaction of the individual's "psyche" and the immediate setting. With careful planning and professional and community support, and acknowledgment of the transactional relationship of individual and environment, Shah maintains that many mentally ill persons can lead nonviolent and productive lives in the community.

NOTE

1. "Report: Arrest Urged in Domestic Disputes," *The Philadelphia Inquirer* (January 27, 1986) Section A, 5.

Chapter 19

Prevention: Some General Approaches

The Violent Offender in the Criminal Justice System

Peter W. Greenwood

THE CRIMINAL JUSTICE SYSTEM'S EFFECT ON VIOLENT CRIME

There are three general ways in which the criminal justice system can attempt to reduce violent crime. They involve the concepts of deterrence, rehabilitation, and incapacitation. Deterrence refers to the inhibiting effect that sanctions may have on potential offenders who would commit crime if it were not for the risk of being caught and punished. Deterrence theory holds that increasing the probability of arrest, conviction, or incarceration, or increasing sentence lengths, will decrease the willingness of potential offenders to commit crimes. Rehabilitation refers to the effect of any postconviction treatment in reducing an offender's propensity to engage in crime. Incapacitation refers to the fact that an offender is physically restrained from committing crimes against the general public while he or she is confined.

The Deterrent Effect of Sanctions

All theories of deterrence predict a negative association between aggregate crime rates and sanctions, with levels of sanctions measured either by severity or by risk. Most of the . . . research on deterrence has involved analysis of natural variations in crime rates and sanctions across sites. With few exceptions, these studies consistently find a negative association between crime rates and the risks of apprehension, conviction, or imprisonment. [As risks increase, crime rates decrease.]

The problem with these studies is that they all use the same questionable data sources—aggregate statistics on crime rates, arrest rates, and prison populations from the few years for which such data are available. Rather than thirty independent studies, the deterrence literature actually represents only two or three basic studies replicated many times over by different authors with minor variations in their statistical methodologies. A National Academy of Sciences panel (Blumstein et al., 1978) that . . . reviewed these studies found that the evidence did not warrant an affirmative conclusion regarding the existence of deterrence because of an inability to eliminate other factors that could account for the observed relationship, even in the absence of deterrence. . . .

The negative associations between crime rates and sanctions found in these studies appear strongest for the probability of arrest and incarceration and weakest for the length of time served. This tentative finding is important for violent crimes, where the question is most frequently not whether a convicted offender should be incarcerated, but for how long. . . . [U]ntil additional evidence on deterrence is forthcoming from more experimental or quasi-experimental studies, the existence and magnitude of any deterrence effect . . . will remain in doubt.

Do Police Prevent Crimes?

One special form of the deterrence issue concerns whether increasing the number of police will reduce crime, aside from any effects on sanctions. Many people apparently believe that it will, and some studies have found this effect.

In 1966, New York City increased the level of police manning in one of its high-crime precincts by more than 40 percent. An evaluation . . . found that outside robberies were reduced by 33 percent (Press, 1971) with the higher level of manning.

During the period 1965–1971, New York City also dramatically increased the number of uniformed patrolmen on its subway system in an effort to cut down on robberies. An analysis by Chaiken et al. (1974) found that the number of subway robberies did indeed drop as a result of the extra police presence.

. . . [O]ne of the questions raised by this type of focused police presence is whether or not the robberies that were assumed to be prevented are simply displaced to another location. Both Press and Chaiken found significant displacement effects to nearby targets.

The most ambitious attempt to determine the impact of additional police presence on crime rates was the Kansas City Preventive Patrol Experiment. In 1972 the Police Foundation and the Kansas City Police Department initiated the experiment, which systematically varied the level of preventive patrol across different areas of the city. In some cases the amount of preventive patrol was doubled, while in others it was completely eliminated. After one year of operation, the evaluators . . . (Kelling et al., 1974) did not find that differences in the level of patrol had any effect on crime rates or on citizens' perceptions of safety. There was not even any displacement of crime. . . . [U]ntil there is additional contrary evidence, it is not clear that additional police presence, over and above that required to supply called-for services, will produce any reduction in crime.

Rehabilitation

Over the past few decades there have been numerous attempts at developing treatment programs aimed at reducing the criminal activity of released offenders. These attempts have included such diverse interventions as psychotherapy, behavior modification, vocational training, work release, and cosmetic plastic surgery.

However, [a] National Academy of Sciences panel (Sechrest et al., 1979) . . . concluded that we know very little about what works and what does not. The general problem with rehabilitation research has been that the evaluation methodology is usually inadequate. However, unlike the research on deterrence, there have been a number of carefully run experimental studies that attempted to measure the rehabilitation effect. The few sound studies that do exist have not found any significant effects of treatment on subsequent recidivism. . . . [A]s with deterrence, until there is . . . evidence that a particular form of treatment (sentence) will result in a subsequent reduction in crime, rehabilitation objectives do not provide any useful guide to establishing appropriate sentences.

Incapacitation

The most certain way that sanctions can affect rates is through incapacitation. As long as there is a reasonable presumption that some offenders will continue to commit crime if they are not confined, and confinement makes them no worse, then crime will be reduced in proportion to the time that offenders' street time is reduced. The magnitude of this incapacitation effect is sensitive to both the current level of sentencing and the rate at which offenders tend to commit crime. . . .

APPREHENDING VIOLENT OFFENDERS

If the criminal justice system can have any effects on violent crime, its effects depend primarily on its success in identifying and apprehending violent offenders. Higher apprehension rates will produce larger deterrent and incapacitation effects. The more the system knows about an offender's violent crimes, the greater is its ability to predict his or her future dangerousness.

In 1979 the percentage of reported violent crimes that were cleared by arrest [(that is, involved the apprehension and taking into custody of a suspected offender)] (U.S. Department of Justice, 1980) was as follows:

	Percentage
Murder	73
Aggravated assault	59
Forcible rape	48
Robbery	25

Although clearance rates for violent crime may vary considerably across departments, there is only limited information about what can be done to change them. There is a clear association between the likelihood of arrest and the number of police officers per capita, but not with the number of detectives or how they are organized (Greenwood et al., 1977). Research on the investigation process indicates why this is so. Most cases are solved by on-scene arrest or because a witness can identify the offender. It is an extremely rare occurrence when a partial identity or physical evidence leads to the apprehension of a suspect (Greenwood et al., 1977). . . . [V]iolent predators who confine their attacks to strangers can do much better than average in avoiding arrest. . . .

WHAT HAPPENS AFTER AN ARREST FOR VIOLENT CRIME

All that the police need to make an arrest is probable cause to believe that a crime was committed and that the suspect was the one who did it. In order for the suspect to be convicted of a specific crime, there must be proof beyond a reasonable doubt. Between . . . arrest and conviction, each case goes through a number of procedural steps in which the strength of the evidence and the seriousness of the alleged behavior are evaluated. At any one of these steps the charges against the suspect can be dropped or modified. . . .

. . . [T]he first disposition choice is made by the police—whether or not to seek a formal complaint from the prosecutor. . . . Figure 19-1 shows the pattern of dispositions for all adult violent felony arrests in California in 1979. The numbers on each of the branch networks are conditional percentages that show what happens to the cases that have survived until that stage in the system. For example, out of 1,813 homicide arrests, the police requested the prosecutor to file charges in 90 percent of the cases. The other 10 percent were released without any court processing. For all those arrests in which a complaint was requested, 90 percent resulted in some charges being filed by the prosecutor. Of those cases filed, 75 percent resulted in conviction on at least one charge, while 25 percent resulted in either dismissal or acquittal.

The percentage of filed cases that result in conviction is remarkably consistent across crimes, varying from a low of 72 percent for robbery and rape to a high of 75 percent for homicide. This consistency in conviction rates across crime types clearly reflects the effects of prior screening by the police and the prosecutor, aimed at weeding out the weaker cases. The lower attrition rate for homicide cases suggests that the police have conducted a more thorough investigation prior to making an arrest.

Of those defendants who were arrested for homicide and eventually convicted on any charges, only 4 percent received sentences that do not involve any incarceration, 19 percent served up to one year in the county jail, and 77 percent are sentenced to state institutions. The percentage of convicted defendants who do not serve any time is also quite small for robbery and rape. Only in assaults, which can be quite minor or involve fights between acquaintances, do we see a substantial percentage who do not serve any time. Among the forcible rape defendants who are convicted and sentenced to state institutions, approximately 15 percent receive civil commitments as mentally disordered sex offenders to a special treatment facility. . . .

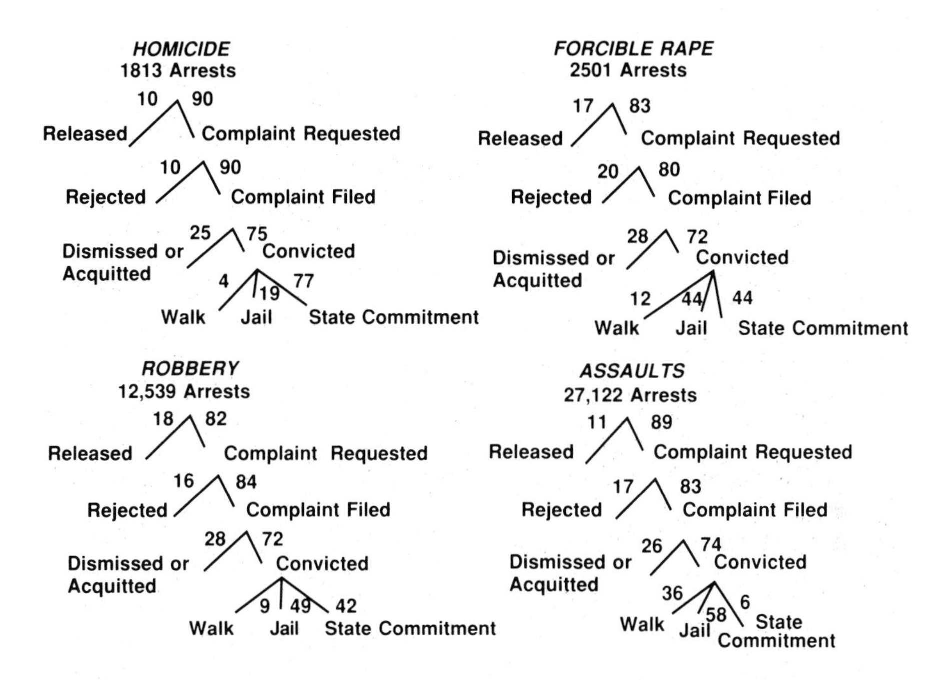

Figure 19-1.
Violent Felony Arrest Disposition Patterns for California, 1979.
Source: California Department of Justice, *Adult Felony Dispositions in California*, 1980.

FACTORS EXPLAINING THE DISPOSITION OF CASES

In the previous section we observed that only about half of the arrests for violent felonies result in conviction. Of those convicted, less than half are sentenced to state prison. In order to understand the adjudication process more fully, we must ask how these extremely divergent outcomes are distributed across different types of cases. Is the probability of conviction affected by the characteristics of the defendant? Are the more serious defendants sentenced to prison, or is sentencing affected more by the strength of the case and hence the prosecutor's plea-bargaining power? . . .

Who Gets Convicted?

We can hypothesize two different patterns of conviction rates, depending on the priorities of the prosecutor. If prosecution manpower is allocated equally among all cases, then we would expect no systematic variation in conviction rates among different types of cases. If, on the other hand, prosecution resources are concentrated on the more serious defendants, we might expect to find lower conviction rates among the less serious cases.

[The Vera Institute (1977), in examining outcomes for a sample of 1971 adult felony arrests in New York City,] . . . found that a prior relationship between the victim and offender had a very strong effect on conviction rates in robbery and assault cases. For robbery arrests, the conviction rate in stranger cases (88 percent) was more than twice that in nonstranger cases (37 percent). This effect is not surprising. In nonstranger cases there is a much larger chance that the crime may involve a dispute between the two parties rather than an unprovoked attack. Also, when the victim and offender are acquainted there is more of a chance that victims will refuse to cooperate with the prosecutor, because they are afraid of further retribution or because of a reconciliation with the offender.

[Williams (1978) and Williams and Lucianovic (1979) analyzed a sample of sexual assault and robbery cases prosecuted in the District of Columbia and found that] . . . prior relationship did not have an effect on conviction rates. Since these studies involve only those cases filed by the prosecutor, it suggests that the prosecutor's screening policy is successful in weeding out those cases where the victim is no longer interested in prosecution.

The principal factors affecting conviction rates that are identified in the Williams studies have to do with the quality of evidence. Cases in which physical evidence or property are recovered and cases involving multiple witnesses are more likely to result in conviction. . . . Forst et al. (1977) demonstrated that some policemen are more successful than others in securing physical evidence and multiple witnesses. This suggests that the frequency with which these items are obtained can be affected by training or other departmental policies.

In . . . one study in which offense seriousness did appear to play a role in determining conviction rates, Cook (1979) found that unarmed robbers were less likely to be convicted than armed robbers. This result might suggest that the charge of robbery is more difficult to prove where a weapon is not involved. Since unarmed robberies are more likely to involve young, unsophisticated offenders, it might be that the lower conviction rate reflects intentionally lenient treatment.

Explaining Sentence Severity

Sentence severity includes both the likelihood of incarceration and the length of time to be served. For violent offenses, length of time served is particularly important, because a large percentage of convicted offenders are incarcerated. . . .

. . . [S]tudies (Vera Institute of Justice, 1977; Cook and Nagin, 1979; Greenwood, 1980) find that prior record has an effect on the likelihood of incarceration. Greenwood found that for robbery arrests in California in 1973, only 5 percent of the defendants with minor records were sentenced to prison, as opposed to 22 percent of those who had been sentenced to prison before. The Vera Institute study showed that in robbery cases involving strangers, the probability of being sentenced to felony time was only 17 percent for those defendants with no prior arrests, as opposed to 42 percent for those with priors.

Both the Vera and the Cook and Nagin studies also found that crimes between acquaintances were less likely to result in incarceration. . . . We would expect more mitigating circumstances in a crime between acquaintances as opposed to a crime between strangers. . . .

In the only study that looks at the issue of arming directly, Cook (1980) found that defendants who were armed with guns were more likely to receive prison commitments than those who were not. Arming with other weapons did not have any consistent effect on sentence severity.

More surprising, Cook found that the degree of injury to victims did not have any effect on sentence severity. One possible explanation of this . . . might be that unarmed robbers are more likely to injure their victims than are robbers who are armed with a gun. But even within each specific weapon category, victim injury did not appear to affect sentence severity. . . .

. . . [O]bserved differences between age-specific arrest rates that peak at around age 18 and age-specific imprisonment rates that peak at around 30 have caused some critics of the system to assert that young adult offenders are treated too leniently. A . . . Rand study (Greenwood et al., 1980) examined sentence severity patterns by age across three jurisdictions and concluded the following:

1. Sentencing breaks for young adult offenders vary considerably across jurisdictions. . . .
2. . . . [T]he degree to which young adult offenders are afforded differential leniency is affected by the maximum age jurisdiction of the juvenile court, the accessibility of juvenile court records to adult prosecutors and the availability of special institutions for young adults.
3. The conviction rate and incarceration rate for older juveniles [are] similar to [those] of young adults who are convicted of similar crimes.

WOULD MORE PROSECUTORS MAKE A DIFFERENCE?

One of the explanations that is frequently offered for the low conviction rates and heavy reliance on plea bargaining usually found in criminal courts is the fact that the system is overloaded, the implication being that if prosecutors had more time to devote to each case, conviction rates and incarceration rates would be increased.

In 1975, the Law Enforcement Assistance Administration (LEAA) initiated a special discretionary grant program to do just that. The program was called Career Criminal Prosecution. It was based on the premise that since a small number of recidivists (career criminals) accounted for a disproportionate share of crime, a concentrated effort to get these recidivists convicted and locked away would lead to a reduction in street crime. . . . A large number of prosecutors received special federal grants to seek increased conviction rates and longer terms for whomever they define as career criminals.

Many of the programs focused on robbers. . . . Others included a mixture of street crimes. Each prosecutor used a different combination of prior record and current offense seriousness to determine whom his program would handle.

The Career Criminal Prosecution (CCP) programs that were developed involved a number of departures from routine practices. . . .

1. A special unit was established within the prosecutor's office. . . .
2. The CCP unit might become involved in a case earlier than normal in order to assist the police with arrest and investigation procedures.
3. A special investigator might be attached to the CCP unit to help expedite case preparation.
4. A single deputy prosecutor was assigned responsibility for each case from start to finish. . . .
5. Plea bargaining was highly circumscribed, if permitted at all. . . .

The system processing objectives of the career criminal program were to: (1) increase conviction rates, (2) increase the strength of convictions, (3) increase the severity of sentences, and (4) decrease processing time for career criminal cases. Evaluations of specific local programs have found conflicting results. . . .

Chelimsky and Dohmann (1980) . . . evaluate[d] four of the programs initially funded by the LEAA. In none of the four did they find that CCP increased conviction rates. In two of the four they found an increase in the likelihood that CCP defendants would be convicted of the most serious charges. In none of the four was there any increase in percentage of convicted defendants incarcerated. In one site there was an increase in average sentence length. In only one site was there a reduction in processing time.

A later evaluation of twelve CCP programs in California (Office of Criminal Justice Planning, 1980) found considerably different results. That study found a small but significant increase in conviction rates, a large increase in the fraction of defendants convicted of the most serious charge, increases in incarceration and imprisonment rates, and an increase in average sentence length. . . .

California prosecutors may simply have more control over the disposition of cases than in other states. . . . Two characteristics of California's criminal justice system suggest that this may be true. In California, prosecutors control plea bargaining with very little interference from the bench. . . . Also in California, sentence severity is directly related to the seriousness of the charges on which the defendant is convicted. The prosecutor can have a direct impact on sentence severity by charging and proving special enhancements, such as gun use. . . .

In summary, the CCP evaluations suggest that in those sites where the prosecutors play a dominant role in determining the severity of sentencing, extra attention devoted to specific types of cases can increase the severity of dispositions.

WHAT HAPPENS IN PRISON?

In comparison to other offenders, defendants convicted of violent offenses are more likely to be sentenced to prison and to serve longer terms. What happens to these offenders as they serve their time? In what kinds of programs do they participate? How are they treated differently from other inmates?

These issues are examined in a . . . study of prison inmates in three states—California, Texas, and Michigan (Petersilia et al., 1980). Information on a sample of prison inmates in each of these states was obtained from official records and through a survey questionnaire.

One of the findings of this study was that neither conviction offense nor prior record had any impact on participation rates in programs or on the rate of disciplinary infractions. In fact, both classification (as to security level) and programming were governed by prior and current institutional behavior rather than by criminal record.

The four most frequent types of treatment programs identified by the study were education, vocational training, alcohol treatment, and drug treatment. . . .

The variation in treatment needs and participation levels across states is considerable. . . . The reason most frequently cited by high-need inmates for not participating in treatment is a belief that they do not need it. More than 60 percent of those with poor educational skills or alcohol problems cited this reason. About 25 percent do not participate because of security reasons or because of discouragement by the staff. Of those with drug problems, 33 percent do not participate because no drug treatment programs are available within their institutions.

. . . [I]t appears that a substantial portion of the inmate population with severe educational, vocational, or drug-related problems are not being treated. Many do not believe they would benefit from assistance. A substantial proportion do not participate because the programs are not available to them.

About half of the inmates claimed to have a work assignment that required about 30 to 40 hours per week. Most of those without work assignments appeared not to want them. Only about 20 percent of those without work assignments reported that no jobs were available to them.

CAN LONGER SENTENCES REDUCE VIOLENT CRIME?

The evidence on deterrence was reviewed in the first section of this chapter. Because of methodological issues in the studies that have been conducted thus far, it is not possible to establish either the existence or the magnitude of deterrent effects of sanctions on crime. To the degree that these studies find relationships that are consistent with the deterrence hypothesis, they suggest that the probability of incarceration is much more important than the length of time served.

The evidence on incapacitation is more positive. As long as there is a reasonable presumption that some offenders would have continued to commit crimes if left on the street, and they are not made any worse by their prison experience, there will be an incapacitation effect. The magnitude of that effect depends on such factors as the types of crime an offender commits, the rate at which he or she commits them, his or her chance of being arrested, and the length of his or her criminal career. . . . Even when these factors are known, it is a very complicated modeling process to estimate the effects of a specific change in sentencing policy. In particular, we do not now have good models for estimating the tradeoffs in crime reduction between a policy of long sentences for a few offenders versus shorter sentences for many offenders.

The issue of appropriate sentence lengths is probably the most important single issue in determining how to deal with violent crime. The natural response to a wave of violent crime is to raise penalties, particularly for recidivists.

The counterargument is economic. The criminal justice system has limited resources for dealing with crime. Sending some offenders away for very long terms ties up resources that might be used more productively in other ways.

Petersilia and Greenwood (1978) analyzed a sample of 625 adult felons who were convicted in the Denver, Colorado, District Court between 1968 and 1970. . . . With this cohort the analysis showed that the imposition of a five-year mandatory term for every conviction would reduce adult violent crime by 31 percent. If the five-year mandatory term were restricted to only those convicted of violent felonies, the reduction in adult violent crime would be 6 percent.

These sentencing options are not cheap. The average sentence for those convicted of a violent felony is only 1.3 years (including those who serve no time at all). If every defendant who was convicted of a violent felony was given a five-year term, the prison population would increase by 150 percent—in order to produce a 6 percent reduction in adult violent crime.

This study also provides some evidence on the "long sentence for a few versus short sentences for many" argument. Two different sentencing policies would result in about the same increase in prison population—about 50 percent. The first involves a five-year mandatory term for every defendant convicted of violent crime with at least one prior. The other involves a one-year mandatory term for anyone convicted of a felony, regardless of priors. The first policy reduces the adult felony crime rate by only 3 percent. The latter reduces it by 11 percent and is clearly more efficient. This . . . suggests that the maximum incapacitation effect for any given increase in prison population can be achieved by imposing modest terms on those who now serve no time.

As a means of collecting data to estimate the distribution of offense rates over the active offender population [the] Rand [Corporation] conducted a self-reporting survey of 625 California prison inmates (Peterson et al., 1980). . . . The responses . . . indicate that most active offenders engage in a variety of different crime types during any one period in their careers. For instance, among inmates convicted for robbery, 60 percent had also committed assaults, 52 percent had committed burglary, 27 percent had committed armed robbery, 60 percent had committed assault, and 46 percent had sold drugs. Given this mixture of crime types, it is easy to see why it becomes difficult to characterize offenders as violent or property offenders on the basis of their records. Most offenders are both.

Another important characteristic of individual offense rates revealed . . . that they are highly skewed to the low side. Among armed robbers, the mean armed robbery rate was 4.6 crimes per year. The median rate was 1.5 crimes per year. About 10 percent committed armed robberies at a rate higher than 30 crimes per year. This same pattern held up for every type of crime that was examined. If it can be shown that these differences in offense rates between offenders persist throughout long periods of the career, then this would argue for a policy that attempts to distinguish these high-rate offenders for longer terms. . . .

Suppose that a jurisdiction decides that it will attempt to reduce violent crime through incapacitation by imposing harsher sentences. How should it proceed? There are basically two approaches:

Under a *generalized* . . . approach, the jurisdiction will attempt to increase sentence severity across the board or for special categories of offenders based on "just deserts" alone. It will not make any attempt to maximize the incapacitation effects of the resulting increase in prison population by concentrating on high-rate offenders. Policies that attempt to achieve this goal might include:

1. eliminating the possibility of probation for anyone convicted of a violent felony;
2. lengthening the base term or minimum eligible parole date for violent offenders; and
3. adding additional time to the terms of violent defendants who have previous felony convictions.

An alternative approach to reducing crime could involve *selective* incapacitation. Under this approach, sentence lengths would be adjusted on the basis of actuarial experience to reflect future risk. The goal of selective incapacitation would be to maximize the amount of crime prevented within any fixed prison population constraint. . . .

Selective incapacitation is based on the knowledge that criminals vary widely in their offense rates. Most commit crimes at very low rates, while only a few commit crimes at high rates. On the average, high-rate offenders can be distinguished from low-rate offenders on the basis of such characteristics as prior record—both juvenile and adult, age, drug use, and employment.

Selective incapacitation involves giving longer terms to some offenders on the basis of their predicted future criminality. It also involves shorter terms for a larger number of offenders. The prediction is based on the experience of other offenders with similar characteristics, not a clinical diagnosis of a particular offender's traits. . . . The amount of crime prevented by incapacitation can be increased by increasing the percentage of offenders who are sent to prison or increasing the length of their terms.

Research on criminal career patterns has established that individual offense rates are distributed so as to make selective incapacitation an attractive option. The critical issue to be determined now is how accurately the high-rate offenders can be identified. . . .

REFERENCES

Blumstein, A., Cohen, J., and Nagin, D. (Eds.). *Deterrence and incapacitation: Estimating the effects of criminal sanctions on crime rates.* Washington, DC: National Academy of Sciences, 1978.

California Department of Justice. *Adult felony arrest dispositions in California.* Sacramento, CA: Bureau of Criminal Statistics and Special Services, September 1980.

Chaiken, J. M., Lawless, M., and Stevenson, K. A. *The impact of police activity on crime: Robberies on the New York City subway system* (R-1424-NYC). Santa Monica, CA: Rand Corporation, 1974.

Chelimsky, E., and Dohmann, J. *Career criminal program national evaluation summary report.* McLean, VA: MITRE Corporation, 1980.

[Cook, P. J. "Reducing Injury and Death Rates in Robbery." *Policy Analysis*, 1980. 6(1), 21–45.]

Cook, P., and Nagin, D. *Does the weapon matter?* (PROMIS Research Project Publication 8). Washington, DC: INSLAW, December 1979.

Forst, B., Lucianovic, J., and Sarah, J. C. *What happens after arrest?* Washington DC: INSLAW, 1977.

Greenwood, P. W. *Rand research on criminal careers: An update on progress to date* (N-1572). Santa Monica, CA: Rand Corporation, 1980.

Greenwood, P. W., Chaiken, J. M., and Petersilia, J. *The criminal investigation process.* Lexington, MA: D.C. Heath, 1977.

Greenwood, P. W., Petersilia, J., and Zimring, F. E. *Age, crime, and sanctions: The transition from juvenile to adult court* (R-2642). Santa Monica, CA: Rand Corporation, 1980.

Kelling, L., Pate, T., Dieckman, D., and Brown, C. E. *The Kansas City Preventive Patrol Experiment: A summary report.* Washington, DC: Police Foundation, 1974.

Office of Criminal Justice Planning. *California career criminal prosecution program: Second annual report to the legislature.* Sacramento, CA: Office of Criminal Justice Planning, 1980.

Petersilia, J., and Greenwood, P. W. Mandatory prison sentences: Their projected effects on crime and prison populations. *Journal of Criminal Law and Criminology*, 1978, 69(4), 604–615.

Petersilia, J., and Honig, P., with Hubay, C. *The prison experience of career criminals* (R-2511-DOJ). Santa Monica, CA: Rand Corporation, 1980.

Peterson, M. A., and Braiker, H. B., with Polich, S. M. *Doing crime: A survey of California prison inmates* (R-2200-DOJ). Santa Monica, CA: Rand Corporation, 1980.

Press, S. J. *Some effects of an increase in police manpower in the 20th precinct of New York City* (R-704-NYC). Santa Monica, CA: Rand Corporation, 1971.

Sechrest, L., White S. O., and Brown, E. D. *The rehabilitation of criminal offenders: Problems and prospects.* Washington, DC: National Academy of Sciences, 1979.

U.S. Department of Justice. *Crime in the United States, 1979.* Washington, DC: Government Printing Office, 1980.

Van Dine, S., Conrad, J. P., and Dinitz, S. *Restraining the wicked.* Lexington, MA: D.C. Heath, 1979.

Vera Institute of Justice. *Felony arrests: Their prosecution and disposition in New York City's courts.* New York: Vera Institute of Justice, 1977.

Williams, K. M. *The prosecution of sexual assaults* (PROMIS Research Project Publication 7). Washington, DC: INSLAW, December 1978.

Williams, K. M., and Lucianovic, J. *Robbery and burglary* (PROMIS Research Project Publication 6). Washington, DC: INSLAW, March 1979.

Wilson, J. Q., and Boland, B. *The effect of the police on crime.* Washington, DC: U.S. Department of Justice, Law Enforcement Assistance Administration, 1979.

Offender Types and Public Policy

Marcia R. Chaiken and Jan M. Chaiken

Faced with high crime rates, fiscal limitations, and a conservative political movement, public officials increasingly long for a simple, encompassing policy that would permit them to deal quickly and effectively with criminals. They have also de-emphasized rehabilitation in favor of longer prison sentences as a means of reducing crime. Unfortunately, an important truth has almost disappeared during these developments: There are many kinds of criminals, and to fix on any single punitive solution to the problem of crime is simplistic, unjust, and inefficient. . . .

This [selection] describes the diversity of criminal behavior in a way that can help the criminal justice system realistically distinguish among various subgroups of offenders. . . .

We aimed at discovering the extent to which official records and characteristics that the records might or might not contain would permit identification of serious criminals.[1] The models we developed rely on information about criminals that is currently or potentially available to the criminal justice system. . . .

Using . . . survey data, we established a framework for classifying criminal offenders. . . . Our results indicate that criminals can be categorized according to the combinations of crimes they commit, and that the resulting typology may be quite useful for prosecution, diversion, incapacitation, and rehabilitation policy. [Subjects] who committed *specific combinations of crimes* were distinguishable from other [subjects] by their crime commission rates, their persistence in committing crime, and their personal characteristics.

One important result of [our] study is our ability to identify and characterize the most serious category of offenders. Criminals in this category reported committing robbery, assault, and drug deals. . . . We found that these criminals, whom we have called "violent predators," usually committed the three defining crimes at high rates, and they often committed burglaries, thefts, and other property crimes at high rates too—sometimes at higher rates than any other type of criminal, including those who specialized in those crimes. Typically, the violent predators also began persistently using hard drugs as juveniles and committing violent crimes before they were 16. In short, these "omni-felons," deeply entrenched in a life of multiple drug use and violence, constitute an important criminal threat to society. . . .

. . . [O]ur analysis showed that information currently available from such sources as official arrest and conviction records does not allow criminal justice officials to distinguish meaningfully between the violent predator and other types of offenders. Better distinctions can be made . . . by collecting complete and detailed information on such factors as specific forms of drug use, employment, and juvenile drug use and violence. Even so, high-rate serious offenders will be poorly identified. Low-rate offenders will be accurately identified, thus giving prosecutors and judges clearer understanding of the type of criminal they are confronting in particular cases. . . .

The characteristics we found associated with the violent predators have been associated with high probability of recidivism in many earlier studies (Robbins and Wish, 1977; Pritchard, 1979; Glaser, 1972; Hoffman and Beck, 1980). We infer that until effective means are found to prevent criminals from repeating serious crimes, the violent predators are better candidates for incapacitation and worse candidates for conventional rehabilitation and diversion efforts than any other criminal types. Conversely, the characteristics we found associated with low-rate offenders have been associated in (the same) past studies with low rates of recidivism. By focusing on the less serious offenders, existing rehabilitation and diversion programs may prove more effective than they currently appear. . . .

Because the violent predators commit a disproportionate amount of crime, it would in principle be prudent to devote a commensurate proportion of criminal justice resources to dealing with them. At present, the only method known to be effective for curtailing their criminal behavior is incarceration. But many of the violent predators . . . stopped doing crime for periods lasting two years and more, so a deeper understanding of these phenomena might point to new programs or policies for producing desistance. In the long run, it would be preferable to develop effective ways of dealing with the young juveniles who are most likely to become violent predators—those under 16 who are committing serious crimes. Finally, . . . even if data eventually become available to permit implementing selective incapacitation policies, they should always allow for broad exercise of judicial discretion. In every identification exercise we performed, there were individuals who neither fit the category nor committed crimes at the rate typically associated with their particular characteristics. . . .

BACKGROUND AND METHODOLOGY . . .

Although we did not attempt to develop a comprehensive typology of criminal offenders, our study indicates strongly that stable, empirically based classifications of offenders can be constructed. The main distinctions between our work and typological research of earlier years are, first, that we defined our subgroups . . . based on self-reported behavior over one- to two-year periods instead of either sequences of officially recorded criminal acts or anecdotal reports, and second, that our sample contained hundreds of offenders from each of three states. An offender who, in our data, appears to have a stable pattern of committing, for example, robbery, burglary, assault, forgery, and auto theft might appear, in official record data, to be switching unpredictably from one type of crime to another. To call such an offender "stable in versatility" is not mere sophistry, because he can be clearly distinguished from other offenders who consistently engage in different combinations of crimes. Moreover, certain stable combinations of criminal activity are substantially more serious than other combinations.

To the extent that criminal behavior is not stable within the classifications we developed, the transitions appear as progressions from less serious to more serious forms of behavior . . . or as temporary interruptions in criminal activity.[2]

The [Rand] survey [(on which this study is based)] included nearly 2200 offenders from three states (California, Michigan, and Texas). . . . The survey questionnaire elicited self-reported information about the following aspects of the inmates' background and activities:

- Juvenile criminal behavior, use of illegal drugs, and incarceration in juvenile facilities.
- Criminal behavior and arrests during a one- to two-year period just prior to the present conviction.
- Other behavior during the same period prior to conviction, including use of alcohol and illegal drugs, employment, and change in residence.
- Types of crimes committed in two earlier reference periods.
- Sociodemographic information.

For prisoner respondents (but not those in county jails), the following additional information was collected from their official records (inmate folders):

- Rap-sheet arrests for the same one- to two-year period covered by the self-reports.
- Details of the current conviction offense(s).
- Prior history of adult convictions.
- Juvenile probation and commitments to juvenile facilities.
- (For California only) details of up to ten juvenile arrests: date, charge, whether convicted, and disposition if convicted.
- Sociodemographic data.

The structure and administration of the survey and associated data collection efforts were intended to provide multiple means for exploring the integrity of the inmate's responses. The questionnaire included pairs of questions, widely separated, that asked for essentially the same information about crimes the respondents had committed and about other topics. This made it possible to check for internal quality (inconsistency, omission, and confusion). Over 83% of the respondents filled out the questionnaire very accurately, completely, and consistently. . . .

Access to official records made possible an external check of the self-reports' validity for prisoner respondents. Although the external comparison of validity of their responses did not yield as favorable results as the check of their internal quality, 59% of the prisoner respondents had an external error rate of less than 20%. . . .

. . . [W]e believe that the data from the self-reports, coupled with official record data and handled conservatively, are sufficiently valid and reliable to serve as a credible basis for our findings.

IDENTIFYING THE SERIOUS CRIMINAL

Most research concluding that criminals do not specialize focuses on *known offenses*. Even when offenses are categorized into broad groups, an individual's arrest history usually shows nearly random shift from one category of offense to another (Figlio, 1981). Moreover, in self-reports, few criminals say that they commit just one kind of offense (Peterson and Braiker, 1981). The self-reports used in this study are no exception. However, we examined the stability over time of the entire complex of crimes committed by an offender. In this way, we found indications of substantial stability in varieties of criminal behavior or very clear and understandable transitions from one variety to another. While it is true that the . . . most criminally active offenders[,] commit a broad range of types of crimes, other offenders commit only specific, limited combinations of crimes. Most offenders commit the same specific combinations of crimes from year to year, or they stop entirely.

When the combinations of crimes are arrayed hierarchically . . . offenders whose behavior puts them in high-level (serious) varieties of behavior are very likely to commit one or more of the crimes that define lower-level varieties.[3] For example, 81% of the offenders in our survey sample who rob and assault and deal drugs also commit burglary, and 71% of them commit theft. The situation is analogous to any profession in which an individual advances through ranks based on cumulative knowledge and adequate performance of tasks at each level. The most highly trained individuals have some facility in performing tasks usually handled by lower-level personnel. . . .

. . . The questionnaire asked about a number of different types of crimes that we summarized into eight: assault, robbery, burglary, drug deals, theft, auto theft, fraud, and forgery or credit card swindles. Counting each respondent as "yes" or "no" according to whether he did nor did not report committing each of these eight crime types, there could have been 256 different combinations. However, examination revealed 17 combinations of crimes reported so frequently that they described the behavior of 59% of the respondents in all three states. Moreover, 110 combinations occurred extremely infrequently (either no respondent or one respondent reported the combination). Examination of the remaining 129 varieties showed that many of them differed from the major 17 varieties by "uninteresting" distinctions among four crimes: auto theft, other theft, forgery, and fraud. (For example, a person who commits robbery, assault, burglary, and auto theft does not seem meaningfully different from a person who commits robbery, assault, burglary, and other theft.)

When these four crime types were joined together, the 17 combinations became 11, . . . obtaining ten varieties plus a default category ("didn't do any of these").

Because of the crimes that define them, we can arrange the ten varieties of behavior in approximate order of publicly perceived seriousness. The most serious category consists of offenders who concurrently rob, assault, and deal drugs. The least serious categories consist of those who commit only property crimes or only drug deals. We must note that some offenders may be misclassified according to seriousness if they committed serious crimes that were not among the eight in the questionnaire. For example, rape and kidnapping were not included, and homicide was not distinguished from assault in defining the varieties of behavior.

These varieties would have little interest for criminological research or criminal justice policy if they were unstable over time. If most criminals switched from one variety of behavior to another during a year, knowing that they belonged to a particular variety at a particular time would not help prosecutors or judges anticipate what kinds of crimes these offenders would later commit or how often. . . . However, the . . . data strongly suggest that criminals do belong to single varieties or naturally related pairs of varieties over extended periods of time. Further, the data give some indication that if they make transitions, offenders usually move to a more serious variety of behavior (or else they stop committing crimes altogether). . . .

Crime Commission Rates

The survey data reveal that the rate at which criminals commit crimes is related to the seriousness of the crimes that define their variety of criminal behavior. The more serious the variety, the more likely the offender to commit the defining crimes at high rates—and to commit less serious crimes at high rates, too.

Most criminals commit crimes at low rates. . . . Most . . . will commit none or a small number of each particular crime, but a small number will commit the crime at very high rates. . . . Even among the subgroup that we call violent predators, there are offenders who commit crimes at low rates. However, this group of robber-assaulter-dealers is much more likely than any other group of offenders to have very high rates for all crimes. These high-rate offenders have a strong influence on the average crime rates for the entire group. Table 19-1 shows nine average crime rates for each variety of criminal behavior. Since violent predators are defined by the fact that they commit robbery, assault, and drug dealing, it is not surprising that they have very high crime rates for these three crimes. But the table also shows that these robber-assaulter- dealers are higher-rate burglars than are offenders who just commit burglary. In fact, burglars who do not commit robbery have an average burglary rate between 36 and 42 burglaries per year, while robber-assaulter-dealers commit on the average 172 burglaries per year. . . .

. . . Even if we allow for the possibility that respondents overestimated their commission rates by factors of three or four[,] . . . the most active violent predators commit hundreds of serious crimes a year. And they commit five or more distinct types of crimes.

The survey's data indicate that the relative representation of the ten varieties of criminal behavior . . . will determine crime rates in any naturally occurring subpopulation of inmates (e.g., all the offenders imprisoned from a given county in a given year). The greater the fraction of offenders in the more serious varieties, the higher the crime commission rates will be. Comparison of data from the three states illustrates this hypothesis. Prisoner respondents in Texas had substantially lower crime commission rates than their counterparts in Michigan and California. For example, the California prisoners had average robbery rates five times greater than Texas prisoners, burglary rates three times greater, and rates for almost all other crimes two times greater. The relative numbers of prisoners in each variety of behavior almost entirely explain these differences—especially the fraction of prisoners who are violent predators. Texas had relatively few of them in prison.

Table 19-1.
Comparison of Crime Commission Rates among Varieties of Criminal Behavior (Average Annualized Rate)

	Robbery		
Variety of Behavior	**All**	**Business**	**Person**
Violent predators (robber-assaulter-dealers)	63	21	40
Robber-assaulters	45	17	24
Robber-dealers	24	11	9
Low-level robbers	7	2	5
Mere assaulters	—	—	—
Burglar-dealers	—	—	—
Low-level burglars	—	—	—
Property and drug offenders	—	—	—
Low-level property offenders	—	—	—
Drug-dealers	—	—	—

NOTE: The annualized crime rate is defined to be the number of crimes committed in a year, if the offender is free from incarceration for the entire year. Respondents in any category who reported not committing a particular crime were counted as having zero rate for that crime. "All" robbery includes some crimes that could not be classified as either business or person robbery.

The Violent Predators

The discussion to this point indicates that the robber-assaulter-dealers commit serious crimes, often at high rates, and typically have done so persistently for a number of years. This combination of traits earns them the label "violent predator." However, if . . . criminal records do not provide enough information for the criminal justice system to identify these offenders, how can they be identified? We can hardly expect criminals to put themselves in jeopardy by volunteering the kinds of information that the self-reports supply. In establishing and addressing this dilemma, the study makes its most potentially important finding and contribution to criminal justice policy. . . .

. . . [W]e collected background information on the inmates that included more than their criminal activities, arrests, and convictions. The questionnaire also asked about juvenile history, drug and alcohol use, employment, and demographic characteristics—information that is currently or potentially available to the criminal justice system. The inmates' responses clearly establish that certain personal characteristics correlate strongly with the various varieties of criminal behavior. These characteristics make it possible to identify the most serious criminals and distinguish them from less serious criminals. Thus, even though criminal records, as now constituted, do not permit identification of violent predators, our results show what kinds of information could improve records to make such identification possible in the future. . . .

Considering their effect on crime rates—especially for serious crimes—the violent predators are extremely young. In the survey, they averaged less than

Assault	Burglary	Theft	Forgery and Credit Cards	Fraud	Drug Dealing
8	172	214	30	35	1252
6	69	185	3	14	—
—	122	117	24	23	836
—	48	63	3	23	—
2	—	—	—	—	—
3	42	145	25	5	713
—	36	175	3	1	—
3	—	442	37	104	791
—	—	171	68	169	—
—	—	—	—	—	1180

23 years of age when coming into jail or prison. Yet, they also averaged considerably more total arrests than any other respondents, including those substantially older, and they had been committing the more serious crimes for at least six years.

The length of their criminal activity is implicit in their juvenile history. The predators typically begin committing crimes, especially violent crimes, well before age 16. They are likely to commit both violent and property crimes frequently before they are 18. They are more likely than other types of criminals to have received and had parole revoked and to have spent considerable time in juvenile facilities. Yet some of those who report the highest juvenile crime rates have no official records of juvenile criminal behavior.

They are also more socially unstable than other types of criminals. Few of them are married or have any other kind of family obligation. They are employed less regularly and have more trouble holding jobs. The more they are unemployed, the more crime they tend to commit. . . .

The violent predators also have characteristic histories of drug use. Most of them begin using several types of "hard" drugs, and using them heavily, as juveniles. Indeed, their use of drugs and their criminal careers usually begin at about the same time. However, this does not indicate that drug use caused them to become criminals. Rather, drug use appears to be just another element of the criminal life-style they have adopted. . . .

In addition to dealing drugs, 83% of the violent predators in our survey also used drugs. . . . As other studies have indicated, using drugs is often synonymous with dealing drugs. Further, heroin addiction has long been seen as part of the criminal subculture, often as the economic cause of crime. However, the survey revealed that certain types of drug use are even more characteristic of the violent predators than heroin addiction. Although they are more likely than other offenders to have high-quantity, high-cost heroin addictions, their more distinctive characteristic is multiple drug use: heroin with barbiturates, heroin with amphetamines, barbiturates with alcohol, barbiturates with amphetamines, amphetamines with alcohol, or multiple combinations of these.

When their drug use is costly and intense, the violent predators are more likely to commit most kinds of crimes and at much higher rates. However, the nature of the drug use seems related to the kind of crime that the user will commit: Addictive use of heroin is more associated with robbery and property crimes than with assaults, and there is some indication that cost, rather than the drug's physiological effect, provides the impetus here. As a matter of fact, heavy but relatively inexpensive heroin use is not associated with high crime rates. . . .

In contrast, multiple drug use, especially use of barbiturates and intermittent, "recreational," use of heroin, is associated with assault; and extremely heavy use of nonopiate psychotropic drugs is strongly related to high rates for all crimes except the nonviolent crime auto theft. This association helps explain an otherwise puzzling finding that white respondents committed assault at much higher rates than black respondents did. The whites used barbiturates more commonly. . . .

Why Violent Predators Cannot be Identified from Official Records Compared with criminals in other varieties of behavior, violent predators seem to be different in kind. Then why are the violent predators so hard to identify from official records? An immediate problem is their youth: Because most of them are so young, their adult criminal records do not usually reveal extensive prior criminal activity. And juvenile records offer little more enlightenment. Many of the violent predators' self-reports describe such heavy juvenile drug use and frequent, violent criminal activity that they must have been highly visible to teachers, neighbors, and schoolmates. Yet, some appear to have no official juvenile criminal records. . . . Even when the violent predators have juvenile records, they rarely indicate the rate or seriousness of their criminal activities. Indeed, where self-reports and juvenile records disagree, the self-reports usually report more crimes and incarcerations than the records do.

When violent predators do have prior adult records, those records do not readily distinguish them from other (lesser) offenders. It might seem that checking an inmate's prior record to see whether he had ever been convicted of the defining crimes—robbery, assault, and drug dealing—would provide an easy method of identifying violent predators. However, this method does not work: Some offenders with convictions for these three crimes in their records are not committing them concurrently at the present time and consequently do not match the definition of violent predator. . . .

Quite apart from whether they are or are not violent predators according to our definition, the inmates whose conviction records include assault, robbery, and drug dealing are not predominantly high-rate offenders. In fact, they are not significantly different from other offenders in their crime commission rates. In order to effectively and efficiently reduce crime, it is crucial to be able to differentiate the violent predators—who are disproportionately high-rate offenders—from others.

Sometime[s] official records show that a criminal has been arrested or convicted of robbery and assault and also has a history of drug use or addiction (usually an indication that he also deals drugs). But this information is not pragmatically useful for identifying the violent predator. Although violent predators are significantly more likely than other inmates to have this kind of history, we found a large number of "false positives"—inmates who use drugs but are not drug dealers. . . .

. . . To sum up, there is no simple, straightforward way to identify robber-assaulter-dealers from the data in their official records—as those data are currently collected. A number of factors explain the records' limitations: plea bargaining, imprecise definition of drug use, and the fact that some offenders successfully evade arrest and conviction for crimes they commit frequently.

The Value of Information not in Official Records We carried out regression analyses to determine what personal characteristics are most associated with a high robbery commission rate. . . . The following characteristics, only three of which can be reliably obtained from inmates' officials records, proved to be the most important in explaining the robbery commission rates of incoming inmates:

- Frequent violent juvenile crime (committing violent crime frequently before age 18).[4]
- Early onset of violent juvenile crime (committing violent crime before age 16)[5]
- Number of prior adult robbery convictions.
- Being young.
- Being unmarried.
- Persistent unemployment or unstable employment.
- General drug use.
- High-cost heroin use (more than $50 daily).
- Use of both heroin and barbiturates.
- Use of both barbiturates and alcohol.

With minor exceptions, the same variables explained robbery rates in each of the three study states.[6]

Offenders . . . whose characteristics indicated their robbery rate "should," according to the regression analysis, be in the highest 20% actually had, on the average:

- Robbery rates 65 times as high as those predicted to be in the lowest 20%;
- Burglary rates 66 times as high;
- Auto theft rates 346 times as high;
- Other theft rates 10 times as high; and
- Drug dealing rates 5 times as high. . . .

We also carried out staged multiple regressions to provide comparisons between the strength of official record information and the strength of other personal information in associations with robbery commission rates.[7] In the first stage, only the inmate's age and officially recorded adult conviction data were considered. . . . In the second stage, we considered all other adult official record items, including what some might consider inappropriate official record information about recent robbery *arrest* rates. [Introducing these variables increased explanatory accuracy.] . . .

The following information in official records of inmates was specifically not predictive of high robbery commission rates:

- Any details of the current conviction crime, such as multiple conviction offenses in conjunction with robbery, use of a weapon, or injury to victim.
- Prior adult convictions for any other types of crime.
- Annualized arrest rates for any other types of crime.
- Information about incidents of probation or parole and/or their outcome (revocation or successful completion).

Next we considered all official record information about juvenile criminal activity, none of which [increased explanatory accuracy]. . . .

To briefly summarize, we can draw a portrait of the high-rate robber, whose characteristics overlap significantly with those of the violent predator. He is a relatively young man who committed violent crimes, and committed them frequently, before he was 16; a long-term user of psychotropic drugs or addictive doses of heroin who has supported his drug habits with property crimes, which he also began committing before 16; a relatively unstable person who does not work very much or assume family obligations and has spent a lot of time in juvenile institutions and/or prison in the recent past. Unfortunately, most of this information that distinguishes high-rate robbers from other incarcerated criminals cannot be found in records the criminal justice system currently has readily available.

Importance of Distinguishing between Violent Predators and Other High-Rate Offenders Violent predators commit so many crimes at high rates that their data overwhelm information about other types of offenders who may also commit some crimes at high rates. For example, analysis shows that the characteristics associated with those committing burglary at high rates are essentially identical with those of violent predators—because violent predators are often also high-rate burglars. Nevertheless, it is interesting to know what kinds of offenders, other than violent predators, commit crimes at high rates. To find out, we . . . examined factors associated with high crime commission rates for these other varieties of offenders. . . .

We believe that the high crime rate of violent predators has overwhelmed official record data and led some researchers to draw conclusions about criminals in general that actually apply only to the predators or that are distorted by their activities. For example, many researchers conclude from arrest records that all offenders switch from committing one type of crime to another in random fashion. If they could identify and exclude the violent predators, as we did, they would probably find distinctly different patterns that reflect the activities of other offenders.

POLICY AND RESEARCH IMPLICATIONS

Much of the information that helps to distinguish the violent predator or other high-rate offender convicted of a crime is currently or potentially available from various sources. But even assuming that our findings prove to be generalizable, serious questions remain about whether and how that information should be used, especially for purposes of criminal sanctions.

As we have indicated, there are always some offenders who do not commit the crimes at the rates that their characteristics would suggest. . . . On the low end, the separation can be considered highly successful: 86% of respondents that the [analysis] predicted to have robbery rates in the lowest 20% reported committing no robberies during the measurement period, and only 3% committed more than 10 robberies a year. Even so, a 3% false-negative rate could be considered a failing of any formula intended for sentencing purposes. At the high end, the false prediction problem is more serious: although the [prediction analysis] also captured the bulk of high-rate offenders, some respondents identified as high-rate robbers reported having committed no robberies. Ten percent of those it predicted to have robbery rates in the highest 20% committed over 63 robberies per street year during the measurement period, but 30% reported no robberies and another 37% reported under 10 per year. Among convicted robbers, 54% of those predicted to have robbery rates in the highest 20% reported under 10 robberies per year. Without recourse to disinterested self-reports, this margin of error allows for considerable false identification of some offenders as high-rate robbers—which is more than just a research problem if the criminal justice system acts upon such identifications.

Even if the models were foolproof, the legal and ethical ramifications of their use by the criminal justice system would be a matter of dispute. Sentencing offenders for past crimes that have never been adjudicated runs counter to principles of just deserts, while sentencing them for predicted future crimes runs counter to tenets of free will and justice. Therefore, we urge that neither our findings nor any other formulas based on these data should be used simplistically as criteria for passing judgment on specific individuals.

The findings do, however, have important implications for criminal justice policy and criminological research, especially concerning these issues:

- Limitations of official criminal records.
- Criminal drug use and drug control.
- Incapacitation effects.
- Diversion programs.
- Rehabilitation efforts.
- Effects of the environment.

Limitations of Official Criminal Records

As we have seen, official records provide a very limited and usually misleading picture of the seriousness of any given offender's criminal behavior. They make some very serious criminals look relatively inoffensive and other, less serious criminals look relatively vicious. Inability to distinguish the violent predators from other offenders may cause the justice system to focus resources on the wrong targets. . . . This study suggests that certain . . . characteristics of offenders could give prosecutors, judges, and other criminal justice officials a clearer sense of seriousness than the nature of the current conviction crime or officially recorded prior offenses. Information on significant juvenile behavior and drug-use history could help identify the violent predator and distinguish him from less serious offenders. It would be possible to collect this information.

Juveniles with long histories of violent crime and heavy drug use can hardly have gone unnoticed by schools, police juvenile officers, probation officers, and juvenile courts. Consequently, when dealing with young *adult* offenders, prosecutors might be able to distinguish between predators and others if they had access to school records and other appropriate information about juvenile activities. We believe that a study is warranted to determine the feasibility of collecting such information and its potential for discriminating violent predators from other offenders. . . .

Criminal Drug Use and Drug Control

. . . [I]nformation about a criminal's drug history can tell more about the seriousness of his criminal activity than the kinds of crimes he is arrested for. If offenders were routinely tested for drug use when arrested, the tests would, in the long run, help to distinguish between more and less serious offenders. We are not suggesting that the drug test would necessarily be relevant for prosecuting the offender on his current arrest, but rather that the history of drug tests would eventually be highly informative.

Use of heroin and multiple drugs can now be accurately and inexpensively determined from electronic urine tests. These technological advancements make possible the specific drug tests needed to make the distinctions described in our study. . . .

Drug use and drug-use patterns cannot only tell criminal justice officials a great deal about the kinds and rates of crime a criminal probably commits, they also have important implications for drug control efforts. Drug use is one of the major factors associated with virtually every type of crime we studied, and specific forms of drug use correlate strongly with crime types and rates.[8] . . .

Although violent predators often have expensive heroin addictions, they more characteristically use combinations of drugs, particularly the alcohol-barbiturate combination. Considering the violent predators' contribution to very high rates of serious crimes, these emerging forms of drug abuse could possibly contribute as much to crime as heroin addiction does. Prosecutors and judges should be wary of leaning toward short sentences for offenders convicted of major, violent crimes who appear to have been acting uncharacteristically because they were "high" on these drugs at the time. The drug use should, in fact, be viewed as possibly indicating that the behavior for which the offender was convicted is characteristic of his deviant life-style. Equally important, drug control agencies should not invest resources so heavily in controlling heroin (and marijuana) traffic that they unduly limit their resources for controlling traffic in these other drugs.

. . . [P]reventing *adults* from beginning use of hard drugs does not appear to be a sensible approach to reducing crime. Relatively few inmates reported simultaneously beginning both crime and drug use as adults. Further, inmates who began using drugs as adults were just as likely to have engaged in crime before using drugs as after. These findings suggest that the relationship between drug use and criminal behavior is *chronic* rather than acute. In our sample, the vast majority of those who had long-term histories of drug use, usually beginning as juveniles, also had relatively long criminal careers. Thus, efforts to reduce crime by reducing drug use should focus primarily on juveniles. . . .

Incapacitation Effects

Many diverse legal and philosophical rationales have been given for imprisoning convicted offenders. At one extreme is the position that prison sentences should be based solely on "just deserts" for the current crime (Von Hirsch, 1976). At the other extreme are utilitarian purposes such as reduction in the amount of crime in society. Wide differences among crime rates of offenders, as revealed in this study, tend to give credence to utilitarian policies, one of which is selective incapacitation: giving longer prison terms to convicted offenders with high crime rates. . . .

. . . [I]dentifications of high-rate offenders from presently available data will yield a large fraction of false positives, typically over half. In our view this is a major failing of any plan to implement selective incapacitation in the near future. Some might nonetheless consider selective incapacitation attractive if it could be shown to have a large crime-reduction value. But it cannot. A long series of studies has shown that the crime reduction effect is likely to be small.

A report by Greenwood and Abrahamse (1982), based on the same jail and prison survey data that we analyzed, is interpreted in some quarters as showing that the crime reduction effect can be large. We do not concur. Their study did not address, much less resolve, the major uncertainties concerning the amount of crime reduction to be expected from selective incapacitation:

- *Crimes committed before first conviction*. A large fraction (around 45%) of the offenses for which prisoners are typically convicted could not have been prevented by any incapacitation policy, because this crime was their first felony conviction.[9]

- *Desistance*. Many high-rate offenders stop committing crimes, at least for extended periods. Incarcerating them during those periods does not reduce crime at all.

- *Group offending*. "The effect of [incapacitating a member of a group which typically offends together] . . . could easily be zero crimes averted, as the co-offenders could continue to account for the same number of crime incidents" (Reiss, 1980).

- *Replacement*. People who cooperate with other offenders in their criminal activity can be replaced if they are imprisoned.

- *Substantial incarceration under present policies.* High-rate offenders are already incarcerated a large proportion of the time. Although they would commit many crimes if left free for an entire year, this may not happen often. . . .

Diversion Programs

Although we find no current basis for implementing selective incapacitation policies that focus on high-rate offenders, our findings do suggest how, by focusing on low-rate offenders, overcrowded prison populations may be reduced at the least probable risk to the public. If more accurate and detailed data are collected in official records, they can be used to permit accurately identifying the lowest-rate convicts. If these offenders are not convicted of serious crimes, they are good candidates for diversion from jails and prisons to alternative community programs.

The rapid proliferation of diversion programs in the last decade has provided a multitude of possible alternatives to incarceration. . . .

. . . [N]ew diversion criteria should concentrate on convicts with the characteristics least predictive of high-rate serious behavior. Focusing diversion programs on them would provide a cost-effective way of dealing with them and would also increase the probability of achieving goals of secondary prevention and correction.

For example, supervised alternatives to incarceration for adult male populations could be focused on individuals convicted of crimes less serious than robbery who are known to have no prior convictions or arrests for robbery (either as adults or as juveniles), who are known to be less than frequent users or nonusers of other hard psychotropic drugs (as adults and as juveniles), and who are known not to have a juvenile history including episodic or frequent violence in which weapons were used or others were harmed. Furthermore, we suggest that incarceration be imposed when individuals in diversion programs are found to be using illegal hard drugs.

The knowledge required for implementation of these recommendations obviously entails improving official records, as we have already discussed. . . .

Rehabilitation Efforts

Our findings suggest that the apparent failure of many rehabilitation programs may be due less to their content than to the nature of offenders in the programs. Standard programs of vocational training and drug rehabilitation are better aimed at criminals who engage only in income-producing rather than in violent crimes. Most of them use crime as a substitute for legitimate sources of income, and we found that their crime commission rates go up when they are out of a job. They could probably benefit from vocational training programs, especially training in the fundamental skill of working steadily at a job. . . . [T]hese less serious offenders appear capable of abstaining from drug use.

Superficially, violent predators seem to be the best candidates for rehabilitation. Most are relatively young drug users with unstable employment who have been convicted of their first adult offense. However, their patterns of criminal behavior were established at such young ages, persisted for so long, and reached such a degree of seriousness that conventional programs of rehabilitation can probably have little, if any, significant effect on their lives.

If our conclusions about the relationship between drugs and criminal life-style are correct, trying to rehabilitate adult violent predators through drug intervention may be tantamount to "curing" tubercular patients by suppressing their coughs. In our sample, drug use alone was not a major reason for becoming involved in a criminal life-style. . . . [A]ny effective program will have to alter not just criminal users' drug patterns but their entire behavioral patterns. . . .

. . . Identifying [violent predators] at a very early age and attempting to control the factors that enhance the chances of their becoming . . . [such predators] might be more sensible and effective than trying to "fix" them after they enter the adult criminal system, or even after they enter high school. . . .

Effects of the Environment

We have said very little about the differences we found among states in our study, but the findings in Texas indicate that there may be environments and criminal justice practices that inhibit development of the patterns through which juveniles become and continue as violent predators.[10] Especially in comparison with the California cohort, the Texas cohort had much lower commission rates for most crimes, lower incidence of serious crime, and a much lower percentage of violent predators. At the same time, the Texas sample reported much less serious drug use and much higher employment rates.

Clearly, Texas sentences to prison less serious offenders than California and Michigan send to either jail or prison. But even after the study accounted for personal factors, including drug use, Texas inmates still appear to have significantly lower rates of robbery than those in the comparison states. . . .

These findings seem to suggest that some environments tolerate life-styles comprising frequent criminal acts and hard-drug use while others condemn them, that these disparate attitudes manifest themselves in different criminal justice policies and practices, and that the differences in those policies and practices explain why some environments have a more serious criminal problem than others. That is a highly conjectural interpretation, but its possible implications for criminal justice policy make it a worthwhile topic for research.

NOTES

1. Our complete findings are in Chaiken and Chaiken (1982). Descriptions of the survey instrument, its design and administration, and response patterns are given in Peterson et al. (1982).

2. Although the data we analyzed were cross-sectional in nature, they included a limited amount of information about criminal behavior of respondents in earlier periods.
3. Individuals who commit only assault are (by definition) an exception.
4. This also implies commission of property crimes as a juvenile.
5. Different coefficients for violent crime and for property crime in the absence of violent crime.
6. Commission of property crime, but not violent crime, as a juvenile was relevant only in Texas. Use of both heroin and barbiturates was relevant only in Michigan.
7. The staged regressions described here were carried out for inmates convicted of robbery.
8. It should be noted that the study sample contained a small but significant number of inmates (16%) who had relatively long criminal careers but had never used drugs.
9. This was demonstrated for prisoners in Colorado by Petersilia and Greenwood (1978). Others reaching similar conclusions include Van Dine et al. (1979) and Cohen (1982).
10. The reader will find considerable material on the similarities and differences among states in Chaiken and Chaiken (1982).

REFERENCES

Chaiken, J. M. and M. Chaiken
1982 Varieties of Criminal Behavior. Santa Monica, CA: Rand Corp.
Figlio, R. M.
1981 "Delinquency career as a simple Markov process," in J. A. Fox (ed.) Models in Quantitative Criminology. New York: Academic Press.
Glaser, D.
1972 Adult Crime and Social Policy. Englewood Cliffs, NJ: Prentice-Hall.
Greenwood, P. W. (with A. Abrahamse)
1982 Selective Incapacitation. Report R-2815-NIJ. Santa Monica, CA: Rand Corp.
Hoffman, P. B. and J. L. Beck
1980 "Revalidating the salient factor score: a research note." J. of Criminal Justice 8: 185–188.
Peterson, M. A. and H. Braiker (with S. M. Polich)
1981 Who Commits Crime: A Survey of Prison Inmates. Cambridge, MA: Oelgeschlager, Gunn & Hain.
Peterson, M., J. Chaiken, P. Ebener, and P. Honig
1982 Survey of Prison and Jail Inmates: Background and Method. Report N-1635-NIJ. Santa Monica, CA: Rand Corp.
Pritchard, D. A.
1979 "Stable predictors of recidivism." Criminology 17, 1: 15–21.
Reiss, A., Jr.
1980 "Understanding changes in crime rates," in S. Fienberg and A. Reiss, Jr., (eds.) Indicators of Crime and Criminal Justice: Quantitative Studies. Washington, DC: U.S. Government Printing Office.

Robbins, L. N. and E. Wish (1977)
1977 "Childhood deviance as a developmental process: a study of 223 urban black men from birth to 18." Social Forces 56, 2: 448–471.
Von Hirsch, A.
1976 Doing Justice. New York: Hill & Wang.

Neighborhood, Family, and Employment: Toward a New Public Policy Against Violence

Lynn A. Curtis

... [This selection serves to identify a national policy to prevent crime] paying attention to ... innovations that are supported by scientific research and to my own practical experience in running public- and private-sector programs—keeping in mind what seems to be politically feasible.

On the basis of these criteria, three words perhaps best suggest a future policy framework that can prevent individual and group violence in a cost-effective way: neighborhood, family, and employment. More specifically, I believe that we need to:

- Demonstrate and evaluate ways in which indigenous inner-city organizations can take the lead in reducing crime and fear—not only as an end in itself, but as a means of developing their neighborhoods economically and creating youth employment, especially among minorities;
- Demonstrate and evaluate how extended families and other personal networks can be a crucial source of support for minority youth in high crime areas; and
- Demonstrate and evaluate the linkage between the employment of minority youths and the reduction of crime committed by these youths

THE HOUSE OF UMOJA AND EL CENTRO

Let me first illustrate how such policies already show signs of working successfully by summarizing a 1981 MacNeil-Lehrer Report on the House of Umoja Boy's Town in West Philadelphia.[1]

Umoja is a Swahili word that means "unity." . . . Sister Falaka [Fattah] describes how, over ten years ago, she and her husband, David, opened the doors of their house on North Frazier Street to provide an alternative extended family for tough youth-gang members from broken homes. . . .

. . . [She] is sitting at a table with several young men. She is leading the *Adella*—a Swahili word for "just" and "fair." It is a vehicle for character building, mediation, and self-government. Problems are raised and resolved. Today Sister Falaka shows her concern that James got fired from a construction job for talking back to the foreman. "If you were hanging on a rope by your mouth, and you just had to get in that last word, you'd be gone. Isn't that right?"

The young men listen to Sister Falaka because they respect her. That is because she listens to and respects them. *Respect* is a word these young men use over and over.

Robert MacNeil comments on the Swahili words and asks Sister Falaka whether she is Muslim. She is not. The words provide an African ethnic identity. The young men are encouraged to take pride in their ethnic origins—and build on them. . . .

Some youths seem to become more willing to channel their interests into building a future for themselves. There are shots of these young men working for high school equivalency tests. Others are shown learning to rehabilitate row houses on Frazier Street. The remodeled houses, named for Martin Luther King and other black leaders, will be used for residences, services, and youth-operated businesses that will provide jobs and bring income into Umoja.

There is also an Umoja Security Institute. On the program, "Brother Rat," a former Umojan, describes to the Adella how he learned private security work through the institute. He now is a detective. "I didn't used to listen. But she [Falaka] turned me around. Now I got a good job, a wife, and a family. I feel real good about myself. And you can do the same thing."

The neighborhood shopping center is being patrolled by young men with Security Institute training. They wear Umoja uniforms, do not carry weapons, and serve as additional eyes and ears to protect the community. The street savvy of these young men is being tapped, not ignored or blocked. . . . They know what suspicious behaviors to watch for, and they use that knowledge to prevent crime. Umoja has contracts with a nearby shopping mall, a 7-Eleven, and a Burger King to help keep crime and fear down. That also encourages businesses to stay in the neighborhood.

What do criminal justice leaders think of all this? On the program, a Philadelphia juvenile court judge says that community organizations like Umoja have made perhaps the biggest difference in reducing crime and gang violence in the city. A member of the Los Angeles Police Gang Unit adds that neighborhood groups are not the only answer but that they have an important role to play.

As for results, Sister Falaka cites a recent study by the Philadelphia Psychiatric Center that reported a 3 percent rearrest rate for Umojans compared to a rate of 70 to 90 percent for young people from conventional juvenile correction facilities. . . .

I do not want to place too much emphasis on Umoja. There are other examples of success—like the Center for Orientation and Services in Ponce, Puerto

Rico [El Centro], which has received national attention. . . . Umoja and El Centro seem to get similar results, drawing on the strengths of their different cultures, black and Hispanic[;] . . . creat[ing] self respect in youth[;] provid[ing] family-like support alternatives when there are broken families[;] motivat[ing] the young men to take action for the benefit of themselves and the community[;] and channel[ing] their energy from illegal to legal market activity.

FAMILY

. . . Currie [discusses] other family programs—like the Department of Health, Education and Welfare's Child and Family Resource Centers of the 1970s—the results of which suggested substantial enhancement of family functioning at very low cost. Although these programs were not explicitly designed to test how family supports can reduce crime, a General Accounting Office assessment predicted that they would reduce delinquency by improving early parent-child relations and school performance.[2] Future federal programs need to build on these centers and evaluate their crime-reducing impact. . . .

New departures are politically feasible if they can be made part of [a] national family policy. . . . We need to overturn the many existing federal policies that still fail to recognize the long history behind the weak black kinship institutions which the Violence and Kerner commissions observed. For example, Comer cautions that "traumatized families often overwhelm institutions and programs based on the notion that no previous trauma took place, that success as families in the economic system is merely a matter of will and hard work. Housing programs that isolate the poor and then systematically remove the best organized and most effective families from the neighborhood or housing project through income limits are an example of such thinking."[3]

MINORITY YOUTH UNEMPLOYMENT

The National Urban League has estimated the unemployment rate during the 1970s among young urban minority men in high-crime groups to have been over 60 percent. The rate, the League says, has risen in the 1980s.[4] Much of this is structural—unemployment that persists despite business-cycle and seasonal fluctuations. Denied jobs directly through discriminating hiring behavior by employers and indirectly through inadequate educational opportunity, many young minority men have become victims of structural unemployment and have thus increasingly become part of the underclass. . . .

. . . [M]any young blacks and Hispanics tend to be excluded from the legal primary labor market, where there are adequate wages and stable jobs. They tend to be limited to the legal secondary market, with low wages and unstable, dead-end jobs as dishwashers, busboys, hotel clean-up workers, and the like. . . .

Yet these are only the *legal* job markets. The competition for the labor of a youth on the south side of Chicago includes offerings in a variety of illegal or quasi-legal job markets. To an intelligent young man in a Watts public housing project, whose education has been substandard and whose heroes include only some participants in the legal primary markets, it can be rational—that is, consistent with his values and experience[5]—to pick up one or more of the illegal options.

. . . [W]hy might public- or private-sector employment not divert an underclass youth from committing crime—especially acquisitive crime and illegal market activity? The most sophisticated answers have come from research by the Vera Institute of Justice, funded by the U.S. Department of Justice.[6] If job training is directed to unrewarding dead-end work in the legal secondary labor market and if local work rules and hiring patterns make even those dead-end opportunities hard to find, competing illegal labor-market activities may be more attractive. . . . [C]ommon sense street-level decisions by young underclass men about pursuing legal opportunities, illegal ones, or some combination depend not only on the money involved. They also can depend on intrinsic satisfaction, what feels best given the values and expectations of the community and how one generates respect among peers. We know that a good number of minority youths earn more money and develop more self-respect from the skills involved in criminal pursuits, and from the autonomous work conditions of criminal business, than from available legal secondary labor-market jobs with low skill potential, limited scope, and arbitrary management.[7]

In addition, Vera found that broken family backgrounds tend to increase commitments to illegal options, whereas strong family supports and reliable kinship networks tend to increase legal market commitments. . . .

There are clear and important policy implications to the Vera findings. We need to demonstrate and carefully evaluate programs that incorporate secure bridges between the secondary and primary legal labor markets; facilitate family, extended-family, and kinship network support; and build employment on interests and street skills that are intrinsically satisfying to the individual, but that previous public-sector programs often denied. . . .

Most of the federal programs of the 1960s and 1970s failed to measure carefully the relationship between employment and crime, but some did. And some *were* successful at reducing crime by those employed. . . . In the most thorough review of the 1970s public-sector employment and training programs, Robert Taggart concludes, "Comprehensive residential training (e.g., Job Corps) for the most disadvantaged youth pays off in earning gains . . . as well as in large reductions in crime and delinquency. . . . Every dollar spent on residential training yields at least $1.45 in social benefits, according to conservative estimates of the current values of benefits and costs and after accounting for the real rate of return on the same resources. . . . Naysayers who deny that labor market problems are real and serious, that social interventions can make a difference, or that the effectiveness of public problems can be improved will find little to support their preconceptions."[8]

We now know from the experience of the Law Enforcement Assistance Administration (LEAA) and various academic studies that a policy of raising illegal market costs has not succeeded in reducing crime or fear. We also know, from the experience of groups like Umoja . . . , evaluations like that of Taggart . . . and research like that of Vera and the Rand Corporation, that there do seem to be ways of increasing legal market benefits that work to reduce crime and fear.

This does not mean that we should reduce the costs of illegal market employment. But the time has come to begin spending our program, evaluation, and research dollars in the more promising direction of increasing legal market benefits. For too long, we have neglected coordinating a targeted, structural federal labor-market policy with a federal crime prevention policy.

CRIME PREVENTION BY INNER-CITY NEIGHBORHOOD ORGANIZATIONS

Organizations like Umoja and El Centro illustrate the great potential for what today is called neighborhood or community-based crime prevention. . . . A program like Umoja both addresses the causes of crime and reduces opportunities for crime. Causes are addressed by employing youth, empowering young men through participatory decision making, providing extended family support, and mediating disputes. . . . The youth patrols are ways of reducing opportunities for crime without necessarily addressing underlying causes. Other examples of opportunity reduction through other neighborhood organizations include block watches, escort services, and home security through hardware. Sometimes the causes of crime can be addressed while opportunities are reduced as in the employment of youth on Umoja's security patrols. . . .

Opportunity reduction *is* needed in the inner city—for example, to help reduce fear and to ensure that businesses will not move out. But opportunity reduction alone can, at best, displace crime to another location. If the displacement is to other parts of the inner city, what have we gained for a policy targeted at the underclass? . . .

Nor can we hope that organizing citizens around reducing opportunities for crime, cleaning up garbage and maintaining order will necessarily lead to later activity that addresses the causes of crime. . . . [S]uch a progression is not inevitable. It is just as likely that the initial organization of citizens around the need to clean up garbage or throw out drunks will lead to other forms of order maintenance and target hardening that never ask why crime is being committed. Ultimately, a strategy of opportunity reduction alone in the inner city may only teach citizens to become better controllers—surrogate police who simply try to keep the lid on. . . .

. . . I believe that the police have a strong role to play—but a supporting role, if and when a capable neighborhood organization is willing to take the lead. At Umoja and El Centro, the community organization runs crime prevention activities, and the police play a backup role as deemed appropriate—not the other way around. . . . In inner-city areas, citizens must take the lead in prevention because the police forces have been institutionalized to *react* to crime after it has been committed, not to *prevent* it from happening. . . .

A reason for encouraging crime prevention by indigenous neighborhood groups is that people are motivated to action if they have a stake in what is happening and if they can control their own turf. . . . In American cities, most police do not live in the neighborhoods they patrol and therefore do not necessarily have a deep personal stake in the community. . . .

Some police departments may resist playing only a supporting role; many other departments will be responsive. The record already shows that successful inner-city organizations can make the work of police much easier and more efficient. For example, key to El Centro's success are advocates, young people who work directly with youth in trouble with the law and often mediate between them and the criminal justice system. . . .

More generally, if citizens believe that they themselves are the initiators rather than the recipients of "help" from outside professionals, and if those professionals—here the police—make themselves available for advice when needed, then the potential exists for more cooperation by citizens with police. This can result in more . . . reporting of crime, more tips on suspects, and improved police apprehension rates. . . .

Using Crime Prevention as a Means to Economic Development

At Umoja and El Centro, crime prevention is not an end in itself. It is used as a means to make the community secure and encourage economic development, housing rehabilitation, the retention of old businesses, and the attraction of new ones. This, in turn, encourages employment, including work for the minority youth who commit so much of the crime.

. . . If we are to integrate neighborhood-based crime prevention in the inner city with a program to reduce the underclass, such prevention needs to be part of the economic development process, not conceptualized as an arm of the criminal justice system. . . . Conceived as part of the development process, neighborhood crime prevention is more naturally made available to the grassroots constituencies that must make the program work, block by block. The jobs and sense of ownership that can be generated by development help address the causes of crime. There also are more opportunities to finance crime prevention—as, for example, when developers and neighborhood organizations set aside a portion of their property-management funds for security. By contrast, crime prevention as an adjunct of the criminal justice system is more vulnerable to the politics of the local police chief, his relationship with the mayor, and their attitudes toward citizen grass-roots leadership. Funding for programs is more dependent on outside grants limited to criminal justice and does not benefit as much from linkages to the economic development process. . . .

. . . [S]elf-sufficient [measures] help keep Umoja and El Centro afloat. To avoid the failures of the past, future national crime prevention programs must understand that creating financial self-sufficiency is as important as addressing the causes of crime and reducing opportunities for crime. Otherwise, new local programs again will go out of business. Local crime prevention programs can promote financial self-sufficiency if they are run by neighborhood organizations that have a sound financial-management system in place, a supportive board, a well-defined constituency, and a good track record in economic development, housing rehabilitation, and youth employment. . . .

A National Plan

To have any significant impact on crime and fear, neighborhood-based crime prevention and the employment and family programs that can be integrated with it need a policy that is national and coordinated in scope for both the private and public sectors.

In the private sector, the Eisenhower Foundation, as the re-creation of the Violence Commission, already is funding and facilitating neighborhood-based self-help among inner-city organizations across the country in the ways I have indicated. An attempt is being made to address the causes of crime while also reducing the opportunities for crime, to use crime prevention as a means of economic development, to create at least partial financial self-sufficiency, to directly fund inner-city organizations in order to ensure their leadership role, to allow programs to "bubble up" on the basis of local circumstances rather than "trickle down" from dictates in Washington, to provide unobtrusive technical assistance when needed, and—for the first time in a national program of this kind—to . . . evaluate what works and what does not through impact and process measures. . . .

. . . [T]he need is too great and resources today are too limited for the private sector to cover more than a part. . . . And even if there were sufficient private-sector monies, it is better to have a public- and private-sector mix of resources in order to avoid the undue influence of any one funding source. In the 1980s, there is much potential for such a mix, especially for using public-sector challenge grants to leverage private-sector matches.

To ensure the link between economic development and crime prevention, it might help to give the national public-sector lead to a development agency rather than to a criminal justice agency. . . . [T]here is a precedent. In the late 1970s, . . . the Justice Department, the Labor Department, and the Department of Health and Human Services transferred discretionary monies to HUD for youth-employment, victim/witness, juvenile-delinquency-prevention, and drug-abuse-prevention components. Within HUD, career civil servants at first conceived the effort as a security target-hardening program but later came to refer to it as an anticrime program and embraced the importance of resident initiatives and employment to get at the causes of crime. . . .

[CRIMINAL JUSTICE AGENCIES]

. . . The . . . federal interest in improving the treatment of victims that began in the 1970s and has expanded in the 1980s would do well to focus on inner-city populations, where the view often is held that the system of justice also has been disproportionately victimizing them. . . .

Although technology often may be the appropriate way to improve the functioning of the justice system, people-oriented programs can be just as efficient—and can serve to employ inner-city minorities. . . . [They] also can redress symptoms of the more underlying issues of race that often serve to trigger group disorder. . . .

As the first major publication to report . . . that a very small proportion of violent repeat offenders commits most violent crime,[9] the Violence Commission . . . began the modern debate on who in fact must be incarcerated. The findings on repeat offenders, plus the acknowledged limitations of deterrence as a national policy, have led many to advocate the currently fashionable policy of selective incapacitation.[10]

. . . [S]ome controversies on criminal justice policy can be minimized and efficiency can be improved by following the implications that flow from a strategy of selective incapacitation. Police and prosecutor resources can be directed toward career criminals and violent juveniles. Judges can set aside outmoded notions of deterrence and simply keep high-risk offenders off the streets. Prison officials and parole authorities need not waste time with emotional and ideological arguments over constructing more prisons versus abandoning them; rather, high-risk offenders can be imprisoned and lower risk offenders diverted to other settings.[11] . . .

. . . But national policy must never lose sight of the limitations to incapacitation.

The most obvious concern is the possibility of unjustly sentencing an offender to a prison term on the basis of a false prediction of his future criminality. After a relatively brief time, most high-risk youth leave high-risk, low-return street crime for less dangerous criminal opportunities and for places in the legal labor market.[12] Selective incapacitation for long periods interrupts the process. . . . [U]nless we keep high-risk youths in prison till they are old men . . . , it is possible that, upon release, they will continue in high-risk crime. They will have been stockpiled in a prison system that reinforces the underclass and teaches violence.

Umoja, El Centro, and other groups are successfully dealing with these same young repeaters in carefully coordinated and managed community programs. . . . [S]uch programs cost less than imprisonment (which is more per year than room, board, and tuition at Yale). Recidivism rates, at least at successful operations like Umoja and El Centro, are far lower than for offenders released from prison. . . .

Even with the experience and empirical findings that support it, the potential of neighborhood, family, and employment as a national policy of crime prevention integrated with a policy to reduce the underclass will be resisted by those who are unable or unwilling to move beyond preconceptions and face the limitations of deterrence and incapacitation. Those who say that the relationship between unemployment and crime is too complex to unite structural labor-market policy and crime prevention policy cannot be paying attention to Taggart's study of federal programs and the Vera and Rand studies funded by the federal government. Those who say that they have never seen the causes of crime and that we cannot create effective extended-family programs have not seen . . . the House of Umoja. . . . Those who believe that police, rather than community organizations, must control neighborhood-based crime prevention appear uninformed of El Centro's good relations with the police and of the cost-effective benefits that . . . can accrue from integrating community regeneration, economic development, and crime prevention. . . .

Political feasibility is no small point when it comes to creating change in our inner cities and recognizing the continuing American dilemma of the underclass. . . . [Let us] . . . hope that we can respond, in a civilized and durable way, to the often overwhelming challenges from within.

NOTES

1. "The MacNeil-Lehrer Report," Public Broadcasting System, December 8, 1981.
2. . . . Elliott Currie, "Fighting Crime," *Working Papers*, May–June 1982 . . . , p. [23].
3. [James P. Comer, "Black Violence and Public Policy," in Lynn A. Curtis, ed., *American Violence and Public Policy: An Update of the National Commission on the Causes and Prevention of Violence* (New Haven: Yale University Press, 1985).]
4. National Urban League, *State of Black America, 1984* (New York: National Urban League, 1984).
5. A great deal of research and policy action is based on misperceptions and inaccurate definitions by mainstream outsiders of what *rational* means in the inner city. In *Dangerous Currents* (New York: Random House, 1983), Lester C. Thurow justifiably criticizes the use of the term in econometric modeling and forecasting on the basis of a definition derived from the nineteenth-century white middle-class notion of economic rationality set forth in the utilitarian economics of Jeremy Bentham.

   Using this definition, Edward C. Banfield, in *The Unheavenly City* (Boston: Little, Brown & Co., 1970), noted deploringly that inner-city minorities could not "defer gratification" (for example, by saving money) but instead seemed wedded to "immediate gratification" (like spending or mugging). In *Behind Ghetto Walls* (Chicago: Aldine, 1970), Lee Rainwater responded that immediate gratification is a very rational goal when, as often is the case in the underclass, the choice is between immediate gratification and no gratification at all. Similarly, a large proportion of robbery is committed by young poor minority men. The most common victims are other young poor minority men, who tend to have the least money and are the most likely to fight back with lethal weapons. To an outsider, it therefore might appear "irrational" to try to rob such young men. But this might be rational behavior, for example, to a young man who seeks the approval of peers in order to gain admittance to a gang.

   Unless researchers and policymakers take more care to understand how their values and experience differ from those of the inner city, federal actions regarding the underclass and crime will continue to be misdirected, to the detriment, of course, of the disadvantaged.
6. James W. Thompson, et al. *Employment and Crime* (Washington, D.C.: National Institute of Justice, October 1981).
7. One evaluation of a federal employment program found that many verbally skillful, enterprising, and intelligent minority youths dropped out of job training because they experienced more personal self-esteem and often derived more economic rewards from work in illegal markets than from the legal secondary markets offered by the federal government. See Nathan Caplan, "Competency among Hard-to-Employ Youths," *Institute for Social Research Newsletter* (Ann Arbor, Mich.: Institute for Social Research, June 1973).

8. Robert Taggart, *A Fisherman's Guide: An Assessment of Training and Remediation Strategies* (Kalamazoo, Mich.: Upjohn Institute, 1981).

9. The study was later published as Marvin E. Wolfgang et al., *Delinquency in a Birth Cohort* (Chicago: University of Chicago Press, 1972).

10. See, for example, Peter W. Greenwood, with Allan Abrahamse, *Selective Incapacitation* (Santa Monica: Rand Corporation, 1982).

11. See Kenneth R. Feinberg, ed., Foreword to *Violent Crime in America* (Washington, D.C.: National Policy Exchange, 1983).

12. Michael E. Smith and James W. Thompson, "Employment, Youth and Violent Crime" in Feinberg, *Violent Crime*.

Chapter 20

Prevention: Specific Types Section 1: Homicide

Intervention Strategies to Reduce Homicide

Margaret A. Zahn

To construct and evaluate strategies that will reduce homicide, it is first helpful to discuss *types* of homicide and their *causes*. Unfortunately, with few exceptions, homicide research and theory do not usually link types of homicides and causes in a systematic way. Further, policy implications have been neither drawn systematically from available evidence nor evaluated after being implemented. The sum effect is that we have little integration of theory, research, intervention strategies, and policy evaluation.

TYPES OF HOMICIDE

A profitable research focus might be to construct different categories of homicide, with policy implications derived for each. Intervention strategies can then be devised that apply either to all homicide types or to specific types. In current research, the typology used most commonly is based on *victim-offender relationships*.

The description of these types of homicides is based on material from the 1980 *Uniform Crime Reports (UCR)* (U.S. Department of Justice, 1981), a national study on the nature and patterns of American homicide (Riedel and Zahn, 1982), and a survey of studies done on each homicide category, including familial murder and murder between friends and acquaintances and between strangers.

Family Homicide

In 1980, family homicide constituted 16.1 percent of the homicides nationally (U.S. Department of Justice, 1981, 12). This represented a slight decrease from the mid-1970s. The bulk of within-family homicides were spouse killings. A second, smaller group of within-family homicides involved children. (See Figures 20-1 and 20-2 for summaries of causal factors and prevention strategies for spousal and child killings, respectively.)

Based on national FBI data (Riedel and Zahn, 1982), approximately 55.0 percent of family-homicide victims are white and 43.7 percent are black. The median ages of victims and offenders are 33 and 32, respectively. A handgun is the weapon used to kill in 40.0 percent of the cases, followed, in decreasing order, by other guns (24 percent), knives (17 percent), and other means (18 percent). Spouse homicides take place most frequently within the home.

According to Luckenbill (1977) and Gelles (1972), these deadly incidents involve a series of dynamic interactional stages which occur after many other previous assaultive incidents. The process generally involves an escalating set of interactions whereby the victim first criticizes the offender or refuses to obey a command; the offender responds to this as an affront and demands that some amends be made—or else threatens violence; the victim agrees that violence is an acceptable way to resolve the confrontation and therefore neither apologizes nor flees; the situation escalates; and a homicide results.

Homicide between Friends and Acquaintances

In 1980, 34.8 percent of all homicides nationally involved friends and acquaintances (U.S. Department of Justice, 1981, 12). Victims of acquaintance homicide are younger than the victims of family homicide and are much more often males. Further, this homicide type is more prevalent among blacks (who comprised 53.3 percent of the victims nationally in 1978). The median age of offenders is 29, which is slightly younger than the median age of their victims, which is 30, and is younger than those who commit family homicide. Handguns are the weapons of choice and are used in 48.6 percent of the cases; knives are used in 19.6 percent of the cases. Homicides between friends are most likely to occur within a private residence. However, one-third of these homicides occur on the street; and many more homicides between friends occur in bars than do other types of killings. We know very little about the arguments that precipitate these homicides or how the events unfold. We also know very little about why arguments between black males are more likely to be lethal than those between white males or between females. (See Figure 20-3 for hypothesized determinants and prevention strategies for homicide between friends.)

Stranger Homicide

A stranger homicide is one in which the victim and killer do not have a prior known relationship. In 1980, 13.3 percent of the homicides nationally were committed by strangers (U.S. Department of Justice, 1981, 12).

Data from the FBI supplemental homicide reports for 1978 indicate that in stranger homicides the victims and offenders are predominantly male. The median ages of victims and offenders are 31 and 25, respectively. Those who kill strangers are the youngest offenders. Most killings of strangers are accomplished with firearms: 53.0 percent with handguns and 13.9 percent with other types of firearms. Robberies comprise 32.0 percent of the stranger homicides. The association of the homicide with a contemporaneous felony (such as robbery, rape, or arson) is higher in urban areas.

Studies by Zimring (1977), Cook (1981), and Block (1977) have indicated an increase in robbery murders in the 1970s. Although the chance of being killed in a robbery is small, it is greater if the robber has a gun: 9.0 per 1,000 with a gun and 1.4 per 1,000 without a gun (Cook, 1981). Furthermore, victim resistance in the presence of a gun appears to be the most significant determinant of a lethal attack during a robbery (Block, 1977). (See Figure 20-4 for a summary of causal factors and prevention strategies for stranger homicide.)

CAUSES OF HOMICIDE

Most studies do not look at causes of homicide by type. An important exception shows that causes may vary by the type of homicide. Smith and Parker (1980) mainly distinguish primary (family and friends) from nonprimary (strangers) homicides. Structural factors are somewhat different for each. Poverty is more strongly associated with primary homicides. Causal studies and explanations have not been restricted in focus to homicide but usually deal with the more general subject of the relationship between aggression and biological, psychological/psychiatric, and sociological determinants and correlates.

Sociological Theories of Homicide

There are three major sociological approaches to explaining homicide: cultural (or subcultural), structural, and interactionist. Cultural theory explains homicide as resulting from learned, shared values and behavioral routines specific to certain groups (e.g., young, black males). Basic causes are the norms and values that are learned and transmitted across generations.

Certain subgroups exhibit higher rates of homicide because they participate in subcultures that subscribe to violence. First developed by Wolfgang ([1958] 1975) and later expanded by Wolfgang and Ferracuti ([1967] 1982), this position assumes that a subculture exists which is characterized by a cluster of values that support and encourage the use of force in interpersonal relations and in-group interactions. Easy access and the actual carrying of weapons symbolically indicate a willingness to participate in violence—to expect and to be ready for its occurrence.

Cultural formulations have also been used to explain higher rates of homicide, especially in the South. For example, Hackney (1976) asserted that the most fruitful avenue for explaining Southern violence is tracing the development of the Southern world-view which defines the social, political, and physical environment as hostile and casts the white Southerner in the role of the passive victim of

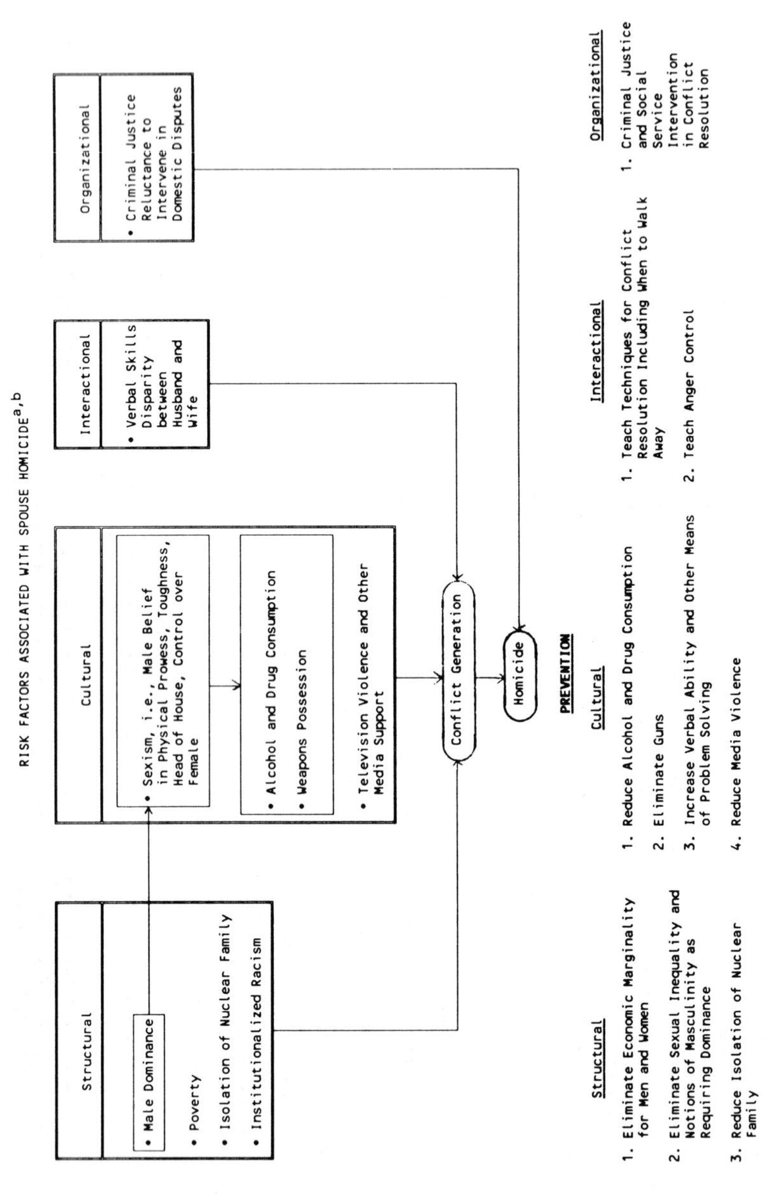

Figure 20-1.
Family (Spouse) Homicides.
Source: Adapted partially from Lynn Curtis, *Violence, Race and Crime.*

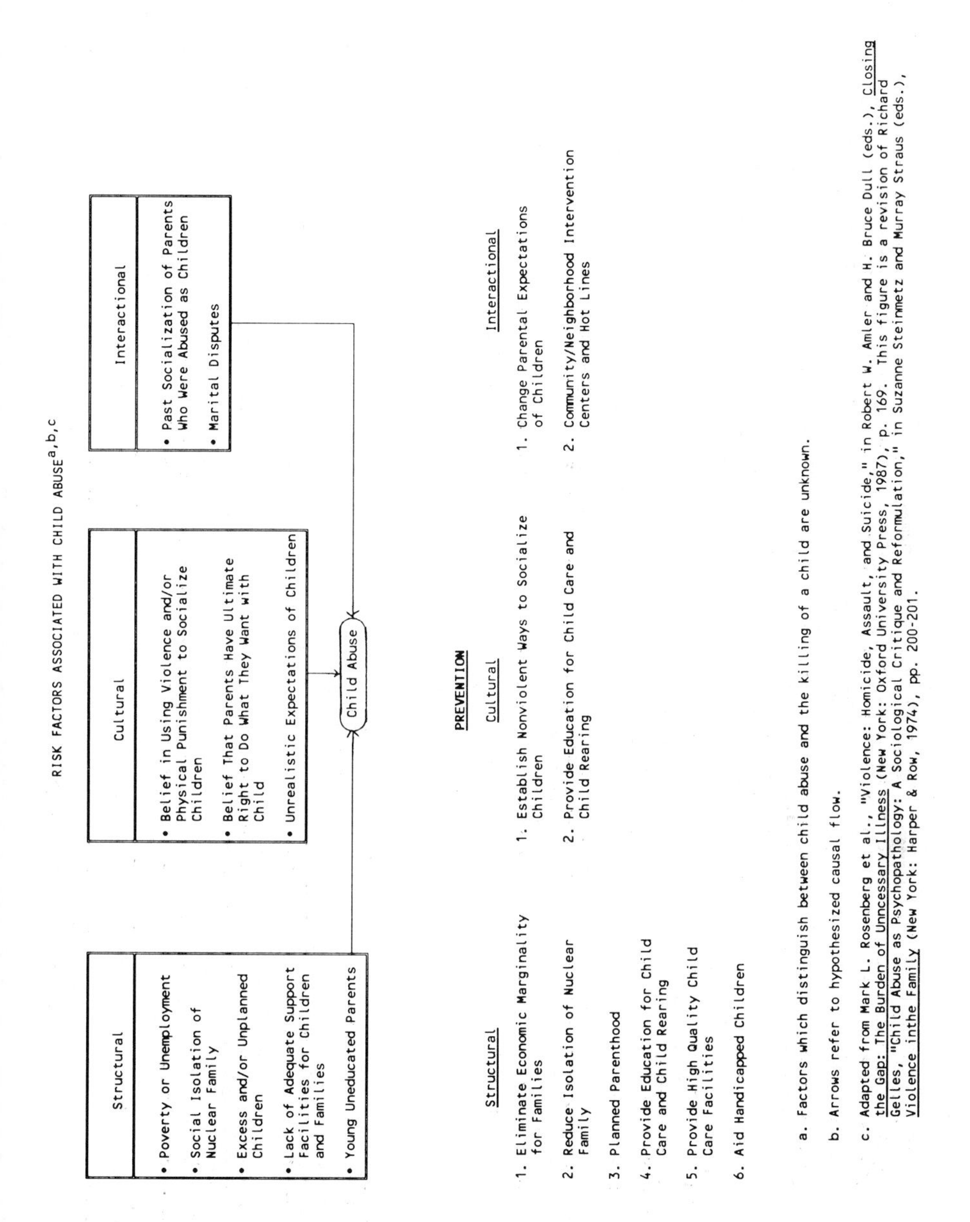

Figure 20-2.
Family (Child) Homicide.
Source: Model partially adapted from Richard Gelles, "Child Abuse as Psychopathology: A Sociological Critique and Reformulation," in *Violence in the Family*, pp. 200–201.

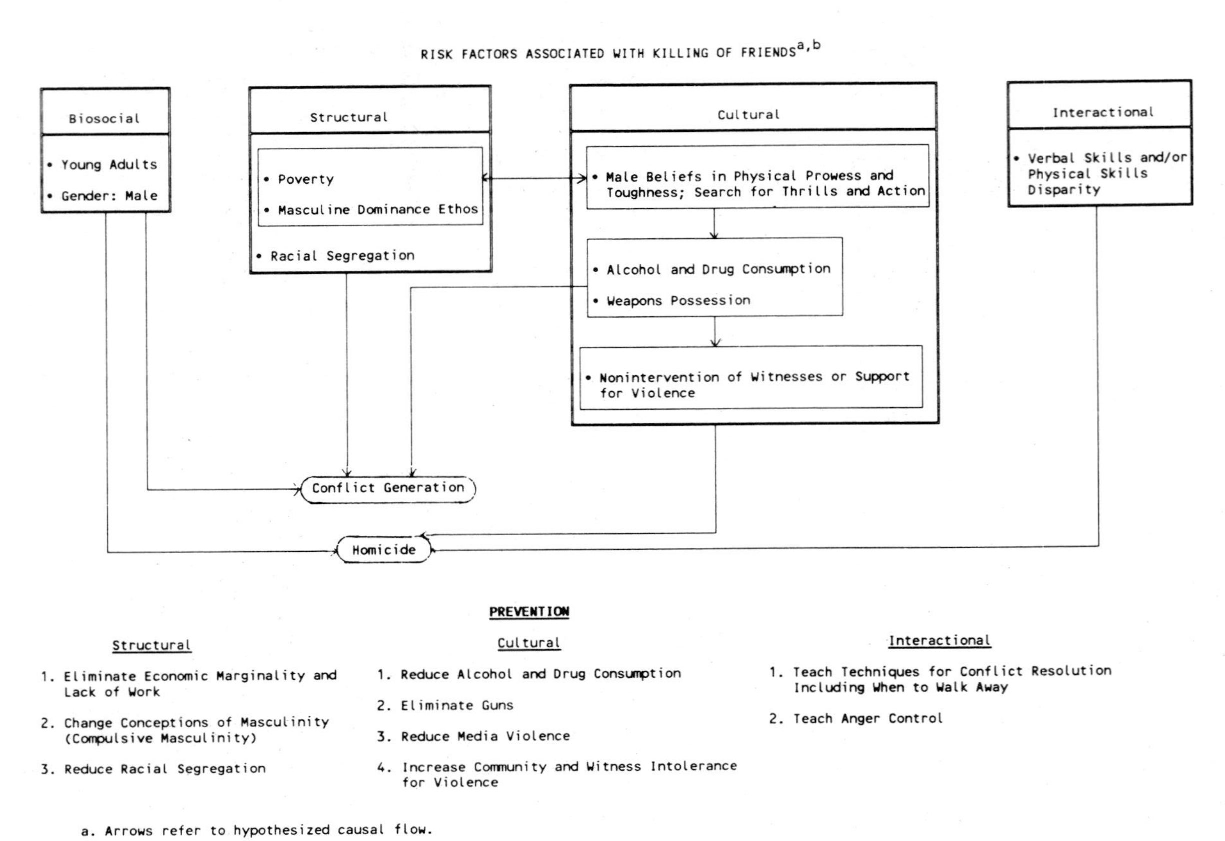

Figure 20-3.
Killing of Friends.

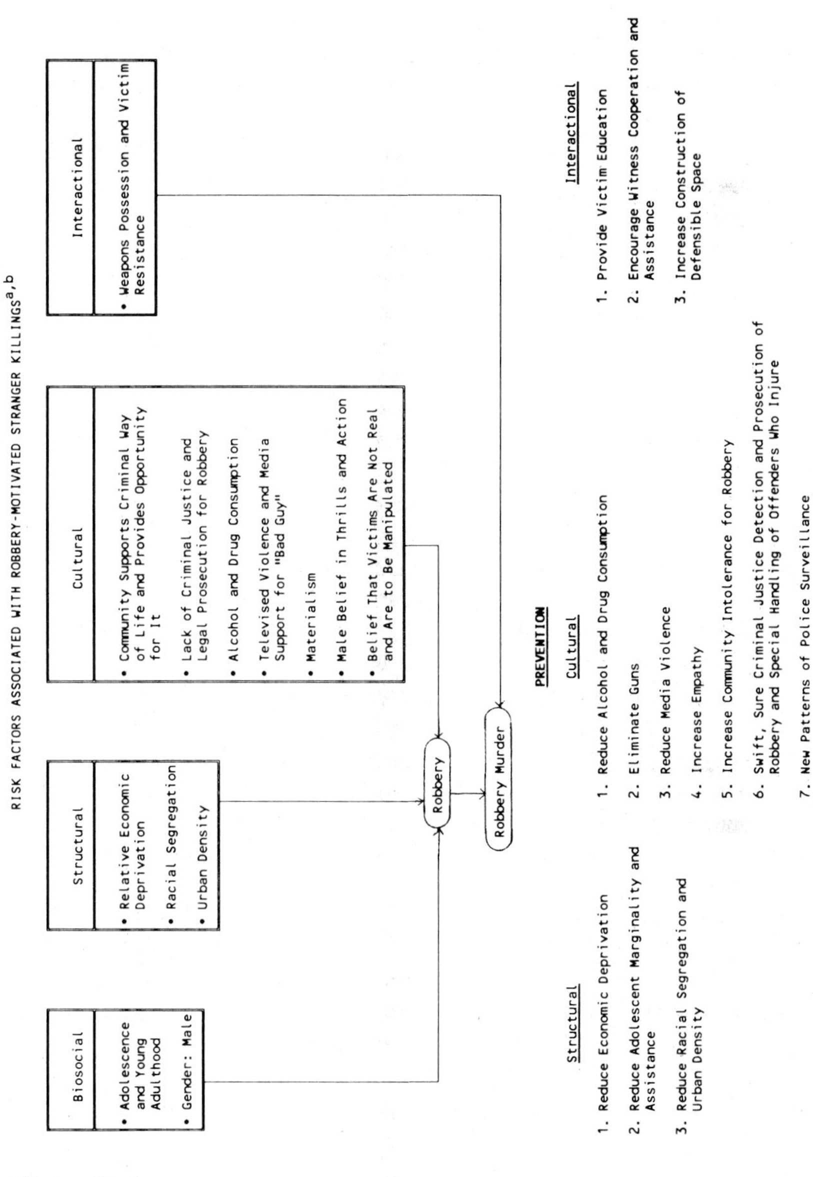

Figure 20-4.
Stranger Killings—Robbery Motivated.

to the need to protect itself from threats arising from outside the region; consequently, from the beginning, Southern identity has been linked to a siege mentality. Such a world-view supports the denial of personal responsibility and locates threats to the region as lying outside the region and, by location, locates threats to the person as lying outside the self. The siege mentality is reflected in high rates of gun ownership—the "paranoid personality"—and in a "paradoxical heritage," one that is both graceful and violent (Hackney, 1976, 534–35). Using rigorous statistical procedures as well as qualitative interpretations, Gastil (1971) supported the culture-of-violence explanation for high rates of homicide in the South.

However, Loftin and Hill (1974) took the Gastil-Hackney thesis to task, noting that Hackney and Gastil had no measure of cultural factors other than the regional variable itself. They examined a structural poverty index and found this indicator to be an important predictor of homicide rates, leading them to conclude that

> there is strong evidence that socio-economic variables are closely correlated with state homicide rates and, at least until new evidence is available, one cannot reject the hypothesis that socio-economic variables are directly involved in the maintenance of high levels of interpersonal violence in the South. (722)

Deficiencies of the cultural perspective have resulted in other theoretical efforts. One of the more influential is the structural perspective which asserts that broad-scale social forces—such as lack of opportunity, institutional racism, poverty, demographic transitions, and population density—determine homicide rates. Illustrations of this approach were offered by Cloward and Ohlin (1960), who related social and economic opportunity and control structures to conflict gangs, and by Van den Berghe (1974), who argued that resource competition leads to aggression. With few exceptions, these explanations fail to examine whether structural forces operate in the same way for family, friend, and stranger killings.

Interactionist theory focuses on the behavioral interaction sequence and how it escalates into a homicide. Luckenbill (1977), in examining the various stages of the "situated transaction" in seventy homicides, described a series of "moves" made by the offender and the victim that are often influenced by other persons who are present. From this perspective, Luckenbill derived several interaction stages that the lethal transactions follow: Violence grows out of a series of provoking arguments which escalate into murder. These arguments often involve threats to identity and self-esteem, with sexual identity often being the most salient.

Integrated Approaches

According to Curtis (1975), culture is the critical intervening variable between structural determinants and violent criminal behavior. Economic marginality and institutional racism are two main structural determinants. These structural conditions are filtered through a series of contra-culture values and behaviors (e.g., physical and sexual prowess, thrill-seeking) which, when coupled with weapon possession or alcohol and drug consumption, can lead to lethal conflict.

The interactions between structural, cultural, and interactional factors comprise perhaps the most instructive way of explaining homicide. The four figures identify variables found to be related to different types of homicide. The arrows in each figure indicate the direction of causal influences.

Despite the extensive literature on violence and homicide, few authors concern themselves specifically with prevention. In an extensive bibliography on homicide (Riedel and Zahn, 1982), only 17 of the 364 bibliographic items dealt directly with prevention; and only one book (Allen, 1980) focused exclusively on this topic.

INTERVENTION STRATEGIES

If we turn to national policies, we find few focusing on violence in general or on homicide in particular. Some states and localities have developed limited programs to deal with violence. By and large, these limited interventions have been in the areas of gun control legislation, criminal justice programs, and social service delivery (e.g., police domestic disturbance teams, crisis centers for battered women, child abuse reporting requirements, career criminal prosecution, and selective incapacitation). There have been fewer attempts to reduce violence through a general reduction in economic or job marginality, support for families raising young children, or restrictions on television shows depicting violence. Each of these "nonspecific" social policies could result in not only fewer homicides but also, more generally, in a less violent and more equitable society.

Specific Interventions

Guns are the most pervasive means of committing homicide. According to the 1980 *UCR* (U.S. Department of Justice, 1981), 50 percent of all murders involved a handgun; 12 percent, another firearm; 19 percent, knives; 13 percent, other weapons; and 6 percent, bodily weapons (e.g., hands or feet).

Although the 1980 *UCR* does not classify types of homicides by types of weapons, Riedel and Zahn (1982) did so for national and city data. Nationally, approximately two-thirds of the family homicides, homicides among friends, and stranger homicides involved guns. Data from selected cities showed the same pattern, although there was a slight tendency for family homicides to involve a wider variety of lethal technologies. Clearly, guns are used in the majority of cases. However, would the elimination of guns reduce homicide rates?

Gun control can mean many things in practice. Three approaches have been evaluated: (1) mandatory prison terms for carrying a nonlicensed firearm (the Massachusetts Bartley-Fox Gun Law, 1975); (2) the prohibition of purchase, sale, and possession of handguns by residents other than law enforcement officers or members of the military (the District of Columbia's Firearms Control

Regulation Act of 1975); and (3) two-year mandatory sentences for felonies committed while possessing a firearm (Detroit, 1977).

To evaluate the Bartley-Fox Gun Law, comparisons were made between assault, gun assault, robbery, gun robbery, overall homicide, and gun homicide rates in Boston before and after the introduction of the law. The evaluation compared Boston's violent crime rates with those of a selected group of other cities. Results showed that the law substantially reduced the incidence of gun assaults (down 13.5 percent) but substantially increased armed assaults not involving guns (up 31.0 percent). The law also appeared to deter some individuals from carrying and/or using firearms. However, it did not prevent people from using alternative weapons in assaults. There was also a short-term reduction in gun robberies and an overall decline in the incidence of criminal homicide (down 38.0 percent) in the two-year period following implementation of the law. The evaluation concluded that the law's effects may have been achieved through the highly publicized nature of the law, rather than from its actual implementation. In any event, the law or its announcement had an impact on homicide, gun assaults, and gun robberies.

While firm conclusions cannot be drawn from case studies, they suggest that gun control can reduce homicide rates. However, gun control legislation must focus on owning or carrying guns rather than on mandatory sentences for crimes committed with a gun.

Gun control policies must also consider which kinds of killing these policies would affect. Cook (1981) predicted that a reduction in gun availability would cause a reduction in homicides that involve victims who are physically stronger than their killers because these victims cannot be killed easily by other means. A reduction in gun availability should therefore reduce the lethal victimization of husbands in spousal killings and the fraction of homicide victims who are youthful males.

Based on an analysis of robbery murder in fifty cities, Cook concluded that "if robbers could be deprived of guns, the robbery murder rate would fall, the robbery injury rate would rise, and robberies would be redistributed to some extent from less to more vulnerable targets" (1981, 78). Robbers, people who kill friends, and mates who kill their spouses are not "determined killers" (e.g., dedicated to committing the murder). Keeping guns out of the hands of these people could therefore save many lives because, without lethal weapons available, these incidents would remain less gravely violent. To accomplish effective gun control requires federal, state, and local cooperation in enacting legislation and the determination of which gun control methods are most influential.

Law Enforcement

The *UCR* routinely notes that "Criminal homicide is primarily a societal problem over which law enforcement has little or no control" (U.S. Department of Justice, 1981, p. 11). The police are faced with limited options, with the exception of employing domestic disturbance teams and patrolling cars as a "general preventive."

Traditionally, when the police were called to the scene of a domestic dispute, they usually responded by either making an arrest or taking no action. Other approaches had not been considered until Morton Bard began the Family Crisis Intervention Unit (FCIU) in the New York City Police Department in 1967. Officers were trained to mediate family disputes and to refer troubled family members to other social service agencies. While the results do not confirm a reduction in family homicides, they do show that changes in police procedures can reduce family assaults and injuries to police officers (Robin, 1980, 100; Steinmetz and Straus, 1974). Few other police departments have such programs. Extending this program should, therefore, be given high priority. Furthermore, extending this method to other dispute situations (e.g., between friends and neighbors) should be explored.

The most comprehensive study to date on preventive patrol (Kelling et al., 1974) examined three types of patrol in Kansas City: high-level patrol (proactive), the usual single patrol car, and no preventive patrol (reactive). The evaluators concluded that after one year of operation, the type of patrol had no effect on crime rates or on citizens' perceptions of safety.

Apprehension rates for homicide have always been higher than arrest rates for other crimes, although they have declined in recent years (dropping from 86 percent in 1970 to 71 percent in 1981). These rates have declined because stranger murders have increased. One study found that most crimes of all types are solved because someone witnessed them, informants reported them to the police, or, in those homicide cases in which the victims did not die immediately, victims identified their offenders (Greenwood, 1982, 324). When there is no social connection between the victim and the offender, as in stranger homicides, the arrest rate is low. The decline in homicide arrests suggests that new and improved apprehension methods must be devised.

Extending police patrol capabilities could be accomplished through informal neighborhood surveillance, for example, as part of town watch programs. Other means of citizen cooperation in offender apprehension and prosecution could also be tried: Silent witness programs and the provision of support and protection for those who testify could be expanded and augmented. However, these programs can prevent homicide only if there is a deterrent effect produced by enhanced apprehension and punishment.

Sanctions: Deterrence and Incapacitation

Generally, responses to homicide involve either enacting and imposing more sanctions (deterrence) or physically restraining offenders.

There is a vast literature on deterrence and incapacitation. One of the most comprehensive evaluations of this literature was conducted by the National Research Council (Blumstein, Cohen, and Nagin, 1978), which reported that a firm conclusion cannot now be made regarding deterrence effects.

Do murderers kill again? Studies on murder recidivism are rare. A summary of the few that exist indicates a low recidivism rate (Wolfgang, private communication). Whether recidivism is low because of long incarceration is currently unknown. Whether the type of social relation (family, friend, or stranger) has an impact on recidivism is also unknown.

An important prevention issue involves recidivism risks among murderers who have not been apprehended. To illustrate, there were 23,967 homicides in 1980 for which 17,975 arrests were made. Most homicides involve a single offender and a single victim. Therefore, there are about 10,000 murderers each year who remain on the streets. Until our apprehension and conviction rates increase, pressing questions pertaining to this group will go unanswered.

Incapacitation, which involves confining offenders so they cannot commit crimes while confined, is almost always used with convicted murderers. Greenwood reported that only 4 percent of those who are convicted avoid incarceration (1982, 329). Use of selective incapacitation to reduce felony-connected homicide merits consideration.

Cohen (1983) quantitatively modeled different sentencing strategies to evaluate their potential impacts and concluded that maximum incapacitative effects vary across both offenses and offender types within an offender category. For example, research must identify which type of robber is likely to commit a robbery murder. A small percentage (approximately 10 percent) of robbers commits in excess of thirty robberies per year (Greenwood, 1982, 341). Whether it is the high-rate or low-rate robbers who eventually kill is unknown and requires further analysis. Until those analyses are conducted, the potential effectiveness of selective incapacitation in reducing homicide will remain uncertain. Indeed, for some groups, selective incapacitation may be counterproductive:

> high risk youth engage in a complex exploration and learning process from their mid to late teens to the mid to late twenties. This age span is rich in transitions . . . from school to labor market and, in the typical sequence, from street crime to employment. Most high risk youths commit some crime while negotiating these transitions. . . . By selectively incapacitating them, we risk interruption of the process by which the bulk of them . . . will shortly abandon it for lower-risk crime and, in time, a place in the labor market. (Smith and Thompson, 1983, 37)

General Intervention Strategies

More general, nonspecific homicide policies would reduce economic and job difficulties, diminish isolation and stress in families, promote healthy development of children, and decrease the amount of violence portrayed by the media. Homicide studies suggest that reduction in lethal exchanges would occur, as do numerous other related studies. Rappaport and Holden (1981) formulated a rationale for the development of "nonspecific" policies to reduce violence, arguing that social policies that generally enhance the quality of life reduce the discontent and frustration which often produce deadly violence.

These policies would have to expand job opportunities at much younger ages, especially for high-risk youth, with schools facilitating work experience. Also, these policies would have to correct the critical shortage of high-quality day care, insufficient knowledge about contraception among the young, and the lack of preparation for childrearing. Furthermore, policies would have to focus on crisis and long-term care centers for children (including handicapped children), parental support groups, early identification of and intervention in child abuse, and education about nonabusive childrearing. Tax, welfare, and business policies and philosophies that promote social isolation and divide families must be reexamined. Clearly we are recommending some fundamental changes in basic social organizations. However, long-term changes, when coupled with shorter-run strategies, could reduce violence and the fear that it spawns.

REFERENCES

Allen, Nancy H. *Homicide: Perspectives on Prevention*. New York: Human Sciences Press, 1980.

Block, Richard. *Violent Crime*. Lexington, MA: Lexington Books, 1977.

Blumstein, Alfred, Jacqueline Cohen, and Daniel Nagin, eds. *Deterrence and Incapacitation: Estimating the Effects of Criminal Sanctions on Crime Rates*. Washington, DC: National Academy Press, 1978.

Cloward, Richard A. and Lloyd E. Ohlin. *Delinquency and Opportunity*. Glencoe, IL: Free Press, 1960.

Cohen, Jacqueline. "Incapacitation as a Strategy of Crime Control: Possibilities and Pitfalls." In Michael Tonry and Norval Morris, eds., *Crime and Justice: An Annual Review of Research*, 1–84. Chicago: University of Chicago Press, 1983.

Cook, Philip J., ed. *Gun Control. The Annals* 455 (1981).

Curtis, Lynn A. *Violence, Race and Culture*. Lexington, MA: D.C. Heath, 1975.

Gastil, Raymond D. "Homicide and a Regional Culture of Violence." *American Sociological Review* 36 (1971): 412–27.

Gelles, Richard J. *The Violent Home: A Study of Physical Aggression between Husbands and Wives*. Beverly Hills: Sage, 1972.

Greenwood, Peter W. "The Violent Offender in the Criminal Justice System." In Marvin E. Wolfgang and Neil A. Weiner, eds., *Criminal Violence*, 320–46. Beverly Hills: Sage, 1982.

Hackney, Sheldon. "Southern Violence." In Hugh D. Graham and Ted R. Gurr, eds., *Violence in America: Historical and Comparative Perspectives*, 393–410. Beverly Hills: Sage, 1976.

Kelling, George, T. Pate, D. Dieckman, and C. E. Brown, *The Kansas City Preventive Patrol Experiment: A Summary Report*. Washington, DC: The Police Foundation, 1974.

Loftin, Colin and Robert H. Hill. "Regional Subculture and Homicide: An Examination of the Gastil-Hackney Thesis." *American Sociological Review* 39 (1974): 714–24.

Luckenbill, David F. "Criminal Homicide as a Situated Transaction." *Social Problems* 25 (1977): 176–86.

Rappaport, Julian and Karen Holder. "Prevention of Violence: The Case for a Nonspecific Social Policy." In J. Ray Hays, Thomas Kevin Roberts, and Kenneth S. Solway, eds., *Violence and the Violent Individual*, 409–40. New York: SP Medical and Scientific Books, 1981.

Riedel, Marc and Margaret A. Zahn. *The Nature and Patterns of American Homicide: An Annotated Bibliography*. Washington, DC: U.S. Department of Justice, National Institute of Justice, 1982.

Robin, Gerald D. *Introduction to the Criminal Justice System*. New York: Harper & Row, 1980.

Smith, M. Dwayne and Robert Nash Parker. "Types of Homicide and Variation in Regional Rates." *Social Forces* 59 (1980): 136–47.
Smith, Michael E. and James W. Thompson. "Employment, Youth and Violent Crime." In Kenneth R. Feinberg, *Violent Crime in America*, 1–43. Washington, DC: National Policy Exchange, 1983.
Steinmetz, Suzanne K. and Murray A. Straus. *Violence in the Family*. New York: Dodd, Mead, 1974.
U.S. Department of Justice. *The Uniform Crime Reports: Crime in the United States, 1980*. Washington, DC: U.S. Government Printing Office, 1981.
Van der Berghe, Pierre L. "Bringing Beasts Back in: Toward a Biosocial Theory of Aggression." *American Sociological Review* 39 (1974): 777–87.
Wolfgang, Marvin E. *Patterns in Criminal Homicide*. 1958. Reprint. Montclair, NJ: Patterson Smith, 1975.
Wolfgang, Marvin E. and Franco Ferracuti. *The Subculture of Violence: Towards an Integrated Theory in Criminology*. 1967. Reprint. Beverly Hills: Sage, 1982.
Zimring, Franklin E. "Determinants of the Death Rate from Robbery: A Detroit Time Study." In Harold M. Rose, ed., *Lethal Aspects of Urban Violence*, 31–50. Lexington, MA: Lexington Books, 1977.

Capital Punishment, 1986

EXECUTIONS

Since 1930, when data on executions were first collected by the Federal Government, 3,927 executions have been conducted under civil authority. . . . Since the death penalty was reinstated by the Supreme Court in 1976, the States have executed 68 persons:[1]

1977: 1

1979: 2

1981: 1

1982: 2

1983: 5

1984: 21

1985: 18

1986: 18

A total of 12 States have carried out executions since 1977. During the period, 43 white males, 24 black males, and 1 white female have been executed. The largest number of executions occurred in Texas (20), Florida (16), Georgia (7), and Louisiana (7).

PRISONERS UNDER SENTENCE OF DEATH AT YEAREND 1986

A total of 32 States reported 1,781 persons under sentence of death on December 31, 1986, an increase of 206 or 13.1% over the count at the end of 1985. . . . States with the largest number of prisoners under sentence of death were Florida (254), Texas (236), California (176), Georgia (111), and Illinois (101).

Although 37 States (covering 77% of the Nation's adult population) had statutes authorizing the death penalty, 5 of these reported no prisoners under sentence of death at yearend (Connecticut, New Hampshire, New Mexico, South Dakota, and Vermont).

Of the 1,781 persons under sentence of death, more than three-fifths (62%) were in the South, 17% were in Western States, 15% were in the Midwest, and 5% were in the Northeastern States of New Jersey and Pennsylvania. Nearly all were male (99%), and most were white (56.5%). . . . Blacks constituted 42.1% of those under sentence of death, and another 1.4% were American Indians or Asian Americans. The States reported a total of 107 Hispanics under death sentence, 6% of the total. The largest numbers of Hispanics were held in States with relatively large Hispanic populations: Texas (36), California (22), Florida (14), Illinois (10), and Arizona (9).

The median age of those under sentence of death was nearly 32 years. Slightly more than 1% were under the age of 20, and 2% were 55 or older. The youngest offender under sentence of death was 17 years old; the oldest was 75 years old. About 1 in 10 of the inmates for whom information on education was available had not gone beyond seventh grade, but about 1 in 11 had some college education. The median level of education was 10.6 years. . . .

The 18 women under sentence of death at yearend 1986 were held in 12 States; Indiana's 3 female inmates were the most of any State. . . . Since . . . 1977, one woman has been executed.

Minimum Age

A total of 22 States specify a minimum age at which the death penalty may be imposed. . . . In some States the minimum age is specified in the capital punishment statute; in others it is, in effect, set forth in the statutory provisions that determine the age at which a juvenile may be transferred to criminal court for trial as an adult. The most frequently specified age is 18 years (9 States). Fourteen States and the Federal system report no minimum age.[2]

Method of Execution

At yearend 1986, lethal injection (17 States) and electrocution (15 States) were the most common methods of execution. . . . Eight States authorized lethal gas; four States, hanging; and two States, a firing squad. Nine States provided for more than one method of execution—lethal injection and an alternative method—generally at the election of the condemned prisoner.

NOTE

1. For the period 1977–86, the FBI reported 204,300 cases of murder and nonnegligent manslaughter and an estimated 197,920 arrests for these crimes. During the same period, 2,419 persons entered prison under sentence of death, and there were 68 executions. In 1986, there were 20,610 reported murders and nonnegligent manslaughters, 19,190 arrests, 297 persons who entered prison under a death sentence, and 18 executions.

[2. The Supreme Court in June 1989 ruled that states must set a minimum age in the application of the death penalty at no lower than 16 years (*Wilkins v. Missouri*).]

Capital Punishment in Perspective

William J. Bowers

Death has been justified as an appropriate retribution and a necessary deterrent for the crimes that most offend the public conscience. Yet in practice we find no evidence of its alleged unique deterrent power, and we observe that as retribution it has been contingent on the offender's race and that of his victim. And, . . . paradoxically, . . . *the death penalty has been most widely prescribed and imposed where its use has departed most conspicuously from standards of just retribution and effective deterrence*. That is, in the South where most executions have occurred its retributive justification is obviously questionable in view of the discriminatory way in which it has been applied, and its deterrent power is plainly doubtful in view of the relatively high rates of criminal homicide in this region. Could it be that the death penalty has other functions in society which outweigh those of retribution and deterrence and which govern where and when it will be most widely employed?

The evidence of racial discrimination in the administration of capital punishment suggests that the death penalty may have served as an instrument of *minority group oppression*—to keep blacks in the South in a position of subjugation and subservience. The fact that the death penalty for rape has been imposed primarily on blacks whose victims were whites suggests that the death penalty was used as an instrument of *majority group protection*—to secure the integrity of the white family and community in the face of threats or perceived challenges from blacks. . . .

Or, the fact that executions in America rose to a high point during the economic depression of the 1930s suggests that the death penalty may have served as a *repressive response* to conditions of social dislocation and turmoil in this time of economic hardship. It is true that the incidence of homicide increased during this period, but the increase in executions was even more substantial—the *execution rate* peaked in this period ([Bowers 1974:] Table 1-4). Perhaps the more frequent use of the death penalty served to relieve public anxiety about high or rising offense rates. . . .

Is it not possible that such extra legal functions as majority group protection, minority group oppression, and repressive response, are more fundamental to the use of capital punishment in society than are the legal functions of retribution and deterrence—that they dictate where and when the death penalty will be most widely used and that they cause the legal functions of capital punishment to be displaced and compromised? . . .

HISTORICAL PERSPECTIVE

The death penalty has an ancient history. The best known of all executions—those of Socrates and Jesus—were performed in the ancient world. However, the impression that capital punishment was particularly favored or common among ancient or primitive peoples appears to be mistaken. The death penalty fell into disuse during the time of the Roman Republic, and indeed it was subjected to many of the same challenges voiced in modern parliamentary debates (Green 1929; reprinted in Sellin 1967).

Ironically, the widespread adoption and use of capital punishment in the Western World came with the ascendancy of the Christendom in the Middle Ages. The pre-Christian Barbaric Codes contained fewer crimes and milder punishments in general than did the codes of the twelfth and thirteenth centuries in western Europe (Sorokin 1937, vol. 2, 584 ff., esp. table 42). . . .

Even more ironically, the most gruesome and torturous forms of execution were invented under religious auspices. The rack, the wheel, the iron maiden, burning at the stake, and impaling in the grave are but a few of the diabolical methods devised and employed in the name of religion to cause protracted suffering before death. Such diabolical tortures were devised especially for heretics and justified as a means of extracting confession and repentance and thus holding out the possibility of salvation for the heretic. . . .

The religious basis for capital punishment was clearly evident in the "Capital Laws" of Massachusetts circa 1641. The first three capital crimes to be named were religious in character [(worshipping other than the true God, witchcraft, and blasphemy).] . . . And indeed, biblical authority was cited for each of the remaining twelve capital crimes, which included murder (premeditated, passionate, or guileful), rape (of a minor or married woman, though execution was discretionary in the case of an unmarried female), bestiality, homosexuality, adultery, kidnapping, false witness, and treason [(Haskins 1956)]. . . .

With the demise of religious hegemony in Europe and the rise of national monarchies, occurring at about the fourteenth century, the number of offenses in the criminal codes again increased and the prescribed punishments appear to have become even more severe on the average (Sorokin 1937, vol. 2, 584 ff., esp. table 42). Furthermore, this change from medieval to early modern times showed another substantial change in the structure of the criminal laws with political crimes displacing religious ones, particularly on the list of capital offenses. Death was still the punishment for those who challenged the basis of authority in society, but the secular state had displaced the Church as the authority that might be offended.

The state rivaled the church in devising ungodly and grotesque methods of execution for those who committed crimes against the primary authority. And such punishment was the executioner's duty as late as 1812 when seven men convicted of high treason were sentenced as follows:

> That you and each of you, be taken to the place from when you came, and from thence be drawn on a hurdle to the place of execution, where you shall be hanged by the neck not till you are dead; that you be severally taken down, while yet alive, and your bowels be taken out and burned before your faces—that your heads be then cut off, and your bodies cut into four quarters, to be at the king's disposal. And God have mercy on your souls. (Quoted in Scott 1950, 179)

The purpose of such a ghastly execution for political crimes was surely not so much to test the beliefs of the victim, as it was to eliminate him and to dissuade his followers from the pretensions to political power. . . .

Notably, executions appear to have reached their highest level in English history during the period of turmoil and political consolidation that followed Henry VIII's break with the religious domination of the papacy. The number of executions annually is believed to have quadrupled after Henry's break with the Catholic Church. . . .

Struggles for control of the state at other times and places have also led to the widespread use of capital punishment. In twentieth century Russia, for example, the unsuccessful Revolution of 1905–1907 brought with it an enormous increase in the use of the death penalty. In the years from 1881 through 1905 there were ordinarily no more than twenty executions per year in Russia. Then, as the Revolution got under way, the annual number of executions increased to 547, 1139, and 1340 during 1906, 1907, and 1908, respectively. . . . Concerning the successful Russian Revolution of 1917, Sorokin (1937, vol. 2, 601) has written:

> According to the most conservative estimate, which certainly understates the real number, during the years 1917 to 1922, at least 600,000 (!) persons were executed. The executions during the subsequent years, especially from 1929 to 1935, have also to be counted by the tens of thousands. . . .

Eighteenth Century England

With the development of commerce and industry in England, the number of capital offenses expanded from eight major crimes at the end of the fifteenth century (including high treason, petty treason, murder, larceny, robbery, burglary, rape and arson) to some 223 offenses by 1819, according to one estimate (as reported by Radzinowicz 1948, vol. 1, 4). At least a hundred capital offenses were added during the agricultural and industrial revolutions of the eighteenth century alone. By and large, new capital statutes extended the death penalty to offenses against property and commerce, evidently to protect economic interests within

English society. . . . [P]roperty offenses accounted for the overwhelming majority of capital convictions and executions in eighteenth century England. . . .

. . . [M]urder constituted less than 5 percent of the capital convictions and only about 10 percent of the executions. Thus, throughout the eighteenth century the application of the death penalty, as well as the statutes providing for its use, seem to have served the interests of private property and commerce.

This unprecedented extension of capital punishment to property offenses occurred at a time of accumulating wealth in the shops and warehouses of England's cities and of growing poverty, idleness, and vagrancy in their streets. . . . In short, the economic growth of the eighteenth century brought with it an impoverished, exploited, and alienated working class which first threatened the property and later the dominant position of the aristocrats and gentry who controlled Parliament throughout this century.

Then, during a period of political reform that included expanding representation for the middle classes in Parliament, emancipation for slaves in the British Empire, and protections for workers in the factories of England, executions for property offenses virtually disappeared. . . .

Convictions for murder remained at 5 percent or less of all capital convictions, as they had throughout the eighteenth century, but executions for murder climbed from their earlier level of about one out of ten to six out of ten in 1835. From this time on, murder accounted for most of the executions in England, and with the penal code revision of 1863, it became the only effective cause of executions, although treason and piracy remained capital offenses, until 1965 when England abolished the death penalty. . . .

Nineteenth [and Twentieth] Century America

In America, too, changing economic and social conditions had a profound impact on the character of the capital statutes. By 1785, when Massachusetts had been transformed from a Puritan colony into a center of trade and commerce and the patriotic sentiments associated with the Revolutionary War were still ripe, treason and piracy had entered and moved to the head of the list of capital statutes of the Commonwealth of Massachusetts, and idolatry, witchcraft, and blasphemy were no longer punishable by death (*Law Reporter* 1846, 387).

But the more dramatic change in capital statutes in America—one that rivaled the expansion of capital statutes in England as a response to changing social and economic conditions—occurred with the growth of slavery and the development of a large scale plantation economy in the South. In contrast with the eight or so capital crimes of Massachusetts and Pennsylvania in the post-revolutionary period, North Carolina, for example, had some twenty-six capital crimes in 1837, including . . . slave stealing[,] concealing a slave with intent to free him[,] inciting slaves to insurrection (second conviction)[, and] circulating seditious literature among slaves (second conviction). These four offenses obviously reflect the character of slaves as valuable property free of outside interference. . . .

Perhaps more portentous than the proliferations of capital statutes to protect the institution of slavery was the differentiation of capital offenses for blacks and whites. Thus, for example, in Virginia in the 1830s there were five capital crimes for whites; for black slaves the offenses punishable by death numbered seventy by one count (Spear 1844, 227–231). In 1848 a blanket statute was passed in the Virginia Assembly requiring the death penalty for blacks for any offense that was punishable by three or more years imprisonment for white freemen. . . .

Still further differentiation by race was provided in rape statutes which specified punishment according to the race of both offender and victim. In 1816, Georgia explicitly required the death penalty for a slave or "freeman of colour" who raped or attempted to rape a white female; while at the same time, reducing the minimum sentence from seven to two years and removing "hard labor" for a white convicted of rape. And, for a white convicted of raping a slave woman or a free woman of color, the punishment was a fine and/or imprisonment at the discretion of the court (NAACP Legal Defense and Education Fund, Inc., brief for *Jackson* 1971, Appendix B). . . .

With the Emancipation Proclamation of 1864[,] . . . [a]ll men were punishable for their crimes according to the codes for white freemen. Yet neither the Proclamation nor the period of Reconstruction that followed seriously altered the long-standing and deeply felt sentiments behind these [discriminatory] Black Codes. . . . And predictably, as Reconstruction ended, the white majority reasserted its dominance. . . .

[L]ynching provided a de facto extra-legal restoration of the antebellum Black Codes. Although we lack data on the use of the death penalty in the antebellum South, we do have relatively comprehensive information on lynchings in the late nineteenth century ([Bowers 1974:] Table 2-3). These data show that such extra-legal executions—directed primarily against blacks in the South—far outnumbered all legally imposed executions under state and local authority in America during the last two decades of the nineteenth century. . . .

For the twentieth century, the characteristics of those who have been executed in America are a matter of record. Most of the executions in this century were imposed in the South and most of those executed were blacks. . . . Particularly in the South, blacks have been executed for lesser offenses, at younger ages, and more often without appeals. . . . And for rape, the death penalty has been reserved out of all proportion for blacks whose victims were white. . . . Other studies . . . have revealed racial discrimination in capital cases at indictment, conviction, sentencing, and execution. And, although the data have been less adequately developed, there are strong indications of discrimination against the socially deprived and impoverished in the administration of capital punishment [(Bowers 1974, chapters 3–4)]. . . .

It is doubtful whether the death penalty has ever been applied in a strictly uniform manner to offenders from all strata of society. Historically, "Benefit of Clergy" and "Royal Prerogative" have protected higher echelons of society and given the Crown discretion to discriminate in its own interests. . . . In this century, American society appears to have tolerated the use of the death penalty only against the racially subjugated and the impoverished. . . .

If the death penalty has been used to protect dominant interests in society, it appears equally to have been used to oppress disenfranchised and dispossessed minorities. . . . The evidence of racial discrimination in capital punishment in twentieth century America is now hardly contestable. And there is mounting evidence that social class may also have served as a basis for the discriminatory treatment of capital offenders within the criminal justice system. Indeed, the research on social class suggests that discrimination against the socially deprived and impoverished may have been quite pronounced outside of the South, and that it may, in fact, account for some of the racial disparity in treatment inside the South.

The essential feature of poverty and racial subjugation is their dehumanizing effect. These conditions breed contemptuous stereotypes which deprive people of their human qualities in the eyes of others and even in their own eyes if they are sensitive to prevailing social definitions. Injustices against them evoke little sympathy, and their deaths cause little remorse. Indeed, the death penalty can be—and surely has been—used even carelessly and arbitrarily against such powerless victims without generating substantial concern or objection. . . .

COMPARATIVE PERSPECTIVE

The legacy of the Enlightenment and its expression in the French and American Revolutions was a new[-]found dignity and newly proclaimed rights for all men. . . . Inspired by the Enlightenment, Caesar Beccaria's attack on the death penalty in 1764 led to criminal code reforms including the abolition of capital punishment in several European countries—Russia, Austria, and Tuscany—in the late eighteenth century. And while these initial reforms did not last, they marked the beginning of a movement that was evident throughout most of the nineteenth and twentieth centuries. In 1848, France abolished the death penalty for all political crimes; in 1863, England effectively restricted the death penalty to murder, though it remained on the books for treason and piracy. Some eleven nations abandoned or abolished capital punishment in the nineteenth century and remained abolitionist thereafter; others, like Italy, abolished it in the nineteenth century, but restored it under fascism for a period in the twentieth century. . . .

The movement away from capital punishment gained momentum in the twentieth century, particularly in the years since World War II. This accelerating pace of abolition is highlighted in the fact that virtually half of the abolitions . . . have occurred since 1940. The rapid expansion of abolitionist ranks after the Second World War was undoubtedly linked to the experience of atrocities and brutality before and during the War. . . .

In addition to the growing abolitionist ranks, many countries that retain the death penalty have used it only rarely in recent years. A survey of the use of the death penalty for the period 1958–1962, with responses from 128 countries, identified some 89 countries which provided for capital punishment. . . .

Of the [535] executions reported annually during this period, [268] were performed in just four of the 89 countries with capital punishment; and the

United States, despite two decades of decline in executions by that time, was one of these four, [contributing 9.2%. (The other three were South Africa, 18.7%; Korea, 12.7%; and Nigeria, 9.5%.)] . . .

. . . [F]ive . . . societal characteristics we have examined are associated, in one way or another, with the availability or use of the death penalty. Political Centralization and [I]ncomplete [I]ncorporation . . . [are related to] the availability of capital punishment with only minor variations between highly and less developed nations. Political Instability . . . [is also associated with] the use of capital punishment. . . . Political Coerciveness displays effects primarily among the highly developed nations; it is the most decisive . . . predictor of trends . . . [against] abolition, and it appears to have a noteworthy effect on the availability of capital punishment as well. Likewise, [G]roup [D]iscrimination shows an effect only among highly developed nations, but in this case it is with respect to the actual use of capital punishment. The ability of these few variables to predict the presence and use of the death penalty is reasonably strong by standards of social science research. . . . [This research is based on Patrick's (1965) survey.]

And what about the fact that around the world capital punishment has been associated with the centralization and coercive use of power, the presence of internal instability and strife, and deprivation and poverty of large numbers of people, and the failure to incorporate or represent diverse social elements in national political structure? In England and America, the use of the death penalty has been historically associated with conditions of servitude and exploitation of labor and political and legal disenfranchisement of oppressed or minority groups. Quite recently in the United States and South Africa, the death penalty has been used against ethnic and racial groups in ways that defy justification by any standard of legal punishment. . . . Tradition, unfamiliarity, and for some the desire for vengeance, may have deadened our moral sensibilities about the inhumane character of capital punishment. . . . The fact that the victims of the executioner have been the most inarticulate and dispossessed members of society may have blinded society to the moral reality of such charges, but it does not refute their validity. . . .

REFERENCES

[Bowers, William J. *Executions in America*. Lexington, MA: Lexington Books, 1974.]

Green, W. M. "An Ancient Debate on Capital Punishment." *Classical Journal* 241 (1929): 267. Reprinted, with some Latin passages rendered in English, in Sellin, p. 46.

Haskins, G. L. "The Capitall Lawes of New England." *Harv. L. School Bull.* 7 (1956): 10.

Law Reporter, "Capital Punishment in the United States." *Law Reporter* (March 1846): 487.

NAACP Legal Defense and Educational Fund, Inc., . . . 69-5030 (1971), Brief for Petitioner in *Jackson v. Georgia*, O.T. 1971 No. 69-5030 (prepared by attorneys for the N.A.A.C.P. Legal Defense and Educational Fund, Inc.).

Patrick, C. H. "The Status of Capital Punishment; A World Perspective." *J.C.L.C. & P.S.* 56 (1965): 397.

Radzinowicz, L. *A History of English Criminal Law and Its Administration From 1750.* London: Stevens & Sons Limited, Volume 1 (1948); Volumes 2 and 3 (1956); Volume 4 (1968).
Scott, G. R. *The History of Capital Punishment.* Ann Arbor, Mich.: Finch Press Reprints, 1950.
Sellin, T. *Capital Punishment.* N.Y.: Harper & Row, 1967.
Sorokin, P. A. *Social and Cultural Dynamics.* New York: Bedminster Press, 1937.
Spear, C. *Essays on the Punishment of Death.* Boston: by the author, 1844; London: John Green, 1844.

The Death Penalty: A Debate [A.] The Abolitionist Rests

John P. Conrad

Whatever the outcome of this debate in the minds of our readers, it is clear to me—and, of course, to my stern opponent as well—that at this stage of our history, capital punishment is a winning cause in America, if nowhere else in the civilized world. Abolitionists may win some of their cases in the courts, in spite of the retentionists' furious denial that the courts should have jurisdiction over the nature and quality of the punishment that the state may impose on criminals. It is still possible for abolitionists to attain high office from the electorate and subsequently to "sabotage" the executioner's craft by commuting the sentences of condemned murderers. Nevertheless, I must gloomily concede that the public opinion polls, in which the hangman now receives a handsome plurality of the respondents' votes, are corroborated in statewide referendums. If the general public has its way, Dr. van den Haag's cause is won, and without the benefit of his robust arguments.

I construe this predilection for the executioner as the outcome of the common man's yearning for a tough stand, a hard line, a crushing response to the nation's surfeit of criminals. The common man may never have met a criminal, but he knows what will deter him and what he deserves—the gallows, no less, or its local equivalent. In this certainty, the electorate is encouraged by demagogues who tell the world that the return of the executioner will signal to criminals everywhere that they can no longer expect leniency from the courts, and that the state will resume an implacable severity that prevented crimes in the old days and will soon prevent it again.

What humbug! Political candidates and their advisors know that, regardless of the deterrent value of the gallows, the death penalty has nothing to do with the nonhomicidal criminal. The arduous and costly tasks that society must undertake if crime is to be prevented still have to be defined and faced—even if we settle on an unswerving program of killing all murderers and stick to it. The signal that is really conveyed by the noose and the electric chair will be understood by thoughtful criminals and ignored by the reckless. That signal will tell those who receive it that Americans do not understand the crime problem in spite of all the exposure they have had. Whether thoughtful or reckless, criminals know that neither the gallows nor the prison awaits them, whatever their offense may be, if they are not caught, prosecuted, and convicted. They know that the police do not catch them often enough (although there is reason to suppose that most are eventually arrested), that busy prosecutors are only too willing to settle for a guilty plea to crimes less serious than those with which they are charged, and that, if they are convicted in court, the chance of probation is pretty good unless the crime is so heinous as to have become a matter of public notoriety.

Under the circumstances, how can the criminal justice system deter any man or woman desperate enough to gamble on engaging in a criminal career? The police solve a higher percentage of homicides than any other crime reported to them, but, as my well-informed opponent never tires of pointing out, the number of murders increases every year at an unacceptable rate. There are plenty of potential killers who will accept the 70–30 odds against them, perhaps because they calculate that well-planned murders by disinterested and anonymous murderers constitute most of the 30% that are uncleared. Spouse-killers and rapist-murderers are usually brought to justice, homicidal robbers and contract hit men almost never.

We distract public attention from the expensive requirements of more police, more courts, and more prisons in the stentorian advocacy of capital punishment as a panacea for violent crime. The public officials responsible for this clamor know better. They also know that the execution of a contemptible killer comes cheap, compared to all the measures that must be taken to combat crime effectively.

I do not include my profoundly reflective opponent among the disingenuous office-seekers, office-holders, and editorialists who have somehow convinced the majority of the public that killing killers is the solution to the crime problem. Dr. van den Haag has for many years been a sincere believer in the efficacy of the death penalty as a deterrent of homicide, just as he has advocated more severe punishment for those who commit lesser crimes. . . . His case for the resumption of the death penalty is rational and well argued. He is undisturbed by the overwhelming rejection of his argument by psychologists, sociologists, economists, and statisticians—with the lonely and generally discredited exception of Dr. Isaac Ehrlich.[1]

What a stark and dismal world my bleak opponent contemplates! . . . In this van den Haagian world, everyone must be on his guard against every neighbor, for everyone is a potential murderer, prevented from committing the most horrible of crimes only by the tenuous threat of the death penalty. Especially likely to commit such crimes are the poor, who enviously observe the comfortable classes and determine to take by force what they could not gain by merit and industry.

The vertiginously rising crime rate must be attributed in very large part to the desperation of the underclasses. It follows that these people must be stringently controlled. The death penalty must be imposed on those of them who carry their crimes to the point of killing.

When pressed for evidence of the superior deterrent effect of capital punishment, as compared with life imprisonment, Dr. van den Haag will first assert that the lack of evidence does not prove that the death penalty does not deter potential killers; it merely means that statisticians and social scientists have yet to discover a methodology to prove what is self-evident to the ordinary citizen with rudimentary common sense. For those who are unimpressed with this reasoning, he invokes the ancient *lex talionis*; it is right that unlawful killers should themselves be killed.

That is a symmetry that cannot be achieved with respect to any other crime. Rapists cannot be raped; robbers cannot be robbed; burglars cannot be burglarized. The state cannot retaliate against these criminals by treating them as they treated their victims. It is nevertheless possible for the state to kill, as it must—in my righteous opponent's opinion—when a man or a woman stands convicted of murder. Only because murder, the crime of crimes, is punishable by death is it regarded with proper horror. Any lesser response would trivialize the death of an innocent victim.

I say that nothing can trivialize murder. Good men and women abhor violence and particularly abhor it when it is homicidal. To suppose that ordinary citizens will accept murder as a matter of course unless the executioner impresses the horror of it upon them is to state a case for which there is not the slightest supporting evidence. It is a misanthropic fallacy that emerges from the most pessimistic misinterpretation of Freudian doctrine—that all human beings are potential killers, restrained from acting on their primitive and destructive urges only by the threat of extreme punishment. The truth is that in this violent country, where the punishment of criminals is more severe than in any other nation except the Soviet Union and South Africa, fewer than 20,000 murderers are found each year—less than .01% of our total population. Even if we adjust the population at risk by discounting the infants and the aged, even if we allow for the murders that take place and are not recognized as such, and even if we allow for the murderous assaults in which the victim survived, our annual crop of killers could not exceed .05% of the population. Perhaps there is another .05% of potential killers who have abstained from murder for one reason or another, and we have 0.1% of the population to worry about. Call for a ten-year cohort of these killers and potential killers and we can elevate the danger level to 1%. But what reason is there to believe that the remaining 99% are restrained only by the threat of the hangman? Is a society imbued with this belief about its members better than a nation of paranoids?

I insist that the murderer is an exceptional person and so is the citizen who can be persuaded only by threats to abstain from acts of violence. Let the reader consider his own experience and his observation of his friends and enemies. How many truly murderous men, women, and children does he know?

The anachronism that is capital punishment originated in an era when physical punishments were all that could be imposed on criminals. In this debate we have both alluded often to the old days when sentences of truly horrifying cruelty were imposed on men and women guilty of crimes far less grave than capital murder. It is a stain on Western civilization that children could be hanged for theft, men could be broken on the rack for robbery, and women burned to death for witchcraft and adultery as recently as the eighteenth and nineteenth centuries, when many of the brightest achievements of European and American culture flowered. It should not have taken so long for a man like Beccaria to emerge with a protest against the evils of punishment as administered in the eighteenth century, or for men like Bentham and Romilly to make their case against the idiocies of nineteenth century criminal justice in England.[2] . . . The only way to understand the diehards of the times is to remember the dread in the upper classes that upheavals like the French Revolution might take place in their own countries if social controls were eased. . . . The impassioned arguments in favor of the hangman in both the English Houses of Parliament exposed the transparent apprehensions of the privileged and their trust in the gallows as the best possible prevention of crime. Those were the days when there were over 200 offenses in the statutes that called for execution.

Romilly and his friends prevailed, as did their counterparts elsewhere in Europe. Their success may be partly laid to Yankee ingenuity, which had contributed the penitentiary to the administration of criminal justice. It was adopted with alacrity throughout Europe. The penitentiary is not the brightest gem of American social technology, but it is a feasible alternative to capital punishment. The whip was eliminated for ordinary offenders, and the gallows was reserved for murderers.

The question that I have raised so often in this debate must be confronted again: *Why should we retain capital punishment when a life sentence in prison will serve the deterrent purpose at least as well?*

Implicit in that question is my complete disbelief that there exists a population of potential murderers who would be deterred by the gallows—or the lethal needle—but would proceed with their killings if the worst they could expect was a life sentence in prison. If such extraordinary people exist, a supposition for which there is absolutely no evidence, they would be balanced by an equally extraordinary, and equally hypothetical, few who are tempted to commit murder to achieve the notoriety of public execution. There may be a few in each of these classes, but in the absence of any positive evidence of their existence in significant numbers, no debating points can be claimed for them by either side.

The adequacy of a life sentence in prison as a deterrent to murder—if deterrence is truly our aim—is obvious to those who know what that experience does to the prisoner. The term begins in ignominy. It is lived out in squalor. It ends when youth is long since gone, or, more often than most people know, in the death of the senile in a prison ward for the aged and infirm. Those who fancy that life in prison bears any resemblance to the gaiety of a resort hotel or the luxury of a country club have been beguiled by dishonest demagogues. Commitment to an American prison is a disaster for all but the most vicious human predators, men who discover a false manhood in the abuse of the weak. The unique combination of ennui and chronic dread of one's fellows, of idleness and wasted years, and of lives spent with wicked, vicious, or inane men and women should be—and for most people certainly is—a terrifying deterrent prospect. Those who find it tolerable are manifesting the meaninglessness of their lives before commitment. . . .

It is natural in our goal-oriented culture to adopt the deterrent theory. It promises to accomplish steps toward the prevention of the worst of crimes with each cadaver hauled away from the place of execution. Some day, the retentionist hopes, science will justify the killing by showing the effectiveness of capital punishment as measured by the numbers of innocent lives saved. This is the hope that Dr. van den Haag and his friends express so ardently. . . .

To suppose that the criminal justice system can or should prevent crime is to expect too much of it and too little of the larger social system of which criminal justice is only a part. I contend that the criminal justice system must be process-oriented, not engaged in achieving goals that are beyond its reach. The police should be efficient in apprehending criminals, the courts should be fair in trying them, and the penal system should be humane but secure. The process-oriented hanging of criminals as their just desert for the crime of murder is an archaism surviving from a bygone and primitive age. The assertion that some day it will be shown that it is a necessary deterrent to murder is, at best, a naïve indulgence in wishful thinking.

Throughout this debate I have insisted on the primacy of retributivism in the administration of justice. My utilitarian opponent scorns retributivism as a theory, and in the strict sense in which that word is used by scientists, he may be right.[3] He supposes that deterrence qualifies as a theory because it may be subjected to verification tests. . . .

I do indeed hold that it is necessary to punish crimes in the interest of retribution.[4] There are enough empirical supports for the notion that punishment will deter in many situations. There are none at all for the notion that the death penalty will deter criminals more effectively than a protracted prison sentence. I do not accept the argument that punishment is intrinsically wrong, but I do hold that punishment must not be inflicted beyond simple necessity. It is not necessary to punish anyone with a sanction more severe than the gravity of the crimes committed and the criminal's record of recidivism for serious crimes. I see no great problem in achieving a consensus on the scale of sanctions, with a life term in prison for the first degree murderer at the apex of the scale.

The rule is that we should punish no more than we must. The death penalty is needless in an age when the maximum-security prison is available. Adherence to the principle of necessity as the limiting factor in determining the nature and quality of punishment will go far toward preventing our nation from ever descending to the horrible depths of degraded justice that are to be seen in Eastern Europe, in South Africa, and in Argentina.

The executioner does what he has to do in behalf of the citizens of the state that employs him. His hand is on the lever that releases the cyanide, switches on the current, or springs the trap. We, as citizens, cannot escape a full share of his responsibility. We voted into office the legislators who make killers of us all. If the deliberate killing of another human being is the most abhorrent of crimes, we are all guilty, even though we shall be scot-free from legal punishment. The pity and terror that an execution inspires in even the most callous is punishment enough for the perceptive citizen. Pity and terror, mixed with the knowledge that what has been done is futile.

As my stoical opponent has repeatedly reminded us, we must all die. Many of us will die in conditions far more painful than sudden oblivion from a whiff of gas or a lethal charge of electricity. None of us has to inflict death on another. The statutes that make such deaths occasionally possible must be repealed in the interest of decency and good conscience. The sooner the better.

NOTES

1. Isaac Ehrlich, "The Deterrent Effect of Capital Punishment: A Question of Life or Death," *American Economic Review* 65 (1975): 397–417.
2. Cesare Beccaria, *On Crimes and Punishment*, trans. Henry Paolucci (1764; reprinted Indianapolis, IN: Bobbs-Merrill, 1963).
3. On the usage, "theories of punishment," to which Dr. van den Haag has objected, see H. L. A. Hart, *Punishment and Responsibility* (Oxford: Clarendon Press, 1968), p. 70: "theories of punishment are not theories in any normal sense. They are not, as scientific theories are, assertions or contentions as to what is or is not the case. . . . On the contrary, those major positions concerning punishment which are called deterrent or retributive or reformative 'theories' of punishment are *moral* claims as to what justifies the practice of punishment—claims as to why, morally, it should or may be used." Hart goes on to write that if we claim that capital punishment protects society from harm, then we should call "this implicit moral claim 'the utilitarian position.'" I agree with Hart's fastidious use of terms, but the word *theory* is by now too deeply embedded in criminological discourse to be summarily uprooted.
4. I readily concede that I am too squeamish to justify punishment for the sake of vengeance. I insist that there is a significant difference between primitive vengeance—the *lex talionis* of Hammurabi, Leviticus, and the Twelve Tables of republican Rome—and the denunciatory, reprobative functions of retribution.

[B.] The Advocate Advocates

Ernest van den Haag

*T*here are two basic arguments for the death penalty; they are independent of, yet consistent with, one another.

The first argument is moral: The death penalty is just; it is deserved for certain crimes. One can explain why one feels that certain crimes deserve the death penalty. But as usual with moral arguments, one cannot show this conviction to be *factually* correct (or, for that matter, incorrect) since moral arguments rest not on facts but on our evaluation of them. My evaluation leads me to believe that, e.g., premeditated murder or treason (a fact) is so grave and horrible a crime (an evaluation) as to deserve nothing less than the death penalty, that only the death penalty (a fact) is proportionate to the gravity of the crime (an evaluation). My widely shared view is opposed by abolitionists, who claim that the death penalty is unjust for any crime, and inconsistent with human dignity. Professor Conrad's arguments in favor of this position seem unconvincing to me. Since most abolitionists believe, as I do, that punishments should be proportionate to the perceived gravity of crimes, the abolitionist claim seems to me logically precarious. It implies either that murder is not so horrible after all—not horrible enough, at any rate, to deserve death—or that the death penalty is too harsh a punishment for it, and indeed for any conceivable crime. I find it hard to believe that one can hold either view seriously, let alone both. But I am wrong: Professor Conrad does, and he is by no means alone in the academic world.

I must confess that I have never understood the assorted arguments claiming that the death penalty is inconsistent with human dignity or that, somehow, society has no right to impose it. One might as well claim that death generally, or at least death from illness, is inconsistent with human dignity, or that birth is, or any suffering or any undesirable social condition. Most of these are unavoidable. At least death by execution can be avoided by not killing someone else, by not committing murder. One can preserve one's dignity in this respect if one values it. Incidentally, execution may be physically less humiliating and painful than death in a hospital. It is, however, morally more humiliating and meant to be: It indicates the extreme blame we attach to the crime of murder by deliberately expelling the murderer from among the living.

As for the dignity of society, it seems to me that by executing murderers it tries to keep its promise to secure the lives of innocents, to vindicate the law, and to impose retribution on those who so horribly violate it. To do anything less would be inconsistent with the dignity of society.

I see no evidence for society somehow not having "the right" to execute murderers. It has always done so. Traditional laws and Scriptures have always supported the death penalty. I know of no reasoning, even in a religious (theocratic) state, that denies the right of secular courts to impose it. We in America have a secular republic, of course, and therefore, the suggestion that the right to punish belongs only to God, or that the right to impose capital punishment does, is clearly out of place. It is not a religious but a secular task to put murderers to death. Our Constitution does provide for it (Amendments V and XIV). However much we believe in divine justice, it is to occur after, not in, this life. As for justice here and now, it is done by the courts, which are authorized in certain cases to impose the death penalty. . . .

The second argument in favor of capital punishment is material, grounded on empirical facts. They are contested, . . . but no one would deny that what is contested are facts. The factual question is: Does the death penalty deter murder more than life imprisonment, or does it make no difference?

I do not agree with Professor Conrad's wishful idea that the work of Professor Isaac Ehrlich has been discredited. I believe that Ehrlich's findings—that the death penalty does indeed deter more than any other penalty currently inflicted, so that each execution saves between seven and nine innocent lives, the lives of victims who will not be murdered in the year of execution because of the deterrent effects of executions—have been confirmed by subsequent studies and have stood up sturdily under criticism competent and incompetent, which Ehrlich has convincingly refuted. However, Ehrlich's work is controversial. Anything is, if a sufficient number of people attack it. It is fair, therefore, to say that although the preponderance of evidence is now supporting the hypothesis that capital punishment deters more than any other punishment, the statistical demonstration has not been conclusive enough to convince everybody. Certainly not Professor Conrad and his friends. They have not changed their pre-Ehrlich convictions, and indeed tend to dismiss his work.

But Conrad's fellow abolitionists have admitted that they would want to abolish the death penalty even if it were shown statistically that each execution does reduce the homicide rate by 500 murders per year. Why then worry about statistical proof? And why take seriously people so irrational that they would sacrifice the lives of 500 innocents to preserve the life of one convicted murderer?

Statistics have their place. But here I think they scarcely are needed. Harsher penalties are more deterrent than milder ones. Not only does our whole criminal justice system accept this view; we all do to the extent to which deterrence is aimed at in our everyday life. All other things equal, we penalize our children, our friends, or our business partners the more harshly the more we feel we must deter them and others in the future from a wrong they have done. Social life would not be possible if we did not believe that we can attract people to actions we desire by giving them incentives, and deter them from actions we do not desire by disincentives. The incentives and disincentives are usually proportionate to the felt desirability or undesirability of what we want to attract to or deter from. Why should murder be an exception? Why should we not believe that the greatest disincentive—the threat of death—is most likely to be the greatest deterrent?

Where there is life there is hope. This certainly is one major argument in favor of the death penalty. The murderer who premeditates his crime—and crimes of passion are not subject to capital punishment—if he contemplates the risk of life imprisonment is not likely to believe that, if convicted, he will remain in prison for life. He knows, however inchoately, about parole, pardons, commutations—he believes above all that he, a smart and superior fellow, will find a way to escape. Few prisoners actually do escape. But practically all "lifers" believe that they will, at least when they start their sentence. So believing, they do not greatly fear a sentence of life imprisonment and are not deterred by it. This is why the rate of stranger-murders—murders in which victim and murderer do not know one another and to which the threat of the death penalty should apply—as a proportion of all murders has steadily climbed in the last twenty years. The murderers knew that in practice they would get away with life imprisonment, from which they would be paroled after a few years. Or they hoped they would escape. . . .

I find it hard to believe, as Professor Conrad does, that most men are incapable of murder. I admire his optimism. But I find it hard to share. I do not see how he can cling to his faith after Stalin and Hitler, in the presence of assorted tyrants and murderers . . .

. . . But faith obviously is not subject to empirical verification. I am optimistic, however, in my own way, which seems more realistic to me: I believe that most men can be deterred from murder by the threat of the death penalty.

Even if Conrad were right, even if his claim that only a few men would ever become murderers in the absence of the threat of punishment were correct, I should continue to advocate the death penalty to deter these few men. And even if only some of these men need the threat of capital punishment to be deterred, while others would be deterred by the threat of life imprisonment, I should advocate the death penalty to deter the very few who, according to Conrad, do, or even just may, require it to be deterred. The lives of the innocents that will or may be spared because of the death penalty are more valuable to me, and to any civilized society, than the lives of murderers. I do not want to risk their lives for the sake of the lives of murderers.

The reader will have to decide for himself on which side he wants to be.

Section 2: Rape and Sexual Offenses

Stopping Rape: Effective Avoidance Strategies

Pauline B. Bart and Patricia H. O'Brien

Women threatened with rape are in a double bind. On the one hand we are told, "Fighting back will only excite him. Fighting back will only get him angry," advice which assumes that the assailant is not already angry and that immediate retaliation is the most dangerous strategy. We are warned as well that resistance will result in serious injury, if not mutilation and death. . . .

On the other hand, rape has traditionally and legally been defined as an adult man's carnal knowledge of a woman *by force and against her will*. . . . According to this definition, it is not enough that a man used or threatened to use force for the act to be considered rape; a man can compel a woman to have sex and still not legally be acting against her will. Therefore, in order to prove legally that what happened was rape, the woman has to prove that it was indeed against her will. The best way to prove that she is not willing to be forced to have sex is *not* by saying "Please don't" or, "I have my period." The best way to prove that the act is not mutually consensual is by physically resisting. In this selection we describe the strategies that have prevented rape and the conditions under which they were effective. . . .

METHODOLOGY

This report is based on an analysis of 94 interviews with women eighteen or older who had been attacked and who had either avoided being raped ($N = 51$) or been raped ($N = 43$) in the two years prior to the interview. We limited the sample to women who experienced either force or the threat of force. The interview consisted of a self-report dealing with demographic variables, and answers to unstructured and semistructured questions about situational and background factors. Because of the exploratory nature of the research, we added questions when unanticipated patterns emerged—for instance, on incest, sexual assault in childhood, or other violence in the woman's life, or on whether the woman was primarily concerned with being killed or mutilated or primarily concerned with not being raped. The first part of the interview addressed such situational variables as the presence of a weapon, the number of assailants, the response of the woman, the acts that occurred during the assault, the degree of acquaintance with the assailant. The second part dealt with background variables, with questions about a woman's sense of competence and autonomy and about her socialization as a child and an adult into a traditional female role. We asked the raped woman about how her significant others responded to the assault and about interaction with institutions such as the police, hospitals, and therapists. We also examined the negotiation process between the woman and her assailant(s) if such negotiation took place.

Because of the nature of our major research question, we could not obtain a random sample. Therefore, following a pretest, we launched a campaign to find respondents and recruited 94 women through newspaper ads (including major Black and Hispanic papers), press releases, public service announcements (the radio announcements were in both English and Spanish), appearances on radio and television, flyers, and contacts initiated through friendship networks of the project staff.

The resulting . . . nonrandom sample, when compared to the female population of the Chicago standard metropolitan statistical area (SMSA), which includes Cook and the surrounding counties, was disproportionately white, young, and unmarried (either single or divorced). Also none of the women who responded was engaged only in domestic labor at the time of the interview; all were either working outside the home or attending school. However, while the sample is not representative of women in the Chicago SMSA, it is not very different from the population of raped women and rape avoiders in national victimization data, except for an overrepresentation of white women. . . . In addition to the demographic bias, the sample is shaped by the fact that the participants were volunteers. A final source of possible bias in our sample was the very high proportion of women who had been raped by strangers or near strangers (approximately 80 percent). An additional 10 percent were attacked by men they had met for the first time just prior to the assault. . . . The problem of defining rape adds further complications; many women who agree that they have been forced to have sex do not label the act as rape.[1] . . .

A serendipitous finding was that while there was no problem in differentiating rape from seduction, there was no hard and fast line differentiating rape from rape avoidance. Since we can conceptualize rape as a continuum starting with the first approach, verbal or physical, and ending with the rapist's penetration and intercourse to orgasm, any interruption in the continuum before the rapist's orgasm could theoretically be considered an avoidance.

In order to address this issue, we examined the data in three ways: the woman's perception of herself as either a raped woman or one who had avoided rape, the nature of the acts that occurred, and the legal definition of them. The acts consisted of genital intercourse, sodomy, fellatio, interfemoral penetration (the assailant masturbating himself between the woman's thighs), cunnilingus, digital penetration, fondling and touching, and kissing. The possible legal definitions coded (using Illinois statutes at that time) were rape, attempted rape, and deviant sexual assault. When we examined the relationship between self-perception and the acts that had occurred, we learned that, for the most part, the women define rape by what is done with a man's penis (genital intercourse, sodomy, fellatio), not by what is done to a woman's genitals (digital penetration, fondling and touching, cunnilingus). . . .

FINDINGS

Defense Strategies

When the women described their assaults, distinct types of defense techniques emerged that were classified in the following way. A woman could

1. flee or try to flee.
2. scream, yell, or talk loudly—usually in an effort to attract attention.
3. use "affective verbal" techniques such as begging and pleading with the assailant in order to gain his sympathy.
4. use "cognitive verbal" techniques, which included attempting to reason with the assailant, "conning" him, trying to make him "see her as a person," and stalling.
5. take advantage of environmental intervention—someone or something in the surroundings that intruded on the scene and either caused the assailant to stop the assault or gave her an opportunity to escape.
6. respond with physical force, the possibilities ranging from a simple push to self-defense techniques to use of a weapon.

Avoiders used a substantially greater number of strategies than raped women. All of the five respondents who employed *no* strategies were raped;

Table 20-1.
Strategies of Rape Avoidance, by Outcome of Attack (%)

	Raped Women ($N = 43$)	Rape Avoiders ($N = 51$)
Fled or tried to flee	9	33
Screamed	35	49
Used physical force	33	59
Used cognitive verbal strategies	72	67
Used affective verbal strategies	33	22
Benefited from environmental intervention	5	20
Used no strategy	12	—

these made up 11.6 percent of the raped women in the sample. Of the respondents who used only one strategy, 30 percent (13) were raped women and 18 percent (9) were avoiders. Of the respondents who used two kinds of strategies, 28 percent (12) were raped women and 29 percent (15) were avoiders. The difference between raped women and avoiders sharply increases after this. Twenty-one percent (9) of the avoiders used four types of strategies. The modal number of strategies for raped women was one, while for avoiders it was three. The mean number of types of strategies for raped women was 1.86 and for avoiders was 2.53, consistent with the results reported in the Queen's Bench study.[2]

Not only did avoiders use more types of strategies, the strategies they used differed from the strategies of the raped women. Avoiders were more likely to flee or try to flee, to talk loudly or scream, to use physical force, and to be aided by environmental intervention. Raped women were more likely to plead. Both were about equally likely to use cognitive verbal techniques, the strategy most frequently used (see table 20-1).

Because we have qualitative data, we can also study the sequence of strategies. Our analysis took particular note of women who used physical strategies since most debates revolve around this response. Six women who stopped their rapes first used physical strategies and then yelled or screamed. Another effective sequence of strategies for women who stopped their rapes involved using cognitive verbal strategies, and when those proved ineffective, changing to physical strategies. Such strategies, then, can convince the assailant that the woman is serious, not just feigning resistance. The modal strategy for women who stopped rapes was a combination of screaming/yelling and physical resistance. . . .

Avoiding Death or Avoiding Rape

A woman's primary focus emerged during the interviews as a factor sharply differentiating raped women from rape avoiders: the women whose primary concern lay in avoiding death or mutilation have been less likely to avoid rape than those who had a gut reaction of rage and were primarily determined not to be raped. Because of the exploratory nature of this study, we were able to add a question to the interview schedule addressing this point after the pattern emerged. Twenty-eight women who were raped and 19 women who avoided rape expressed fear of death or mutilation as their foremost concern, while 3 women who were raped and 26 women who avoided rape were primarily determined not to be raped.... This response was surprising since we had originally thought that if there were a weapon no resistance would be possible. At the same time, the women who feared death should in no way be blamed, since descriptions of rape in the media emphasize the more lurid rape/murders and give scant attention to the women who stopped their rapes.

Psychological and Bodily Consequences of Physical Resistance

The effectiveness of using physical force to resist rape proved to be our most controversial finding, albeit one that is replicated in other studies.[3] We have suggested above that its effectiveness may lie in its communicating a clear message to the assailant, in addition to any physical injury he might receive or be in danger of receiving. Some assailants were not convinced by other strategies, presumably because they subscribed to the ideology prevalent in pornography and other media that women, whatever they might say, really want to be sexually assaulted. But what of the effect of this strategy on the women? We found that raped women who used physical strategies were less likely to be depressed than raped women who did not. The largest number of women who said they were depressed or who had symptoms of depression such as insomnia and weight loss were among those who were raped but did not use physical strategies. There was no difference in frequency of depression among women who avoided rape by fighting back and those who avoided rape without using physical strategies. Thus we can say that one of the most important functions of physical resistance is to keep women from feeling depressed even if they have been raped.

If what we are tapping were merely personality differences between those who physically resisted and those who did not, then we would not find differences in depression only for those women who were raped. We think the results stem from the traditional vocabulary of motives used in our society to account for rape, a vocabulary many women have internalized. In this vocabulary, rape is provoked by women through their dress, their carelessness, their foolhardiness in going to a "forbidden" place, such as a bar. Women are told, moreover, that they cannot be raped against their will—that, indeed, women really want to be raped and enjoy it. By resisting rape, however, women demonstrate to themselves and to others that this vocabulary does not apply to them. They are less likely to attribute their rape to their "personality defects"—weakness, cowardice, ineffectiveness—and thus less likely to say, "If only I had fought back it wouldn't have happened." They are less likely to blame themselves and to feel depressed, more likely to gain strength from the belief that they did everything they could in that situation.

We are told that if we fight back, if we physically resist, we will pay the price through severe injury or death. This admonition is not supported by our findings or in the studies reported above. Furthermore, advising women to comply or risk injury assumes that rape in itself does not result in injury, physical as well as mental. Several women who talked to us reported serious injury from rape. One woman had a psychotic breakdown which resulted in her hospitalization. Her rapist also tore the area between her vagina and her anus so badly that it required surgical repair. In addition she became pregnant and had an abortion. Since she was not conscious during the attack, the injury did not stem from her resistance. Another contracted venereal disease, which led to pelvic inflammatory disease; she is now permanently sterile. She screamed and tried to reason with her assailant but did not resist physically.

We know that women who resist physically are more likely to avoid rape. We also know that there is little relationship between women's use of physical resistance and rapists' use of additional physical force over and above the attempted rape. . . .

Women who fought back sustained the following kinds of injuries: bruises and bite marks on the neck, soreness for a few days, strained muscles, bruises and minor cuts, more serious cuts, back injury, and aching the next morning. While we asked the women about the assailant's tactics including physical abuse, we did not systematically ask about their own injuries and so there may have been minor injuries not reported. It is likely, however, that all the women who had serious injuries told us of them.

To judge the correlation between injury and physical resistance we must consider the interviews of the 5 women who were brutally beaten or suffered serious injury. Three were raped and 2 avoided being raped. Both avoiders' injuries resulted from their having fought back. However, for one of them, the resistance delayed the rape long enough for a train to pull into the platform where the assault was taking place, and the assailants fled. A third woman who was raped fought back even though her assailant had an ice pick as a weapon. It is unclear whether her beating was in response to her fighting back or to her screams. A raped virgin, attacked by two armed assailants, fought back and was seriously injured. But the injury was a result not of her struggle but of her seven rapes and her escape method. . . .

These experiences suggest that by fighting back a woman significantly increases her chances of rape avoidance and somewhat increases her chance of rough treatment. However, not resisting is no guarantee of humane treatment.

Degree of Acquaintance with Assailant

Do women respond differently when attacked by men they know than when attacked by strangers? If so, is such difference in response associated with whether the outcome of the attack is rape or rape avoidance? Being assaulted by a stranger results in different patterns of response than does being assaulted by an acquaintance. . . . Raped women were more likely to yell or scream as well as to use both cognitive and affective verbal strategies when the assailant was a stranger than when he was someone they knew. Women who stopped their rapes did not respond differently to their assailant whether or not they knew him—except that they were more likely to yell or scream when the assailant was a stranger. There was also environmental intervention more often among women who were not raped. . . .

Presence of a Weapon

Conventional wisdom would suggest that the most important variable in a woman's response to attack is the assailant's possession of a weapon. And indeed, presence of a weapon does influence the outcome. Of the group of women who were attacked by an unarmed assailant, 37 percent (19) were raped and 63 percent (32) avoided rape. Of the group of women who were attacked when an assailant had a weapon, when a weapon was presumed to be present, or when the assailant used a weapon to threaten or wound the woman, 56 percent (24) were raped and 44 percent (19) stopped the rape. The last point needs emphasis, however; even where there was some indication of a weapon, 44 percent of the women avoided being raped. . . .

Since much of the debate about rape avoidance focuses on whether women should use physical force, it is important that one of the most striking differences between raped women and rape avoiders occurred in the case where the assailant did not have a weapon. In such situations, three-quarters (24) of the avoiders used physical strategies while one-quarter (8) did not; about half (9) of the raped women used such strategies, and about half (10) did not.

Being Attacked While Asleep

. . . Two of the 5 women who were asleep used no strategies. How did the women who were not raped manage to avoid the assault? None pleaded, although all used cognitive verbal strategies. One, whom we call the "Super Negotiator," screamed, talked, and fought. Another talked, used physical force, and took advantage of environmental intervention. Their assailants were armed in both cases, and yet both women physically resisted. A third screamed and used cognitive verbal strategies, while a fourth was one of the few women who was able to avoid rape simply by persuading the man that she was not interested. The latter case is particularly striking because the assailant was later apprehended on numerous rape charges. . . .

CONCLUSIONS AND POLICY IMPLICATIONS

Much of what occurs in any assault depends on the woman's interaction with her assailant. In our interviews we discovered that women were able to negotiate parts of the scenario. Although it was difficult to avoid genital intercourse itself through negotiation, some of the women whom we interviewed were able to negotiate their way out of other sex acts after intercourse was completed; several through argument avoided sodomy, fellatio, and multiple acts of intercourse. Women also made bargains involving money or credit cards, negotiated regarding the place of assault, and modified some of the conditions of their assaults—arranged to be tied up in a more comfortable position, got assistance in walking from one place to another. . . .

Women who avoided rape used more kinds of strategies in response to the assault than women who were raped. They also used different strategies. Strategies associated with avoidance were fleeing or trying to flee, yelling, and using physical force. In cases where rape was avoided, there was also more likely to be environmental intervention. Women who were raped were more likely to use no strategies (no woman who avoided rape fell into this category) or to rely on affective verbal strategies. The most common strategies used were cognitive verbal—reasoning, verbally refusing, threatening, and conning. Use of such tactics, though they are frequently advised, did not differentiate raped women from those who avoided rape, and those strategies alone were rarely effective. The modal response which resulted in avoidance was a combination of yelling and using physical force. While the assailant's having a weapon made rape the more probable outcome, 37 percent of the women who avoided rape did so when the assailant was armed or claimed to be armed.

Because of the exploratory nature of the study and because ours was not a random sample, caution should be used in interpreting these results. Nonetheless, four empirical studies comparing the strategies of raped women and rape avoiders came up with similar findings. It is no accident that these findings, which suggest that women should physically resist their assailants, run counter to official ideology that women can avoid rape by behaving in ways more consonant with traditional socialization. Since rape is, after all, a paradigm of sexism in society,[4] it is not surprising that male advice to women on how to avoid rape also reflects that paradigm. . . .

NOTES

1. Irene Hanson Frieze et al., "Psychological Factors in Violent Marriages" (Pittsburgh, PA: University of Pittsburgh, Department of Psychology, 1979); Irene Hanson Frieze, "Investigating the Causes and Consequences of Marital Rape," *Signs*, no. 3 (1983): 532–53.
2. Queen's Bench Foundation, "Rape: Prevention and Resistance" (San Francisco: Queen's Bench Foundation, 1976).
3. Ibid.; William B. Sanders, *Rape and Woman's Identity* (Beverly Hills, CA: Sage Publications, 1980); Jennie J. McIntyre, "Victim Resistance to Rape: Alternative Outcomes" (final report to National Institute of Mental Health, grant R01MH29045); Richard Block and Wesley G. Skogan, "Resistance and Outcome in Robbery and Rape: Non-fatal, Stranger to Stranger Violence" (Evanston, IL: Northwestern University, Center for Urban Affairs and Policy Research, 1982).
4. Pauline B. Bart, "Rape as a Paradigm of Sexism in Society," *Women's Studies International Quarterly* 2, no. 3 (1979): 347–57.

Treatment of Sex Offenders with Antiandrogenic Medication: Conceptualization, Review of Treatment Modalities, and Preliminary Findings

Fred S. Berlin and Carl F. Meinecke

. . . The sexual deviation disorders, or paraphilias, include voyeurism, exhibitionism, erotic sadism, and pedophilia (sexual attraction to children). They are considered psychiatric syndromes by the medical profession and are listed as diagnostic categories in the official psychiatric nomenclature. However, persons who manifest the behaviors characteristic of these syndromes often come into conflict with society, which considers them criminal offenders. This paper examines the rationale for treating these conditions medically rather than punitively and reviews the treatments available, especially use of the antiandrogenic agent medroxyprogesterone acetate (Depo-Provera). . . .

DIAGNOSIS OF A PARAPHILIAC SYNDROME

One way of arriving at a diagnosis is to appreciate the presence of a syndrome, which is a cluster of features that appear together consistently. . . . Mania, for example, can be diagnosed by recognizing a syndrome that includes delusions of grandeur, sustained mood change, hyperactivity, and prolonged insomnia. Disease syndromes such as these tend to follow a relatively predictable course and often respond in a predictable way to treatment.

. . . [A] diagnosis of paraphilia can be made by identifying such a syndrome. This is done by examining a person's cognitive, emotional, and behavioral state. Cognitive examination reveals recurrent persistent fantasies about deviant sex. Examination of the feeling state discloses erotic cravings perceived as noxious when frustrated. The frustration can be relieved temporarily if deviant fantasies are carried out. Behavioral examination shows relatively stereotyped sexual activity because erotic pleasure is maximized only when deviant fantasies are enacted precisely. The exhibitionist, therefore, exposes himself in response to his fantasies and urges on repeated occasions, often in a stereotypic manner. The pedophile, frequently impotent in adult sexual relationships, seeks out young children, sometimes of a particular age, sex, and appearance, in keeping with his fantasies. One would not ordinarily expect a pedophile to develop some other paraphiliac syndrome, such as exhibitionism or erotic sadism, any more than one would expect an adult with conventional heterosexual desires to suddenly begin fantasizing about and seeking out young children. . . .

Paraphiliac syndromes typically manifest themselves initially at puberty and follow a chronic course that may, however, be altered by treatment. At present their etiology is unknown, although certain types of early life experiences are thought to be possible contributory factors in some instances. The etiology of erotic desires and fantasies that influence conventional heterosexual behavior, as well as knowledge about what makes a stimulus sexually appealing, is also poorly understood.

In addition to the triad of cognitive, emotional, and behavioral findings, physical and laboratory examinations may reveal associated organic pathologies. Preliminary data from our center suggest that there may be an unusually high frequency of genetic, hormonal, or neurological anomalies. . . . It may be that biological vulnerabilities in some individuals predispose them to develop unconventional sexual desires (1). However, this hypothesis requires further confirmation by comparison with a control population.

Diagnosis of a paraphiliac syndrome cannot be made on the basis of sexual behavior alone because similar behaviors can occur for a variety of reasons. For example, rape could be committed in response to recurrent urges and fantasies about having coercive sex; in such cases the diagnosis of paraphilia would be appropriate. However, rape could also be initiated by a hallucinating person in response to voices telling him to do so, by a mentally retarded person with conventional rather than deviant sexual desires who "doesn't know any better," or by a hostile, angry individual to humiliate a woman. Such differential diagnosis is important because treatment may be different for a hallucinating, retarded, or impulsive angry person than it is for a paraphiliac. Not all sex offenses (a legal term) are committed by persons manifesting a sexual deviation disorder or paraphilia (a medical term).

METHODS FOR TREATING PARAPHILIAC PATIENTS

Our review of the relevant literature revealed over 230 references pertaining to treatment of sexual deviations. In addition to the medication therapies, psychodynamic therapy, behavior modification, and surgery have been tried.

Psychodynamic theory generally assumes that sexually deviant behaviors occur because of unresolved unconscious conflicts, and treatment is directed at uncovering such conflicts (2–4). To our knowledge there have been no well-controlled clinical trials to demonstrate that any of the individual or group psychodynamic methods result in sustained behavioral change in these conditions, and achieving insight into how they may have developed does not necessarily alter them. In point of fact, most of us have little understanding about why particular things arouse us sexually (5, 6). The causes of sexual cravings are probably multifactorial and are often unknown. . . .

Behavior therapists are often less concerned with the antecedent causes of unconventional sexual behavior than with what can be done about it (7–9). A number of techniques, including hypnosis and biofeedback, have been advocated. Usually the principle is to try to make an unacceptable erotic stimulus less appealing while the person is trained to become sexually aroused by a formerly neutral, or aversive, stimulus. This can be done in the case of pedophilia by following erotic thoughts about children with a mild electric shock and by instructing the patient to masturbate while looking at pictures of a nude, age-appropriate partner. Although this approach is occasionally successful, results are more often disappointing. Most of the literature on psychodynamic or behavioral treatment of sex offenders has consisted of uncontrolled individual case reports without long-term follow-up. It appears that brief changes in behavior are relatively easy to accomplish, but long-term maintenance of such change is achieved far less frequently. Nevertheless, behavior therapy has on occasion been helpful, and it should not be dismissed entirely. . . .

Biological therapies have included surgical castration, intramuscular injections of medroxyprogesterone acetate, or oral administration of cyproterone acetate (the latter is currently unavailable in the United States) (10–12). Forced castration is clearly not acceptable as treatment in this country but has met with some success elsewhere (13–15). . . . Brain surgery has also been attempted as a treatment for sexually deviant behaviors, presumably with the idea of ablating pathways thought to be involved in sexual desire, but this approach has met with only limited success (16).

When medication has been used to try to reduce sexual cravings, efforts have been made to titrate the dosage so as not to cause total impotence. The medication currently in use investigatively in the United States is medroxyprogesterone acetate (17). It is an antiandrogenic agent that can be administered once or twice per week intramuscularly to be gradually absorbed into the bloodstream, causing a reduction in circulating levels of the male sex hormone, testosterone. Effects appear to be fully reversible within a few months after the medication is stopped, although it has not yet been used widely enough for us to be sure this is entirely true. Major side effects are weight gain and mild lethargy; cold sweats, nightmares, dyspnea, hyperglycemia, hypogonadism, and leg cramps have also been reported. High doses can cause breast cancer in female beagle dogs, but the drug does not appear to do so in humans, and it does not cause men to become feminized in appearance (18). . . . Besides decreasing testosterone secretion by the testes, the medication appears to act centrally on the brain as well. This hypothesis is supported by two observations. First, increasing doses of medication seem to decrease erotic fantasies even when serum testosterone levels remain unchanged. Second, there is no compensatory . . . [secretions of] the pituitary gland as a response to lowered levels of testicular testosterone production. Because medroxyprogesterone acetate is given by injection, it is easy to monitor treatment compliance. Psychiatric counseling is ordinarily given in conjunction with the medication to help patients cope with the difficulties encountered as a consequence of their unconventional sexual desires. Most men are hospitalized during the initial phase of treatment.

EVIDENCE THAT MEDICATION CAN BE HELPFUL

Because of difficulties in carrying out research with persons whose behaviors, if untreated, can cause others distress, a controlled double-blind study on the use of medication has not been done. This is necessary before firm conclusions about therapeutic efficacy, or mode of action, can be made. . . . [T]here are some data available in support of the hypothesis that medroxyprogesterone acetate can reduce the intensity of deviant sexual urges and the frequency of accompanying erotic fantasies. . . .

In one study (19) conducted at Johns Hopkins Hospital under the direction of Dr. John Money, 10 paraphiliac men were given medroxyprogesterone acetate intramuscularly approximately once per week. Data were gathered from structured personal interviews with patients and family members who made themselves available and from social agencies and institutional records. Evaluations made before and after treatment suggested that medroxyprogesterone acetate decreased the reported frequency of erotic imagery, as well as the frequency of erection and ejaculation. In addition, some men stopped offensive sexual behavior entirely, sometimes for as long as a couple of years, reporting relief from the psychological pressure to act on their paraphiliac urges. Presumably the decreased frequency of erotic thoughts comes about, at least in part, as a consequence of lowered levels of testosterone.

In a follow-up study to the one just cited, 20 men with histories of chronically recurrent paraphiliac behaviors were placed on medroxyprogesterone acetate for varying lengths of time. . . . Only 3 of the 20 patients showed recurrences of sexually deviant behavior while taking medication; in one such case, relapse was clearly related to alcohol abuse. The recidivism rate jumped dramatically when patients discontinued their medication regimen. Of the 11 patients who discontinued medroxyprogesterone acetate against medical advice, 10 relapsed. . . . Whether the marked number of patients in this study who eventually relapsed would have remained symptom free had they been required to continue taking medication (perhaps, for example, as a condition of parole) is not known. . . .

The preliminary impression based on these data and other cases now being analyzed is that in general, these men appear to do well in response to antiandrogenic medication as long as they continue taking it and as long as their problems are rather clearly confined to unconventional sexual cravings. They seem to do less well if they have been noncompliant about taking the medication or if in addition to having such cravings they abuse drugs and alcohol, are sexually impulsive, or have a history of other sorts of sociopathy or violence. . . . [P]rognosis may depend not only on the effects of medication on the deviant thoughts and cravings comprising the syndrome, but also on other features of the person manifesting the syndrome, such as his attitude about treatment and commitment to it. . . .

CASE REPORTS

Case 1 (sadistic paraphilia). Mr. A, a 47-year-old man, complained of being unable to obtain sexual satisfaction unless he hurt his wife. His preoccupation with sadistic fantasies made it difficult for him to concentrate, even at work. He believed his actions to be wrong and consistently felt disgusted and remorseful afterward, often working overtime to avoid the opportunity to harm her. However, every few weeks his cravings would build up to a point where he could not control them. During 25 years of marriage, he had frequently handcuffed his wife, shaved her head, stuck pins in her back, and struck her—although never so forcefully as to require medical or legal attention. Alternative means of obtaining sexual satisfaction such as masturbation led to erection, but ejaculation could not be achieved unless he hurt her. Neurological examination showed evidence of nonprogressive basal ganglia dysfunction, and he had a mild gait disturbance.

Mr. A began treatment voluntarily 4 years ago after he became frightened he might seriously harm or even kill his wife. Since that time there has not been even a single recurrence of the sexual sadism that had occurred previously for nearly 25 years. Conventional sexual activities have become a regular part of Mr. A's marriage, and as before, there has been no extramarital involvement. He believes he can control his paraphiliac desires, which he said have become much less intense, only with help from antiandrogenic medication. He has found considerable relief from the obsessive erotic urges that he had previously experienced as noxious rather than pleasurable. With treatment his serum testosterone has been maintained at below-normal levels. . . .

Case [2] (paraphiliac rape). Mr. C, a 32-year-old man with adult-onset idiopathic epilepsy since age 19 but seizure free for the past 3 years, was referred for treatment after committing two rapes. Although never charged previously, he admitted to a lengthy history of similar behavior satisfying legal criteria for rape, beginning at age 20. His first sexual experience was at the age of 6 or 7 with a 14-year-old babysitter who had asked him to watch her masturbate while clothed in her undergarments. Since then, he has fantasized several times daily about similar encounters, often masturbating while doing so. At the age of 15 he broke into the office of a gynecologist who had been dating his sister to steal textbooks to "learn more about the female body." He had a steady girlfriend at the time of hospital admission, but he had never found sexual activities with her sufficiently satisfying and usually masturbated about four or five times per day while fantasizing about various women performing autoerotic acts. In his fantasies he would always imagine forcing a woman previously unknown to him to masturbate while clad in her undergarments. He had been too embarrassed to ever tell any of his regular girlfriends about his erotic preoccupation, and he rarely sought a second encounter with any women whom he had forced to have sex, feeling compelled instead to repeat the episode with a fresh partner.

The patient maintained an apartment separate from his girlfriend. Three or four times per week he would try to meet a new woman (preferably slim and wearing pants rather than a skirt) whom he would persuade to join him at his apartment to smoke marijuana; he never used threats up to that point. Subsequently, however, he would threaten to harm the woman unless she removed her panties and masturbated while he watched and masturbated himself. On some occasions he would have intercourse, but this was the exception rather than the rule. Each episode invariably followed this same pattern; he estimated that there had been more than 60 such episodes since he was age 20. On some occasions he would threaten his victim with a knife as well as verbally, but in those instances when she refused to be intimidated, he always allowed her to leave without becoming physically assaultive. As far as we could determine, on no occasion did he injure a woman physically, and none of his erotic fantasies was sadistic in the sense of wanting to inflict pain. After each episode he would escort the woman out, "trying to be kind, apologizing, and making sure she was okay," with no further threats. He reported that he would then invariably vomit, feeling "disgusted, sick, and remorseful" and vow never again to act in such a manner. However, in a few days his fantasies and urges would recur with renewed intensity and the whole pattern would be repeated.

Mr. C believed coercion of another person was wrong, worried about the troubles his actions could cause him, and appeared to have some concern for his victims. Nevertheless, he stated that his erotic thoughts and cravings consistently proved to be more than he could resist. In his words, "It's like an insatiable drive, like a pressure that is always on me. Sometimes I can push it off by masturbating, but eventually I feel driven to repeat this thing over and over." His serum testosterone level was found to be . . . well above the reported normal 2 SD range. . . . Because we are only now beginning a careful, rigorously supervised treatment protocol, it is too soon to know whether success can be achieved.

DISCUSSION

. . . Some persons undoubtedly misuse other people with little concern for them and may require quarantine or punishment. Others (just as is true of some drug addicts, cigarette smokers, or overeaters) may be in a sense victims of intense cravings that are quite resilient and therefore difficult, if not impossible, to resist. Such persons must still assume responsibility for their own actions, but when they seek medical help they should be treated with an appreciation for their difficulties rather than with stigmatization, scorn, or contempt (20). . . . Although many treatments, including psychodynamic and behavioral therapies, have been tried in the past, only recently has the potential for help in the form of medication become available. Some might argue that in a way paraphiliac behavior is no more a reflection of disease than is conventional sexual activity. In a nonjudgmental sense, this may be true. However, syndromes are often labeled diseases when they impair functioning or cause suffering. Since paraphiliac behaviors can infringe on the rights and well-being of nonconsenting persons, causing suffering, it seems proper to make a value judgment about them, that is, that they must stop and because the cravings associated with such behavior can often be alleviated by medication, the term "treatment" still seems appropriate. Unconventional sexual activities between consenting adults that cause no harm do not ordinarily require psychiatric care. . . .

[S]ociety as well as the sex offender will likely benefit if the offender can be treated successfully rather than being imprisoned and then released unchanged. There is no evidence, except in the case of the paraphiliac sadist or rapist, that having a paraphiliac syndrome increases the probability of physical violence, and some paraphiliacs seem reasonably well adjusted at work and in other spheres of social endeavor (21).

People do not decide voluntarily what will arouse them sexually. Data presented here suggest that non-learned biological as well as learned environmental factors may play an etiological role in the development of sexually deviant behaviors. Better understanding of causal factors may eventually lead to more specific forms of treatment. At a symposium at the Massachusetts Institute of Technology Goy and McEwen (22) reviewed evidence suggesting that nonlearned biological factors may be more important determinants of human sexual behavior than is generally appreciated. Improved understanding of possible genetic, hormonal, or neurochemical bases for human sexual pathology should be sought in pursuing further the rationale for treatment with medication. . . . Currently, treatment with medroxyprogesterone acetate involves using it as a suppressant of sexual desire in general. It seems to decrease the intensity of sexual urges but does not change them qualitatively. If there is an unlearned biological basis for deviant sexual activity, an ideal medication might suppress deviant sexual cravings alone without affecting more conventional erotic interests. When medroxyprogesterone acetate is discontinued, allowing the sexual appetite to heighten or return, behaviors engaged in to satisfy that appetite are also likely to be reinstituted. . . .

Given our present level of knowledge of the paraphiliac, it is still too soon to predict with confidence the future of hormonal treatment programs. It is unclear whether the compliance problems evidenced by some patients can indeed be solved. It is possible that even with improved compliance, future results may yet fail to support preliminary impressions of good therapeutic efficacy. Certainly many more data are needed. Even so, it is already clear that several patients have experienced marked reductions in sexually deviant activity and fantasy while taking medroxyprogesterone acetate. This suggests that the idea of considering at least some sexual offenses to be a behavioral manifestation of intense aberrant drives, possibly related to a dysfunction in brain and representing a condition that is potentially treatable with medication, merits continued investigation. It is hoped that legal demands for justice can be reconciled with medical concerns for understanding care.

REFERENCES

1. Regestein RR, Reich P: Pedophilia occurring after onset of cognitive impairment. J Nerv Ment Dis 166: 794–798, 1978
2. Loland S, Balint M (eds): Perversions: Psychodynamics and Therapy. New York, Random House, 1956
3. Salzman L: The psychodynamic approach to sex deviations. Int Psychiatry Clin 8:21–40, 1971
4. Karpman B: The sexual psychopath. JAMA 146:721–726, 1951
5. Sexual behavior and the sex hormones. Lancet 2:17–18, 1979
6. Gadpaille WJ: Cross-species and cross-cultural contributions to understanding homosexual activity. Arch Gen Psychiatry 37:349–356, 1980
7. Bancroft J: The behavioral approach to treatment, in Handbook of Sexology. Edited by Money J, Musaph H. New York, Elsevier Scientific Publishing Co, 1978
8. Ince LP: Behavior modification of sexual disorders. Am J Psychother 17:446–451, 1973
9. Serber M, Wolpe J: Treatment of the sex offender: behavior therapy techniques. Int Psychiatry Clin 8:53–68, 1971
10. Cooper AJ, Ismail AAA, Phanzoo AL, et al: Antiandrogen (cyproterone acetate) therapy in deviant hypersexuality. Br J Psychiatry 120:58–64, 1972
11. Van Moffaert M: Social reintegration of sexual delinquents by a combination of psychotherapy and antiandrogen treatment. Acta Psychiatr Scand 53:29–34, 1976

12. Schumann HJ: Resocialization of sexually abnormal patients by a combination of antiandrogen administration and psychotherapy. Psychother Psychosom 20:321–332, 1972
13. Bremer J: Asexualization: A Follow-Up of 244 Cases. New York, Macmillan Publishing Co, 1959
14. Sturup GK: Treatment of Sexual Offenders in Herstedvester Denmark: The Rapists. Acta Psychiatr Scand Suppl 204, 1968
15. Taus L, Susicka L: Five year follow-up study of five sexual deviants after therapeutic operation. Cesk Psychiatr 69:51–55, 1973
16. Dieckmann G, Hassler R: Treatment of sexual violence by stereotactic hypothalamotomy, in Neurosurgical Treatment in Psychiatry, Pain, and Epilepsy. Edited by Sweet WH, Obrador S, Martin-Rodriquez JG. Baltimore, University Park Press, 1977
17. Money J: Use of an androgen depleting hormone in the treatment of male sex offenders. Journal of Sexual Research 6:165–172, 1970
18. Physicians' Desk Reference, 35th ed. Oradell, NJ, Medical Economics Co, 1981, p 1819
19. Money J, Wiedeking C, Walker P, et al: Combined antiandrogenic and counseling program for treatment of 46 XY and 47 XYY sex offenders, in Hormones, Behaviors, and Psychopathology. Edited by Sachar EJ. New York, Raven Press, 1976
20. Money J: Ideas and ethics of psychosexual determinism. British Journal of Sexual Medicine, May 1979, pp 27–32
21. Groth AN: Men Who Rape: The Psychology of the Offender. New York, Plenum Publishing Corp, 1979, pp 147–148
22. Goy R, McEwen BS (eds): Sexual Differentiation of the Brain. Cambridge, MIT Press, 1977

Section 3: Domestic Violence

The Specific Deterrent Effects of Arrest for Domestic Assault

Lawrence W. Sherman and Richard A. Berk

with 42 Patrol Officers of the Minneapolis Police Department, Nancy Wester, Donileen Loseke, David Rauma, Debra Morrow, Amy Curtis, Kay Gamble, Roy Roberts, Phyllis Newton, and Gayle Gubman

POLICING DOMESTIC ASSAULTS

Police have been typically reluctant to make arrests for domestic violence (Berk and Loseke, 1981), as well as for a wide range of other kinds of offenses, unless victims demand an arrest, the suspect insults the officer, or other factors are present (Sherman, 1980). Parnas's (1972) qualitative observations of the Chicago police found four categories of police action in these situations:

negotiating or otherwise "talking out" the dispute; threatening the disputants and then leaving; asking one of the parties to leave the premises; or (very rarely) making an arrest.

Similar patterns are found in many other cities. Surveys of battered women who tried to have their domestic assailants arrested report that arrest occurred in 10 percent (Roy, 1977:35) or 3 percent (see Langley and Levy, 1977:219) of the cases. Surveys of police agencies in Illinois (Illinois Law Enforcement Commission, 1978) and New York (Office of the Minority Leader, 1978) found explicit policies against arrest in the majority of the agencies surveyed. Despite the fact that violence is reported to be present in one-third (Bard and Zacker, 1974) to two-thirds (Black, 1980) of all domestic disturbances police respond to, police department data show arrests in only 5 percent of those disturbances in Oakland (Hart, n.d., cited in Meyer and Lorimer, 1977:21), 6 percent of those disturbances in a Colorado city (Patrick et al., n.d., cited in Meyer and Lorimer, 1977:21) and 6 percent in Los Angeles County (Emerson, 1979). . . .

An apparent preference of many police for separating the parties rather than arresting the offender has been attacked from two directions over the last fifteen years. The original critique came from clinical psychologists, who agreed that police should rarely make arrests (Potter, 1978:46; Fagin, 1978:123–24) in domestic assault cases, and argued that police should mediate the disputes responsible for the violence. A highly publicized demonstration project teaching police special counseling skills for family crisis intervention (Bard, 1970) failed to show a reduction in violence, but was interpreted as a success nonetheless. By 1977, a national survey of police agencies with 100 or more officers found that over 70 percent reported a family crisis intervention training program in operation. . . .

By the mid-1970s, police practices were criticized from the opposite direction by feminist groups. Just as psychologists succeeded in having many police agencies respond to domestic violence as "half social work and half police work," feminists began to argue that police put "too much emphasis on the social work aspect and not enough on the criminal" (Langley and Levy, 1977:218). Widely publicized lawsuits in New York and Oakland sought to compel police to make arrests in every case of domestic assault, and state legislatures were lobbied successfully to reduce the evidentiary requirements needed for police to make arrests for misdemeanor domestic assaults. Some legislatures are now considering statutes requiring police to make arrests in these cases.

The feminist critique was bolstered by a study (Police Foundation, 1976) showing that for 85 percent of a sample of spousal homicides, police had intervened at least once in the preceding two years. For 54 percent of the homicides, police had intervened five or more times. But it was impossible to determine from the cross-sectional data whether making more or fewer arrests would have reduced the homicide rate.

In sum, police officers confronting a domestic assault suspect face at least three conflicting options, urged on them by different groups with different theories. The officers' colleagues might recommend forced separation as a means of achieving short-term peace. Alternatively, the officers' trainers might recommend mediation as a means of getting to the underlying cause of the "dispute" (in which both parties are implicitly assumed to be at fault). Finally, the local women's organizations may recommend that the officer protect the victim (whose "fault," if any, is legally irrelevant) and enforce the law to deter such acts in the future.

RESEARCH DESIGN

In response to these conflicting recommendations, the Police Foundation and the Minneapolis Police Department agreed to conduct a randomized experiment. The design called for random assignment of arrest, separation, and some form of advice which could include mediation at the officer's discretion. In addition, there was to be a six-month follow-up period to measure the frequency and seriousness of domestic violence after each police intervention. . . .

The design only applied to simple (misdemeanor) domestic assaults, where both the suspect and the victim were present when the police arrived. Thus, the experiment included only those cases in which police were empowered (but not required) to make arrests under a recently liberalized Minnesota state law; the police officer must have probable cause to believe that a cohabitant or spouse had assaulted the victim within the last four hours (but police need not have witnessed the assault). Cases of life-threatening or severe injury, usually labeled as a felony (aggravated assault), were excluded from the design for ethical reasons.

The design called for each officer to carry a pad of report forms, color coded for the three different police actions. Each time the officers encountered a situation that fit the experiment's criteria, they were to take whatever action was indicated by the report form on the top of the pad. We numbered the forms and arranged them in random order for each officer. The integrity of the random assignment was to be monitored by research staff observers riding on patrol for a sample of evenings. . . .

Anticipating something of the victims' background, a predominantly minority, female research staff was employed to contact the victims for a detailed face-to-face interview, to be followed by telephone follow-up interviews every two weeks for 24 weeks. The interviews were designed primarily to measure the frequency and seriousness of victimizations caused by the suspect after the police intervention. The research staff also collected criminal justice reports that mentioned the suspect's name during the six-month follow-up period.

CONDUCT OF THE EXPERIMENT

The experiment began on March 17, 1981, with the expectation that it would take about one year to produce about 300 cases (it ran until August 1, 1982, and produced 330 case reports). . . .

There is little doubt that many of the officers occasionally failed to follow fully the experimental design. Some of the failures were due to forgetfulness, such as leaving the report pads at home or at the police station. Other failures derived from misunderstanding about whether the experiment applied in certain situations; application of the experimental rules under complex circumstances was sometimes confusing. Finally, from time to time there were situations that were simply not covered by the experimenter's rules. . . .

. . . Ninety-nine percent of the suspects targeted for arrest actually were arrested, while only 78 percent of those to receive advice did, and only 73 percent of those to be sent out of the residence for eight hours were actually sent. One explanation for this pattern, consistent with the experimental guidelines, is that mediating and sending were more difficult ways for police to control the situation, with a greater likelihood that officers might resort to arrest as a fallback position. . . .

Such differential attrition would potentially bias estimates of the relative effectiveness of arrest by removing uncooperative and difficult offenders from the mediation and separation treatments. Any deterrent effect could be underestimated and, in the extreme, artifactual support for deviance amplification could be found. That is, the arrest group would have too many "bad guys" *relative* to the other treatments. . . .

. . . We applied a multinominal logit formulation (Amemiya, 1981:1516–19; Maddala, 1983:34–37), which showed that the designed treatment was the dominant cause of the treatment actually received. . . . However, we also found that five other variables had a statistically significant effect on "upgrading" the separation and advice treatments to arrests: whether police reported the suspect was rude; whether police reported the suspect tried to assault one (or both) of the police officers; whether police reported weapons were involved; whether the victim persistently demanded a citizen's arrest; and whether a restraining order was being violated. We found no evidence that the background or characteristics of the suspect or victim (e.g., race) affected the treatment received.

Overall, the logit model fit the data very well. For well over 80 percent of the cases, the model's predicted treatment was the same as the actual treatment (i.e., correct classifications). . . . In summary, we were able to [account for] the assignment process with remarkable success simply by employing the rules of the experimental protocol (for more details, see Berk and Sherman, 1983).

We were less fortunate with the interviews of the victims; only 205 of 330, counting the few repeat victims twice, could be located and initial interviews obtained, a 62 percent completion rate. Many of the victims simply could not be found, either for the initial interview or for follow-ups: they either left town, moved somewhere else or refused to answer the phone or doorbell. . . .

The response rate to the bi-weekly follow-up interviews was even lower than for the initial interview, as in much research on women crime victims. After the first interview, for which the victims were paid $20, there was a gradual falloff in completed interviews with each successive wave; only 161 victims provided all 12 follow-up interviews over the six months, a completion rate of 49 percent. . . .

There is . . . no evidence that the experimental treatment assigned to the offender affected the victim's decision to grant initial interviews. . . . In short, while the potential for sample selection bias (Heckman, 1979; Berk, 1983) certainly exists . . . , that bias does not stem from obvious sources, particularly the treatments. This implies that we may well be able to meaningfully examine experimental effects for the subset of individuals from whom initial interviews were obtained. The same conclusions followed when the follow-up interviews were considered.

In sum, despite the practical difficulties of controlling an experiment and interviewing crime victims in an emotionally charged and violent social context, the experiment succeeded in producing . . . cases with complete official outcome measures and . . . apparently unbiased . . . responses from the victims in those cases.

RESULTS

The 205 completed initial interviews provide some sense of who the subjects are, although the data may not properly represent the characteristics of the full sample of 314. They show the now familiar pattern of domestic violence cases coming to police attention being disproportionately unmarried couples with lower than average educational levels, disproportionately minority and mixed race (black male, white female), and who were very likely to have had prior violent incidents with police intervention. The 60 percent suspect unemployment rate is strikingly high in a community with only about 5 percent of the workforce unemployed. The 59 percent prior arrest rate is also strikingly high, suggesting (with the 80 percent prior domestic assault rate) that the suspects generally are experienced lawbreakers who are accustomed to police interventions. But with the exception of the heavy representation of Native Americans . . . , the characteristics in Table 20-2 are probably close to those of domestic violence cases coming to police attention in other large U.S. cities.

Two kinds of outcome measures will be considered. One is a *police-recorded* "failure" of the offender to survive the six-month follow-up period without having police generate a written report on the suspect for domestic violence. . . . A second kind of measure comes from the *interviews with victims*, in which victims were asked if there had been a repeat incident with the same suspect, broadly defined to include an actual assault, threatened assault, or property damage. . . .

[Police data indicate that t]wenty-six percent of those separated committed a repeat assault, compared to 13 percent of those arrested. The mediation treatment was statistically indistinguishable from the other two. To help put this in perspective, 18.2 percent of the households failed overall[, that is, resulted in a written police report.] . . .

[W]hen self-report data are used[, we find] . . . a different ordering of the effects, with arrest still producing the lowest recidivism rate (at 19%), but with advice producing the highest (37%). Overall, 28.9 percent of the suspects . . . "failed" [in terms of victim reports of assaults.] . . .

An obvious rival hypothesis to the deterrent effect of arrest is that arrest incapacitates. If the arrested suspects spend a large portion of the next six months in jail, they would be expected to have lower recidivism rates. But the initial

Table 20-2.
Victim and Suspect Characteristics: Initial Interview Data and Police Sheets

A. Unemployment			
Victims	61%		
Suspects	60%		
B. Relationship of Suspect to Victim			
Divorced or separated husband		3%	
Unmarried male lover		45%	
Current husband		35%	
Wife or girlfriend		2%	
Son, brother, roommate, other		15%	
C. Prior Assaults and Police Involvement			
Victims assaulted by suspect, last six months		80%	
Police intervention in domestic dispute, last six months		60%	
Couple in Counseling Program		27%	
D. Prior Arrests of Male Suspects			
Ever Arrested For Any Offense		59%	
Ever Arrested For Crime Against Person		31%	
Ever Arrested on Domestic Violence Statute		5%	
Ever Arrested On An Alcohol Offense		29%	
E. Mean Age			
Victims	30 years		
Suspects	32 years		
F. Education		Victims	Suspects
< high school		43%	42%
high school only		33%	36%
> high school		24%	22%
G. Race		Victims	Suspects
White		57%	45%
Black		23%	36%
Native American		18%	16%
Other		2%	3%

N = 205 (Those cases for which initial interviews were obtained)

interview data show this is not the case: of those arrested, 43 percent were released within one day, 86 percent were released within one week, and only 14 percent were released after one week or had not yet been released at the time of the *initial* victim interview. Clearly, there was very little incapacitation, especially in the context of a six-month follow-up. Indeed, virtually all those arrested were released before the first follow-up interview. Nevertheless, we introduced the length of the initial stay in jail as a control variable. . . . [T]he story was virtually unchanged.

Another perspective on the incapacitation issue can be obtained by looking at repeat violence which occurred shortly after the police intervened. If incapacitation were at work, a dramatic effect should be found in households experiencing arrest, especially compared to the households experiencing advice. Table

Table 20-3.
Speed of Reunion and Recidivism by Police Action

Police Action	Time of Reunion: Within One Day	More than One Day but Less Than One Week	Longer or No Return	(N)	New Quarrel Within A Day	New Violence Within A Day
Arrested (and released)	38%	30%	32%	(N = 76)	(2)	(1)
Separated	57%	31%	10%	(N = 54)	(6)	(3)
Advised	—	—	—	(N = 72)	(4)	(1)

N = 202 (Down from the 205 in Table 20-2 due to missing data)

20-3 shows how quickly the couples were reunited, and of those reunited in one day, how many of them, according to the victim, began to argue or had physical violence again. It is apparent that *all* of the police interventions effectively stopped the violence for a 24-hour period after the couples were reunited. Even the renewed quarrels were few. . . . Hence, there is again no evidence of an incapacitation effect. There is also no evidence for the reverse: that arrested offenders would take it out on the victim when the offender returned home.

DISCUSSION AND CONCLUSIONS

The experiment's results are subject to several qualifications. One caution is that both kinds of outcome measures have uncertain construct validity. The official measure no doubt neglects a large number of repeat incidents, in part because many of them were not reported, and in part because police are sometimes reluctant to turn a family "dispute" into formal police business. . . . This is not to say that the self-report data are flawless; indeed there is some reason to believe that there was undercounting of new incidents. . . .

The construct validity of the treatments is more problematic. The advice and separation interventions have unclear content. Perhaps "good" mediation, given consistently, would fare better compared to arrest. The more general point is that the treatment effects for arrest are only relative to the impact of the other interventions. Should their content change, the relative impact of arrest could change as well.

. . . [W]e noted earlier that a few officers accounted for a disproportionate number of the cases. What we have been interpreting, therefore, as results from different intervention strategies could reflect the special abilities of certain officers to make arrest particularly effective relative to the other treatments. For example, these officers may have been less skilled in mediation techniques. . . .

Finally, Minneapolis is hardly representative of all urban areas. The Minneapolis Police Department has many unusual characteristics, and different jurisdictions might well keep suspects in custody for longer or shorter periods of time. The message should be clear: external validity will have to wait for replications.

Despite these qualifications, it is apparent that we have found no support for the deviance amplification point of view. The arrest intervention certainly did not make things worse and may well have made things better. There are, of course, many rejoinders. In particular, over 80 percent of offenders had assaulted the victims in the previous six months, and in over 60 percent of the households the police had intervened during that interval. Almost 60 percent of the suspects had previously been arrested for something. Thus, the counter-productive consequences of police sanction, if any, may for many offenders have already been felt. In labeling theory terms, secondary deviation may already have been established, producing a ceiling for the amplification effects of formal sanctioning. However, were this the case, the arrest treatment probably should be less effective in households experiencing recent police interventions. No such interaction effects were found. . . .

. . . For those who theorize that a metamorphosis of self occurs in response to official sanctions over a long period of time, our six-month follow-up is not a relevant test. For those who argue that the development of a criminal self-concept is particularly likely to occur during a lengthy prison stay or extensive contact with criminal justice officials, the dosage of labeling employed in this experiment is not sufficient to falsify that hypothesis. What this experiment does seem to falsify for this particular offense is the broader conception of labeling implicit in the prior research by Lincoln et al. (unpubl.), Farrington (1977) and others: that for every possible increment of criminal justice response to deviance, the more increments (or the greater the formality) applied to the labeled deviant, the greater the likelihood of subsequent deviation. The absolute strength of the dosage is irrelevant to this hypothesis, as long as some variation in dosage is present. . . . [T]he experiment does . . . seem to falsify this [hypothesis].

The apparent support for deterrence is perhaps more clear. While we certainly have no evidence that deterrence will work in general, we do have findings that swift imposition of a sanction of temporary incarceration may deter male offenders in domestic assault cases. And we have produced this evidence from an unusually strong research design based on random assignment to treatments. In short, criminal justice sanctions seem to matter for this offense in this setting with this group of experienced offenders.

A number of police implications follow. Perhaps most important, police have historically been reluctant to make arrests in domestic assault cases, in part fearing that an arrest could make the violence worse. Criminal justice sanctions weakly applied might be insufficient to deter and set the offender on a course of retribution. Our data indicate that such concerns are by and large groundless.

Police have also felt that making an arrest was a waste of their time: without the application of swift and severe sanctions by the courts, arrest and booking had no bite. Our results indicate that only three of the 136 arrested offenders were formally punished by fines or subsequent incarceration. This suggests that arrest and initial incarceration alone may produce a deterrent effect, regardless of how the courts treat such cases, and that arrest makes an independent contribution to the deterrence potential of the criminal justice system. Therefore, in jurisdictions that process domestic assault offenders in a manner similar to that employed in Minneapolis, we favor a *presumption* of arrest; an arrest should be made unless there are good, clear reasons why an arrest would be counterproductive. We do not, however, favor *requiring* arrests in all misdemeanor domestic assault cases. Even if our findings were replicated in a number of jurisdictions, there is a good chance that arrest works far better for some kinds of offenders than others and in some kinds of situations better than others. We feel it best to leave police a loophole to capitalize on that variation. Equally important, it is widely recognized that discretion is inherent in police work. Simply to impose a requirement of arrest, irrespective of the features of the immediate situation, is to invite circumvention.

REFERENCES

Amemiya, Takeshi
1981 "Qualitative response models: a survey." Journal of Economic Literature 19: 1483–1536.

Bard, Morton
1970 "Training police as specialists in family crisis intervention." Washington, D.C.: U.S. Department of Justice.

Bard, Morton and Joseph Zacker
1974 "Assaultiveness and alcohol use in family disputes—police perceptions." Criminology 12:281–92.

Berk, Richard A.
1983 "An introduction to sample selection bias in sociological data." American Sociological Review 48:386–98.

Berk, Richard A. and Lawrence W. Sherman
1983 "Police responses to family violence incidents: an analysis of an experimental design with incomplete randomization." Unpublished manuscript, Department of Sociology, University of California at Santa Barbara.

Berk, Sarah Fenstermaker and Donileen R. Loseke
1981 "Handling family violence: situational determinants of police arrest in domestic disturbances." Law and Society Review 15:315–46.

Black, Donald
1980 The Manners and Customs of the Police. New York: Academic Press.

Emerson, Charles D.
1979 "Family violence: a study by the Los Angeles County Sheriff's Department." Police Chief 46(6):48–50.

Fagin, James A.
1978 "The effects of police interpersonal communications skills on conflict resolution." Ph.D. Dissertation, Southern Illinois University. Ann Arbor: University Microfilms.

Farrington, David P.
1977 "The effects of public labeling." British Journal of Criminology 17:112–25.

Heckman, James
1979 "Sample selection bias as a specification error." Econometrica 45:153–61.

Illinois Law Enforcement Commission
1978 "Report on technical assistance project—domestic violence survey." (Abstract). Washington, D.C.: National Criminal Justice Reference Service.

Langley, Richard and Roger C. Levy
1977 Wife Beating: The Silent Crisis. New York: E. P. Dutton.
Lincoln, Suzanne B., Malcolm W. Klein, Katherine S. Tellmann and Susan Labin
unpubl. "Control organizations and labeling theory: official versus self-reported delinquency." Unpublished manuscript, University of Southern California.
Maddala, G. S.
1983 Limited, Dependent and Qualitative Variables in Econometrics. Cambridge: Cambridge University Press.
Meyer, Jeanie Keeny and T. D. Lorimer
1977 Police Intervention Data and Domestic Violence: Exploratory Development and Validation of Prediction Models. Report prepared under grant #RO1MH27918 from National Institute of Mental Health. Kansas City, Mo., Police Department.
Office of the Minority Leader, State of New York
1978 Battered Women: Part I (Abstract). Washington, D.C.: National Criminal Justice Reference Service.
Parnas, Raymond I.
1972 "The police response to the domestic disturbance." Pp. 206–36 in Leon Radzinowicz and Marvin E. Wolfgang (eds.), The Criminal in the Arms of the Law. New York: Basic Books.
Police Foundation
1976 Domestic Violence and the Police: Studies in Detroit and Kansas City. Washington, D.C.: The Police Foundation.
Potter, Jane
1978 "The police and the battered wife: the search for understanding." Police Magazine 1:40–50.
Roy, Maria (ed.)
1977 Battered Women. New York: Van Nostrand Reinhold.
Sherman, Lawrence W.
1980 "Causes of police behavior: the current state of quantitative research." Journal of Research in Crime and Delinquency 17:69–100.

Section 4: Collective Violence

Alternatives to [Collective] Violence in a Democratic Society

Ted Robert Gurr

The belief that democratic societies are insulated by their political values and institutions from violent conflict is historically a myth. Events of the 1960s laid it to rest in the United States and most European societies. The paradoxical character of violence in democracy . . . is on its way to being recognized as a truism:

disruptive conflict is as common in democracies as elsewhere but ordinarily it focuses on limited issues and rarely threatens dominant political and economic institutions. Or so it seems. Since Western democracies have fallen before the onslaught of revolutionaries, for example in Germany in the early 1930s and Czechoslovakia in 1948, even this generalization has limited applicability: democracies are resistant to revolutionary challenge but not wholly immune to it.

Meanwhile citizens and officials in democratic societies, the United States in particular, must deal with hard questions about how to cope with the recurring fact of violent conflict. Group violence has a private face and a public face: it is used by those out of power and those in power. So there are two sets of questions. First, when are private groups warranted in the use of violence in a society that professes democratic procedures, and what consequences should they expect? On the public side of the equation of conflict are questions about whether and when it is legitimate for those in power in a democratic society to respond violently to the opposition of private citizens, and what practical alternatives they have to meeting force with force.

The answers to these questions in the United States are constrained by constitutional theory. The United States is not a pure, majoritarian democracy. Its constitution guarantees a "republican form of government," and hence its political institutions were designed not only to ensure the majority a decisive voice in most political decisions, but also to protect the rights of minorities against potential abuse by majorities. The constitutional concern for minority rights constrains the use of force by majorities against minorities, even if the majority wills it, and by implication it gives minorities an ultimate right of self-defense against an abusive majority.

The realities of political power also limit answers to questions about responses to violence. A government in power is always tempted to tilt its policies to favor its own interests and those of its supporters. There are privileged minorities as well as disadvantaged ones, and the ever-present risk is that when conflict comes to a violent head, especially empowered minorities will be better served than other groups. Constitutional prescription and institutional checks-and-balances limit but do not eliminate the possibility of favoritism; the ultimate redress is the electoral success of a majority in opposition. So it must be recognized at the outset that, constitutional democracy being imperfect in practice, public responses to private challenges will often be less than even-handed.

From the viewpoint of both constitutional theory and democratic practice, responses and alternatives to violence can be judged only by reference to the issues and groups involved. Neither justice nor public order are served if the same public response is meted out to a large aggrieved minority demanding reform and a band of revolutionaries using armed violence against the state. . . .

ORIGINS OF GROUP VIOLENCE

The disorderly skein of violent conflict in American history is more understandable if we concentrate on three of its major themes. Some groups have organized for the purpose of defending a threatened status quo, others have sought limited or "reformist" ends within the existing system, while still others have declared themselves in open rebellion against it. All these objectives can be pursued without leading inevitably to violent conflict; conflict turns violent when a group pursuing one of these objectives encounters the resistance of another, public or private group. The potential for violence and the prospects for reducing or avoiding it depend most fundamentally on who is seeking what from whom.

Defensive Groups

Defense of the status quo has been the most common source of group violence in American history. A central theme of the growth of the American Republic has been flight from external oppression and resistance to its reappearance in the New World. Thus colonial settlers in America resisted British, French, or Spanish imperialism, settlers on the Appalachian frontier opposed seaboard authorities, and enthusiasts of local or states rights fought against metropolitan or national encroachment—as in New England during the late eighteenth century, in Texas in the 1840s, and in the South during the Civil War era. . . . Shays' Rebellion in Massachusetts, 1786–1787; Fries' Rebellion in eastern Pennsylvania, 1798–1799; some of the activities of the Grangers, Greenbackers, and Farmers' Alliance after the Civil War; and the "Green Corn Rebellion" of Oklahoma farmers during the First World War: Most of these frontier rebellions and rural uprisings were centered on the hinterland's opposition to change in the form of onerous political restrictions or economic centralization and its attendant dislocation. . . . The farmers' march on Washington in spring 1978 and their threat of withholding cropland from production was one recent manifestation of collective rural resistance to threatening external conditions.

For more than two centuries America's aboriginal settlers, the Indians, resisted the encroachment of white settlers in a series of raids, wars, and "disturbances." . . . [I]t is well-nigh impossible to find a major episode of conflict in which the Indians sought anything more than preservation of their territory and way of life. Whites too saw themselves in a defensive role, defending the outposts of expanding civilization against the depredations of "savages," whose very right to existence they were prepared to deny.

The Indian wars contributed to a strain of aggressive vigilantism that has been a recurrent response of white middle- and working-class Americans toward outsiders or lesser classes who seemed to threaten their status, security, or cultural integrity. The most celebrated examples come from the expanding frontiers, where more than 350 vigilante movements existed between the 1760s and 1900. They were found in almost every state and territory outside the Northeast and claimed the lives of more than 700 men. All were organized by private citizens who concluded that they had no other effective way of establishing and preserving law and order. . . .

The frontier vigilantes are distinguishable more in style than substance from the Ku Klux Klan, which rode three times in less than 100 years. Each time the Klan sought to defend a way of life that was threatened, not by crime but by social change. . . .

The spirit of vigilantism is far from dead in contemporary America. Racial tensions in the 1960s spurred the rise of neo-vigilante organizations among urban Americans, both black and white. . . . These brief flashes of violent resistance to social change were followed by vigilante-style opposition to court-ordered school busing and midnight raiding on behalf of environmental causes. Most of these were isolated, local episodes and seldom had the deadly consequences of nineteenth-century vigilantism, but they shared much of its style and spirit of group defense.

All these defensive movements were based on deeply felt grievances. But some of the movements were long-lived and intensely violent, while others were short-lived. There were two crucial differences among them: their extent of support and the responses of political authorities. . . . Vigilantes usually had the support of the "better sort" of citizens in the territories where they operated, and they were numerous and effective as a result. . . . [V]iolence arising from defensive movements is likely to be a serious and persistent occurrence to the extent that it is based on grievances that are deeply and widely felt, and go unremedied.

Reformist Groups

The demand for reform has been the second most common source of violent conflict in American history. Whereas defensive violence originates among groups that have mobilized to resist change, reformist violence arises from the organized advocacy of change. . . .

American history is studded with ethnic violence but rarely before the 1960s did it arise out of the organized demands of ethnic minorities. It is true that American society has been especially vulnerable to the frustrations of rising but disappointed expectations, for Americans proclaimed their country the "land of opportunity" and invited millions of destitute immigrants to partake of its fulfillment. Many sought and achieved individual mobility, others failed. But rarely did those who felt excluded organize and press their demands collectively to the point of violence. Anti-Irish and anti-Italian riots of the nineteenth century and race riots before the Second World War were initiated by groups further up the socioeconomic ladder who felt threatened by the prospects of Catholics or blacks getting "too big" and "too close." . . .

The first large-scale mobilization of an ethnic group for collective action occurred among blacks in the 1950s, in the form of the civil rights movement. It has since inspired many emulators among other ethnic and segmental groups, including Hispan[ic]s, Indians, women, and even some traditional white ethnic groups like the Italian-Americans. . . . Almost all organized advocates of minority and woman's rights in the United States have advocated peaceful dissent, and their activists have seldom initiated violence. The civil rights marchers, for example, were frequent targets of violence but never its agents. When massive violence did erupt, in the ghetto riots and rebellions of 1964 to 1970, it was the unorganized who rioted, not the organized. Even during these years, civil rights demonstrators outnumbered rioters and looters by a large margin. . . .

The history of American labor conflict between the 1870s and 1930s illustrates more clearly the path from group mobilization on behalf of reform, to confrontation between organized forces for change and organized resistance. Each decade saw hundreds of bloody clashes between workers and employers. They often claimed dozens of lives a year, 200 of them between 1902 and 1904 alone. . . . [V]iolence in these labor-management conflicts was seldom a deliberate tactic of working-class organizations. Usually it was the result of forceful employer resistance to workers' efforts to organize and the use of nonviolent but then-illegitimate tactics, like the strike and picket line. Companies repeatedly resorted to coercive and sometimes terroristic activities against union organizers and used violent tactics to break strikes. . . .

Another source of violence on behalf of reform has been opposition to war. . . . In the War of 1812, the pacifist citizens of Plymouth, Massachusetts, seized their prowar congressman and kicked him down the main street of town. During the Civil War, Southerners violently resisted the draft in half a dozen states. In New York City, antidraft mobs of 50,000 fought police and troops for five days in July 1863 at a cost estimated as high as 1,300 lives. Pacifists were more often violated than violent, though. During the First World War pacifist meetings and marches were attacked time and again by "patriots." . . . In the 1960s an estimated three million Americans took part in hundreds of demonstrations against the United States' involvement in the Vietnam War. Almost all the 1,600 people injured in these demonstrations were activists who were attacked by angry supporters of the war and, occasionally, by police. . . .

The pattern which emerges when we look at reformist movements is that their members are more often victims than attackers. . . . [T]he seriousness of violence arising out of reformist movements does not depend directly on how deeply and widely felt the reformers' grievances are. It depends largely on how violently the reformers are opposed, and by whom. Reformist protest on behalf of widely supported causes is not likely to cease until some change has been achieved. Reformist violence is minimized when those who oppose the reformers use nonviolent means.

It is not difficult to understand why reformers are usually less violent than those who defend the status quo. Most reformers in the United States have thought they had more to lose and less to gain from violence. This is one of the ironies of democracy as practiced in America: reformers have been hopeful enough of success to try to avoid violently antagonizing the Establishment, while the Establishment has often felt so threatened by the reformers' chances of success that coercion was necessary.

Rebellion

The essence of rebellion is complete rejection of superior political authority in favor of a new political system. . . . With the exception of the Revolutionary and Civil Wars, serious separatism and revolutionary movements have been remarkably rare in American history. I suggest above that the Shay, Whiskey, and other "rebellions" were defensive movements with limited objectives, not full-fledged attempts to secede from the Union. Much the same can be said of two briefly successful "revolutions" at the state level: Dorr's Rebellion in Rhode Island (1842) and the White League's armed seizure of power in New Orleans (1874). But the historical landscape contains no serious attempts to carry out a populist or socialist revolution in the United States, despite the precedents provided by France in 1789 and again in 1848 and 1871, or by Russia in 1917, or China in 1949. Nor have the South or the West or New England or even Hawaii talked seriously of seceding from the Union, not since the 1860s. . . .

Some political terror in the 1970s has had revolutionary objectives, just as it did for a handful of radical labor organizers at the turn of the century. Police in black ghettos were attacked in a short-lived campaign of the Black Liberation Army because they were symbols and agents of a white Establishment. . . . [A] small band of Puerto Rican nationalists continue a sporadic 30[-plus] year campaign of symbolic violence on behalf of a cause supported by less than a tenth of natives of the island. In none of these campaigns have the terrorists received significant support from the group for whom they claim to act, no more than did labor terrorists three generations ago. Most of their potential supporters have been too apolitical or too deeply committed to reformist movements to be attracted by revolutionary martyrdom.

On the Outcome of Group Violence

The outcomes of private resorts to violence are problematic. The most visible mark of success is the capitulation of government in the face of rebels, but this is not the only or necessarily the best criterion of "success." . . . A . . . more precise criterion is the extent to which the grievances which give rise to collective protest and violence are resolved. Even revolutionary victories do not necessarily lead to complete success in these terms. The American Revolution placed effective political control [in] the hands of the colonists, but eventually led to an expansion of state and federal authority that diminished local autonomy to the point that uprising broke out in frontier areas over essentially the same kinds of issues that had caused the revolution. . . .

If revolutionary victory is unlikely in modern democracies, and uncertain of resolving the grievances that give rise to revolutionary movements, are there any circumstances in which less intensive private violence is successful? . . . I suggest that private violence can succeed when both the tactics and objectives of violence are widely regarded as legitimate. The vigilante movements of the American frontier had widespread public support as a means of establishing order in the absence of adequate law-enforcement agencies, and were generally successful. The Ku Klux Klan and similar organizations of the Reconstruction era similarly had the sympathy of most white Southerners and were instrumental in reestablishing and maintaining the prewar social and political status quo. Both movements occurred in regions whose inhabitants were acclimatized to violence. Southerners had just fought a much bloodier Civil War to defend privileges they now sought through interracial and anti-Republican violence, while probably the majority of Western vigilantes were veterans of the Mexican-American, Civil, or Indian wars.

The chronicles of American labor violence, however, suggest that violence was almost always ineffective for the workers involved because their objectives usually were not widely supported. In a very few instances there was popular and state governmental support for the grievances that had led to violent confrontations with employers, and in several of these cases state authority was used to impose solutions that favored the workers. But in the great majority of cases the public and officials did not accept the legitimacy of labor demands, and the more violent the conflict, the more disastrous the consequences for the workers who took part. . . .

A similar principle applies, with two qualifications, to peaceful protest. If demonstrations are regarded as a legitimate way to express grievances, and if the grievances themselves are widely held to be justified, protest is likely to have positive effects. One qualification is that if public opinion is neutral on an issue, protest demonstrations can have favorable effects. . . . If public opinion is negative, however, demonstrations are likely to exacerbate popular hostility. . . .

The second qualification is that when violence occurs during protest activities, it is rather likely to alienate groups that are not fundamentally in sympathy with the protesters. I mentioned above the unfavorable consequences of labor violence for unions and their members, despite the fact that violence was more often initiated by employers than by workers. . . .

The evidence supports one basic principle: force and violence can be successful techniques of social control and persuasion when used for purposes which have extensive popular support. If such support is lacking, their advocacy and use are ultimately self-destructive, either as techniques of government or of opposition. The historical and contemporary evidence of the United States suggests that popular opinion tends to sanction violence in support of the status quo: the use of official violence to maintain public order, the use of private violence to maintain popular conceptions of social order when government cannot or will not. If these assertions are true—and not much evidence contradicts them—the prolonged use of force or violence to advance the interests of any segmental group may impede and quite possibly preclude reform. This principle is a fundamental trait of the American character. . . .

ALTERNATIVE RESPONSES TO POLITICAL VIOLENCE

Different types of political violence call for different types of public response. The first question is just what an ideal "democratic response" might be. Presumably it is the set of policies that restores civil peace with the least pain, and the most gain, for society at large. In the United States the major constitutional constraint on this principle is that minority rights are to be respected in the process, which means that majorities may sometimes be required to accept a modicum of discomfort in order to ensure equity to minorities. The practical political constraint is that majorities, and privileged minorities, will seldom surrender significant advantages without putting up a fight themselves. So there is no one ideal strategy. That which restores civil peace in one circumstance may foment civil war in another. Three basic kinds of strategy have been used historically by American officials in response to political violence: acquiescence, control, and reform.

Acquiescence

The easiest response to political violence is sometimes to do nothing. Federal and state officials seldom interfered with vigilantes; the vigilantes were often doing state and territorial governments a favor, even if outside the limits of the law. During the same era that Westerners were violently ridding their new towns of undesirables, Southern lynching parties were disposing of some 2,000 blacks who had transgressed the white social code. The lynchings rarely attracted any more governmental attention than did vigilantism, perhaps less. . . .

Passivity in the face of violence may have been practicable in nineteenth-century America; it can be decisively rejected in the late twentieth century. Public and private interests both oppose such a policy. First, contemporary society is less tolerant of private violence than it once was and is more likely to learn of the occurrence of serious incidents via the mass media. . . . Second, the United States is a much more thoroughly governed and policed society now than in the nineteenth century. Officials even more than the public are committed to maintaining public order, and they have most of the necessary means of control at their disposal. . . .

Control: The Official Uses of Force

The more common official response in America has been to suppress outbreaks of violence, not to ignore it. The more threat violence has posed to the nation's political and economic institutions, the more likely it is that authorities will attempt to contain it. But there are two quite different strategies of control, as well as intermediate strategies that combine elements of both.

Events at Kent State University, Ohio, in the spring of 1970 were typical of a strategy of control that has been employed hundreds of times over the past century. The clash began with the actions of a disruptive, sporadically violent group of protesters. Outside forces were called in to restore order. The inevitable confrontations occurred and finally fatal shots were fired. . . . Kent State was typical of *reactive control* and distinct from a strategy of *preemptive control.*

Preemptive control of political violence involves two governmental tactics. One is the use of intelligence activities to anticipate violent confrontations, the other is preventive force to keep those situations cool. The details of these tactics became quite familiar in the 1960s and early 1970s. They included surveillance of potential "trouble-makers," infiltration of activist groups by informers and agents provocateurs, the harassment and arrest of influential activists, and saturation police tactics during demonstrations and incipient riots. . . . [T]he use of spies, harassment of activists, and massive preventive force have ample American precedents, especially in labor-management conflicts.

Neither reactive nor preemptive responses to group violence may satisfy liberal ideals about how democratic governments should deal with dissent, but force is widely believed to be effective. . . .

The two most fundamental human responses to the use of force are to flee or to fight. This assertion rests on rather good psychological and ethological evidence about human (and animal) aggression. Force threatens and angers people, especially if they believe it to be illegitimate or unjust. Threatened, they will defend themselves if they can, flee if they cannot. Angered, they have an innate disposition to retaliate in kind. Thus people who fear assault attempt to arm themselves. . . . Governments facing violent protest often regard compromise as evidence of weakness and devote additional treasure to counterforce. Yet if a government responds to the threat or use of violence with greater force, its effects may be identical to the effects that dictated its actions: its opponents will resort to greater force.

There are only two inherent limitations on such an escalating spiral of violence and counterviolence: the exhaustion of one side's resources, or the attainment by one of the capacity for genocidal victory. There are societal and psychological limitations as well, but they require tacit bonds between opponents: one's acceptance of the ultimate authority of the other, arbitration of the conflict by neutral authority, recognition of mutual interest that makes bargaining possible, or the perception that acquiescence to a powerful opponent will have less harmful consequences than resisting certain death. In the absence of such bases for cooperation, regimes and their opponents are likely to engage in violent conflict to the limit of their respective abilities.

To the extent that this argument is accurate, it suggests one more kind of circumstance in which violence succeeds: that in which one group so overpowers its opponents that they have no choice short of death but to desist. This was the point to which American Indians had been pushed a century ago. . . . Not surprisingly, the list of successful official violence against opponents is much longer than the list of dissident successes against government, because most governments have much greater capacities for violence, provided they keep the loyalty of their generals and soldiers. Some dissident successes include the American Revolution, and white Southerners' successful resistance to the first Reconstruction. Among the many governmental successes in the United States are the North's victory in the Civil War and the quelling of riots of the 1960s.

Official violence is likely to be successful in quelling specific outbreaks of private violence except in those rare circumstances when the balance of force favors its opponents, or the military defects. But the historical evidence also suggests that governmental violence often succeeds only in the short run. . . . The North "won" the Civil War, but in its very triumph created hostilities that contributed to one of the greatest and most successful waves of private violence in our history. The 17,000 Klansmen of the South in the 1860s were neither peaceable nor content with the outcome of the "War of Northern Aggression." . . .

The long-range effectiveness of public force in maintaining civil peace seems to depend on three conditions: public belief that governmental use of force is legitimate, consistent use of that force, and remedial action for the grievances that give rise to dissidence.

Remedial Strategies

Remedial strategies are those that are directed at the cause rather than the symptoms of political violence . . . and are of three distinguishable types.

The *paternalistic strategy* is to attack the immediate symptoms of grievance. If people are unemployed, as millions were during the Depression of the 1930s, the paternalistic approach is to put them on the dole or public assistance. . . .

The *accommodation strategy* is to increase opportunities within the existing system for discontented individuals. The accommodation approach to unemployment is to create new jobs, directly by work projects, indirectly by "pump-priming" and job training. It is essentially the approach taken by the federal government to black Americans' demands for improvement in their economic status. . . .

The strategy of accommodation may lead to gradual but ultimately very substantial changes in the distribution of economic and political power. Those who have wealth, power, and status in American society today are far more heterogeneous in ethnic background than they were 100 or even 50 years ago. But this is the result of individual mobility. The *radical reform strategy* requires a direct adjustment in the structure of political and economic power by improving the status of collectivities as such. The collectivities may be communities, associational groups, people with a common ethnic origin, classes, or even biologically defined groups—women, the elderly, the handicapped. The crux of the radical reform approach is that groups acquire some of the means necessary to resolve their grievances themselves. Just what those necessary means are depends on the collectivity and its needs. They may include rights: to organize, to be represented in decision-making, to raise and spend funds. They may also include more tangible benefits: government grants, group-administered service programs.

The radical approach has the sanction of American political tradition. It was colonial Americans' solution to their painful dependence on Britain: by seizing power they improved their capacity to help themselves. . . . The struggle of the labor movement to obtain recognition and rights was the great breakthrough, and demonstrates aptly how radical reform can resolve some kinds of conflict. . . . The movement toward recognition and negotiation was strongly reinforced when workers in most occupations were guaranteed the right to organize and bargain collectively by the National Labor Relations Act of 1935. . . . It is worth emphasizing that in this situation the long-range consequence of radical reform was a decrease not increase in violent conflict. In fact, violence was chronic so long as union recognition was denied. The outcome suggests the inadequacy of arguments that concessions inevitably breed greater violence. . . .

The principle of conferring rights and resources on quasi-autonomous groups has its limits as a means of conflict resolution. The stronger and more self-assertive each newly empowered group, the more likely it is to collide with the individual and collective rights of outsiders. If the principle is applied too widely and well, the likely consequence is an increase in intergroup conflict. But the social costs of such routinized conflict between more or less equal collectivities are probably less than the persistence of festering pockets of poverty and powerlessness.

OPTIMUM STRATEGIES FOR CIVIL PEACE

Each strategy of response to group violence has disadvantages that must be weighed against its historical successes. If one asks which is most desirable for democracy as planned and practiced in America, again there is no single, unambiguous answer. The most appropriate strategies depend on the social basis of violence. It is necessary to consider the underlying cause—revolutionary, reformist, or defensive—and how much popular support it commands. . . .

[T]he grievances of political revolutionaries can seldom be satisfied by nonrevolutionary means. If they are incompetent or isolated, they deserve little attention. When they threaten public safety or confidence, though, preemptive control is likely to be both necessary and sufficient. This strategy presents problems for democracy only when police agencies exercise too much zeal and too little discrimination. It is particularly important that police, prosecutors, and judges dealing with revolutionaries and other dissidents follow due process and respect democratic liberties. . . .

What if revolutionaries have potential large-scale support? They may give voice to widely shared grievances of people who otherwise disavow the tactics of violence and would prefer the slow certainties of reform to the disruption and uncertain outcome of revolutionary conflict. This has been the situation of much of the black community and many students in times recently past: they have sought radical reform but rejected violent, revolutionary means to achieve it. In this circumstance preventive control can work only if remedial strategies are also followed. . . . If an Establishment does use all force and no reform, revolution is indeed one step closer.

The solutions to violence in defense of the status quo depend on who is violating the status quo. If it is government itself, the alternatives are only to back off, or to persist. If some larger justice demands persistence—which it does for civil rights, for example—then preventive control over violence is needed first of all. Second to that is remedial action to compensate for the pain of change. It requires only a little social insight to see that poor Southern whites or urban blue-collar workers would be less opposed to racial equalization if their own life prospects were better.

Reformist movements are the other common stimulus to status quo violence. In this case reformist and status quo violence are two sides of the same coin: a democratic solution to one must embody a solution to the other. This situation is always the most difficult because whatever mix of strategies is used, some substantial group is likely to get hurt. Doing nothing can be quickly ruled out as a response because it means that the contending groups will go on fighting until one wins—which may be never. . . .

When the status quo and reformist movements meet head on in violent conflict, the optimum response must be a mix of control and remedial strategies. If control alone is used, both groups will likely be at one another's throats whenever control is relaxed. This was for many decades the official American response to violent industrial disputes: to send in the National Guard. . . .

If remedial strategies are used alone, the contending groups are likely to go on fighting, which makes reform more difficult if not impossible. Reforms cannot be introduced if order is wholly lacking, and reforms will not be made if those who have the means to make them are constantly in jeopardy. . . .

In summary, democratic leaders who are charged with responsibility for outbreaks or threats of group violence can respond in two ways. They can forcefully tighten up social control, or they can exert public effort and encourage private efforts to resolve the issues that give rise to violence. Increased control is usually necessary to reestablish peace. Remedial strategies must be followed simultaneously if enduring civil peace is sought. . . .

Grudgingly and with much tumult, the dominant groups in American society have moved over enough to give immigrants, workers, and women better—not the best—seats at the American feast of freedom and plenty. Many of them think the feast is bounteous enough for dissatisfied students, Indians, blacks, and the Hispan[ic]s. Whether there is a place for young militants who think the feast has gone rotten, no historical or comparative evidence we know of can answer, because absolute, revolutionary alienation from society has been very rare in the American past and no less rare in other prosperous democracies.

Section 5: Weapons Use

The Bartley-Fox Gun Law's Short-Term Impact on Crime in Boston

Glenn L. Pierce and William J. Bowers

A comprehensive gun control strategy designed to reduce the incidence of gun-related crime would need to address the successive decision points leading to the use of a gun in crime: the decision to acquire a gun, the decision to carry it, and the decision to use it for criminal purposes. Existing gun control efforts have typically focused on one of these decision points at the exclusion of the other two.[1]

The approach that casts the broadest net is the one that attempts to restrict the acquisition of guns. This includes laws that regulate or limit the importation, manufacture, sale, transfer, ownership, and/or possession of firearms. Such laws will, in principle, reduce the pool of potential gun offenders; fewer people will be in a position to carry a gun or to use it for criminal purposes.

Opponents of acquisition control laws argue that, in practice, such laws will not stop serious criminals—presumed to be responsible for most gun crime—from acquiring, carrying, and using guns. Instead, they say, such laws will deprive law-abiding citizens of the guns they want and need for sport and self-protection. . . .

At the other end of the spectrum are approaches aimed narrowly at the decision to use a gun for criminal purposes. Gun-use laws, commonly referred to as "weapon enhancement" statutes, typically impose an additional term of imprisonment for crimes committed with a gun. Michigan's "felony firearms statute" which adds a mandatory two years to the sentence imposed for offenses such as aggravated assault, armed robbery, forcible rape, and criminal homicide when they are committed with a gun is an example of this approach.[2]

A law of this kind is more attractive politically; it specifically targets the "criminal element," those who have been convicted of violent felony offenses. . . . But the effects of these weapons enhancement laws are doubtful. . . . The problem with this approach may be that it targets too narrow a group of potential offenders who are too committed to criminal activity and too dependent on guns in such activity.

Perhaps the optimal approach from the standpoint of both deterrent effectiveness and political feasibility is the one that targets the decision to carry a gun outside of the home or place of business. It may be that a substantial proportion of those who become involved in gun-related crimes carry guns but do not anticipate the specific situations that will precipitate their use and do not have the time or presence of mind when confronted with these situations to weigh the punishment if caught against the immediate advantage of using a gun.

The Massachusetts legislature took this approach when it enacted the Bartley-Fox gun law, which mandated a one-year minimum prison term for the unlicensed carrying of firearms. The law was explicitly intended to reduce the incidence of gun-related crime as well as the illicit carrying of firearms. . . .

The law is unlikely to be effective against those who decide to carry a gun for a specific, short-term purpose, such as robbing a bank. The target group is rather those who carry guns on their persons or in their cars without specific criminal purpose in mind, but as a matter of life- style—those Beha has called the "casual carriers."[3] The cumulative risk of apprehension for such people may be substantial over an extended period of time, especially if police employ proactive search-and-seizure tactics.

The law confronted this group with a dramatic apparent increase in the legal risk associated with carrying a gun without a license. A concerted campaign for two months prior to the law's effective date characterized the impending consequences in the following terms, "If you are caught with a gun, you will go to prison for a year and nobody can get you out." Carrying without a license had previously been punished with a fine or suspended sentence, and only occasionally with a brief incarceration.

For its intended impact on gun-related crime, this kind of law may be said to rely upon a derivative deterrent effect. That is, by increasing the punishment imposed for one offense—carrying a gun without a license—the law is intended to reduce the incidence of other crimes: gun assaults, gun robberies, and gun homicides.

The Massachusetts gun law could, conceivably, have still further deterrent effects on gun assault, gun robbery, and gun homicide if offenders were charged for carrying without a license and had a year added to the sentence imposed for assault, robbery, or homicide. Such an application of the law follows the model of a weapons enhancement statute. The available evidence suggests, however, that the approach will have little or no impact on gun-related crime.[4] Moreover, the publicity surrounding the implementation of the law gave no indication that it would be applied in this way, nor has this approach been adopted in subsequent practice to any noticeable degree.[5]

The Bartley-Fox Amendment became effective on 1 April 1975. Gun-related violent crime rates fell dramatically in Massachusetts between 1974 and 1976, suggesting that Bartley-Fox had an extraordinarily large deterrent effect. But before we accept this conclusion, it is necessary to rule out other possible explanations for the observed reductions in gun violence. Our rather extensive analysis of violent crime patterns in Massachusetts and other jurisdictions has convinced us that the Bartley-Fox law, and/or the publicity that attended its implementation, was indeed a highly effective deterrent—at least in the short run. . . .

ARMED ASSAULT

A large proportion of assaults are the result of spontaneous arguments, which the antagonists are unlikely to have foreseen. Gun assaults may typically be committed by those who are carrying guns without criminal intent and find themselves provoked or threatened. A law that dramatically increases the punishment for illicit carrying may cause a substantial proportion of these casual carriers to leave their guns at home, and thus may produce a substantial reduction in gun assaults.

To the extent that armed assault is situationally provoked rather than purposeful and preplanned, the removal of guns from the situations in which assault occurs cannot be expected to reduce the overall number of assaults. In assault-provoking situations, those involved will presumably resort to whatever weapons are available at the scene. Hence a reduction in the public's propensity to go armed with guns may increase the number of nongun assaults. Indeed, with fewer guns being carried into assault-prone situations, potential assaulters may feel less restrained, and hence the increase in nongun assaults could more than offset the decrease in gun assaults.

Our analysis of armed assault focuses on the complementary issues of deterrence and weapon substitution. The presentation of our results is organized into three parts: (1) an intervention point analysis, using [time series] techniques, to examine when and if the level of gun and nongun armed assaults change; (2) a control group comparison of changes in Boston against those in selected control jurisdictions; and (3) an analysis of the impact of the law on citizen reporting.

Intervention Point Analysis

[Intervention point analysis draws upon statistical techniques associated with time series analysis.[6] The techniques permit us to test] . . . whether the actual observed crime trends after the gun law exhibit statistically significant departures from the predicted future of the crime time series based on its history prior to the policy intervention.

A major advantage of this method is that the techniques are capable of incorporating the type of seasonal cycles that is often found in crime data. This is particularly important because seasonal fluctuations can obscure or be mistaken for immediate or short-term effects of a policy intervention. . . .

For gun assault, we found that a statistically significant downward shift occurred in March 1975—the month prior to implementation of Bartley-Fox. Since implementation was preceded by a vigorous publicity campaign of several months duration, it is not surprising to find evidence that the law began to influence behavior even before it was officially in effect. Our analysis found that the downward shift that occurred in March was sustained in subsequent months.

The same type of analysis yielded a statistically significant increase in nongun armed assaults in Boston, beginning in May 1975. We interpret this result as reflecting a tendency for people to substitute other weapons for guns in assault situations following implementation of the law. . . .

Control Group Comparisons

As noted, intervention point analysis, by incorporating information on the pre-Bartley-Fox history of gun and nongun armed assaults, controlled for the effect of ongoing trends that might otherwise obscure or be mistaken for an impact of the law, or its publicity. These methods, however, do not control for those instances where exogenous events or socioeconomic factors intervene and result in departures from prior trends in crime. The Bartley-Fox law, of course, represents one such event, but the issue is to isolate the effects of the law from the effects of other possible factors.

To address this issue, we introduce control groups into our analysis. . . . The control group design employed here allows us to compare the level of violent crime in Boston over time with the levels of crime in comparable jurisdictions over the same period.

The logic of this type of analysis is, of course, strengthened to the extent that an investigator can select control groups that are truly similar. That is, we want to be able to identify control jurisdictions that would be subject to the same exogenous factors . . .—except for the Bartley-Fox law—as those in Boston, Massachusetts.

Since Boston's population has averaged 600,000 inhabitants over the last decade, as control jurisdictions we have selected cities in two size categories: 250,000 to 500,000 inhabitants and 500,000 to 1,000,000 inhabitants for the United States, the North Central region, and the Middle Atlantic states. . . . In addition, we have drawn on the set of all cities within a 750-mile radius of Boston and that are equal to or larger than Boston in population: Washington, D.C.; Baltimore; Philadelphia; New York; Cleveland; and Detroit. . . .

In addition to these control groups, we also selected Chicago as a control jurisdiction. Chicago serves a dual purpose because (1) it is a northern industrial city, although somewhat farther away than the other individual cities selected; and (2) along with Boston and Washington, D.C., it was chosen . . . to be one of the sites for . . . an experimental program designed to reduce the illegal sale of firearms. This program was initiated in Boston and Chicago in July 1976 and in Washington, D.C., in February 1976. Thus Chicago—and Washington, D.C., to a lesser extent—becomes a useful reference point for measuring the impact of an alternative intervention . . . whose effects could be confounded with the Bartley-Fox law. . . .

. . . Three sets of annual statistics [were collected] . . . : (1) gun assaults per 100,000 inhabitants, (2) nongun armed assaults per 100,000 inhabitants, and (3) the percent gun assaults of all armed assaults for the years 1974, 1975, and 1976. This last measure, because it combines both potential deterrent and displacement effects, is a particularly sensitive indicator of the law's impact. . . .

Between 1974 and 1975, Boston showed a 13.5 percent decline in gun assaults, a decrease greater than that occurring in any of the [control] jurisdictions. Indeed, of the control jurisdictions, only Chicago showed a decline in gun assaults approaching that of Boston. . . . In the following year, 1975 to 1976, however, Boston showed a slight increase in gun assaults while a number of the control groups showed declines. Over the two-year period following Bartley-Fox—1974 to 1976—Boston showed an overall decline in gun assaults of 11.7 percent. Unlike the first year change, 1974 to 1975, where Boston showed the greatest decrease, 4 of the 13 control jurisdictions—Philadelphia, Washington, D.C., Cleveland, and Chicago—showed a two-year decline greater than that of Boston. . . .

Looking at nongun armed assaults, we find that Boston shows a 31.1 percent increase between 1974 and 1975 and a 40.4 percent increase over a two-year period, 1974 to 1976. Importantly, these increases are more than twice those exhibited by any of the control jurisdictions. . . .

Examination of the measure that combines potential deterrent and weapon substitution effects shows that the weapon-related character of armed assaults in Boston changed following Bartley-Fox. Between 1974 and 1975—the first year following Bartley-Fox—the percent that guns represented of all armed assaults in Boston dropped from 25.9 percent to 18.8 percent. This decrease was almost four times greater than that shown by any of the control jurisdictions. In the two-year period—1974 to 1976—Boston showed a 30.4 percent decline in the percentage that gun assaults represent of armed assaults versus a maximum 16.1 percent decline occurring in the control group. . . .

Review of the impact on assault findings reveals a strong pattern of evidence supporting the hypothesis that the Bartley-Fox law reduced the likelihood of gun assault in Massachusetts. When the first year—1975—following the introduction of the law was examined, we found that relative to each of the control jurisdictions in both Boston and non-Boston Massachusetts communities, (1) gun assaults decreased, (2) non-gun armed assaults increased, and (3) the percent that gun assaults represent of all armed assaults declined. In the two years following

Bartley-Fox—1974 to 1976—this same pattern of results held up with one exception: between 1974 and 1976 gun assaults in 4 of Boston's 12 control jurisdictions showed larger declines than Boston had exhibited. Thus in 5 of 6 possible comparisons made, the results consistently indicate that the gun law affected the character of armed assault in Massachusetts.

The [results] . . . suggest the rather surprising conclusion that the weapon substitution effect of Bartley-Fox was larger than the deterrent effect—that is, the increase in nongun assaults more than compensated for the reduction in gun assaults. However, closer scrutiny of these data convinced us that deterrent effects of the law are underestimated in Boston. Implementation of the Bartley-Fox law and its attendant publicity appears to have increased the likelihood of citizens' reporting gun assaults. . . .

ARMED ROBBERY

As with our analysis of the Bartley-Fox law's impact on armed assaults, the armed robbery analysis will examine the dual questions of deterrence and weapon substitution. . . . To the extent that robbery is more often the result of planned purposeful action than is assault, we would expect a law like Bartley-Fox to have less deterrent impact on robbery because this law is specifically aimed at the carrying rather than the using of a firearm. Under these circumstances, individuals who carry firearms with a specific use in mind have relatively less to lose than offenders who are not planning to assault or to rob someone. Quite simply, although the costs are the same in terms of the gun law—a one-year prison term—the benefits of carrying a gun are less for the person who carries a gun, but who has no specific anticipated use for it.

Compared with assault, we also expect the magnitude of the displacement effects to be less. . . . Robbery with a gun is generally a much easier task than robbery with other types of deadly weapons, unless an offender chooses to rob highly vulnerable targets. However, there is also a disincentive to switch to more vulnerable targets because these also tend to be much less lucrative, for example, a street robbery of an elderly person is generally much easier but also less lucrative than a robbery of a drug store.

Control Group Comparisons

Data restrictions prevent our conducting an intervention point analysis of gun and nongun armed robberies. The . . . available data are sufficient, however, for a comparison group analysis. As in the assault analysis, we examined the law's impact on (1) gun robbery, (2) nongun armed robbery, and (3) the percent that gun robbery represents of all armed robbery for Boston. . . .

. . . When we initially examined Boston's first-year (1974 to 1975) post-Bartley-Fox change in gun robbery, there appeared to be little evidence of an immediate deterrent effort of the law. Indeed, between 1974 and 1975, gun robberies declined by only 1.8 percent in Boston. However, when Boston's first change in gun robberies—1.8 percent—is compared to the changes occurring in the control jurisdictions, we find that in 9 of the 12 sets of control jurisdictions, gun robberies increased more than they did in Boston. Thus although the law failed to reduce the level of gun robbery in Boston between 1974 and 1975, it may have been responsible for suppressing what would have been a substantial increase.

This impression is reinforced when the two-year (1974 to 1976) post-Bartley-Fox change in gun robbery is examined. Between 1974 and 1976, Boston showed a 35.5 percent decrease in gun robberies. Boston's two-year post-Bartley-Fox decline was exceeded by only 2 of the 12 control groups. . . .

. . . [A]nalysis of Boston's nongun robbery statistics reveals strong evidence indicating substantial first-year (1974 to 1975) displacement effects. In the first year following the Bartley-Fox law, we find nongun armed robberies in Boston increased by 35.4 percent between 1974 and 1975—an increase of 40 percent greater than that occurring in any of the control jurisdictions.

One measure—the fraction of robberies involving guns—incorporates both the potential deterrent and displacement effects of the law, and hence is an especially sensitive indicator of the gun law's impact. When this measure is examined, Boston unambiguously shows the greatest post-Bartley-Fox change in the weapon-related character of armed robbery. In the first year following Bartley-Fox—1974 to 1975—the percent that gun robbery represents of all armed robbery declined in Boston by 14 percent—a decline twice that shown in any of the control jurisdictions. In the two-year period—1974 to 1976—following Bartley-Fox, Boston showed a 23.3 percent decline versus a maximum 14 percent decline—Chicago—shown in any of the control jurisdictions. . . .

CRIMINAL HOMICIDE

To the extent that homicide is a function of an offender's premeditated willful intention to kill his victim, we would have little reason to expect that the Bartley-Fox law would deter gun-related homicides. The assumption is that an offender who is willing to risk the legal sanction for murder would also be willing to risk the sanction for a Bartley-Fox offense. On the other hand, if as Richard Block proposes, homicides occur not primarily as a result of an offender's planned determination to kill, but rather as something that sometimes happens as the unanticipated consequence of other criminal or life-style activities,[8] then the introduction of the gun law might have a derivative deterrent effect on gun homicide. . . . [T]he gun law might prevent some gun-related homicides by affecting the decisions that potential offenders make regarding whether or not to carry a firearm, and/or whether or not to use a firearm to commit a robbery or an assault.

Indeed, we have already observed that the Bartley-Fox law appeared to reduce gun-related assaults and robberies throughout Massachusetts. Thus we should not be surprised if gun-related homicides also show a decline following the Bartley-Fox law.

There also appears to have been an increase after the law in nongun armed assaults and, to a lesser extent, nongun armed robberies. However, for at least two reasons, we also do not expect to find similar displacement effects for criminal homicides: (1) we would expect to find that an increase in nongun armed assaults or robberies did not result in a proportionate increase in nongun criminal homicides because guns are likely to be more deadly than other types of weapons and (2) offenders who switch from guns to other deadly weapons may generally be those offenders who are least intent upon physically harming their victims. Thus an increase in the use of other deadly weapons by those offenders might very well not result in an increase in homicides.

Comparison Group Analysis

Criminal homicide statistics for Boston and the control jurisdictions are presented in Table 20-4. . . . In the first year—1974 to 1975—following the gun law's implementation, gun homicide in Boston declined by 21.4 percent—a decrease greater than any of the jurisdictions experienced except Baltimore. In the two years—1974 to 1976—after Bartley-Fox, gun homicides in Boston declined by 55.7 percent—a decrease greater than that exhibited by any of the control jurisdictions. . . .

We, of course, want to address the issue as to whether the Bartley-Fox law . . . produced displacement effects similar to those observed for nongun armed assaults and to a lesser extent nongun armed robberies. However, when nongun criminal homicides for Boston are examined we find that in the two years—1974 to 1976—following Bartley-Fox, nongun homicides actually dropped in Boston by 20.3 percent. Moreover, only one of the control jurisdictions—Washington, D.C.—exceeded this decline. . . . Thus we find no evidence suggesting a displacement effect of the Bartley-Fox law on nongun criminal homicide.

The pattern of impact where gun homicides appear to have been deterred while nongun homicides do not appear to have increased has important implications because it suggests that the Bartley-Fox law may have had an overall effect of reducing incidence of criminal homicides in Boston, at least in the short run. Indeed, if the gun homicide and nongun homicide statistics . . . are added together, we can see that the overall level of criminal homicides showed a greater decline in Boston . . . than in any of the control jurisdictions in the two years following the introduction of the gun law.

Finally, further evidence of the Bartley-Fox law's impact on criminal homicide in Boston is available when the percent of gun homicides . . . is studied. Here we find that between 1974 and 1976, Boston showed a greater decrease in this measure than any of the control jurisdictions. . . .

CONCLUSION

This analysis has focused on the Bartley-Fox law's impact on armed assault, armed robbery, and homicide. For each type of crime, we independently examined the law's impact on gun-related offenses and nongun-related offenses in Boston.

Introduction of the gun law had a twofold effect on armed assaults. First, the law substantially reduced the incidence of gun assaults. Second, it resulted in a

Table 20-4.
Gun Homicides, Nongun Homicides, and Percentage of Gun Homicides of All Homicides in Boston in Comparison to Cities Grouped Regionally and for Selected Eastern Seaboard and North Central Cities

Regions	Gun Homicides			Nongun Homicides			Percentage of Gun Homicides of All Homicides		
	Rate, 1974	1974–75, Percentage Change	1974–76, Percentage Change	Rate, 1974	1974–75, Percentage Change	1974–1976, Percentage Change	1974	1974–75, Percentage Change	1974–76, Percentage Change
Boston	70	−21.4	−55.7	64	0.0	−20.3	52.2	−11.5	−27.6
Comparison cities grouped regionally: 250,000–500,000 inhabitants									
All United States cities except Boston	3140	−6.5	−23.0	1379	9.3	−0.7	69.5	−4.9	−8.2
North Central cities	470	−9.1	−26.1	139	3.4	−5.7	77.2	−9.7	−9.1
Middle Atlantic cities	164	−0.6	−28.0	171	−1.3	−11.6	49.0	6.9	−10.4
Selected eastern seaboard and north central cities									
New York	794	9.1	−2.5	822	0.2	3.0	49.1	4.3	−2.9
Philadelphia	248	−24.2	−32.7	171	−4.1	−13.5	59.2	−9.8	−10.5
Baltimore	204	−23.5	−45.6	90	15.6	−4.4	69.4	−13.5	−18.9
Washington, D.C.	170	−14.7	−30.6	106	−16.0	−33.0	61.6	0.6	1.3
Detroit	510	−14.7	−3.5	200	−13.5	−12.5	71.8	−0.4	2.8
Cleveland	254	−15.7	−34.6	52	42.3	−11.5	83.0	−10.5	−5.7
Chicago	668	−17.4	−25.0	301	−11.3	2.7	68.9	−2.2	−10.2

substantial increase in nongun armed assaults. Thus while the law appears to deter some individuals from carrying and/or using their firearms, it did not prevent them from using alternative weapons in assaultive situations.

Introduction of the Bartley-Fox law also resulted in a short-term reduction in gun robberies, and a concomitant increase in nongun armed robberies. However, the magnitude of the weapons substitution effect for armed robbery appears to be less than what we observed for armed assault.

The law also deterred some gun-related criminal homicides in Boston, but did not result in a corresponding increase in nongun criminal homicides. Thus the gun law produced an overall decline in the incidence of criminal homicide.

Our analysis also suggests that the law may have achieved its effect primarily through its "announced" intent, rather than its actual implementation. Importantly, in the assault analysis where the effects were most pronounced, we observed that the decline in gun assault in Boston started one month prior to the effective date of the law—suggesting that offenders, at least initially, were responding to the publicity attendant with the introduction of gun law rather than mandatory imposition of its sanctions. Hence, we conclude that the observed reduction in gun crime was the result of an announcement effect, rather than the product of sanctions actually imposed—the traditional definition of a deterrent effect. . . .

For this reason, we draw no conclusions about the effect of the "mandatory" nature of the law. That is, the observed effects of the law do not depend on its having been applied in a mandatory fashion. At this point in our analysis, we simply know that it was advertised as imposing a "mandatory one-year prison term."

NOTES

1. The recent New York state gun law that became effective in 1980 is an exception that focuses on both carrying and use of a firearm.
2. Colin Loftin and David McDowall, "'One with a Gun Gets You Two': Mandatory Sentencing and Firearms Violence in Detroit," *The Annals* of The American Academy of Political and Social Science, 455: 150–67 (May 1981).
3. James A. Beha, III, "And Nobody Can Get You Out: The Impact of a Mandatory Prison Sentence for the Illegal Carrying of a Firearm on the Use of Firearms and the Administration of Criminal Justice in Boston, Part I–Part II," *Boston University Law Review*, 57 (1977).
4. Loftin and McDowall.
5. David Rossman, *The Impact of the Mandatory Gun Law in Massachusetts*. (National Institute of Law Enforcement and Criminal Justice, Law Enforcement Assistance Administration, United States Department of Justice, 1979).
6. G. E. P. Box and G. M. Jenkins, *Time Series Analysis: Forecasting and Control* (San Francisco, CA: Holden-Day, 1977).

7. Philip J. Cook, "The Effect of Gun Availability on Violent Crime Patterns," *The Annals* of The American Academy of Political and Social Science, 455: 63–79 (May 1981).
8. Richard Block, *Violent Crime: Environment, Interaction and Death* (Lexington, MA: Lexington Books, 1977).

Section 6: Mental Disorder

Dangerousness and Mental Illness: Some Conceptual, Prediction, and Policy Dilemmas

Saleem A. Shah

Concerns about the alleged or presumed dangerousness of an individual are raised in a variety of sociolegal contexts, e.g., involuntary commitment of the mentally ill, adjudication and commitment of defective delinquents and sexual psychopaths, the confinement and release of persons acquitted of criminal responsibility by reason of insanity, and the sentencing and release of "dangerous" offenders. The dangerous behaviors of greatest social concern in the above situations are those which are believed to pose a threat to members of the community, viz., dangerousness to others. However, commitment laws for the mentally ill typically use the phrase "dangerous to self or others." Thus, two conceptually different bases for State intervention (viz., to protect the individual's welfare under the parens patriae powers of the State and to protect the community against harm under the police power authority) tend to get thoroughly confounded. . . .

Definitional Issues

. . . *[D]angerousness* refers to a propensity (i.e., an increased likelihood as compared to others) to engage in dangerous behaviors. *Dangerous behavior* refers to acts that are characterized by the application or overt threat of force and are likely to result in injury to other persons. The above statement would also define violent behavior. Thus, . . . dangerous behavior is considered synonymous with violent behavior. . . . [According to t]he *Uniform Crime Reports (UCR)* of the FBI, . . . [t]he category of violent crimes includes: murder, aggravated assault, forcible rape, and robbery. Along with these offense categories are the so-called inchoate crimes, viz., attempts to commit violent crimes.

Of course, one could well go beyond these categories of violent crimes and include various other criminal acts such as assault and battery, arson, kidnapping, extortion, all serious felonies, or even lesser categories of criminal conduct. . . . In any event, the range of "dangerous" acts to be included under formal legal and other societal responses remains basically a matter of public policy and has to be addressed by appropriate policymakers, viz., legislatures and courts.

Consideration of an individual's dangerousness is raised at many decision points in the criminal justice and mental health systems:

1. Decisions concerning the granting of bail (or release on personal recognizance) to persons accused of crimes; also the level at which bail is to be set.
2. Decisions concerning the waiver of juveniles charged with serious crimes to adult courts.
3. Sentencing decisions following criminal convictions, including decisions about release on conditions of probation.
4. Decisions pertaining to work-release and furlough programs for incarcerated offenders.
5. Parole and other conditional release decisions for offenders.
6. Decisions pertaining to the commitment and release of persons handled via a number of quasi-criminal statutes concerned with "sexual psychopaths," "sexually dangerous persons," "mentally disordered sex offenders," "defective delinquents," and the like.
7. Determinations of dangerousness for all indicted felony defendants found incompetent to stand trial (e.g., in New York State[1]).
8. Decisions regarding the special handling (including transfer to special prisons) of offenders who are disruptive and dangerous in regular penal settings.
9. Commitment of drug addicts because of fears that they will commit violent crimes to support their drug habit.
10. Decisions concerning the emergency and longer term involuntary commitment of mentally ill persons considered to pose a "danger to self or others."
11. Decisions concerning the "conditional" and "unconditional" release of involuntarily confined mental patients.
12. Decisions concerning the hospitalization (on grounds of continuing mental disorder and dangerousness) of criminal defendants acquitted by reason of insanity.
13. Decisions regarding the transfer to security hospitals of mental patients found to be too difficult or dangerous to be handled in civil mental hospitals.
14. Decisions concerning the invocation of special legal proceedings or sentencing provisions for "habitual" and "dangerous" offenders.

15. Decisions concerning the likelihood of continued dangerousness of persons convicted of capital crimes, as a basis for determinations regarding the use of the death sentence.[2]

Despite the serious consequences for persons officially designated as "dangerous," it is astonishing to note the absence in far too many instances of clear and specific definitions and criteria for use of the key terms in the various relevant laws. . . . Moreover, even though "dangerousness," as used in various laws and regulations, is clearly a *legal* term requiring determinations by courts and other designated triers of fact, often such crucial determinations are actually made by mental health experts. This situation has been criticized with regard to the apparent arrogation by psychiatrists and other mental health professionals of determinations that are fundamentally legal. However, it must be noted that the above problem is a reflection more of judicial default than of the arrogance of mental health professionals (Shah 1974).

SOME CONCEPTUAL ISSUES

A major consideration in efforts to assess, predict, prevent, and change dangerous behavior pertains to the manner in which behavior is conceptualized. Behavior—whether defined as dangerous, friendly, constructive, or antisocial—is often viewed as stemming largely, if not entirely, from *within* the person, i.e., as being a stable and fairly consistent characteristic of the person. In other words, behavior is viewed in the traditional *trait* perspective, determined largely by the individual's personality. Thus, the assumption often is made that the samples of "dangerous" behavior are fairly typical of the individual and are likely to be displayed in other situations. . . .

. . . The trait model assumes that the rank order of individuals with respect to a specific personality variable will tend to be the same across different settings and situations. Thus, even though the model recognizes the impact of situational factors, there is an assumption that persons described as "friendly" or "dependent" or "honest" or "aggressive" will tend to display such behaviors across a variety of situations. . . .

In contrast to the foregoing, a *situation-focused* model places major emphasis on the external stimuli and variables in the setting and situation as the basic determinants of individual behavior. Although recognizing individual differences, *situationism* is basically a stimulus-response (S-R) approach which focuses major attention on the stimulus factors influencing subsequent response (Endler and Magnusson 1976). However, the weakness of this model lies in the fact that it tends to ignore, or at least to underemphasize, individual-related factors as they influence the perception, interpretation, and response to the environment.

Much theoretical and empirical work has been done in recent years with respect to an *interactional* model of behavior. This model emphasizes the importance of ongoing person-situation interactions in efforts to understand both personality and behavior. It is held that behavior involves an indispensable and continuous interaction between individuals and the various situations that they encounter (Shah 1966, . . . Endler and Magnusson, . . . 1976). . . .

During the past decade, there has been a major resurgence in the fields of personality and social psychology with regard to the interactionist perspective. . . . [T]he accumulating empirical evidence has demonstrated rather clearly that individual-situation interactions need to be considered and are much more useful in helping to understand and to predict behavior, than either of these sets of variables alone (Endler and Magnusson 1976). . . .

. . . [S]ome social settings are highly structured in that the rules and prescriptions for enacting specific role behaviors impose rather narrow limits on the range of possible behaviors (e.g., in church, at school . . .). In other situations (e.g., informal social gatherings, a party . . .) the range of possible behaviors and roles is broad, and individuals have much more leeway in selecting and cognitively constructing and reorganizing situations with minimal external constraints. . . .

. . . Relatively little attention is focused on the particular setting and situational factors, and on the patterns of individual-specific interactions which may differentially affect the occurrence of certain behaviors. Use of an interactionist perspective . . . requires that greater attention be focused upon the particular setting and situational conditions which have in the past and which are likely in the future to elicit, provoke, and maintain certain violent or other problematic behaviors. More attention also needs to be focused on the particular social settings and contexts in the community in which the person will live; assessments of likely functioning and problems must consider the availability and nature of the supportive, stressful, and other relevant factors likely to affect the person's functioning. . . . It has been shown, for example, that accurate predictions of posthospital adjustment of mental patients in the community hinged on knowledge of the particular environment in which the expatients would be living, the availability of jobs, family and related support systems—rather than on any measured characteristic of the individual's personality or his inhospital behavior (Fairweather 1967). . . .

[TECHNICAL PROBLEMS]

Traditionally there appear to have been two major assumptions underlying most laws authorizing indeterminate (and even preventive) confinement of the mentally ill, and also of persons variously designated as "sexual psychopaths," "sexually dangerous persons," and the like (Brakel and Rock 1971). The first assumption is that dangerousness (to self and others) is a characteristic typically, or at least frequently, associated with mental illness. Secondly, it is possible to make reliable and reasonably accurate assessments of persons likely to engage in dangerous behavior. While there has been a paucity of sound empirical evidence to support these assumptions, in recent years increasing evidence has accumulated to challenge such beliefs. These assumptions do not have the degree of empirically supported validity that would provide necessary and reasonable support for related public policies and practices. . . .

. . . [T]here still remain many problems with the underlying assumption that the mentally ill constitute one of the most dangerous groups in our society. For example, analysis . . . indicates that higher arrest rates for exhospitalized mental patients are associated with some of the same factors that are related to criminal recidivism, viz., prior criminal record, personality disorders, and problems with alcohol and drug abuse. Thus, if indeed the major societal concern is with identifying groups that are clearly and demonstrably the most dangerous, then there is considerable evidence indicating that persons with repeated arrests and convictions for drunken driving (Alcohol and Highway Safety 1968; Mulvihill and Tumin 1969; Shah 1974) and offenders with three or more convictions for serious misdemeanors and felonies are quite demonstrably, not just presumably, very dangerous in terms of the probabilities of further involvement in serious crime (PROMIS Research Project 1977a, 1977b; Shinnar and Shinnar 1975; Wolfgang et al. 1972).[3]

With regard to the second assumption, the ability to make reliable and reasonably accurate predictions of dangerousness, there is impressive and convincing evidence pointing to the considerable technical difficulties inherent in predicting very infrequent events. Typically in such prediction situations there occur huge rates of "false positive" errors, i.e., persons predicted as likely to be dangerous but who will *not* in fact display such behavior. . . .

[CONFOUNDING OBJECTIVES]

It has been pointed out that there are several instances in the handling of the mentally ill and certain other categories of social deviants where our legal system tends to confound social control objectives designed to protect the community (viz., police power concerns) with the asserted parens patriae aims of providing proper treatment for the deviant individuals (Shah 1975, 1977). Rather typically, the individual whose fate is being determined pays a heavy price as a result of the confounding of the stated purposes. . . .

. . . [T]he doctrine of exculpatory insanity derives from certain moral, social, and legal considerations which hold that in our system of justice it is neither fair nor proper to punish individuals who cannot be held blameworthy for the commission of criminal acts. . . . [T]he rationale for use of the insanity defense is provided by relevant legal doctrine and the finding of "not guilty by reason of insanity" (NGRI) constitutes a *legal* determination with respect to prescribed sociolegal processes involved in criminal adjudication.

It should also be noted that courts have repeatedly pointed out (e.g., *McDonald* v. *United States*[4]), that the concepts of mental disease or defect, as used by legislatures and courts for certain public policy and legal determinations, are *not* synonymous with the psychiatric meanings and uses of these terms.

The defense of insanity raises questions about the defendant's mental condition at the time of the alleged offense. And, there has been much recent judicial opinion that a determination of exculpatory insanity does not automatically nor even necessarily imply *present* "insanity" (i.e., following the NGRI adjudication). Thus, applying principles derived from the Supreme Court's decision in *Baxtrom*,[5] the U.S. Court of Appeals in *Bolton* v. *Harris*[6] held that a finding of "not guilty by reason of insanity" (NGRI) could *not* lead to an automatic commitment of the individual (acquitee) to a mental hospital. Rather, the Court held that

> After acquittal by reason of insanity there is also need for a new finding of fact: the trial determined only that there was a reasonable doubt as to the defendant's sanity in the past, present commitment is predicated on a finding of present insanity. (p. 650) . . .

Is the NGRI acquitee committed to the mental hospital for treatment of his "insanity," and/or for his offensive conduct? [For example, suppose the acquitee is a paranoid-schizophrenic who committed an assault with a dangerous weapon. Should he] be treated for the paranoid schizophrenia—which condition provided the basis for the insanity acquittal, or [should] he . . . also . . . be treated for his offensive behavior (viz., assault with a dangerous weapon) and for any criminal propensities[?]

We might recall that the legal determination resulting in the insanity acquittal was based upon a finding of a mental disorder adjudged to constitute "insanity," and a further finding that there was the legally required connection between the "insanity" (paranoid schizophrenia) and the offensive behavior. However, . . . it does *not* necessarily mean that once the person's schizophrenic disorder has effectively been treated there will be no further criminal behavior. Clearly, the vast majority of persons who engage in various types of aggravated assaults and other serious criminal acts do not suffer from paranoid schizophrenia, nor any other psychotic disorder (. . . Guze et al. 1969). Likewise, the great majority of persons suffering from paranoid schizophrenia do not engage in criminal behavior. Moreover, if there are public policy and legal concerns that the NGRI acquitee be successfully treated for his offensive and dangerous behavior . . . then it should be evident that mental hospitals are not the facilities which either claim, or which could even reasonably claim, to provide effective treatment for criminal behavior. There is no sound empirical research indicating that mental hospitals have had any demonstrated success in "treating" criminal behavior. . . .

. . . It must be remembered, however, that the adjudication resulting in the insanity acquittal was related to certain moral values and legal doctrine—and *not* to considerations of psychiatric treatment (nor even the treatability) of the mental disorder and the hoped for effects on subsequent criminal behavior. Yet, *legal* decisions involving criminal adjudication and insanity acquittals tend rather typically to be confused and confounded with mental health and psychiatric consideration relevant to effective treatment. . . .

In sum, the confusing and confounding of police power and parens patriae objectives, and also of legal and mental health concerns, serve to place the mental hospital in a role much like that of a maximum security prison, but with the added feature of allowing indeterminate periods of confinement and using rather stringent standards for release. Thus, to paraphrase Justice Fortas, the NGRI acquitee can end up receiving "the worst of both worlds"—he receives neither the full range of protections and the determinate confinement accorded to criminals, nor the adequate and effective treatment sought from the mental health system.[7] . . .

IMPLICATIONS FOR CLINICAL PRACTICE

Earlier . . . , traditional personality trait and psychodynamic perspectives on behavior were described as being insufficiently cognizant of the setting and situational aspects influencing behavior. . . . It was suggested that an interactionist perspective provides a distinct improvement in the conceptualization of behavior. . . .

This section outlines some major questions and provides some suggestions relevant to the assessment, prediction, and handling of dangerous behaviors. [Foremost,] there needs to be some clear notion as to which specific acts (behaviors) fall within the legal definition of "dangerousness."

Determinations about the specific range of behaviors judged to constitute "dangers" to the community, within the meaning of the relevant laws, have to be provided by appropriate policymakers, i.e., legislatures and courts. These are fundamentally normative and public policy judgments, and they should *not* be left, whether directly or through default, to "experts." Thus, expert witnesses should not be asked by courts or other decisionmakers whether an individual is likely to be "dangerous," without some clarification and specification as to the range of behaviors of legal concern (e.g., acts of violence against persons, felonious crime, etc.). . . .

Once dangerous behaviors have been defined, [other questions need to be addressed:] . . .

1. *What is the likelihood (probability) that the feared dangerous behaviors will occur or recur?* This is the crucial and most difficult question with respect to predictive assessments. Rather typically, the answer seems to depend pretty much on the subjective, intuitive, and often "seat-of-the-pants" impressions of various experts. Moreover, there is often a failure to provide some objective description of the assessment process, of the specific criteria used, and of the cues and "clinical signs" used for making predictions of dangerousness. Thus, even though some clinicians may well be good predictors, it is very difficult to know precisely how they go about making their assessments. . . . To reduce inconsistencies and disagreements among mental health professionals in predicting "dangerousness," Schwitzgebel (1977) has suggested that two or more experts be asked to make such assessments—but *independently*. . . .

   With respect to determining the likelihood of future violent behavior, as well as the frequency and likely social context of such behaviors, it is most essential to carefully ascertain the relevant history and pattern; e.g., whether there have been any such behaviors in the past; and, if so, whether the previous violent act(s) was part of a consistent or persistent pattern . . . , or whether it was a rare and possibly one-time event. If the violent behavior was quite untypical, the predictive task may well be impossible. The best that one could do would be to try to determine the particular person- and situation-specific factors which appear to have elicited the past violent act. . . .

In some . . . cases the likelihood of repeated violent behavior may relate to some clearly discernible sequence of circumstances that can be ascertained from the relevant history. For example, in a case of child battering it was determined that the unmarried young woman was usually a very attentive and capable mother to her three small children all under 6 years of age. However, it was when her boy friends began to lose interest in her and she was left alone to care for the children in her state of worry and resentment, and also when she began to drink, that incidents of child battering had typically occurred. Such knowledge can be of much value to persons charged with assisting the woman under some form of [therapeutic] community supervision. . . .

. . . [T]he individual's past pattern of behavior and functioning, as well as knowledge of the social setting and circumstances in which he will be living, will typically provide more relevant and reliable information than the person's psychiatric diagnosis. In short, the situation with respect to determining the "dangerousness" of mentally disordered persons is not basically different from that faced in evaluating criminal recidivism for offenders. . . .

Indeed, it appears that the . . . probabilities associated with serious criminal recidivism will have factors in common for convicted offenders and for many mentally disordered offenders. Predictions of future dangerous behavior can reasonably be made when there exists a long pattern of serious criminal behavior and associated factors (e.g., youthful age, alcohol problems, and absence of stabilizing and supportive resources) remain in effect. It remains to be determined whether variables such as psychiatric diagnoses (other than personality disorders) and a history of serious mental illness help by themselves to distinguish particular subgroups with respect to their future dangerousness. Based upon current knowledge, it might even be that, by focusing *primarily* on the person's mental condition and on vague and often very speculative psychodynamic factors, mental health professions may well tend to *decrease* their predictive accuracy. . . .

2. *Who are likely to be the victims of the expected or feared "dangerous" behaviors?* Decisionmakers may wish to know whether the dangerous acts are more likely to occur against some *particular persons* (e.g., a spouse or girl friend, the individual's own children,) . . . and/or against some *broader group* of people (e.g., minor boys or girls in the case of a pedophile, adult women in the case of certain exhibitionists or rapists, etc.), and/or against a *more dispersed segment of the community* (e.g., the likely victims of "purse-snatchings" and other street robberies, . . . etc.). Here, again, the previous and longstanding pattern of behavior will typically provide relevant information. Even if there is a long pattern of

previous assaultive behavior, but this behavior is very person- and situation-specific . . . , preventive interventions may be feasible. Such person-specific criminal acts could possibly be prevented by means of explicit and closely monitored conditions of release. . . .

3. *What is the severity of harm or injury likely to be inflicted IF the dangerous acts were to recur?* Relevant case law . . . has pointed out the need to carefully balance the severity of harm likely to be inflicted by an individual and the loss of liberty to be suffered as a result of confinement. In order to undertake such balancing, courts need to have some idea of the severity of harm or injury that particular persons (or the community more generally) are likely to suffer if the released person engaged in further dangerous behavior. . . . [T]he past history and pattern of criminal or other dangerous behavior (mostly reflected by arrests, prosecutions, convictions, and penal incarcerations) will tend to provide the most relevant information. . . .

4. *Is the feared dangerous behavior of a nature that could appreciably be decreased, modified, or even prevented by certain environmental changes?* The conceptualization of behavior as a product of person-environment interactions has certain clinical and other practical implications. For example, in the case of an elderly and somewhat senile person who is being considered for involuntary hospitalization because he forgets to turn off the gas jets on his stove after cooking, such lapses could endanger not only the man himself in the event of a fire or gas explosion, but also his neighbors in the apartment building. Thus, he could be considered as "dangerous to himself and others." However, it is obvious that the "dangerousness" does not lie *within* the person; rather, it results from certain characteristics of the person and their interactions with a particular environment. The "dangerous" situation in this particular case might readily be corrected by replacing the individual's gas stove with an electric one. . . .

   . . . It would be fair to say that a large number of hospitalized mentally disabled persons, as well as incarcerated offenders, could very likely be handled in the community *if* our society were willing to provide the necessary resources to develop a wider range of less drastic alternatives for handling such persons and the problems that they present. It should be evident that the sociolegal decision to involuntarily confine a person considered to be "dangerous to himself or others" is *not* simply a reflection of the degree of danger posed by the person. It is also a reflection of the tolerance levels in the community for deviant behaviors, and of the lack of less restrictive alternatives available in the society. The latter relates very directly to the resources the society is willing to allocate to such social needs.

5. *Are there certain treatment alternatives which relate more directly to the behaviors of specific concern, and which could more predictably reduce the likelihood of certain dangerous behaviors?* It has been noted that . . .

questions arise whether mental hospitals are the appropriate social institutions for treatment of *dangerous behaviors*—as contrasted with the treatment of serious mental disorders. Questions also arise about how the treatments typically used for psychiatric disorders relate to specific and episodic dangerous behaviors.

During the last two decades, various behavioral approaches to treatment have been developed and many of these can more specifically be related to the particular behaviors and problems of concern. . . .

. . . For example, exhibitionists are subject to indeterminate confinement under provisions of various "sexual psychopath" and "sexually dangerous persons" laws. Assuming a societal interest in providing treatment, certain less drastic treatment approaches could be used in outpatient settings, rather than relying on indeterminate confinement [for example, "covert sensitization"]. . . .

CONCLUSION

. . . [D]iscriminatory practices vis-a-vis the mentally ill tend to reinforce and to maintain longstanding social prejudices. For to the extent that policymakers, courts, and mental health professionals concentrate their concerns with "dangerous" behavior largely on the mentally ill, they help to perpetuate the myth that the mentally ill, as a group, are the most dangerous persons in our society. However, there is abundant empirical evidence to demonstrate that certain other groups (e.g., drunken drivers and recidivistic criminals) are clearly and convincingly more dangerous to the community. . . .

. . . [I]f the basic object of a legal system in a society is to achieve the "idea of justice" for its members, its success at any given moment cannot be measured by the ideas it professes nor the constitutional or legal rules to which it pays lipservice. Rather, success must be measured in terms of the *actual achievement* of the guiding values and objectives. When societal institutions are found to be dysfunctional in reference to professed values and policy objectives, society must either modify the institutions or be forthright enough to abandon the professed values or strive diligently to bring the values closer to the reality which it wishes to preserve. [W]hen the policies themselves deviate from major societal values, appropriate changes in such policies must also be made—else the underlying goal values will tend to be depreciated and weakened.

Mental health professionals need, therefore, to consider very carefully the roles that they find themselves playing as agents of social control with respect to various categories of the mentally ill, rather than as caregivers and therapists. With better awareness of their own roles and with greater attention to ways in which empirical research findings can help to improve various clinical tasks, mental health professionals should join with lawyers, behavioral and social scientists, and other concerned citizens to make societal policies and practices with respect to the mentally ill more accountable and less hypocritical.

NOTES

1. Section 730.50 of New York State's Criminal Procedure Law (Sept. 1971) mandates a determination of dangerousness for all indicted felony defendants found incompetent to stand trial.
2. Texas Code of Criminal Procedure, Art. 37.071, effective June 14, 1973. Section (b)(2) states, "Whether there is a probability that the defendant would commit criminal acts of violence that would constitute a continuing threat to society" (p. 278).
3. The ongoing PROMIS research project in the District of Columbia sought to determine ways of predicting the likelihood of criminal recidivism. It was found that if a defendant had five or more arrests prior to the current arrest, the probability of subsequent arrest began to approach certainty. (PROMIS Research Project, 1977a, page 12.)
4. *McDonald* v. *United States*, 312 F.2d 847 (1962).
5. *Baxstrom* v. *Herold*, 383 U.S. 107 (1966).
6. *Bolton* v. *Harris*, 395 F.2d (1968).
7. *Kent* v. *United States*, 383 U.S. 541, at 556 (1966).

REFERENCES

Brakel, S. J., and Rock, R. S. *The Mentally Disabled and the Law*. Rev. ed. Chicago: University of Chicago Press, 1971.

Endler, N. S., and Magnusson, D. Toward an interactional psychology of personality. *Psychological Bulletin*, 83:956–974, 1976.

Fairweather, G. W. *Methods in Experimental Social Innovation*. New York: Wiley, 1967.

Guze, S. B.; Goodwin, D. W.; and Crane, J. B. Criminality and psychiatric disorders. *Archives of General Psychiatry*, 20:583–591, 1969.

Mulvihill, D., and Tumin, M. *Crimes of Violence*, Vol. 12. A staff report to the National Commission on the Causes and Prevention of Violence. Washington, D.C.: Superintendent of Documents, U.S. Government Printing Office, 1969.

PROMIS Research Project. Highlights of interim findings and implications. Publication 1. Institute for Law and Social Research. Washington, D.C.: The Institute, 1977a.

PROMIS Research Project. Curbing the repeat offender: A strategy for prosecutors. Publication 3. Institute for Law and Social Research. Washington, D.C.: The Institute, 1977b.

Schwitzgebel, R. K. Prediction of dangerousness and its implications for treatment: A speculative overview. Unpublished paper, 1977.

Shah, S. A. Treatment of offenders: Some behavioral concepts, principles, and approaches. *Federal Probation*, 30:1–9, June 1966.

Shah, S. A. Some interactions of law and mental health in the handling of social deviance. *Catholic University Law Review*, 23:674–719, 1974.

Shah, S. A. Dangerousness and civil commitment of the mentally ill: Some public policy considerations. *American Journal of Psychiatry*, 132:501–505, 1975.

Shah, S. A. Dangerousness: Some definitional, conceptual, and public policy issues. In: Sales, B. D., ed. *Perspectives in Law and Psychology*, Vol. 1. New York: Plenum Publications, 1977.

Shah, S. A., and Roth, L. H. Biological and psychophysiological factors in criminality. In: Glaser, D., ed. *Handbook of Criminology*. Chicago: Rand McNally, 1974.

Shinnar, R., and Shinnar, S. The effects of the criminal justice system on the control of crime: A quantitative approach. *Law and Society Review*, 9:581–611, 1975.

U.S. Department of Transportation. *Alcohol and Highway Safety:* A Report to the Congress from the Secretary of Transportation. Washington, D.C.: The Department, Aug. 1968.

Wolfgang, M. E.; Figlio, R. M.; and Sellin, T. *Delinquency in a Birth Cohort*. Chicago: University of Chicago Press, 1972.

Copyrights and Acknowledgments

The authors are grateful to the following publishers and copyright holders for permission to reprint the selections in this book.

Academic Press, Inc. "The Violent Face of Television and Its Lessons" by George Gerbner and Larry Gross. First published in *Children and the Faces of Television: Teaching, Violence, Selling*, edited by Edward L. Palmer. Copyright © 1981 by Academic Press, Inc. Reprinted by permission of Academic Press and the authors.

American Psychiatric Association "Adaptive Strategies and Recovery from Rape" by Ann Wolpert Burgess and Lynda Lytle Holmstrom, from *American Journal of Psychiatry*, vol. 136, pp. 1278–82. Copyright © 1979 by the American Psychiatric Association. Reprinted by permission of the American Psychiatric Association and the authors.

"Treatment of Sex Offenders with Antiandrogenic Medication: Conceptualization, Review of Treatment Modalities, and Preliminary Findings" by Fred S. Berlin and Carl F. Meinecke, from *American Journal of Psychiatry*, vol. 138, pp. 601–7. Copyright © 1981 by the American Psychiatric Association. Reprinted by permission of American Psychiatric Association and the authors.

American Society of Criminology "Trends in Violent Crime among Ex-Mental Patients" by Joseph J. Cocozza, Mary Evans Melick, and Henry J. Steadman, from *Criminology*, vol. 16. Copyright © 1978 by the American Society of Criminology. Reprinted by permission of The American Society of Criminology and the authors.

American Sociological Association "The Specific Deterrent Effects of Arrest for Domestic Assault" by Lawrence W. Sherman and Richard A. Berk et al., from *American Sociological Review*, vol. 49 pp. 261–72. Copyright © 1984 by the American Sociological Association. Reprinted with permission of the publisher and authors.

The Free Press "Homicide: Behavioral Aspects" by Marvin E. Wolfgang and Margaret A. Zahn, from *The Encyclopedia of Crime and Justice*, vol. 2, edited by Sanford Kadish. Copyright © 1983 by The Free Press, a division of Macmillan, Inc. Reprinted by permission of The Free Press, a division of Macmillan, Inc.

"Rape: Behavioral Aspects" by A. Nicholas Groth, from *The Encyclopedia of Crime and Justice*, vol. 4, edited by Sanford Kadish. Copyright © 1983 by The Free Press, a division of Macmillan, Inc. Reprinted by permission of The Free Press, a division of Macmillan, Inc.

"When Battered Women Kill" by Angela Browne. Copyright © 1987 by The Free Press. Abridged and reprinted by permission of the author and The Free Press, a division of Macmillan, Inc.

Giuffre Editore "Il Comportamento Violento. Teorie Esplicative" by Marvin E. Wolfgang and Neil Alan Weiner, from *Trattato di Criminologia, Medicina Criminologica e Psichiatria Forense*, ed. by Franco Ferracuti & M. C. Giannini. Copyright © 1987 by Giuffre Editore. Reprinted with permission of Franco Ferracuti and Dott G. Giuffre, the publisher.

Hoover Institution Press *"Terrorism: Threat, Reality, Response* by Robert H. Kupperman and Darrell M. Trent; abridged and reprinted with permission of Hoover Institution Press. Copyright © 1979 by the Board of Trustees of the Leland Stanford University.

Morton Hunt *The Mugging* by Morton Hunt. Copyright 1972 by Morton Hunt. Reprinted by permission of Morton Hunt and his agents Lescher & Lescher.

Law and Society Association "Corporate Homicide: Definitional Processes in the Creation of Deviance" by Victoria Lynn Swiggert and Ronald A. Farrell in Volume 15:1 of *Law and Society Review*. Copyright © 1981 by Law and Society Association. Reprinted by permission of the Law and Society Association.

Lexington Books, D. C. Heath "Capital Punishment in Perspective" by William J. Bowers from *Executions in America*. Copyright © 1974 by Lexington Books, D. C. Heath. Reprinted by permission of Lexington Books, D. C. Heath and Company.

"The Shape of Police Violence" by Hans Toch, from *Peacekeeping: Police, Prisons, and Violence*, ed. Hans Toch. Copyright © 1979 by Lexington Books, D. C. Heath and Company. Reprinted by permission of the publisher.

National Council on Family Relations "Societal Change and Change in Family Violence from 1975 to 1985 as Revealed by Two National Surveys" by Murray A. Straus and Richard J. Gelles, from *Journal of Marriage and the Family*, vol. 48. Copyright © 1986 by the National Council on Family Relations. Reprinted and abridged with the permission of the publisher.

Northwestern University School of Law "Blind Justice: Police Shootings in Memphis" by James J. Fyfe, from *The Journal of Criminal Law and Criminology*, vol. 73, Issue 2. Copyright © 1982 by Northwestern University School of Law. Reprinted and abridged with permission of the publisher.

"Human Violence: A Comparison of Homicide, Aggravated Assault, Suicide, and Attempted Suicide" by Alex D. Polorny, from *Journal of Criminal Law and Criminology* Vol. 56, Issue 4. Copyright © 1965 by Northwestern University, School of Law. Reprinted by special permission of Northwestern University, School of Law.

Pennsylvania Prison Society "The Anatomy of a Prison Riot" by Israel Barak-Glantz from *The Prison Journal*, vol. 63 (Spring-Summer 1983). Copyright © 1983 by the Pennsylvania Prison Society. Reprinted with the permission of the publisher.

Plenum Press *The Death Penalty: A Debate* by John P. Conrad and Ernest van den Haag. Copyright © 1983 by Plenum Press. Reprinted and abridged with the permission of the author and the publisher.

Mass Murder: America's Growing Menace by Jack Levin and James Alan Fox. Copyright © 1985 by Plenum Press. Reprinted and abridged with the permission of the authors and the publisher.

Sage Publications, Inc. "Alternatives to Violence in a Democratic Society" by Ted Robert Gurr, from *Violence in America: Historical and Comparative Perspectives*, edited by Hugh Davis Graham and Ted Robert Gurr, rev. ed. Copyright © 1979 by Sage Publications, Inc. Reprinted with the permission of the publisher.

"American Labor Violence: Its Causes, Character, and Outcome" by Phillip Taft and Philip Ross, from *Violence in America: Historical and Comparative Perspectives*, edited by Hugh Davis Graham and Ted Robert Gurr, rev. ed. Copyright © 1979 by Sage Publications, Inc. Reprinted with the permission of the publisher.

"The Bartley-Fox Gun Law's Short-Term Impact on Crime in Boston" by Glenn L. Pierce and William J. Bowers, from *The Annals*, vol. 455. Copyright © 1981 by Sage Publications, Inc. Reprinted with the permission of the publisher.

"Convenience Stores, Armed Robbery, and Physical Environmental Features" by Dennis C. Duffala, from *American Behavioral Scientist*, vol. 20. Copyright © 1976 by Sage Publications, Inc. Reprinted by permission of the publisher.

"Crime and the Mass Media: A Selective Review of Research" by James Garafalo, from *Journal of Research in Crime and Delinquency*, vol. 18. Copyright © 1981 by Sage Publications, Inc. Reprinted by permission of the publisher.

"Domestic Criminal Violence" by Richard J. Gelles, from *Criminal Violence*, edited by Marvin E. Wolfgang and Neil Alan Weiner. Copyright © 1982 by Sage Publications, Inc. Reprinted by permission of the publisher.

"Drugs and Violent Crime" by Paul J. Goldstein, from *Pathways to Criminal Violence*, edited by Neil Alan Weiner and Marvin E. Wolfgang. Copyright © 1989 by Sage Publications, Inc. Reprinted by permission of the publisher.

"The Experiences of Violent and Serious Victimization" by Gary Gottfredson, from *Violent Crime and Violent Criminals* edited by Neil Alan Weiner and Marvin E. Wolfgang. Copyright © by Sage Publications, Inc. Reprinted with permission of the publisher.

"High-Risk Children" by David Finkelhor and Larry Baron, from *Sourcebook on Child Abuse*, edited by David Finkelhor. Copyright © 1986 by Sage Publications, Inc. Reprinted by permission of the publisher.

"Historical Patterns of American Violence" by Richard Maxwell Brown, from *Violence in America: Historical and Comparative Perspectives*, edited by Hugh Davis Graham and Ted Robert Gurr, rev. ed. Copyright © 1979 by Sage Publications, Inc. Reprinted with the permission of the publisher.

"Offender Types and Public Policy" by Marcia R. Chaiken and Jan M. Chaiken, from *Crime and Delinquency*, vol. 30. Copyright © 1984 by Sage Publications, Inc. Reprinted by permission of the publisher.

"On Being Mugged: The Event and Its Aftermath" by Robert Lejeune and Nicholas Alex, from *Urban Life and Culture*, vol. 2. Copyright © 1973 by Sage Publications, Inc. Reprinted by permission of the publisher.

"Social Dynamics of Terrorism" by Austin Turk, from *The Annals*, vol. 463 (September 1982). Copyright © 1982 by Sage Publications, Inc. Reprinted with the permission of the publisher.

"The Violent Offender in the Criminal Justice System" by Peter W. Greenwood, from *Criminal Violence*, edited by Marvin E. Wolfgang and Neil Alan Weiner. Copyright © 1982 by Sage Publications, Inc. Reprinted by permission of the publisher.

Society for the Study of Social Problems "Criminal Homicide as a Situated Transaction" by David F. Luckenbill from *Social Problems*, vol. 25, no. 2. Copyright © 1977 by the Society for the Study of Social Problems, University of California Press. Reprinted and abridged with permission of the author and publisher.

"The 1980 New Mexico Prison Riot" by Mark Colvin, from *Social Problems*, vol. 29, no. 5. Copyright © 1982 by the Society for the Study of Social Problems, University of California Press. Reprinted and abridged with the permission of the author and the publisher.

South End Press *The Real Terror Network: Terrorism in Fact and Propaganda* by Edward S. Herman. Copyright © 1982 by South End Press. Reprinted by permission of the publisher.

The University of Chicago Press "Historical Trends in Violent Crime: A Critical Review of the Evidence" by Ted Robert Gurr from *Crime and Justice: An Annual Review of Research*, vol. 3, edited by Michael Tonry and Norval Morris. Copyright © 1981 by The University of Chicago Press. All rights reserved. Reprinted and abridged with permission of the publisher.

"Stopping Rape: Effective Avoidance Strategies" by Pauline B. Bart and Patricia H. O'Brien from *Signs: Journal of Women in Culture & Society*, vol. 10. Copyright © 1984 by the University of Chicago Press. Reprinted and abridged with the permission of the publisher.

"Violence in School" by Jackson Toby, from *Crime and Justice: An Annual Review of Research*, vol. 4, edited by Michael Tonry and Norval Morris. Copyright © 1983 by the University of Chicago Press. All rights reserved. Reprinted and abridged by permission of the publisher.

University of Miami Press "Minimanual of the Urban Guerrilla" by Carlos Marighella, from *Terror and the Urban Guerillas*, edited by Jay Mallin. Copyright © 1971 by the University of Miami Press. Reprinted and abridged with permission of the publisher.

University Press of America "Patterns and Recent Trends in Black Homicide" by Patrick W. O'Carroll and James A. Mercy, from *Homicide among Black Americans*, edited by Darnell F. Hawkins. Copyright © 1986 by the University Press of America. Reprinted by the permission of the publisher.

Victimology Inc. "Wife Beating: How Common and Why?" by Murray A. Straus, from *Victimology: An International Journal*, vol. 2, 1977–79, nos. 3–4. Copyright © 1978 by Victimology Inc. All rights reserved. Reprinted by permission.

Yale University Press "Collective Violence: The Redress of Grievance and Public Policy" by Sandra J. Ball-Rokeach and James F. Short, Jr., from *American Violence and Public Policy*, edited by Lynn Alan Curtis. Copyright © 1985 by Yale University Press. Reprinted and abridged with permission of the publisher.

"The Extent and Character of Violent Crime in American, 1969 to 1982" by Neil Alan Weiner and Marvin E. Wolfgang, from *American Violence and Public Policy*, edited by Lynn A. Curtis. Copyright © 1985 by Yale University Press. Reprinted and abridged with permission of the publisher.

"Neighborhood, Family, and Employment: Toward a New Public Policy against Violence." by Lynn A. Curtis, from *American Violence and Public Policy*, edited by Lynn A. Curtis. Copyright © by Yale University Press. Reprinted and abridged with permission of the publisher.

Margaret A. Zahn, "Intervention Strategies to Reduce Homicide." Copyright © 989. Reprinted by permission of Margaret A. Zahn.

Index

B C D E 3 F 4 G 5 H 6 I 7 J 8